Some of the c...
rienced by ev...
neously. Eve...
thirty, for instance, is examining the ...
they've built in their twenties—relationships,
career, life direction. This process occurs at
the same time that the planet Saturn, which the
ancients associated with time and the matu-
ration that it brings, is completing a full orbit
and returning to the natal birth position.

In addition to charting personal cycles,
ASTROCYCLES also presents numerous col-
lective cycles that hint at who will sit in the
White House and large-scale global changes
that may emerge in years to come. For in-
stance, the 172-year cycle that renews itself in
1992–93 coincides with many of the changes
foreseen in Alvin Toffler's *Third Wave*.

The 1990s will see more of the need for hu-
mankind to embrace a worldview that ac-
knowledges the interrelationship of all life.
Cracks in the ozone, dwindling rain forests,
epidemics such as AIDS, and the erosion of the
American economy are just some of the hints
that restructuring of external—and internal—
life systems are mandated.

VIVIAN MARTIN
From ASTROCYCLES

ASTROCYCLES

How to Make the Major Planetary Cycles Work for You

Vivian B. Martin

BALLANTINE BOOKS • NEW YORK

Grateful acknowledgment is made to the following:

Tom Savarese of Heaven Knows!, Post Office Box 3314, Burbank, California, 91504 for permission to use the Ephemeris tables which he generated from AGS's Nova Software program and which he then reprogrammed into table format.

Library of Congress Catalog Card Number: 90-93464

ISBN 0-345-34864-8

Manufactured in the United States of America

First Edition: February 1991

For my parents, Rutrell and Ruth Martin, who through the years have come to understand this Aries's need to do it "my way."

CONTENTS

Contents

Contents

CHARTS/TABLES

INTRODUCTION

Astrology, and whether there is anything to it, is one of humankind's oldest debates. At one time or another it has been banned in virtually every place it has surfaced, and it would seem that astrology should have died out by now. Considering the drastic ups and downs of its acceptance, it may be surprising that in the present age of technological advances respect for astrology is growing. In fact, history books of the twenty-first century will surely be remiss if they don't mention the growing numbers of serious students, some armed with training in statistics, psychology, and other disciplines, who were refining and devising new techniques and working to gain more acceptance for this ancient craft as the twentieth century ended.

Astrology took its earliest steps in the Tigris-Euphrates valley of the second millennium B.C., with objections to the practice growing as it became more entrenched in society. In 139 B.C. Roman leaders banned astrology from all of Roman Italy in order to keep the lower classes and slaves from taking action against their oppressors. But at some point "the people" began looking at their horoscopes again. Augustus Caesar, in A.D. 11, prohibited citizens from consulting astrologers, although he, like many leaders, continued to consult astrologers about his personal and public life. Giovanni Pico della Mirandola had much to say about astrology in his late-fifteenth-century twelve-volume attack on it. He may have converted some people, but had he been alive for the rest of the Renaissance (of astrology and all forms of knowledge), he would have realized that he'd wasted his time. The seventeenth century's increased focus on "rationalism" and presumably more "scientific" ways of thinking would eventually force astrologers out of the papal courts and universities of Europe, but astrology survived. Late-nineteenth-century England, France, and the United States, and pre–World War I and II Germany, saw a rebirth of astrological ideas. By the 1960s, throughout most of the Western world, the question "What's your sign?" no longer had to be explained.

In 1975 a group of 186 scholars (18 of whom were Nobel prizewinners), thought they'd lick this astrology thing with a press conference. Actually they did a bit more. The scholars signed a manifesto that appeared in the 1975 fall issue of *Humanist* magazine. It said, in part, "We the undersigned . . . wish to caution the public against the unquestioning acceptance of the predictions and other advice . . . by astrologers. Those who wish to believe in astrology should realize there is no scientific foundation for its tenets." The "Objections to Astrology" manifesto was publicized around the world, yet the press rarely examined the fact that some of the ringleaders openly acknowledged that they'd never really studied astrology. As Bart J. Bok, a leading astronomer at the time, contended, astrology was too silly and in violation of existing scientific laws and hence didn't merit serious study. Instead of questioning whether known scientific laws themselves adequately expressed the nature of the Universe, the debunkers assumed that they were in the right. The manifesto, for the most part, refused to acknowledge even the most stringently controlled statistical studies that suggest correlations between planetary activity and life here on earth.

The most significant body of evidence is the result of more than thirty years of studies conducted by Michel Gauquelin and his former wife, Françoise Schneider Gauquelin, both of whom were Sorbonne-trained statisticians and psychologists. While still in his twenties, Michel Gauquelin, who'd been curious (and skeptical) about astrology from an early age, discovered that a statistically significant percentage of people who become physicians are born sometime within the first two hours after Mars and/or Saturn have either risen or reached their highest points in the sky during their daily travels. The Gauquelins' work over the years has shown correlations between a range of planets and temperaments, as demonstrated by career choice. Their work has been consistently challenged by skeptics from around the world. But although the data have always been replicated—even in hostile hands—academics in leading American universities and other positions of influence sought to discredit it and have successfully kept the controversy out of sight of mainstream scrutiny. If the debate had concerned any subject other than astrology, the Gauquelins' findings and their subsequent ramifications would be the source of much open talk worldwide. As was observed by Grant Lewi, a former Dartmouth professor and eminent astrologer of the 1930s, astrology is believed and disbelieved by people who know absolutely nothing about it.

It is impossible to live on earth and in a human body and not develop an appreciation for the law of cyclicity as it is expressed in the changing of the seasons, the regular coming and going of the tides, the beat of the human heart, and each breath we take. Our conversations take this concept further. Businessmen speak of "cycles," people talk of going through phases, the economy expands and contracts, the stock market, as well as many life ventures, busts and booms.

Often this appreciation of cycle gets more specific. We think about changing jobs every two and a half years, and we've all heard of the seven-year itch. Political commentators say they see trends coming back every twenty years. Psychological researchers have shown that specific ages—turning thirty or the so-called midlife crisis of the mid-forties—are characterized by specific urgencies and behaviors. In short we believe in cycles.

Astrocycles will show how the seven-year itch and other conventional rhythms have been documented by scientific and traditional forms of research. It will also explain how these cycles correlate to particular astronomical phenomena, and the specific schedules kept by the planets.

Some of the cycles or rhythms we will explore are experienced simultaneously by everyone of the same age. Everyone between the ages of twenty-eight and thirty, for instance, is examining the structures they've built in their twenties—relationships, career, life direction—and they are asking whether or not these structures accurately reflect the identity they're now beginning to perceive more acutely than they did as they began their twenties. Many of the circumstances of this age group are a result of thinking of oneself in a way that is often colored by inaccurate messages from friends, relatives, and society at large. Now they find that it's time to define who they really are. Like Henry David Thoreau, who spent his entire 28 to 30 year-old period at Walden Pond, it's important to take a trip to the woods (inside oneself) before setting up new structures in the outer world.

This process occurs at the same time that the planet Saturn, which the ancients associated with time and with the development and maturation that it brings, is completing a full orbit. Saturn takes approximately 29.5 years to return to the portion of the sky it was tenanting when a person was born. The Saturn

Return, from ages 28–30, is one of the most significant periods of time in terms of maturation and psychological development (and often of career and situational changes as well). At approximately ages thirty-five to thirty-six Jupiter, the largest planet in the solar system, completes an 11.8-year orbit and makes its third ''return'' to the place it tenanted at birth. This planet of expansion and opportunity seems to oversee the new level of social participation and integration that we move into through job promotions, new types of relationships, and a greater contentment and faith in the Universe and our place in it. The downside of this is a lack of perspective and balance that can cause life to get further out of kilter, but foreknowledge of the Jupiter Return and the many other age cycles can limit the chaos.

In addition to age cycles, *Astrocycles* will present numerous rhythms that are tied to the day and year of birth, as well as cycles that hint at who will sit in the the White House and larger-scale global changes for years to come. A 172-year cycle that renews itself in 1992–93 suggests the onset of even larger shifts than the unification of the European Common Market suggests and it will bring about many of the changes foreseen in Alvin Toffler's ''Third Wave.'' The 1990s will see more open acknowledgment of the need for humankind to embrace a worldview of the interrelationship of all that exists in the Universe. Cracks in the ozone layer, dwindling rain forests, epidemics such as AIDS, and the erosion of the American economy are just some of the hints that a restructuring of external (and internal) life systems is mandated. *Astrocycles* will explain cycles, such as the 172-year rhythm, which last renewed itself in 1820–21 as industrialism's momentum was becoming more apparent, and show how its quarter phases help build on the changes that now await us. The cycle involves the coming together of Uranus, the planet of revolution and awakening, and Neptune, the planet of ideals that dissolve with an eye toward eventual unification. These two planets meet every 172 years.

As you read this book, keep in mind that the rhythms I am speaking about—whether they be of 172 years, the 29.5 years of the Saturn Return, as well as smaller rhythms of 7 or 2 years—are all periods that are based on indisputable astronomical phenomena recognized throughout the world. Saturn's orbit is 29.5 years, whether the person talking is an astrologer or an astronomer. Astrologers have studied the activities and psychological states that occur with planets' "returns" in the same way that scientists first observed that high tides always correlate to specific lunar activity. The 29.5 days between one New Moon and another is an astronomical fact; astrologers, drawing on observation as well as conventional research that shows that the phases of the Moon correlate to increased rainfall, births, and other activity, view the 29.5-day period as being a truer "month" than the calendric month. Once the rhythm of the lunar month is understood, it can add perspective to one's short-term activities.

I've found over the years that being able to test astrological ideas upon immediate contact is something that cuts through the "to believe or not to believe" debate. The initial "tests" I ran when I first encountered astrology through a chance reading of a paperback while in my second year of college seemed to have validity in relation to my life, and that is what kept me investigating. This "discovery" of the more detailed aspects of astrology ironically coincided with a career in journalism. Like many budding journalists in the mid and latter 1970s, I saw Bob Woodward and Carl Bernstein's intrepid pursuit of a morally corrupt president as an indication that most everyone else had been lying to us, too. As I read more about astrology and saw it at work around me, I got the same feeling and sense of surprise, disbelief, and "aha, so that's what they're up to" that I get as I research and write about more conventional matters in my work as a journalist. My feeling about astrology in those early days was, "If this is true, this is a good story."

Over the past twelve years, as I've continued to track down more traditional good stories, I've led another life with astrology. My prime interest has been research, vocational consulting, and lecturing. I view astrology as a field of knowledge that helps inform a larger worldview rather than being a worldview in itself. And so I'm not one who spends much time planning the more routine details of my life by the stars. I prefer to look at the broad picture that astrology brings into focus.

Grant Lewi said that astrology "isn't something to believe in, it's something to know about." *Astrocycles* attempts to give intelligent people additional perspective rather than presenting a way of life.

The book is divided into four parts, including an appendix that presents more advanced astrological techniques for which an exact birthtime (preferably from your birth certificate) is necessary. Part I introduces cycle theory as it is being developed in areas ranging from biology to economics and presents the concept of astrocycles and the basic elements of astrology. Part II is a trip through the solar system that discusses cycles ranging from monthly trends, to the yearly rhythm that is renewed with each birthday, to the longer-term age cycles involving Saturn, Uranus, Neptune, and Pluto. Part III presents chapters on cycles as they affect politics and long-term socioeconomic trends. Part IV includes instructions for constructing a basic birth or natal chart. It also includes an ''advanced class'' for those who want to discover their personal Saturn ''boom and bust'' cycle and the way it relates to periods of major life transition. (Help is also provided for those without an exact birthtime.)

We are entering a time in which the fragmented worldview that separates human life from the rest of the Universe—and, more directly, personal aims from politics, economics from sociology, mathematics from poetry, daily life from spirituality—is shifting to a more integrated view. Synthesis is what Alvin Toffler says the next predominating worldview will seek. Humankind has been making tiny steps toward this anticipated paradigm shift, but the 1990s will see a greater push toward critical mass. ''The hundredth monkey'' phenomenon, which essentially says that at a certain point a given view is held by enough people to make a total shift in human consciousness occur, will awaken humankind to the future that awaits us. The concept is derived from a study conducted in the 1950s, and the story is that one monkey's technique of washing the dirt off sweet potatoes before eating was eventually picked up by other monkeys. At a certain point the one hundredth monkey adopted the habit and a shift occurred. In his book, *The Hundredth Monkey*, Ken Keyes writes, ''Then it happened. By that evening almost everyone in the tribe was washing sweet potatoes before eating them. The added energy of this hundredth monkey somehow created an ideological breakthrough!'' Soon monkeys throughout neighboring islands and on the mainland were also washing their potatoes.

This is how a new world consciousness, the paradigm shift, will come about. Nobody knows precisely when it will begin. Those who have christened the new age ''the Aquarian Age,'' in anticipation of the Vernal Equinox point eventually aligning with the Aquarius constellation after moving backward through Pisces, give a variety of starting dates, ranging from the eighteenth century to as many as two or three hundred years from now. The precise date even eludes astronomers because of disagreement about the technical measurements involving the constellations and other celestial points.

But we shouldn't be sidetracked by the technicalities. Those who have studied the calendars from Aztec and Mayan civilizations say that the Earth is now moving through the eye of the storm and that its inhabitants are being called upon to raise the planetary consciousness and vibrations and forge a relationship with higher intelligences in the solar system. *Astrocycles* introduces a field of knowledge waiting to be integrated into the new worldview that is forming. Awareness that the solar system, of which we are a part, provides signposts that can only deepen experience and understanding of life on Earth, both for individuals and for the collective. Astrology has in many ways been forced to live on the run during the last two thousand years, but it is one of the survival tools humankind must carry with it as it moves warily toward the twenty-first century.

Vivian B. Martin

ACKNOWLEDGMENTS

To Cheryl Woodruff, my editor whose Sun in Aries gives her the vision to see the possibilities and who is also blessed with the right doses of Earth sign business acumen and Water sign sensitivity to make it all come together.

To William Giese, whose cover art gives those of us on Earth a fabulous view of our solar system. To Tom Savarese, who came through with a much-needed ephemeris to make this journey easier for readers who are first-time travelers.

To Marie Brown, my literary agent, who was an important link in the chain of serendipitous events that brought this book to life.

To Arch Crawford, Barry Lynes, Bill Meridian, and Norman Winski, who shared pieces of their astroeconomic expertise.

To Capel McCutcheon, who gave special attention to the data for computerized birthcharts appearing in this book.

To the people who've shared stories about how they've weathered various life cycles.

To my siblings for a variety of reasons: Rutrell Yasin, my brother and writing colleague, who helped to provide important contacts; Valerie Martin, my baby sister, who helped research birthdates of famous people and prepare the manuscript; Maxine and Sonya Martin, who as artists understand the problem with "day jobs" and were supportive; Anthony Martin, who always remained open-minded and curious despite his Taurean practicality.

ASTROCYCLES

PART I

Cycles: Natural Rhythms

ONE

Cycles: A Matter of Time

In these waning years of the twentieth century, scientists are increasingly documenting the existence of cycles, the rhythms of expansion and contraction, peaks and troughs, underlying life throughout the Universe. Studies of biological clocks— blood-pressure and body-temperature rates that rise and fall at regular intervals in a 24-hour period, for instance—are the most familiar. But investigators are also discovering that rules of regularity guide the increase and decrease of phenomena as varied as marriage rates, animal populations, economic trends, agricultural crops, riots, full-scale wars, creativity, barometric pressure, river water tables, psychological moods, and real estate prices, to list just a smattering of the hundreds and hundreds of areas under study.

In the same way that a roller coaster would be nothing without the alternating steep hills and valleys that define it, the inherent structure of most phenomena is one of expansion, contraction, stabilization, and rebuilding phases that all grow out of one another at predictable and regular intervals. The cycle is self-sustaining and -perpetuating. Those who thought the freer life-style of the 1960s and 1970s would render marriage obsolete had only to wait a few years longer to gain perspective on an 18.2-year marriage cycle that federal census data make verifiable back to 1869. Marriage declines in popularity for nine years, hits a low, and then moves up, reaching a peak nine years later. It's all a matter of time.

Cro-Magnons of thirty-five thousand years ago carved the various quarters of the Moon's monthly cycle on animal horns and other artifacts, indicating an understanding and appreciation for the regular return of the Moon's crescent and of its full-grown phase in the sky. An impression of the regularity at work in the Universe no doubt could just as easily have been fostered by observing the change of seasons or the change between day and night. We may never know where humankind got its first cue, but there's no doubt that cyclical thinking is more than just an arbitrary concept.

Count how many times the word *cycle* is used in a week. It won't always sound the same way. Some people talk of "phases"; of coming back to square one; of always coming back to where they started; of booming and busting, then booming again.

In his book *Talking Straight*, corporate leader Lee Iacocca draws from this wisdom of the ages when he writes, "As far back as I can remember, I've always been a strong believer in the importance of cycles. You'd better try to understand them, because all of your timing and often your luck is tied up in them." Donald Trump's *Art of the Deal* casts a vote for the cyclical view as well. "Everything moves in cycles, and real estate is no different." Buying property during the low point of New York City's fiscal crisis in the 1970s helped put Trump on top when he hit the general upward trend in the 1980s. Before, of course, heading down again.

People concerned with personal planning may feel a certain affinity with rock diva Tina Turner, whose autobiography *I Tina*, written with rock critic Kurt Loder, speaks about a seven-year rhythm underlying the major stages in her life. "She began to see her life in Sevens. From birth to age seven, childhood . . . From 7 to 14, first love . . . and then meeting Ike and becoming a singer. From 21 to 28, falling in love with Ike and then becoming his prisoner . . . 28 to 35, she had now come to hate the man," Loder wrote.

Some may dismiss Turner's speculations about the number seven as superstition. But life-cycle researchers, particularly Yale psychiatrist Daniel J. Levinson, have found that people need to to make structural changes in their life approximately every seven years. Moreover, Levinson has shown that the critical ages outlined by Turner have special developmental significance for all people.

J. H. Douglas Webster, a medical researcher interested in cycles, studied diaries and monthly records of creative people and found that many of them—Victor Hugo, Wolfgang Amadeus Mozart, Katherine Mansfield, Henrik Ibsen, John Keats, Percy Shelley, Anne Brontë, and Franz Schubert, among others—had peaks of creativity approximately every 7.6 months. Daydreamers, meanwhile, don't necessarily have overworked imaginations; they're responding to a rhythm in which brain patterns and other inner stimuli cause the mind to drift toward other realms every ninety minutes, a time period that is also evident in sleep cycles, the recurrence of hunger pangs, and the craving for oral satisfaction (a toothpick, thumb, gum, or cigarette) every ninety minutes.

Real estate investors can benefit from examination of a general national average 17- to 18-year cycle in both real estate transfers and construction activity. Cycle researchers correctly predicted the lows of 1974 and 1990 and also foresaw the mid-1980s boom, and are projecting a high for late 1993 and early 1994. Bull markets and optimism can distort the picture, and local and regional markets often lag behind the national "big picture," but cyclicity is the rule. While the force of the San Francisco earthquake in October 1989 that killed more than two hundred people took most people by surprise, cycle researchers, who noted that the weekend prior to the earthquake had one of the highest tides in the decade, were in the uncomfortable position of seeing some of their worst predictions (and fears) come true.

Cycles: A Matter of Time

The *Random House Dictionary of the American Language* says a cycle is a "recurring period of time . . . in which certain events or phenomena repeat themselves in the same order and the same intervals." The human heart, which beats on a one-second interval, and breathing, which occurs at six-second intervals, are among the more precise examples of periodicity, a concept synonymous with cyclicity. Visually, a series of similar-sized waves with peaks and troughs spaced at regular points best illustrates the idea. *Kyclos*, or circle, the Greek word from which *cycle* is derived, implies regularity. The trip around the circle presumably will always be the same length and duration, but a circle doesn't accurately portray the unit of time that will be of such concern throughout *Astrocycles*.

Yet, no natural cycles, not even those that never deviate or have no irregularities, are as precise as the musician's metronome. As those studying fertility and other issues related to the menstrual cycle have learned, few women are as regular as the average 29.5-day rhythm from one New Moon to another. Since the 1930s, the existence of a "desire" rhythm within the menstrual period has been observed. Dr. Marie Stopes, a medical researcher, discovered that women have an increased sexual desire just before menstruation begins and again eight or nine days after the end of menstrual flow. A University of Pennsylvania study by Rex Hersey was among the first to verify the existence of a male emotional cycle lasting four to six weeks. Feeling elated (or content, agitated, or sad) today would correspond to feelings about five weeks prior and five weeks hence. Hersey also found a four-to-six-week emotional rhythm for women that exists apart from their menstrual cycle. Whether there is truly a precise connection between the menstrual/emotional rhythm is not certain; subsequent chapters in this book will allow both men and women to examine this matter as it pertains to individual emotions.

Longer-term "moods" that relate to peaceful or riotous times among the masses also respond to rules of periodicity. A. L. Tchievsky, the late Russian historian, traced historical events from 500 B.C. to A.D. 1922 and found a rhythm of human excitability that peaks every eleven years. Tchievsky left limited files and was circumspect in some of his writings because of the repressed environment in which he worked. Nonetheless it's interesting to note that Tchievsky uncovered about nine peaks (toward the end of the decade) in each century. Tchievsky held that each eleven-year period has four phases: The first phase, of approximately three years, hosts a minimum of excitability and is characterized by peace, passivity; during the following two years excitement grows; the third phase contains the maximum excitability. But while revolutions and wars abound, some of the era's most pressing concerns are met. Riots and anarchy are the catalysts for change. The final period, lasting three years, shows a gradual decrease in excitability that eventually leads to apathy. A recent example of the eleven-year cycle at work would be the buildup in the sixties and heightened third-phase activity, followed by the apathy of the seventies with the rhythm building up again to its peak around the time of the hostage takeover and revolutions of the late 1970s. An apathetic phase set in with the early 1980s, with tension building again as the decade ended.

Though the eleven-year rhythm deals with approximate time periods, it, too, adheres to laws of periodicity. A similar idea was developed by the late Raymond Wheeler, a professor at the University of Kansas. Wheeler found that there were 1,000- and 500-year climatic cycles that, in addition to relating to the earth's overall temperatures, also spoke to trends in human activity. Especially warm periods, such as the Warm/Dry phase in force in the 1930s, relate to the uprise of dictators and other authoritarian terrors visited upon the world's citizens. Cold periods cause creativity and individuality to flourish. Because we are currently in a transition into a cold period, Wheeler's theories point to a flourishing of culture and the promotion of human rights and collective goals for humankind. The transition also coincides with the end of a 500-year-cycle around the year 2,000. The trends point toward a new world order, but don't look for leadership to come from Washington. Writing in the early 1950s, Wheeler pronounced unequivocally that Western civilization would decline in importance and that the new world would belong to Asia.

Wheeler's work extends backward to 600 B.C. The rather uneven size of each of the phases can make it difficult to visualize a rhythm at work. However, Wheeler's idea embraces many of the arguments underlying Arthur M. Schlesinger, Jr.'s theory of fifteen-to-twenty-year "cycles of history" that favor public-policy periods like the 1960s and then shift into private-interest periods such as the 1980s. Schlesinger's historical rhythms will be discussed in more detail later on.

Numerous other long-term cycles are being explored, including more esoteric theories, such as those based on the Mayan calendar, which holds that Earth civilizations as we know them will dissolve through the 1990s, during which time Earthlings will become more attuned to the presence of a galactic intelligence. These theories are introduced in slightly more detail in Part III. For now it is important just to note that the cyclic view expands to include a range of worldviews and areas of life.

The Foundation for the Study of Cycles

Since 1941 the Foundation for the Study of Cycles, which recently moved from Pittsburgh to Irvine, California, has been a clearinghouse for cycle research from around the world. To date, the foundation has verified the existence of more than four thousand cycles, some of the most common rhythms being the 9.3 years/18.6-year rhythm noted earlier for real estate and marriage ups and downs. Cycles of 9.6 to 9.7 years are the most common on file with the foundation. Cotton prices, wheat acreage, and abundance in the population of lynx, owls, hawks, and grouse in Canada are examples of many different expressions of the nine-year cycle. Cycles of 18.2 to 18.6 years are also especially fruitful in such areas as real estate, building activity, and wholesale prices.

"The student of periodic rhythms in human affairs has a tool which the Law of Averages . . . puts into its hands. If trends have continued for decades, or if the oscillation of cycles around the trend have repeated themselves so many times and so regularly that the rhythm cannot be the result of chance, it is unwise to ignore the probability that those behaviors will continue . . ."

So wrote the foundation's founder, Edward R. Dewey, in *The Science of Prediction*.

It was Dewey, a Harvard-trained economist, who ensured that "cycle research" would become a field of science in its own right. Dewey was among those who wanted deeper answers to questions about why a Great Depression could occur and grind the American economy to a halt. As he amassed information, Dewey became increasingly in awe of the forces at work in the Universe. That many cycles—for instance, 9.6-year cycles involving various crops and animal populations—turn (reach highs and lows) at the same time at the same latitudes, and also turn later as one moves southward toward the equator, is just one of the findings that only made him more intrigued and interested in pursuing cycles further. Dewey died without finding out the cause of the cycles he discovered, but his search continues. The foundation he left behind receives support from those in academia, as well as business leaders such as Chicago millionaire W. Clement Stone who, through the years, has unabashedly spoken of how knowledge of cycles has helped him get rich.

For this reason, it is probably fitting that one of the most active areas of cycle research involves business and the economy. Since the mid-nineteenth century, scholars, economists, and others have talked of business and economic cycles. Bona fide rhythms range from 40 to 41 months, 5 years, a 7-to-11-year rhythm; 9-, 18-, and 22-year cycles. Prior to his eight-year tenure as head of the Federal Reserve, Paul A. Volcker penned a discussion about a ten-year business rhythm and its implications for government policies. But the very rules of cyclicity raise questions about the extent of influence that governments or business leaders truly have on the economy. The economy would seem subject to the same "seasonal" phases affecting the earth: spring follows winter, winter follows fall, which moves out of summer that is born of spring. Contractions are needed to realign forces, to strip a situation to bare essentials before rebuilding and expanding again. The work of Nikolai Kondratieff, who detected a 54-year economic cycle in industrial nations, reflects this understanding. Like Tchievsky, Kondratieff was forced to work cautiously out of fear of Russian leaders who didn't care for his conclusions. Kondratieff was sent to Sibera, but his work is being reviewed and taken further by researchers around the world. Those who support his theories most staunchly contend the depressionlike conditions that Kondratieff's theories would have set in the 1970s did occur and continue to be upon us, despite modern-day manipulations that camouflage the extent of some economic downturns until it is too late.

And herein lies a major misconception about cycles. Humankind, though enterprising, does not create cycles. Oh, we can have five-year plans and attempt to impose those on top of our lives, but the plan won't take if five years isn't the underlying trend. Contrariwise, as the cycle research collected by the foundation shows, a war or particularly benevolent government policy might distort a cycle like the one involving real-estate trends for a year or two, but then something clicks and the true cycle overtakes those aberrations on the graph. This is why Dewey and other cycle researchers only accepted as valid cycles that repeated themselves 10 to 15 times. An enterprising person taken with the idea of cycles might discover that there were flu epidemics in 1972, 1976, and 1980, but these would not necessarily constitute a cycle. Cycle researchers would want to know what happened every four years prior to 1972 and every four years after 1980. Like the body rhythms that we can alter only slightly—day larks whose body temperatures decrease as the day progresses will never be night owls, and night owls will always prefer to sleep during the day—cycles are self-sustaining, and the seeds for each bust and boom are contained within the cycle.

The Natural Tendency of Things

In speaking of the natural flow of life, cycles contain the secrets of the structure and process of change. A single cell, an economy, a small business, an individual—all are organisms that move through identifiable phases in just the same way as the ever-changing Moon. The principles that hold the organism together will always remain the same, but this continuity is contained within an unfolding process that illustrates that life is neither linear nor static.

Time, which can't be possessed, has a nature that is constantly changing. If this were not so, then the 9.6-year rhythm identified in the life span of stock prices or various animal populations would not be so specific. Why not nine years, or eight years, or why doesn't the cycle just round itself off to an easy ten? But it doesn't do that. It renews itself every 9.6 years, and each time it does, these phenomena go through predictable stages related to their process of growth. Cycles are broken down into phases, intervals, seasons. Time and cycles don't stand still, even if the changes within them are subtle. Each wave builds upon what went immediately before; the highs and lows take their cue from an internal dynamic within the cycle so that the true past is never revisited. Although the marital-rate cycle has been evident for nearly a century and a half, the highs and lows conform to cyclical rules, but also reflect the changing nature of time. As a result, the highs of the marital cycle that will be reached in the early 1990s will not be as high as the highs of decades past, while the low points we will see at the end of the century will be lower than troughs of decades past.

Cycles work within other cycles and in conjunction with trends, which are the long-term patterns that we in Western society are so often accused of never stretching our necks to

see. Like subways and connecting flights, cycles help phenomena move toward the long-term trend, which more often than
not remains hidden from view. It may not reveal itself until
scores and scores of cyclic renewals; decades and decades,
hundreds of years. Most trends ultimately result in an entity
dying out and giving way to something else. An example is
the way various manufacturing industries that were so potent
in the nineteenth century are dying out, giving way to service
economies. As the industries are on their final legs, the growth-
and-expansion portions of the cycle are becoming smaller and
smaller. And those who in the late 1980s were viewing the
bank failures, spiraling domestic and trade deficits, and limited
production growths as evidence that America's economy is in
need of an overhaul, were basing some of their ideas on the
fact that no system lasts forever.

Pinpointing Specific Cycles

But before these "ends" come, there are a series of recurring
peaks and troughs to move through. Studying the timing of
these cycles and the accompanying phases can provide perspective similar to a road map, which includes the upcoming
mountains, highways, and detours to be encountered in the
journey. The longer view is regarded as being more important
than short-term gratification and remedies, an attitude that can
only enhance activities for the individual and society as a whole.
Dewey has helped lay the groundwork for locating cycles
by applying scientific method to such studies. *Astrocycles* is
also concerned with specificity in the determination of cycles.
But it seeks to take the approach of Dewey and other researchers
farther in two different ways. First, the cycles presented in this
book will have direct applicability to all areas of an individual's
life, from monthly moods, to long-term changes in life direction, to special insights into the political and socioeconomic
trends under way all around us. Second, you will be given
specific road signs that will allow you to plot these rhythms of
boom and bust as far back into the past or future as you desire,
sometimes locating turning points within specific months. A
frustrating aspect of the "cyclical" view taken by so many
people—whether in regard to trends in business or to their
personal lives—is that while a rhythm may be sensed, it usually

can't be pinpointed or defined. To some people a cycle simply indicates the end of one activity and beginning of another rather than the periodicity emphasized here.

For our purposes, and especially because we're concerned about forecasting future cycles, it is important to maintain stricter guidelines. Earlier, the more quantifiable cycles were described as being akin to waves. Most people have seen these ideal cycles drawn in magazines and annual reports; the graphs with waves and several peaks and troughs that register uniform highs and lows. When the data of what actually happened are thrown onto the graph, we often have the same set of waves, with the same general outline, but peaks and troughs may be a bit early or late at some points, and the extent of the highs and lows may vary. The important message is that the general "wave" outline, or direction, has been borne out.

After learning about Dewey's scrutiny of proposed cycles— and the foundation's rejection of many proposed cycles—it might seem nearly impossible to chart specific cycles in any given individual's life or in the world at large. A human life is full of many intangible phases and moments that don't appear measurable in the same way that one could measure cycles of the water table levels of the St. Louis River. You might think that it's best just to chalk up those two-to-three-year job changes you go through to random restlessness, not something within a life that calls out for new activity and projects every two years. Maybe talk of seven-year itches means that we're a little more superstitious than we'd like to admit.

Astrocycles is about natural rhythms ranging from a month in the life of an individual to hundreds of years in the life of a society. All of these rhythms can be charted in advance, which gives us the opportunity to take advantage of the accompanying phases of contraction or expansion. The rhythms are as natural as the seasons, the daily rising and setting of the Sun, the phases of the Moon. As we head toward the twenty-first century, science is increasingly presenting data that suggest that we take some cues from ancient civilizations and look out on the horizon and other parts of the sky at some of the phenomena that, in their keeping of ever-precise schedules, do more than drop hints about cycles moving through all of life.

TWO

Astrocycles

In its two hundred years of publication, the *Old Farmer's Almanac* has distinguished itself with year-in-advance weather predictions. Informal surveys in various regional newspapers and other periodicals have often credited the *Almanac* with 80 percent accuracy, a better track record than high-powered government-financed weather bureaus, whose forecasts become increasingly vague with each day they attempt to extend their predictions.

What is the secret of the *Almanac* makers' success? They're discreet up in Dublin, New Hampshire, but editor Susan Peery reveals that "natural cycles" are at the heart of the "secret formula" that almanac founder Robert B. Thomas developed and passed down to the *Almanac*'s meteorologists. The tradition continues. Dr. Richard Head, formerly a chief scientist with NASA, looks to the recurring sunspots—dark splotches that break out on the Sun on a regular basis—and other recurring astronomical phenomena to guide his almanac forecasts. Says Peery, Dr. Head believes that the astronomical phenomena "are the main determinants of our weather. Because these cycles are predictable, we believe that the weather associated with them is also predictable."

In other words, the weather-prediction secret lies out there in the cyclical solar system of which we are a part. As Mark

Twain wrote, "By the Law of Periodical Repetition, everything which has happened once must happen again and again and again—and not capriciously, but at regular periods . . . the same Nature which delights in periodical repetition in the skies is the Nature which orders the affairs of the earth." If recurring astronomical phenomena correlate to weather—as those affiliated with NASA apparently do more than suggest—couldn't the same principle be applied to other recurring phenomena on earth?

Consider this:

J. Danforth Quayle at age twenty-nine stumbled onto the news that Republicans in his congressional district were looking for a candidate to campaign for a vacancy in the House of Representatives. Quayle volunteered and launched a new career—actually, his first real career—and by now the rest of the story is known. Michael Dukakis was elected to his state senate at twenty-nine, whereas the death of a major love caused Abraham Lincoln to slip into a depression at this age.

This age found Spike Lee, the young filmmaker, taking his first major risk: Creating, producing, directing, and acting in his first national film, *She's Gotta Have It.* Playwright Wendy Wasserstein was getting national attention for her *Isn't It Romantic,* effectively launching her career as an artist. A number of popular entertainers we've now become used to seeing—Tom Hanks, Cyndi Lauper, Oprah Winfrey—got big breaks at twenty-nine to thirty years of age that allowed them to show off all the work they'd been doing in their twenties.

But this age period in life isn't always so wonderful. Mary Beth Whitehead, the infamous surrogate mother of Baby M, gave birth to the little girl two weeks before her twenty-ninth birthday and spent the next year in a custody fight with the adoptive parents. Steven Jobs, wizard behind Apple Computers, was forced out of managerial authority at the company he founded and subsequently resigned from at age thirty.

Readers of popular psychology books will quickly recognize these "turning-thirty" stories as inevitable points of transition on the road to becoming an adult. The average person doesn't make transitions as publicized as those of celebrities, but they nonetheless mark the period with career changes, special health problems, the beginnings and endings of important relationships, and other commitments they will build on in their thirties. Yale psychiatrist Daniel J. Levinson, who has studied age cycles, tracked the lives of forty men and discovered a period of transition that "typically began at age 28, with a range of 26 to 29. It ended between 31 and 34, most often at 33."

Like the sunspot cycles and other regularly recurring natural phenomena associated with specific weather patterns, turning 30 correlates with specific astronomical activity. As stated earlier, every 29.5 years the planet Saturn returns to the point in the sky it tenanted 29.5 years ago. The completion of this full orbit means that Saturn is back at the point where it was located when those who are 28 to 30 years old were born. Chronos (Saturn's name in Greek mythology), god of sowing, reaping, and the passage and results of time, presides over a class reunion of sorts.

But the purpose of this reunion isn't to give an accounting of the first thirty years of life in order to impress other people. As Saturn returns, people find that they've been spending too much time thinking and caring about the role others have assigned them. Now it's time to strip off these fake identities and restructure their lives. It's time to get closer to their true identities and find ways of preserving and further developing them as the move is made into the thirties and full-fledged adulthood—rather than the dress rehearsal of the twenties—and deeper life commitments begin.

Drawing such connections between what Levinson has referred to as the "age thirty crisis" and the 29.5-year orbit of Saturn may seem subjective for some, particularly if they quibble with the concept of conventional life cycles as documented by psychologists and others. But the planets in our solar system offer other types of examples.

David Williams, a retired naval officer and former Con Edison executive, conducted extensive research through which he discovered that 80 percent of the time since 1792, major dips in stock prices have occurred every 9.3 years, when the tilt of the Moon's orbit crosses 0 degrees Aries or Libra. In 1974, noting that the Moon's orbit would cross this point in July 1978, Williams accurately predicted that a major drop would follow. During October 1978 it dropped 14 percent in two weeks in what became known as the October Massacre. Noting that the 0 Aries/Libra points had also been crossed prior to major drops in 1932 and 1970, Williams described the recurring 9.3 rhythm as an "advance warning indicator." His summation of data noted that the next low point was due December 1987, a date that, like others on his list, showed that even the months before the indicator is reached can be viewed as "borrowed time."

History repeats itself in many other ways.

Roughly every twenty years the political and legislative climate in the United States alternates from public-oriented and public-spirited policies to those aimed at promoting private interests. Compare the differences between the 1980s and of the 1960s. Midway through each of these twenty-year periods—in this case 1970 and 1990—there are discernible attempts to balance some of the more aggressive initiatives launched at the beginning of the twenty-year cycle. Often, Schlesinger found, the moderating actions are necessitated by socioeconomic circumstances such as the Great Depression, which required a hands-on approach that differed sharply from the laissez-faire 1920s.

Schlesinger's cycle moves quite evenly with the coming together (or conjunction) of the planets Jupiter and Saturn every twenty years, most recently in 1980–81. Jupiter (expansion and liberalism) and Saturn (restrictions and conservatism) make a 180-degree angle (definitely at odds from one another) ten years after the conjunction, forcing the expansion and contraction principles to negotiate a more balanced expression of the twenty-year trend. The period of late fall 1989 through 1990 represents the negotiation period for the 1980–81 cycle.

The stock market, psychology, history, weather—all have been shown to display cycles synchronous with natural planetary rhythms. While Williams describes his work as "astro-economics," his studies, the "secret" weather formula, the Saturn/turning-30 connections, as well as any other planetary cycle with terrestrial connections, can be placed under the broader heading of "Astrocycles." The term embraces the astronomical phenomena and their terrestrial correspondences.

The Pattern of Astrocycles

Unlike man-made "cycles," such as annual holidays, Astrocycles have their basis in the reality of the solar system, where planets stick to schedules so exact that once the general orbit lengths are known, it's almost possible to throw away the printed schedule. Right around the annual birthday, the Sun is always at the approximate position where it was located at birth. The Moon's orbit is 27.5 days; it moves in tandem with the Sun and forms a majestic Full Moon every 29.5 days. Jupiter takes 11.8 years to go from one point and return again, Saturn 29.5 years. While Neptune takes 168 years to complete a full trip, rest assured that it is going about its business, even though it'll take several generations to ensure the job is done. In the meantime Neptune meets up with Saturn every thirty-six years, with Jupiter every thirteen years, and with Mars about every two years, while the Sun, Mercury, and Venus meet up with Neptune annually.

These are indisputable astronomical facts. The Astrocycles concept, as demonstrated by the almanac forecasters, determines the pattern of activities that recur simultaneously with the recurring astronomical phenomena. An Astrocycle researcher, finding that Jupiter and Uranus come together every fourteen years, would determine the years and approximate dates—the relatively slow movement of these planets would cause the influence to span throughout most of the year—and look for a pattern in the activity. Definite patterns would emerge. Moving back in history, the Jupiter/Uranus configuration would show up as entrepreneurial energy was being renewed in 1983; men walking on the Moon in 1969; invention/expansion activities like McDonald's launching a fast-food revolution in 1955; Pearl Harbor, World War II, and defense-industry expansion in 1941; Lindbergh's transatlantic crossing, Babe Ruth, and other heroics in 1927; World War I began in 1914 and major strikes and rebellions such as those of the Boers and Boxers were among the outbreaks and out-of-control expansion efforts in 1900.

The configuration can be tracked back through other centuries as well. It showed up after the French and Indian War and the American Revolution. But an exhaustive list isn't needed for our purposes. The fourteen-year rhythm has already revealed itself to be connected to attempts to break out of routine and tradition, as well as activities that can get out of control, unfettered growth, recklessness.

What has just been offered is a simple introduction to the workings of Astrocycles. As the subject is explored in more detail, it becomes more complex, particularly as various cycles are shown to be the result of more than one cycle working simultaneously. The rhythms, meanwhile, must also be monitored between each successive renewal. We'd want to check in on our 14-year Jupiter/Uranus configuration halfway—seven years—into each 14-year period because the midpoint of any rhythm, like the fall harvest season six months after the spring planting, is a turning point, a reckoning phase in the rhythm. Also important are the quarter periods or phases, which fall 3.5 years after the 14-year cycle begins, and then 3.5 years before it ends. That sort of fine-tuning is a skill that will be explored later in this book. For now the concept of the larger 14-year rhythm, when the cycle begins, is the most important point to stay fixed on.

Early Precedents

Humankind was making organized efforts to find correlations between celestial activity and earthly concerns in the second millennium B.C., which is the period during which scholars believe that full-time omen watchers began developing the "Enuma Anu Enlil," a series of cuneiform tablets excavated from the site of Assyrian King Ashurbanipal's palace at Nineveh in 1853. The text was subsequently found during excavations of other Mesopotamian sites, indicating its popularity as a source for omen interpretation. Historians infer that Ashurbanipal, who ruled in the seventh century B.C., apparently employed full-time omen watchers. Upon observing various planetary phenomena, they would search the "Enuma" to guide interpretation of upcoming events or activities that would affect the king and the state. One of the "Venus" tablets now in the British Museum uses the appearance of Venus for three days in the west and its subsequent reappearance in the east as an omen of rain.

While these early tablets demonstrate what scholars say is rather crude astronomy and mathematics, more detailed tables—and hence more detailed correlations between celestial and earthly activity—started showing up as the fourth century gave way to the third century B.C. The almanac-type publications, which list astronomical and meteorological data, commodity prices, and important political and religious events, were found in Babylon, now under Greek rule. This more extensive codification presumably made it possible for more detailed Astrocycle studies to be made. By the time the political and socially conscious Jupiter and Saturn came together for their twenty-year reunion and shared the sky with an eclipse and lineup of Mercury, Venus, and Mars near the eclipse in the spring of 7 B.C., sky watchers thought an important child was to be born and started out toward Bethlehem. Today several planetariums around the country produce slide shows that show what the sky would have looked like to the omen watchers and also suggest that the star seen "rising in the east"—the Christmas star—was most likely a combination of the eclipse and several planets sharing the same portion of the sky.

Fine-tuning Cycle Research

A. L. Tchievsky, the Russian historian mentioned earlier, left behind extensive studies of eleven-year cycles of human excitability. He used the eleven/twenty-two-year sunspot rhythm as an indicator of the trends. The periods when sunspots were at their maximum every eleven years—the official high was expected to occur in spring 1990—relate to anxious times. This was certainly the case at the end of the 1970s and 1960s, two recent maximum periods. People are more complacent during the eleven-year low points, such as the fall of 1986.

Tchievsky also linked maximum sunspot periods to epidemics (cholera, typhus, small pox) that struck around the world in eleven-year cycles through the nineteenth century. More sophisticated medical practice has made this pattern less visible in the twentieth century. Work by Tokyo biologist M. Takata, in the 1930s, showed a connection between sunspot cycles and other activity on the Sun and changes in blood-serum levels. Further related research around the world in the 1940s and 1950s caused Takata to conclude that a cosmic connection was the only solution to the puzzle. "Man is a living sun dial," he said. The changes in blood-serum levels, which Takata measured through a chemical procedure, show how biological systems adapt to their environments. Sunspots and other disturbances on the Sun in the second half of the twentieth century have been correlated to a sudden increase in health problems, blood clotting, industrial and automobile accidents, and economic trends, carrying on ideas that had also captured the interest of Uranus discoverer Sir William Herschel, who examined connections between sunspots and wheat prices.

Though the precise cause of sunspots has not been determined, among the more popular theories are those that link the increase and decrease in sunspot activity to various combinations of recurring planetary orbits. In other words, various planetary combinations correlate to sunspots, which, in turn, relate to specific terrestrial activity. The cycles all reverberate in and out of one another. While the connections outlined so far have only involved the Sun, the Moon is just as popular among researchers.

Arnold Lieber, a Miami psychiatrist, has found that more homicides occur at Full Moon than other lunar phases. A study conducted by Frank J. Guarino for his master's thesis examines the Dow Jones index and lunar phases. Both of these studies will be discussed in Chapter 6. The movement of the Moon during the day and month is increasingly being linked to weather fluctuations, particularly rainfall. In an article in *Weatherwise*, a meteorological journal, Alfred K. Blackadar, professor of meteorology at Pennsylvania State University, provided a computer program for tracking the Moon's position for studying its weather connections. "Twenty-five years ago most scientists scoffed at the idea that the moon and the weather might be related. Today, many scientists are cautiously open-minded on the subject." Blackadar briefly notes research findings showing that precipitation at each of the 1,100 stations in the United States from 1900 to 1950 was heaviest during the three days after the New Moon and Full Moon. Stations with records dating back prior to 1900 also show wet New and Full Moon periods, while studies in New Zealand produced similar results. A study of thunderstorms from 1953 to 1963 in the United States showed this phenomenon occurred most frequently during the two days following the Full Moon. The Full Moon has been viewed as a possible trigger for earthquakes as well—one occurred three days prior to the October 17, 1989, San Francisco quake—but no certain pattern has been determined. Some investigators have found Uranus at its highest point of the day during the moments of a quake, but the pattern is not consistent.

Solar and lunar eclipses have also been studied. Archibald Crawford, who got his initial training as a technician for Merrill Lynch, was juggling a number of conventional and astronomical techniques back on August 8, 1987, when his newsletter, *Crawford Perspectives*, informed subscribers that a series of planetary configurations indicated a "wild speculative ride . . . and we pick the top for August 24, give or take three days. Then a horrendous crash into the Eclipse of the Sun." The top came August 25. On October 10, four days after a lunar eclipse and eighteen days following the solar eclipse, Crawford issued a memo headlined, "No Sign of Bottom." Drawing on past history of eclipses and recurring planetary configurations, Crawford wrote,

> Look for a temporary Low on the 22nd or 23rd of this month [October] followed by a top on Wednesday, the 28th. Then down again into a more stable formation in the first two weeks of November. Our technical tools are still not showing any improvement!!! Oscillators . . . show up as deeply oversold and we feel that this condition will mirror that of the Bull Market rise, inversely, of course. That means they will continue oversold all the way down. . . . Continue to short any rallies until October 22.

Some can quibble with the exactitude of the dates that Crawford offered, but clients who took his advice would have been better off than those relying on more conventional prognosticators, more than 95 percent of whom were looking for the bull market to move unfettered through 1987. Crawford's techniques are assessed as having been more reliable than the conventional wisdom of John Rosenthal, who tracked the advice of several Wall Street prognosticators in *A Fool and His Money*. Further evidence of how far the observational practices of the Mesopotamian cycle researchers have come can be found in the work of Bill Meridian, the pseudonym of a vice president at a national brokerage firm, who also includes astronomical cycles in his analysis. Meridian helped develop a computer program, Astroanalyst, that shows the correlations between Dow Jones activity and every planetary configuration back through 1789. The information ranges from short-term cycles to longer-term configurations, such as the Jupiter/Pluto conjunction that occurs every thirteen years. During the summer of 1988, Meridian was giving special attention to a cycle that was renewing itself every twenty-two days, as Mercury drew into a configuration with Saturn and Uranus. That Saturn and Uranus are only conjunct every forty-five to forty-six years, as they were in the summer of 1988, shows the complexity of such research as some cycles seem to die out or are overtaken by more potent ones. Meridian began recording such data manually in 1973. The computer program, developed with Astrolabe of Orleans, Massachusetts, will now make inquiries easier and help modern-day researchers get closer to the X factor for which the Mesopotamians searched. Meridian publishes a newsletter, *Cycle Research*, and his economic perspective will be discussed in more detail in Part III of this book.

Edward R. Dewey, the cycle research pioneer introduced in the previous chapter, conducted similar research and was aware of connections made between phenomena such as real estate and stock prices and the nine/eighteen-year rhythm created by the crossing of the ecliptic by the Moon's orbit. He also studied reports connecting sunspots to planetary activity, and planetary orbits to other terrestrial phenomena. But he wasn't entirely convinced.

Dewey, after considerable research, didn't necessarily think most of the cycles could be tied to the singular orbit of one planet, or even the intersecting orbits of two planets, but wasn't closed to the possibility of intricate webs of cycles related to a variety of planetary, sunspot, and still-to-be determined cosmic phenomena. Jeffrey Horowitz, former executive director of the foundation that Dewey founded, says in a letter to the author that astrophysical cycles are a "major interest of study. We are continually comparing the frequencies of astrophysical cycles to terrestrial cycles. Although we have no clear statistical correlation at this time, there does clearly seem to be some kind of association between the two."

Astrology—A Science by Any Other Name

The obstacles to finding statistically significant connections between planetary activity (astrophysical) and terrestrial events extend beyond the complexity of the subject matter. Most conventional cycle researchers set off on their investigations with presumptions that limit the scope (and findings) of their labor. At the heart of the problem is the cycle researchers' limited knowledge about the history behind cosmic-cycle inquiries and the way the topic relates to (is actually part of) the broader field of astrology. And it is in their relationship that we find a controversy rages.

While the astroeconomists encountered in this chapter—David Williams, Arch Crawford, and Bill Meridian, for instance—are astrologers and use the symbolism and other practices adopted by the field to enhance their conventional work, most cycle researchers believe that they and astrologers share no common ground.

Full Moon researcher Arnold Lieber, who has presented data on the increases in homicides at Full Moons that connect with astrological tradition, is typical in his efforts to distance himself from astrology. A Connecticut psychiatrist I contacted for information about his work linking lunar phases and biological changes said he feared having his research discussed in a book that dealt with astrology because his attempts to receive funding were already hindered by colleagues' belief that his work smacked of astrology. Frank Guarino, whose master's thesis at Pace University showed links between lunar phases and the Dow Jones Average, observed that the discovery of the connection between geomagnetic activity and the world of finance "has been retarded by its similarity to astrology. However, just as alchemy was transformed into chemistry, perhaps astrology may yield to biomagnetics and science." But today most of those who try to make connections between astronomical phenomena and terrestrial activity refuse to look to the past and acknowledge their heritage.

Gifts from the Greeks

It was the Greeks who invented astrology as it is now in use in the Western world.

As most of the handful of astrological history books attest, astrology began thriving throughout the Tigris-Euphrates valley in third century B.C. The Babylonians were especially advanced and shared their knowledge with inquiring Greeks. Numerous texts credit Berossus the Chaldean with introducing astrology to the Greeks around the third century through a school on the island of Kos, which was also the home of Hippocratic medicine. By the time the Greeks began conquering societies in Egypt and the neighboring Tigris-Euphrates valley, the Egyptians had divided day and night into twelve hours each and created the twelve-month year, while the libraries of Babylonian kings were full of astrological literature. The Greeks, who oversaw the creation of Alexandria as an intellectual capital of the ancient world, acted as synthesizers of the different astrologies they encountered; their development of more scientific astronomy (in contrast to its cruder prototypes in Mesopotamian society) gave them the tools for dividing the sky and creating horoscopes similar to the ones pictured in this chapter.

Classics scholar Jim Tester, observing that those who revere the ancient Greeks for their rational approach to life might find it hard to accept that these were the very same people who created astrology as it is still practiced today, says it's important to understand astrology and its appeal to the Greek mind.

> It was not the uneducated and superstitious who accepted and developed it. It was the philosophers, like Plato, who prepared the ground, and the Stoics—who were among the greatest logicians and physicists of their times—who most fully worked it into their system. It was the doctors and the scientists, like Theophrastus, who accepted it and developed its associations with medicine and plants and stones, and with the science of alchemy, which was then nearer to chemical technology than to the magical search for the philosopher's stone it has become.

The Greeks' extensive curiosity and keen critical nature allowed them to separate the more scientific pieces of the Babylonians' work from the more ridiculous, Tester argues. When astrology, with its thesis of connections between observable astronomical phenomena with terrestrial activities, was stacked alongside many of the religions of the day, Tester observes that it would have appeared highly rational to the ancient Greeks.

Rome's military contact with Greece resulted in astrology being spread to Italy by the second century B.C. Jim Tester reports that unrest among the lower classes and the large immigrant slave population caused city leaders to ban astrologers from Rome and Roman Italy in 139 B.C.

Astrology, however, could not be contained. It thrived in centers of learning such as Alexandria and spread to Spain and other parts of Europe. The mid–second century A.D. was the era of Ptolomy, the famous Greek geographer and astronomer who followed up his *Almagest* astronomical text with *Tetrabiblos*, a work that is still read for insights into the way astrology had developed by this period of history. A major turning point in astrology's shifting locale took place in the sixth century as Greek astrologers and intellectuals, often in an attempt to avoid the growing hostile Christian environment, headed east toward Persia and Syria. Tester holds that these people adopted Greek astrology and spread it to other Arab groups, most widely during the eighth and ninth centuries. Arabs brought various techniques to astrology as well, and when they brought astrology back into the West, where practice was at its most dormant during the tenth and much of the eleventh centuries, they offered what Tester describes as a "late Greek astrology."

Astrology was debated, ridiculed, and banned as it reared its head in public again. One of the most infamous series of attacks was Giovanni Pico della Mirandola's twelve-volume attack. The criticism came at a time when astrologers were in their prime at the Italian court. Pico viewed astrologers' competitions for princes' patronage and favor as fraudulent because he felt astrology was a false science. Yet even as he attacked the application of astrology to the lives of individuals, it should be noted that Pico accepted the idea that the planets have an effect upon weather and medicine. It seems that even astrology's most vociferous critics weren't able to wage a full frontal attack against it.

The Renaissance gave the field a new life and increased acceptability among academic circles and the educated populace that it hasn't seen since. However, the discoveries of Newton and the shift in the worldview toward a more mechanistic view of the Universe increasingly caused society to adopt a rationalistic approach that was unable to integrate astrology into its philosophy.

As recently as the seventeenth century, when Johannes Kepler tracked rainfall and other activities and noted their correlations to planetary phenomena, the mathematicians/scientists of the day were unembarrassed about what it was they were studying. Kepler's "On the More Certain Fundamentals of Astrology" removes any doubt that, telescopic inventions and the development of "astronomy" aside, there was more to be done in the area of astrology. The almanac makers of the seventeenth and eighteenth centuries—including Benjamin Franklin's pseudonymous Richard Saunders—would keep astrology in front of the general populace. Such pamphlets were all that many people read, which is why Benjamin Franklin chose to make Poor Richard offer bons mots of self-improvement to his readers.

Some astrologers claim that several of the United States'

Founding Fathers were astrologers and elected to create a new nation at a time that would be most auspicious, although, to date, there has not been any documentation of such claims. Garry Wills's *Inventing America* raises questions along this line. In addition to reporting about the extensive astronomical interests among the educated elite, he discusses Thomas Jefferson's curious habit of recording the exact times of rainfalls and other phenomena.

America's modern-day astrological history, like that of England and other parts of Europe, doesn't become visible until astrology's late-nineteenth-century revival, a movement that occurred alongside the resurgence of spiritualism. Astrology would gain steady popularity with the public in the 1920s and 1930s (when the general horoscope columns began), and flamboyant personalities such as J. P. Morgan and other financial leaders openly used the services of Evangeline Adams, who worked out of a studio at Carnegie Hall. Adams was a descendant of John Adams.

Astrology and the Propaganda Machine

Germany saw a twentieth-century revival of astrology, which has given modern astrology some of the cleanest, most precise methods of astrological analysis and prediction. But Germany's contribution is tainted by World War II. The rise of Hitler resulted in some astrologers attempting to curry special favor by establishing Aryan astrological societies. Yet, to this day, rumors and assertions that Hitler directly hired astrologers have never been documented, as Ellic Howe writes in *Urania's Children,* which traces the rise of astrology in Germany. The Third Reich hired astrologers to disseminate false predictions that were allegedly based on prophecies by sixteenth-century occultist Nostradamus, who used astrology along with a range of divining practices. The predictions of these astrologers-for-hire were intended to make it appear that the stars were on the side of Hitler and Germany. Some of these employees languished in prison camps alongside other astrologers who had been rounded up after Hitler, upset about Rudolf Hess's presumed consultations with astrologers who told him to flee the country, signed an order imprisoning occult practitioners. Great Britain got wind of Hitler's supposed use of astrology and hired their own astrologers to assess the type of information Hitler was receiving and to issue propaganda pamphlets that also cited Nostradamus as a source.

Despite a history of dishonorable associations, Germany's astrological contributions are today highly regarded. As in England, it's not uncommon to find many more Germans who combine astrological knowledge with scholarship and mainstream professional success—law, psychology, engineering, journalism—than in the United States. Since the 1960s, when astrology saw its most recent revival, increasing numbers of people have been making attempts to rid astrology of its more ludicrous tenets. One of these is the erroneous assumption that astrologers are saying that planets "cause" changes on Earth. Astrologers have been wrongly accused of holding the belief that planets zap people into love affairs, accidents, or other life events. While those in more distant times may have been in possession of such worldviews, astrologers today talk of correlations. The view is that there is an acausal connection between planetary movements and human endeavors, an association that extends beyond being merely synchronous.

In exploring the concept of "synchronicity," Carl Jung drew correlations between events and the psychic states people were undergoing. His "Synchronicity: An Acausal Connecting Principle" tells of one patient, a know-it-all type, who questioned whether her therapy was working, but who dreamed of a scarab, a mythological association with renewal and regeneration. Just as the woman recalled the dream during a session with Jung, a golden beetlelike insect—the nearest thing to a scarab at that particular latitude—alighted on the outside windowsill and tapped for attention. Jung, who studied astrology as well as other "occult" topics such as the Tarot, felt that the concept of synchronicity governed these fields, as well as the ancient *I Ching*. Jung wrote the introduction to the English translation of Richard Wilhelm's popular German translation of the *Chinese Book of Wisdom*. Comparing the acausal (synchronistic) view with causality, Jung said that the latter represented "statistical truth and not absolute . . . whereas synchronicity takes the coincidence of events in space and time as meaning something more than mere chance, namely, a peculiar interdependence of objective events among themselves as well as with the subjective (psychic) states of the observer or observers."

The idea that events occurring at a specific moment in time hold the quality of the moment is not so unusual, Jung observes, if one thinks of wine experts who, with only a fingerprint of a sample, can name the grove and year of a particular wine, or antiquarians who can date a book rather precisely. Martin Shallis, an Oxford-trained physicist and researcher of astrological theories, demonstrated the evidence of synchronicity at work in two seemingly unrelated places: he observed that a quarter of the winning horses at the racetrack around the world near the hour of the royal wedding between Prince Charles and Lady Diana had names such as Royal Princess or Lady.

Every Moment is Unique

Astrology assumes such relationships between moments of time and planetary configurations. All activities—whether a business venture, a horse race, or a marriage—bear the quality of the moment of their birth, and no two moments are alike. Today natal astrology, which focuses on the lives of individuals, is the most widespread branch of astrology. A personalized horoscope is based on the exact date, place, and minute of a person's birth. Without all of these precise details, the life, timing, and less obvious features of a person's psychological makeup and destiny remain hidden. Every moment in time has its unique quality; no two horoscopes are precisely alike. The earth's relationship to the rest of the solar system makes measurable changes every four minutes, so no two people—not even twins—would draw their first breath at the same precise moment.

The natal horoscope, or birthmap, drawn for a specific moment in time is derived through trigonometric calculations that, until the advent of computers, could require a few hours of mathematics for each chart. The calculations involve various points in space, as well as the positions of the Sun, Moon, and planets in relation to the view from earth. Once the astronomical work is completed, the astrologer's special skill of interpretation is put to use. While basic meanings of the planets are easy to learn—the Moon's connection to emotions and feelings, Mars's to aggression and action, Neptune's to elusiveness and defeat—they are, at the very least, "short phrases" that require several years of study before the chart can be synthesized and its meaning put into flowing sentences that speak to the unfolding story depicted in the chart. The complexity of the chart is much like a one-of-a-kind soup whose creator closely guards the recipe. Carrots and beets (a particular planet at a specific point in the sky) have their own special tastes, but when they're thrown into a soup, the tastes take on different nuances. The Universe cooks up a special stew for each of its children.

The idea that synchronicity can be applied to this stew in the sky at the time of birth and establish a level of predetermination in a life is one that seems less ludicrous as "science" catches up with some of the Universe's secrets. A highly complex web of unknowns is linked to human DNA and the increasing discovery that diseases such as depression and schizophrenia are hereditary. Moreover, temperaments, gestures, and proclivities toward certain hobbies and talents are also in the family bloodline. One body of studies bolstering genetic arguments is the University of Minnesota project through which identical and fraternal twins were reunited after decades of being reared apart. Twins, such as the brothers who were both firefighters and had the same tastes in women and hobbies, are typical of the researchers' discovery. Genes overruled environment in the lives of numerous reunited twins.

What is essentially being said by the University of Minnesota researchers is that at the time of birth of the twins, various conditions existed that would be present throughout their lives, no matter where they lived. Such genetic rules must affect all humans. And while some people may feel uncomfortable making a leap that links genetics to astronomical configurations, there is the more than thirty years of statistically significant research initiated by Michel and Françoise Gauquelin. Since the mid 1950s, Gauquelin has shown that eminent people in specific fields have a statistically significant preference for being born when certain planets are rising and culminating. For instance, sports champions favor Mars; members of eminent associations, such as the French Academy of Medicine, favor Mars and Saturn; actors, politicians, and journalists, Jupiter; writers and artists, the Moon. The true connection here isn't really the link between planets and careers but the link between planets and temperaments. Because certain professions require certain personality traits—aggression and strong will for sports champions (Mars), for instance—those who achieve eminence presumably have an abundance of the necessary characteristics. Approximately 22 percent of the Olympic-quality athletes in various studies were born with the so-called Mars

Effect, whereas only 16 percent would have been expected due
to simple laws of chance, and the odds of such findings being
due to chance have been one to a million in various runs of
the tests.

The Gauquelins' research is especially dependent on the use
of specific birthtimes, since planets rise and culminate at precise
moments. To conduct their investigations, the Gauquelins spent
years visiting birth registries throughout Europe to take exact
birthtimes from certificates. Their files of more than sixty thousand birthtimes are testaments to their fastidiousness. Unlike
France, where Napoleonic law required the recording of a specific birthtime, the United States does not have uniform requirements for birth certificates. This factor, combined with
privacy laws in the United States that prohibit everyone but an
individual from directly obtaining his or her birth certificate,
has made data collection difficult for the Gauquelins, as well
as for many other individuals who would like to discover their
own true moment in time.

While the United States has not yet produced astrological
researchers on the level of France's Gauquelins, there are increasing efforts to build a ''neo-astrology'' through research
and more systematic examination. One example is Mark Urban-
Lurain's work for a master's thesis in social-science research
at the University of Michigan. Through the employment of
multivariate statistics, Urban-Lurain has been able to predict
alcoholism in a birthchart with more than 80 percent accuracy.
The use of multivariate statistics is a breakthrough of sorts
because it allows the consideration of several variables simultaneously, which is closer to what astrologers actually do than
most previous researchers have attempted.

Robert Hand, one of astrology's opinion leaders, a world-
renowned teacher/lecturer and author of various texts, says
astrology must take four steps if it is to become a mature
discipline. It must first define itself. This step, Hand notes,
should eventually incorporate the many related sciences and
research endeavors (various forms of cycle research, for instance) that are trying to hide under more acceptable names.
Second, astrology must create an institutional base (these range
from libraries, research institutes, support in universities).
Third, astrology must prove the efficacy of its techniques. And
finally, a theoretical framework must be developed.

Astrology is still trying to find itself. Marcello Truzzi, a professor of sociology at Eastern Michigan State University, offers a way of putting the current evolving body of astrological information into a larger context. He says astrology and other occult sciences are "protosciences" that have often been known to make their way into the mainstream. "These groups serve important functions for science. They often act as repositories and reminders of the existence of anomalies for the expanding and adapting legitimated sciences."

While this process—which has been under way for a few thousand years—continues, individuals can take up personal studies to determine whether astrological theses are relevant to their lives. Numerous years of study are needed before a horoscope can be understood at a glance. *Astrocycles*, however, offers the opportunity to study the basic cycles that outline the life of individuals and their societies. Cycles are astrology's building blocks; the Sun, Moon, and planets are always moving in relation to some earlier point, are always in some phase of a cycle that has special meaning to a given individual or country. The following chapter provides all the tools necessary for readers to discover the points on the map of time that have special meaning for their lives. We'll begin by examining the significance of date of birth and the way in which it affects us throughout our lives.

THREE

Astrological Shorthand

Learning astrology is not unlike learning a foreign language. Initially we pick up words or phrases, that keep us interested while we're learning the alphabet or parts of speech that make up the language. Most of those first words or phrases can't really be put to practical use. But eventually, if we stick with it, we'll be able to have conversations with natives from our adopted country and start reading and comprehending more subtle aspects of the language.

And then there's the major breakthrough. One night, while asleep, we find ourselves in one of our usual dream scenarios, only everybody is speaking our "foreign language" and we understand exactly what's being said.

Astrology, too, has the various states of rote understanding before students are at the point where they can pick up a chart and have the entire horoscope come to life. With time and practice our eye is trained to understand where the patterns are taking us.

It probably takes much longer to master astrology than it does a foreign language. Yet our study of Astrocycles is designed so that a limited amount of knowledge can allow people to pinpoint the natural rhythms in their lives. Only three features of astrology will be necessary to accomplish this goal:

1. Planets
2. Aspects
3. Zodiac signs

The categories will all be introduced in rather shorthand form in this section and then expanded upon throughout the book. However, before the brief lesson begins, its important to introduce two technical areas, which will be encountered throughout the book as well.

Key Power Points: Loosely speaking, this is your password. Every horoscope has a multivaried connection of factors at work, but the three most important points in the chart are as follows: The Sun, the Moon, and Ascendant, or Rising, sign.

The Sun, as we have discussed, is the part of astrology to which almost everyone has been introduced. Your Sun sign is a result of your month of birth. Saying I'm a Leo or I'm a Taurus means you were born when the Sun was in this portion of the zodiac. The Sun, as readers will increasingly become aware of, represents your evolving self, the personality under development and expression throughout your life. Many people can be born under the same Sun sign because the Sun spends approximately one month in each sign. If you haven't read the description of your Sun sign, the information is located at the end of this chapter.

The Moon is a lesser-known quantity to laypeople. The Moon changes signs every 2.5 days. The Moon shows how people respond emotionally; it's the habitual reactions they've been operating out of all of their lives.

The Ascendant/Rising sign is the third power point in the chart and is dependent on the exact minute of birth. Rising signs change every two hours as the horizon intersects with the band of space known as the ecliptic. The Rising sign is the segment of the zodiac that is rising at birth. The position shows the qualities we use to adapt to our environment; it's the face we show to the world and therefore may have little to do with who we are inside. At astrological conventions, the three sign positions of the Sun/Moon/Ascendant are shared with acquaintances in much the same way that one might say, "Hi, I'm Mary Jane Sullivan." This should illustrate how critical they are to our personal identity.

Houses: Once the Ascendant is discovered, astrologers can then set up a horoscope, the outline of which is defined by the twelve-spoke wheel in which the birth planets are scattered. For those who want to follow Astrocycles in their own life as they are explored in the following chapters, there are simple guidelines in Part IV beginning on page 375 of the book to help you find your Ascendant/Rising sign and set up an approximate chart.

Loosely speaking, the Rising sign is placed at the nine-o'clock position of the wheel. It is said to represent the "First House," which is concerned with image and the way a person presents himself or herself to the world. All of the houses speak about life circumstances and situations—money, romance, education, friends, self-undoing, and hidden enemies—in much the same way as a game board. The horoscope wheel is a two-dimensional attempt to show the relationship of the time and place of birth to the rest of the solar system. Though all horoscopes have twelve spokes, the areas between each spoke, as well as the concentrations of planetary contents, can vary, depending on birthtime and location. Each section represents an area of the sky. The Sun or any other planet that was rising at the time of birth would be placed in the part of the sky or horoscope allotted to the First (image, identity) or sometimes the Twelfth House (hidden limitations). When planets reach their highest point during the day, they are in the part of the sky designated as the Tenth House (career, status, prestige). When the Sun or any planet reaches the lowest point during the day, it's at the horoscope's Nadir, the Fourth House (home). Beautiful sunsets and other setting planets are moving through the Seventh House (one-to-one relationships).

Basic Astrology at Work

Astrology views every minute as precious and distinct, and a difference of an hour can vastly alter the horoscope interpretation, particularly as it relates to the timing of key events in a life. To illustrate, I've chosen the charts of two active public figures who were born on the same day. (See Figures 3.2 and 3.3). Former president Jimmy Carter and Chief Justice William Rehnquist were born on October 1, 1924, but 3.5 hours apart and in different time zones and latitudes (Georgia and Wisconsin). As stated earlier the horoscope and its accompanying twelve-spoke wheel is a two-dimensional representation of the sky's relationship to a specific time and place on earth. Without knowing anything about the intricacies of the horoscope, it is immediately obvious that the sky around the two men differed, despite the fact that the planets (as symbolized by the glyphs, or symbols, in each section of the horoscope wheel) were in the same sequential order.

Carter and Rehnquist both display concentrated interests in negotiating relationship matters and issues of justice. Both of them have some of the reformer's zeal and have, during their public lives, been known to raise stinger tongues at those who would attempt to threaten them. Both started major new jobs—Carter, as governor of Georgia; Rehnquist, as Supreme Court Justice—in 1971. Each has a crisp intellect, but they usually diverge in their conclusions on issues such as civil rights and the intent of the Constitution; but then, astrology doesn't claim that everyone born the same day will join the same political party.

Birthcharts—Road Maps with Alternate Routes

As we've discussed, astrology doesn't necessarily make absolute claims about many areas of life. The horoscope for the moment of birth contains potentialities. Some of the possibilities speak to innate talents that can be developed; others point to predilections for violence and other negative traits. Each soul is more attuned to some traits than to others, which is why multitalented people can share the same birthdate with people who live more ordinary lives. The birthmap shows choices that are available. That certain roads will be more appealing to some people than to others is part of the mystery of each individual, something that astrology (at least as it is currently understood by Western astrologers) can't pierce entirely. In the same way that figure skaters or ballerinas are born with certain physiques that are compatible with their work, horoscopes feature "signatures" that are more often than not apparent in the charts of certain careers and life orientations. Thousands of people nurture fantasies of being champion athletes, actresses, or great American novelists, and many of them find ways to express their interests. Few, however, are born with the combination of drive, ambition, persistence, and talent (all of which are exhibited in the birthchart) needed to win

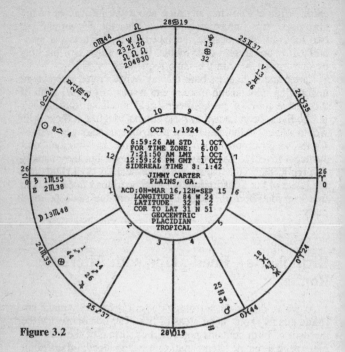

Figure 3.2

eminence in their chosen endeavors. And as noted earlier, genes, which are partially reflected by common astrological factors between the charts of parents and their children, also can't be overlooked.

Yet, in the same breath that we speak about predetermined temperaments, we must acknowledge the presence of free will, which, like that of the seemingly fickle finger of fate, is draped with an invisible cloak, making it difficult to discern the difference between the two. Carl Jung's observation that free will is the ability to undertake gladly what must be done is perhaps the best expression of the complex interplay between the two X factors. Further accepting the dictum that "character is fate" bolsters the argument that all actions grow out of who an individual truly is; individuals reveal themselves through their actions (or inactions). So let's take a brief look at the charts of Jimmy Carter and William Rehnquist and see what they reveal.

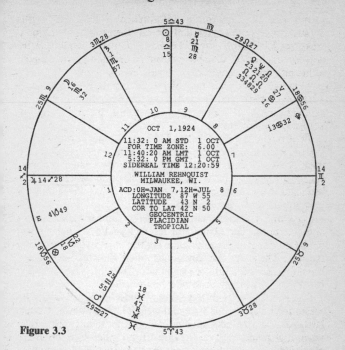

Figure 3.3

By checking the planetary glyphs, or symbols, noted in both charts on pages 36 and 37, the following glimpse of astrology at work should be easy to follow.

Jimmy Carter and William Rehnquist, both born October 1, 1924, have the Sun in relationship-oriented, negotiating Libra and the Moon in intense, probing Scorpio.

Being born at different times of the same day gives Carter and Rehnquist different adaptive strategies in their lives. Carter was born near sunrise, when the Rising sign is the same as that of the Sun (Libra). This intensifies his need to seek balance in his interactions with the world; it adds to his Libran indecisiveness, while also pulling him into various "fights" directly. Carter's campaigns for justice and peace are boosted by the double Libran emphasis.

Rehnquist, on the other hand, was born when Sagittarius was rising, a position indicating a life where a person constantly seeks to understand the big picture, to put himself and the experiences of others into a philosophical context. Sagittarius is much more opinionated and zealous than Libra, so it would make sense that this would be the Libran who would get involved with law and also be in the midst of controversies related to his attempts to impose his worldview on others.

Although Carter has two of his three power factors in the same sign, most people will have the Sun, Moon, and Ascendant each in a different sign, illustrating the complexity of horoscope interpretation.

The houses in figures 3.2 and 3.3 are numbered. Rehnquist, as can be seen by looking at his First House (the nine-o'clock position) was born as Jupiter, planet of journeys and expansion, was on the rise. Look up at the noon position, where the Sun has reached its highest point of the day. He has the Sun in the very important career house.

Look at the Carter chart. He has the somber planet Saturn rising at birth. The Gauquelin research had a special interest in planets rising and reaching the highest point in the sky during the day. These are the key zones where athletes have Mars. Rehnquist's rising Jupiter, signature planet of politicians and judges, makes him a bona fide Jupiterian.

Carter's Jupiter is in the Second House of money and possessions, indicating the financial wealth he has known. Carter, however, is a somber-minded Saturnian, having been born when that planet was on the rise. But a quick look up at the Ninth House of worldviews finds the power planet Pluto moving through after culminating (reaching its high point) an hour earlier. This is also significant by Gauquelin standards, which has found Pluto to be an investigator, reformer. Many world leaders are born with Pluto in the culminating position in the chart.

The visual differences between the Carter and Rehnquist charts show the important role timing plays in a horoscope. Readers should also have a sense of all the pieces of the puzzle that must be assimilated when a chart is interpreted.

Planets

Planets are the engines that run astrology. It's entirely possible to disregard houses and the zodiac and still make accurate assessments using just the planets. Understanding the function of each planet is the basis of astrological study. Planets have jobs to do. In much the same way that the human heart has a function, or the liver or kidneys have specific tasks, each planet is always working on specific tasks within us. Just as no body function is isolated from the rest of the body and the health of the entire biological system depends on each organ doing its share, the planets within each of us must pull their weight and mix with one another so that we can each evolve as humans. Because the planets are encountered throughout *Astrocycles*, this initial introduction is brief and is aimed at bringing on the players. (see "Planetary Players" chart on page 41).

Planets are divided into the following categories: personal, social, and outer.

Personal planets are closer to earth and deal with basic life-survival issues. For instance, Mercury is the thinking function, Mars the ability to go out and take action. The Sun and Moon, which for purposes of simplicity are considered "planets," represent the conscious developing self and the unconscious reactions respectively. Venus is the personal value system, personal tastes, the ability to give and receive in life.

The *social* planets Jupiter and Saturn involve relations to the larger world. They involve the internal dynamics related to the ability to grow and thrive in the world (Jupiter), while maintaining a sense of self as separate from others. They also deal with understanding and obeying inner regulations in the form of one's ego system, as well as outer authorities, such as the police and government.

The *outer* planets were all discovered in comparatively recent times: 1781 (Uranus), 1846 (Neptune), and 1930 (Pluto). They move slowly and hence, while related to poignant dramas in some individual's lives, are more timed to the collective tasks of generations, as larger groups of people are born with these planets in the same locations. In the bigger picture of history, these three planets are the most important when it comes to determining long-term trends for humankind.

A Word About Planetary Symbolism

Planets can symbolize emotional states and experiences, as well as specific ypes of people or activities. The Sun, for instance, relates to each individual's personal self, but when politics is concerned, it relates to the head of state (Bush, Gorbachev). It relates to male figures. The Moon represents individual emotions, but also mass emotion. Neptune, the dissolver and escapist, represents spirituality and fine art, as well as drugs and mental instability. Its veil of illusion is involved with advertising as well as with the CIA. Its attempt to achieve universality and unification causes it to oversee the plight of society's disadvantaged as well as the plight of racial minorities in given societies.

Initially these multiple associations can be confusing, which is why it's first important to know the basic principle each planet represents. When Pluto's underground connotations are recognized, its relation to everyone from 1930s gangsters to Adolf Hitler and current hate attacks in the United States is better understood. These links will all be explored throughout *Astrocycles*, giving you ample opportunity to begin stretching your mind to come up with some of your own associations. Astrology is an emerging, constantly evolving art. The increasing levels of intelligence and experiences of new students brings more practical and profound insight.

Asteroids and Other Things in the Sky

Astrologers employ a range of other techniques to better understand the Universe. Increasingly this includes various asteroids (they exist between the orbits of Mars and Jupiter) and other celestial points. The four asteroids discovered in the early 1800s (Ceres, Pallas, Juno, and Vesta) are the most popular, but numerous other asteroids are being employed to study both individuals and the stock market. Other celestial points—such as the Moon's Nodes—and celestial bodies—such as Chiron, the planetoid discovered between the orbits of Saturn and Uranus—are in steady use. *Astrocycles*, while making passing references to some of these points and providing brief explanations, does not include these more advanced procedures. The basics will require enough time to master.

Aspects

Once the job descriptions of each of the planets are understood, it's important to know how any particular planet works with the rest of the solar system. This is accomplished by examining the geometric angles it makes with each of the other planets. Officially, these angles are called aspects.

An aspect essentially shows how the specific principles and

Planetary Players

Planet/Principles	Primal Urges
Sun Vitality; selfhood; creativity; life force; inner radiance; ego expression	To be, to create
Moon Emotions, feeling, habitual responses; unconscious memory	To feel inner support
Mercury Conscious mind, communication; thinking, speech; attitudes	To express intelligence, to make connections
Venus Values; tastes; giving, receiving	To express affection, love, tastes
Mars Desire; will to act; drive; physical energy; sex	To act, to assert oneself
Jupiter Expansion; seek; integration; assimilation; opportunity; faith	To integrate self with larger order
Saturn Contraction; discipline, effort; self-preservation; structure	To defend and define self-structure
Uranus Revolution; originality; nonconformity; individualistic freedom	To individualize and differentiate from tradition
Neptune Dissolution of ego-self and boundaries; inspiration; illusions; transcendence; universal concerns	To escape from earthly limitations
Pluto Death/rebirth; elimination; transformation; power/powerlessness; healing	To regenerate

functions represented by a given planet "get along" with co-worker planets. Aspects are a way of discovering how the various psychological functions represented by the planets are integrated into a personality. Sometimes two principles—for example, the Mars principle of action and the Saturn principle of restrictions—work together smoothly, like moving men sharing the load of a large piece of furniture they are carrying into a van (trine). In other circumstances the same two principles may be pulling in different directions (an opposition), or one planet may be looking to lay down the piece of furniture while the other planet is struggling to lift it (square).

Aspects are formed in two different ways:

1. Natal: At the birth of an individual or business venture, that is, the configurations the planets in the sky made with one another at that moment.
2. Transiting: The angular relationships that the positions of the planets as they move through their orbits make to the original planetary positions in the birthchart. For instance, Saturn traveling through Capricorn in the fall of 1989 was transiting Mars in Capricorn in Ronald Reagan's birthchart, coinciding with the increased criticism being aimed at his former administration.

LIFE IN A CIRCLE   Aspects are derived by divisions of a 360-degree circle. Most astrologers stick to aspects that are derived by dividing the circle by two and four, or three and six. The effects of these aspects, as will be shown, are direct and often speak to specific situations in a life. Since the principle underlying aspects is the same found in geometry and music theory, it is easy to think of these more traditional aspects as being like John Philip Sousa marches or perhaps like more conventional music written in common time (4/4) or 3/4 or 2/4 time.

Dividing the 360-degree circle by 3 produces an angle of 120, by 4, an angle of 90. Aspects that are precise are at their most potent, but astrology recognizes an "orb of influence" or allowable inexactitude of 5 degrees on either side of the precise point. An orb is like describing Alexandria, Virginia, as the "Washington, D.C., area." Charleston, South Carolina however, is not an orb, but Silver Springs, Maryland, is. As for aspects, planets would be considered to be at right angles to each other when they are anywhere from 85 to 95 degrees apart, although 90 degrees is exactitude. In some cases the orbs can be extended, as will become more evident when this book takes up longer-term sociopolitical issues. Personal-chart interpretation sometimes requires wider orbs as well.

Because this book is for newcomers, technical measurements will not be employed. Instead, aspects will be determined by counting between zodiac signs (See "Sign-to-Sign Relationships" on page 50). Zodiac signs, as will be discussed in the following section, have "aspect" relationships with one another. Being three signs apart is the same as being in the 90-degree-angle position. The sign approach is suited for the various cycles discussed in this book and it will be presented in the succeeding section.

In the meantime the nature of the major aspects are as follows:

Conjunction (zero degrees, same sign): Planets come together like two people looking to sit in the same chair simultaneously. As it would be with people, the coming together can be either positive or negative depending on the planets involved. Mars with the Moon would produce emotional upsets, irritation, and emotionally defensive actions. Venus and Jupiter would be very sociable, party loving, possibly too much of a good thing.

Sextile (60 degrees, two signs apart): Two friends walking along hand-in-hand, the sextile relates to opportunities, social exchanges, communication. The planets talk over coffee. For example, Saturn gives Mars support and discipline; Mars doesn't question Saturn's authority. The Sun (conscious self) and Moon (unconscious self) support each other.

Square (90 degrees, three signs apart): Planets blindside each other and work at cross-purposes. They're two people who want the same job and are scheduled for an interview at the same hour. They talk behind each other's backs. There's an element of sabotage. People paint themselves into corners. Venus wants to be sociable, to give and receive love; Saturn is more apprehensive, hesistant, more comfortable with tasks. Venus plays when it's time to work; Saturn is rejecting at social affairs, probably thinks Venus is a bimbo.

Trine (120 degrees, four signs apart): It's summertime and the living is easy . . . sometimes too easy. Planets here are like third- and fourth-generation heirs of wealthy families who haven't had to work or worry. The planets' comfort with each other can mean that the energies are never spurred into action. People who have Venus trining Jupiter may be used to being given gifts, money, affection, opportunities; the better ones know enough to say thanks everyday and put out a little effort for what they get. Moon trine Pluto can result in an ability to understand and empathize with many different people, a quality that can obviously be abused.

Opposition (180 degrees, six signs apart): A tug-of-war. Need for moderation, reconciliation of competing interests, search for common ground. Oppositions are often acted out through relationships with other people, who seem to take on the characteristics of an individual's "other half." But because the opposing sides sit directly across from one another, there is a greater chance for balance and a solution; the planets agree to disagree. Mars/Venus is the make-war-or-love quandary. Jupiter/Saturn oscillates between expansion and restriction. The Sun and Moon pit ego expression against receptivity, masculine against feminine urges.

Inconjunct/Quincunx (150 degrees, five signs apart): Increasingly this is being viewed as a major aspect. It relates to situations that require alterations and adjustments; people have to give up something to make circumstances work. Yet the source of the problem is not as direct as that outlined in the opposition. The United States, for instance, is pretty clear on the distinction between capitalism and Russian communism, but is puzzled by the economic philosophy of Japanese and other Far Eastern businesspeople. The standoff is not direct, but rather a catty-corner glance at each other. The negotiation and adjustment needed are not as directly obvious, requiring an initial pulling back, analysis, and implementation of some technique.

Zodiac Signs

The signs will appear in varying forms throughout *Astrocycles*, so they're being presented here in an introductory chart form, which should be reviewed. The twelve-sector zodiac has various subcategories that better explain the intrinsic nature of the signs and their relationship to one another. Three concepts that are briefly outlined here include *elements, modalities, and polarities*.

ELEMENTS   The elements are the building blocks of life. Fire, Earth, Air, and Water are the life-giving forces, all of which are needed for survival.

The **Fire** signs (**Aries, Leo, Sagittarius**) are hard to contain. They are spontaneous, self-expressive, always seeking larger-than-life experiences. Highly idealistic, they can be more wedded to ideals than to people. They can be very impractical, too. They're propelled by spirit and are often intuitive visionaries.

The **Earth** signs (**Taurus, Virgo, Capricorn**) prefer to deal with matters that they can touch, being highly alert to the realities of the material world. Physical security is important. They're practical and attuned to their five senses and bodily needs, but are not generally open to more perceptive, intuitive approaches.

The **Air** signs (**Gemini, Libra, Aquarius**) need social interaction and mental stimulation to survive. They are comfortable with abstractions and concepts and quite literally can be guilty of always having their heads in the clouds. They can seem cold, detached, unfeeling.

The **Water** signs (**Cancer, Scorpio, Pisces**) live in the realm of feeling and are more reactive than proactive. They react on the basis of the instincts and emotions and often bring a highly subjective and sometimes overly sensitive posture into the world. They are empathetic where other elements might be brusque or openly unsympathetic.

MODALITIES   Each sign has a modus operandi that describes how it goes about getting what it wants. Signs in the same element—fire, for instance—have similar goals but don't share the same tactics. The three modalities link signs that, while pursuing interests that are at cross-purposes, can knock up against one another, because they have the same style. It would be similar to having a room full of people who were the Mike Tysons or Donald Trumps of their respective fields. Everyone would want to talk at once.

The **Cardinal** signs (**Aries, Cancer, Libra, Capricorn**) occur at the beginnings of the seasons (spring, summer, fall, winter) and are born initiators. They're action oriented in their specialty areas. For instance, Aries is a self-promoter; Libra constantly takes actions related to its relationship needs (even though many of these actions are self-negating); Cancer leads on the home front; Capricorn sets up structures in the outer

Zodiac Signs

Planets will have following qualities/concerns when in:	Element	Modality	Ruler	Polarity
Aries Beginnings; creativity; identity; self-assertion; pioneering; impulsive; bold; independence	Fire	Cardinal	Mars	Libra
Taurus Physical security; sustenance; values; personal resources; sensuality; perseverance; building	Earth	Fixed	Venus	Scorpio
Gemini Communication; interaction; dualistic thinking; scattered; neighborhood affairs; related interchanges; siblings	Air	Mutable	Mercury	Sagittarius
Cancer Emotional security; home; family; personal life/foundation; parents; dependence; nurturance	Water	Cardinal	Moon	Capricorn
Leo Self-affirmation; self-expression; love given; creativity; drama; recreation; radiation of warmth; magnanimity	Fire	Fixed	Sun	Aquarius
Virgo Adjustment; daily survival; need for order/routine; analysis; discrimination; health; service	Earth	Mutable	Mercury	Pisces

Sign	Ruler	Quality	Element	Opposite	Keywords
Libra	Venus	Cardinal	Air	Aries	Relationship; accommodation; balance and moderation; social approval; passive-aggressive behavior; warfare
Scorpio	Pluto	Fixed	Water	Taurus	Power/powerlessness; regeneration; death/rebirth/manipulation; control; purging; intensity; healing
Sagittarius	Jupiter	Mutable	Fire	Gemini	Expansiveness; spiritual quest; idealism; beliefs; aspirations; journeys; assimilation; foreign cultures
Capricorn	Saturn	Cardinal	Earth	Cancer	Structure; limitations; definition; authority; social standing; discipline; parental influence; rigidity
Aquarius	Uranus	Fixed	Air	Leo	Social participation; social causes; ideology; perverse; radical; detachment; networking; friendship
Pisces	Neptune	Mutable	Water	Virgo	Oneness; dissolution; illusion; surrender; escape; inspiration; spirituality; universality; glamour, deceit

world. Cardinal signs are crisis-oriented people and are always jumping out of the pan and into the fryer.

The **fixed** signs (**Taurus, Leo, Scorpio, Aquarius**) are hard to move. They get stuck in ruts and habitual patterns that can be unhealthy. On the positive side, they're conservative and know how to build on what has gone before. Their special concern involves attachments and the need to know when to hold on and when to let go. For Taurus the issue shows up in money; with Leo it's ego. Scorpio has many power concerns; while Aquarius, whose detachment can often belie their attachment needs.

The **mutable** signs (**Gemini, Virgo, Sagittarius, Pisces**) are highly adaptable. This is why Gemini is such a good go-between and professional communicator, teacher, or salesperson. Sagittarius is open to the big world. Pisces seeks to become one with all it encounters. Virgo is trying to specialize in adjusting to the realities of daily existence, such as holding a job and paying the rent. The problem for these people is that they can get so adept at adjusting to situations that they never confront problems head-on; they just move down the street, and the problems eventually follow them.

POLARITY The concept of polarity recognizes that the existence of any force creates its opposite. In effect there are really only six pairs of zodiac signs. The polarities are:

Aries (I)	**Libra** (Partners)
Taurus (Having)	**Scorpio** (Releasing)
Gemini (Thinking)	**Sagittarius** (Understanding)
Cancer (Private life)	**Capricorn** (Public life)
Leo (Love expressed)	**Aquarius** (Love Received)
Virgo (Adjustment to daily reality)	**Pisces** (Transcendence)

SIGN-TO-SIGN ASPECTS When we introduce concepts such as elements and modalities, we begin to get a better idea of the aspects that signs make to one another. Sign-to-sign relationships (See "Sign-to-Sign Relationships" on page 50) will be the framework used throughout *Astrocycles* to help readers plot individual and world cycles.

> **Conjunction:** Planets in the same sign
> **Sextile:** Planets two signs apart
> **Square:** Planets three signs apart
> **Trine:** Planets four signs apart
> **Opposition:** Planets six signs apart
> **Inconjunct/Quincunx:** Planets five signs apart

Signs in compatible elements (Fire/Air) (Earth/Water) are two signs away from one another and are in the sextile relationship. For instance, Aries (the first sign in the zodiac) is two signs away from Gemini (the third sign in the zodiac) and two signs away from Aquarius (the eleventh sign in the zodiac). Taurus (the second sign in the zodiac) is two signs away from Cancer (the fourth sign in the zodiac) and two signs away from Pisces (the twelfth sign in the zodiac).

Signs in the same element (Gemini, Libra, Aquarius for instance,) are in the 120-degree trine aspect of ease.

Signs within the same modality clash. They are all either three or six signs from one another. Three signs separate Cancer and Libra; Taurus and Leo; Scorpio and Aquarius, for instance. Three signs are equal to a 90-degree square aspect, which relates to a blockage of energy because the two sides are working at cross-purposes.

A six-sign separation, related to the need for balance, is represented by the 180-degree opposition aspect. Signs in opposition are in a polarity relationship to one another (Aries/Libra, Taurus/Scorpio, etc.).

The following chart on zodiac signs gives a clear summary of many of the points we have touched on in this chapter.

Sign to Sign Relationships

	Ar	Ta	Ge	Ca	Le	Vi	Li	Sc	Sa	Cp	Aq	Pi
Ar	Co		Sx	Sq	Tr	In	Op	In	Tr	Sq	Sx	
Ta		Co		Sx	Sq	Tr	In	Op	In	Tr	Sq	Sx
Ge	Sx		Co		Sx	Sq	Tr	In	Op	In	Tr	Sq
Ca	Sq	Sx		Co		Sx	Sq	Tr	In	Op	In		Sx
Le	Tr	Sq	Sx		Co		Sx	Sq	Tr	In	Op	In
Vi	In	Tr	Sq	Sx		Co		Sx	Sq	Tr	In	Op
Li	Op	In	Tr	Sq	Li		Co			Sx	Sq	Tr	In
Sc	In	Op	In	Tr	Sq	Sx		Co		Sx	Sq	Tr
Sa	Tr	In	Op	In	Tr	Sq	Sx		Co		Sx	Sq
Cp	Sq	Tr	In	Op	In	Tr	Sq	Sx		Co		Sx
Aq	Sx		Sx	In	Op	In	Tr	Sq	Sx		Co	
Pi		Sx	Sq	Sx	In	Op	In	Tr	Sq	Sx		Co

ASPECT KEY Co (Conjunction), **Sx** (Sextile), **Sq** (Square), **Tr** (Trine), **In** (Inconjunct), **Op** (Opposition). The aspect called the semisextile does not appear on this chart but is designated by the vacant spaces. The semisextile is considered a minor aspect of stress and refers to signs that are adjacent to one another (for instance, Pisces is semisextile Aquarius and Aries). Some texts refer to inconjuncts (which are five signs apart) as semisextiles, but this is changing as astrologers take the inconjunct's demand for adjustments more seriously.

PART II
Cycles in Your Life

FOUR

The Birthday Cycle

Whether a birthday is spent in celebration or it is a quiet stay-at-home, we can expect to undergo a series of predictable feelings as we look forward and backward, trying to put the present moment and our life in perspective. As author Linda Randall Lewis observes,

Mention a birthday and charge the atmosphere. No wonder. These occasions stir emotions that have long been buried, ones we wish would stay buried as well as ones we wish we might experience again. . . . High hopes and bitter disappointments, terrible reminders and fears about the future, pride and self-doubt all may come up on a birthday unbidden. Astonishing things seem to happen on these love feasts that link birth and death.

Certain birthdays—turning twenty-one and "legal" in every state; hitting the "big three-oh," the "four-oh," and so forth— are often draped with more importance. And there are people who claim to not pay any attention to the coming and going of birthdays. They'd like to have everyone believe that their mind can erase all thought of birthdays and age as easily as government officials can shred incriminating documents or a word processor can hit a delete button on the computer. It's not that easy. While some modern-day societies, such as the Soviet Union, don't put celebratory emphasis on their leaders' birthdays, it's impossible for Americans to open a newspaper or turn on the radio without hearing about the "famous people celebrating their birthday today." And even if people don't pay attention to such "news" most days, they'll take a few seconds out of their routine to hear about the famous and infamous with whom they're sharing a birthday.

But even if birthday parties and all references to age were suddenly outlawed, a "birthday" would still hold special significance and would be different from the 364 "unbirthdays" in the year. Whether it falls on July 1, October 15, or whenever, a birthday marks the start of each individual's "New Year." A need for agreed-upon reference points requires that modern industrial societies start counting the year on a date, such as January 1, but each individual resonates to a more personalized schedule (which is why January 1 New Years' resolutions are tough for anyone who wasn't born around that time). With the arrival of a birthday, we renew a year-long rhythm that will reach critical turning points (and often challenges) in approximately ninety-day intervals. These points come about three months to the day after the birthday, six months to the day after the birthday, and nine months to the day after the birthday. And then, three months later, it's another birthday again, another personal New Year. We've changed and now are looking to give new expression to this continually evolving self. Each ninety-day phase has nuances that separate it in purpose from the other. All parts contribute to the overall meaning of the one-year cycle, which sheds light on who each individual is in the process of becoming. The year-long rhythm—as well as shorter-term interval periods—can't be utilized to maximum benefit until the trend's connection to ongoing activity in the sky is understood in some detail.

It All Revolves Around the Sun

This emerging self and the general ways in which we express it is symbolized by the Sun, whose heat and energy is essential to life on earth. In the horoscope, the Sun is important, for it symbolizes the life force and vitality of each individual. That some Eastern religions often include rituals requiring adherents to pray while facing the direction of sunrise (the east) expands on the idea of the Sun as symbol of spirit that is renewed with each breath, each day.

Sunrise, in true astronomical terms, is essentially how the Sun appears to us as the Earth revolves around the Sun and simultaneously rotates on its own axis. Whereas the axial rotation is a twenty-four-hour process and causes the shifts between day and night, it takes the earth a full year to complete its orbit around the Sun. As humankind learned to appreciate early, the Sun is a constant and appears in the same part of the sky approximately every 365 days (give or take a day or two). In other words, the Sun, personification of the self, always returns to the exact point in the sky where it was located at an individual's birth, within a day or two of the annual birthday.

Aside from providing people with two choices from which to choose an "official" birthday—the traditional calendar date or the astronomically precise date and time—the more technically derived chart gets special attention from people who see it as a way of determining the trend for the upcoming year. By drawing a chart for the precise minute that the Sun reaches the birth position, an astrologer comes up with a Solar Return chart. The birthday greeting "many happy returns," like "mazel tov," which means "may your constellations be good," contains some of the hopes with which some approach the Solar Return chart. Despite debates about the validity and technical basis for these charts, some people take them so seriously that they search the globe looking for the best latitude and longitude at which to experience the most positive Solar Return, where the combination between the planets and the Sun's movement to the birth position produce the most favorable configuration. That was the intent of one well-regarded Michigan astrologer, who rushed from a workshop he gave in Connecticut to take his wife to Maine, where presumably better stars awaited her.

There's nothing wrong with planning a special trip for the Solar Return day, but Solar Return charts should be drawn for the city where you live most of the year. Even if the plans for the evening are just to sit in front of the television, it can be interesting to know when the bell goes off. The Solar Return chart will be a snapshot of the moment, which can sometimes contain mini-epiphanies that can turn your head a bit.

The big trends in a life show themselves in the birthchart. Sometimes the Sun's return to its birth position will act as a trigger, along with Mars and the fast-moving Moon, and bring to a head the sudden job changes, accidents, or other activities that come around the birthday. But events such as Mikhail Gorbachev's election as general secretary of the Soviet Union within a week of his birthday; Michael Dukakis's presidential loss five days after his birthday; Madonna and Sean Penn's ill-fated wedding/birthday parties; or Debbye Turner's crowning as Miss America 1990 three days before her birthday *always* correspond to other major planetary energies.

The Solar Return is a way of replacing the bulbs that have cast the light guiding us over the past year. This light shows general direction and interest over the next 365 days. Despite its metaphysical importance, the Solar Return, as well as upcoming (see subsequent chapters) cycles, such as those involving the transiting Moon, Mercury, Venus, and Mars, can be compared to the outer-edge ripples that occur when a pebble is thrown into the middle of a pond. More important are the interactions that the traveling Saturn, Jupiter, and the slower-moving planets Uranus, Neptune, and Pluto make to the Sun, Moon, and other planets in the horoscope that was determined at your exact time of birth.

Though lower on the hierarchical rung of cycles, the birthday rhythm provides a renewal in consciousness that can work in tandem with larger trends for positive growth. People certainly react to it. Even before the Sun returns to the exact address it tenanted at birth, they sense the revitalized energy as soon as the Sun moves into the general neighborhood of the birthday Sun.

The "neighborhood" here is defined by the zodiac, which is the path along which the Sun appears to travel. The zodiac is the subdivision or address that the Sun appears to move through during the course of the year. Technically it corresponds to the ecliptic, which is an imaginary band of space. The ecliptic should not be confused with the constellations, many of which have similar names as the zodiac. The ecliptic, or zodiac, is broken into twelve sectors (Aries, Taurus, Gemini, Cancer, Leo, Virgo, Libra, Scorpio, Sagittarius, Capricorn, Aquarius, and Pisces). By saying, "I'm a Pisces," for example, a person is saying that he or she was born during the part of the year when the Sun was moving through that part of the sky. Each sign of the zodiac, which is represented by a 360-degree circle, contains 30 degrees, with the Sun moving through the entire sign in a little over thirty days. In other words, the Sun remains in Aries for approximately thirty days before moving into Taurus for a one-month stay, and so on.

A birth at the beginning of the sign would equate with having the Sun in one of its rawest forms and in the earliest degrees—one to nine, for instance—while the final days of a sign relate to higher-degree numbers.

Knowing whether a person was born at the end of one sign or the beginning of another—whether he or she is a Leo or a Virgo, for example—is confusing to newcomers to astrology because much misinformation has been promoted about the idea of the "cusp." In reality, people are born in one sign or the other, but astrology columns can't provide specific information for ending- and beginning-of-sign people. (The Sun Sign Appendix contains a table.) The Sun's entrance into any of the zodiac signs can vary by a day or two depending on the year. While many people who were born on September 23 are Virgos, Bruce Springsteen, born September 23, 1949, 10:50 P.M. in Freehold, New Jersey, is a Libra. The Sun moved into that sign at 5:06 A.M. EDT.

In taking up the plight of the cusp-born, we're flirting with the quicksand of zodiac signs. To astrologers trying to get more people to take their craft seriously, zodiac signs are a bugaboo, a red herring that has made people the world over assume that astrology's sole concern is throwing people into twelve categories and making predictions based on these limited assumptions. When Sun-sign columns first debuted and were popularized in England in the 1920s and 1930s, the approach seemed like an effective way of making general astrological information available to the masses. As the format spread around the world, it began to trivialize astrology since most who encounter newspaper and magazine horoscopes are not aware that the Sun is just one of numerous factors to be read in an individualized horoscope cast for the exact date, location, and time to the nearest minute of birth. But zodiac signs add some specifics that the more primary factors—the planets and their aspects—don't supply. Planetary symbolism states that Mercury rules the mind, one's ability to communicate. The zodiac sign shows whether that communication will be fast-talking and spontaneous (Aries) or more deliberate (Taurus). The Moon and planets continually change zodiacal addresses. The zodiac supplies qualities and issues for its tenants to deal with. For example, when Jupiter moves through Leo, it expands through creative projects and flamboyant personality presentations. Like people moving from Manhattan to Dubuque, it takes on a different color and expression when moving through routine-conscious Virgo. Jupiter, a hard planet to contain, proceeds to expand Virgo's work load, but it also brings opportunities to better appreciate the beauty of daily routines and the joy of work.

When astrologers meet people whose only exposure to astrology is Sun signs, they are in a political predicament. They want to remove themselves as far as possible from the limited twelve-category format, but can't ignore the fact that the Sun is the life force around which the chart is built. Even when all the variables are taken into account in the chart, the Sun and the configurations it makes with the Moon and the planets steer the chart. The zodiac sign in which the Sun is placed adds additional coloring to a general life theme. The 300,000 Americans born under the same zodiac sign in a year all draw charts unique to their birth location and time, but these people share common experiences with those born under the same sign in any given year. Aries typically experiences a life in which the road toward identity is strewn with fights and challenges to traditional authority; Virgo typically struggles to find and perfect a relationship with work and life that is rhythmic and flowing. Certainly those born under other Sun signs will have routine and work-related experiences similar to those confronting Virgo—this is especially true if the Moon, Rising sign, or key planets are in Virgo—but the search for order permeates life for Virgos such as Stephen King or Mother Teresa.

Finding Your Place in the Zodiac

Capsule descriptions of each of the twelve Sun signs begin on page 60. Locate and read the description of your Sun sign before taking up the following section.

Seasons in a Year

Astrologically, the New Year starts at the vernal equinox, the first day of spring. And in the same way that spring means renewal, your individual birthday begins your new year or annual renewal. Viewing the birthday year as being broken down into four seasons—spring, summer, fall and winter (see the Birthday Year Chart on page 70—will help you understand how your solar will develops over the course of 365 days.

Spring: The birthday and the Solar Return represent a seeding period where new trends and life are emerging. You are in your metaphorical spring and will be for the next ninety days. It's time to sit down and write your objectives for both the first ninety days of your new year and the entire year. Some people will see immediate action in their environments in the form of new jobs and other activities. Mostly, this is an internal recentering period: the blooming comes later with help from the other planets.

Summer: Things take root as the Sun moves three signs ahead of the birthday Sun. Newcomers can find the especially critical day by counting about 90 to 91 days from the birthday; on this day, the Sun will be 90 degrees from the birthday Sun. The ''summer'' position places the Sun in a sign that, while in the same mode as the birthday Sun (Cardinal, Fixed, Mutable), has different priorities, resulting in tension.

During this second critical point, people often take some action, or there are environmental challenges to one's sense of self. Examples include a woman who began going out on job interviews and a man who suffered a car accident during this time.

Fall: The major turning point/harvest in the year. The Sun is six signs (180 days) from the birthday Sun. People report either a high-energy time, where projects are coming to a head, or unexpected events come about. Others report fatigue, low energy. In both cases this phase is a point of illumination where the year's trend is put into perspective, because the Sun is in the sign that is the polar opposite of the birthday Sun (polar opposites seek a balance between their competing viewpoints of the world).

Winter: This is about 270 days after the birthday. The Sun is three signs (90 days/90 degrees) behind (and en route toward) the birthday Sun. A mop-up period begins. Possible head-turning events that cause some reorientation in thinking about the year that is soon to end, and the new one due to begin in three months. Time-out for hibernation.

"Happy Birthday to You": The Song and the Cycle

It is crucial that every solar renewal be started with a conscious attitude. Because a year is such a short span of time, it is possible to fall out of harmony with the rhythm. The structure of the birthday song—and the difficulty people have singing it—speaks to some of the nuances of the cycle and the importance of starting at the right pitch from the beginning. Even when adults are singing "Happy Birthday to You," most of them miscalculate the key in which they begin singing the song, so that by the third line—which in its structure is like the "Fall" six months after the birthday—the sounds can cause many earaches (and sore throats).

Harnessing Solar Energy

1. Find a biography or autobiography about a man or woman born under your Sun sign.
   a. What is the common theme throughout the story?
   b. Compare it to your own life experiences.
   c. Read up on your polar-opposite sign (six signs away)
2. Keep a "Seasons Diary" for a year.
   Use the "Birthday Year" chart on page 73 to show how to locate the "summer," "winter," and other seasons for your Sun sign. Take special notes on your priorities and experiences during this time.

Sun Signs

Aries: March 21–April 19
Fire/Cardinal/Mars

Even as they admired his drive, competitiveness, and daring, sportswriters over the years had also noted that Pete Rose was one of those people who couldn't be told anything. It was difficult for anyone to put brakes on the impulsive, combative Rose. His inability, or unwillingness, to cooperate and compromise were particularly evident when he was suspended from baseball for life. Instead of apologizing directly and showing a desire to make amends, the swaggering Rose kept his arrogant "make my day" pose and, though the decision certainly wasn't up to him, indicated that he expected to be back playing ball in a year.

There you have it, Aries' high and low. The pioneer of the zodiac, Aries jumps in where none dared jump before. Sometimes the result is a heightened sense of identity and the courage, independence, and commitment to true self-assertion and expression that that entails. Gloria Steinem, Bette Davis, Thomas Jefferson, Andrew Lloyd Webber, Sandra Day O'Connor, Liz Claiborne, Madalyn Murray O'Hair, and the erudite Bart Giamatti, who died nine days after censuring Pete Rose, are all Aries.

Inherent in the sign's strengths are its weak points, such as impulsiveness, impatience, limited self-reflection, selfishness, disrespect of others, which can make life difficult for Aries and everyone around them. It's the sign of beginnings—the vernal equinox in the Northern Hemisphere—and this results in many self-starters. But Aries always likes to be starting things and often doesn't have the genes for going the distance, which is why their ideas are often appropriated and developed by more persistent and patient signs. The life story of those in this sign often involves challenges and breaks with authority and father figures. Aries goes out and finds his or her own way. Marlon Brando's use of the Academy Awards as a vehicle for protesting the treatment of Native Americans is an example. Some, like Eddie Murphy, may not have a cause, but they have a fierce individuality. Some in the sign are sheep; others recruit heroes to lean on. But they eventually get confronted with the need to stand up and be counted as individuals.

Taurus: April 20–May 20
Earth/Fixed/Venus

After its debut in Aries, the spring in the Northern Hemisphere settles in for a calmer, steadier ride through Taurus, the sign where things (from plants to money) grow. These are creatures of earth and habit. Taurus wants to build a secure foundation on steady ground, so it often rejects the schemes hatched up in Aries. Taurus is practical, pragmatic, more comfortable with what can be verified through touch and the other senses. Often, these traits can produce true builders, such as acclaimed architect I. M. Pei, who also demonstrates the sign's appreciation for form. But many Taureans are so bound to the material world that they can't sense the beauty of the unseen.

They're often greedy and only interested in physical comfort and pleasure.

Actor Jack Nicholson is often associated with some of the more hedonistic sides of this sign, both on and off screen. He's also known as a solid artist in command of his craft. He might not have the same values as Taurus stalwart Katharine Hepburn, but he answers to values that are purely his own, which is what all the best Taureans learn to do. Karl Marx's values involved redefining economic systems and the distribution of personal money and possessions. But money matters aren't the only values at issue in this sign, as Pope John Paul II and Sigmund Freud's concern with hidden realities show. As a sign that loves both beauty and form, Taurus helps Shirley MacLaine, and people like Barbra Streisand, Irving Berlin, and Cher, build solid careers in the arts. Taureans don't exactly go out of their way to bring change in life, but sometimes their unwillingness to take any steps that might jeopardize their security forces continual changes upon them.

Gemini: May 21–June 21
Air/Mutable/Mercury

The spring will soon give itself to summer, which is why the energy in the air is more changeable when the Sun moves into Gemini, which represents the daily communication and exchanges that we experience in life, our attitudes, how we take in and give out ideas. As a result, the sign contains Bob Hope, Joan Rivers, Mario Cuomo, John F. Kennedy, and many other people with a good rap. George Bush displays the good-natured and scattered aspects of the sign. Harriet Beecher Stowe, Joyce Carol Oates, and Ralph Waldo Emerson are just a handful of those who show the sign's active role in written and verbal communication.

Gemini's connection to "The Twins," siblings and near relations, is a shorthand attempt at expressing the duality of the sign. The idea of the good and bad twin is reflected in the sign's need to acknowledge both sides of itself, to understand that much of what it encounters in the face of its sibling (twin) are mirror images. Perspective and focus elude many in this sign. They often exhibit an amorality that favors expediency and the use of tricks, much like those employed by public relations people. They can be mental pickpockets, plagiarizers of other people's ideas.

But intellectual stimulation is their oxygen, which is why those who know astrology weren't surprised when supermodel Brooke Shields entered (and then graduated from) Princeton. Anne Frank's father was obviously aware of the need for mental exercise when he gave his young daughter a diary to help her pass the time as the family hid away from the Nazis. Anne's daily accounts of her family's life in an attic show a young Gemini interacting with her environment with wit, humor, insight, and poignancy.

Cancer: June 22–July 22
Water/Cardinal/Moon

While Taurus is concerned with physical and material security, Cancer is the sign of the home, both literally and physically. The sign is concerned with emotional security, what's needed to feel emotionally safe. People bond here, form clans. When emotional security (in the form of home or family) are threatened, Cancer can become a pit bull, or at least as ferociously protective as Nancy Reagan reportedly was at the White House.

Cancer's domesticity brings Betty Crocker to mind, but it's also important to recognize that Cancer is also happy doing business in the world, particularly if it's his or her business. H. Ross Perot, Bill Cosby, and the moody George Steinbrenner are all Cancers known to bring the sign's tenaciousnous, protectiveness, and nurturance (in varying degrees) to business. Elizabeth and Bob Dole have both found homes in government. Faye Wattleton, head of Planned Parenthood, works on issues of special concern to women. Twins Eppie and Poppo Friedman ("Dear Abby" and "Ann Landers") nurtured on a large scale. Even the "tough guys" like Ernest Hemingway or boxer Mike Tyson often act macho to cover up their emotionalism and attachment to the past. Sometimes nostalgia is harmless; other times it stifles forward growth. It's not unusual to find Cancers who can't see the future because they relate everything to past experiences. They do this with situations and people alike, and this can make them appear to have petty prejudices. The higher expression of this is the Cancer who picks up the mood of the moment or takes a talent for emotional perceptions and mimicry and turns it into artistic expression—Meryl Streep's acting or Gilda Radner's comedic talents, for instance. Mel Brooks and Dan Akroyd also have the lunar touch.

Astrologer Betty Lunsted has suggested that Cancer children are often not nurtured by their parents and that they grow up compensating. Family issues, for better or worse, are a major theme in Cancer's identity development. Some, such as Mike Tyson, spend their lives trying to find a family. Others, particularly in these times, are looking to break away from parental influence and build their own families. The need to have a home and family are a common theme.

Leo: July 23–August 22   *Fire/Fixed/Sun*

Theirs is the self-styled, signature touch: Henry Ford's car company that bore his name, Lucille Ball, Mick Jagger, Madonna (and Sean Penn), Connie Chung. All of these people are known for their highly self-expressive lives. Born under the Sun-ruled sign of Leo in high summer, they all reflect the sign's need to express itself, to find what is truly the self, and project it through creative endeavors, love affairs, recreation. All of these "creations" are affirmations or extensions of an individual. In Leo, people become their own art form, after taking that Aries identity and adding on to it through the other signs. The journey to one's roots in Cancer gave the foundation needed before this self took the stage. Pride, vanity, and arrogance can stunt Leo's growth and detract from the sign's essential giving and loving nature.

Carl Jung's journeys and examinations are an example of Leo taking his inner self to heart and expressing it through forms that have helped thousands of others look for the essence of who they are so that they, too, can find a truer level of self-expression, which is the Leo byword. When Leo is understood as the sign where you do what you do because that's who you are, its flamboyance can be viewed as more than just an attention-getting ploy. Certainly there are many Leos whose clowning and attempts to push their way into the spotlight represent a very superficial grasp of their deeper needs. These are the people who (like those in many other signs) are content with dressing up and making the rounds of the latest nightspots, just to be seen. But the Leo need is deeper and it is violated every time a person adopts someone else's style or panders to the crowd, or when the applause and attention are priorities. This latter problem becomes especially evident in the area of love affairs, where Leo's need for self-affirmation can cause preoccupation with romance. Self-love and appreciation are needed before Leo's magnanimity and outpouring of love can really be genuine, as Leo Sun-sign Whitney Houston's rendition of "The Greatest Love" shows.

Virgo: August 23–September 22
Earth/Mutable/Mercury

All of that Leonine self-expression can be excessive, and the Virgo period is for analyzing this new self to see what needs to be improved, what skills must be perfected. A season is ending and is ready to give way to another, so a certain amount of reflection is in order. Virgo wants to bring order to life, to establish a routine, to master the details. The sign's concern with working and getting it right is symbolized by Debbra Fields, who perfected her chocolate chip cookies while still a teenager. Lily Tomlin's character portrayals are so powerful because of her well-developed technique and timing. Agatha Christie shows the intricacies of technique, as do Michael Jackson's dance routines. Despite his megastar status—or maybe because of it—Jackson also exhibits some of Virgo's penchant for worrying and for odd habits. Since her creator is a Virgo, it's fair to view the angst of "Cathy," the comic-strip heroine, as Virgoan as well.

Long known as the lint-and-nit pickers of the zodiac, the better Virgos simply see God in the routine of everyday living. Many in the sign follow the path of pioneer social worker Jane Addams or Mother Teresa. While Leo is the sign of "stars," Virgo, with its quiet countenance, is a worker, as Stephen King prolifically shows. It's a perfect sign in which to celebrate a holiday such as Labor Day, but this shortchanges the idea of right vocation and the daily rhythm of life, with which Virgo is trying to find harmony. There are plenty of Virgos who aren't good at the jobs they hold, ones whose lack of perspective and overemphasis on details cut them off from what's really going on. Many of them also have self-worth problems—all that internal criticism—which causes them to adapt to boring, go-nowhere jobs or to take abuse from employers or lovers. Sometimes the only way they can relate to other people is to try and fix or improve them; hence they attract a fair share of friends and associates who are social misfits or have problems that keep them out of the mainstream. Virgos who are most concerned with bringing order, rhythm, and daily reverence to their own lives don't have to worry about this.

Libra: September 23–October 23
Air/Cardinal/Venus

"I wouldn't be where I am today if I were as nice as everyone says I am. I can be very diplomatic, but if you make me angry, I can easily become difficult and stubborn," says actor Michael Douglas, whose Libran face and charm caused directors to cast him in "nice guy" roles for many years until the movie *Wall Street*. Douglas wasn't saying that he was as nasty as Gordon Gekko, the role for which he won an Oscar, but his point in the quoted interview in *Ladies Home Journal* was that he can't be pushed around.

Believe the man. Like most Librans, Douglas goes through life with a fairly pleasant demeanor; this is the sign of relationships and partnerships, after all. But while some Librans want to be liked so badly they'll agree with everyone, Douglas has developed a sense of self and identity that doesn't always come easy to many in this sign. Some astrologers believe that Librans are among the angriest people in the zodiac because many would never dare even to admit to anger, much less express it.

There are some Librans, of course, who can be mistaken for the opposite sign, Aries. These are the Lee Iacocca types, who seem self-directed and don't back down from fights. Margaret Thatcher couldn't be described as anything but tough. Jesse Jackson likes to get things going. Jimmy Carter, known for indecisiveness and an inability to lead, is more typical. Most Librans prefer to be advisers and confidants to the leaders, and accomplish this goal because of their ability to accommodate others and compromise. Astrologers, who've long thought of Libra as a peace-making sign, have attributed this sign's representation among the ranks of military generals and military elite—Dwight Eisenhower or Oliver North—to Libra's political skills. But the real truth to this is that Librans have a lot of fight in them. At some point in their lives they learn that while relationships with others are important, it's even more important to have a self. And those are the Librans who won't be ashamed to say that they're not as nice as everybody thinks.

Scorpio: October 24–November 22
Water/Fixed/Pluto/Mars

In Scorpio the idea of relationships is taken deeper—everything is deeper in Scorpio. Scorpio is where an individual confronts his or her own power and powerlessness. A key area where these issues are confronted is in the realm of intimate emotional connections. As a result Scorpio involves experiences—money, sex—that are shared with other people. It is through these interactions that we come to know ourselves on more intimate levels and confront the matters of power and, sometimes, crass manipulations.

While opposite sign Taurus seeks out money and sex as signs of physical security and pleasure, Scorpio's involvement with these commodities speaks to the conscious and unconscious power issues at work. Unlike Taurus, Scorpio could walk away from the money and other accumulations. It's all part of the sign's perverse courting of death. Death is another area over which individuals have no power; neither their own death or that of a loved one or acquaintance. News of the death of even a distant acquaintance takes something away from us. It's a vulnerability that can't be avoided. Death, however, also takes on more abstract and figurative meanings in Scorpio, the sign in which activities, situations, and ego states come to an end. This allows for the possibility of regeneration and transformation. Whether the new beginning is moved toward depends on the individual Scorpio. As most people with even a passing acquaintance of astrology know, Scorpio is the most maligned of the signs, with older astrological texts accusing them of everything from murders to sex crimes. But even Henry Miller made up some of the sexploits in his novels.

Yes, it's difficult to be a Scorpio, but it's unfair to name Scorpio Charles Manson as the sign's poster child. That the sign can be symbolized by the lowest of lizards or the self-destructive scorpions that sting themselves to death, or the more evolved eagle or the mythological phoenix, which rises anew from its ashes, hints at the depths and complexities of the sign.

The intense Ted Turner displays the sign's ability to consolidate resources and exercise power through CNN and the more recent Turner Network. Marie Curie's long, painstaking years of research and Pablo Picasso's life and art show the concentration and passionate involvement that the sign can bring to its investigation of life's mysteries. Billy Graham's passionate evangelical work shows a Scorpio summoning his inner resources to reform others. Robert Kennedy was a man with a mission. A pack of media celebrities—Dan Rather, Jane Pauley, Bryant Gumbel, Pat Sajack—have the solidity of purpose and accompanying charisma to become "anchors." Roseanne Barr has the sting down well.

The wins and losses that Michael Dukakis has taken during his political career show that the strength of this sign lies in its coming to terms with the only true area of life over which it has some control—inner resources. Through the examination of its own inner motivations and machinery, Scorpio gains the power it seeks and the phoenix rises again.

Sagittarius: November 23–December 21
Fire/Mutable/Jupiter

One thing about Sagittarius people: They don't shy away from making news. Ed Koch, former mayor of New York, is known for his blunt speeches. He's no Mark Twain, but then again Twain—novelist, essayist, lecturer, world traveler—was a Sagittarius extraordinaire. Bette Midler's comic sense and versatility show her to be a true child of Sagittarius, while Phil Donahue's talk of all things topical is an example of this sign at work.

Sagittarius, which follows the transformative Scorpio experience, seeks to develop a philosophy of life and spread it to others. While opposite sign Gemini is concerned with moving around and communicating for his or her own sake, Sagittarius has to see the big picture. Sagittarius represents man's aspirations, both tangible and ontological. The sign's association with religion, higher education, and wisdom result in Sagittarians spending their lifetimes searching for the real meaning of life. Some do it in Sagittarian professions: lawyer, clergy, college professor, publisher, tour guide, travel agent, lecturer, sports. All of these careers, whether it's filmmaking for Steven Spielberg, Chris Evert on the tennis court, or politics for an erudite Paul Simon, allow physical, intellectual, spiritual expansion.

On the surface Sagittarians seem to have a good time. But a self-righteous streak, a belief that their ideas are the last word for the planet, and a certain amount of hypocrisy can turn this Sun sign's ethical concerns into mere abstractions and theories. The world witnessed a rather large—Jupiter rules Sagittarius— example of this in Gary Hart's downfall. Despite his "new ideas" and quest for the big picture, Hart failed to show ethics and honor in his personal life. Frank Sinatra is another Sagittarian who wants everything "my way." As biographer Kitty Kelly has shown, Sinatra's way has often been a reckless disregard for others, particularly women. Sagittarius must learn to integrate the two ends of the centaur (the mythological creature that was half man/half beast) so that their arrow (another Sagittarian symbol) of higher aspirations and quests will be more on the mark.

Capricorn: December 22–January 19
Earth/Cardinal/Saturn

Benjamin Franklin, one of the country's first and most popular self-help writers (*Poor Richard's Almanac*) had the sort of initiative, discipline, political skills, and business acumen that generations of Americans have admired. Elizabeth Arden and Diane Von Furstenberg are Capricorns who had the stuff needed to go the distance in life, to allow them to build the systems and structures in the outer world the sign values so much. And as Diane Sawyer, Marlene Dietrich, and actor Ted Danson show, the sign, which rules the skeletal system, can also bestow good bones.

Even Capricorns who are involved with illegal matters— such as the exclusive call-girl service run by the so-called Mayflower Madam, an industrious Capricorn if there ever was one—have a seriousness and an air of respectability and elitism that's very to-the-manner-born. David Bowie veers from the often-traveled road, but with Capricorn discipline and skill. Martin Luther King, Jr.'s humanitarian and religious interests show that the sign has concerns beyond money and status, but it should also be noted that King's approach to civil rights was more conservative than that of various radicals of the 1960s.

The sign's concern with status can produce a perverted sort of person who wouldn't waste his time with anything or anyone who couldn't help him promote his interests. At their best, however, Capricorns are the respected businesspeople who are also able to build a healthy personal domestic life. It's impossible to talk about Capricorn in modern times without noting that the most fascinating and infamous person in the tribe is Richard Nixon. His life epitomizes the perseverance, determination, and hard work that took him from humble beginnings to the most powerful leadership position in the world. And then he lost it all when paranoia and the need for control turned against him. A cloud of moroseness follows many Capricorns, even Elvis Presley. Edgar Allan Poe's life showed these strains. The sign can cut itself off from its emotions and instinctual life. These people can build walls between themselves and others—even family members, whom they're often working very hard (even if unconsciously) to please. Like their opposite sign, Cancer, Capricorns are usually working out significant issues related to parents and other authority figures in their lives. Their rigidity can cause them to snuff out their true identity and uniqueness. There's nothing wrong with ambition and building steady structures, but self-respect is more important than the more temporal prestige offered by the outer world.

Aquarius: January 20–February 18
Air/Fixed/Uranus/Saturn

Oprah Winfrey, Helen Gurley Brown, Ronald Reagan—what they have in common is the way they interact with the human community. On the one hand, they're a part of it; on the other hand, they stand alone amid the crowd. It's hard to know which of these things you want to do when you're an Aquarius. The sign cherishes freedom, but it also believes in participating in society. *The Arsenio Hall Show* is one of those ways. Before politics became his vocation, Dan Quayle was known for being out among the crowds, even if only on a social level.

Their detachment, even as they stand amid the masses, makes them difficult to know, as those in Reagan's cabinet have said in their kiss-and-tell books. Usually they have a hard time fitting in, no matter what they do. The sign is home to both those who work to promote mankind, as well as rebels without a cause. The better ones have their mind on the future, which allows them to visualize and obtain goals for themselves and society. Thomas Edison, and Mark Goodson, the television producer who created most of the game shows on the air, show the creative range. The Aquarian bent for the perverse and radical can produce rabid conservatives as well as liberals. Franklin D. Roosevelt's membership in the sign makes sense to those who fall for the publicity kit proclaiming Aquarius as the sign of brotherhood. But the Aquarian interest in societal goals is often characterized by ideology and dogma. They know what's best for the community, as Ronald Reagan more or less said for eight years.

The typical Aquarian, of course, doesn't play such a consequential role in the life of the planet. Some act as community organizers, mobilizing people to take on the government or other powers that be. But frequently these Aquarians display the manipulative and authoritarian tendencies of the sign. Unlike Leo, who isn't afraid to take center stage and who is pretty up front about his or her pride and ego, Aquarius likes to appear to be above all of it. In addition to being in need of some of the Leo warmth and love for life, Aquarians need to understand who they really are, apart from the roles they take up in society.

Pisces: February 19–March 20
Water/Mutable/Neptune/Jupiter

Whereas all of the other signs were looking to discover their true identities through various earth activities, Pisces would really prefer to get out of here altogether. The sign seeks to transcend all limitations, the body and its responsibilities. These people are E.T. waiting for the ride home. In the meantime they seek ways to merge with God or the Universe, something larger than themselves. Michelangelo and Leonardo da Vinci are Piscean legends. Elizabeth Taylor, Rudolf Nureyev, and Alice Walker are people who can transcend the earth by means of their art; Albert Einstein, by trying to understand man's relationship to it all. Others find work in the healing/counseling professions. Pisces businessmen and government officials, such as Alan Greenspan or Mikhail Gorbachev, might appear to be contradictions but the sign has a relation to institutions that address man's collective ills and problems. A number of insurance executives have this sign prominent, which probably speaks to the societal "safety net" that insurance provides against life's perils.

At the risk of stereotyping signs, we can't overlook the many Pisces people who have trouble finding a niche in life. Life can be overwhelming and unbearable for them, so they seek solace in alcohol, drugs, or various other addictions. Certainly all the signs have their share of addicts, but the Pisces experience expresses some of the motivations and issues surrounding addictions, mental illnesses, and various delusions or confusions about daily living, so the sign is said to have a special affinity with these matters. Older texts describe Pisces as the zodiac's "dustbin" and say that it contains elements of all the other signs as well as anything that has been discarded. What is being spoken to is the diffuseness of the sign. Pisces knows no borders and often doesn't differentiate.

Patty Hearst's abduction experience, her "love affair" with one of her militant captors and assumption of the identity of Tanya, as well as her subsequent marriage to her bodyguard, is an extreme expression of the unusual twists of victimization, class, and race that can crop up in the personal lives of some Pisces (as well as in its opposite sign, Virgo). Both signs host a fair number of people with patterns of mates who are from strikingly different social classes or have physical handicaps that might set them apart from the rest of society—the social worker who dates prison inmates, for instance. People with this Sun sign must find expressions that allow them to merge with the essence of the Universe, but they must also come to learn that meeting the demands of daily existence can have a special magic to it, too.

Birthday Year Chart

The following chart divides the "year" by seasons. The individual "spring" begins with the birthday. Summer is three signs away and begins about 90 days after the birthday. Fall is six months, or about 180 days, after the birthday. Winter begins three signs (and about 90 days) prior to the next birthday.

Birthday/Spring	Summer	Fall	Winter
Aries Mar/Apr	Cancer Jun/Jul	Libra Sep/Oct	Capricorn Dec/Jan
Taurus Apr/May	Leo Jul/Aug	Scorpio Oct/Nov	Aquarius Jan/Feb
Gemini May/Jun	Virgo Aug/Sep	Sagittarius Nov/Dec	Pisces Feb/Mar
Cancer Jun/Jul	Libra Sep/Oct	Capricorn Dec/Jan	Aries Mar/Apr
Leo Jul/Aug	Scorpio Oct/Nov	Aquarius Jan/Feb	Taurus Apr/May
Virgo Aug/Sep	Sagittarius Nov/Dec	Pisces Feb/Mar	Gemini May/Jun
Libra Sep/Oct	Capricorn Dec/Jan	Aries Mar/Apr	Cancer Jun/Jul
Scorpio Oct/Nov	Aquarius Jan/Feb	Taurus Apr/May	Leo July/Aug
Sagittarius Nov/Dec	Pisces Feb/Mar	Gemini May/Jun	Virgo Aug/Sep
Capricorn Dec/Jan	Aries Mar/Apr	Cancer Jun/Jul	Libra Sep/Oct
Aquarius Jan/Feb	Taurus Apr/May	Leo Jul/Aug	Scorpio Oct/Nov
Pisces Feb/Mar	Gemini May/Jun	Virgo Aug/Sept	Sagittarius Nov/Dec

Five

The Moods of the Moon

The mysterious Moon has entranced humankind since we first saw it sweeping across the sky, moving through the rhythmic changes that make it all the more awe-inspiring. People worship the Moon, write poems about it, and yearn, dream, and fantasize under its watch. Walking on the Moon may have made it more familiar, but that feat hasn't totally demystified it. On nights when the Moon is at its fullest or in perfect crescent form, we can't help but fall for its seduction act, even as we rush to the video store, automated bank teller, or other high-tech errands.

Growing up, however, requires accepting some facts about the Moon and its hold on our life: The Moon isn't made of cheese, and those craters really aren't the outline of a "man in the Moon." It represents the way we've registered experiences and, hence, how we react to new ones. Like the mood rings popular in the 1970s, the Moon is emotions, and feelings, and the way we accept (or reject) and handle them. This function can be applied to mass psychology as well, and Chapter 6 will explore the Moon's role in phenomena such as rainfall, stock market fluctuations, murder rates, and the menstrual cycle. But its connection to individual emotions and daily responses to life are the point from which we're going to begin our discussion.

At the risk of conjuring up annoying images of singers who never seem to be able to hit the high notes but insist on crooning the popular tune from *Cats*, the Moon is memory. The Moon's association with memory should not be confused with the kind of mental process that helps us remember addresses or phone numbers. Memory here involves the range of sense impressions that we exhume when revisiting moments in our lives. It's the pictures, tastes, smells, feelings, and images that come to mind when we attempt to recall our earliest encounters with our mother or the earliest of our childhood experiences. The Moon should be viewed as the way we've assimilated the past and, hence, suggests our habitual responses today.

Carol, a twenty-nine-year-old musician, had an ample supply of mental snapshots to share when asked to recall the very first moments from her childhood. "My first memories are pre-school. I felt stupid. . . . feeling I couldn't do anything right. I didn't fit in there. . . . Whenever I felt like I wanted attention, I would go in the corner and sulk, and this teacher would always come to me. I was always feeling I was going to do something wrong and get laughed at . . . feeling dumb like. Everybody had their family names, and mine was Dizzy, Dumb. Even Ma called me those names: Dummy, Old Dizzy, Stupid, Dense. Those names stick with you. You really feel like you're stupid, and then whenever people wanted to compliment you, it was hard to accept. My mother and sister remember me as being good at softball, running around the bases. But I remember being afraid to hit the ball and finally striking out and letting everybody down. I never liked sports. I always felt klutzy. I was the last person to be picked for kick ball. I guess I made up for it with creative things, writing poems and stories and music. But the names stuck for a long time. It's probably why I didn't want to go to my high school reunion. It was like all these memories coming up again."

Leafing through snapshots from the past can be emotionally overwhelming. Even without actual photographs in hand, the imprints from past experiences can be deeply embedded within us. They affect the way we feel about ourselves, handle our emotions, and carry on in daily life. Like Carol's mother and sister, whose memory contains pictures of her being adroit at softball, other people around us may have viewed our life situations differently than the way we were feeling them. But since we're talking about "our" feelings, "our" memories, the recollections, sense impressions, smells, colors, and images that come to mind when we recall past experiences carry more weight because those are the pictures that are affecting our lives today. As playwright Harold Pinter wrote, "The past is what you remember, imagine yourself to remember, convince yourself you remember or pretend to remember."

Craig Barclay, a University of Rochester psychologist, says that while many of these autobiographical memories may diverge from reality, they are tied to our belief about ourselves. Barclay asked people to keep a diary of three daily events for four months, and their memories of these events were examined over two and a half years. Five months into the experiment the subjects generally began accepting "false memories" (Barclay had altered diary records) with a high level of confidence. Futher research comparing women who suffer from premenstrual syndrome (PMS) with those not subject to it found that the PMS group were more error-prone than the control group in distinguishing between accurate records and altered ones. Barclay theorized that mood swings might be the cause. The control group, who in psychological tests were shown to have a more positive view of themselves, had trouble remembering negative events in their past and therefore were more optimistic and confident about their future.

Astrologers start with the Moon when they want to excavate details about the past—and, often, the future. Because it relates so much to early conditioning, the Moon has an indirect connection to our self-image. As the second most important factor in the horoscope, generally speaking, the Moon performs a life function similar to its astronomical role of acting as the reflector for the Sun's light. Our Gemini, Taurus, or Leo energy, as indicated by our Sun sign, works in tandem with and can be viewed as reflecting off of our Moon. An especially embattled Moon isn't going to allow the Sun to move forward in its glory. A Moon that by sign and other configurations is not sympathetic to the Sun's cause can also make it difficult for people to feel comfortable or secure with themselves. Because the Moon moves through the entire zodiac in 27.5 days, it spends no more than 2.5 days in each sign. While the Sun stays about 30 days in one sign, the Moon's movement will produce different Sun/Moon combinations every 2 or 3 days. A Taurus, at one point in the week, might be born with a practical-minded, though fussy, Virgo Moon. Another Taurus, born in the same year 17.5 days later, will have adventurous, restless Sagittarius for a Moon sign. The later Taurus is faced with more contradictions than the Virgo Moon, which shares the Earth element with Taurus. But even compatible Moon signs require study for insight into their responses to life and the reasons behind them.

Exploring the Moon can often be like lifting an old Band-Aid off a wound that hasn't healed, despite a seemingly lengthy period of time. Over the last decade, in particular, we've heard much about the need to rediscover who the inner child is, since these are the needs we are unconsciously trying to have met for once in our lives. People who didn't feel nurtured may seek this in relationships; or conversely, may unconsciously feel unworthy and continually reject partners because that feeling is so familiar. The dilemma—and the need for reparenting—form the basis of many self-help guides in today's bookstores. Even books that aren't directly about healing childhood hurts but are more concerned about teaching us how to find a mate or build a healthy corporate career usually spend a chapter or two looking in on the children we once were.

Familiar Connections

Not only does the Moon help lead astrologers to the answers about early emotional conditioning, the variety of Moon sign expressions also explains how siblings form unique personalities and relationships with their parents. Sometimes they draw the same Moon signs. Both of Aristotle Onassis's children—Christina, who died at thirty-seven in 1988, and Alexander, who died in a plane crash at the age of twenty-five in 1973—were born with the Moon in Capricorn. That Adolf Hitler also had his Moon in this sign is a piece of shorthand often used to convey the difficulties of this position. Obviously, most people born with the Moon in Capricorn aren't like Adolf Hitler, but they do close off their feelings from others and themselves. Abraham Lincoln's lifelong struggle with depression was a result of complicated horoscope configurations, but having the Moon in Capricorn didn't ease the problem. Astrologer Donna Cunningham quotes a Moon in Capricorn woman whose mother was fond of saying, "I'm not raising children, I'm raising adults." Those with this Moon put their energy into playing their strengths, which are a persistence and organizational sense that allow them to build the place in the world that brings about the respect and authority they need for emotional security.

Since the Moon is most often associated with the female parent, let's consider the brood of Lillian Carter, a double Leo (both the Sun and Moon in this very proud sign) from Plains, Georgia. The family produced very different personalities. As her youngest child, Billy (born in 1937) was to observe, "I have a brother who wants to be President, one sister who rides motorcycles, and another who is a holy-roller preacher. That makes me the only sane one in the family." Sister Gloria did ride a motorcycle with her husband, but her life displayed many of the Moon in Taurus concerns for stability, pragmatism, and comfort. Younger sister Ruth had the Sun in Leo need for expression, and her Moon in Virgo caused her to want to analyze and bring order to things. She wrote a book explaining her "Brother Billy" (and the rest of the family) to the world when brother Jimmy ascended to the American presidency. It wouldn't surprise most people to learn that Jimmy's Sun in Libra was nearly 180 degrees from Billy's Sun in Aries; the two seemed at direct odds, polar opposites. But emotionally the two brothers were similar and drew the same intense, probing, brooding, but inherently resourceful Moon in Scorpio to prove it.

The Moon in Scorpio is one of the more misunderstood (and commented upon) Moon positions. Those born under it are often bogged down with resentments about the slings and arrows from the past. They often grow up feeling manipulated, cheated, and overly sensitive to hints of betrayal. Billy Carter, born eight years after Jimmy, grew up dreaming of taking over his father's peanut business. His father always told Billy the business would be his since oldest son Jimmy had chosen the navy. But when Earle Carter died in 1953, Billy was only fifteen. Jimmy was forced to abort his career as a naval officer to oversee the family business. As Ruth Carter Stapleton notes in her account of the period, not one of the brothers (nor Jimmy's wife, Rosalynn) was initially pleased with the turn of fate. Billy, in particular, felt cheated out of the family business. Feelings that combined with his grief over his father's death cast a shadow over his life that would never lift, even as he struggled in his final living days to fight alcoholism. On many levels he got even with life and his family for the hand he'd been dealt, and in doing so, as the self-destructive side of Scorpio would have it, he got himself, too. In his fight against

his addiction, Billy Carter displayed some of the Moon in
Scorpio's tremendous power for self-healing and transformation (witness the lives of people like Jean Nidetch, Weight
Watchers' founder, or Elizabeth Taylor's fight against food and
drug addiction, or the work of feminist lawyer Gloria Allred,
a former rape victim). Jimmy Carter showed the position's
reformer instincts, as well as the inherent adeptness at gathering
and consolidating a number of resources to put oneself in a
position of power. The commingling of resources also involves
issues such as sex, which some in this Moon group abuse. This
is the Happy Hooker's Moon sign. While Raquel Welch shows
the sign's ability to project sexuality and animal magnetism,
she has fought successfully in recent years to downplay her
sex-symbol image and be taken seriously as an actress. But
even after overcoming tremendous obstacles, this Moon sign
isn't immune to certain levels of bitterness. Jimmy Carter,
Libran smile aside, was known to make cutting remarks every
now and then.

Moon signs set the response to life from birth and possibly
even before that. Baby M, subject of a bitter custody battle
when her biological mother, Mary Beth Whitehead, backed out
of a surrogacy agreement, was born with a Scorpio Moon.
Given what we know about Baby M's life and past—as well
as the conditions that resulted in her conception—it's not difficult to imagine the Moon in Scorpio at work in her life as
she matures. Baby M was born with the Sun in fighting Aries,
just like her biological mother. Mary Beth Whitehead's Moon
is in Cancer, the Moon's natural home.

Natural should not be mistaken for "better" or "best." In
the same way that the Moon is concerned with the past and
where one comes from, Cancer is where people nest, set up a
home, and live, both in a literal and an emotional sense. In
setting up one's home, Cancer sets boundaries—defining who
is in the family or clan—and defends, protects, and nurtures.
People with this Moon sign will fight crab-claws and nails with
anyone who poses a threat to the home life. This is where
astrologers get all those adjectives about the "nurturing, sensitive" Cancers and why it's considered the sign of motherhood
and parenting. Those with Moon in Cancer (and the Sun, too)
like to cook and tend to the needs of those around them.

All signs have their negative sides. While astrologers commonly point out the more negative traits of signs such as Scorpio
(ruthless) and Virgo (picky, picky, picky), Cancer's weak

points are often couched in words that don't accurately reflect the damage they can do to themselves and others. This need to nest, to revel in one's home, literally and figuratively speaking, can often produce people with little objectivity. Sometimes it's harmless nostalgia, where conversation with a friend might get someone with a Cancer emphasis to start recalling a special dessert Mother used to make or the family's regular summer trips to Nantucket. But often the Cancer Moon's feelings or impressions prejudge or misinterpret people and situations based on past experiences that either they or someone from the family has had. In Part III you will encounter the notion of horoscopes for nations and see how being "born on the Fourth of July," and therefore with the Sun in Cancer, helps foster the clannishness, insecurity, and defensiveness of the U.S.A.'s national character. In much the same way that the U.S.A.'s protectiveness toward other countries carries certain strings, Cancer's nurturing instincts can sometimes be as much for Cancer to handle as they are for the recipient of his or her attention. This is why an emphasis on Cancer in the birthchart can just as often indicate a difficult home life as it does a comfortable one. As the Baby M case indicated, mothering might have been what Mary Beth Whitehead desired and needed, but she probably wasn't the best mother for the baby.

In fact, many astrologers give Taurus higher marks in the parenting/domesticity department (the ancients believe the Moon was exalted in Taurus). These people know how to create comfortable surroundings without the emotional trip that Cancer puts on people around them. Taurus also rates high as a sign of professional chefs. Their relationship with cooking and food is more of a sensual experience than is Cancer's, which is really a feeding of feelings and emotions. As most weight-control experts attest, people shouldn't eat when they're upset or looking to adjust their feelings, they should eat when they're hungry. A Moon that is under stress in a birthchart can relate to eating disorders or bad habits learned as far back as childhood. Sometimes what's passed down from Mother or the family isn't just an attitude but a way of living that children need to deprogram themselves from or reconcile within themselves in order to thrive. Liza Minnelli is an example of a Cancer Moon who has blossomed, despite having had a mother (Judy Garland) who bequeathed her both talent and tragedy.

Which Came First? Mother or the Moon?

But mothers can't be totally blamed for the ways we grow into our Moons. Christina Crawford's Moon in Aries would have needed to learn independence, to stick up for itself, to take charge in life. Moon in Aries can also suggest an angry, harsh mother. But Crawford, an adopted child, had an Aries Moon before Joan Crawford's (Sun in Aries/Moon in Aquarius) abusive mothering. For some reason we don't understand, Crawford's Aries Moon learned some of its inherently necessary independence needs from the movie star. Crawford's emotional need to lead and fight is now being expressed on behalf of abused children. Other Moon in Aries people—baseball manager Billy Martin, Marlon Brando, Lily Tomlin, Jacqueline Kennedy Onassis—pick their fights in other arenas. Founding Father John Adams was an Aries Moon who was notorious for agitating his colleagues. The musical *1776* does a comical take on this, with a song "John, Won't You Sit Down." Even if Joan Crawford had been June Cleaver, Christina Crawford would have internalized an emotional need to stand up for herself and take charge of her life. Ideally, of course, it's always nice to have a cheering squad rooting on your behalf.

The 27.5-Year Mood Cycle

Another area of emotional development that should be briefly noted is a 27.5-year cycle of emotional maturation. This cycle, known as the Secondary-Progressed Moon, is derived from the idea that every day beyond birth is equal to a year of life. According to this theory, the ephemeris listing for the tenth day after birth—for example, July 27, 1957 for someone born July 17, 1957—tells us some about a person's subjective life experiences during the tenth year of life. Because the Moon takes 27.5 days to make a full trip through the zodiac, the ephemeris shows it returning to the exact point it was located at a person's birth, 27.5 days—or by extension, 27.5 years—after birth. People begin responding to life more objectively, setting the stage for the critical age-thirty changes that will be discussed in the chapters on Saturn.

While the 27.5-year Lunar Return is especially important,

emotional reactions take on a change in "shading" every 2.5 years, when the Secondary-Progressed Moon changes signs. For instance, Sean was born with the Moon in Taurus, a sign that likes to stay put. Some forty-three days after Sean's birth, the Moon was in Sagittarius. Now, in his forty-third year of life, he's traveling and getting more interested in philosophy and the larger world. His Taurus Moon is still the dominant influence—he makes sure any hotel he checks into has all the comforts a Taurus requires—but his current emotional need is to explore the world more than he has before. During the previous two years, when the Moon moved through Scorpio, he underwent a divorce and got some therapy. While larger cycles indicate some of the major changes he's undergone, his Progressed Moon shows his emotional reactions and some of his evolving emotional needs. Michelle, meanwhile, is a Sagittarius Moon who is becoming more interested in giving form to her aspirations and philosophy now that her Progressed Moon is in Capricorn.

You can track your Progressed Moon once you have become more acquainted with your natal Moon sign and the different qualities that all the other zodiac signs bring to the Moon. Although it's a technical undertaking, I mention it for those of you who may choose to carry your study of the Moon further.

The Moon Out in the World

Discussion so far has been limited to the Moon's operation on an individual level, but its effect can be observed in a more general way in the population at large. The Moon's swift movement means that it forms configurations with the rest of the solar system throughout each day. Those who clock the Moon's movement in connection with stocks often find discernible shifts during stressful configurations, such as sudden reversals with an aspect to Uranus (provided other indicators are at work), or maybe a drop with Saturn. Astrometeorologists track the Moon in a similar manner. The configurations that correlate to the hourly weather changes are the same ones that might trigger a shoot-out or other event that makes the local or national news. To simplify its effect, the Moon is being isolated from the rest of the sky and viewed as a solitary traveler. When this is done, the sign in the zodiac through which it is moving will be the "something in the air" that causes people to be especially outspoken one day (the Moon in Sagittarius) or more emotional and concerned with domestic matters (Moon in Cancer) on another. It's not accurate to assign specific types of activities to the Moon's travels through the signs. Much more important than the Moon's zodiac sign are the angular relationships (aspects) among the Moon, Sun, and planets.

Yet despite the secondary importance of the zodiac signs, the Moon placement colors the event. The opening of the New York subway, for instance, occurred when the Sun was in underground Scorpio and the Moon in Gemini, the sign of short trips. Pearl Harbor and Hiroshima involved threats to emotional security, family, home and country, pride, and dignity as the Moon moving out of Cancer and into Leo on the days of both the bombings shows. John F. Kennedy was killed as the Moon traveled through socially conscious Aquarius. An Aquarian placement could also indicate an event that would affect the masses emotionally. The Moon was in Aquarius when the Founding Fathers adopted the Declaration of Independence back in 1776. The big break away from the crushing foot of authority had been taken on a Full Moon two days earlier, when the Moon was in Capricorn. That was when the debate was at its most critical, when sides had to be drawn and a decision made. The Founding Fathers had to confront their feelings about authority, homeland, and tradition. Then, in radical Aquarius, it was time to band together around common goals and a vision for the future.

Emma Goldman, Angela Davis, Margaret Mead, Prince, and Daniel Ortega were all born on days when the Moon was in this cause-oriented sign. Richard Nixon, despite the corrupt Watergate antics, displayed the Aquarian Moon's visionary and social engineering talents through his history-making trip to China and creation of agencies like the Occupational Health and Safety Administration. These activities were more progressive than those advocated by many other Republicans. The Moon shows his detachment from the masses but also his desire to participate in its destiny. Many astrologers wrongly assume that everything Aquarian has to be politically radical, or at the very least Liberal-Democrat. Sandra Day O'Connor, a political conservative, is an Aquarian Moon, which, working along with a Sun in Aries, has been evident in her struggle for equality as a woman working in male-dominated arenas. Aquarius is concerned with community and social goals for the future. And all Aquarians think that the future has been revealed to them; they believe that they know what's best for group interests.

That Inconstant Moon

The Moon's speed—an average of 13 degrees a day—makes it a source of research that can provide ample information in a short amount of time. The following chapter will acquaint you with Moon phases; how they affect individual personalities at birth and how they provide a monthly rhythm in life. Because the Moon changes signs so frequently, it's impossible to include a Moon ephemeris in this book. However, Donna Cunningham's MOON SIGNS (Ballantine) records all Moon sign locations for this century and provides a good introduction to the Moon's meaning in each sign. The book and/or a birth chart will enhance your personal research efforts.

But research must be undertaken carefully. The natal Moon position is a major player in the psychological makeup of an individual. The transits that planets—particularly Jupiter through Pluto—make to the Moon, as well as the progressions of the Moon and other planets, will be significant throughout life.

However, the transiting Moon, which is now under study, stands at the lower end of transits affecting the birthchart. It's important for students to learn the general mood they're in each month when the Moon is in Leo, Gemini, or any other sign. But the daily movement of the Moon through the sky *does not* in itself denote any specific event. The Moon might let us know whether the hot temperatures being predicted for tomorrow would be offset by balmy breezes or stifled by humidity. The transiting Moon would be among the last in the hierarchy of factors studied, acting as a timer in interaction with larger forces.

But even in a chart such as that of serial killer Ted Bundy, where the traveling Moon had made a 90-degree (tension) angle to his Sun about two hours before his execution, the Moon was merely helping pull the curtain down over a highly intensified story line between numerous planets. The meat of the story lay in the full birthchart, in the progressions, and in the transits of the slower-moving planets.

Isolating the Moon's zodiac location during public events involving the famous and infamous is more misleading than revealing. People lose jobs, walk out on relationships, and die when the Moon is in signs that on first sight seem quite friendly (two or four signs away from the birth Moon and Sun). The Moon was moving across Patty Hearst's Sun sign—no doubt causing useless newspaper horoscopes to proclaim much good for everyone born under Pisces for February 4, 1974—as well as her Venus when she was abducted. Several once-in-a-life-time planetary rhythms were being activated when Pete Rose was suspended from baseball. The traveling Moon was moving in opposition to his natal Moon during the time of the press conference announcing the decision, indicating a possible emotional upset. The Moon was in Michael Dukakis's Sun sign and directly across from his Moon sign on election day, which came five days after his birthday. The Moon's travel through the Sun sign is considered an energizer. The Moon's transit right across from the natal Moon sign can be viewed as stressful, but its movement over the Sun would have balanced this. Astrologer Debbi Kempton Smith has called the days when the Moon moves over one's Sun sign "green light" days. In theory this would seem to be true, but since the traveling Moon can never act alone, be careful about applying such information. The presidential election on November 7, 1989, is a perfect example of this. By daily Moon standards Dukakis looked better than Bush.

Before resting this argument about the highly transitory nature of the daily Moon's influence and the importance of knowing the bigger cycles in effect, I'm going to move over to the tennis court, where the kind of emotional ups and downs indicated by the Moon's travels have important ramifications. Martina Navratilova lost to teen whiz Steffi Graf in the finals at the 1989 U.S. Open, with the Moon returning back to the older champion's natal birth position in Capricorn and starting a new monthly emotional cycle. The traveling Moon was in a challenging position to her natal Sun. Having the traveling Moon return to intense, calculating Capricorn would suggest a chance to focus emotionally and give extra impetus to the game, or it might also cause initial diffusement.

But Steffi Graf rewrites any previous definitions of "good" and "bad" days. Graf had survived the Moon moving in unfriendly angles (three and six signs away) to her Sun and Moon during her win against Navratilova and during other portions of the Open. It's almost ridiculous even to think that the possible discomfort or emotional unevenness suggested by the traveling Moon would be significant enough to set her back. She has given astrologers much to think about before giving dismal forecasts or discouraging clients from putting out their best in any given situation. Her 1988 series of tournament and grand-slam wins came in the midst of the kind of astrological configurations that cause some people to withdraw from life or stumble along for a while. Graf showed that people have the ability to excel despite the most difficult of energies, and to win. Other champions show this same ability to be "on" and in the moment, even though many astrologers would have recommended they lie low for the day.

Know Your Chart

Understanding the general energies symbolized by the traveling Moon's zodiac position is important. But knowing what the position means for you personally requires study of the birthchart. You may indeed find that Moon in Sagittarius truly causes optimism and good feeling. But such information can only be determined if you keep a log on how you respond to each Moon sign over a period of time. Numerous books contain lists indicating which Moon signs are best for certain types of activities—meetings, socials, and sales pitches, for instance— and these lists are good to scan to get a sense of the general public mood for the day. But there are limits to this sort of thinking. Once again, the configurations that the Moon is in with the rest of the solar system are important. And even this information isn't enough. The Moon in Libra (an arts sign) for *A Chorus Line*, which opened off-Broadway May 21, 1975, was being battered around by Saturn, among other planets, and there are many other configurations that astrologers in their limited wisdom would have counseled producers to avoid. Any new venture has difficulties—some of them necessary for purposes of momentum and further development—so daily Moon-sign watching has to be kept in perspective. *Saturday Night Live* (October 11, 1975) debuted with the Moon in dour Capricorn in strained relationships with the Sun and other points in the sky.

Several people with a yen for gambling and lotteries have sought help by using "lucky day" charts that name days that are supposedly the best for playing lotteries and engaging in other gambling activities. Some of these mass-produced charts are keyed to the Moon's travel through certain zodiac signs and advise people to buy lottery tickets and other chances when the Moon is in risk-taking Leo or Sagittarius. But in truth, people also win lotteries when the Moon is in nongambling signs, such as Virgo or Capricorn. It all depends on the natal predilection. One lucky winner who comes to mind is a "professional contestant" I interviewed for a women's magazine. This woman, who lives in the Denver area, regularly wins trips to the Cayman Islands, New York, California, ten-thousand-dollar lotteries, and has a strong, bountiful Jupiter (Sun in Pisces/Moon in Sagittarius), among other patterns, which causes her to spend more than forty hours a week seeking opportunities on radio call-in shows, coupons, and anywhere anyone is giving something away.

People with the Moon in Sagittarius shouldn't take this as a suggestion that they should head to Las Vegas. Not all people with this Moon sign expand through gambling. As the lives of Neil Armstrong, Albert Einstein, and Mike Tyson show, the Sagittarian journey can take many forms. Oprah Winfrey calls her television show her "ministry," a word reflecting the Sagittarian's liking for preaching. The general meanings and roles of the Sun, Moon, and planets aside, every person responds differently and reacts to some combinations more than others. Some charts will be particularly sensitive to every movement the Moon makes, others won't. The challenge for anyone looking to read a chart is to get a good sense of how all of the energies interact with one another. A horoscope is a painting. Blue is blue of course, but when it is placed next to red or mixed with green, it shows something that wasn't there before.

Individuals can begin to answer some of the questions about the role of the Moon for themselves by undertaking several projects related to the Moon's travel through the zodiac.

The 27.5-Day Rhythm

The Moon moves through the whole zodiac in 27.5 days, meaning that it will always return to a given sign 27.5 days later. This allows for several different projects.

1. **Mood Log:** Keep a diary of the Moon's effect in each sign. Of particular interest will be personal reactions to specific Moon signs (this will ultimately have something to do with the

way the Moon interacts with the specifics of the birthchart).
But initially, simple observations of activities, dreams, and
other phenomena associated with the sign are important.

2. Monthly Ups and Downs: Cycle studies show a four-
to six-week emotional cycle. The "Monthly Mood/Moon
Cycle" chart on page 96 will allow the tracking of moods, as
well as help readers determine whether certain moods are more
likely to be associated with a given Moon sign. Ideally, moods
should move through the range of stages in a given month.
Should you find yourself alternating between elation and
depression, with no stages in between, on a regular basis you
may want to read *Moodswing*, by Dr. Ronald R. Fieve, a leader
in the treatment of manic-depressives and others with significant mood shifts.

3. The Moon's Return: During its monthly trip through
the zodiac the Moon returns to each individual's birth Moon.
Some branches of astrology have found much information
on general emotional trends by studying charts drawn for the
exact moment of this so-called Lunar Return. Even without a
monthly Moon chart, those who have an especially prominent
Moon always know when the Moon has returned. One Cancer Moon woman is usually in a depression funk, while a
Scorpio Moon man says his already seething emotions become
even more intense. "It gets scary," he says.

There's a monthly trend at work, which would have a trigger
point 14 days from the Lunar Return. The concept is similar
to the 14.5-critical-emotional-day period noted by biorhythms,
and sometimes they overlap. But the intent here isn't to mix
up the biorhythms with astrology. Little convincing work has
been done to correlate the two systems, and biorhythms are as
overlooked as astrology is when it comes to mainstream researchers.

The Moon cycle stands alone for now. The fourteen-day
period from one's monthly Lunar Return would put the Moon
at about 180 degrees away from the personal Moon position,
which would highlight personal emotional matters.

4. When the Moon Meets Your Sun: Watch these days,
because you often have extra energy and may be able to focus
on a special task in your environment. A Libran who spent one
of the days when the Moon was in Libra lining up a string of
new business opportunities described it as his "power day."
Some astrologers feel that when the Moon is six signs, or 180
degrees, away from one's Sun, it brings about emotional upsets

and other obstacles. But this is not always true, as examples earlier in this chapter showed (the rest of the chart must be studied). When the Moon is in Aries, the Libran mentioned above says he's often in situations that require compromise and negotiation. "But I still win," he says.

Moon Void-of-Course

Some astrologers place much weight on the times when the Moon, while traveling through any given zodiac sign, falls out of communication with the other planetary travelers in the sky. Because of its current location, the Moon is not able to make any of the traditional aspects or mathematical relationships, so it in essence is in a world of its own. This is called a Void-of-Course Moon. On Earth these voided periods, which can last anywhere from two hours to 2.5 days, are viewed as times when there is a high degree of error in decision-making. Activities take on a diffuse quality until the Moon moves into a new sign and begins making special angles to the rest of the planets all over again. Because the Moon changes signs every 2.5 days, it can get a renewed charge and start having relationships with other planets once it gets into a new sign. It's sort of like changing tables at a party or leaving your favorite neighborhood pub and coming back when you have more steam. The most basic (and least disputed) example of a voided Moon would be one moving from 29 degrees of one sign to zero (the beginning of another). The Moon is in this state for about two hours every 2.5 days.

When the Sun moves to 29 degrees, it means it's getting ready to go into a new sign. At 29 degrees, 59 minutes Pisces (where the Sun can be anywhere from March 19 to March 21, depending on the year), the Sun is throwing off it's winter mindset, and the next stop, zero (0 degrees Aries) is the first day of spring.

The Moon can go Void-of-Course within minutes after entering a sign. It depends on what the rest of the solar system's tenants are up to at the time. Each zodiac sign has thirty degrees. Moon could enter Taurus and find itself in an angular relationship with the Sun and planets throughout most of its Taurus ride. So it may just be looking to dust itself off during the 29th degree of Taurus before heading into Gemini. But then it may move into the sign only to find that it has a difficult time getting in touch with other planets through the traditional angular relationships—it can't make a square, trine, sextile, opposition—and we all know what happens when E.T. can't call home.

The recommended antidote for Moon Void-of-Course is meditation and reflection. Those in creative work say the period is good for incubation. New York astrologer Al H. Morrison has promoted observance of the Void and says it's not a good time to launch a project. Its full effect, however, is not known. Some writers have attributed the fate of various political campaigns to the Void, but the theory falls apart under inspection. Both George Bush and Michael Dukakis (who was born on a Voided Moon) announced their candidacy on a Voided Moon if traditional definitions are utilized.

This brings up technical matters that result in disputes about when the Void actually begins. Astrologers universally agree that since there are thirty degrees to a sign, the 29th degree is particularly important as one phase of a cycle disintegrates and moves into the start of another period. This concept applies to the Moon, Sun, and all the planets in chart interpretation. The Moon would take about two hours to move from 29 degrees to 29 degrees 59 minutes, so these two hours would be expected to show subtle shifts in the public mood and, by most definitions, would be a Void-of-Course Moon period if the Moon made no major aspects during those final two hours. More controversial and complex is the matter of Moons that might get to 5 degrees of a zodiac sign and not make any major aspects (conjunction, sextile, square, trine, opposition) to the Sun or planets before leaving the zodiac sign, say, two days later. To diehard Void watchers, these would be take-it-easy days. Yet to more technically minded astrologers—particularly those who watch the Moon for the stock market or business applications—the Moon might make several uncommon (but valid) angles (72, 135, or 150 degrees, for instance) before leaving the sign. To those who apply the more technical aspects, there would still be time to do business. Aspects such as the 72-degree angle, which indicates the urge to give form to something, sometimes talent, are particularly meaningful in the interpretation of some birthcharts. People disagree, however, about whether they should be applied to general trends.

Astrologers often embrace theories without testing them or thinking through their technical ramifications. It would be remiss to ignore some of the Void-of-Course theories. The usual advice to meditate and try to avoid making major plans or decisions deserves attention. Such advice is not practical for many people, however. You'll have to do your own research to decide whether any of this works for you. Morrison has published a handful of anecdotes about Voids, including the case of a bank loan officer who stopped accepting loans during the Void because most of the applications had insufficient or inaccurate information. The officer's boss eventually rewarded him for his efficiency. A more methodical study showing whether there is a connection between faulty applications and the Void would be instructive to many industries. Testing how the idea truly works—or doesn't—can result in strategies for getting the most from the energy.

Moon Signs

Moon in Aries: Quick reactions distinguish members of this group from more placid Moons. They instinctively feel that people have to fight for their rightful place in line and may view some of the most innocent behaviors from others as a direct challenge to their being. Anger is often strong and un-acknowledged, since deep personal reflection doesn't come naturally. Witness Billy Martin. One of the parents—most probably the mother—had a lot of fight and gave the Moon in Aries baby early training in the need to be independent and to do for themselves. Some of the men will have to spend extra time working through angry feelings toward women, but others, such as Alan Alda, are avowed feminists. Jacqueline Kennedy Onassis's Moon in Aries is part of the secret of her resilience. Lily Tomlin, Marlon Brando, and Dick Gregory have the Moon in Aries. It's where Sally Field gets her pep-club energy.

Moon in Taurus: Their emotions are fixed, and they rarely change their minds about certain likes and dislikes. Bad habits are especially hard for them to break. Many have an especially healthy relationship with their body and the rest of the material world; others have to develop this trait. Strong values and overall solidity are trademarks. Katharine Hepburn, Carol Burnett, and Pope John Paul have the Moon in Taurus. Nature and physical comforts are important to their well-being. Michael Dukakis shows the steadiness and frugal side of this group. Prince Charles epitomizes the Moon in Taurus who is born amid all the earth's comforts. Ronald Reagan's early years as a child of an alcoholic threatened his Taurean comfort needs. Jesse Jackson's start in life, as the son of a poor, unwed teenage girl, also correlates to some of the self-worth and other problems that this Moon sign confronts when material and financial security are missing from their lives.

Moon in Gemini: Shallow? A lot of them are. Astrologers don't like overgeneralizing about any given sign, but this Moon group is notorious for pushing feelings away. They can rationalize anything, and when you leave the room, they'll change their argument to suit the next situation. Congresswoman Pat Schroeder showed she had a good cry or two in her when she decided against pursuing the U.S. presidency. But this Moon's initial reaction is one of intellectualization. Gary Hart's amoral handling of his infidelities—the rationalizations and lies—should give an idea of some of the low moments of this group. But many are great dinner companions and conversationalists. Goldie Hawn's humor is an example of the bright spots. Sigmund Freud shows that this position can work with other configurations and put the Gemini communication skills to use by helping others talk about the emotional and hidden aspects of their lives, though even Sigmund was accused of a certain voyeurism and intellectualism in his approach, which reflects his Moon sign.

Moon in Cancer: Having the Moon in its natural sign puts people right on the front when it comes to the battle of trying to develop a sense of emotional security. Phyllis Diller shows that this emotional concentration is not without humor. There's a caring, tender, nurturing side to these people, both the men and the women, even sizzlers such as Mae West or Farrah Fawcett Majors, it would seem. Dan Rather and Willie Nelson have a certain hominess about them. This Moon can get caught up in dependencies, exhibited by clinging and whining, that can drive people away. They seem to want either to be babied or to play mother, neither of which is usually appropriate in adult-to-adult situations. Many may have had the stereotypical mother who smothered her children with guilt, while others may have been ignored by the mother figure in their life. Whatever the reason, they're often very caught up in family-related dramas and must work extra hard to reprogram themselves from the past. They have a not-always-healthy habit of judging current and future experiences by the past, and this subjectivity can limit growth and integration with the wider world. Benjamin Spock, Franklin D. Roosevelt, Eleanor Roosevelt, and Liza Minnelli are other examples.

Moon in Leo: They can be such babies, especially when they don't get enough attention. The dramatic mode of emotional expression of this Moon is evident in personalities such as Barbra Streisand, Geraldo Rivera, Gloria Steinem, and Mikhail Gorbachev. All of these people are noted for the flamboyant self-presentation that is habitual. Everybody has the need to feel good about themselves and to respond to life with the love and joy felt internally, but it's oxygen to Leo. Arrogance, vanity, and excessive self-aggrandizement can distort their personalities, making emotional exchanges with others difficult. But the dignity and proud bearing of some with this Moon are admirable (Queen Elizabeth, Jane Fonda, Nancy Reagan). Dan Quayle shows how the confidence of this position can take people far. His mother, a newspaper heiress, was from a line of "royalty" of sorts. Marlene Dietrich epitomizes the grandeur.

Moon in Virgo: They try to dissect everything that comes at them. Why? Why? Why? These "inquiring minds" want to know. Extensive discussions about the details of their dirty chores can certainly bore most onlookers, but much of this is necessary for Moon in Virgo's development. Disturbances in their daily routine can throw them off significantly. An especially critical nature—possibly inherited from a fussy, critical mother—can result in worry and health problems. Bill Cosby has shown that there is much humor in life, and his fellow Virgo Moons would be wise to keep this in mind. Even though she was running a band of hookers, Sidney Biddles Barrow (the Mayflower Madam) exhibited this Moon sign's concern with cleanliness and orderliness by giving her "girls" extensive written lessons on ways to check clients for sexual disease. Emily Post, another member of this tribe, would be proud. Madonna shows the workhorse side, while Alexander Graham Bell showed Virgo's ability to refine technique. Shirley MacLaine's Moon here suggests that she has some sense of earthly realities, despite what her critics may charge.

Moon in Libra: Relationships and interactions with other people have a hold on this Moon. Much of their self-image and emotional well-being is tied to their relations with another person. Moon in Libra gives the kind of skills that make for able public relations specialists and other advisers such as Henry Kissinger. But the need to accommodate the wants and emotions of other people can keep them off balance, and this is what makes George Bush and others with this Moon fence sitters. Burt Reynolds and Sylvester Stallone show how balancing interpersonal relationships with one's identity can come to the forefront (and headlines), while Elizabeth Barrett Browning is a historic example of someone whose name is often said in the same breath as her partner. Vanna White readily displays charm and sociableness. Maria Callas, the opera singer, had that world-class diplomatic refinement that this Moon is able to use to great advantage. It is crucial that the public relations skills of this Moon be combined with self-awareness and independence elsewhere in the chart. Ted Turner and Billie Jean King exhibit autonomy, showing it's not precluded from this placement.

Moon in Scorpio: It's like going deep down into a never-ending cave. These people are always asking questions—there is a desperate need to get to the bottom of things—as the life of Pierre Curie suggests. Phil Donahue takes the high-tech route for his search. The perceptions are sharp. They're especially attuned to power plays and sexual undercurrents—see the works of Henry Miller—but are also overly suspicious and see slights and threats where none exist, as assassin James Earl Ray demonstrated. People with this Moon approach the world as if they were unwanted and they hide their feelings from others. Often they aren't even sure what they're getting at because so many buried resentments and repressed feelings are welling up inside of them. They often succumb to self-destructive habits. But those same people who have the power to do much self-destruction also have pools and pools of inner resources that allow them to transform their lives, and heal themselves from addictions and other negative patterns. Helen Gurley Brown came up from a life of poverty and invented herself. She wrote a book (*Sex and the Single Girl*) and became editor of a magazine (*Cosmopolitan*) aimed at helping young women live happier, more with-it lives. Elizabeth Taylor's fight with drugs and food is another example of transformation.

Moon in Sagittarius: The Oprah Winfrey Moon. They have opinions on everything and are often moralistic and philosophical. The desire to explore can take them all over the globe. Sally Struthers, for instance, is concerned about saving children around the world. Albert Einstein, Thomas Jefferson, and Neil Armstrong give hints of the expansive nature of this placement. But a desire to be free makes it difficult for them to form commitments. Some observers say this Moon has a problem with intimacy, that it can't get close to people. Many grew up in home situations where religion, philosophy, or some educational theory was invoked to explain away the hurt or feelings that were causing discomfort.

Moon in Capricorn: They feel, get hurt, and have emotions. As Mia Farrow and her large family of adopted children show, this Moon has nurturing instincts and needs. Most times, though, it doesn't show. They've grown up learning to be cautious when expressing their feelings or fears. In their early years such vulnerability may have resulted in ridicule, annoyance, or denial by parents. One parent might not have been around at all. They're hard people, as Adolf Hitler grew up to show the world. But Lucille Ball showed they have humor and a good, efficient business sense. Indira Gandhi and Johnny Carson exhibit this in different ways. Even though she deals with the realm of imagination and emotion, writer Joyce Carol Oates is known for the apparent discipline and steady work habits that sometimes cause her to produce as many as two novels a year. Oliver North shows how this Moon seeks the mantle of authority and prestige. Some Moon in Capricorns have a fancy for May-December relationships—Sonny and Cher, now Cher and younger men—reflecting some of the parent-child-authority-control issues they're working through.

Moon in Aquarius: This is the Moon sign of people who are known for uprooting themselves from society and from others around them, but who also need the community and a role in it for their emotional well-being. They grow up feeling that they are on the fringes, and they aren't comfortable with emotional expression. It is the home of many radicals, ranging from Daniel Ortega to Angela Davis, Jerry Rubin, Betty Friedan, and Emma Goldman. These are the pioneers, from Sally Ride and Sandra Day O'Connor to Jean Paul Sartre. Antisocial people, as well as outright outlaws, such as David "Son of Sam" Berkowitz, are in this group, but most people are not overtly extreme. The presence of such people as former Speaker of the House Jim Wright and Richard Nixon show that this Moon is concerned with interacting with and participating in society. Even as it stands off to the side, detached and observing, it needs to be a part of some community or social order in order to feel secure. But while many are known for their large network of friends, they, too, are hard to get to know. Woody Allen, for instance, touches on anxieties that

The Monthly Mood/Moon Cycle

Researchers have found a four-to-six-week mood cycle. Each cycle ends and another begins when the mood—the day's overall emotional state—returns after having moved through the other stages in varying intensities. To determine how this rhythm works in your life, and whether there are any connections to the Moon's travels, chart the mood rhythm for a few cycles and use a moon sign ephemeris to compare the Moon's positions to your moods. Do you always feel the same way when the Moon is in Leo? Does another Moon sign always get you down? You won't know unless you start keeping mood records.

Cycle Days*

	1	2	3	4	5	6	7	8	9	10	11	12	13	14	15	16 30

Moods
Elation +
Pleasure +
Contentment +
Neutral
Discomfort −
Frustration −
Sadness/Depression −

*For purposes of data keeping, the first day of the cycle begins when the data recording starts. A tip: Assigning each month its own separate wave or line will give a visual presentation of your emotional ups and downs.

move many of us, but his work also has a detached quality. Richard Nixon is another example of this cerebral Moon. Nixon often seemed to be very much the loner amid society, even though he's spent much of his life concocting big plans for it.

Moon in Pisces: They're sponges who pick up on all the neuroses and yearnings going on around them. Michael Jackson has the talent to turn this empathy into an international music reputation. Sissy Spacek trades on it, too. Others are overwhelmed by the constant stimuli and can't separate the outer world from who they are and what they're feeling. They can be paranoid, overly sensitive, and escapist, and are especially vulnerable to addictions, as Betty Ford's life indicates. Ford, however, also fought back, to show that even this Moon sign doesn't have to allow itself to become a victim. The compassion, creativity, and humaneness can be utilized to the benefit of the individual and society. Barbara Walters, Lloyd Bentsen, Martin Luther King, Jr., Leonardo da Vinci, Michelangelo, and Toni Morrison are examples.

SIX

New Moons, Full Moons: A Monthly Planning Guide

Stories about Full Moon lunacy have become such a cliché that it's difficult to get people to listen to some of the real evidence. A series of news clippings for February 1–3, 1988, can't help but make one wonder. Two men, claiming to be members of a Native American tribe protesting discrimination against blacks and Native Americans by a county sheriff, took 17 people in a North Carolina newsroom hostage. Down the coast a day later, on February 2, a man, looking to call attention to the plight of the nation's homeless, held eighty schoolchildren and their teachers hostage in Tuscaloosa, Alabama. Across the Atlantic, some 6,000 nurses joined a countrywide labor strike in Great Britain, while a group of gay activists was arrested following a protest against antihomosexual bills passed in the House of Commons. Down under, in Australia, officials announced that they were investigating 225 persons suspected of taking part in Nazi crimes in World War II.

Is it just coincidence that a wild group of Iranian students stormed a wall and took over the American embassy on a November Full Moon in 1979, or that a ban of rebels gathered in Philadelphia on a Full Moon of July 2, 1776, and voted themselves independent of the English crown?

Stories about extra-active police scanners and hospital emergency rooms on the Full Moon have been exaggerated; many a Full Moon has gone by with no news to report. Of course certain characters in town don't need a little light from the Moon to encourage their lunacy; they act up all the time. But while most skeptics have simply dismissed any suggestion that the increased emotionalism and intensity at the Full Moon is exaggerated, others have tried putting such claims to the test. The general result is some support for claims that the Full Moon (and New Moon) increase rainfall, hemorrhaging, epileptic seizures, births, homicides, and other activity. The extent—and sometimes the methodology—of most of these studies have been limited and haven't been replicated by other researchers.

Another problem for researchers is that the mechanistic nature of our society is such that many of the more natural rhythms have been obscured. Claims that more babies are born around Full Moon might have been valid fifty years ago, but the large numbers of C-sections and other forms of intervention at birth change birth patterns. Recently, while I was collecting data for a project for which I needed a 365-day breakdown of births, a statistician at the National Center for Health Statistics cautioned me against giving any particular credence to especially low numbers for weekend and Monday births because of the C-section and other scheduling factors. Similarly, the practice of medicating people with emotional problems means that it is ever more difficult to get a clear picture of what really goes on under a Full Moon.

Evidence for the Moon's Effect

Fortunately some phenomena have escaped distortion. Perhaps the most lauded work on the Moon's influence on earthly activity was logged by Frank Brown, a Northwestern University professor who, in the 1950s, took twelve oysters out of Long Island Sound in New Haven and placed them in a laboratory in Evanston, Illinois. Oysters open and close at high and low tides, which are related to the Moon's travels through different points in the sky. For ten days, the New Haven transplants responded to the schedule they kept back on Long Island Sound. But eventually their rhythm adjusted to what would have been low and high tides if Evanston had been on a seashore. Brown extended his studies of twenty-four-hour rhythms and the Moon to plant and animal life. He put caged hamsters in a room that was artificially lit and made to appear like a twenty-four-hour day—alternating light and dark—and found that the animals were active at night and inactive during the day. Brown also found that the hamsters were more active on their treadmill during the Full Moon, and to a lesser degree during the New Moon, than at other portions of the month.

More practical applications are suggested by work such as Frank J. Guarino's study on the correlation between Moon phases and changes in the Dow Jones Industrial Average from 1950 to 1973. Guarino conducted the study as partial fulfillment for a master's degree in business administration at Pace University. His hypothesis was that "if the phases of the moon and investor psychology are interrelated, then the influence of the Moon should be evidenced in man's most sensitive financial instrument, the stock market." Guarino found that "changes in the stock market during the period from the Full Moon to the Last Quarter Moon are the least favorable for investors." But the periods around the New Moon are the most beneficial for investors.

Anyone looking to conquer Wall Street obviously needs more than information on Moon phases. The best astroeconomists combine conventional techniques with astrological/astronomical knowledge. Guarino's study is mentioned here to illustrate the many different areas that have been under study. Other activities of the human species have also been examined for possible lunar-phase connections.

Miami-based psychiatrist Arnold Lieber has a continuing interest in several studies he has conducted that showed an increase in murders in Cuyahoga (Ohio) and Dade (Florida) counties around the Full Moon. In Ohio the murders peaked three days after Full Moon, while the Florida murders peaked right at the height of the phase. Lieber's work has undergone extensive criticism from his fellow psychiatrists, and he is vehemently against astrology. In an analysis of lunar-phase work by Lieber and other studies of planetary influences, Hans Eysenck, professor of psychology at the Institute of Psychiatry, University of London, notes that other work on the same topic has produced similar results. But Eysenck, who is among the more open-minded supporters of unbiased research into astrology, says that the correlations have been slight, not statistically significant. Some studies have also linked suicides to the Full Moon, but separate experiments showed more suicides at New Moon.

Moonstruck

But people shouldn't let the conflicting data keep them from trying to gain insight into the way this rhythm might work in their lives. Allow yourself to become a little "moonstruck" for a while. The three days of breakups, reconciliations, and new love that take place under the Full Moon in the Academy Award–winning movie of the same name are highly illustrative of the intense emotionalism of this period of the Moon. Losing a fiancé and gaining a new one all under one Full Moon—the experience of the heroine, played by Cher—is not a routine scenario during this time of the month, but is certainly an example of the "coming to a head" situations people often encounter in their environment.

But it's not just the Full or New Moon that have special significance and define the monthly rhythm. This chapter will explore six additional phases—each of the eight phases lasts about 3.5 days—that speak to the Sun/Moon-relationship cycle. While most readers are familiar with the First and Last Quarter portions of the cycle, such concepts as the Crescent, Gibbous, Disseminating, and Balsamic moons are less publicized. But the insights that are often gained at the Full Moon illumination often have no relevance until put into practice in the succeeding Disseminating Moon phase. In the same manner, the Full Moon green light that might be needed for a project might never come unless the Gibbous phase, which occurs during the three days prior to Full Moon, is used for analysis, preparation, and making needed adjustments.

The first half of the 29.5-day cycle—the time from New Moon to Full Moon—is for momentum and is the waxing stage. Following Full Moon the cycle starts to wane, and there is a release and clearing-out period of 14.5 days before the next cycle begins. The beauty here is that the cycle can be watched from Earth, through the different faces that the Moon takes on each month. At New Moon, the start of the cycle, the Moon and Sun are located in the same place in the sky from the viewpoint of earth. There's no apparent distance between the two bodies; they are, figuratively speaking, one. The Sun and Moon pull apart with the Moon carrying the Sun's light out into the world, building upon the seeds planted at New Moon. By Full Moon, the two are lined up in opposition, demanding a reconciliation. At Full Moon, the Sun and Moon are in opposite signs: Sun in Pisces, Moon in Virgo and vice versa.

Related to, but less common than New and Full Moons, are eclipses, of which there are two to seven a year. A solar eclipse can only occur at New Moon, a lunar eclipse at Full Moon; but several other astronomical factors also must be present for an eclipse to occur. One criterion is that the Sun and Moon must be near the two diametrically opposed points in the sky where the plane of the Moon's orbit intersects with the plane of the ecliptic. These meeting points or intersections are the Moon's Nodes. (These technical features are particularly important when studying 9.3- and 18.6-year rhythms like the real estate and other cycles cited in the first chapter of this book and also relate to turnpoints and important personal connections in our individual lives). Lunar Eclipses occur fourteen days before or after solar ones though some solar eclipses don't come with an accompanying lunar period.

In the same way that the eclipse temporarily blocks out light, astrologers have long related the phenomenon to turning points and intensified activity on earth. In the early days, of course, they got a bit wild, predicting deaths to kings and other catastrophes. Observation has calmed them down. An eclipse never works alone and can generally be viewed as shaking loose pent-up energy or trends indicated by other planetary cycles. An eclipse of September 22, 1987, near the autumnal equinox, worked along with an October 6, 1987, Lunar Eclipse to trigger the October 19, 1987, stock market crash. During the March 3, 1988, Lunar Eclipse, which took place a month after the February 1–3 Full Moon activity detailed above, leaders in Panama were forced to shut down the banking system as the economic crisis worsened. On the March 17, 1988, Solar Eclipse, America sent troops to Honduras. Eclipses occur at the same point in the zodiac every nineteen years—for example, the 1987 eclipses of March 29 and September 23 took place on March 28 and September 22, 1968—making the subject especially accessible to researchers. The September 1, 1989, Solar Eclipse shook up the drug czars in Colombia and the United States.

Eclipses often relate to crises or changes in individual lives. Some astrologers insist that major events can't happen in a life unless an eclipse is activated at some point in the chart. An eclipse was in the exact degree of John F. Kennedy's Saturn, falling in his house of public standing, four months prior to his assassination. Nixon's power planet Pluto, up at the top of his chart, was activated two months prior to his resignation. Sandra Day O'Connor's natal Moon in Aquarius was turned upside down by eclipses in February and July 1981, possibly announcing the coming changes that would take place in her life with her ascension to the Supreme Court that year. Eclipses really should not be considered without a thorough understanding of a birthchart. Astrologers disagree among themselves about the power of eclipses. One matter of debate is the duration of an eclipse's effect or whether an eclipse that occurs six months before an event can be viewed as having a relationship to it. Eclipses also come and go in people's lives without any corresponding external event, though there may be a connection to ongoing inner matters. Lunar Eclipses, in particular, are believed to relate to emotional, rather than objective concerns. Many eclipses can seem just like another New or Full Moon.

But a simple New or Full Moon isn't something to ignore. At birth not only did we have a specific Sun/Moon combination—by sign there are 144 different Sun/Moon combinations—but the relationship between them, known as the Moon phase, also has a bearing on how our personality and identity will manifest. Some people are certified Full Mooners, though this can be a real blessing. Full Mooners as diverse as Michael Jackson, Michael Dukakis, and Dan Quayle show how this phase gives people an opportunity to integrate a range of competing components within their personality. New Mooners like Pope John Paul, Katharine Hepburn, and Ludwig van Beethoven have the conscious self (the Sun) working on the same concerns as the unconscious emotional system (the Moon), and the result is a focalized personality that is able to leave its imprint on its surroundings.

During various periods of the month, when the Moon is in a phase that makes 180-degree (six signs away) or 90-degree (three signs) angles to the birth Moon phase, people may experience noticeable emotional disruptions. (A chart to help you determine your Moon phase can be found at the end of this section.) Some researchers have tried to link the start of a woman's monthly menstrual cycle to the phase of the Moon under which she was born, but the speculation hasn't held up under statistical scrutiny. Dr. Eugene Jonas, a Czech psychiatrist, conducted the most popular studies in this area and claimed to be able to link peak fertility as well as predict the time most conducive for conceiving a boy or girl. But review of his research has prompted Eysenck, as well as astrologers with a particular interest in this subject, to suggest that people stick to more conventional forms of birth control. But even if a fertility link cannot be made with a high degree of certainty, it is in your best interest to locate your birth phase and determine how you respond emotionally during other phases.

The Sun/Moon cycle is a good tool for understanding the "month," but it also gives a framework for viewing the structure underlying the many other Astrocycles to be encountered in this book. The cycles under examination include *cycles of position*, which involve a planet's takeoff from a particular point and its subsequent return. A cycle of position would be the Sun's 365-day ride from one birthday to another, or the Moon's 27.5-day travel through the zodiac. The second category is *cycles of relationship*, which involve the ongoing relationship between two planets (including the Sun and Moon) as they move through the sky. The 29.5-day Sun/Moon cycle falls under this heading and gives us some of the general "rules" for viewing other cycles of relationships.

All cycles can be broken down into two stages: waxing and waning. The cycle builds until it reaches its midpoint, and then it wanes. The midpoint of each cycle, like the Full Moon, involves bodies standing 180 degrees (an opposition, six signs) away from one another. In the case of cycles of position—such as the birthday cycle—the midpoint occurs when the Sun (or planet) is six signs away from its own starting point. In the case of cycles of relationship the traveling celestial bodies—at Full Moon, the Sun and Moon, for example—are 180 degrees (six signs) away from one another. All cycles have critical First Quarter/Last Quarter jolts. It was the late master astrologer Dane Rudhyar who pioneered cyclic approaches to astrology. He did extensive work on lunar phases and is responsible for assigning descriptions such as "crisis of action" to the First Quarter, or "crisis of consciousness" to the Last Quarter, and "illumination" to the Full Moon phase of a cycle. Some of his insights will guide us as we dissect the monthly Sun/Moon rhythm.

The Cycle

Who hasn't been told to put together a report, proposal, or other project and get back to the boss in a month? Even if the speaker is vague about dates, there's an implicit understanding about what is being said. If the request is made on May 15, we're looking at a June 15 deadline. Being asked to come up with a project for the first of the month, means just that, give or take a day or two.

But many times, the turning points needed to pull off the project don't seem to present themselves until the deadline has passed, or it takes longer than expected to build the right momentum for what must be done. Part of the problem is that everyone's been using the wrong calendar: It's time to turn the clock back to Lunar time.

That's the way true time is kept, anyway. Each month begins with the New Moon. While the Chinese, Muslims, and Hebrews are among those who've looked to the lunar cycle to schedule holidays—for example, the sighting of the crescent of the New Moon is widely known to be the call to start Ramadan in Muslim countries—the modern Christianized world, aside from the scheduling of Easter, does not do this. Farmers have used certain phases for planting. The period from New Moon to Full Moon is the time for planting aboveground crops. The building of Stonehenge and other astronomical edifices speaks to the desire of humans to chart the comings and goings of the New Moon. When it arrived, they curtsied to it in Scotland, while others danced, sang, and prayed. And even though most people today haven't been taking notice, something inside each individual has always been renewed with each New Moon, the seed for all beginnings.

The New Moon's coming, of course, is not as visually awe-inspiring as the Full Moon, but that, too, speaks of the inward fecundation of the period, which will reach a climax at Full Moon. The waxing phase of the cycle is the first fourteen to fifteen days; the cycle begins waning after Full Moon reaches technical exactitude (precisely 180 degrees from the Sun).

The cycle is generally broken down as follows, though in actual practice each phase may run plus or minus half a day:

1. New Moon—Days 0 to 3.5 of the cycle
2. Crescent Moon—Days 3.5 to 7

3. First Quarter Moon—Days 7 to 10.5
4. Gibbous Moon—Days 10.5 to 14
5. Full Moon—Days 14 to 17.5
6. Disseminating Moon—Days 17.5 to 21
7. Last Quarter Moon—Days 21 to 24.5
8. Balsamic Moon—Days 24.5 to 28–29*

Like any beginning, the New Moon, where the Sun and Moon come together, starts with a promise, both in the world and in our personal lives. It is the time when people propose or begin to think of new possibilities. Religions whose calendars are built around the New Moon prescribe fasting and meditation, practices that recognize the benefits that inner calm can bring to this period. The intensity of the month is determined by the way the New Moon and its subsequent phases interact with each individual birthchart. Some New and Full Moons will make significant configurations to points where planets are placed in a chart, and this will heighten the month's activities. A similar point should be made about New and Full Moons and world events.

Tracking the lunar phases in world events can actually be more difficult than might initially appear. It's certainly easy to flip through the ephemeris and find Supreme Court rulings, such as the curb on abortion rights or Oliver North's jury, being announced on New Moons. But government actions related to a specific issue are rarely contained within one 29.5-day cycle. The more obvious New and Full Moon–related events are those that take people by surprise, such as news that Nancy Reagan employed an astrologer and the simultaneous death of astrologer Carroll Righter, a longtime Reagan family friend. But all of the monthly trends combine with more potent forces. The Full Moon that occurred in the middle of the October 13, 1989, 200-point stock market dive and the October 17, 1989, San Francisco area earthquake that killed about 200 people, aligned with a highly disillusioning Saturn/Neptune configuration that was already up to no good.

*(The cycle includes two subcycles which will be explained later in this chapter.)

Don't Get Lost in the Short-term

It's also important to go into the Sun/Moon cycle knowing specifically what is under examination. And with this said, I have a confession to make that will put into perspective some of the views I have about the use of small cycles like this one, or the tracking of the Moon in its monthly ride through the zodiac. Though I strongly advocate gaining an understanding of the 29.5-day lunar rhythm, I don't feel that it's necessary to look constantly for an astrological correlation for everything that happens during the day. I know too many purposeful, dynamic people who don't check out the day's Moon sign. I never try to convert them because I don't necessarily believe that astrology will make them any more effective. What I see astrology doing is adding perspective and explaining the natural rhythms that these people move through, more particularly the long-term trends. If you can handle the more potent demands of Saturn, Uranus, Neptune, and Pluto, you won't need to look up the daily location of the planets before leaving the house. At a certain point everyone—including astrologers—needs to throw out the ephemerides and live life with all of its intricate twists and turns.

In the same way that the Full Moon makes people more vulnerable to certain types of crime and causes more rain to fall, Full Moon energy in a chart can often relate to unforeseen experiences. And this doesn't have to be viewed as negative. People fall in love, get great job offers, have interesting experiences that give them different perspectives about their daily routine. Too much ephemeris watching hinders life's natural rhythm.

Once these limitations are accepted, the Sun/Moon cycle can be examined with purpose. And rightfully so, since it packs more of a wallop than the singular study of the Moon's ride through the zodiac each month. While we can view the Moon's zodiac ride as relating to moods in effect for less than an hour, the 29.5-day Sun/Moon cycle targets an area of life—as determined by which of the twelve houses in the horoscope the New Moon and Full Moon occur—for a month-long focus. It's not always overt, and sometimes all the movement of the New Moon in a house may do is cause us to be more conscious of changes we may want to make in time. Sometimes the force of the New Moon is so strong we find a quickened pace in activity. A New Moon in the fourth might correlate to a concern about a parent or our home life; two weeks later, with the Full Moon hitting house four and opposite house ten, our concerns come to a head, or we're trying to balance this sudden need to deal with some private, personal matter with career or public responsibilities that are indicated by the tenth house. New Moon in the tenth might have caused us to start the month giving extra thought to both short and long-term career plans.

Since New Moons and Full Moons fall within approximately the same houses of a person's birthchart at the same time each year, it's easy to see why they would correspond to the more intensified work, or domestic, health, or relationship matters people might experience every September or May, for example. It should also be obvious that some years are more intense than others. A New Moon can set up the right inner process to expedite change, and Mars moving through the same house will put more action behind the inner focalizing. Longer-term trends in the chart would reveal the bigger plan at work, whether this will truly be the year when you paint the garage, take that vacation to St. Croix, or go back to school. Because it's always too easy to say, "I'll do it next September," knowing about the monthly New Moon cycle as it pertains to your birthchart is very important. With knowledge that the New Moon and Full Moon are focusing on your daily routine, your finances, or other specific issues, you can write down goals and take more directed action. Astrologer Sophia Mason has done extensive work on this cycle. Her ideas, as well as information in Donna Cunningham's *Moon Signs*, can be used to gain more detail. But a precisely timed horoscope will be needed to truly benefit from the Sun/Moon cycle planning advocated by astrologers.

The New Moon at the start of one cycle may be used to lay the groundwork for changes realized on a Full Moon or other critical lunar phase several months later. Subsequent chapters on practical cycles ranging from the Sun/Mercury rhythm to the 2-year Mars trend to longer-term 7-year, 11.8-year, and still longer cycles will make readers aware of the complexities involved. A particular Sun/Moon phase can be used to organize finances, to undertake a housecleaning, or to implement a short-term routine or health-regime change. But even when people are consciously using New Moon/Full Moon information, there are limits to what they'll accomplish in one 29.5-day period.

A New Moon in the part of the horoscope concerned with the image you project outward, the initial way people experience you (the first house), could highlight image concerns in a positive or negative way. I've seen numerous cases of people whose life regularly brings them into greater public view when the New Moon hits this point in their chart annually. Negative experiences may cause people to feel they need to refine their image, so a seed is planted for future work. But nobody can change an image in a month. A true image change—something beyond color-coordinated clothes and makeup—more commonly would come when Saturn or Pluto moved through the "image" sector, or house, of the horoscope. The same is true for any of the other eleven horoscope houses.

Such specificity is not the focus of this book. However, by dipping briefly into more technical and philosophical concerns, I've established some of the parameters for viewing this monthly cycle. We can now detail the eight phases of the cycle, assign some strategies, and also look briefly at how it relates to personality.

The "Month"

The section on each Moon phase starts by listing the number of celestial degrees between the Sun and Moon. Such information is only important to those with a technical bent. New Moon begins with the Sun and Moon in the same exact degree (the tightest conjunction possible), and the Moon then moves on. The number of zodiac signs between the Sun and Moon are given to help newcomers get a sense of the Sun/Moon relationship. The Moon moves ahead of the Sun in the zodiac until Full Moon, when it then passes behind and then moves ahead en route to its next conjunction with the Sun.

1. New Moon: Sun and Moon 0 to 45 degrees apart; Sun and Moon are in same sign, Moon sometimes moving ahead in the adjacent sign.

With the start of each New Moon some people mistakenly think that the New Moon will allow them to run with the ball and accomplish things right away. But what is symbolized here is the seeding, with the results dependent on what actions are taken elsewhere during the cycle. Listing your goals or priorities for the month is a good way to start the month. Your ideas will go through revision along the way, with specific actions

coming to bloom in many cases around or just after the Full
Moon. People often aren't aware when they've started something. This was evident when I asked some people who aren't
aware of astrology to share portions of their personal journals
and work-related logs or other records for certain dates. Entries
around the New Moon were often tentative. An administrator
in the advertising/public relations division of a midsize corporation writes of a lunch meeting at which she and the boss
"kicked around some thoughts" about an "in-house training
program that will help some of our people make better presentations." Those seeds took on a larger form and became a
live proposal a few days after the Full Moon. Entries of others
tended to focus on various emotional and psychological issues
raised by the New Moon as it fell in specific houses in their
birthcharts. We might not see dynamic activity, but the cycle
is always at work. If you wanted to list "green light" days on
the calendar, this would definitely be one of them. Even if
you're not able to dive into a project head first, it's good to
take even the most symbolic of steps. Do some research, make
some telephone calls, put out feelers, just to make some use
of the energy.

2. Crescent Moon: The Moon is 45 to 90 degrees ahead of
the Sun, in the sign adjacent to it or two signs away (for
example, Sun in Aries, Crescent Moon in Taurus/Gemini; Sun
in Scorpio, Crescent Moon in Sagittarius/Capricorn).

In the same way that the Moon's crescent seems to struggle
to appear out of the darkness in the sky, the time of the Crescent
Moon is one when people start taking tiny steps to feel out the
environment's reactions to the ideas and plans they've begun
seeding at the New Moon. By the Crescent Moon, some of the
dimmer inklings of the New Moon have taken form and are
being looked at in terms of practicality and possibility. In other
words, you can still be talked out of it. The steps forward come
a little more easily when the Moon is in a sign that sextiles
(two signs away) the Sun.

Janet, the advertising/public relations woman who "kicked
around" ideas for a training program, spent the Crescent phase
looking around the office and assessing possible supporters.
She also started collecting information about similar ventures.

3. First Quarter Moon: The Moon is 90 to 135 degrees
ahead of the Sun, three signs (square) ahead of it, then moves
four signs ahead making action a little easier (for example, Sun

in Aries, Moon in Cancer/Leo; Sun in Libra, Moon in Capricorn/Aquarius).

Janet, somewhat reluctantly, plunged into a series of meetings with people who would be involved with what was still only an idea. She became more aware of some of the logistical and political issues at stake. The First Quarter is the "crisis of action" phase. After getting their toes wet in the Crescent stage, now people plunge in, often headfirst. Action at First Quarter is impulsive as people try to break away from the past. It's like running away from home; sometimes people just do it without thinking of the consequences. Janet jumped into plans for the training program without being mindful of office politics and others who might be threatened by the plan. "I let word out about the idea too soon," she writes. "My field correspondents report minor confrontations in the environment."

4. Gibbous Moon: The Moon is 135 to 180 degrees ahead of the Sun, four and five signs (mainly five signs) away from it (for example, Sun in Aries, Moon in Leo/Virgo; Sun in Pisces, Moon in Cancer/Leo).

Janet writes, "I was avoiding Bill, who had put me on the project. I stayed away from the water cooler and was doing pretty good, but then he tapped me on the arm unexpectedly and asked about the project. I gave him a brief rundown and told him some of the objections from other departments. He said he'd need a written report in a week or so. Nothing too detailed, but an outline of the problem and some projected numbers and dates."

The Gibbous phase starts three days before Full Moon and often gives people a chance to make changes, tidy up, and put things in order. It's a "leave this one in, take that one out" type of energy.

THE TURNING POINT

5. Full Moon: The Moon and Sun are 180 degrees apart, the Moon six signs ahead of the sun (for example, Sun in Aries, Moon in Libra; Sun in Leo, Moon in Aquarius; and vice versa).

"I'm tired of these people messing with me; I'm sick of men who think they know more. If that idiot had himself together, he would have known that somebody higher up would want a rundown on what I was up to. What does he care? I'm the one who looks like a jerk, unprepared. A few more months and I'm out."

In the same way that world events can seem to come undone, things get a little crazy both at the office and at home. Janet was particularly upset because her boss's boss sought her out for a quick oral progress report on the proposed training. "I was just getting the idea fixed in my mind, what I would recommend as feasible to pursue, the limits and other possibilities," she says. "I figured I could wing a memorandum in two days or so. I wasn't ready to talk with anyone and wasn't as sharp as I like to be. I was tongue-tied in fact and resented the hurry, since I was just beginning to get some sense of where I was going."

Michael is an account executive who was fired on a Full Moon five years ago. To this date he cringes and grimaces when he recalls the way his voice became especially emotional, how he thought he had almost cried in front of other men. "I often wonder if I would have been smoother if it hadn't been a Full Moon, even though I don't really believe in any of that," he says.

But too often the Full Moon is viewed as a time of firings and no-gos. Some people report job offers, promotions and sudden opportunities or breakthroughs. Marjorie needed a job, showed up at a personnel agency that desperately needed an administrative assistant, and was hired on the spot. Pam and Mark met on a Full Moon and married six months later. Dane Rudhyar, the late master astrologer, said that the Full Moon can relate to illumination and fulfillment, or separation and divorce. The midpoint phase of any cycle relates to the release of the cycle's deeper meaning or intention setting the stage for full manifestation and completion.

5. Disseminating Moon: The Moon is 135 to 90 degrees behind the Sun, five and four signs (mainly four) away from it (for example, Sun in Aries, Moon in Scorpio/Sagittarius; Sun in Gemini, Moon in Capricorn/Aquarius).

Anyone familiar with a graduate of est (now called the Forum) knows that there's no convincing these people that the seminar isn't for you. Once they've gone through it, they think everybody in the world should. The same can be true of people who sell Amway, Herbalife, and other products. The Disseminating Moon brings out all the salespeople and others who've lived through the Full Moon illumination who now want to share the experience. This phase (sometimes called the Waning Gibbous) is an ideal one for living out what has been learned.

It's the ideal time for activities that require communication and interaction with people. The use of energy is easier, without the buildup of tension that precedes Full Moon. Janet drew up a memorandum on the proposed training program, and though her information was sketchy, she and others were able to discuss the weak and strong points they'd detected over the past week.

6. Last Quarter Moon: The Moon is 90 to 45 degrees behind the Sun, three signs behind the Sun, but then moves two signs away, which eases some of the tension (for example, Sun in Aries, Moon in Capricorn/Aquarius; Sun in Taurus, Moon in Aquarius/Pisces).

Janet's boss didn't really like her memo. He didn't think she covered all the important bases. She's not sure if anyone higher up saw that first memo. The Last Quarter coincides with crises that cause changes in the thinking or attitude one has been carrying through the cycle. It's a "head turning" period. Dane Rudhyar called it the "crisis of consciousness," in which people start evaluating what has been done and what's left to be done. It's not a time for a new start, though it's clear the current trend is not forever.

8. Balsamic Moon: The Moon is 45 to 0 degrees behind the Sun. This phase has two subphases within it. Dane Rudhyar included both energies under the Balsamic heading, an approach that makes it easier for people using the nineteen-year Moon phase chart at the end of this chapter. Donna Cunningham's *Moon Signs*, however, separates the Waning Crescent from the Balsamic Moon, which is often called the Dark Moon.

The Waning Crescent starts with the Moon moving two signs behind the Sun. As Cunningham writes,

> Here the Moon is two signs behind the Sun, in a complementary element—fire with air and earth with water. Thus, the emotional reactions and needs are in harmony with the basic sense of self. These are I'm okay people who feel their own perspective is right and wise. They believe the world should see things as they do from their enlightened perspective.

Cunningham was discussing the type of personality born at the Waning Crescent. The late John Belushi was in this group. Oprah Winfrey (Sun in Aquarius, Moon in Sagittarius) is an example of the energy at work. A *New York Times Magazine* article quoted Winfrey as saying of her take on life and her relationship to the Universe, "I have total comprehension," after which the writer observed in parentheses, "She is 35."

The personality correlation reveals this particular period as one when there is a feeling that work in some particular area has been completed. There's a certain emotional sense of a cycle ending. And then the phase slides into the Balsamic/Dark Moon period, where the Moon is not visible for two days before New Moon. At Balsamic Moon new seeds are being readied for planting at New Moon, which is why the time is associated with visionary personalities (Karl Marx, Betty Friedan). The Moon is in the sign just before the Sun, or in the same sign as the Sun, en route to making an exact conjunction.

As for Janet's project, a few more discussions with her boss and they both realized that what Janet really needed was a committee to hash things over with. There was also a chance that the original idea would be combined with another department's plans to bring in outside consultants for special training. During the last three days of the cycle, people were looking toward the future. In many ways, this part of the month contains downtime as the transition from one cycle to another is made.

The last two days of the Balsamic Moon have a special quality that make it a subphase. The time is also known as Hecate's Moon (named for the Greek Moon goddess). During these periods the Moon may be in the same sign as the Sun, but coming from behind and not yet at the exact point at which it will create New Moon. This phase is also future-oriented, and seeds are planted.

Janet's proposal was transformed into a special training program about six months later. But she wasn't around to oversee the final details, having quit in a huff in the midst of a Full Moon that set off a number of planetary cycles in her birthchart. Like many situations in life, Janet's plan needed several more "months" to play itself out. Even though it's not always possible to get closure on matters that come up around the phases of a 29.5-day month, there are points worth summarizing. The following summary should assist those looking to use the ideas in this chapter. But remember, the phases last 3.5 to 4 days, so there is an overlap beyond the schedule listed below.

Planning Your Monthly Moons

1. **New Moon** (Days 1 to 3.5 of the cycle): Start something. At the very least make lists of priorities for the month (knowing that the birthchart will determine which house in the horoscope is affected by the New Moon). Pay attention to dreams and spend time reflecting on the content of your conscious thoughts. This is a good time to write out a personal inventory.

2. **Crescent Moon** (Days 3.5 to 7): You must take some action related to the New Moon goal, even if it's simple research, for instance, reading a career guide if you have special job concerns this month. This is a "building" time.

3. **First Quarter Moon** (Days 7 to 10.5): This is an impulsive time, when people feel compelled to take action that can get them into trouble later. The environment usually poses situations that need response. Keep your head clear.

4. **Gibbous Moon** (Days 10.5 to 14): This is a time for analyzing and organizing. Turn a critical eye to the short-term plans initiated at the New Moon.

5. **Full Moon** (Days 14 to 17.5): Tension either comes to a head or is released. This is a good time to reflect on the meaning of the month-long cycle and gain perspective. It's also a good time for projects that need public support, particularly as the Disseminating phase begins.

6. **Disseminating Moon** (Days 17.5 to 21): Publicize your ideas. Go on job interviews. Attempt to integrate the strains of proposals and plans that have been vying for attention this month.

7. **Last Quarter Moon** (Days 21 to 24.5): Situations (and internal thinking) cause you to look back on recent initiatives and newly hatched ideas. Immediate tasks are getting completed, but some ideas are being rejected. The desk is being cleared. The cycle is in its last week. There's a better sense of strategy.

8. **Balsamic Moon (Waning Crescent/Dark Moon)** (Days 24.5 to 29.5): Some short-term issues and plans are completed or are dying out. There's a sense of completion during the first two days, then the energy eases into a period of limbo as the cycle is new cycle is about to begin. Some people will respond to the new "month" a day or two earlier as the Dark Moon/Balsamic phase begins. But this phase is mainly for clearing

out, not for new beginnings. Plan New Moon rituals (fasting, meditation, and so on).

Full-Mooners and Other Phases

The various energies assigned to the lunar phases can also be detected in the way people express their personalities, in the way the Sun and Moon express themselves. Because Moon phases recur on the same date every nineteen years, it is not difficult to put together a chart by which the moon phase can be determined for any day in this century. While a brief capsule of the personality/lunar-phase correlations is listed below, your growing knowledge of the nuances of the 29.5-day month will help augment your own interpretation. It's important to be aware that the chart is an approximation. Moon phases are not as neatly tied to specific Sun/Moon arrangements as it might appear. For instance, all New Mooners do not have the Sun and Moon in the same sign. Some, like Sigmund Freud, have the Sun late in one sign (in this case Taurus) and the Moon fairly early in the succeeding sign (Gemini). Agatha Christie's Virgo Sun and Libra Moon share a New Moon relationship. The same situation holds for other lunar phases. Dan Quayle was born hours before Full Moon, but his Sun in Aquarius/Moon in Leo are in the Gibbous configuration. Gloria Steinem, while demonstrating some Gibbous skills, is still under the First Quarter influence. People who straddle two phases by virtually a few hours will reflect the idea of one phase giving way to another.

1. New Moon (from the moment Sun and Moon are at exact degree, up to 3.5 days later): They are able to project themselves into the environment in a spontaneous, personalized way. With the energies of the Sun and Moon working so closely together, their personalities often have a vivid impact on their surroundings. Examples would be Irving Berlin, Angela Davis, Bruce Springsteen, Henry Ross Perot, Martin Sheen, Katharine Hepburn.

2. Crescent Moon (3.5 to 7 days after New Moon): They struggle to break away from the past and to build new forms, like the baby chick that struggles to knock away the eggshell enclosing it. Examples would be: J. Edgar Hoover, Anne Tyler, Bette Davis, Bill Cosby, Maria Montessori.

3. First Quarter Moon (7 to 10.5 days after New Moon): A repudiation of the past that often has a "running away from home" quality to it. There are impulsive breaks, a rebelliousness. They are anxious about the future and the past, yet not certain where they should be, so the break away comes without reason. Often the running away from home is real, as these people are often moved by intense domestic/parental struggles. Margaret Trudeau, Herman Melville, Marie Curie, Barbra Streisand, and Sylvester Stallone are examples.

4. Gibbous Moon (10.5 to 14 days after New Moon): Lifelong apprentices, this group is always analyzing, preparing, trying to better understand the circumstances in which they're involved. They often have special skills or a solid understanding of a technique. Constant need to make adjustments in life. Franklin D. Roosevelt, Josephine Baker, Jack Kemp, Louis Pasteur, and Madalyn Murray O'Hair are examples.

5. Full Moon (14 to 17.5 days after New Moon): Personalities are pulled between two equally competitive modes of expression (one more direct and conscious and related to the Sun; the other more habitual and unconscious, due to the Moon's influence). The struggle to gain balance can bring about illumination, a person who is able to develop the male/female polarity in an enlightening fashion. The downside is a feeling of always being "pulled apart" in two different directions and being particularly off center in relationships and other situations. Examples are, Jean-Jacques Rousseau, Judy Garland, Henry Ford, Amy Carter, Gary Hart, and Eugene Fodor.

6. Disseminating Moon (17.5 to 21 days after New Moon): They seek lives that allow them to demonstrate the inner enlightenment they've received (they were born after the Full Moon illumination). They want to share it with others through teaching, lecturing, writing, for example. Some are still trying to discover a philosophy or a "why" for their existence, and their life is characterized by this restless search. Vincent Van Gogh, Jesse Jackson, Thomas Jefferson, Cher, Lauren Bacall, and Francis Ford Coppola are examples.

7. Last Quarter Moon (21 to 24.5 days after New Moon): Dane Rudhyar called it the "crisis of consciousness," as a way of describing the "head-turning" experiences that cause reorientation in this group's thinking and approach to life throughout most of their living days. They often go through a range of careers and other life expressions as they alter their life direction. Unlike the "crisis in action" group, the Last Quarter is more detached and reflective, not given to rash changes. Their changes of consciousness grow more evenly and directly out of one another. Examples are Albert Einstein, George Lucas, George Sand, Mother Teresa, John Hancock, George Washington, and Philip Roth.

8. Balsamic Moon (Waning Crescent/Dark Moon Balsamic Moon) (24.5 to 29.5 days after New Moon): Donna Cunningham's observation on the two subgroups within this phase has already been noted. The first group (*the Waning Crescent*) is self-satisfied and has a certain attitude that they feel the rest of the world should adopt. Mahatma Gandhi, Harriet Beecher Stowe, and Amelia Earhart are examples. By contrast, dark Moon/Balsamic (27–29.5 days) are futuristic people. They're looking for the new cycle to start. This results in people whose work is pioneering. It also produces personalities who don't feel connected to their surroundings and hence don't participate in it. Dianne Feinstein, Ludwig von Beethovan, Bob Dylan, Gwendolyn Brooks, Karl Marx, and Ted Turner are examples.

How to Find Your Phase of the Moon

To determine your moon phase, find your Sun sign in the left-hand column and then move across the page until you find your Moon sign. Your Moon phase will be listed at the top of the column on which you've landed. For instance, someone born with the Sun in Taurus and Moon in Aquarius was born in the Last or Third Quarter (Last Q) phase; Sun in Aquarius with Moon in Taurus is the First Quarter (First Q) phase.

Moon

Sun	New	Cr	First Q	Gib	Full	Dissem	Last Q	Cr	Dark
AR	AR	TA-GE	CN	LE-VI	LI	SC-SG	CP	AQ	PI-AR
TA	TA	GE-CN	LE	VI-LI	SC	SG-CP	AQ	PI	AR-TA
GE	GE	CA-LE	VI	LI-SC	SG	CP-AQ	PI	AR	TA-GE
CN	CN	LE-VI	LI	SC-SG	CP	AQ-PI	AR	TA	GE-CN
LE	LE	VI-LI	SC	SG-CP	AQ	PI-AR	TA	GE	CN-LE
VI	VI	LI-SC	SG	CP-AQ	PI	AR-TA	GE	CN	LE-VI
LI	LI	SC-SG	CP	AQ-PI	AR	TA-GE	CN	LE	VI-LI
SC	SC	SG-CP	AQ	PI-AR	TA	GE-CN	LE	VI	LI-SC
SG	SG	CP-AQ	PI	AR-TA	GE	CN-LE	VI	LI	SC-SG
CP	CP	AQ-PI	AR	TA-GE	CN	LE-VI	LI	SC	SG-CP
AQ	AQ	PI-AR	TA	GE-CN	LE	VI-LI	SC	SG	CP-AQ
PI	PI	AR-TA	GE	CN-LE	VI	LI-SC	SG	CP	AQ-PI

SEVEN

Mercury: Communicator, Mediator, and (Sometimes) Spoiler

When the mythological tales involving Mercury/Hermes get stacked up alongside accounts of the exploits of Jupiter/Zeus or the trysts between Venus/Aphrodite and Mars/Aries, our fleet-footed god appears rather commonplace. He had a few good tricks up his sleeve, and access to Jupiter, the leader of the pack. But Mercury's role as errand boy to the more dynamic personalities on Mt. Olympus makes it easy to take the planet of communication for granted. That is, of course, until it moves backward.

Backward? Well, not exactly, but that's the way it looks from our seats here on Earth. It's an astronomical phenomenon known as *retrogradation*, something all the planets from Mercury on out to Pluto go through at varying times in the year (the Moon, not a planet, is the exception of course). The planets first appear to slow down to a standstill (termed going stationary) and then they retrace their steps before standing still again and then once again moving forward—or so it seems. When a planet is retrograde, all of the issues over which it has rulership need to be reexamined with an eye toward making repairs and refining circumstances.

Being born with a planet in retrograde can sometimes result in a person spending a good deal of his or her life internalizing special strategies for using the planet. Unlike a forward-moving planet, a backward one is not immediately accessible, at least not for use in traditional forms. It's like the difference between having a pencil and a piece of paper right next to the telephone when a caller wants to leave a message and being caught off guard and having to scurry a bit before being able to record the necessary information. Mercury Retrograde not only provides communication challenges (and sometimes subsequent triumphs) for the many people born under its influence—people as diverse as Benjamin Franklin, Anne Frank, Anne Tyler, Whoopi Goldberg, Philip Roth, Sam Donaldson, Michael Jackson, and Ralph Nader—but its frequency requires the rest of us to develop strategies for getting through the phase. Since Mercury is so close to both the Earth and the Sun, Mercury goes backward for twenty-one to twenty-eight days every three to four months, compared with the two months that Mars takes off about every other year. Venus moves backward for about forty days every twenty-one months, while the planets Jupiter through Pluto spend four to six months in a backward direction per year. Because of its frequent interruptions, as well as the planet's affinity with much in our daily routine and functioning on earth, Mercury Retrograde periods are especially notorious for bringing confusion, delays, and misdirected communication (lost mail, memos). The retrograde phenomenon is important to study but it is also a good way to gain more nitty-gritty insight into the workings of Mercury, a planet whose speed and seeming "ordinariness" make it more difficult for people to track.

Illustrative of Mercury's role in daily affairs is the case of Elizabeth, who moved to England a few days after Mercury had turned Retrograde. She had planned to live there with a new lover on a three-month trial basis, but within three weeks she was flying back home. Not being sure of what she wanted to do, Elizabeth literally got caught up in Mercury's backward movement. Mercury's role as communicator indicates an affinity with interchanges between people—from ground transportation to conversation—and it also refers to the process of thinking. Intelligence and quality of mind involve a number of planetary functions, but Mercury is the transmitter between our inner antennae and the messages it sends out to and receives from the world. As the go-between, it has a relationship to the nervous system that works throughout the body, and it is in steady contact with the brain.

Can We Talk? (Some Mercuries Do More of It Than Others)

It was Mercury in conjunction (same sign) with somber Saturn at the time of his birth that caused people to think poor Albert Einstein was a dolt, but Saturn was quietly adding depth and caution to the natural originality and inventiveness found in his Mercury in Aries. The combination needed time to come into its own. The Mercury profile of any individual is intricate, and Einstein's genius signature is much more subtle and complex than an annual Mercury/Saturn conjunction. But a good point from which to start studying Mercury's influence is through its zodiac placement, which suggests general speech and thinking style. Mercury in Sagittarius, for example, helps Ted Turner say exactly what's on his mind. You don't like his colorized films? "Well, last I checked, I owned them," he's said. Geraldo hits the airwaves with talkative Mercury in Gemini. Oprah Winfrey's Mercury is in iconoclastic and opinionated Aquarius. Mercury in Capricorn makes competitor Phil Donahue a cautious, well-informed interviewer.

The zodiac placement of Mercury shows some of the basic communication problems between people. Those with Mercury in a Fire sign (Aries, Leo, Sagittarius) are tuned to ideals and aspirations. Their minds are motivated by self-expression, future plans, and they often have a difficult time talking with those with Mercury in the more methodical, practical Earth signs. The latter are people who learn best by concrete example; they need to see and touch the evidence, while the Fire people are more perceptual. Mercury in the Air signs (Gemini, Libra, Aquarius) produces people fond of ideas and intellectual stimulation. They grasp theories, concepts, and logic. Mercury in the Water signs (Cancer, Scorpio, Pisces) is motivated by the unconscious and the emotions. When trying to sell them on something, appeal to their feelings, to nostalgia.

Mercury has been given rulership over two signs, Gemini and Virgo, both of which are concerned with adapting to the immediate environment. As new planets are discovered, Mercury will eventually reside over only one of the signs. Gemini seeks to make connections through mind and communication, while Virgo is concerned with developing a routine and a sense of order. Both signs are concerned with the information gathering and mental dexterity that comprise what are often known as life skills. We learn to speak, read, think, and tie our shoes in Gemini. In Virgo we develop an appreciation for efficiency and responsibility. We learn to nurse our bodies, what to do if the plumbing goes, how to show up for a job.

Things Move Toward Disorder

Mercury, as you can see, has much daily responsibility. Because of this it always runs the risk of overload, which is why Mercury Retrograde is so necessary for restoring balance. As the Second Law of Thermodynamics goes, things move toward disorder (and necessarily so for the sake of momentum, rebuilding, and refinement). Mercury Retrograde is where situations reach the point where they must go through a period of diffusion in order to get stronger. Without Mercury Retrograde, things would probably get even more messed up, and both people and the planet would experience the kind of mental exhaustion and fatigue that come after several days of concentrated work with no interruptions for sleep. Sometimes Mercury Retrograde is the reprieve needed from jammed schedules and ill-thought-out demands from bosses. Madeline, a manager of pension accounts who has been watching retrogrades for three years, says she now knows that she can "pretty much ignore the half-baked stuff that comes up in the office just a day or so before Mercury goes retrograde. It seems like all the really stupid people are in prime form and have all these ideas that need to be done right away. I put them in my circular file and wait for Mercury Retrograde to end. Most times all the really bad ideas have died out too."

The problem with Mercury Retrograde isn't from any one major thing that happens. Rather, it's the cumulative effect of three weeks of canceled meetings, botched plans, miscommunications, and dumb ideas that seemed to make sense when you first thought of them. Sometimes we're bombarded with especially ludicrous communications, such as Barbara Walters using prime-time television on two consecutive Fridays to let actress Robin Givens discuss her marital difficulties with Mike Tyson (the reason for the second interview was to clear up the confusion from the first interview, but the problem was only compounded). Often events like the student revolt in China begin unraveling shortly before Mercury is due to go retrograde, and the subsequent backward period is beset with confusion and lies, such as the attempts by Chinese leaders to discredit those who called for more democratic rule. The October 2–3, 1989, confusion over whether or not a coup had ousted Noriega occurred the day Mercury was moving forward after a three-week retrograde period.

The Iran/Contra scandal, for which Oliver North eventually stood trial, had Mercury Retrograde footprints during critical meeting dates, and arms shipments throughout the entire undercover operations. The plan first got off the ground on August 31, 1984, when security adviser Robert MacFarlane suggested the White House reconsider its previous policy of shunning Iran. News of the Irangate scandal first appeared in a Lebanese magazine as Mercury turned retrograde in November 1986, and the Tower Commission issued its damning report on the scandal during the following Mercury Retrograde period in February 1987. Oliver North's trial began with Mercury moving backward, making jury selection especially difficult and controversial. The jury finished its work and found North guilty of only three of the charges a week before Mercury went retrograde in May. George Bush's inauguration on a Retrograde Mercury— the same one that took North to trial—announced that the administration will always be trying to catch up with itself. Had Mercury not been Retrograde, our Founding Fathers might not have gone through with the Declaration of Independence, because the risks were so great.

Personal and Political Matters Go Awry

Celebrities and politicians aren't the only people out spinning their wheels when Mercury goes backward. For the purposes of astroscience, I asked several non-believers to keep a diary during various Mercury Retrograde periods. Kathy McKula, a newspaper librarian who is not unfamiliar with hectic activity, filed the following report of unusual occurrences in her office.

February 18: Person with serious medical test was supposed to get results and call me; did not call. She was not at home when I tried to call her. When I reached her, she said her doctor was on a week's vacation, but hadn't told her when he had set up the appointment for her to come in and discuss the results.

February 19: Every file has been missing. Received notice saying gift items are on back order, but on the same day the recipient of gift said it had arrived.

February 20: Another person with another doctor. Doctor called late Friday with the test results and then went on vacation.

February 23: A neighbor was supposed to call in to report a delay in employee's arrival due to weather; she was an hour late, but neighbor never called.

February 24: Medical test (see February 18) was negative. Notice was delayed. Someone in office said she'd do something in two weeks on March 2 (two weeks is March 9).

February 25: Two foot-high photocopies, which were a rush job for a meeting today. Meeting was canceled.

And this was just one week of entries. It shouldn't be difficult to understand why Kathy gets an anguished look in her eye whenever she hears that Mercury is about to go retrograde. Sometimes she can smell it a week away, without even looking at an ephemeris. There's a certain built-up tension and scattered feeling in the air as plans and meetings aren't coming together.

Early on, we must concede that the best-laid plans do indeed get messed up. Bad things do happen to good people, as they say. To those who always seem to be retracing their steps, Murphy's Law may seem to be much more reliable than a Mercury Retrograde theory. But screwups all have their own unique features. Things break down for different reasons. While canceled meetings, lost medical tests, and vacationing doctors can cause frustration during any time of the year, such occurrences during Retrograde Mercury are tied in to a larger picture and meaning that is best understood by studying the entire three-to-four-week period. Moreover, a year of Mercury Retrograde diary entries will give insight into the way individuals go about making changes in their daily routines, as well as dealing with the more ontological issues of their lives. When Mercury retrograde is appreciated as the necessary turning-inward and reorientation period that it is, people will find themselves gladly adjusting to the change in pace, and eventual focusing, that this period can represent. You'll be less apt to spin your wheels by launching ill-fated projects or expecting to nail down all necessary details at the last minute when Mercury is retrograde. Instead the time will be consciously used for sorting out glitches and rethinking plans and aims that had been so consuming during the last three or four months before Mercury started moving backward.

Getting Beyond Superstition

Don't mistake this as permission to slack off, to just do nothing. Unfortunately too many astrologers, and hence their clients, students, and friends, give advice with little regard for the fact that most people must go out and conduct business no matter what Mercury is doing. The way some of the more superstitious people talk, one would think that newspapers, radio stations, the post office—all of which are Mercury-type functions—simply go out of business when Mercury is retrograde, that people aren't able to address letters and mail them properly, or that every contract negotiated at this time will cost people their jobs. There's also a lot of misinformation about travel accidents increasing during these times, though data on airline, motor vehicle, and train accidents, which the Federal Aviation Administration and its transportation counterparts all willingly supply, don't support this claim. In making wild, unresearched claims, people put this cycle into the realm of "Friday the 13th" and destroy the possibility of finding practical truths that will help put Mercury Retrograde periods to better use.

Strategies are definitely needed. My respect for the power of the Mercury Retrograde period was increased by experiences that took place during the writing of this book. Prior to this project I'd scoffed at reports of increased cases of disappearing mail and important documents when Mercury moves backward. My own personality had long ago made me a faithful customer of Express Mail and other special mail services. I just assumed most Mercury Retrograde stories were fish stories spread by some Pisces who needed an excuse.

But the writing of this book intensified my experiences of cycles, including Mercury Retrograde. Several checks and manuscripts en route to and from my mailbox, papers in need of my signature, all took a detour. The people involved were not irresponsible people. And then the Express Mail service, in whom I had entrusted more faith than I place in any person, let me down. I was finally ready to concede that Mercury Retrograde does have special qualities that must be dissected and understood if people are to adopt techniques that will allow for practical use of this time. Such strategies range from simply double- and triple-checking contracts that must be signed during this period, to recognizing that some parts of the three-to-four-week period are more diffuse than others. The retrograde period contains both an old clearing-out phase (the first ten to twelve days) and then a new phase that, the backward-moving direction of Mercury aside, is very good for refocusing and starting out again.

The Sun/Mercury Cycle

Astronomically speaking, Mercury Retrograde concerns something more significant than a planet making an about-face. Just as the Moon-phase cycle involved the relationship between the Sun and Moon, the Mercury Retrograde phase is part of the larger cycle in the relationship between the Sun and Mercury. What essentially happens is that every time Mercury gets some 28 celestial degrees away from the Sun, we on Earth witness an optical illusion similar to what occurs when a fast train passes a slower-moving train. The slower-moving train—Mercury—appears to stop, then back up to those of us on the fast track (Earth).

By the time this phenomenon—retrogradation—starts, Mercury is nearly finishing a cycle with the Sun that began about two weeks after Mercury had last gone retrograde, some four months earlier. The new trend begins two weeks into the Retrograde Mercury period we are now viewing. What happens is that Mercury comes together with and makes a conjunction with the Sun. Officially known as an *inferior conjunction*, it is similar to what occurs both astronomically and symbolically at New Moon. This is ''New Mercury,'' time for new approaches and initiatives. New Mercury continues to move backward for about twelve days, and then it turns forward. Two months later Mercury will make another conjunction, called a *superior conjunction*, with the Sun. This conjunction, which occurs while Mercury is moving forward, works something like a Full Moon in that it often coincides with New Mercury's initiatives coming to a head or completion. Mercury's role as mediator in our daily affairs and in connection with our environment makes it an important rhythm to watch for clues to the way various projects will evolve over the course of several months. It is more evident in the life span of many projects than is the Sun/Moon cycle.

Ronald Reagan's Secret Strategy?

Ronald Reagan, who won his first term on a Retrograde Mercury, danced in step with the New Mercury/Full Mercury rhythm and managed to win his 1981 tax cut and other initiatives. Reagan announced plans for the tax cut during his first State of the Union address in 1981. The address coincided with the retrograde inferior conjunction, or New Mercury. The normally slow wheels of government began turning almost immediately, and (despite the assassination attempt on March 30, 1981), Reagan's first appearance before Congress and the public, slightly less than a month later, coincided with the full-term superior conjunction. Reagan told Congress he wanted his tax cut by summer's end, and though political glitches correlated to other portions of the Mercury/Sun rhythm when the planet went retrograde in June 1981, Reagan signed the bill into law under the August 13, 1981, superior conjunction.

The astrohistory of the passing of the tax cut, which proved to be ill considered and did its share toward increasing the budget deficit, is as follows:

Mercury Retrograde February 8	February 7—Reagan signs to raise debt limit
Sun/Mercury Inferior Conjunction February 17	February 18—Tax cut announced in State of the Union address
Mercury Direct March 2	No significant public action. (Conjunction proved more important.)
Sun/Mercury Superior Conjunction April 27	April 28—Reagan pleads with Congress
Mercury Retrograde June 9	June 9—Revised tax bill submitted

Sun/Mercury Inferior Conjunction June 21	Entire retrograde period a time for committee votes and other procedural steps related to the bill
Mercury Direct July 3	No significant public action.
Sun/Mercury Superior Conjunction August 10	August 13—Reagan signs bill into law

Later sections of this chapter will provide readers with data to track some of their future Sun/Mercury experiences. Initially the tax bill example can be simply used to show how Mercury changes faces during various portions of its retrograde phase. Whether Reagan's astrologer friends had any role in helping him make practical use of Mercury Retrograde—and in particular the Sun/Mercury rhythm—to get his tax cut is somewhat doubtful. Reagan, whose 1980 election was on a Retrograde Mercury, stumbled as much as any other president during these periods, though the Great Communicator was usually able to talk himself out of the holes he dug. Ideas about the nuances of the Mercury Retrograde phase have not been developed or researched to any degree, so most astrologers would have been inclined to steer him away from speaking during this period. Reagan, like most people, probably ended up making his announcements on the Sun/Mercury conjunction in spite of himself or of any advice he may have received.

Mercury Loved Lucy

The Sun/Mercury pattern can show up in a range of places. *Saturday Night Live* first aired two days after a Retrograde Sun/Mercury conjunction. Another experimental television show where people made up rules as they went along was *I Love Lucy*. Rehearsals began on September 3, 1951, a Monday. Despite limited support from television executives and a betting pool aimed at guessing the amount of dollars the show would lose before dying out after its first season, and logistical problems that caused delays during that first week, the audience that watched the first taping loved the Ricardos and Mertzes. And so did the rest of the country when it aired on Monday, October 15, 1951, two days after the forward-moving Mercury and Sun formed a superior conjunction.

Mercury Retrograde's unpredictability did surface, however. The first segment that was taped, "The Diet," was aired as the third show in the series because television executives felt it had strong ratings appeal and would help the show continue its momentum. Lucille Ball's second series was initially broadcast as *The Lucille Ball Show*, on October 1, 1962, six days into a retrograde phase and five days before the New Mercury (inferior conjunction), connoting beginnings; the show was re-titled *The Lucy Show* a month later.

Despite the chances for an early self-correction hinted at by the example of the renaming of the 1962 *Lucy* show, it's best to understand the nuances of the entire retrograde period, just in case. The changes coinciding with Mercury's move backward become obvious almost immediately. The day or so before the actual move backward or forward usually marks the times when Mercury, like any retrograde-prone astronomical body, is stationary (or seems to be). A standstill is needed to change directions. Those following the stock market say the shift in direction—either backward or forward—often coincides with a discernible change in the Dow Jones Average. Mercury went retrograde the Friday before the October 19 market crash, working with several other planets, of course. Friday saw a 108-point drop, and then there was Black Monday.

Three Weeks of No-Gos

But the weeks in between the days that Mercury shifts direction are also important. A series of rumors and misunderstandings among newspaper colleagues during one Mercury Retrograde period epitomizes some of the pitfalls of this cycle: An editor received a tip about the misuse of government funds, and this prompted the establishment of a fifteen-person reporter/editor task force charged with shaking the story out of the city. With Mercury just a few hours away from turning backward, the first meeting of the task force was convened, and things went retro. The task force meeting unleashed a wild stream of speculations and theories, which reporters then went running around town trying to check. Nobody they interviewed had any knowledge about the rumors, but by the time the second reporter turned up with the same questions, those being interviewed gladly shared the scuttlebutt they were now hearing around town. In other words, the reporters were falling over their own rumors. This comedy of errors fizzled out as Mercury started moving forward again.

It's hard to get the answers you need when Mercury is retrograde. While some people experience a string of miscommunications and misplaced telephone calls, others note that their telephone simply stops ringing. "It's like nobody else is out there," was how one astrologer described an especially quiet period. People wait nervously for the results of mortgage applications and other inquiries and hear nothing, sometimes not until the day Mercury moves forward again. But if things seem to be at a temporary standstill in our lives, we can be entertained by world leaders. Reagan's approach was to say or announce something while Mercury was retrograde that he'd have to undo or explain further once Mercury started moving forward again. This is what happened when, under Mercury Retrograde, the White House said that Reagan was going to visit Bitburg, the Nazi cemetery. When Jewish groups and others decried the lack of sensitivity Reagan was displaying, the president tripped over himself again a few days after Mercury went forward by announcing plans to include a concentration camp on his excursion to Europe. These periods were Jimmy Carter's Waterloos, as histories of the period now show. Carter's often-criticized energy initiatives, which were blocked and watered down in Congress, were rushed to legislators with several technical flaws under a Mercury Retrograde in 1977. And some of his more ridiculed speeches were made as the planet was changing direction or was well established in the Mercury Retrograde phase. Such periods certainly can be like stubbing one's toe every three or four steps if the nature of the time is ignored. While labor doesn't need Mercury Retrograde to cajole it into calling a strike—such actions don't rise and fall with the planet's movement—the baseball strike of 1971 began on a Mercury Retrograde. It lasted for most of the season, causing the loss of millions of dollars to each of the host cities, and subsequently forced the change in strike ground rules. Some of the owner-player standoff may have been due to Mercury moving backward. At the very least, labor leaders should keep in mind that Retrograde Mercury may make negotiations more difficult. Reflection and solo research seem to be more in order. Things move slowly.

Harnessing the Mercury Cycle

But it's obvious that we can't shut out the world for three weeks. People must get up and out and make decisions, no matter what Mercury is doing. To be able to move effectively in the world, it is necessary to first understand one's past history with Mercury Retrograde. Next, it is important to know where the loose ends are in one's life.

For the most part, these issues relate to daily effectiveness. These would be situations such as several involving Bill, who spent most of 1988 trying to clear up a messy credit history and obtain financing for a house, which he eventually bought a year after the property was first offered to him. Each retrograde period in 1988 advanced and set back portions of Bill's planning. The turning points were confined to the times Mercury was Retrograde, or the day it conjoined the Sun in the superior-conjunction configuration that occurs when Mercury is moving forward.

Elizabeth's aborted relocation to England gives information about how several consecutive Mercury Retrograde phases contained related issues. We will also review a full retrograde phase to better understand how to make such periods work better in our lives. Elizabeth was having troubles dealing with several larger cycles in her life, but Mercury Retrograde was the point at which things began to unravel. The drama of the overseas romance was not unrelated to other retro phases. The previous 1987 March period found her contacting and going to lunch with a man with whom she'd had another short-term relationship. With Mercury moving backward, she wanted to retrace her steps and find out why the relationship had fizzled. She'd last seen the man during the November retrograde period of 1986. The prospect of a trip to England to visit a man with whom she had a fairly light dalliance in 1987 had originally been a whim, something she might do in late summer or early fall. Sometime in mid-June, however, she found herself making reservations and then quitting her job and giving up her apartment. Five days after Mercury had gone backward, Elizabeth left for England. Within a week she was telephoning friends in the United States to tell them of her misery. She finally got back on a plane and was flying into Kennedy Airport as Mercury was stationary and readying to move forward again.

The following list breaks down the June–July 1987 phase and Elizabeth's experiences of it.

Mercury Retrograde—June 20, 1987 (11:45 P.M. EDT)
Elizabeth left for England June 26

Sun/Mercury Conjunction—July 4, 1987
Phoned friends in the United States to say she was unhappy

Mercury Direct—July 15, 1987
Flies into JFK

Elizabeth and her lover debated the issue, but she was back in Connecticut on the evening of July 15. "I woke up that morning knowing I was going to leave, even though I didn't do anything about it right away. . . . But then I just got my things together and wrote him a note." Mercury went direct at 7:27 A.M. in London. Many astrologers don't think there's a "green light" until Mercury gets to the degree of the zodiac at which it began its backward movement, a point that is too technical for our discussion here. While there are cases that bear such thinking out, the example of Ronald Reagan's tax cut suggests that the Sun/Mercury conjunction ten to twelve days after the retrograde period begins, as well as the days when the planet actually changes direction, are particularly noteworthy.

The Sun/Mercury conjunction seems to be a point of clarity, where people have a better focus on what projects need to be overhauled and launched. I began viewing the cycle this way after finding that many of the work assignments I received as Mercury turned backward were usually revised on the conjunction; the person assigning the project either refocused or altered it in some way. The people making assignments after the conjunction had more clarity about what they wanted. This should be instructive to others, particularly the self-employed, who don't want to waste valuable billing time. Unless it's a quick, temporary assignment, work before the conjunction can cause more trouble than its worth. Because real estate closings and other business often can't be put off until Mercury starts moving forward, it makes sense to try to schedule necessary transactions on or after the Sun/Mercury conjunction. The planetary configuration symbolizes the coming together of the solar will (Sun) and its secretary (Mercury), which is why presidents seem to end up holding press conferences or making significant announcements during these periods. The floundering during the two weeks leading up to the conjunction causes some inward principle to get hold of things and get down to business. Seeds are planted, and as the planet starts to move forward, it's time to step out refreshed, with bigger and better projects.

Those who decide to take up further study of Mercury Retrograde will also find that some periods are more potent than others. This is partially due to the workings of other planets, but there are certain Mercury Retrograde periods that are a power unto themselves. Such potency was in the air in November 1986, when the Irangate stories first broke. Mercury started moving backward on November 2 as the first leaks were getting attention. From then on, there was no keeping a lid on it. The November phase was especially important because it was a SuperRetro, only thirteen of which occur each century. SuperRetro is a loose way I have of describing the astronomical phenomenon called *Mercury Transits*, during which the planet appears like a spot against the Sun. These times have always coincided with news leaks, lies, and miscommunication that seem to throw the planet into a tizzy. Prior to 1986, the most recent SuperRetros worked with bigger cycles and coincided with Nixon's 1970 move into Cambodia and the 1973 start of impeachment proceedings against Nixon. The Mercury Transits—an even less common Venus Transit also took place in November 1986—are a side issue. Any Mercury Retrograde can have qualities of déjà vu or find people going to their past and bringing forward long-forgotten elements. Sometimes the past can come to you. Pick up the telephone when Mercury is retrograde and the next voice you hear may well be someone you haven't talked with in years. Some Cosmic Reporters say that Mercury Retrograde and Venus Retrograde—it helps if they're happening at the same time—are great for reconciliations with lost lovers and friends. But don't sit by the telephone waiting for a call; Mercury is needed to bring back a major love that got away.

We often hear from Mercury-ruled people, those with Gemini and Virgo prominent in their charts. These Mutable (adaptable) people seem to come and go with the planet. Mercury-ruled people may appear even more scattered or anxiety-ridden when their planet is moving backward. Even if they're not Mercury-ruled, people can expect changes and delays in the area of their birth-chart where Mercury is located or where the signs Gemini and Virgo are placed (we all have some of it somewhere).

Does time move backward? That's one question that physicists may be toying with for a long time. At the very least, Mercury Retrograde makes you wonder about things like time warps. "I don't have a problem when Mercury is retrograde because finally everybody is operating at my speed," says one retrograde Mercury, who often seems to be out of sync in conversations with forward-moving Mercury types because of the way Retrograde Mercury tends to let ideas and thoughts settle in before responding or assaulting them in "normal" Mercury fashion. When Mercury is retrograde, it's not that people are out to lunch, but a little maintenance work is under way. In its seeming eccentricity Retrograde Mercury may tap the essence of time, change, and cycle better than most astronomical phenomena. Simultaneously the planet's comings and goings, back and forth over various areas of life, provide concrete information about how we can refine the way we communicate with our environment. All planetary energies must be developed to higher and higher levels. Because we are always in the midst of using one or the other of our Mercury-related functions, we can get complacent, and think that we've learned all there is to know about responding to the stimuli around us or making connections with the world in which we live. Retrograde Mercury allows us to play the role of utility lineman by cleaning out our antennae and transmitting signals. More importantly, we're allowed—encouraged actually—to pull back and spend time talking with ourselves until it's time to go back out into the world again.

The Backward Checklist

In order to glean helpful information about this cycle, it is necessary to track it through several phases. A chart detailing future Mercury Retrogrades through this century appears on page 136. A more detailed ephemeris is necessary to find the precise date and hours for other points in the cycle, such as the Sun/Mercury inferior conjunction that occurs ten to twelve days after Mercury goes retrograde. Tables in this book can be of general assistance, and you can call an astronomical observatory to hear a recorded message about conjunctions to the Sun. Several general-interest astrology magazines (*American Astrology, Dell Horoscope*) list important planetary conjunctions and other configurations each month. Also helpful is the Skywatchers report presented by the Smithsonian Institution (1–202–357–2000), where new taped information is offered each week and phenomena such as retrogradation and Moon phases, among many other celestial activities, are addressed.

To summarize:

1. Mercury stationary and ready to move backward.
2. The Sun/Mercury inferior conjunction ten to twelve days later. New cycle starts.
3. Mercury turns stationary direct (a pause before definite actions).
4. Some people will want to continue tracking the phase by keeping an eye on the Sun/Mercury superior conjunction six weeks after the Sun/Mercury inferior conjunction.

Mercury Retrograde

1989
January 16 to February 2
May 12 to June 5
September 11 to October 3
December 30 to January 20
(90)

1990
April 23 to May 17
August 25 to September 17
December 14 to January 3
(91)

1991
April 4 to April 28
August 7 to September 31
November 28 to December
18

1992
March 17 to April 19
July 20 to August 13
November 11 to December 1

1993
March 27 to April 9
July 20 to August 13
November 11 to December 1

1994
February 11 to March 5
June 12 to July 6
October 9 to November 30

1995
January 26 to February 14
May 24 to June 17
September 22 to October 14

1996
January 9 to February 3
May 3 to May 27
September 4 to September 26
December 23 to January 12 (97)

1997
April 16 to May 8
August 17 to September 10
December 7 to December 27

1998
March 27 to April 20
July 31 to August 23
November 21 to December 11

1999
March 10 to April 2
July 12 to August 6
November 5 to November 25

2000
February 21 to March 14
June 23 to July 17
October 18 to November 8

Sun/Mercury Conjunctions

A Matter of Details

A new Sun/Mercury cycle begins each time that Mercury is retrograde and makes a conjunction with the Sun; this cycle (and issues related to the cycle) meets its culmination point two months later when Mercury is Direct and makes a conjunction with the Sun. The technical word for the Retrograde Conjunction (known as RC below) is an Inferior Conjunction; the Direct Conjunction (DC) is known as a Superior Conjunction.

1. March 1, 1991   (Direct Conjunction, culmination of cycle that began in December 1990)

2. April 14, 1991   (Retrograde Conjunction; New Cycle)
   June 17, 1991   (Direct Conjunction, culmination.)

3. August 21, 1991   (RC)
   October 3, 1991   (DC)

4. December 8, 1991   (RC)
   February 12, 1992   (DC)

 5. March 25, 1992   (RC)
    May 31, 1992   (DC)

 6. August 3, 1992   (RC)
    September 15, 1992   (DC)

 7. November 21, 1992   (RC)
    January 23, 1993   (DC)

 8. March 9, 1993   (RC)
    May 16, 1993   (DC)

 9. July 15, 1993   (RC)
    August 29, 1993   (DC)

10. November 6, 1993   (RC)
    January 3, 1994   (DC)

11. February 20, 1994   (RC)
    April 30, 1994   (DC)

12. June 25, 1994   (RC)
    August 13, 1994   (DC)

13. October 21, 1994   (RC)
    December 14, 1994   (DC)

14. February 3, 1995   (RC)
    April 14, 1995   (DC)

15. June 5, 1995   (RC)
    July 28, 1995   (DC)

16. October 5, 1995   (RC)
    November 23, 1995   (DC)

17. January 18, 1996   (RC)
    March 28, 1996   (DC)

18. May 15, 1996   (RC)
    July 11, 1996   (DC)

19. September 17, 1996 (RC)
    November 1, 1996   (DC)

20. January 2, 1997   (RC)
    March 11, 1997   (DC)

21. April 25, 1997   (RC)
    June 25, 1997   (DC)

22. August 31, 1997   (RC)
    October 13, 1997   (DC)

23. December 17, 1997   (RC)
    February 22, 1998   (DC)

24. April 6, 1998   (RC)
    June 10, 1998   (DC)

25. August 13, 1998   (RC)
    September 25, 1998   (DC)

26. December 1, 1998   (RC)
    February 4, 1999   (DC)

27. March 19, 1999   (RC)
    May 25, 1999   (DC)

28. July 26, 1999   (RC)
    September 8, 1999   (DC)

29. November 15, 1999   (RC)
    January 16, 2000   (DC)

30. March 1, 2000   (RC)
    May 9, 2000   (DC)

31. July 6, 2000   (RC)
    August 22, 2000   (DC)

32. October 30, 2000   (RC)
    December 25, 2000   (DC)

Mercury Signs

Mercury in Aries: The mind moves rapidly, speech is often staccatolike. They're original and inventive, as Albert Einstein showed, and film director Francis Ford Coppola and Philip Roth continue to show. Candice Bergen has the straightforwardness that can come with the position. With Mercury here, Diana Ross wouldn't have settled for less than lead singer. Neither would Liza Minnelli.

Mercury in Taurus: They might appear to be developmentally slow to faster wits, but this Mercury simply believes in taking its time in order to methodically reach conclusions. They have to see, touch, and taste things for themselves and are not comfortable with theories and abstractions that have no application. It steadies Gemini George Bush. This Mercury can get boring and uninspired, but George Lucas and Miles Davis show the potential to build on solid foundations. Cher's voice demonstrates the Taurean slowness but musicality and sensuality as well.

Mercury in Gemini: If only they could all have their own talk shows like Geraldo Rivera, or the literary talents of Joyce Carol Oates. You get the point. Words can seem to be their raison d'être. Some talk too much and say very little. This Mercury's need for mental stimuli, to interact with its environment, to express and share ideas, is usually quite evident. They can be amusing and clever. They must take special pains to learn to focus.

Mercury in Cancer: Emotions and feelings color their thinking and communication process. They react to situations and people who stir their memories. Bill Cosby uses this ability to tap moods and emotions in his comedy. Pauline Kael, the *New Yorker* film critic, also demonstrates the way this Mercury can sense and communicate moods and impressions. Carly Simon's music often deals with emotional exchanges and other Cancer-inspired interests.

Mercury in Leo: Flamboyant, creative, they usually let people know they're around. Michael Jackson shows their ability to put their own personal stamp on their communications. Lily Tomlin and Zelda Fitzgerald show the flair. There's a vanity and self-centeredness that can block this group's ability to communicate. Sometimes they can also take the drama too far. Jerry Falwell has shown the more arrogant, self-important side of this Mercury.

Mercury in Virgo: The Paul Volcker Mercury. They're analytical, cautious, frugal, discriminating types. Their minds seek order and prefer routine over potluck. Talented editors and able critics, as well as craftsmen whose calling requires a special reverence for technique, have this placement. Barbara Walters's to-the-point questioning draws on this Mercury. They go in looking to get the job done, but as Neil Armstrong showed, they can also quip a few memorable lines while they're working.

Mercury in Libra: They're wonderful diplomats whose tact and charm can open doors, but they can also be argumentative. Sometimes, as historian Arthur Schlesinger, Jr., and reporter

Jack Anderson demonstrate, truth and justice is the goal. Libran logic can help get a balanced view. It didn't hurt Agatha Christie's work either. Bruce Springsteen, whose Sun and Moon are also in Libra, meets his public with the Libran pleasantness of speech and concern about justice and peace.

Mercury in Scorpio: Probing, resourceful, intense. Dan Rather's days as a reporter were helped by this Mercury's dogged persistence to get to the bottom of things. Johnny Carson shows the bent for sarcasm, while writer Anne Tyler's explorations of the undercurrents in human interactions demonstrate the perception abilities.

Mercury in Sagittarius: Michael Dukakis's juggling of several foreign languages shows some of the good ways this Mercury can be put to use. The mind is expansive, always reaching for knowledge and adventure. The best become true citizens of the world. Some are opinionated and don't let the facts get in the way of their beliefs. Their statements can generalize too much. Ted Turner has the bluntness, Bette Midler the comic touch.

Mercury in Capricorn: They have minds like steel traps. They are calculating and are always looking for situations that can be pressed to their advantage. They look for ideas to fuel their ambition and are careful about what they say or put in writing. Phil Donahue's Mercury is evidence; he is more erudite than his counterparts, better informed, more careful. Jane Fonda's activism gets some steadiness and direction from this Mercury. Richard Nixon (whose Sun is also in Capricorn) is perhaps the best living example of the combination of depth, drive, and opportunism of this placement.

Mercury in Aquarius: Minds are focused in the future, often on goals that further society. Mark Goodson, producer and creator of popular game shows and other television fare, demonstrates some of the more inventive aspects of the sign. Whoopi Goldberg shows the offbeat, eccentric side. Some are highly scientific, almost clinical. Oprah Winfrey shows the mass-media instincts. Dan Quayle may ultimately be stimulated by some of the more progressive, creative qualities of the sign.

Mercury in Pisces: Their minds are often so attuned to the static and mixed signals thrown around the planet that they have a hard time focusing on their own thoughts. Others have a difficult time differentiating between reality and fantasy or are overcome by irrational fears and paranoia. Artists such as

William Hurt and Alice Walker display some of the higher possibilities. Though his routines are often antifemale and vulgar, Eddie Murphy's comedic talent owes some of its appeal to this Mercury, which is able to read the collective mind.

EIGHT

Venus: The Things We Like and Want

Those glossy, seductive advertisements in the shopping catalogs make everything—even telephone receivers shaped like shoes or cartoon characters—seem necessary for a happy existence on Earth. But while it may seem as if we could take two of everything from the catalog, we have visceral reactions that would ultimately determine what we truly want to buy. Those items, whether understated pumps or a pink-and-purple polyester jumpsuit, could be said to embody what it is we value, what it is we like. This embodiment is extended to all the furniture, jewelry, houses, styles of relationships (open or monogamous), or bodies that we look at and say, "That's for me." When we pursue certain life-styles, activities, or people—or when we run away from them—we're acting on something in us that has made a good/bad assessment.

That something in us is Venus, most commonly known as the planet of love. Certainly romantic trysts in both their more exciting and humdrum states fall under the watch of Venus (with assistance from most of the other planets). But Venus's involvement with things we "love" and don't love is much more encompassing than reports on the alleged indiscretions of the love goddess might suggest. The concern of Venus with affairs of the heart is a by-product of her deeper overall concern with an individual's value system, which is a collection of abstract and emotional states out of which blooms issues ranging from self-worth to interpersonal relationships to feelings (and hence, experiences) about possessions and money.

Venus's rulership over matters around which we build our sense of personal contentment would seem to give it an affinity with the Moon, but Venus is more consciously cultivated than the Moon. Its concerns are more aesthetic and abstract. The Moon shows daily survival needs as well as types of emotional nurturing; Venus picks the restaurant. This shortcut explanation might seem to downgrade Venus's worth, but it is intended to show the difference between needs, as defined by the Moon, and general preferences, as defined by Venus. The Moon in a person's chart might seek security through the development of long-term emotional bonds with a small circle of people, but Venus may be less discriminating and eager to befriend everyone in town. Striking a compromise would be a challenge. Woe unto those who mistake some of Venus's more superficial preferences—check out the personal ads detailing the expected height, weight, hair color, and eyes of Mr./Ms. Right—for true "needs." But a life that gave no homage to Venus would be barren and off center. The process of assigning worth or investing in something must occur before anything of substance manifests. It will be up to Mars to go out and bring back the goods for Venus, and the rest of the chart also affects eventual contentment. But Venus is the place where the process begins.

Here are some quick exercises to help you begin isolating the Venus Factor. Sit back and quiet yourself and try to hear your inner responses to the following:

1. Five things I want for my life:

2. My ideal relationship would have the following qualities:

3. These are a few of my favorite things (activities, objects):

4. My ideal lover is:

5. Major turnoffs (in lovers and otherwise):

6. Happiness (personal contentment) is:

What It All Means

Venus's zodiac placement—the sign it is in—in the birth-chart shows the style and qualities favored by our Venus. Venus is either in the same sign as our Sun or no more than two signs away in either direction; the planet never moves more than 48 celestial degrees from the Sun. (Jacqueline Onassis is an example of someone born with the Sun (Leo) two signs away from Venus (Gemini). Dan Quayle has Sun in Aquarius and Venus in Sagittarius. We can see Quayle's Venus working in his love of sports and rowdy party-hardiness in his college days; he'd seek freedom in all of his relationships, which is just fine with his Sun in Aquarius as well. Jackie O.'s Venusian pursuits are more obvious. With Venus in Gemini, a person would be expected to value a life infused with a steady flow of intellectual stimulation, communication, and environmental interaction promoting variety and versatility. Jackie O, a former "inquiring photographer," is multilingual, works in book publishing, and is connected to some of the world's most sophisticated and urbane social circles. She epitomizes many of the ideas behind this Venus placement. The more typical citizen would have some interest in his or her surroundings and may be up on the trendiest places to eat in town. Intellectual hobbies—trips to the museum or much leisure-time reading—are ways people with this position would express themselves. Venus in Gemini also produces a fair share of media groupies, who get a charge out of circulating among those who work in the communications industry.

Onassis's love of intellectual stimulation and communication with her environment, as represented by Venus in Gemini, does not conflict with the developing self-expression indicated by her Sun sign, Leo. Gemini, which is Air, and Leo which is Fire, are two signs apart and hence have empathy for each other. But many people are born when the Sun and Venus are in signs that have contrasting views on life, requiring special adjustments if both energies are to receive their proper due. George Bush is a Gemini with Venus in family-oriented, emotional Cancer. Liz Claiborne, the highly successful fashion designer/entrepreneur, is an example of someone born with Sun and Venus signs that feel uncomfortable around each other. But she has managed to bring both energies into her life with megasuccess. Claiborne was born with the Sun in pioneering, dare-to-be-courageous Aries, a sign that allows its natives to take the risks and accomplish feats many others didn't realize existed. Most people with the Sun in Aries, however, never live up to their leadership and entrepreneurial skills, lacking the patience, persistence, and follow-through to implement their plans.

Claiborne's Venus in Taurus provides some of the staying power that allowed her to develop a designing career and then have the persistence and practicality to put together a multimillion-dollar company. Claiborne and her businessman husband retired from active management in 1989, but solid building over the previous thirteen years brought the company to the point where it will be a strong money-maker for years to come. Liz Claiborne, Inc., epitomizes all of the Venus in Taurus concerns with steadfastness, devotion, finances, form, and art.

Aphrodite Consciousness

Art's connection to Venus helps illuminate the planet's meaning further. Those in the creative professions (musicians, painters, dancers, writers), develop a certain relationship with their work that can be compared to love relationships. Author and therapist Jean Bolen describes the involvement necessary to give life to a lump of clay or use a healing art to help a client's "Aphrodite consciousness." On the subject of the attraction/union/fertilization/incubation/birth process, as it relates to sexuality (specialty of goddess Aphrodite/Venus), she says,

Creative work comes out of an intense and passionate involvement—almost as if a lover, as one (the artist) interacts with the "other" to bring something new into being. This "other" may be a painting, a dance form, a musical composition, a sculpture, a poem or a manuscript, a new theory or invention, that for a time is all-absorbing and fascinating.

Creativity is also a "sensual" process for many people; it is an in-the-moment sensory experience involving touch, sound, imagery, movement, and sometimes even smell and taste. An artist engrossed in a creative process, like a lover, often finds that all her senses are heightened and she receives perceptual impressions through many channels.

Venus's rulership over Taurus and Libra heightens the planet's meaning in the lives of those born with the Sun or Ascendant in Taurus and Libra, or who have these signs (or the planet) emphasized in other ways. Like Mercury, Venus has been assigned rulership over two signs, but astrologers feel that the discovery of other planets will eventually take care of this dual-rulership problem as well. Yet within astrological circles there is debate over which planet (Taurus or Libra) will lose the Venus rulership. Taurus is concerned with discovering and building a life based on personal values, security, and comfort. The physical is important to them, and this manifests in areas such as possessions, money, and enjoyment of their physical bodies and senses. In the more refined Taureans this can translate into a persona of integrity, strong self-worth, comfortable surroundings, and a good eye for art and other forms. Yet while Venus has proven itself to be concerned with all of these matters, some astrologers argue that the Earth rules Taurus because it displays an innate appreciation and understanding of Mother Nature at work.

On the other hand, as we move into the realm of balance-seeking Libra, we have to question whether that sign's main concern with one-to-one relationships that ideally become equal partnerships once all the competition and self-negation are worked through thoroughly embraces the deeper, value-seeking face of Venus. Libra has the artist's eye for color and balance, pointing to a Venus connection. But some astrologers feel that the asteroids Juno (who was concerned with women's equality within marriage) and Pallas (strategist/negotiator/warrior) speak to Libran concerns better than Venus does. The asteroids, which are gaining wider use among astrologers, do seem to highlight the concerns of Margaret Thatcher, Jimmy Carter, Jesse Jackson, Oliver North, and Barbara Walters better than Venus. Older astrology texts have pushed the idea of the sweet-faced Libran, yet this sign often produces very assertive women. And while Oliver North and Dwight Eisenhower show how Libra can combine political and tactical skills, the sign is also known for producing noticeable numbers of more passive men who seek strong, assertive female partners.

Venus—For Women Only?

Maybe we'll be better able to assign Venus's rulership when we work out our male/female conflicts and move toward greater gender equality. It may also cast another face on the argument over the different ways men and women use Venus in the chart. One guiding rule of interpretation is that Venus (and the Moon) in a man's chart indicates the type of women he would be attracted to, in the same way that Mars (and the Sun) indicates what a female is seeking in a relationship. Mars in a man's chart is related to his sense of manliness, while Venus in a woman's chart relates to her concept of femininity. While such guidelines are valid, women's better integration of their so-called masculine energies and men's increased exploration of their femininity is changing the rules of interpretation, particularly for people who came of age after the women's movement. It's important for men and women to become thoroughly familiar with the workings of their Venus.

The Cycle

One active way to study the planet's role in our life is to watch its various movements in the sky, both generally and as it relates to our birthday. Unlike the more dynamic cycles of Mars, Jupiter, or Saturn, Venus cycles can seem to come and go with little announcement. The cycle can't be tracked as concretely as others in this book, which is why we will examine it differently.

Venus's annual return to its natal position takes a little less than a year, depending on whether or not it goes into retrograde motion between one return and another. The Venus Return day can happen within a month or two before or after the annual birthday or Solar Return. Check the Venus ephemeris at the back of the book. This will be the week when you will want quiet time and a journal. Friend and fellow astrologer James Santa-Mo has made a point of taking the entire day of the exact return off from work to "think about my ideals and values."

Others report being conscious of questioning whether they're getting what they want from relationships and other activities.

The return day is the time to ask yourself questions like "What makes me happy?" "What in my life (right now) makes me happy?" "What am I not happy with?" Go back to the earlier Venus exercise in this chapter and quiz yourself again. The annual return is one of the best times for separating true values from media messages. Some Venuses may never love a poor man or woman, while others are naturally faithful in areas of romance. And, cultural conditioning aside, some have always preferred Venus de Milo's more statuesque build to models with adolescent figures. You do have the right to get a little risqué about this. Venuses can be very specific about likes and dislikes in the lovemaking department—some are more tactile than others—and this is your time to take notes.

Venus can move through an entire sign in less than a month. For this reason we won't be dwelling on some of the seemingly important pit stops the planet makes in relation to your natal position as it moves through the zodiac. The day that Venus is 90 degrees (three signs) away from your specific natal Venus position can bring some subtle insights to areas of your life, but separating the useless messages from truth will take years of Venus watching. The day when Venus is exactly 180 degrees (the opposition, six signs) could be a little more revealing, but all of this comes with time. Venus is a passive, internalized function that needs other energies to help it give form to itself. The following chapter will explore Mars and also include information showing how Mars and Venus work together. But Venus's movement in relationship to the Sun's ongoing position in the sky is another revealing cycle.

The Sun/Venus Cycle

Approximately every ten months the traveling Venus and Sun are conjunct in the sky. The conjunction marks a time when people can purge themselves of unneeded and culturally conditioned values that are blocking personal growth. Because this cycle involves the transiting relationship between the Sun and Venus, everyone on the planet will have some connection to the rhythm simultaneously. But the specific meaning for each individual's life depends on the birthchart.

Venus Retrograde

Like the Sun/Mercury cycle, the relationship between the Sun and Venus is built around the periods of retrograde motion, as well as the two conjunctions between the Sun and Venus that are related to the turning points. Venus goes retrograde every eighteen to nineteen months, when it gets about 48 celestial degrees away from the Sun. Like Mercury Retrograde, the backward movement is an optical illusion, but once again, the effects are real. When Venus is retrograde, people pull within themselves and begin reexamining relationships, personal likes and dislikes, and other Venusian elements of their lives. Many relationships go awry during a retro. The trend is one of detachment and reorientation, not cuddling. It's good to spend time alone. When couples aren't aware of the changing direction of Venus (and hence their relationship), there are special discomforts. Good relationships obviously survive the many comings and goings of the Sun and Venus, but when there are fermenting issues, Venus Retrograde will coincide with tension-filled scenarios. Some lovers walk out the door in such sharp timing with the planet's turn of direction that one would think they're going out to meet it. Relationships started at this time may have difficulty getting on track.

Since the planet is retrograde for forty to fifty days every eighteen to nineteen months, a good number of people were born with the backward-Venus condition. Their way of relating to other people often seems to go against more traditional or "normal" socialization. Elizabeth Barrett Browning was a forty-year-old invalid who was isolated from most people until she met the younger man who became her husband. Some Venus Retrograde people wear their social isolation like a badge of honor. Serial killer Ted Bundy had smooth moves, but obviously had social-adjustment problems. Venus Retrograde worked with a complex of other planets. Some Venus Retrogrades are sincerely introspective souls who prefer a solitary life in order to explore personal and more universal ideals than those ordinarily experienced in daily life. Acquaintances ranging from a Buddhist priest to established artists come to mind.

People born under the Retrograde Venus, as well as those with prominent Taurus and Libran energy, will have a special interest in the Sun/Venus cycle. But the rest of us must also be on guard. We are affected in a number of ways: The areas of our charts that are ruled by Venus and the Sun, the part of the birthchart where our Venus is located, and the part of the chart where the Sun/Venus conjunction falls.

The first Sun/Venus conjunction in a cycle occurs with Venus Retrograde, and it is technically an inferior conjunction. Like the New Moon, the inferior conjunction is a seeding period when new values begin to take form. The values being reevaluated and re-formed meet certain internal and external challenges during the superior conjunction that occurs ten months later as forward-moving Venus conjoins the Sun.

In one eight-year period there are ten Sun/Venus conjunctions, or five full Sun/Venus cycles. Venus returns to the same point in the zodiac on the same date every eight years. Those who study correlations between the stock market and Astrocycles find the eight-year Venus cycle useful in their forecasts. Individuals can adapt this technique to their own lives by watching the Sun/Venus cycles and recording the internal changes (and ultimately external ones) that relate to this rhythm. It may be difficult to look back and dig up the feeling that was operative during past Sun/Venus cycles. But do record future ones. Below is an example from Tom, a Boston man who has a basic understanding of astrology and also keeps a journal. (The conjunction dates are in boldface.)

Finding What You Really Want

April 3, 1985 (Retro): Tom had a job interview for a position in another department at the financial services corporation where he worked. He was turned down for the job and was particularly depressed because he was growing increasingly frustrated in his position. He made several ill-conceived attempts to find a comparable job.

January 19, 1986: Got a poor performance evaluation around this time. Knew he was going to have to make some short-term attitude adjustments, but also come up with a plan for his future.

November 5, 1986 (Retro): Tom and his wife separated about a week after this conjunction. The job situation was still frustrating.

August 23, 1987: Started working for a recruitment firm

and also began consulting on the side, about two weeks after this conjunction. His marriage was moving into the divorce stage.

June 14, 1988 (Retro): "I'm feeling more clear about my goals for the next five to ten years. I haven't felt that way in a long time," he writes.

Tom's crises correlate to configurations involving Saturn, Uranus, and Mars, among other sensitive points in his chart. However, the transiting Sun/Venus cycle, which everyone experiences in some way, provides helpful information about the process of incremental inner regrouping that was necessary to meet the bigger challenges. The April 1985 conjunction listed above was the new start, while January 1986 was the culmination period that would have put the matters on the table more directly. The June 1988 beginning will culminate with an April 4, 1989, conjunction. January 18, 1990, will start another new cycle, which will culminate November 1, 1990.

As another example of the way a general cycle like Sun/Venus can have specific applications in some people's lives, we'll take a brief look at the August 23, 1987, conjunction, which was part of the so-called Harmonic Convergence lineup. On August 24, the Sun, Moon, Mercury, Venus, and Mars were close together at the end of Leo and in early Virgo, and formed the tightest five-planet conjunction in the century. The grouping trined Jupiter in Aries, and Uranus and Neptune in Sagittarius. Archibald Crawford, the world's premier financial astrologer, in an August 8 newsletter, predicted that the Dow Jones would reach a high within three days of August 24. The high came on August 25 and then crashed, as Crawford had also predicted.

On a personal level the potent conjunctions related to many people orienting themselves toward specific goals. Several people in an astrology course I conducted that month were buying properties and taking advantage of various opportunities that had suddenly materialized. Many of the projects people were undertaking had been forming in their consciousnesses for the past year. Mars's involvement with Venus in the August 1987 conjunction caused more activity than usual. But before Mars gets the stage, something has to happen to other parts of us. We have to know exactly what it is we want.

Harnessing Venus

1. Read the capsule description of your natal Venus sign (the descriptions begin on page 154.). Expand on it by finding out more about the meaning of the sign (element, mode, etc.). Read the description for Venus six signs away. As the polarity sign into your natal placement, it gives further insight to the matters you're trying to balance.
2. Be ready for the annual Venus Return by checking the date in the Venus ephemeris at the back of the book. Spend time reflecting on what gives you pleasure.
3. Where is Venus in your life? What areas is it missing from? What form would you like it to take in those areas?
4. Compare the style of your Venus sign to that of your Sun sign. In what ways are they alike? How are they different?
5. Compare Venus's style to that of your Moon sign. What are the conflicts?
6. Take an inventory of your favorite clothes, art, and jewelry and explain to yourself (preferably in writing) the meaning that each holds for you.
7. Locate dates of Sun/Venus conjunctions (past and future) and take notes.

Sun/Venus Conjunctions

The Sun/Venus cycle opens with a Retrograde Venus conjuncting the Sun (Inferior Conjunction, IC) and culminates with the Superior Conjunction (SC).

1. August 22, 1991 (IC); June 13, 1992 (SC)
2. April 1, 1993 (IC); January 17, 1994 (SC)
3. November 2, 1994 (IC); August 21, 1995 (SC)
4. June 10, 1996 (IC); April 2, 1997 (SC)
5. January 16, 1998 (IC); October 30, 1998 (SC)
6. August 20, 1999 (IC); June 11, 2000 (SC)

Venus Signs

Venus in Aries: Both the men and women enjoy the chase and conquest in love and in other areas of life. They place much stock in independence, self-assertion, and competition. There's a self-centeredness that can sometimes block out the desires and needs of others. They like flash, excitement, and nice sports cars, but still believe in true love, as Elizabeth Taylor, head of this pack (with considerable help from Uranus in Aries), consistently shows. Joan Crawford, Marilyn Monroe, and Katharine Hepburn also relate in this fashion. Albert Einstein showed that this Venus's love of adventure can take on lofty goals (while simultaneously pursuing sometimes combative or difficult relationships with loved ones and peers).

Venus in Taurus: They are looking for things of quality that are going to last: objets d'art, a nice home, good jewelry, and one faithful love. This Venus sign doesn't like to waste time with trifling sorts (unless of course they're paying the way). Their love of physical beauty and sensual nature is strong, though they're practical as well. Materialism, possessiveness, and values are major themes. Billy Joel's first wife, for instance, was his business manager, giving money matters special prominence in the relationship. His second wife, supermodel Christie Brinkley, is also an artist. Liz Claiborne's art and money are bound up in her marriage relationship as well.

Venus in Gemini: They like to gad about and talk with people, exchanging ideas and information. Can you imagine Bill Cosby sitting quietly? This Venus placement puts much value on diversity and social intercourse. They're often accused of flirting, leading others on, and sometimes that's exactly what they intended to do. But often, they're just satisfying a need to have some connections to the environment of the moment. They are highly cerebral, and sometimes superficial. Cher displays this Venus's mercurial side as well. Amelia Earhart took her Venus on the road, so to speak.

Venus in Cancer: The need for emotional security characterizes their relationships and life preferences. Often, unmet needs from childhood are crying to be fed. Relationships frequently have a mother-child aspect to them. At times they play both parts. But the self-aware members of this Venus group can be warm, caring lovers who don't mind doing the cooking. Despite her extensive career demands, Meryl Streep (who is also a Cancer) is known for her close family bonds. It's Robert Redford's more homespun side, and Raquel Welch's as well. Ditto, George Bush.

Venus in Leo: They like drama, intrigue, and romance. Geraldo Rivera's professional and personal life have the Venus in Leo dash. Michael Jackson shows how this Venus can infuse one's work. Pride and vanity can cause some setbacks. Love affairs can be especially painful if these people don't look for something deeper than the affirmation they seek in such trysts. Once they pierce the mysteries of self-love, they can be truly giving without expecting applause. Margaret Trudeau's joie de vivre draws from this Venus, and Coco Chanel wore it well, too. Mother Teresa's life demonstrates that self-expression can be used for a higher good.

Venus in Virgo: Even before AIDS, many of these people were worried about getting germs from sex partners. Although many of them are noted for their discriminating nature, others relish mates they can make over. Virgo's connection with health matters and the disadvantaged often pull this Venus group into relationships with people with special illnesses or other problems that can have major bearing on the relationship. Many approach life with a genuine desire and need to serve others. Lee Iacocca's first wife, Mary, was a diabetic, and her illness and subsequent death caused the car baron to set up foundations and make other contributions to help cure the disease. Rosalynn Carter and Julia Child have the discriminating air that comes with this Venus.

Venus in Libra: Social niceties—manners, for instance— turn this group on. Human relations are important, so they're attracted to displays of refinement and other pleasantries. Sometimes, of course, they can be superficial and snobbish. But they shine when a diplomatic, tactful touch is needed. Woody Allen's angst aside, the man has formed partnerships with several attractive actresses, many of whom remain his friends. (Longtime love Mia Farrow has her Venus directly opposite in Aries.). The balancing act between the needs of self and others is always underneath most experiences, and sometimes they're not up-front about what they want because they value harmony at all costs. A percentage of them openly display the competitive concerns of Libra. Billie Jean King, Grace Kelly, and Prince Charles are examples.

Venus in Scorpio: Intense feelings make these people especially passionate in most of their dealings in life. Henry

Miller is an example. They often get caught up in love triangles, betrayals, and intrigues from which it takes them a long time to recover, and then they'll go back for more. Goldie Hawn's longtime bitterness toward an ex-husband has resulted in headlines, while Bruce Springsteen gets press for messy partings. Some people with this Venus willingly work through the resentments and more unconscious residue that keeps them from receiving their due in life. The pathos of this placement can be put to use in art, politics, and the healing professions. Whatever the activity, this Venus infuses depth, and Gandhi shows that some take the high road. Marie Curie's working partnership with husband Pierre and his death in a traffic accident prior to her receiving the second Nobel prize have all the elements of power and intimacy that come with this placement (and with her Sun sign, Scorpio).

Venus in Sagittarius: They operate out of beliefs and philosophies that may always be in flux, because these people are always moving toward still-larger beliefs, ideals, and adventures. The restlessness makes it difficult for this Venus to make commitments in relationships. And if you do get them to commit, chances are they'll soon be commuting to a job on the opposite coast. Emily Dickinson's long-distance pining for a married minister she saw only three times is an example. Intimacy problems can underlie some of this Venus's penchant for people from other cultures, vastly different religious backgrounds, or brother-sister type of relationships. But some are honest seekers of truth and adventure who need freedom. People who can make the stretch with them usually get asked to come along. Dan Quayle's social expansiveness—his wife has said he'd rather play golf than have sex—is boosted by this Venus placement. Jane Fonda and Bette Midler (both of whom are also Sagittarians) have this freedom-loving signature.

Venus in Capricorn: Meet the consummate social climber. This Venus, of course, wouldn't describe itself that way. "I'm just selective" is what you'd hear. At the very least, they like to be around people and activities that are socially respectful, have prestige and status, and will get them somewhere. They bring the rule book into many of their life dealings. Structure is important to them. The conditions they're always placing on their love can cause barriers that are difficult to tear down. They place value on achievements, which often never seem to be enough. Though the rest of his chart indicated a wilder sort of guy, Gary Hart's "traditional" marriage corresponded to the desires of this conservative Venus placement. This Venus would also indicate a mate who would also be concerned about social status and position. Gorbachev's Venus hooked him up with an elegant mate who is a public asset. Indira Gandhi knew how to put this Venus to use, too.

Venus in Aquarius: They are often known for their huge network of friends, but their detachment and contrariness has many people wondering if they really know anything about love, at least the individual, personal kind. Social participation and affiliations based on shared goals and causes (the environment group, astrology club, etc.) are important to this Venus, and they receive much benefit from such associations. But they're always trying to set themselves apart from the crowd to prove their individuality (mostly to themselves). The more self-aware ones know how to show warmth, and they can simultaneously share with peers while maintaining a unique place in the crowd. Gloria Steinem, Franklin Delano Roosevelt, Whoopi Goldberg, Bruce Willis, and William Hurt are examples.

Venus in Pisces: They live for love, and may even sacrifice themselves for it. But it's not simply the romance of it all that they crave. Love is tied up with ideas, such as religion and God. In fact, some people will take their love to a spiritual level and go live in a monastery. Others get caught up in self-destructive relationships with druggies, drunks, and other louts. It's the Patty Hearst syndrome. These are very imaginative, impressionable, sensitive souls, as the lives of Barbra Streisand and Betty Ford reveal. Some can have imaginary lovers. Ronald Reagan showed how those with this placement see their loved ones and the world as they want. Never mind the truth, thank you. Tom Selleck brings this ethereal touch to his value system and life.

NINE

Mars: Moving Forward

Sports champions who break Olympic records and grace the Hall of Fame have the right stuff, and it's called the Mars Effect. The most eminent European—and more recently, American—champions have shown a statistical preference for being born when the planet Mars is at a key point in the sky. Moreover, famous people whom biographers and others frequently describe as aggressive or iron-willed also show this high statistical connection to Mars. These are the findings of more than thirty years of research by the French statistician and psychologist Michel Gauquelin. The part of his work that shows planetary connections to temperaments has been replicated around the world, including experiments run by scientific committees in Belgium and the United States.

That the red planet, for whom the war god Mars/Aries was named, should show such an affinity for the best of champion athletes (as well as high-ranking soldiers and, with help from Jupiter and Saturn respectively, industrial leaders and surgeons) is more than a mere suggestion about the self-assertive, competitive, challenge- and action-oriented nature of Mars. The Mars function within us is like a battery, and it gets recharged every two years when the planet returns to the place it visited at an individual's birth. Astrologers have speculated on the possible connections between the first Mars Return of life and the onset of the "Terrible Twos" phenomenon, identified in toddlers who suddenly show a desire to stake more of a claim in their environment at this age. Future Mars Returns will be less dynamic, more low-key, than this rite of childhood, but the raw assertion and attempts to "take one's show on the road" gives insight into the concerns to which Mars will speak throughout life.

Mars is our capacity to move forward in life, to put our goals and intentions into action. Back in Venus we admired all manner of items in the catalog, but it is Mars that will determine whether or not we will actually go out and get any of these things for ourselves. Like the quarterback who calls actions on the field, Mars puts the chart into play. It must read the other player-planets for signals—and usually there are many conflicting messages—but it has a special relationship with Venus, which is on the other side of the Earth and holds the key to what we want and value. Mars has its own agenda and motivations as well. When its game piece disagrees with Venusian values and other needs expressed in the chart, Mars can turn around, in General MacArthur fashion, and carry out its own aims and policies while ignoring the dictates of the hierarchical demands of the chart. The result is high levels of discomfort, agitation, and sometimes outright warfare between Mars and the other planetary energies. Mars will be especially hot then, showing its angry, bullying side. Sometimes there will be an attempt to suppress, ignore, or displace the anger, but it eventually disrupts in the form of physical abrasions, anxiety attacks, or stress. After decrying the dangers of Type A behavior several years ago, researchers found themselves retracing their steps to say that Type A behavior in itself doesn't cause heart attacks—anger does. Less outwardly active people can be just as angry (sometimes more so) than those who are achievement-oriented. Antidotes to anger range from therapy, to meditation, to projects aimed at correcting a condition that might have caused anger. Anger, when properly channeled, produces many a purposeful muckraker or activist. Physical release is often necessary, and that's when you head for the (nonliving) punching bag.

In addition to anger, Mars contains much energy that needs to be regularly released. Those who have sedentary jobs often remark that they feel groggy, unable to move forward in their lives, if they don't devote some time to exercise or a physical regime that will allow the energies within their bodies to move more freely. Intellectual work, in particular, often needs intermittent bicycle rides, dance classes, or other activities to bring the knowledge from the head down to the rest of the body, allowing it to be translated into a form or act.

When discussing Mars's need for release, we can't ignore the sex act or desires, which beg for expression through the planet. Feelings like love or closeness are provided by the other planets, but Mars is the sex act itself. Mars, at its basest level, is looking to reproduce itself. Most people are familiar with the traditional Mars symbol that is often used to represent testosterone (male hormones) and other male interests, while a reverse-side handmirror-type drawing is used to represent Venus and female concerns, particularly as both these planets relate to sexual-reproduction issues. Mars is literally connected to fecundation, though the ways in which gender affect this matter are as debatable in astrology as they are in conventional literature. Mars's role in the chart of sexual partners at the time of conception has not been studied to the same degree as the connection Moon phases and female fertility has. This is most likely because Mars is viewed as representing the male who presumably has greater freedom in his expression. Females must be concerned about pregnancy and, as the thinking most likely goes, could benefit from research linking fertility with various lunar phases.

The sexuality expressed through Mars also suggests the planet's figurative association with reproduction. Mars carries our animus—this is true for both sexes—and helps us get our agenda on the table. It helps us make contact with the environment through activity. It's like an emblem we wear. It's the Nike cry of "Just Do It." If the chart is viewed as the executive board discussing life direction, aims, and current priorities, Mars is the planet the rest will look to in order to get out and start implementing these management decisions.

Running Backward

What's been described here is Mars working under the most ideal of conditions, which unfortunately doesn't represent the real world most people face. Difficult configurations between Mars and other planets will color its expression. But there is another phenomenon that adds a subtle and sometimes quirky expression to Mars: retrogradation, which we also encountered in the Mercury and Venus chapters. Because they are the faster-moving personal planets, Retrograde Mercury, Venus, and Mars affect daily functioning more than the other planets. While a direct Mars can be as straightforward as getting into a car, sticking the key in the ignition, and speeding off, a Retrograde Mars is like the diesel engines that require a minute or so to warm up before takeoff. A high-powered finish is still possible—and possibly more probable than with a direct Mars, because of the special strategies involved—but often a backward Mars can appear noticeably hesitant, reluctant to jump into situations. Shakespeare characterized this phenomenon expertly in *All's Well That Ends Well*, which, like many of his works, contains astrological symbolism. Here's an excerpt of dialogue from that play:

Helen: The wars have so kept you under that you must needs be born under Mars.
Parolles: When he was predominant.
Helen: When he was retrograde, I think rather.
Parolles: Why think you so?
Helen: You go so much backward when you fight.
Parolles: That's for advantage.
Helen: So is running away, when fear proposes safety. But the composition that your valor and fear makes in you is a virtue of a good wing, and I like the wear well.

It takes time to be comfortable with Retrograde Mars. Having the planet in charge of "getting us into the game" moving backward means that there is some frustration in making contact with the environment. During the times when Mars is retrograde, there's a general feeling of being blocked, often by something that can't be pinpointed. People can feel boxed into corners or as if they don't have control of situations.

For those born with the retrograde, an eventual life-achievement award may be an ability to assess and apply precise actions in a timely manner. Martin Luther King, Jr.'s preference for civil disobedience over violence reflects his Retrograde Mars at work. Sigmund Freud's Retrograde Mars was a porthole through which he explored ideas, such as the human sex drive and its role in human development. Mikhail Gorbachev's backward Mars may make him more reflective about the use of aggression to achieve his country's aims. But it should also be noted that people with this Mars are not always direct about their intentions and can also seem to shoot themselves in their own feet at times. Being born with Mars in rash, dynamic, impulsive Aries gives Jesse Jackson spontaneity, energy, and a desire to be at the head of the line. But the Retrograde Mars calls for a more conscious application of energy, something that Jackson often refuses to accept. While his speeches have much appeal for the disenfranchised, his actions, though headline grabbers, often fail to meet the true needs of the situation. He also has a history of having to retrace his actions to make amends or various corrections, having been off target the first time around.

Older astrological literature has held that a Retrograde Mars is more of a problem for men than it is for women. Some of this thinking is related to cultural stereotypes. We obviously judge men by their ability to take action, to appear in control, and move forward, so they may experience a special despair as a result of being born when Mars is retrograde. Yet when I examine the charts of women with backward Mars, I find them especially frustrated in their efforts to move directly toward what they want in life. Some of the frustration is gender-related, but the backward Mars is causing internalized anger and other problems. As one woman told me, "Whenever I decide that I'm going to go in and just be bold and on top of things, it always backfires, and then I have to go back and sit in my corner." The ranks of famous women with Retrograde Mars include someone who is particularly inner-directed, as Pulitzer Prize–winning writer Anne Tyler; the talented but self-destructive Judy Garland; and tennis superstars Steffi Graf, Martina Navratilova, and Billie Jean King, who taught Bobby Riggs (a Retrograde Mars himself) something about the power of a woman's Mars. That such phenomenal female athletes are born under Mars Retrograde would indicate that the position is not weak, but there is an indication here that the internal and mental conditioning that these athletes are known for reflects the elevated use of Mars Retrograde. Julius Erving (Dr. J), the basketball player, was known for a highly individualized dancelike court style that also shows a Mars Retrograde finding its own way.

To many people Mars is male, action-oriented, dynamic. Marlon Brando was born with the Sun, Moon, and Mercury in Mars's natural sign, Aries. And while you'd have to live in a galaxy far out of sight of Mars not to agree that the planet's propensity for violence can make it unpleasant company, the planet has admirable traits that women, when given the chance, wear just as well as men. It's become fashionable to view women who are active in the world as denying their nurturing side and femininity. But the list of Aries women (Mars rules Aries)—Gloria Steinem, Liz Claiborne, Sandra Day O'Connor, as well as fashion models such as Paulina Porizkova and Elle Macpherson—undermines such arguments. Sandra Day O'Connor and Liz Claiborne combined childrearing with their outer-world success. What these examples show is that people develop best when they are allowed to express the energies that are true to themselves, rather than the predetermined ideas about what any sex should be like.

Going to Acapulco

Both sexes seem to need to learn something about the effective uses of Mars. The truth is that Mars, despite its seeming straightforwardness, is more like a foot soldier gone AWOL in most charts. There is some poetic license here, of course, since Mars, like other planets, is always doing something. But the abundance of motivational books, tapes, and courses intended to get people to take more profitable action in their lives, as well as the many others that address problems such as crime and the level of general animosity on the planet, would indicate that people generally don't know what to do with Mars. In one of his well-attended talks, motivational speaker Zig Ziglar said that several factors keep people from achieving what they want. The major ones are the following:

1. They aren't sold on specific goals.
2. Not being sold on anything, they can't set specific goals in realistic increments and time frames.
3. They are fearful.
4. They have a poor self-image which makes them feel they don't deserve what they want, thus insuring they'll never get it.

As an exercise to get this point across, Ziglar asks participants to imagine being invited on an all-expenses-paid vacation at a private home in Acapulco. All anyone has to do is be on the plane when it leaves at 8:45 A.M. the next morning. Making the plane, of course, requires jotting down a list of tasks that must be completed before the plane takes off. A similar process is required before we can meet any goal. So, Ziglar asks, ''Why don't you go to Acapulco tomorrow, every day of your life?'' To do so would require attentive cooperation from natal Mars. While the trip to Acapulco might seem too remote to get Mars's process across, try the following exercise:

List a recent goal or accomplishment (something concrete, such as a new project, weight loss, the implementation of a new routine or practice, etc.).

Answer these questions:

a. What was the goal?
b. Why and when did you set it?
c. What was the first step you took toward the goal? Now list the subsequent steps you took until the goal was reached, no matter how routine they appear.

One way to make the information particularly graphic is to make one column headed ''*Action*'' and another headed ''*Result*.'' Making a telephone call or taking any other step would fall under the Action heading, while the receipt of particular information or other help leading to the goal would fall under the Result heading. Also crucial to this accounting is a category I usually mark ''*Obstacle*.'' This column includes specific problems that arise en route to the goal. Each ''obstacle'' requires specific ''actions,'' which relate to negative or positive ''results.'' Some people prefer to forgo the multicolumn approach and instead list all actions, obstacles, and results in chronological order. Valerie, a nineteen-year-old student, chose the chronological approach in order to outline her goal to get her first job.

Goal: To get a job for spending money.

It was my idea (with encouragement from my older sister) to get a job.

1. Went across street to day care center to fill out application. (There were no openings; school schedule had caused her to put off project for several months.)
2. At the urging of mother and sister, inquired about the status of my application—no job.
3. Decided to go to chain family restaurant, which was up the street from my house.

4. Ate at restaurant to check out the place.
5. Asked if manager was present. Was told to come back the following day.
6. Later that same day went with sister to bookstore café. Liked the feel of it and the environment.
7. Sister and I talked about advantages of my working there.
8. Talked to my mother about it.
9. Next day went back to bookstore café and applied for job. Talked to manager.
10. Got job three days later.

When Valerie reviewed the steps she'd taken to reach her goal, she realized a couple of things: "I sometimes need to be prodded, but when I'm interested in something (like the bookstore café), I can be persevering. I was initially reluctant about the day care center because of a fear that they would reject me. Being rejected in person is hard." That Valerie is young and her goals are less complex than those of older people doesn't detract from this example. Many older people have described similar approaches to goals. The preceding exercise works best if several goals are diagrammed (the obstacles and successes met on the way to the goal and your specific response to each should also be listed).

What emerges from these exercises is information about how Mars works in a specific life. Such information becomes particularly important if people are to get the most out of the cycle we're soon to dissect. While the Mars profile in the natal chart is always complex, the zodiac sign in which the planet is located shows its style and motivations. The sign shows "how" we do what we do.

Valerie's Mars is in the easily disoriented sign of Pisces, a Water sign, a group that is often motivated by unconscious stimuli. Those who have Mars in a Water sign aren't as obviously self-expressive as a fiery Mars in Leo (Cher), or as reliant on mental exchanges and social interaction and activity like the Air sign Mars in Aquarius (Jimmy Carter and George Bush) or as result-oriented like the Earth sign Mars in Taurus (George Steinbrenner). But this doesn't make Water signs any less effective, though it might initially appear that way. Water, remember, moves in and out of places that Fire could never enter. Air often can't touch ground, while Earth can have difficulty dealing with anything that isn't spelled out right in front of it. Tennis champions Chris Evert and Martina Navratilova, who were doubles partners and fierce competitors with one another, both have Mars in Pisces, and they are both near the same zodiac degree. While both women on and off the court have gone through periods where the Piscean vagueness and insecurities have set them back, they've managed to tune into the psychic aspects of this Mars and condition themselves to win. Sandra Day O'Connor and U.S. Senator Lloyd Bentsen show how the universal concerns of Pisces can be put to use in government and the larger world. Listening to the inner promptings makes the difference.

Mars in Cancer, a sign especially concerned with emotional security, can result in both men and women acting on the defensive even when it isn't necessary. When Henry Ford II fired Lee Iacocca, he apparently didn't hesitate to respond when asked for a reason: "It's personal," Iacocca has quoted him as saying. "Sometimes you just don't like somebody." But Liz Claiborne is a businesswoman who wears thè fit well. Mars does have special challenges when called upon to work in the sensitive, moody Water signs. But at the same time, Mars in Scorpio ranks as one of the most effective placements at least in a strategic, productive sense.

There are people who'll succumb to the self-destructive, manipulative side of Mars in Scorpio, but others become real king makers and power mongers. Oprah Winfrey's status as the richest woman in television owes part of the credit to a Mars in Scorpio that knew enough about power to shun the usual agents and managers who give bad advice and take too much of a performer's money. Bill Cosby is another example of someone who knows how to position himself and what to do with his own money. Mars in Scorpio is usually ranked right up alongside calculating Mars in Capricorn, which has the placement with the surest, steadiest footing in the work of nine-to-five success.

Even though his handling of his eight years in office will come under criticism for many decades, you have to admire Ronald Reagan's persistent, determined, and of course ambitious move through broadcasting, the movies, and the White House. It took him nearly two decades to land the final job, but like many a Mars in Capricorn, he kept plugging away toward the goal. Boris Becker and Diane Von Furstenberg have put this strategic and initiating Mars to good use. Unlike Earth brethren Taurus and Virgo, Capricorn is an initiator and has a shrewder view of the big picture, the political concerns. The sign is motivated by prestige and respect from authority figures and society. Taurus, though built for the long haul, believes in giving the body a rest. The sign loves money, and Mars in Taurus (George Steinbrenner) shows they know how to make it. With money in the bank, planets in Taurus are content to lull about and are not as interested in kissing up to the boss as Capricorn. Writer Joan Didion, who has said she'd want to die "on the case," taking notes and making observations, is a good example of the hardworking, detail-minded people with Mars in Virgo. But Virgo's need for greater and greater efficiency can sometimes backfire and make them among the least efficient people around. Their concern with getting it right and handling the details makes them task-oriented, but often tasks don't add up to the kind of big goals that Capricorn, the long-distance runner, was eyeing.

The Mars ephemeris will reveal the planet's location at birth, and the section at the end of this chapter describes the zodiac placement.

The Cycle

Several different Mars cycles are at work in everyone's chart. Of particular concern in this chapter, however, are Mars's regular returns to the place where it is situated in the natal chart. Mars goes over the birthday Sun every two years and energizes the sense of self (Sun) and bestows a revitalization of martial energies (Mars). It should also be noted that every venture or enterprise in life has its own Mars cycle; a business, new job, or relationship—each is linked to Mars's location at the launching date. The numerous intertwining cycles that can result by looking at a chart from the cyclical perspective can become as difficult to unravel as the legendary Gordian knot. Newcomers will want to put most of their energies into understanding the two-year rhythm that is renewed every time Mars returns to the birth position.

The Mars rhythm renews itself every 1.5 to 2.5 years. The retrograde periods cause the planet's orbit to fluctuate, but the orbit lasts an average of two years. Like the year-long Sun cycle, the Mars energy, as we can think of it because of the reverberations it sends out, can be viewed as going through four seasons before renewing itself. Spring occurs as the planet returns to its birth position; the building and critical "summer" period takes place when Mars is three signs ahead of the birth Mars. The time is similar in cycle, structure, and impulsive action to the First Quarter/Opening Square phase of the Sun/Moon cycle. Like the Full Moon, the "fall/harvest" period comes when Mars is 180 degrees (six signs) away from the birth position; while "winter" (when Mars is moving three signs behind the birth Mars position) is the change-in-thinking phase that is similar to the Last Quarter/Closing Square Moon phase, a clearing away/withdrawal period. A chart showing the phases, or "seasons" for each Mars sign appears on page 179. (When natal Mars is in Capricorn, Aries is summer, Cancer is autumn, and Libra is winter, for example).

As important as the Mars cycle can be in gearing up for projects, it (like cycles involving the Sun, Moon, Mercury, and Venus) is a small piece of the planetary equation relating to major life events. Mars can act as a trigger as it aligns itself with various other configurations. But its relationship to the birth Mars position cannot be viewed as a direct correlation to any activity in itself, at least not beyond the short-term challenges that people experience. The critical points in the two-year Mars cycle often come and go without any obvious external activity. Also, the phases don't necessarily portend positive or negative activity.

Famous people who are in the news around the time of the beginning of one of their four critical Mars seasons are often in hot water—Zsa Zsa slapping a Beverly Hills policeman, Sean Penn having fisticuffs with photographers—showing the short-term agitation that can result at the Mars Return or subsequent phases. Former head of the Department of Housing and Urban Development (HUD) Samuel Pierce pretty much sat out his eight years at the helm of the megabureau, letting politicians and aides loot the place. But Pierce's Mars was in high gear in mid-September 1989, when he canceled an appearance before a congressional committee investigating the escalating HUD scams. With traveling Mars exactly 90 degrees (in the winter position) from his natal Mars, Pierce, obviously under all sorts of political and other major planetary pressures, said that his lawyers needed more time to prepare his case. But the congressional committee sent Pierce a subpoena.

People are often throwing down the gauntlet or being kicked

in the rump when Mars is starting one of its four "seasons." It's like the common dream experience of riding in a car that is being driven by someone we don't particularly like or trust. It's your dream, your Mars cycle. To get the most out of it, you must navigate as carefully as you would on a freeway. The behaviors on display during both the negative and the positive events indicate that all four phases of the Mars cycle are hosts to an outbreak of energy that can and must be brought under control for greater effectiveness. Those who directly take up specific activities don't seem to get into the trouble that goes looking for those who are either hanging out or stumbling around without goals and priorities. Rolling Stone Mick Jagger (Mars in Virgo) and Cher (Mars in Leo) were launching national concert tours on Mars Returns in the summer of 1989. Since both move around so much onstage, they probably need this extra charge from Mars. But even if we have no desire to follow Cher into the gym to lift weights, we can take a cue from her about the type of agenda making and goal specifying that should be done on a Mars Return, as well as at other points in the cycle.

People feel the need to get on with something when Mars returns to its natal place. "I want to do something, but I don't know what" is how three different people recently described this period in their lives. The personal confusion often resulted in frenzied and ill-conceived activities that eventually caused problems, such as car accidents and uncomfortable confrontations at other critical points in the cycle. One woman moved from Florida to Connecticut to start a job on a Mars Return, while another woman started a job search that didn't pay off until Last Quarter (winter) Mars, three months before the next Mars Return. "I had a lot of starts and stops because I really didn't know what kind of job I wanted," she now says philosophically.

All of the phases or seasons within each two-year period contribute to the overall meaning of the cycle. A magazine editor plunged into so many new work projects at the Mars Return that the summer "season" demanded relaxation to avoid exhaustion and physical fatigue. A new job opened up for her when Mars moved six signs away from the birth Mars. A Mars in Aries who spent her Mars Return contemplating a range of part-time jobs and social activities was in a car accident during the week that the First Quarter (summer) Mars influence was at its most potent. The woman, who had flipped over her car in an accident less than eighteen months earlier, is always quick to point out that she was not at legal fault during her most recent action. But she misses the real point.

All Phases Can Be Put to Good Use

While all the phases of the cycle can correspond to events that may seem similar—people get hired and fired on all of them—the conjunction (same sign, or spring) and opposition (six signs away, or fall) are more direct than the squares (three signs away, summer and winter). With a square, people often trip over themselves, unaware of their self-destruction. They don't relate to the role they themselves have played in the situation. The opposition, on the other hand, is like sitting down at the negotiation table, where opposing parties confront one another face-to-face. The obstacles are more direct and the opposition offers more of a chance for a reconciliation. Yet Steffi Graf and Mike Tyson aren't always stopped by squares or oppositions of Mars to their natal Mars. Other champions—Lendl, Evert, Navratilova, and Becker, for example—exhibit potency during difficult Mars aspects as well, showing the potential of all these configurations for those who are disciplined, prepared, and willing to take action.

Situations definitely come to a head, or an understanding, around the opposition. The job that had seemed to overwhelm Tom at his Mars Return became notably easier at the halfway point a year later; he got an extra bonus from his boss. Sue got a call from a headhunter and a new job on the Full Mars. Mara entered her first body-building contest after working out for a year. John went on vacation; Andy proposed. Derek, who has a tendency to change women at the critical points of all his Mars cycles, had a brief four-word scare from a new girlfriend—"I think I'm pregnant"—but that blew over, and he moved on to someone new. Mars, remember, can get into some rather primitive stuff about proving manhood and masculine insecurities.

And sometimes it seems that if our leaders don't adequately deal with their Mars assertiveness and anger, they can attract all kinds of trouble for themselves, as well as for the rest of us. Jimmy Carter was mishandling a number of planetary energies during his last two years in office. Mars was one of the smaller influences, but important just the same. The transiting Mars was six signs away from Carter's natal Mars in Aquarius when the Iranian students stormed the American embassy in Tehran. The planet moved forward and then went retrograde a few months later, moving back to make that 180-degree (six signs away, fall season) angle to Carter's natal Mars again. Five days after it stopped going retrograde, Carter planned the ill-fated rescue mission in the desert. By Carter's next Mars Return, it was time to leave the White House to Ronald Reagan.

The opposition/fall phase makes a left turn into the Last Quarter (winter) period. People get to thinking that what they set out to do at the start of the Mars trend may need to be overhauled or aborted. The perfect phrase to describe this time was a political lesson that David Stockman, Reagan's former budget director, learned several years ago. Stockman privately felt that Reagan's White House had made a mess of things and that they were fudging budget numbers to make it appear as if the budget deficit was declining, though in truth it was continuing to grow. Stockman shared these views in a series of informal talks with friend and journalist William Greider, who eventually included the information in an article for *Atlantic Monthly*. Stockman was definitely a man on the outs when the article appeared, and he was forced to visit Reagan for a special dressing down over lunch. The White House and Stockman portrayed the meeting as a "trip to the woodshed."

The "trip to the woodshed" plays a role in positioning for the future Mars Return, sometimes as soon as four months away. Some people start things in the woodshed that are either ill-fated or that don't come into their own until the new cycle gets under way. Sometimes short-term moves or job experiences—trainee programs, for instance—where people don't take on full responsibilities until near the time of the upcoming Mars Return, mesh perfectly with the nature of Last Quarter (winter) Mars.

But sometimes we're still not ready. If people aren't able to negotiate the bigger cycles, Mars will just aggravate things further. Timothy showed how wise use of a small Mars cycle helped support a bigger cycle. He relocated for a new start during his most recent Mars Return. After finally acknowledging and accepting his homosexuality at his Saturn Return, he used the Mars Return prior to the move to start dating and setting up a life-style and consciousness that reflected his new identity. Mars helped guide him through a series of social interactions, as well as job changes that, on the start of the next cycle, worked along with other relocation-oriented astrological indicators. Mars was the trigger for him to try for a fresh start in a new environment. Mars is basic to our movements about town, but this two-year cycle is just one of many that affects Mars energies.

The Mars profile of any individual is complex. The Mars Return is sometimes easier to implement if Mars moves over one's Sun sign within the same few months. Then there are all the configurations—which aren't the subject of this book—that other traveling planets make to natal Mars. For example, it was Saturn moving in and making a 180-degree angle to Lee Iacocca's natal Mars that corresponded to his getting fired from Ford. But the 180-degree aspects, as noted earlier, indicate a time for balance following illumination. Saturn, through confrontations with authority, was calling on Iacocca to redefine how he was using his energies and to restructure the way he was doing things. In hindsight he recalled that his instincts had been trying to get him to leave Ford long before the firing. Wait long enough, though, and the issue has to be forced. Iacocca was able to rise to the Saturn challenge to Mars at Chrysler.

The Mars/Venus Relationship

Once the Mars sign is studied, it will be important to see how its style compares with that of the natal Venus. The two are a team, and we can find the going stressful when they are three or six signs away from each other. Communication is easier when the planets are two or four signs away from each other (that is in the same or empathetic elements: Fire/Air, Earth/Water).

Mars and Venus are conjunct every two years and renew a cycle related to values, purpose, and goals. The portion of the horoscope where the conjunction falls would be reawakened. (Some conjunctions are prolonged when one of the planets is nearing retrogradation.)

The complexity of this cycle in relation to the overall horoscope—especially a precisely timed chart—makes it difficult for newcomers to plot and interpret it without further study or guidance. Mars/Venus conjunctions are good for setting goals after reflection on short-term aims. The type of ongoing process during which people find themselves discarding certain types of lovers, possessions, and experiences because they don't want them any longer has a relation to this cycle. The energy can cause people to get suddenly turned off about singles bars or dating through the Personals, for example. But the configuration usually works more subtly and in connection with a number of other energies in the chart. A fairly in-depth understanding of how the natal Venus and Mars work in the chart is also critical for further analysis. Extensive effects of this cycle, as well as critical phases, usually can't be determined without interviewing people about its effect. And several renewals of the rhythm (several consecutive cycles) would have to be studied for a true picture of the rhythm's meaning in an individual's life. Once again, the cycle is mentioned to give newcomers a taste of the complexity of this art/science. The rest is up to you.

The Thirty-two-Year Compound Rhythm

During our thirty-second birthday the Sun, Venus, and Mars all make their returns around the same week. Sometimes the Solar Return chart can find them all right at their natal position. While compound cycles such as these haven't been given much study, this particular cycle may be important because they occur soon after the important turning-thirty transition period discovered by psychiatrists and other cycle researchers. The astrological connection to this transition is Saturn, which completes a full orbit every 29.5 years and marks a coming into adulthood. The time right after the first Saturn Return is the first part of life when people begin to operate with a greater and deeper sense of their true identity.

Daniel Levinson, the Yale psychiatrist who has pioneered modern-day age-cycle work, says people typically undo structures of their life between the ages of twenty-eight and thirty-four. They cast off the careers, relationships, and other situations that no longer define them and settle into new structures around age thirty-three (and no sooner than thirty-two, Levinson says). The return of such life-maintenance planets as the Sun, Venus, and Mars all in the same week, sometimes the same day, can be like receiving CPR after the sometimes sobering reality alerts sounded at the age-thirty crisis. The symbols of the evolving self, values, and self-assertion returning together at thirty-two resuscitate us and help us as we set a course through the first true decade of adulthood. Again, these cycles are not life-altering in themselves, but the fact that these three important returns come together when they do suggests that at this time we're ready to move toward (Mars) what it is we seek and want to become in this life.

The Two-Year Mars Cycle

The Mars cycle has four important phases that begin with the return of Mars to the natal position. Phase I is akin to spring; Phase II, the "Opening Square," is summer; Phase III, the midpoint, is the fall harvest; Phase IV is the "Closing Square," or winter position.

Natal Mars	Phase II	Phase III	Phase IV
Aries	Cancer	Libra	Capricorn
Taurus	Leo	Scorpio	Aquarius
Gemini	Virgo	Sagittarius	Pisces
Cancer	Libra	Capricorn	Aries
Leo	Scorpio	Aquarius	Taurus
Virgo	Sagittarius	Pisces	Gemini
Libra	Capricorn	Aries	Cancer
Scorpio	Aquarius	Taurus	Leo
Sagittarius	Pisces	Gemini	Virgo
Capricorn	Aries	Cancer	Libra
Aquarius	Taurus	Leo	Scorpio
Pisces	Gemini	Virgo	Sagittarius

Examples:

1. Michael rehabbed a house with help from his Mars Return.

Mars in Taurus	Mars in Scorpio
(Mars Return March 1987)	(November 1987)
Began gutting Victoria	Project completed
House a week later	

2. How Janet (finally) got a new job.

Mars in Capricorn (Mars Return, June 1986) Resumé blitz	Mars in Aries (February 1987) Job interviews	Mars in Cancer (June 1987) More interviews	Mars in Libra (November 1987) Reluctantly took in-house transfer
Mars in Capricorn (Mars Return, April 1988) Offered and accepts post	with employer who had interviewed her a year earlier		

Mars Signs

Mars in Aries: They seem to assault their environments, jumping in impulsively, even recklessly. Sometimes it can be so important for them to just get out and do something that they don't take time to think first. Their independence, combative spirit, and desire to assert their identity can result in fearless pioneers or people everyone tries to avoid. Gloria Steinem, Elisabeth Kübler-Ross, Billy Martin, and Jesse Jackson are all known for exhibiting traits of this Mars sign in varying degrees. Norman Mailer, his literary abilities aside, has often displayed the fight within this sign.

Mars in Taurus: It's not important that they be first in line. They're interested in building something that lasts. Catherine the Great, George Steinbrenner, and H. Ross Perot are examples of the "builders" of empires and wealth. Where some signs might use up all their energy for a fast, splashy start, Mars in Taurus starts slowly and builds up steam like a locomotive. Michael Jackson and Shirley MacLaine have built careers with this approach. Bette Davis showed the staying power in this group. It's important for these people to feel that they aren't advancing at the expense of what they've already built; security is a prime motivator.

Mars in Gemini: They're known for juggling several projects or relationships at the same time. Unfortunately the need for constant intellectual stimulation and diversity can cause these people to fritter their energies away. The choices and possibilities are so varied that they can't settle on one thing. Often they just end up talking about all the actions they want to take. The upside are people like Lena Horne whose activities keep her young and vibrant, and Penny Marshall (Laverne), who moved into film directing once her acting career ended. Astronaut Neil Armstrong showed that the sky wasn't the limit.

Mars in Cancer: Their actions are directed by their emotions and they approach life in a highly personalized manner. As a result, they can be defensive and lose objectivity in their dealings. Yet Toni Morrison and Joyce Carol Oates show how some with this position integrate their feelings and actions in a productive fashion. If a major study is ever done of people who start and run their own businesses, Mars in Cancer will place strongly. Rupert Murdoch, for better or worse, shows how these people grab hold of a business and keep building it. Frank Lorenzo shows they can be tough. Liz Claiborne has applied the nurturing side of this Mars to her business. The business is their life, their family, their security. Concerns about security cause many with this position to moonlight at other jobs. Mikhail Gorbachev takes the personal concerns to a broader audience. The entire Soviet Union is his family, and something he fights to protect.

Mars in Leo: For these people, it's just not worth it if they can't express themselves and put their stamp on things. Cher, Bette Midler, and Bruce Springsteen are examples. The position helps those who are already predisposed to originality and creativity to take the bold steps that help them realize their dreams. The downside here is the position's need for applause and admiration. People can get caught up in ego concerns and excessive displays of vanity and pride. The position is among those highly vulnerable to fixed patterns that are difficult to change.

Mars in Virgo: They're the craftspeople and other apprentices who spend years learning a trade or skill. Writer Joan Didion is an example of how this position can spend years working in a constantly evolving craft that requires attention to detail. Mother Teresa's lifelong service on behalf of the poor and the sick shows the devotion and humility associated with this sign. Astronomer Carl Sagan's expertise in his chosen field reveals other forms of exactitude and discrimination. They're workhorses. Many, like Madonna, find that their work becomes a joy; it's both routine and an affirmation of life. Donald Trump's birth, as reported in his autobiography, would give him this Mars position. We must also mention the nitpickers who can be counted on to ruin deals and slow down overall efficiency because they can't cut through the nonsense and focus on what's important. But the conscientious nature can be counted on in a pinch.

Mars in Libra: The planet of action and war has difficulty resigning itself to hanging out in the sign of partnerships. While Mars normally seeks free movement and independence, its placement here means that it is motivated by personal inter- actions, sociability. In other words, these people need to feel the approval of others, and both the men and women can be excessive flirts as they attempt to achieve these ends (Gary Hart, for instance). Their partnerships are often disrupted as they seek to achieve a balance that allows them to assert their identity. Sometimes they push; sometimes partners push them around too much. Their affinity with relationship issues makes them able advisers, negotiators, public relations people, and diplomats. Ted Turner shows both the argumentative and the socially accommodating sides.

Mars in Scorpio: Lots of entertainers make money and squan- der it, but it is appropriate that Oprah Winfrey and Bill Cosby know how to keep increasing their wealth. With this Mars placement the two have a strategic sense that may not always be evident to people who know them only superficially. This position likes money and power and seeks to accumulate it so that they can control their destiny. Control is a big thing with them. If you try to increase your control at their expense, there will be problems. They know your weak spots and aren't above being underhanded to advance their cause. Robert Kennedy, his dream for social justice aside, was known for pursuing his goals ruthlessly.

Mars in Sagittarius: They're restless and always in search of an adventure. It's part of the reason why Prince Charles didn't marry early, despite pressures. He needed time to explore, and he still seeks the independence and expansiveness indicated by this position. Charles, in recent years, has been expressing opinions on architecture, urban ills, and mysticism. Like many with this Mars, he wants to act upon his ideas. Michael Dukakis and Richard Nixon show how this placement can carry its beliefs through various incarnations (political and otherwise). Sally Fields and Steffi Graf both have the open-faced tomboyishness shared by many in this group. Dan Rather is textbook.

Mars in Capricorn: Calculating, tactical, they've got five-year plans for most areas of their life. Even if Ronald Reagan wasn't your idea of a statesman, he has to be appreciated as someone who pursued a goal (the presidency) until it was his. They're long-distance runners, as Katharine Hepburn's career shows. People might write them off, but they never leave the track until they cross the finish line. They can be coldhearted, especially if what you're proposing has nothing to do with the goals they've set for themselves. Exceptionally competitive, they can be cut off from some of the warmer human exchanges. Their rigidity and preference for sticking to schedules can cause them to miss out on the success they so desperately seek. Steven Spielberg shows the sign's power to combine creativity and discipline.

Mars in Aquarius: They're goal-oriented. They often prefer goals that are related to society or, at the very least, the general direction of the community in which they live. Jimmy Carter, Chief Justice William Rehnquist, George Bush, J. Danforth Quayle—all are social engineers. Lee Iacocca's work as the president of a company looking to give cars to the world also illustrates the way this Mars can rally around a cause and goal. The placement can be overly detached and hold itself apart from other individuals, even those on the same team. There can also be disruptions or problems where friends and affiliations are concerned. Even as this Mars works for "the people," it can appear to be apart from them. There's a need for warmth and an understanding that people are not props to use toward some social or corporate end. Some in this group have a knack for losing their identity to the cause for which they're working.

Mars in Pisces: The duality of this placement is illustrated by the fact that the position produced both Sandra Day O'Connor and Marilyn Monroe. Mars here has the ability to draw on inspiration to read beneath life's undercurrents. The result can cause people to take inspired action—right place, right time— in all their undertakings. It can also result in people receiving confused messages and sending mixed signals. Even as she pouted and hammed it up for the camera, Marilyn complained that she was misunderstood. This position is adept at self-destruction. Steady navigation is required. Lloyd Bentsen used the position to inject his actions with compassion and under-

standing. Former House Speaker Jim Wright experienced the
self-deceiving lows attributed to misuse of this Mars.

Mars/Venus Conjunctions
1991–2001

The conjunctions of Mars and Venus can seem erratic because if either planet is in or about to go retrograde, there will
be more than one conjunction within a few months. Such conjunctions are part of the same cycle and will relate to the same
issues in a life.

1. June 23, 1991– July 26, 1991 (Venus goes retrograde on
   August 1)

2. February 19, 1992

3. January 6, 1994

4. November 22, 1995/June 29, 1996 (Venus Retrograde, turns
   Direct on July 2)

5. October 26, 1997/December 22, 1997 (Venus goes retrograde on December 26)

6. August 4, 1998

7. June 21, 2000

8. May 19, 2002

TEN

Saturn and the Seven-Year Itch

Call it superstition, but the number seven has a special meaning for all of us. There are seven vices and seven virtues. Joseph's interpretation of the baker's dream foretold seven years of plenty and then seven of famine. It's easy to dismiss the notion that broken mirrors lead to seven years of bad luck; but what can't be ignored is that seven years has long been viewed as an appropriate time for paying off debts or making other amends. Indentured servants in the American colonies gave up seven years of freedom in exchange for passage to the New World. For some time, seven was viewed as a reasonable period between the filing of bankruptcy and creditworthiness. It's also the official time allowed for the ratification of proposed amendments to the U.S. Constitution.

Early humankind developed many of their beliefs about the number seven simply by watching the world around and above them. After observing that there were a Sun, Moon, and five planets in the visible sky, with the moon wearing different faces every seven days, the impulse was to name the days of the week after the gods associated with each planet. The seven-day week has prevailed in industrialized countries. The words for "seven" in many different languages are closely related. And remember the Sabbath, the seventh day, which, while varying from religion to religion, has the same connotation of reverence, reevaluation, and completion.

"God has blessed the seventh day and Hallowed it," the *Westminster Press Dictionary of the Bible* notes. "Seven did become a sacred number, and the seventh portion of time a sacred season; and not merely was the recurring seventh portion of time sacred, but it involved a benediction. It was cherished in hoary antiquity as a season of divine favor toward man, when the manifestation of God's Will was to be expected."

People in modern-day society may not be as quick to draw connections between their lives and the number seven. But by his seventh year as president of Ford, America folk hero Lee Iacocca was finding it increasingly difficult to come out ahead in his clashes with Henry Ford II. In 1978 Iacocca was thrown out the door, though he soon landed on the steps of Chrysler. Seven years into that job, Iacocca was a household presence and fighting new battles, both at Chrysler and in his role as chairman of the Statue of Liberty restoration project, a position from which he resigned amid controversy. Paul Volcker started getting itchy and talked about leaving his post as the head of the Federal Reserve around the seven-year mark, and stepped down during the eighth year. And Carly Simon needed seven years away from live performances to grapple with the emotional issues that caused her to collapse during a major stage performance. The stage fright and other emotional turmoil that kept her away for seven years have been highlighted in numerous articles discussing her return to the stage and record making, in particular the appropriately named *Coming Around Again* album.

Sevens in Your Life, Too

You, too, will find a 6.5-to-8-year rhythm—a seven-year average—at work when plotting a graph of your life. The circumstances won't necessarily be the same, but a certain symmetry will exist between phases of expansion and contraction in your life today compared with what it was 7 years ago. The case of Frances, who was undergoing both career and domestic moves in 1980 and 1987 will sound familiar to many of you. A father and son who were estranged over religious differences reconciled seven years later. Seven years into a personnel-related job, Maureen began seeking graduate schooling to increase her presence in her field. Her studies took about 3.5 years, but she founded a consulting/recruiting business seven years after starting school.

When seven-year rhythms of change are examined, we find that we're dealing with the structures of a life. We set the stage for future activities perhaps by moving to a new part of the country or embarking on a new career. ''The concept of life structure provides a tool for analyzing what is sometimes called 'the fabric of one's life.' Through it we may examine the interrelations of self and world—to see how the self is in the world, and how the world is in the self,'' writes Daniel J. Levinson, the Yale professor who has studied the ''life structures'' of men. The men in Levinson's study underwent situational changes on an average of every seven years. Some of Levinson's cycles were tied to specific age periods, such as the infamous mid-life crisis that marks the forties decade. In general, seven years seems to be a time at which structures need to undergo some review, or else risk collapse before the next seven-year period ends. This may be why American presidents generally limp through the final half of their second terms. At the very least, Levinson's work, and the actual substance of people's lives, shows why five-year plans don't have enough momentum and ten-year plans are a disastrous drain.

Seven and Saturn

A more final authority on the idea of seven-year cycles, however, comes from the planet Saturn, for which Saturday (Saturn's day) is named. Saturn's uncompromising 29.5-year orbit, when viewed in quarter sections, coincides with several overlapping seven-year cycles in any given life, institution, or situation. Ever since man became interested in correlations between planetary movements and life on earth, the planet Saturn has been associated with the passage of time and, indirectly, with the aging and developmental stages that man moves through. In Greek mythology he's known as Chronos (Time), who ate his children. In modern society the equivalent is Father Time, who, at the first stroke of the New Year, is replaced by Baby New Year, who will also be changed by the passage of time.

Saturn and the Seven-Year Itch 183

But time is just one aspect of Saturn. To the ancients, Saturn, which seemed to sit at the top of the planetary hierarchy, represented concepts such as reaping and sowing, both in the agricultural and in the karmic sense. Saturn was affiliated with society's rules and customs, with the established and accepted order of things, and with government and authority figures. Such connections are still made by astrologers, but the concept is broadened to include ideas such as reality, both our everyday experience of it as well as what's really going on. People who don't get a clear hold on the saturnine reality of living within certain rules of modern society—the checks and balances of everyday life—run into trouble with the law, their employers, and their communities. On the other hand, Saturn's connection with elders, family lineage, and fathers can relate to conditioning from which people must be deprogrammed in the same way that Zeus was forced to overthrow child-eating Chronos. (Though Jupiter [Zeus] is closer to Earth than Saturn, *Astrocycles* is bowing to Saturn's authority and presenting it first because it is necessary to understand Saturn's role as structure builder before you can receive any of Jupiter's largesse.)

Much psychological matter is contained within Saturn, and the shorthand to which newcomers to astrology are initially introduced can obscure this. People start out learning that, in contrast to Jupiter's expansiveness and optimism, somber Saturn is the planet of delays, restraints, and limitations. This is especially true when Saturn is being viewed in political or economic affairs. Its influence is one of constraints and contractions.

But "limitations," as a concept, is tied into an internal dynamic that allows an individual to set up necessary boundaries between himself and others. It's where one's sense of self as separate from others begins. This function can be too loose or else be represented by steel walls that keep everyone away, resulting in arrested development. A healthy Saturn can allow us to set realistic goals and limits that are neither too rigid nor too loose. It's the healthy superego that psychologists say we all need in order to thrive.

A professional astrological reading will help you determine all the various roles that Saturn is playing in relation to the other planets in your birthchart, but *Astrocycles* contains information on some specific Saturn cycles that can be put to use immediately. The main seven-year rhythm that will be outlined in this chapter involves the traveling Saturn's relation to one's Sun sign, a 29.5-year cycle that coincides with the shaping of a sense of identity and often is involved with career changes and other redefinitions and reformulations of self.

Jimmy Carter lost his reelection bid and was sent home as Saturn moved through his Sun sign. It was time to do something new. Lech Walesa founded Solidarity with Saturn moving across his Sun sign. Mother Teresa won the Nobel Peace prize as Saturn neared the end of its ride through her Sun sign. Sandra Day O'Connor was appointed to the Supreme Court as Saturn moved through the sign opposite (180 degrees) her Sun sign. George Bush won the presidency as Saturn moved into the 180-degree opposition to his Sun. In contrast, Richard Nixon was forced to resign the presidency when Saturn moved across from his Sun, fourteen years after it had moved over his Sun in 1960–61. (Most readers will recognize this as the time when he lost his bid for the presidency to John F. Kennedy.) Kennedy experienced Saturn moving into the 180-degree post from his Sun in 1957–58 as he fought to make himself a political contender. Lyndon Johnson's 1964 run had Saturn sitting across in opposition to his Sun sign. Saturn moving through his Sun sign gave Gerald Ford power by default. George Washington was cajoled into accepting responsibility in the form of the presidency with Saturn moving through his Sun sign. Franklin Delano Roosevelt came to the rescue of the country with Saturn moving through his Sun sign.

Changes in career directions are generally related to ongoing redefinitions of the self, which lies at the core of Saturn's movement in relation to the birthday Sun. The Sun speaks to our evolving self, where we must shine, what we must project into our environment. All planets moving in relation to the Sun—in other words, making transits to the Sun—will affect our self-expression. Some, such as Venus and Mercury, move so quickly through the zodiac that the only correlations may be a day of pleasant or especially communicative encounters at the grocery store. The big ones, such as Pluto moving over the Sun, uproot and relate to irreversible life changes that take people onto new levels of being and self-expression.

Jimmy Carter's gain and loss of power coincided with Pluto moving over and near his Sun. Michael Dukakis's run for president correlates to a time when Pluto was asking him to purge himself of the more unconscious motivations, resentments, blocks, control, and power issues that were keeping him from being a truly powerful person in a way that heals himself and others. That Dukakis felt it was a badge of honor not to have sought therapeutic treatment after the death of his brother is a hint that psychological residue may keep him from being as effective as he can be. Previous political losses prior to the presidential race have been attributed to a limited ability (and willingness) to interact with people and make the horse trades necessary in politics.

Though it took us off track, using the example of Pluto moving over the Sun sign is a way of continually alerting the reader to the fact that a horoscope is a very intricate design, with planetary actions being as concrete and subtle as the workings of the human body. But this chapter is mainly concerned with Saturn transits to the Sun for a number of reasons. As was noted earlier, Saturn represents the structure of a life. It is also the planet of maturation and time.

Saturn deals with specifics. Run a red light and expect the police (saturnine authority figures) to pull you over. There's not a lot of fine print. Saturn crystallizes and relates to particular circumstances requiring attention. It defines and sets parameters. As a result, Saturn's transits to the Sun, or any other point in the chart, demand a period of contraction before further development or expansion can occur. It's the foreman who comes to inspect the work, asking, ''What are we doing here in this area of life? Are we up to speed, meeting quota?'' Since there is always room for improvement, it is necessary to slow down, contract, take stock, add and throw out what's unnecessary. Further expansion or building is then possible. Saturn sends its pupils back to school—it'll even send them back a few grades—because relearning the basics provides a firmer foundation. By basics, I mean the issues of discipline, preparation, structure, and definition in connection with one's career, home life, self-expression, and relationships. The specific area of life depends on the planet or other important horoscope point that Saturn is transiting directly or indirectly through aspect. Unlike Pluto, which takes 248 years to travel the entire zodiac and hence can't be studied in terms of a full cycle in a human lifetime, Saturn provides a workable timetable. Its 29.5-year orbit causes it to spend 2 to 3 years in a zodiac sign or specific sector (house) in the birthchart. Saturn is one of those teachers who walks you through the lesson from start to finish. You could also say that it stays on your back.

Saturn Cycles

Before investigating Saturn's ongoing movement in relation to the birthday Sun, it's good to introduce some of the other Saturn cycles that will have a bearing on life.

- Age: A generic cycle involving Saturn affects everyone at seven-year intervals beginning at birth and coinciding with the "developmental tasks" that have been studied and documented by researchers, most notably that of Erik Erikson, Bernice Neugarten, and Daniel Levinson. The socialization issues faced by seven-year-olds, the rebellion and identity crisis of the 14- and 15-year-olds, the young adulthood that is marked by the launching of careers and other positions in life around 21 and 22, and most significantly, the popular turning-30 crisis that coincides with the return of Saturn to the place it was at birth are the most obvious examples of Chronos in action. The seven-year periods continue throughout life, with the 58- to 60-year-old experiencing the 29.5-year return of Saturn for the second time.

The chronological cycles are studied in-depth in the following three chapters.

- Personalized Boom-and-Bust Cycle: Saturn's movement through the twelve-house horoscope will show whether the current trend is one of inner-directed or outer-directed (public life and responsibilities) activities. An exact birthtime is needed to derive this information, which is discussed in the appendixes.
- Saturn Transits to Natal Planets: Saturn's travels through the individualized birthchart of each person, developing relationships with the Moon (as well as the Sun) and all other planets and critical points. In the same way that Saturn makes seven-year waves in one's solar life, it has intertwining 29.5-year cycles with the Moon and each of the planets and horoscope points. This is the type of information one can get through a consultation with an astrologer.
- General Seven-Year Cycles: This seven-year rhythm simply involves the information first encountered in this chap-

ter. Every seven years the planet Saturn moves three signs
away (a stressful position), to the point where it was located
some seven years earlier. As a result jobs, marriages, and
any number of structures are always undergoing seven-
year adjustments. Prince Charles and Lady Diana's marriage underwent special strain at the seven-year point, or
at the very least it got much public scrutiny.

A cycle of 3.5 years, as well as 14 to 15 years, may have
significance for some people. The 3.5-year cycle would be half
of the Saturn quadrant, while the 14-to-15-year rhythm would
put Saturn exactly opposite the position it tenanted 14 to 15
years earlier. The case of a man who has just left a 15-year
marriage that he says went bad around the seven-year mark is
a reminder that people don't always make revisions or
changes—even on a psychological level—until things reach
critical mass.

Saturn Meets the Sun

As noted in the chapter on the Sun, astrologers are uncomfortable discussing Sun signs, but the Sun is a very important
point in the horoscope.

Loosely speaking, the Sun represents a sort of center in the
chart. It is the identity that humans are consciously striving to
develop, and the zodiac sign in which it is located (Sun sign)
shows the issues that people consciously struggle with as this
identity is developed. For example, Sagittarius is the sign of
man's aspirations and search for the bigger truths in life. To a
Sagittarian like Chris Evert, the search, or journey, is taken
through international sports, while Phil Donahue lets the rest
of the world in on his process on television each day. Mark
Twain wrote and lectured, as did Louisa May Alcott. Beethoven
composed truths.

Saturn, moving through Sagittarius from late 1985 through
1988, forced the redefinition of such Sagittarian ideas as ethics
as religious leaders and public officials were caught not living
up to their pledges and vows. Battles over proposed appoint-
ments to the Supreme Court focused on philosophy and worldviews, while the United States was forced to deal with the
matter of trade restrictions and imports and exports, since Sagittarius rules our relations with foreigners and our attempts to
expand. The news media saw a steady stream of newcomers,

but there were many cutbacks and layoffs related to declining revenues. The publishing industry saw mergers and restructuring related to Saturn's move through the communication sign.

The lives of individual Sagittarians, who were beginning a new 29.5-year cycle, reflected the call for redefinition.

Saturn's position in this part of the zodiac, especially during 1986, put special focus on Sagittarian Bette Midler, who was finishing several movies and now has a new husband and baby. After years of exile and hard work, Midler, who has started her own production company, is restructuring a change-in-life direction that has put more responsibility on her shoulders, but that is also allowing her to take on more of Saturn's mantle of authority. Sagittarian Richard Pryor seemed to be in a more of a reflective mood as Saturn, moving near the exact degree of his Sun sign, coincided with the release of *Jo Jo Dancer, Your Life Is Calling*, a film based in large part on Pryor's tragicomic life. Phil Donahue, getting a run for his money from Oprah, went real Sagittarian (international) and developed a series of shows from Russia. Chris Evert announced plans to play the last legs of her pro-tennis career. As Saturn moved back and forth in the last degrees of Sagittarius, along with upstart Uranus, Jane Fonda, whose Sun is at 29 degrees of Sagittarius, headed to Connecticut to film a movie and found organized groups of Vietnam veterans and others in protest of her presence in their community. As Saturn moved on into Capricorn in 1989, Fonda's fifteen-year marriage ended, forcing her to set up new relationships.

Gary Hart showed himself to be very familiar with one end of the centaur that is associated with Sagittarius. He tried to be a statesman with new ideas and high ideals and was in full force when Saturn went over his Sun sign for the first time in late 1985. But before Saturn left the sign, we were to find that Hart's sense of ethics and principles were lacking.

These examples from the lives of well-known Sagittarians show how the coming together—or conjunction—of Saturn with a Sun sign starts a new cycle in which people are forced to clarify and redefine their sense of identity, and how they handle the issues represented by their Sun sign. This can range from gaining tenure at a university, to the birth of a first child, to the death of a father, to a major promotion or a marriage. Many people feel like Donald, who started the new cycle frustrated, knowing some changes needed to be made, but not sure what to do first. "I felt put upon, burdened, overworked, and unappreciated," he said. "I began thinking about how cramped I felt by my job and toyed with some changes. I'll never work for jerks again." As Saturn moved into Capricorn, he was in a new job and laying the groundwork for a relocation that would suit him better.

The 29.5-Year Rhythm in Parts of Seven

The coming together, or conjunction, of Saturn with the Sun or any sign every 29.5 years marks a period when new seeds are planted and sown for a cycle of development that will last until Saturn visits the sign again. Before Saturn returns, it continues to move in the sky and will make challenging contacts to one's Sun.

Seven years following the conjunction, Saturn will make the 90-degree Opening Square aspect to the Sun. In the loose language of our cyclic approach, Saturn will move into the summer season that is three signs away from the Sun sign. This is similar to the "crisis of action" found at the First Quarter Moon. Liz Claiborne was launching her highly successful design/manfacturing company at this time.

Seven years after the Opening Square, Saturn makes the 180-degree aspect (six signs away) to the birth Sun. Like the Full Moon, this fall or harvest point of the cycle relates to separations, turning points, and illuminations that put the meaning of the cycle more sharply into focus. Nixon's resignation can be instructive, but so is Bush's win. Faye Wattleton, head of Planned Parenthood, Inc., has her work cut out for her with antiabortion forces gaining ground and Saturn moving 180 degrees across from her Sun through 1990 and part of 1991.

The Closing Square (winter) portion of the cycle occurs about 7.5 years later, when Saturn is moving three signs behind the Sun. This relates to the "crisis of consciousness" or change of mind that causes a simultaneous moving forward to complete the cycle, but also a withdrawal to remove what no longer works for this or future cycles. Tasks are still at hand, but are tackled differently than 14 years before; people are oriented to the future and go through changes in attitudes that will help create the new future when Saturn conjoins the Sun in 7 years. Ronald Reagan won his second term with Saturn in the winter Closing Square post to his Sun. Alan Greenspan went to the

Federal Reserve, while Bork, the Supreme Court nominee, was sent home on the Closing Square.

This rhythm is evident in all lives and is best studied by understanding the ongoing relationship between one's birth Sun and transiting Saturn. While traveling through any given zodiac sign, Saturn starts a new cycle for the sign, but also signals the start of various phases for other tenants of the zodiac, depending on Saturn's distance from them. Those most critically affected will have the Sun in signs that are either square (three signs away) or opposition (six signs away) the current Saturn position. For instance, Saturn in Sagittarius was the midpoint of the 29.5-year cycle for Geminis, and for this reason late 1985 to early 1989 would have been a time of illumination and turning point in terms of self-definition and expression. George Bush won the presidency at this point, although the cycle started in 1971–72, when Saturn was in Gemini and Bush was taking on positions of power in government and the Republican party. In 1978–80, seven years into the new rhythm and with Saturn in Virgo three signs away from Gemini, Bush made his presidential ambitions known and got on the Reagan ticket. The winter portion of the 29.5-year rhythm comes in 1993–96 with Saturn in Pisces.

From 1985–88 other Geminis were also visibly contending with the midpoint of the phase. Gemini Joan Rivers's stock soared for a while, with Saturn in opposing sign Sagitarrius. But she also lost her husband and her talk show, and was forced to reassess and realign her sense and display of self. She fought back and launched a new talk show and life after Saturn left Sagittarius. For Virgos, Saturn moving through Sagittarius in 1985–88 was the challenging summer part of the cycle. Former vice-presidential contender Geraldine Ferraro, who first went to Congress when Saturn moved through her Sun sign, was home trying to recover from the failed national-ticket run of 1984, but she wasn't able to hide from public scrutiny. Her son's arrest for drug dealing and the continued examination of her husband's business dealings made Saturn's ride through Sagittarius stressful. Pisces Gorbachev took the lead job in the Soviet Union in 1985, with Saturn still in Scorpio. But he did his major stepping out into the world as Saturn moved in and through Sagittarius, the winter, Closing Square phase to the cycle, which began in 1964, when he was a young man on the move in the Communist party. The cycle for Gorbachev and other Pisceans is renewed in 1993–95.

A Need for Context

The "29-Year Self-Definition Cycle" chart on page 197 will help you see the Saturn/Sun rhythm for the twentieth century. It is imperative that the 29.5-year rhythm be studied in its entirety, as this is the only way to thoroughly understand the critical events that so often correlate to the 7-year intervals along the way to completing the cycle. An illustration of the importance of seeing a cycle in context is presented by events described in the book *Dancing on My Grave*, by Gelsey Kirkland, former prima ballerina with the New York City Ballet.

Kirkland says she was introduced to her calling by ballet classes that began when she was eight years old. At the time, 1960–61, Saturn was conjunct her Sun in Capricorn, and the presence of George Balanchine and his formula for the training of dancers demanded a way of being and thinking from which Kirkland would later fight to deprogram herself. At 15, with Saturn three signs away (a square) from her birth Sun, Kirkland joined the ballet company. When Saturn moved through Cancer and opposed Kirkland's Sun, she left Balanchine in search of a more expressive style of dance. She was also having difficulty in several other relationships with men, including Mikhail Baryshnikov. At the winter phase of the 29.5-year rhythm, Kirkland hit a low; she was institutionalized for psychological problems and drug abuse. Since the crisis also coincided with the 30-year return of Saturn to the place where it was located at Kirkland's birth, this Saturn crisis involved much more than the increased work burden or extra months of responsibilities that some people report. Kirkland says she would have died or been lost to a mental institution for good had she not been able to understand the insecurity and self-esteem problems that had always driven her. Saturn square (three signs away) the Sun, a configuration under which Kirkland was born, often coincides with a difficult relationship with the father, and the return of Saturn to set off this birthchart configuration forced Kirkland to examine how her relationship with a rejecting and alcoholic father had hindered her adult relationships with men. Somewhere in the midst of all of this, a healthy man, a writer (like her father), came into her life. She fell in love, married him, and now they're dancing together. Kirkland began a new 29.5-year journey as Saturn moved into Capricorn in 1989.

Another point: We've talked about Saturn moving through

the Sun sign in a general way. However, the Saturn influence starts to get stronger as Saturn moves within 5 degrees of making an exact conjunction, square, or opposition to the birth Sun. Remember, there are 30 degrees to each sign. Someone born with the Sun in the earliest degrees of a sign (1 or 2 degrees) would experience the full weight of Saturn almost as soon as it entered a sign, while those born in the final days of a sign, at degrees 28 or 29, might wait for 2.5 years before feeling Saturn's full effect. But the growth process indicated by Saturn will be evident during Saturn's entire trek through the zodiac sign.

These points are particularly important when more detailed astrological analysis is being done. But it is also evident that the simple occurrence of Saturn moving into a zodiac sign will cause the natives of the Sun sign—as well as those with the Moon or any planets in the sign—to feel Saturn's call for clarity. Readers with a more advanced understanding of aspects can look to the "Sign-to-Sign Relationships" chart at the end of Chapter 3 or in the Appendix to see other important points in the Sun/Saturn cycle. When Saturn is in signs that *trine* (two signs) and *sextile* (four signs) the Sun, there is an easier flow between the two energies; attempts to build and take on projects that express the self may move more smoothly. But the significant results and work seem to be more identified with the so-called hard aspects, namely the conjunctions, squares, and oppositions. The Sun/Saturn sextiles and trines may work as helpful mediating factors when more dramatic cycles involving Uranus, Neptune, and Pluto start shaking things up.

Saturn, moving through signs that make a so-called *quincunx or inconjunct* (five signs) 150 degrees to one's Sun, needs some mention since astrologers are starting to take it more seriously. You will remember from Chapter Three that signs that are inconjunct are like people sitting at a conference table who are wary of one another but don't know exactly why. Unlike the opposition, whose signs—Virgo and Pisces, for instance—understand why they get on each other's nerves and often agree to disagree, or signs in square that use their energies similarly but have different priorities, inconjunct signs often feel anxiety around one another without being able to put their fingers on the problem. They often don't know how to begin to talk with each other. Each planet has to make some adjustments, but often the thing that needs to be fixed isn't obvious. This is the item that needs to be placed in the box, but unless the object or box is altered, there will be no resolution. Inconjuncts are stressful, some even say fateful. When Saturn is five signs away from the Sun, it requires that each planet give something to make adjustments. One man who was looking for ways to scale back his life-style after overextending himself on mortgages for three different properties moved in with a friend to get caught up and save more money. Cher received her Academy Award when Saturn was 150 degrees from her Sun, showing the reward for her increased technique and skill, but she also had to adjust to new scrutiny of her self-expression. After the award, the media became more interested in her personal life and loves.

Newcomers to astrology will want to limit their initial inquiries to the four phases of the 29.5-year Saturn/Sun rhythm before tackling more advanced configurations. The plot and theme that unfolds at the beginning of each of the four phases provides a fairly detailed look at who we are becoming and also hints at some of the other tests that Saturn will bring to this emerging self as it moves on through the zodiac and we move on in our lives.

Saturn Signs

Saturn's 2.5-to-3-year stay in a zodiac sign makes it important in world affairs, which, in turn, highlights the lifelong issues that people born during each of the twelve Saturn signs face.

Saturn in Aries: Feeling cut off from, and a fear of experiencing and projecting, their identity characterizes this group. They must learn to be independent (and like it) and to stand up for themselves. Saturn in this sign in the late 1930s and late 1960s corresponded to increased aggression and assertion and assaults on individual identity as wars escalated. There is much fight in this group—and a special courage—once they meet and conquer the fear and shame many experienced as children. Albert Einstein, Helen Keller, and Amy Carter are examples. 1909–11, 1937–40, 1967–69, 1996–99.

Saturn in Taurus: A search for clearly defined values that will sustain their lives is a major preoccupation of this Saturn group. Most, of course, wouldn't describe their journey that way. The usual manifestations are intensified concerns about money and possessions. These are symptoms for the root problems of self-worth. World economic problems and other struggles through 1940 and 1941, and then again from late 1969 through the spring of 1971, hint at some of the angst. Jesse Jackson and Ronald Reagan have Saturn in Taurus. 1910–13, 1939–42, 1969–72, 1998–2001.

Saturn in Gemini: Personal mobility was seriously hindered when Saturn was here as World War I and World War II began, and the wage freezes and other constraints in the 1970s are, in part, related to this placement. The daily frustration factor corresponds to people who feel cut off from their environment and have difficulty interacting with it. They constantly make commitments, then pull away. The development of thinking and communication skills will provide the focus needed to establish more responsible links to the people and ideas around them. George Lucas and Angela Davis represent this group. 1912–15, 1942–44, 1971–74, 2000–2003.

Saturn in Cancer: They feel especially insecure about their foundations and home lives, and must spend much of their life debugging themselves of some of the programming of their early lives. Many are cut off from their emotions and basic nurturing, while others overdo it. Both world wars, as well as the Watergate scandal and oil embargo, coincide with this placement, speaking further to the precariousness that many in this group have about their place in the world. Mick Jagger, John F. Kennedy, and Cher are examples. 1914–17, 1944–46, 1973–75.

Saturn in Leo: It's not that these people don't want to jump in and touch their inner divinity and use it to express themselves in the world. There's a brat pack within this cohort whose self-expression revolves around parties and superficial activities. But many in this group don't know it's all right—not selfish— to be who they are and be proud. (They were born right after both the world wars.) The best in this group learn how to affirm themselves in responsible, constructive ways and understand that self-love is necessary before they can truly cast their light about. Donald Trump, Dan Quayle, Indira Gandhi, and Lizzie Borden are examples. 1916–19, 1946–49, 1975–78.

Saturn in Virgo: Some deliberately try to avoid work or any semblance of a daily routine; others are consumed with schedules, work, and health. Events like revolutionary activities in China in 1949, when the downtrodden started fighting back, the takeover of the American embassy in Tehran, as well as the increased economic and other problems that marred Jimmy Carter's last two years of office, epitomize the way this Saturn placement infringes on daily existence in the world and the life of those born with it. The key is to develop daily-survival skills and learn to make adjustments. When this is done responsibly, life stops becoming as stressful as some have made it. Emily Dickinson, Bruce Springsteen, and Eugene Fodor represent this group. 1919–21, 1948–51, 1977–80.

Saturn in Libra: Ultimately they'd like to mate with another; they'd like a partnership of equals. But before that happens, this Saturn groups goes through much alienation—1951–53, like late 1980–82, hosted much friction and hostility—before they're able to relate to others with some comfort. They take relationships seriously, but sometimes wonder if it's for them after all. They're conscious of having to ''give up'' something to be part of a coupling, and it takes time to get the balance just right. George Bush, Jane Austen, and Christina Onassis are examples. 1921–24, 1950–53, 1980–83.

Saturn in Scorpio: In the same way that bank failures and STDs (sexually transmitted diseases) increased through 1984–85, people with this birth placement go through periods of either feeling that they're surrendering too much to others or feeling cut off from the support and ''resources'' (financial, spiritual, and physical) of others. They don't always talk about it—with Saturn in this placement in the 1950s the agitation between the superpowers was called the Cold War—but deep-seated concerns and problems with intimacy drape this group. Much of it boils down to power issues, concerns, and fears about surrendering to any person or force. Jimmy Carter, Chris Evert, and Marie Curie are examples. 1923–26, 1953–56, 1982–85.

Saturn in Sagittarius: In early January 1929, when Saturn was in this spot, Albert Einstein announced that he had refined ten years of thinking about a way to unify electricity, gravity, and magnetism into one theory. It was to be shown later that the theory needed further refinements, but Einstein's announcement and attempt epitomizes the lifelong quest of this group. They want a theory or philosophy of life that can be applied to daily living. The more urbane spend lifetimes moving through other religions, cultures, and universities to find it. Even the Joe Six-Packs wonder what it's all about. Many, of course, hate travel, foreigners, and anything different. Others carry the need for freedom so far that they never commit themselves to anything. As the Saturn in Sagittarius news events of 1986–88 have shown, many people treat personal ethics as an abstraction rather than something to live by. Martin Luther King, Jr., and Jacqueline Kennedy Onassis are examples. 1926–29, 1956–59, 1985–88.

Saturn in Capricorn: The financial scene is fairly austere when Saturn comes into the sign of the goat. The years 1901–02 and 1930–31 certainly were not happy times for most, while 1960–61 were downers too; 1989–91 won't be happy times either. The frugality and fear that characterized these times placed a stamp on the babies born. The parental influence is especially strong, increasing the need for this group to break away and build their own lives and places in the world. There is a need to learn discipline and apply it to specific ends. Liz Claiborne, Sandra Day O'Connor, and Mikhail Gorbachev are examples. 1900–03, 1929–32, 1959–62, 1988–91.

Saturn in Aquarius: A New Deal. FDR's first two years, most of JFK's days, and portions of Teddy Roosevelt's administration were under this Saturn influence. The time calls for individuals to reorder their relationship to society and its long-term goals. People with this placement spend much time trying to understand how they fit into society. Some move right in and become leaders of organizations or groups with a cause; others try hard to show how they're not like everyone else. Michael Dukakis, Gloria Steinem, Shirley MacLaine, and Mario Cuomo represent this group. 1903–06, 1932–35, 1962–64, 1991–94.

Saturn in Pisces: Some people with this Saturn are misfits who are forced to isolate themselves from life's activities; others simply worry a lot. The worriers and those with special compassion put their feelings and thoughts into fields ranging from art to social work. Saturn in Pisces times, such as the mid–1930s and 1960s, require governments and society to take steps to help the disenfranchised and, in doing so, to understand universal humanity. For many born with this position, getting through the day can be tough because the universal undercurrents and early life experiences can overwhelm them. Spiritual activities are important for this group—they need to feel a connection with a higher power to get through life—but they must not use such practices as an escape from the stark realities and requirements of daily living. Woody Allen, Jack Kemp, and Jane Fonda are examples. 1905–08, 1935–38, 1964–67, 1993–96.

The 29-Year Self-Definition Cycle
And Its Seven-Year Intervals

The 29-year self-definition cycle and its four "seasons" of 7.5 years each are a result of Saturn traveling through the sky in relation to the Sun sign. To track the rhythm, look at the left-hand column to find when Saturn was last in your Sun sign; this was the start of a 29-year cycle. To find the other key periods in the cycle move toward the right where the subsequent phases (summer, autumn, winter) are listed as they affect each Sun sign. The appropriate Saturn placement and dates (the month and year it enters a sign, and then the month/year it exits) are listed through the year 2026.

New Cycle/Spring (Saturn in Sun Sign)	Opening Square/Summer (Sat three signs ahead of Sun)	Illumination/Autumn (Sat six signs across from Sun)	Closing Square/Winter (Sat three signs behind Sun sign)
ARIES			
mo/yr	mo/yr	mo/yr	mo/yr
1. 3/1909–1/1911	8/1914–6/1917	10/1921–9/1924	3/1929–11/1932
2. 4/1937–3/1940	6/1944–8/1946	11/1950–10/1953	1/1959–1/1962
3. 3/1967–4/1969	8/1973–9/1975	9/1980–8/1983	12/1988–2/1991
4. 4/1996–2/1999	6/2003–7/2005	11/2009–10/2012	12/2017–3/2020
TAURUS			
mo/yr	mo/yr	mo/yr	mo/yr
1. 5/1910–3/1913	10/1916–8/1919	12/1923–12/1926	1/1903–1/1906
2. 7/1939–5/1942	8/1946–5/1949	8/1953–8/1956	2/1932–2/1935
3. 4/1969–2/1972	9/1975–7/1978	12/1982–11/1985	2/1991–12/1994
4. 6/1998–4/2001	7/2005–9/2007	10/2012–9/2015	12/2020–3/2023

New Cycle/Spring (Saturn in Sun Sign)	Opening Square/Summer (Sat three signs ahead of Sun)	Illumination/Autumn (Sat six signs across from Sun)	Closing Square/Winter (Sat three signs behind Sun sign)
GEMINI			
1. 7/1912–5/1915	8/1919–8/1921	12/1926–11/1929	2/1935–1/1938
2. 5/1942–6/1944	9/1948–8/1951	1/1956–1/1959	3/1964–3/1967
3. 6/1971–4/1974	11/1977–9/1980	11/1985–11/1988	5/1993–4/1996
4. 12/2000–6/2003	9/2007–8/2010	9/2015–1/2018	3/2023–3/2026
CANCER			
1. 8/1914–6/1917	10/1921–9/1924	3/1929–11/1932	4/1937–3/1940
2. 6/1944–8/1946	11/1950–10/1953	1/1959–1/1962	3/1967–4/1969
3. 8/1973–9/1975	9/1980–8/1983	12/1988–2/1991	4/1996–2/1999
LEO			
1. 10/1916–8/1919	12/1923–12/1926	2/1932–2/1935	7/1939–5/1942
2. 8/1946–5/1949	8/1953–8/1956	1/1962–12/1964	4/1969–2/1972
3. 3/1975–7/1978	12/1982–11/1985	2/1991–12/1994	6/1998–4/2001
VIRGO			
1. 8/1919–8/1921	12/1926–11/1929	2/1935–1/1938	5/1942–6/1944
2. 9/1948–8/1951	1/1956–1/1959	3/1964–3/1967	6/1971–4/1974
3. 11/1977–9/1980	11/1985–11/1988	5/1993–4/1996	12/2000–2/2003

LIBRA
1. 10/1921–9/1924   3/1929–11/1932   4/1937–3/1940   6/1944–8/1946
2. 11/1950–10/1953   1/1959–1/1962   3/1967–4/1969   8/1973–9/1975
3. 9/1980–8/1983   12/1988–2/1991   4/1996–2/1999   6/2003–7/2005

SCORPIO
1. 12/1923–12/1926   2/1932–2/1935   7/1939–5/1942   8/1946–5/1949
2. 8/1953–8/1956   1/1962–12/1964   4/1969–2/1972   9/1975–7/1978
3. 12/1982–11/1985   2/1991–1/1994   6/1998–4/2001   10/2012–9/2015

SAGITTARIUS
1. 1898–8/1900   4/1905–3/1908   7/1912–5/1915   8/1919–8/1921
2. 12/1926–11/1929   2/1935–1/1938   5/1942–6/1944   9/1948–8/1951
3. 1/1956–1/1959   3/1964–3/1967   6/1971–4/1974   11/1977–9/1980
4. 11/1985–11/1988   5/1993–4/1996   12/2000–6/2003   9/2015–1/2018

CAPRICORN
1. 1/1900–1/1903   3/1909–1/1911   8/1914–6/1917   10/1921–9/1924
2. 3/1929–11/1932   4/1937–3/1940   6/1944–8/1946   11/1950–10/1953
3. 1/1959–1/1962   3/1967–4/1969   8/1973–9/1975   9/1980–8/1983
4. 12/1988–2/1991   4/1996–2/1999   6/2003–7/2005   11/2009–10/2012

AQUARIUS
1. 1/1903–1/1906   5/1910–3/1913   10/1916–8/1919   12/1923–12/1926
2. 2/1932–2/1935   7/1939–5/1942   8/1946–5/1949   8/1953–8/1956

New Cycle/Spring (Saturn in Sun Sign)	Opening Square/Summer (Sat three signs ahead of Sun)	Illumination/Autumn (Sat six signs across from Sun)	Closing Square/Winter (Sat three signs behind Sun sign)
3. 1/1962–12/1964	4/1969–2/1972	9/1975–7/1978	12/1982–11/1985
4. 2/1991–1/1994	6/1998–4/2001	10/2012–9/2015	12/2020–3/2023
PISCES			
1. 4/1905–3/1908	7/1912–5/1915	8/1919–8/1921	12/1926–11/1929
2. 2/1935–1/1938	5/1942–6/1944	9/1948–8/1951	1/1956–1/1959
3. 3/1964–3/1967	6/1971–4/1974	11/1977–9/1980	11/1985–11/1988
4. 5/1993–4/1996	12/2000–6/2003	9/2007–8/2010	9/2015–1/2018

ELEVEN

Saturn's Return

From July 4, 1845, to September 6, 1847, Henry David Thoreau conducted a bold experiment through which he structured his inner vision and gave others inspiration to search for their own. Thoreau's decision to go to the woods and live a solitary Spartan existence in a ten-by-fifteen-foot hut allowed him to shut out the daily distractions that tend to drown the quieter truths of life. As he wrote in the now-famous *Walden*,

> I went to the woods because I wished to live deliberately, to front on the essentials of life, and see if I could not learn what it had to teach, and not, when I came to die, discover that I had not lived. I did not wish to live what was not life. Living is so dear; nor did I wish to practice resignation, unless it was quite necessary. I wanted to live deep and suck out all the marrow of life . . . and, if it be proved to be mean, why then to get the whole and genuine meanness of it, and publish its meanness to the world; or if it were sublime, to know it by experience, and be able to give a true account of it in my next excursion.

Thoreau indeed had many excursions after he left the woods. But the time at Walden would always be a frame of reference for the rest of his life. To those of us living on the cusp of the harried twentieth and twenty-first centuries, Thoreau's period of reflection and transition might be viewed as a luxury only allowed philosophers or professional intellectuals. Yet the lives of all people contain these clearly delineated times when the issues of identity and of what one must be in life are overiding themes. One of the most critical periods in terms of the structure and development of adult life begins between the ages of twenty-eight and thirty, Thoreau's Walden years.

In the same way that Thoreau communed and forged a relationship with nature, we, too, must look to natural rhythms for insight into the start of the fourth decade of life. Saturn, which keeps a 29.5-year orbit, is the basis for our discussion and analysis. Sometime around 29.5 years after it first moved through a particular point in the sky, the planet returns, coinciding with the 28–30-year period of an individual's life. The planet of identity development, maturation, and crystallization, in making a full orbit since the birth of the individual in question, is saying, "It's time to start a new cycle of maturation. We must take an accounting of where we are, where we've been, and how this relates to what our identity is seeking. We have officially come into adulthood and must repudiate what no longer works for us, and at the same time keep what is working." At ages 28 to 30 there are things one knows about oneself—as well as much misinformation that is a result of programming from family, friends, and the world around us. The task is to separate inner truths from the distractions and distortions. Certainly there are societal responsibilities that must be met. But within these structures we now carve out a truer version of ourselves. Life seems to get narrower, but within the limitations there is freedom and a stretch of new possibilities as people make the passage into full-fledged adulthood. The completion of one Saturn cycle and the beginning of another—in astrological terms the Saturn Return—requires us to "live deliberately, to front on the essentials of life," as Thoreau suggests.

Prolonged Adolescence

Talk of people reaching adulthood at thirty will not set well with those who feel that today's young adults are taking too long to "get their lives together." The idea of predictable age-related crises or turning points will also be an uncomfortable idea to some. But these concepts are being developed and refined through extensive research by psychologists, psychiatrists, and others interested in the ways in which the human species matures. To these researchers the turning-thirty-crisis/transition into adulthood is just one of several clearly defined phases in a human life. Of course life transitions in themselves are inevitable at any age; job changes, relationships beginning and ending, deaths, and relocations affect all our lives without warning. What life-cycle researchers are saying is that certain ages in life coincide with predictable psychological and structural demands that often result in career, relationship, or other life changes. Further, the death of a parent or other significant alternation to one's life takes on an added dimension and meaning when it occurs during critical phases of the age cycle. As mentioned earlier, of particular interest in recent years has been the work of Daniel J. Levinson, who headed a team of Yale University researchers tracking the personal and work lives of forty men over a ten-year period. From this and other research Levinson, a psychiatrist, found that these men underwent discernible psychological, emotional, and life-circumstances transitions as they moved into their thirties, forties, fifties, and beyond.

The Life Cycle

As Dr. Levinson writes,

> The life structure evolves through a relatively orderly sequence during the adult years. The essential character of the sequence is the same for *all* the men in our study and for the other men whose biographies we examined. It consists of a series of alternating stable (structure-building) periods and transitional (structure-changing) periods. These periods shape the course of adult development.

As they turned thirty, the men in Levinson's study were moving either into or out of new careers. Some were just beginning to take careers seriously and settled into them between thirty-three to forty. Prior to the "settling down" time, people were in the "novice" adult phase, getting their feet wet in the "real world." After observing young adults in modern society leave home, go off to school, and set up their own lives, researchers began detecting a period of transition around ages twenty-one to twenty-two. As a result, most textbooks used in human development or personality courses now cite adolescence as lasting until the age of twenty-two. Levinson has synthesized primary and secondary research to form the following phases:

Ages 17 to 22: Early-adult Transition
22 to 28: Entering the adult world
28 to 33: Age-30 transition
33 to 40: Settling down
40 to 45: Mid-life transition
45 to 50: Entering middle adulthood
50 to 55: Age-50 transition
55 to 60: Culmination of mid-life adulthood
60 to 65: Late-adult transition
65 +   : Late adulthood

According to Levinson, all of these stages are marked by specific "developmental tasks" (a wonderfully saturnine phrase), which range from creating a niche for oneself in society in the "settling-down" phase, to greater individuation in the forties. The poignancy of the tasks make themselves known in each of the transition intervals, "which terminates the existing life structure and creates the possibility for a new one." Perhaps the most popular of these phases is the so-called mid-life crisis, which has come to be associated with men looking to renew their youth with flashy sports cars and very young girlfriends. Most men in their early forties don't go to second-childhood extremes, but Levinson says, "for the great majority of men this is a period of great struggle within the self and with the external world. They question nearly every aspect of their lives and feel that they can't go on as before. They will need several years to form a new path or modify the old one."

Just as the turning-30 crisis has a planetary connection, the mid-life crisis and other transitional phases studied by Levinson correlate to planetary configurations, most of them involving several planets simultaneously. As we discussed in the previous chapter, Saturn correlates to important life adjustments every seven years following birth. Life experiences at 7.5, 14, 21–22, and 28–29 are all interrelated because these periods represent quadrants of a full 29.5-year Saturn cycle. The two succeeding chapters will focus on age cycles beyond 30 and their planetary associations, including the second return of Saturn to the natal place at ages 59–60, a time when concerns become more universal and ontological as we make the transition into later life.

The present chapter is primarily concerned with the turning-thirty transition and the first Saturn Return, when first adult commitments and structures that were built up through the twenties are often discarded, refined, or consolidated into structures more in harmony with the emerging self. The decisions committed to in the turning-thirty transition set the tone for the thirty-three-to-forty-year phase. While thirty-six to forty takes "settling down" to a different level—ideally more integrated and satisfying than thirty-three to thirty-six—a failure to understand and grapple with important issues during the transition time will allow less room for growth throughout the thirties decade.

Gender and the Life Cycle

The most detailed life-cycle studies, such as Levinson's, have focused primarily on the lives of white middle-class men. Psychologist Bernice Neugarten included females in her studies, and author Gail Sheehy used extensive female examples in her popularized account of life cycles. While no researcher has focused on women as extensively as Levinson scrutinized the stages of men's lives, the planetary cycles we're about to study are just as active in the lives of women. But there are important distinctions to be made along the way. The barriers women have faced decrease the pool of historical female characters to study and hence limit the sharing of dramatic Walden-type stories. We can find the turning-thirty Indira Gandhi sitting at the negotiating table and helping India make the transition from colonial to independent status; on subsequent phases she becomes prime minister. Her role is similar to that of Thomas Jefferson, who in his late twenties and thirties was laying the groundwork for a new nation. He wrote the Declaration of Independence at thirty-three. Lifelong politicians usually begin setting up shop around the turning-thirty transition. Michael Dukakis's election to the Massachusetts House of Representatives at age twenty-nine is typical. Ronald Reagan was leading the actors' union. George Bush was founding and running his own oil business, but was involved in local politics. Dan

Quayle's stumble into a career in politics at the age of twenty-nine differs from most career politicians in that he had no previous interest or trench-work experience.

Even the best and brightest women have had difficulty consolidating a position in the world. Sexism, cultural conditioning, and childrearing responsibilities cause women's turning-thirty transitions to have more twists. Sandra Day O'Connor started her own law firm because none of the male-run firms would hire her. The need to attend to a growing family kept O'Connor from making an aggressive go of it. But as the thirties and forties wore on, she held state political office and legal jobs and was appointed a federal judge on various age-related cycles in her late forties. Elizabeth Dole had received a master's degree in education from Harvard before realizing that what she really wanted was a career in government. She stayed on in Cambridge and got a law degree and by age thirty was in Washington, D.C., where she took on the first of many government jobs. Former congresswoman Barbara Jordan was running a law practice out of her parents' kitchen at the Saturn Return and won election to the Texas State Senate at the age of thirty after an unsuccessful earlier bid. She went to Congress at thirty-six. Geraldine Ferraro got her law degree at the usual age of twenty-five, but because of childrearing and family responsibilities she didn't take a full-time job until the age of thirty-nine and then went to Congress four years later.

At thirty-four Margaret Thatcher was just beginning the "settling down" phase of life when she was first elected to Parliament. During her twenties, she tried unsuccessfully to get elected, though she held important organization positions with the Conservative party. She began practicing law during her turning-thirty transition. Marie Curie married and had a child during her turning-thirty transition, but still managed to win Nobel Peace prizes at thirty-six and forty-two, ages that will prove important in subsequent chapters.

But for the most part, we can't dig into the biography section of the library and throw out the names of female inventors every time we note that an Alexander Graham Bell invented the telephone during his Saturn Return or that contemporary (and sometime patent competitor) Thomas Edison built his Menlo Park laboratory at his Saturn Return. Most of these men achieved what we remember them for after age forty. And women—Harriet Beecher Stowe writing *Uncle Tom's Cabin* or Mother Teresa—follow the same pattern. But even when the factor of early experience is taken into account, women have traditionally made their moves later than men. The highly talented and financially successful Liz Claiborne, for instance, didn't start her design/manufacturing company until age forty-seven. While subsequent chapters will explain the significance this age phase has always had to CEOs and other corporate leaders, it's easy to speculate that if Liz Claiborne had been born in more liberated times, she might have started a company in her mid-twenties like Calvin Klein. Surveys of female entrepreneurs show that most of them start their businesses after forty (the planet Uranus's connection with this is discussed in a subsequent chapter), but female entrepreneurs are getting younger, as many readers who know women with their own businesses can observe.

It's obvious that even in more repressive decades, some women haven't needed special permission or movements to strike out and seek their identity and freedom. Katharine Hepburn was so tired of the limited female roles that RKO Pictures was forcing her to perform that she bought out her contract during her turning-thirty transition. Bette Davis was fighting the sexism and shallowness of Hollywood's moguls, too. The Warner Studio heads were forced to censure her during this turning-thirty transition phase because of her refusal to do certain films and the convenient way she had of suddenly falling ill when she was scheduled to appear in one she particularly loathed.

"She Who Comes with Her Own Things"

When the lives of women like Hepburn, Davis, or Margaret Sanger, who was writing and campaigning for birth control in her late twenties and formed Planned Parenthood in her early thirties, are viewed in context with the highly publicized 1987 turning-thirty-transition stories of Donna Rice, Fawn Hall, and Jessica Hahn, it's clear that individual character and orientation are more important than gender. Ntozake Shange's *For Colored Girls Who Have Considered Suicide When the Rainbow is Enuf* was a Saturn Return success and initiated its creator into the world as a playwright and artist. The work grew out of an increased commitment to writing during her twenties, after a failed marriage and identity crisis caused Shange to alter her life direction. As she moved through her twenties, she began to feel that life had taken her away from her true identity as a woman of color, and this eventually led to a consultation with the *Xhosa* of South Africa, who helped her choose a new name for herself. They baptized her Ntozake Shange, "She Who Comes with Her Own Things" and "She Who Walks Like a Lion." Other women—such as playwright Wendy Wasserstein, who was gaining national prominence at the Saturn Return, and the prolific Joyce Carol Oates, who picked up a series of national writing awards through the turning-thirty transition—gain the spotlight for their accomplishments. But just as typical in recent years have been situations where the media spotlight focuses on women whose predicaments would seem to indicate an inability to move beyond cultural conditioning and come into their own.

Surrogate mother Mary Beth Whitehead gave birth to Baby M at twenty-nine and lost her in court at thirty. A rocky marriage to an alcoholic, a past as a go-go dancer, and other activities that wouldn't exactly make her a welcome member of the Junior League hurt Whitehead's public appeal. Deciding not to go forward with an agreement that called for her to give birth to a baby for ten thousand dollars may have won Whitehead some sympathy, but various media reports and commentaries indicated that the initial involvement in such a project and accounts of her past tended to sway public opinion against her.

Mary Cunningham lived through a Saturn Return story in the late 1970s and early 1980s that many felt showed women had a long way to go in their understanding of how one goes about being in the world, and that the workplace had far to go toward allowing women to develop. Cunningham was the Harvard MBA who went to work as executive assistant to William Agee, CEO of what was then Bendix Corp., in Michigan. Book-length examinations, such as *Billion Plus One*, claim that Cunningham intercepted the work of others and insulated Agee from colleagues. After a year as his assistant, he made her a vice president, a boost in status that raised eyebrows because of the twenty-seven-year-old's limited work experience. Gossip about an office romance eventually became front-page news after Agee took it upon himself to denounce rumors at an annual meeting. Cunningham was ousted and Agee was subsequently forced out as well. Hers is a very instructive Saturn Return story for any career person, regardless of sex. But it also reveals some of the internal and external problems women have in establishing an identity and building a life. Even an educated activist such as Winnie Mandela, whose husband, Nelson, fifteen years her senior, was imprisoned for life during her turning-thirty transition, found that she had never thought about her own identity and political power apart from those of her husband. "I had ideas and views of my own. I had my own commitment and I wasn't a political ornament," she began to realize.

The Saturn Return in the Lives of Ordinary People

While the theme of giving up one's identity to another is a problem sometimes faced by men—Abraham Lincoln sank into a depression at twenty-nine years of age after a lover died—painful relationships that strip them of a sense of self are often common Saturn Return experiences reported by women. For Louise Lewis, a supervisor in a utilities company, the turning-thirty transition was a time of agony. A marriage early in her twenties proved particularly burdensome. Her husband brought only bills and other headaches to her life. Today she's able to accept personal responsibility for her part in her pain, but the road to financial solvency, as well as a more content relationship with her singular self in her thirties led to a greater liberation and love for life by the time she reached forty.

The time of the Saturn Return is more than a resumé builder or a chance to call in political chits, though careers allow one to set up a life structure and are among the concerns of Saturn. But even in the lives of average people, the matter of career and daily routine relates to identity formation. The Saturn Return, as we will see, takes up the matter of identity by focusing on a variety of issues from unresolved conflicts with parents, sexuality, religion, appearance, health, and subtle attitude shifts. All of these seemingly separate issues eventually get traced back to questions of identity. Examples from private citizens will help us explore some of the subtler and more complex matters of the Saturn Return. As much as we think we have it all under control, that we've been adults ever since we passed our driver's licenses, the process of maturation requires adjustments all along the way. More than just a refresher course, the first Saturn Return reveals issues and lessons that we often hadn't even known pertained to our lives. It also brings out of hiding the tasks we were aware of but chose to ignore, which is why Levinson has often found that the turning-thirty transition is "an age thirty crisis," a phase that rarely ends or stabilizes before the settling-down-into-adulthood phase begins at thirty-three.

"I don't think I really was able to get a hold on who I was until around my twenty-ninth birthday," says Karl, now in his mid-forties and the owner of a computer software company in Massachusetts. "I've made a lot of changes in my thirties and forties, like getting married, going into business for myself, and just a lot of things that were going on around the time I was turning thirty. It was like you've been coasting along, buying time, hanging out with the guys, some women. All of a sudden you wake up and start realizing that a lot of the things in your life have nothing to do with who you are, and you have to make decisions, and it's like, 'Are you adult enough?' "

The form these questions took in Karl's life had to do with his father, who was trying to force him to take over a string of family hardware stores and make more of a commitment to the family circle. "I wasn't sure exactly what I wanted, but I knew I didn't want my father's stores. His idea was to retire, spend time in Florida, and give me the family business. Everyone expected that. I was managing the stores, but also doing some computer graphics and software on the side for a local company. I liked computers and had studied it while getting my business degree. My parents just thought, 'Oh, he's going to be able to computerize the business.' But I was really interested in creating with computers." This realization came as Karl's father began talking of passing the hardware stores on to his son. "I couldn't confront him with what I really wanted to do. I had been making noises since around age twenty-seven and they just pretended they didn't hear. A few weeks before my thirtieth birthday I turned to my father and said, 'We've got to talk to a broker about selling the stores. I want to get into computers full-time.' " Karl admits that this probably wasn't the best way to get a discussion going; his father gave him the cold shoulder for about two weeks. Karl's mother got the two to the negotiation table. "My father talked about family legacies, what he'd worked for and how hard it is to start a business, how most fail and how I didn't need a computer company when I had a hardware business. But he did say he'd look into selling the family stores, and in the end a third cousin and friend bought them. We sold them around my thirty-second birthday, and I got a nice sum to help launch my business."

Karl worries that people might assume that the happy ending suggests that his turning-thirty transition was easier than it actually was. "It was a very heavy time in my life, heavier than anything I can recall. It was about everything I'd been living up until then, though I didn't know that then. There was a lot of man-to-man stuff, too. I guess I was just beginning to see who I was, a person separate from the family, the family stores. I was changing in my act with women, too, getting more serious instead of one-nighters and light stuff, and nobody seemed to understand any of that when they were pushing the family on me. It was almost like an initiation, which made everything else possible. I often wondered what would have happened if I had failed or hadn't started out to make any changes at all."

The answer seems to be that life would have become more and more unbearable, a bigger lie. It's important not to roll over and sleep through the wake-up call of Saturn return. This often means breaking away from family position or challenging parents for the sake of one's own life.

During his Saturn Return, Donald Trump was moving farther away from his father's Brooklyn-based real estate interests and taking bold steps to establish himself as a real estate mogul and deal maker. At twenty-nine, Trump began pushing plans for a convention center at West Thirty-fourth Street, a project that was finally approved two years later and that was eventually transformed into the Jacob Javits Convention Center. Hotels and other business ventures were also forming in Trump's mind. His autobiography aptly titles this chapter of his life "On to Manhattan." "If I hadn't managed to make one of those first projects happen . . . I'd probably be back in Brooklyn today, collecting rents," he writes.

Sins of the Father and
Other Breaks from the Past

Women, too, must decide whether to carry on the family business or name. Benazir Bhutto was twenty-six and living abroad when her father, Pakistan prime minister Ali Bhutto, was executed. The daughter began taking a leadership role in her country's reform during her turning-thirty transition. Though those she is attempting to oust have corrupt pasts, she is also forced to contend with a backlash from those who recall her father's brutal excesses. As leader of the Opposition party, she was detained and jailed as she entered the "settling down" period of her thirties.

Fate seems to play a strong hand in guiding people in a particular direction at this time of life. We can fight it, but listening to the special message it has for us will prove more productive. Ralph Waldo Emerson had several inklings that the fit between himself and those he was hired to minister to at the Second Church was not entirely comfortable. Emerson, whose father was also a pastor, believed in the need for a person to listen within for God's guidance, as opposed to the more "correct," doctrinaire approach of the day. The death of his first wife, Ellen Tucker, sank Emerson into deeper contemplation and unease during his Saturn Return. A journal entry says, reflectively, "Every man hath his use no doubt and every one makes ever the effort according to the energy of his character to suit his external conditions to his inward condition. If his external condition does not meet admit of such accommodation he breaks the form of life, and enters a new one which does." Before the year was out, a conflict between Emerson and his flock would result in Emerson leaving the church. After a trip to Europe, he came back and launched a lecturing career that allowed him to "preach" what he believed.

Beethoven is another person whose life might have sunk into ultimate misery had he not accepted some inner truths in 1800. The thirty-year-old was going deaf. Up until this point Beethoven had been among the group of pianists who vied to perform for the aristocracy. His repertoire at the time didn't depart from eighteenth-century tastes and techniques, though he'd been sketching the outlines of ground-breaking compositions. But his age-thirty crisis forced him to accept impending deafness, which would certainly eliminate chances of his making a living as a performer. He went to the countryside to sketch music compositions and think about his life. He considered suicide, but then realized the crime of giving into such despair. ''It seemed to me unthinkable to leave the world forever before I had produced all that I felt called upon to produce.''

A modern example of someone who accepted the limitations of his situation and then grew into something he hadn't imagined is that of the talented young filmmaker Spike Lee. He made his national film debut at the age of twenty-nine in 1986 with *She's Gotta Have It* and followed this up with the controversial *School Daze* and *Do the Right Thing*. Like many aspiring film students, Spike Lee went to New York University Graduate School for filmmaking. His work impressed the prestigious ICM agency, which signed him as a client. But as an African American, Lee didn't attract the directorial assignments that a white counterpart might. The independent Lee knew to gather his resources and strike out on his own, raising money for and writing, directing, producing, and acting in his projects. He experienced both creative and financial success in a genre—films featuring African-American leads—that Hollywood had ignored or generally dealt with in an exploitative or stereotypical manner. Like others who've suffered discrimination or felt locked out, Lee could have sat back, become bitter, and let his Saturn Return harden this attitude, but he chose the road less traveled and moved into his thirties as a filmmaker. The same could be said for director Susan Seidelman, another New York University film grad and director of the popular *Desperately Seeking Susan*. Independent producing was the only way for Seidelmann to share her vision with the world. Though certainly talented, Francis Ford Coppola's early movements through the clubby corridors of Hollywood decision making were aided by others. At age thirty, on the heels of success with *Is Paris Burning?* and *You're a Big Boy Now*, Coppola started up an independent production company, but the enterprise failed and debts piled up, forcing him into bankruptcy. As a way out, he accepted an offer to direct *The Godfather*, which brought him much acclaim in his mid-thirties (under a Jupiter cycle).

Overnight Success After Thirty Years

In the same way that it can be difficult to sweep Saturn Return decisions under the bed or overlook them, the lessons and skills won under Saturn will always be ours to keep. The Saturn Return can often equate to what has come to be known as "overnight success." Of course there's no such thing. Oprah Winfrey hit it big in Chicago after a decade of forward moves and setbacks. Cyndi Lauper, the offbeat singer, was written off by music executives who met her during her teen years and twenties. Lauper nearly ruined her voice trying to take opera lessons and other training to make it sound deeper and more conventional. But she plugged away, believing in herself, and around her thirtieth birthday she had a "chance" backstage meeting with someone who wanted to launch her career and subsequently marry her. Joan Rivers's pre–Saturn Return life was a Thirty Years War of personal and professional rejections. But Rivers managed to keep going to auditions and attempting to find her own voice. The turnaround came during a last-minute appearance on the Johnny Carson show. She made the audience laugh, had Johnny chuckling, too, and quit her day job the next morning.

"It had been thirty-one years of knowing that's what I should be doing, of knowing I was right when everyone was saying, 'No, no, no, no. You're not meant for this.' Thirty-one years of people saying, 'You're not right.' And, by God, I *was* right."

Speaking with a True Voice

Roseanne Barr found her comedic voice during her Saturn Return, too. She'd been a housewife who, as age thirty approached, felt the restrictiveness of her life and looked for new ways of expressing herself. Her initial attempts at amateur comedy nights were unsuccessful because she tried to pander to audience tastes. Initially her feminist slant was too strong and offensive, but then she found the right nuances and timbre, and her life as a comedienne took off. Feeling that life is particularly narrow as thirty approaches is part of the transition process that allows one to accept the realities of one's life. It helps us understand the various restrictions at work, yet within those limitations find new ways to expand and be more free.

A common experience is the one reported by Marie, who never thought she'd be one of those schoolteachers who'd burn out. But the fall of her twenty-ninth year arrived and it was especially difficult going back to school. "I was tired of the routine, the complacency and security, though that was part of the reason why I'd decided to teach. Kids are fine, but I decided I wanted to be in a more challenging adult environment." Marie began taking courses in human behavior and started a job in the human-resource department of a major corporation the next fall while continuing to work for a graduate degree. But the decision to bring about changes was not without struggle. The career change stirred up resentments in a rather stagnant live-in relationship with a male co-worker whose experiences and ambitions were limited to teaching high school, a job he holds to this day. "I felt it was fine for him, but I wanted to do some different things and eventually I moved out. It was difficult because we had been together off and on for several years. It was part of the life we had both built in our twenties, and I had assumed we'd marry. The life I'd built was too small, but from my twenty-two-year-old viewpoint it seemed like it would be enough."

As the relationship ended, Marie saw that the two had never really been suited to each other. "I remember how I had tried to get out so many times before, but my self-esteem—I like to be with a man—kept me from leaving. I think that my late twenties was the first time I started to begin to get a sense of security about myself."

While Marie's life was too rigid, just as common are the Saturn Return experiences of people who have not committed themselves to any life structure during their twenties. Donna Rice made stabs at being a model and an actress, but various agents and others familiar with her career told author Gail Sheehy that Rice never took courses like other would-bes, and failed to develop discipline and strategies for a career. She was waiting to be discovered, it seemed.

Some people drift with no particular expectations. Jonathan is an example of someone who drifted through many different lives during his twenties and early thirties. "You only go around once, and I figured I'd experiment with different things. I wanted to work with people, do something meaningful, but I didn't want to teach, didn't have the grades for law." Jonathan taught for a year, returning intermittently as a substitute teacher and working at a variety of other jobs when his funds were low. He had a string of girlfriends and one-night encounters, and had several male friends as roommates over the years. He had neither the inclination nor the financial resources to set up a home. His life aptly illustrates the way people have described their twenties to me. "It's kind of potluck," I've been told. "In the twenties you're just trying to find out what the deal is."

Jonathan says he simply wasn't in a hurry. It seems he might not have been rushed to make long-term decisions if his friends hadn't started marrying or moving in with "significant others." Around his thirty-first birthday, Jonathan took a temporary fund-raising assignment that turned into a job he's held for the past seven years. "I'm not particularly aggressive or ambitious . . . but now I do feel more stable and secure. I assume it's just what happens when people get older."

The early success of rock and movie stars, as well as media focus on whiz kids, causes many people to think that success and love must happen at specific times. While genius often expresses itself early, most success is tied to experience. Early success can often seem to make people ignore Saturn's reality alert. Mozart was composing symphonies at age five. He continued composing until his death in his mid-thirties, but his Saturn Return, though musically productive with enduring works such as *The Marriage of Figaro, Don Giovanni*, and the *Jupiter Symphony*, was marred by a mounting debt that he was never able to repay. Writer Sylvia Plath extinguished the early promise she showed when she stuck her head in an oven and committed suicide at thirty. Vincent Van Gogh's suicide at age thirty-seven ended a life that showed intense artistic development throughout his mid- and late twenties. Despite an early interest in art, Van Gogh was dissuaded from pursuing a career. He studied for the ministry, but wasn't good at it. The despair of the poverty-stricken mining town where he worked, as well as what he viewed as the Church's aloofness to the people's plight, sent him into a period of confusion and bitterness. But his drawings of the miners and their families reawakened his artistic interests. He was to experience highly intense work periods, and an accelerated artistic development in the Saturn Return period. But bouts with depression, paranoia, and various medical complications would ultimately lead to a short life. Some people like to speculate about what Van Gogh's life might have been if he'd been encouraged to pursue

art at fourteen or fifteen. Such speculation, however, is futile.
Taking up art in his teens obviously didn't fit in with Van
Gogh's personal timing. The religious attitude he took to his
painting during the short time that he was an artist represented
a vision that had been shaped by the pain, disappointment, and
hopelessness in his life. As Michael Ruffin, a Cleveland writer
notes, "I really don't like it when people talk about somebody
being a late bloomer. There's no such thing. People do things
when it's time for them."

Reckoning Time

And that goes for facing personal inner conflicts, too. The
Saturn Return dredges up the unfinished business from childhood that we might not have been ready to accept or understand
earlier. Karen, who was institutionalized after trying to commit
suicide at twenty-nine, says that being rejected by a man with
whom she'd been infatuated seemed to hit her much harder at
twenty-nine than it had at any other time in her life. "It was
as if every button got pushed. I had been abandoned and rejected before, but I always got over it. This time I thought it
was going to work and I tried to take it slow. When he told
me he wanted to just be friends, it was like he stuck a knife
through my heart, but I still don't understand why I couldn't
recoup the way I had before." Therapy is allowing Karen to
understand how the rejection dredged up twenty-nine years of
pain caused by men, ranging from her father to past boyfriends,
that had been repressed. Karen is also drinking more today
than she did prior to her Saturn Return, indicating the depth
of some of her troubles.

An increasingly common Saturn Return story involves
"coming out" for men and women who either ignored their
homosexuality or weren't aware of it. Changing sexual mores
have made it a little easier to come out, but prejudices and
discomfort with homosexuality still make it risky for people to
assert their new identities; they still face rejection, ridicule,
and hostility. However, some step forward to meet their new
selves despite the difficulties.

"I was always attracted to women, but never thought much
about it," says Catherine, an employee in a large multinational
insurance company. "I would notice if a woman was pretty,
and now I realize I would get aroused by other women, but I

thought all women reacted that way." Catherine grew up reading girl magazines with advice about what to wear and "how
to get him to notice you," and she fantasized about various
men. "I dated in high school, college, and in my twenties, but
nothing ever worked out. There was no big love of my life. I
thought it wasn't time for Mr. Right yet." What did emerge
in her environment, however, was a Ms. Right of sorts. A
fellow volunteer in an arts group befriended her, and the relationship started moving in other areas. "This was all happening around twenty-nine, thirty. I had read *Passages* and
knew that this was a time for change. At first I think I might
have been into it for the sex, which was good. I didn't have
to worry about getting pregnant or anything like that." Once
Catherine accepted this part of herself, she had to fight off old
friends who felt she was being too hasty in her diagnosis. They
said she was just going through a phase.

Tom, a real estate investor, is Catherine's male counterpart.
However, he was aware of his attraction for men as early as
fourteen. But he pursued women. A sexual encounter with
another man in college revealed that he enjoyed being with
men. Further encounters caused him to think he might be homo-
sexual, but he erased the thought from his mind and vowed
never again to have sex with men. To those who watched him
in his twenties Tom was Don Juan, though he says the actual
sexual act with women was uncomfortable. His life changed
at twenty-eight when a hard-to-diagnose disease that doctors
initially mistook for mutiple sclerosis knocked him off his feet.
He lost his job in real estate and moved back in with his parents.
His life didn't get better until he stopped "playing the field"
with women. He had a few liaisons with other men and eventually moved from Philadelphia to the West Coast to start a
truer, freer life. At thirty-nine Tom says he doesn't advertise
his sexual orientation, but he doesn't go out of his way to
appear heterosexual either. "I feel like I bottomed out and was
given a new start. It was like being born and starting life again,
like learning to walk, taking baby steps again."

Like many people, Tom got his warning that something was
amiss a few years before his thirtieth birthday. Two other significant cycles were at work then, too. Current generations
experience transiting Pluto (the planet of death and transformation) moving over the place where Neptune (the planet of
ideals) was located at birth. The death of illusions and various

perceptions about life are related to this configuration around ages twenty-seven to twenty-eight. Meanwhile, age twenty-seven and a half coincides with a detectable shift in emotional awareness and reactions. This is a result of the Progressed Lunar Return briefly introduced in our study of the Moon.

The Saturn Return interacts with all past and future Saturn phases. Changes made around ages thirty-six to thirty-seven usually relate to one's life back at the Saturn Return. Even those who make courageous passages must make some adjustments seven years after the return because Saturn is three signs away (a square) from the birth position. People who willingly take the journey at the return will have more fruitful experiences at the thirty-seven-year mark than those who refuse to change. The thirty-seven-to-forty-four corridor can be especially debilitating and painful if people don't begin important inner work at the Saturn Return.

Saturn Sometimes Returns on Tiptoes

But assuming that all Saturn Returns must be the stuff of Greek tragedy would also be a mistake. Susan, a paralegal who married her high school sweetheart at twenty-four and now has two children, describes her Saturn Return as being "nothing major or serious." The experience suited her life at the time. "I think thirty was the first time I felt comfortable with myself as a woman; I started dressing better and wearing makeup and a more becoming hairdo," she says.

Saturn is the planet of material reality. In many people's lives the planet can relate to simple adjustments to an everyday routine, and to knowing how to act in the adult world. Doug, a police officer in a New England community, is also one of those people who, when asked what was going on in his life between ages twenty-seven and thirty-one, wasn't sure that much out of the ordinary had happened. And it didn't, really. But Doug's everyday routine and experiences were providing lessons that shaped his outlook. The return coincided with a range of societal changes in the late 1960s and early 1970s. Doug, a rookie at the time, remembers being shocked to learn that fellow officers smoked marijuana and that other pillars of society liked drugs and other illegal vices as well. "I was disillusioned by that. At first I didn't believe it. It was against the law." Another lesson came as a result of the urban riots that were taking place in the city that bordered the suburban town where Doug worked and attempts by town officials to decrease chances of confrontations if rioters crossed the town borders. "We were told that the people were disadvantaged and weren't all criminals," recalls Doug. Being simultaneously exposed to police officers who broke the law and to information showing why inner-city residents were thumbing their noses at police caused a reorientation in Doug's approach to his job and life. "I think it all made me see that everything wasn't either black or white, that every case was different, and that the people in authority weren't all good guys. Probably after that I was more willing to give some citizens the benefit of the doubt. You can't always go by the book."

At his Saturn Return, Doug made the transition into adulthood in a way that, while not as melodramatic as some tales, is no less instructive. Because his experience was an integral part of his ordinary daily routine, it demonstrates quite poignantly how structures must constantly be retested and clarified, and many times altered to meet the ever-changing demands of our lives. To accomplish this transition, this new level of maturation, various aspects of reality must be confronted.

Actress Susan Sarandon, who underwent an emotional breakthrough in her late twenties, described the period in an interview in *New Woman* in terms that express most of the demands of the Saturn Return.

> It wasn't so much about finding [my] identity as it was about admitting certain things about myself and the world, about the fact that there was such a thing as evil and that love doesn't conquer all. You are raised with a certain set of values. "Be a good girl and this will happen." And you are a particularly good girl, but things don't fall into place. You can't figure it out, and so you just love harder, and still things happen that shouldn't. So what does that mean? It means life isn't totally in your hands, and that's a tough lesson. That can be very unsettling. . . . You can do everything right and be a loving and giving person, and bad things [still] happen to you.

Yet Sarandon and the rest of us can and do find our separate peace within the Saturnian limitations, and this is what makes the first Saturn Return as empowering as it can be bitter. In taking our trip to the woods, we, like Thoreau, find what is essential to our life and build on it, knowing that the strength and the ability of this foundation to support us through life's future twists and turns will depend on how close to the marrow we're willing to get.

TWELVE

Jupiter and the Wonder Years

Gustav Holst, the composer, developed a special affinity for energies suggested by the planets that he expressed in his famous symphony, entitled *The Planets*. He always saw Jupiter, which is the solar system's largest planet, as "one of those fat, jolly people who enjoys life." For some time astrologers had viewed Jupiter as a Santa Claus of sorts—the ancients, after all, called it the planet of luck—but years of chart watching have caused many astrologers to be less enamored of the bountiful planet. Not only are astrologers coming to realize that Jupiter usually doesn't correlate to luck in the traditional sense of windfalls or lotteries, but the planet can be the too much of a good thing in drink, food, extravagance, confidence, and optimism.

Jupiter can't be blamed for this. Our limited understanding of the Jupiterian function is the cause of the confusion. Many people study and learn astrology through the use of key words, such as action for Mars, love for Venus, and luck for Jupiter. The shorthand method has come down to us over centuries. Those who first made the connection between Jupiter and a certain attitude that often resulted in positive outcomes had the bigger picture in mind when they equated Jupiter with luck. Newcomers to astrology, as well as some longtime practitioners, often never move beyond key words into the deeper underlying principles behind various issues in astrology. As part of their more than thirty years of statistical research into the subject, Michel and Françoise Gauquelin discovered that while the key words for most of the planets can be verified when the biographies of famous people are studied, astrologers have failed to grasp many of the negative aspects of Jupiter and hence some of the key elements of its nature.

Jupiter's different faces are particularly important to our on-going life-cycle discussion because after the Saturn Return, people are better able to use the integrative and assimilative functions designated by Jupiter to broaden their lives. That is why we've changed the natural order of the solar system a bit and tackled Saturn before Jupiter. Jupiter returns to its natal placement in birthcharts every eleven to twelve years, so life at ages twelve and twenty-three to twenty-four, thirty-five to thirty-six, forty-seven, and so forth sounds a call for further integration. The Jupiter return of the mid-twenties helps us get ready for the Saturn Return. Moreover, Jupiter makes challenging configurations to its birth position every three years and helps us take more of the world into our outlook and life. Midway through each eleven-to-twelve-year cycle, Jupiter, like Saturn, makes a 180-degree opposition (six signs away) from its birth position. Such configurations occur at the Saturn Return (as well as at ages forty-two and fifty-three) and give us some of the inner confidence and faith needed to face up to Saturn. As a fellow astrology student observed years ago during a discussion of the interaction of the two planets, ''Jupiter writes the check, but Saturn signs it.'' Jupiter needs to get a certain amount of approval from Saturn before it can move forward with its expansion plans. Saturn can be a hard sell. In the best cases it keeps the more extreme plans of Jupiter in check, but also helps them grow. Once we've moved through the Saturn Return, the Jupiter Return of thirty-five to thirty-six will be the first return with which we're able to approach the world with more inner confidence and self-understanding. Hence, that time of life can be particularly important in terms of taking on a fuller role as a citizen of society.

Expansion, based on a truer sense of identity and direction, was the trend in the life of Colleen Pendleton during the summer of 1987 as she prepared to open the Oneta Gallery, a crafts store. In starting her business, Colleen was acting upon previous art-gallery experience as well as broader psychological knowledge she'd gained, particularly during her Saturn Return.

The breakup of a painful long-term relationship made her more aware of her own problems with self-esteem. She began further self-exploration, which also made her more aware of her need to be her own boss. And this was the consciousness that led to the opening of her store as Jupiter moved through Aries, the sign it had occupied at her birth.

Interactions between Jupiter and Saturn cycles are detectable in all lives. Fashion designer Donna Karan, a leading Anne Klein designer at twenty-nine, started her own company at thirty-five. After teaming up with Pierre Curie in both work and marriage in her twenties, Marie helped the couple win their first Nobel prize on her third Jupiter Return (she was thirty-six; Pierre, forty-four). The award was for the couple's work on radioactivity. Madame Curie was the first woman ever awarded the Nobel prize, and she picked up another one at age forty-four in the midst of important phases in the Saturn and other planetary cycles for her discovery of radium and polonium.

Bruce Springsteen released his first album, *Born to Run*, on his first Jupiter Return. He worked the road through his twenties and stepped onto magazine covers in full bloom at his next Jupiter Return. The Jupiter Return at twenty-four coincides with many people's first job promotions or opportunities that, if handled properly, can make a person into a wunderkind. Steven Spielberg moved to more serious fare, such as *The Color Purple*, as well as fatherhood and married life with his Jupiter Return in his mid-thirties before moving into his forties with a divorce and other life changes. He successfully directed *Duel*, some television shows, and then *The Sugarland Express* (which he also wrote) in his early twenties, winning the respect of older money men, who then entrusted him with *Jaws* and other big pictures. *Close Encounters of the Third Kind* clinched Spielberg's reputation by his late twenties. Cybill Shepherd's fall from grace forced Saturn Return stock taking and more study and work on her craft, leading to her reincarnation as Maddie Hayes on the television show *Moonlighting* at her mid-thirties Jupiter Return. The birth of her twins, her marriage, and her divorce a few years later were the Saturn-square crisis that all thirty-seven-year-olds must face. Whoopi Goldberg's blitzkrieg of movie making came with the Jupiter Return in her mid-thirties. Mark Twain was a roving newspaper columnist in his twenties and then began expanding into his novel-writing life as his Jupiter returned in his mid-thirties.

Madonna's career was speeding in the twenty-three to twenty-four-year-old Jupiter cycle, and it consolidated and took on a deeper, more mature level during the Saturn Return. Steven Jobs founded Apple, from which he was ousted during the Saturn Return. Marilyn Monroe was twenty-four when her appearance on film caused Hollywood moguls to take notice. Marilyn Monroe's death on the following Jupiter Return speaks as much to the nature of this cycle as the success stories. Her declining clout as an actress, as well as other problems around the time of her death, in part reflected her inability to assimilate various parts of herself and expand into another role. Mozart, though a musical genius, also died on the Jupiter Return. Van Gogh, who manically alternated between periods of high productivity and deep depression, committed suicide on a stressful phase of the Saturn cycle that clicks off at age thirty-six to thirty-seven.

Average Expansion

The average person doesn't usually experience Jupiter's extremes. While this same cycle finds ordinary people opening businesses or marrying in greater numbers at twenty-four and thirty-six—some people really aren't ready to marry until the third return—less obvious adjustments in one's personality or relationship to society are also common. Scrully Blotnick, the industrial psychologist, has made some observations about careerists in their mid-twenties that coincide with the Jupiter Return. He said that by age twenty-five people develop a type of personality they feel will suit them in the workplace. People who don't make this transition, who aren't able to understand their niche or read the signals, fall into particular trouble as the twenties end. For instance, those who harbor desires to be salesmen but who haven't shown good interpersonal skills have difficulty making the change if they stay in the same company. The "manager types" have also made themselves known by their mid-twenties. In other words, people who can't meet the social demands of the Jupiter Return at age twenty-four have some catching up to do. Take the idea further: What if Spielberg had really messed up the opportunities he was given around twenty-three and twenty-four? It happens. Spielberg would have been able to move into other projects, but somebody else would probably have done *Jaws*. Francis Ford Coppola's award-winning *The Godfather* occurred on the third Jupiter Return, following Saturn Return bankruptcy. After a string of projects of limited success, taking up the *Tucker* project on his fourth Jupiter Return was particularly significant because of his stated identification with Tucker, an impulsive visionary whose projects often failed to meet commercial tests.

Jupiter can be viewed as a synthesizer that helps shape myriad factions into a whole. The cycle that takes place in a person's mid-thirties is especially important because it's about halfway between the Saturn Return and the so-called mid-life crisis. As a result, it is a point where the real person inside is in full bloom. This is when people begin to tell those stories of waking up and realizing that they have to take some specific actions in order to make good on their dreams and whims if they're to become realities. There was time in the twenties, and there will still be time in the forties, fifties, and sixties, but for reasons both biological and psychological, the options change. At the same time, the false starts and misconceptions of the twenties, and the adjustment period of the early thirties, were necessary to help build the integrated personality that emerges at the Jupiter Return of thirty-five to thirty-six.

Molly Dodd, the lead character in the television show of the same name, explained the cycle perfectly in an episode in which she celebrated her thirty-fifth birthday: "I am content. I mean, I'm not clicking my heels, laughing out loud, but I am content for the first time in a long, long while. It's very odd because I'm not at all where I thought I'd be . . . I'm not rich, I'm not famous, I'm not the youngest kid on the block anymore. . . . But there are other things—things that I've done right, things that I have, that are mine." Blair Brown, who was born in 1949 and hence had gone through a Jupiter Return, has spoken of an identification with many elements of the character she portrays. Molly's dialogue could have been recited by a number of people in their thirties, and usually is.

Inner Dialogues

"The morning I turned thirty-five, I sat in bed for several hours just thinking about all the things I wanted to do and would never accomplish unless I made some immediate changes," says James. These changes included showing more of a willingness to get involved with long-term relationships and possibly marriage, as well as starting his own computer software company, both of which he'd accomplished by forty. The Jupiter Return around forty-seven saw the company expand into the area of computer graphics and gain more accounts and a higher profile. Levinson describes thirty-six to forty as a time when a major concern is ''becoming one's own man.'' ''The major developmental tasks of this phase are to accomplish the goals . . . to become a senior member in one's world, to speak more strongly with one's own voice, and to have a greater measure of authority.'' But this need exists for women, too, though women say they think societal pressures are such that they usually aren't ready to take their show on the road, in relationships or careers, until after age thirty-five. ''It happens later for women,'' says the very successful owner of a financial-planning center. ''My life didn't begin until I was thirty-five.'' While this remark was made by a woman in her mid-forties, women in the baby-boom generation also say they aren't comfortable with themselves until thirty-five. Women who experience their third Jupiter Return in the twenty-first century may have different reports. Yet women should not be viewed as moving through the third return missionless. It was on the third Jupiter Return that Mother Teresa, after receiving her vows and encountering poor people in several countries, got her ''call within a call.'' As she was to say later, ''The message was clear, I was to leave the convent and help the poor while being among them.'' The Living Saint went out to live in the slums of Calcutta, setting up a home for the indigent at age forty (an important age, as the following chapter will reveal) and becoming the inspiration for an international effort at her second Saturn Return at age sixty. She won the Nobel Peace prize on the fifth Jupiter Return, at age sixty-nine.

The 11.8-year Jupiter cycle can be quartered to show that the Jupiter function gets a special kick just about every three years, beginning around age 3. But whether or not the planet enriches the life of a 3-, 35-, or 60-year-old depends in large part on how well this planetary principle is functioning every day in a given life. The Jupiter principle often works much more subtly than Saturn, and as a result Jupiter is misunderstood. Some extra study into the nature of the planet is necessary if people are to know whether to open up to the Jupiterian impulses that come knocking at their lives.

What Does Luck Have to Do with It?

Jupiter's essential meaning is simple; it represents one's overall relationship with society, the world. It is our general philosophy and it guides the actions that Mars takes. While Venus represents one-on-one interpersonal relationships, Jupiter is how one embraces the world, which is somewhat related to our belief or faith in it. This is the planet that tells whether you're the sort who follows your intuition, with the belief that things will ultimately work for the good, or whether Saturnian fear has your better instincts under siege. Of course Jupiter's association with exaggeration and excess is well earned. The planet is related to zealous missionaries who try to foist their views on everyone else. But initially, we're discussing a balanced Jupiter.

That might seem somewhat contradictory, since Jupiter is about leaps. Listen to the Mozart symphony named for this planet: the music is the kind to which one takes large steps. Like the music, Jupiter is boundless, open. On many levels, this is what the Jupiter function within man encourages, but not foolhardy leaps out into a nameless void. Jupiter is also the planet of judgment, a faculty that is developed through interaction with the world. It further requires assimilation of all inner competing needs and desires in such a way that one is in tune with those hunches and insights that will allow greater mobility and opportunity in life. And when all that is clicking just so, people on the outside will call it luck.

In fairness to the more literal among us, Jupiter does have a connection with the type of "luck" that wins in Las Vegas. But luck in its broader sense is symbolic of one's relationship with the Universe, and more specifically with a code of ethics and philosophy that is applied to daily living. Such a philosophy or weltanschauung grows out of a sense of self and attunement with God, or whatever force is recognized as being at the center of the Universe. When these functions are all operating smoothly, aims, thoughts, and actions are correet and successful because they are in harmony with both personal and universal demands. Such people would not have to excuse themselves from political campaigns because of "bad judgment," as some American politicans were forced to do in recent years. Bad judgment isn't something that overtakes a person like a hiccup and then quickly disappears. Right action grows out of an integrated personality that is also not tinged with Jupiter's self-righteous feeling. Of all the planets, its tilt has the slightest inclination; in other words, it is the most upright of the planets. The Gauquelin research, to which we've made reference, has shown that the most eminent actors, politicians, and journalists have a statistical preference for being born when the planet Jupiter is rising, setting, or reaching its highest or lowest points in the sky. This correlation speaks to the reaching-out nature of these vocations, where a sense of the bigger picture is necessary, and on a crasser level, success often depends on contacts and social access. But the Jupiterian connection also relates to temperament and highlights the sense of calling, rightness, and often arrogance, of people in Jupiterian professions. Those holding positions of prestige in business or the community often have prominent Jupiters.

Jupiter, as we started out saying, is connected with goodies. But the solar system isn't running a welfare program. Good things go to people who earn them. The positive manifestations of Jupiter indicate that rewards come when people have adequately undertaken the personal and social assimilation the planet represents.

Jupiter's connection to growth and expansion has caused astrologers to link it to journeys (both mental and physical). It is the "journey" aspect that some astrologers believe is at work when Jupiter shows up so prominently, as it often does, at the time of death. While Pluto oversees death, Jupiter's metaphysical concerns are always present. When we look at the deaths on the Jupiter Return of famous people such as Marilyn Monroe and the genius Mozart, we can also see problems with inner assimilation. Van Gogh had difficulty moving on to another Jupiter level at ages 35–36, and had been in a sanatarium during part of this time, before ending his life a year later as another critical phase in the Saturn cycle began.

For every story of someone who is feeling happier and more content under the third Jupiter Return, there's someone else whose life is out of control in Jupiterian fashion.

Jupiter Says, "Get Perspective"

Leon got a promotion a few months before his Jupiter Return was in full force. But instead of viewing the promotion as an incentive for further development, Leon mistakenly thought that a move up into middle management was special permission to become more arrogant and disrespectful of others. He became romantically involved with a subordinate, who filed a sexual-harassment complaint against him when he tried to break off the affair before his wife learned about it. Leon's supervisors began leaning on him more, and his promotion was looking as if it might be one of his last, at least at that company.

Leon's situation needs little comment; a foolish Jupiter is easy to spot. More complex is the frustration expressed by Margaret, who said she wanted to "stretch, expand more in my life," but who was being overly cautious around the Jupiter Return. She refused a couple of opportunities to relocate "because I just don't know what I'll find at the other end. Maybe the job won't pan out, or maybe I just won't like a new town. I do like my house and things." Margaret probably won't make any major changes until her early forties, when Uranus pulls up the van in front of her house and boots her out unexpectedly some night while she is asleep.

Margaret is very proud of her stability, her saturnine qualities. But while Saturn is certainly important to life, the planet often works overtime. Because it holds the skills for dealing with life's realities, Saturn, like the voice of any authority, can be given more reverence than it is due. It can sabotage Jupiter, both directly and behind its back. Jupiter certainly has been known to thumb its nose at Saturn's ways, but when Saturn, in the form of the accepted modes of being in society, smirks at Jupiterian hunches and faith in the bigger plan, the bountiful planet backs down.

The result can be stifling, suffocating. Jupiter needs a daily voice in a life. It's also important not to confuse the seemingly religious aspects of Jupiter with the more elusive mystical yearnings and castles-in-the-air talk of Neptune. Jupiter shows belief systems and the way they are applied and integrated in daily living. Jupiter differentiates at the same time that it assimilates. Neptune's efforts to dissolve boundaries and transcend structures, to give oneself over to higher ideals and forces, is beyond three- and four-dimensional experience. Jupiter can be compared to the positive-thinking tapes and other success-oriented techniques so popular in today's culture. A religious correlation is the Nichiren-shō-shū Buddhist sect's practice, which calls for daily chanting of Namu Myōhō Renge-Kyō, as well as various morning and evening prayer rituals as a way of getting in tune with the rhythm in life and building the faith that can allow one to attract better life circumstances. My exposure to this group for more than a year allowed me to see people whose life conditions seemed to be elevated through the practice. But in many cases the belief in something—chanting—was enough to inspire them to take more aggressive action to overcome the obstacles that, up until their introduction to this form of Buddhism, had always gotten the better of them. The chanting almost acts as a lube job, cleaning out filters and portions of one's inner being to allow for greater opportunities, awareness, and assimilation. Jupiter can't work unless one commits oneself to a philosophy on which one can build a life. Unless one's Jupiter is able to distill the many different personality components and show one's true self, the highest personal rewards that Jupiter represents in the birthchart cannot be realized.

The Cycles of Reward

Now that we've examined the age-related Jupiter cycles, another fertile area of study involves Jupiter's 11.8-year return to the Sun sign, which coincides with personal expansion on both inner and outer levels. A chapter on transits to the Sun, as well as the Jupiter ephemeris, at the back of this book, will help people track this 11.8-year cycle, which is separate from the current age-related phases we're examining.

Also important are the 11.8-year cycles unique to a job, marriage, or other activity. The clock starts ticking at the "birth" of the activity and can be viewed as reaching important turning points in relation to its growth and integration whenever Jupiter is three or six signs away from the place it tenanted when the cycle began. For instance, a woman sold her real estate company in 1989 with Jupiter in Gemini making an opposition six signs away from the point where it was located in 1984 when she had first opened the business. Other cycles were involved, but in this case the Jupiter cycle was particularly sensitive. Phil's two marriages have occurred with Jupiter's return to Pisces (1975, 1986). A biologist went back to graduate school twelve years after completing her undergraduate studies. A math teacher started a career as an engineer after twelve years of teaching high school.

To track personal Jupiter cycles, use the "Seasons of Jupiter" chart on page 236 that, like the chart used in the Mars chapter, shows the "seasonal" relationship between various Jupiter placements. Then check the ephemeris to see when Jupiter was in the sign. For instance, if a cycle begins with Jupiter in Virgo, the summer (Opening Square) would find Jupiter in Sagittarius. At midpoint (fall harvest) it would be in Pisces. And the winter (Closing Square) would find Jupiter in Gemini. The chart would be useful for tracking phases of the cycle that start with Jupiter moving over one's Sun sign or any other starting point.

Zodiac Placement

The zodiac sign in which an individual's Jupiter is placed at birth shows the style one uses to approach the world, as well as the areas through which one can find special benefits. Astrologer Stephen Arroyo, noting astronomical theories that speculate that giant Jupiter may be a second Sun in the solar system, suggests that the Jupiter zodiac sign is often as evident in the personality as the Sun sign. You will have to test this idea when you locate your Jupiter sign in the ephemeris and read the related capsule descriptions on the Jupiter placement. Self-expressive, flamboyant Jupiter in Leo gets custom designed in the lives of Diana Ross and Dan Rather. Socially conscious Jupiter in Aquarius is evident in Jane Fonda's causes, as well as in Jerry Lewis's telethons. Both Jesse Jackson and Muhammad Ali have put loquacious Jupiter in Gemini to good use.

The issues related to the zodiac sign in which Jupiter is located at birth are highlighted during the Jupiter Return, when inner desires to take in more of the world and also play more of a part in it have a special potency. With the right dues-paying to Saturn and with special attention to Jupiter's aims and needs, the Jupiter Return can be as exhilarating as a ninth wave is to a surfer. Riding the wave requires faith, judgment, and perspective for the long term. And then, you just may get lucky.

Jupiter Signs

Jupiter in Aries: These people do best when pursuing projects that require self-promotion. Freedom to approach the world in a bold, self-assertive manner appeals to this group, which envisions itself as pioneers. Individual efforts in which they lead the way are "lucky" for this Jupiter. Lily Tomlin's unique "selves" show some of the talents of this Jupiter, while Rosalynn Carter's independence and activity as First Lady are also examples of Jupiter in Aries in action. Mae West did it her way. Baseball manager Billy Martin was one of this tribe, while Paul Volcker is a quieter example.

Jupiter in Taurus: Money, possessions, and security are the areas that these people seek to expand in this lifetime, and it's also where they find some of their biggest rewards. A strong value system must be developed if material gains are to last for any length of time. Some overdo it and get greedy. Richard Pryor's drug problems and other difficulties show how an exaggeration of the hedonistic side of Taurus can nearly bury some. But Joan Baez shows the down-to-earth side of Taurus at work. International architect I. M. Pei expanded through Taurus areas in a very literal way. "Talking Head" David Byrne is a Renaissance man who is forever expanding in creative areas from music to art, films, and more recently, anthropology.

Jupiter in Gemini: These people love to throw ideas out and have good conversations. They seek variety, mobility, and that's pretty much what they get from the world. Betty Ford shows the involvement they seek in the immediate environment; Jesse Jackson does, too. Barbra Streisand's many roles in the entertainment field show the versatility at work. They must avoid inherent superficiality and scatteredness. Some are ready to go on to another adventure before the project they've just started is completed.

Jupiter in Cancer: Running the family business would be a prime outlet for this Jupiter. These people need to feel that they belong, and also work best when they have an emotional investment, something they can nurture. But like the family business that suffers from special turmoil caused when the blood and emotions get too thick, this Jupiter can also overdo by overpersonalizing life situations. Author Toni Morrison expands through stories that deal with family connections and the past. George Steinbrenner expands by mothering his business ventures, most notably the Yankees. Mikhail Gorbachev has a country.

Jupiter in Leo: Put them on a stage and they shine. This Jupiter works best when it is allowed to be creative and self-expressive. Here's a hot one; the flames are always ready to burn bright. Vanity, arrogance, and pride can block true creativity and love, but this becomes less of a problem as they tap into their own true style and can take or leave the applause in their lives. Diana Ross, Dan Rather, and Elizabeth Taylor are examples. Simone de Beauvoir showed that intellectuals can have dash, too.

Jupiter in Virgo: They have a knack for mastering the details and demands of daily living without being overwhelmed. Somehow those trips to the cleaners, quick stops for milk, and all the things on the "to do" list get done, and without much stress. These people understand the true beauty of a daily rhythm. If Jupiter is really clicking, they've also found the "right livelihood" or way to spend their working hours. Joan Rivers and Larry Bird are two examples. Yoko Ono was the "details" person behind her husband's music career.

Jupiter in Libra: Relationships are bountiful and important to one's life pursuits. Michael Dukakis, Gloria Steinem, and Cher show the variety in this group. Many rely on the mutual backscratching aspect of relationships. Jack Anderson, the investigative reporter, has this Jupiter, too. Many with the position—Goldie Hawn, Madonna—are often thought of in connection with a partner. But these women also show that the best in this group know how to hold their own as individuals as well. That's when they're really "lucky" and able to have equal partnerships.

Jupiter in Scorpio: They understand the body language, the politics, and the hidden agendas at work in any situation. Donald Trump has shown that this group can also use all that special "inside information" for negotiating deals. Diane Von Furstenberg didn't do too badly for herself, either. Lucille Ball's comic talent was worth much more than a few laughs; she was a very sharp business lady. Jack Kemp has shown the strategy-mindedness of this sign. *Nice* probably isn't a word people would apply to this group, but some have such a shrewd reading on the psychology of others that they don't have to be ruthless. Some in this group are especially attuned to Scorpio's reforming and life-transformation aspects.

Jupiter in Sagittarius: The big picture and big endeavors turn this group on, and many are usually trying to push some philosophy or idea on everyone else. For Lee Iacocca, it's his company's cars. Chief Justice William Rehnquist shows how some in this group apply concerns about the law to their life and ours. Theories can get in the way of application, and self-righteousness is also a pitfall. Maria Callas and Lauren Bacall are examples of the "Citizens of the World" born with this Jupiter.

Jupiter in Capricorn: They meet the authority people and others who can help them; they expand through hard work, investments, and the traditional play-by-the-rules approach. Sylvia Porter learned this lesson (and gave similar advice to others). As the lives of Bill Cosby and Bruce Springsteen show, even the artists in this Jupiter group know how to become businesses (and the Boss) unto themselves. Paul Newman sells salad dressing and other food products in between acting stints. Jupiter here makes right contacts and hooks up with the right people in authority, but their growing influence puts them in the driver's seat. Real snobs and social climbers are among this crowd, but most people eventually can spot them from afar.

Jupiter in Aquarius: Jane Fonda. Isn't it obvious? This Jupiter is lucky when it's involved with causes and ideas that will further society and mankind. Many of Fonda's works are known for their "messages." Jerry Lewis's telethons show this Jupiter at work. The pitfalls are obvious: Some people with "causes" think they have a license to do as they please, or they start to think they're bigger than the cause. Ted Turner has used his network to showcase socially progressive ideas, sometimes without the benefit of advertisers' backing.

Jupiter in Pisces: Judy Collins's songs show how this Jupiter group expands and participates in society by accessing the unexpressed, but deeply felt currents of feeling, emotion, and yearnings that pass in and out of our consciousness. She comforts, inspires, and shows the universality of all of our experiences. Joyce Carol Oates, who writes fiction, draws from a similar well. Walter Mondale tapped the same source for his humanitarian appeals and causes. When people with this Jupiter seek to inspire and serve, they uplift themselves and the rest of the world.

The Seasons of Jupiter

The following table can be used in conjunction with the ephemeris to track Jupiter's travels from one 11.8-year period to another, as well as in relation to the natal Sun sign. The concept of four critical stages (spring, summer, fall, and winter, loosely speaking) that was used in previous chapters also applies here. The critical phases of Jupiter will be much more subtle than the seven-year cycles of Saturn that were studied. Often all that occurs is a shift in viewpoint.

To use the table listed below, locate a given Jupiter sign in the left-hand column. The sign you choose will depend on which cycle is being tracked. If it's the 11.8-year return of Jupiter to the Sun, find the Sun sign in the left-hand column. If it's the Jupiter Return cycle, check the ephemeris and locate the Jupiter sign in the left-hand column. If the Jupiter cycle is being tracked for a marriage, education, or business venture, make note of the date and check the corresponding back-of-the-book table for the Jupiter placement.

Natal Jupiter	Phase II	Phase III	Phase IV
Aries	Cancer	Libra	Capricorn
Taurus	Leo	Scorpio	Aquarius
Gemini	Virgo	Sagittarius	Pisces
Cancer	Libra	Capricorn	Aries
Leo	Scorpio	Aquarius	Taurus
Virgo	Sagittarius	Pisces	Gemini
Libra	Capricorn	Aries	Cancer
Scorpio	Aquarius	Taurus	Leo
Sagittarius	Pisces	Gemini	Virgo
Capricorn	Aries	Cancer	Libra
Aquarius	Taurus	Leo	Scorpio
Pisces	Gemini	Virgo	Sagittarius

Examples:

1. Martha's academic rise. Martha's Sun is in Cancer, a sign Jupiter visited as she started graduate school, so we'll chart that cycle.

Jupiter in Cancer (1978)	Jupiter in Libra (1981)	Jupiter in Capricorn (1985)	Jupiter in Aries (1987)
B.A. in English; entered graduate program	Teaching Assistant	P.h.D.	Part-time professor

Jupiter in
Cancer
  (1989)
Associate
professor

2. Joseph's experience in the restaurant business shows how
   some people expand too quickly under Jupiter. Here's the
   Jupiter cycle of that venture.

Jupiter in Gemini (1977) Opened restaurant	Jupiter in Virgo (1980) Got new partners	Jupiter in Sagittarius (1983) Restaurant closed	Jupiter in Pisces (1986) Opened bistro that closed in a year

Planetary Seasons

The Moon and all planets as they move in the sky form "seasonal" relationships to the Sun in the same manner as Saturn
(Chapter 10) and Jupiter (Chapter 12). Any planet in the same
sign as the Sun is starting a new cycle and is in "spring"
relationship, planting seeds; three signs ahead of the Sun is
"summer," where we build on challenges; six signs away, in
opposition, is "fall," where matters cry out for reconciliation;
three signs behind the Sun sign is winter, where it's time to
mop up the cycle and prepare for a new one. Mars's seasonal
relationships to the Sun should provide data about short-term
trends, but none of these seasons are as significant as trends
indicated by Jupiter and Saturn.

SUN SIGN	SUMMER	FALL	WINTER
Aries	Cancer	Libra	Capricorn
Taurus	Leo	Scorpio	Aquarius
Gemini	Virgo	Sagittarius	Pisces
Cancer	Libra	Capricorn	Aries
Leo	Scorpio	Aquarius	Taurus

Virgo	Sagittarius	Pisces	Gemini
Libra	Capricorn	Aries	Cancer
Scorpio	Aquarius	Taurus	Leo
Sagittarius	Pisces	Gemini	Virgo
Capricorn	Aries	Cancer	Libra
Aquarius	Taurus	Leo	Scorpio
Pisces	Gemini	Virgo	Sagittarius

THIRTEEN

Turning Life Upside Down and Inside Out with Help from Uranus, Neptune, Pluto (and Saturn's Second Return)

Henry Ford began tinkering with machines very early in life. While perfecting his engineering skills, he perceived that the prototype model cars with which inventors on both sides of the Atlantic were experimenting could find a market among working-class Americans. His view differed sharply from his counterparts of the day, who believed the car could only be a luxury for the wealthy. Ford began following his dreams and made a few ill-fated attempts to build a company that would mass-produce automobiles for Everyman. A few months before his fortieth birthday, he started the company that would revolutionize America and the world.

Rosa Parks is a private citizen whose life was turned upside down and took on broader meanings of freedom in her early forties. A seamstress in Montgomery, Alabama, Parks was an active participant in community affairs and secretary of the local NAACP, where members were upset with city laws restricting blacks to the back seats of the bus. One day in December 1955, Rosa, following a hard day's work, was sitting in the first row of the all-black section. When a bus driver barked for the people to move still further back to make room for a white man, Parks refused to get up and was arrested. The action sparked a year-long boycott of Montgomery's transit system by blacks, who, through the courts, won the right to choose their own seats on the bus.

Uranus

The initial jolt that led to Ford's and Park's liberation involved the planet Uranus, whose transits through the signs furthers individuality and breakthroughs in the lives of all people, particularly those between the ages of forty and forty-two, when Uranus moves directly across from the place it tenanted at a given individual's birth. At that time Uranus, whose full orbit is eighty-four years, can be viewed in its usual stance— on its side and rotating on its axis. You could say that Uranus is the rebel of the zodiac that works to further the cause of progress. Discovered at a time when people all over the world were striking out against authority and calling for more individual freedom and expression, Uranus is the planet that pushes us to find and exhibit our uniqueness. It's the light bulb that goes off, the moment of intuitive insight. Uranus is the planet of genius, inventiveness, and high technology. When Uranus moves through a zodiac sign, it urges revolution. Moving through the sign of Gemini from 1942 to 1949, it shook up concepts having to do with communication and education by correlating to increased use of television, mass education, and paperback books. When it moved through Cancer from 1949 to 1956, it brought more technology into the home (Cancer) and continued the buildup of tract homes and suburbs begun in Gemini (the sign of neighborhoods).

Like Neptune and Pluto, which will shortly be introduced, Uranus is viewed as a "generation" planet. It stays in a sign for such a long time that waves of people share the same Uranus position. Uranus shows how entire subgenerations of people behave and pinpoints the areas of life and concepts they must "revolutionize" in order to find their unique, individual selves. Rosa Parks was born in 1913, when Uranus was moving through Aquarius and calling on each individual to find a way to contribute and participate in goals that move society forward. When Uranus was 180 degrees across from that post in 1955, her self-expression and freedom were challenged, and she rose to the time in a history-altering way. Ford was born in 1863, when Uranus was in Gemini, the sign of communication, mo-

bility, and transportation. In 1903, when Uranus was in jour-
neying, expansive Sagittarius, directly across from Ford's natal
Uranus, he started the Ford Motor Company with the idea of
opening up the world with cars for the masses.

The many other people born around the same time as Ford
and Parks also faced Uranian challenges that were unique to
their lives. Today situations such as those described by Jeff
are particularly common: Recently divorced, he was changing
his career and life-style with an eye to reversing the stagnant
state of the previous years of his life. His wife's demand for
a divorce when he was thirty-seven, plus a corporate reorgan-
ization two years later that put him out of the favor he'd known
for so long, were the first visible signs of the unraveling that
was under way in the life he had built. But the seeds had been
there for some time, possibly since age thirty-five, when he
began thinking about the compromises and postponed decisions
that had set him on the road he was walking. He was an artist
and a fairly independent, freewheeling soul who had found
security and some prestige in an engineering degree. By twenty-
four he was heading toward the altar and then eagerly began
giving his parents the grandchildren they wanted. He was a
freethinker who'd become a yes-man to corporate policies and
bosses for whom he had no respect.

Of course, that's how he's telling the story now, some years
later, as he's approaching his mid-forties. He's lived a few
more chapters and seen how some earlier scenarios ended. He
is wiser, but none of this came without difficulty.

For one thing, his wife was just as tired of it all as he was.
But she wasn't one to give a lot of warning. One day she
announced plans to take a graphic-arts job some 125 miles
away in another state. The punchline was that she didn't want
Jeff to come with her. She was giving him no hassles, she said.
She was taking the children and all he had to do was put the
house on the market, give her a share of the profits, send child
support, and visit the kids every now and then. Although Jeff
hadn't been that happy with his life or his wife, his pride was
now at stake. He spent about two years trying to change her
mind, but finally the pressures at work were getting so intense
that he couldn't fight two wars at once.

The standstill broke when Jeff started taking advantage of
his corporation's Employee Assistance Program, where employees with problems (sometimes referred to as bad attitudes)
were sent to discuss their declining productivity and other dif-

ficulties. It didn't take Jeff many sessions to see that he no longer cared to be with his company, his wife, or the counselor. He saw that he was being given a chance for a new start, to look into the possibility of self-employment, live in a cabin in Vermont, be something different. Almost immediately the palpitations he was feeling in his chest stopped, giving him the calm and strength he needed to contact an art-supply franchise that was looking for partners to open a store. It took some negotiation, as well as the borrowing of more start-up cash than he'd cared to sign his name to, but Jeff soon joined the increasing numbers of people who are working for themselves. Many of the employees in the professional department where Jeff worked lost their jobs in a major layoff six months later.

"I liberated myself just in time," says Jeff, whose big phrase at this point is, "I've got to try new things." He walks and talks faster and seems to move toward things in life. He's more curious, and is painting, dating, getting around more. "It's like my life started over at forty, but I was smarter and wiser and just happier once I got used to the changes. I feel like things will keep working as long as I'm myself and moving with the flow. I always thought the mid-life crisis was supposed to be kind of bad, but I don't feel as old as I thought I'd feel. I certainly know I'm not going to live forever, but right now I feel alive. I can't explain it."

This phase of life is often viewed with snickers as people recall images of forty-two-year-olds chasing eighteen-year-olds. While such scenarios are not uncommon, they eclipse the deeper issues at stake in this period of life. Levinson describes this as perhaps the most critical—and painful—in the lives of the men he studied. As Carl Jung's break from Sigmund Freud at age thirty-seven showed, there is a critical need to find one's own voice. Astrologically life between thirty-seven and forty-four correlates to one of the most complicated overlays of concentric cycles, all working simultaneously. Uranus, the planet we've been exploring, has a significant role. But ages thirty-six to thirty-seven and forty-three to forty-four are important interval points along Saturn's orbit. At thirty-six to thirty-seven the Saturn Return changes come up for review and adjustments, while ages forty-three to forty-four find Saturn directly across from the natal position. This Saturn phase had last occurred at ages fourteen to fifteen, when Saturn made a direct assault on one's sense of identity, and it now becomes critical to find a place in the world. The teenager then shares something with the forty-three-to-forty-four-year-old, who is attempting to actualize himself or herself more fully. This chapter will discuss several planetary connections to later years, including the second return of Saturn to its birth position. But the current phase under scrutiny cannot be fully dissected without introducing the last two outer planets—Neptune and Pluto—for their presence becomes particularly powerful in one's life.

Neptune

Within all of us is that yearning for the "Somewhere" that is the ideal place for us, where our highest aspirations and ideals can be realized. While some of these yearnings may be realized, others are castles in the air that can imprison us if we don't keep our feet on the ground. Venus deals with our conscious loves and likes. Neptune is a higher expression, for it symbolizes the ultimate, which can usually only be reached in music, at the movies, in our fantasies, religion, drugs, alcohol, and in genuine or fraudulent mystical experiences. We need to seek and experience Neptune—dreams are an example of this need—but we must integrate it with more common earthly realities.

Neptune takes fourteen years to move through a sign, consequently affecting masses of individuals born under specific Neptune placements. Neptune, moving through Capricorn from 1984 to 1998, is causing society to idealize (Neptunize) the older traditions (family, status, structure) symbolized by Capricorn. But then society will eventually see a distortion of such principles as Neptune dissolves previous concepts to make way for new visions. Neptune moving through Capricorn will initially idealize tradition and the past, but it will eventually cause us certain pains and disappointments as it makes us more ready to think of families, authority, and corporations in different ways. One positive expression already visible is the way in which corporations are increasing day care for employees and taking other steps to humanize the workplace. But a good deal of America is currently using work as a drug. People born between 1984 and 1998 will exhibit the same Capricornian fantasies before they're able to visualize new possibilities. The process will be similar to that undertaken by the Neptune-in-Virgo Great Depression generation, which idealized the work ethic, the daily routine, and carried anxieties about having it slip away from them through most of their adult lives.

Between ages forty and forty-three, Neptune makes a square (three signs away/90 degrees) to the birth position and forces people to question their ideals and faith. The timing coincides with Uranus's reaching the midpoint of its cycle, so the questioning comes at the same time that pieces of the life are being discarded. Rosa Parks and Henry Ford's lives at this time raised the issues of faith and ideals and included the bouts of disappointment and lost faith that relate to Neptune. Franklin Delano Roosevelt was struck with polio and left paralyzed for the rest of his life as he began his forties. His fight to get back on crutches and take on the governorship of New York, and subsequently to lead America through the Depression and World War II, place him above mere politicians in the collective memory. Illnesses cause people to ask the universal questions about God and their existential relationship to everything around them. Paul Tsonga, the former United States senator, left public life to battle cancer, a fight that changed him forever. Comedienne/actress Gilda Radner was struck with cancer during this age phase, and though she never recovered, she openly discussed the initial lost faith and fear that she had to fight in order to keep on living.

Pluto

Radner's story was especially poignant and was marked by the issues of personal power and transformation because she, like others born since World War II, experienced a major phase in the Pluto cycle in tandem with the Saturn, Uranus, and Neptune configurations of ages thirty-seven to forty-four. Pluto is the planet of death and life. It is the process of change, indicating the extensive stages that we must go through to claim a new life. The repressed, unconscious motivations—our shadow, many therapists would say—is represented by Pluto, which also holds the power to purge the darkness once we are willing to confront it. Pluto must be confronted if we are to tap our personal power and share in the collective evolution of the Earth. Because it moves so slowly, Pluto isn't able to figure into age cycles as often as Saturn. In previous generations Pluto's first square (three signs away) to its birth position came at a person's retirement, when elders were passing the torch to young people. Richard Nixon's fall from power coincided with the Pluto Square, among other cycles. But Pluto picked up speed—as it always does—once it moved into the second half of the zodiac in 1957, causing the Pluto Square to occur earlier. A 1930 baby would have experienced the square at forty-nine. More recently the Pluto challenge has been coming as the first crop of baby-boomers turn forty to forty-two; the mid-1950s babies will experience the Pluto challenge around ages thirty-five to thirty-seven.

As Pluto squared the birth position for those born in the mid-1940s, we saw issues of manipulation and power (Plutonian concerns) blowing up in the face of Oliver North. Donald Trump was dueling with Merv Griffin over a corporate take-over, and Prince Charles was dealing with his inability to exercise power at all. Many others in the age group are dealing with the corporate downscaling that will force baby-boomers to find different modes for self-expression, as explained in more detail in Chapter 18, "The Astrology of Generations." Several similarly aged people—Pat Sajak, Connie Chung, and Diane Sawyer—were cutting deals to give them more freedom and personal power. Cher's Academy Award and expanded role as an entertainer coincided with the Pluto Square, while Penny Marshall (Laverne Defasio on *Laverne and Shirley*) used the Saturn, Uranus, Neptune, and Pluto cycles to harness her position as a respected director. Other actresses, such as Bette Midler, were trying to control a bigger share of power in Hollywood, though the fantasy factory still remains a male game.

The early Pluto Square made Dan Quayle a household name and through him displayed the many ways in which the current generation must grow up if it is to assume the scepter of power with integrity and effectiveness. Quayle's past as a party boy and his limited record of substance have made him the butt of jokes for comedians. While the Pluto Square is happening earlier than ever before in this century, generations who preceded the planet's discovery also experienced the first square relatively early in their lives. Notable examples include Thomas Jefferson and John Adams, who used the energy to start a new government. Adams was forty-one and experiencing the square in 1776; Jefferson was forty-three, nearing the end of his first square, when the U.S. Constitution was adopted in 1787. George Washington, born in 1732 and several years older than Adams and Jefferson, saw the square at ages forty-one to forty-three as well. It may be that generations who face the square earlier are forced to play special roles in helping society make transitions into new eras.

Critical Times

Pluto adds urgency to what the record shows is an already difficult time to negotiate. Michael Dukakis started this period at thirty-seven by losing his bid for lieutenant governor. At thirty-three he had failed to get on the Democratic ticket as the candidate for attorney general, but he recouped by getting re-elected to the House of Representatives. Losing his bid for lieutenant governor in 1970 put him out of office for the first time since his election at age twenty-nine. But Dukakis used the time well by practicing law and building a coalition that helped him win the governorship in 1974 at the age of forty-one.

The same cycles that helped Dukakis gain more prominence eventually led to his demise as he failed to meet the political demands of his office and incorporate others' views in his agenda. Honesty, hard work, and reform were all part of his bag of tricks, but he was to learn that a successful politician needs more. He alienated voters and the inside political leaders, whom Dukakis had refused to go behind closed doors with to lobby for his programs and ideas. In 1978, after garnering only 42 percent of the vote, he lost his reelection bid to Edward King. The loss, which came at age forty-five, is considered the most significant defeat in Dukakis's life. But Dukakis is a man who has learned from his mistakes. He spent three years teaching at the John F. Kennedy School for Government at Harvard. Coalition building and reconciliation allowed him to wrest his seat back from King in 1982. Dukakis made his transition into his fifties as a mature politician and he gained a third term in 1986. His run for the presidency in 1988 came just a few years before his second Saturn return in Aquarius in 1991–92.

Many of the issues that were blocking Dukakis were personality and character matters left unresolved from his early life. The mid-life-transition period can dredge up many uncompleted childhood tasks that must be tackled before people can truly bloom. A dramatic example was presented by Michael Douglas when he accepted his Academy Award for best actor in *Wall Street* in 1988. Prior to the role of a greedy takeover artist, Douglas's acting had been limited to either nice guy (*Streets of San Francisco*) or wimp (*Fatal Attraction*) roles. He'd built his niche in Hollywood through producing, in particular *One Flew Over the Cuckoo's Nest*, around the time of his Saturn Return.

As Douglas moved through his late thirties, he had to acknowledge that he'd deliberately avoided playing the intense characters associated with his father, Kirk Douglas. "It's true that I've shied away from playing the kind of roles my dad has played, shied away from the comparisons," Douglas told a magazine writer. "That limits you obviously, but now I'm changing. I'm forty-four now, so it's a good time to evaluate. I've always thought I would be a late bloomer and that my forties would be good for me. Maybe it's part of having a famous father. It takes longer to establish your own identity." When accepting his Oscar, Douglas thanked his wife, child, and "Kirk Douglas for helping a son move out of his shadow."

Like Kirk's son, we are always grappling with our sense of self and identity and how we will express it. The Uranus revolution, working with the phases of other planetary trends, can help us break out of the old patterns, to move beyond the planet Saturn in our consciousness and life. Certainly we must always render unto Saturn its due, but after forty-two the need is to move to different levels of awareness. People who negotiate the demands of the mid-life transition are in an especially good position to benefit from the Jupiter Return that takes place at ages forty-six to forty-seven. In past times many men—Lee Iacocca, for one—have ascended to corporate presidencies with the Jupiter Return that follows the mid-life crisis. Women haven't been as fortunate.

Marie Curie won Nobel Peace prizes at thirty-six and forty-four (and also raised children), but was never elected to the prestigious French Academy of Sciences because of her sex. Indira Gandhi became prime minister at forty-nine and kept the job for eleven years, but few women lead corporations or countries unless they are family businesses. Barbara Walters signed her first much-talked-about million-dollar contract at forty-four. Lucille Ball got her first television show at age forty, and her entertainment stock soared through most of the rest of her life. Some of the more memorable mid-life successes by women have been ones they've carved out by themselves.

Liz Claiborne, Inc. was started in 1976 when the clothing designer was forty-seven. Claiborne had always been an independent-minded woman. She pursued a design career against her father's wishes. She was among the minority of "career women" of the 1950s. At her Saturn Return she signed on as a designer with a firm, Youth Guild, where she stayed for fifteen years, a tenure extended because of childrearing responsibilities. Working along with her second husband, Arthur Ortenberg, Claiborne took $250,000 in savings and money from family and friends to build a financial phenomenon that is moving up in the Fortune 500. Saying she and her husband wanted to pursue "environmental, social and other personal interests," the couple retired from active management of their company in 1989 as Saturn returned to Claiborne's birth position.

That women like Claiborne find themselves running major corporations after raising families is an example of how Uranus can cause "reversals" in one's life direction. Theoretically those who have led active external lives become more receptive, while the wallflowers break out more. Surveys showing that a majority of the many women starting up businesses today do so after forty adds some support to theories about Uranus's tendencies. Simultaneously, the increasing number of career women who are choosing to have babies in their forties also shows a similar life reversal.

Men experience the same reversal, usually through a desire to get more in touch with their emotional, nurturing needs. Sigmund Freud put himself in therapy at age forty-two and began deeper exploration of his dreams. Often, as former Senator Paul Tsongas learned, it can sometimes take a major illness to force men to appreciate family life and interpersonal relationships. While multimillionaire Bill Cosby is someone who has been able to combine myriad artistic, business, educational, and philanthropic interests in addition to a close home life, many men spend their first forty years putting most of their energy into building structures in the outside world and neglecting their emotional life. The mid-life transition is intended to dissolve and integrate the various compartments of a life. Much of what happens will depend on what has occurred during the turning-thirty transition and the mid-thirties. The more extreme cases, where people are met with crisis after crisis and have a hard time getting back to their center, occur when the warning signals have all been ignored along the way.

There is no such thing as a final chance in life, at least not until the last breath. But it can be sensibly argued that the turning-forty transition has extreme weight, simply because the physical stamina and other functions aren't going to allow for certain activities and changes once a body gets older. Getting stuck in the mid-life crisis, by allowing Saturn to intercept the messages from other planets, may have much to do with the increased instances of heart attacks and negativity experienced by people who refuse to change or don't see that it's possible. In the novel *The Fortune Teller*, Marsha Norman, the Pulitzer prizewinning playwright, writes of a middle-aged woman who has gotten so used to life with a hurtful, rejecting, cheating man that she thinks she really needs him. The woman lives an isolated, reclusive existence represented by the Hermit in the Tarot deck.

> The picture is of a bearded, robed recluse, who leans on a shepherd's crook for support and holds up a lantern to light his solitary path. But he is not searching for his sheep in the darkness. He is just alone, sentenced to life in exile for an unpardonable crime. It is the Hermit himself who has pronounced the sentence. [Hermits] said they'd rather be alone, or couldn't handle the demands that other people made on them, or could only work or live where it was quiet. And some of these people actually did move to remote areas. But most of them just went so far inside themselves that they weren't reachable by ordinary human means, like physical contact or conversation.

Those familiar with the Tarot deck are also aware that the Hermit looks very much like illustrations of Saturn or Father Time. And while this card may sometimes represent the idea of wise counsel, it can also suggest the way that an overprogrammed Saturn function can lock people into life. We've spent much time discussing the lives of famous people, but everyone must respond to the call to see beyond Saturn. And like other phases, many people find that making subtle shifts in thinking are enough for them to find the inner guidance they need to go on with life.

Judith came to a realization on her fortieth birthday: There was no Mr. Right in her life. Ten years earlier she would have been upset about it. But at age forty she had a career she enjoyed, friends she cared about, the money to vacation in foreign countries. "I remember having a drink, looking around, and telling myself, you can deal with this."

Mark, who is now forty-eight, said he felt more deadlines at forty. He had been very clear about what he had not yet accomplished and what he wanted to do. He remembers feeling as if these goals were second to some of the emotional satisfaction he was beginning to feel with his family, volunteer work on community boards, and other projects. "I hadn't given up. In fact I started a mail-order business and made some of the investments I always wanted to make. The difference was that it wasn't done at the expense of my family relationships. There was more balance, more give-and-take."

Neither Judith nor Mark should be viewed as people who won't make further changes in their lives. Numerous age and personalized cycles will provide both people with the opportunity to expand in any way they might desire. Judith may find that she will marry after all.

While people can spew out their first Saturn Return stories during ages twenty-eight to thirty with some detail, the second return is more subtle and universal in scope. People are less concerned about what they're getting out of society as an individual and start talking about broader spiritual or community goals. Like anyone who has invested time in a career, Robert had seen high periods as a chief political reporter and respected editor. He had also seen low periods when he felt pushed aside by younger and less experienced managements. The Jupiter Returns in his thirties and forties had all been strong periods, but he was now talking about doing something of worth, something for society. While many younger reporters would define their daily assault on the world as "doing good," Robert was talking about "giving something back to the community." He had fantasies of a newspaper that would train racial minorities for careers in journalism. He talked of he and his wife chucking their life and working for the Red Cross. "I want to do something good, something more spiritual," he said.

Such feelings are common to many of this age. Some people talk about what they will leave for their families; others, their community. The Betty Ford Clinic was started after the former First Lady's bout with substance abuse. That it became a full-fledged, acknowledged program around her second Saturn Return is an example of the way personal and universal needs can merge with this cycle. It's what Marjorie, a 63-year old woman, is trying to achieve. In the same way that Robert rejected the idea that his efforts to disseminate information to the public weren't "doing good," Marjorie doesn't feel as if she's made a contribution to the rest of the world, even though she raised four children.

Marjorie has found some of the connection she's seeking by acting as a buddy for AIDS victims. "Working with them, I feel so much more life, because I'm helping them make this crossing that we'll all have to make eventually. I didn't know this would happen. At first I was scared, but all the other volunteer work I was trying to do didn't move me the same way. I'd gone to church and been a good Christian, I guess, but I had never really felt the 'brotherhood of man' until I became an AIDS buddy."

Such experiences have always been there for those who sought them, but people need them at different times in their life. People in their late fifties know that their years are limited. At the very least a person of sixty has experienced the loss of close family members and other loved ones. "At a certain point I think you make peace with your death and then try to do the best with the rest of your years," says a man in his sixties. Cycles involving Neptune, as well as more activity from Jupiter and Uranus, force people to have to think about ideas such as God and the meaning of life. The second Saturn Return may be the first time when people feel comfortable putting some of these broader concepts—such as love for humanity—into action.

Increasingly we are coming to accept the fact that people often do their best work when they're older. Such potentialities should make society more willing to alter retirement ages, as it will no doubt be pressured to do, particularly by the 75-million-strong baby-boom generation. Economic necessities—and the precariousness of pension plans and Social Security—will be part of the impetus, but some of the backlash toward mandatory retirements will come simply because people won't be finished creating and being participants in the world. Producer Norman Lear, whose Act III Entertainment company started as he moved through his sixties, speaks to the desire of the best and brightest to keep working well past their second Saturn Return. Given the cycles they've weathered, this can only be to society's benefit.

A third Saturn Return occurs in the late eighties. Prior to that there's a Uranus Return around age eighty-four. Ideally speaking, this cycle should be like a lightning bolt that brings the whole picture together. But the physical limitations of most people of this age decrease the chances of the reality being ideal. Certainly some minds are still active in their eighties and nineties. Joseph Campbell, the brilliant mythologist who died as Uranus returned, completing an 84-year orbit, was very much in command of his thoughts and work, as evidenced by the PBS series that featured him in conversation with Bill Moyers. George Burns, who turned ninety-three in 1989, is booked to perform at London's Palladium on his one-hundredth birthday. Mother Teresa, born in 1910, untiringly carries out her vision, working among the sick and poor in India. Not everyone can implement a vision on such a large scale. But anyone who takes up the tasks of all their individual cycles has done their part for the bigger plan.

Planetary Age Cycles

The following chart is a checklist intended to assist study.

Jupiter: Calls for social expansion and integration. Key phases every 3 years.

Jupiter Returns: 11–12, 23–24, 35–36, 46–47, and so on. Each renewal calls for a different societal role.

Jupiter Square Jupiter (First Quarter): 3 years following Jupiter Return (14–15, 26, 38, etc): Reassessing life philosophy, opportunities.

Jupiter Oppose Jupiter: 6 years following Jupiter Return (17–18, 28–29, 41–42, etc.): Expansion impulses seek expression, moderation needed. Ethics, philosophy at odds with daily routine.

Jupiter Square Jupiter (Last Quarter): 9 years following Jupiter Return (32–33, 43–44, 55, etc.): Cycle waning; some postures and approaches to life abandoned. Success for those who made adjustments throughout cycle

Saturn: Calls for the establishment of structures. Key phases every 7 years.

Saturn Returns: 28–30, 58–60, 88–90.

Saturn Square Saturn (First Quarter): 7 years following each Saturn Return (7, 36, 62–63, etc.). Decisions and attitudes that prevailed at the return are challenged, and some changes are usually in order.

Saturn Oppose Saturn: 14–15 years following Saturn Return (14–15, 43–44, 72–73). Identity issues often reflected in crises. Confrontation with old structures (either psychological, authoritative, or physical).

Saturn Square Saturn (Last Quarter): 21–22 years after the Saturn Return (21–22, 49–51, 109–110). Adjustments needed; possible crises related to life goals.

Uranus: Calls for a move toward greater individuality. Key phases every 21–22 years.

Uranus Return: 84. Theoretically a reawakening or illumination, but little conventional or astrological research has been done with this age group.

Uranus Square Uranus (First Quarter): 21–22. Rebellion. Attempt to express individuality, but often as defined by peers.

Uranus Oppose Uranus: 40–42. Life reversals. Liberation. Who are you going to be?

Uranus Square Uranus (Last Quarter): 63. Crisis in circumstances or activity forces new roles and consciousness.

Neptune: Evokes personal and collective ideals and dreams. Key phases every 42–43 years.

Neptune Return: 164 years.

Neptune Square Neptune (First Quarter): 42–43. Confusion about one's ideals and reality; a search for something to believe in.

Neptune Oppose Neptune: 82. A forced confrontation (in the best of cases, eventual illuminations) between ideals and reality. Usually a generation is seeing many of the ideals it held dear dissolve in the outer world.

Pluto: Forces change through psychological and/or physical death.

Key phases: erratic

Pluto Return: 248 years.

Pluto Square Pluto: Sometime between 35–60, depending on generation. Individuals forced to confront issues of personal/collective power. Purge. Self-transformation. Repressed matters surface.

Pluto Oppose Pluto: 70–80, for some born after World War II. Direct power confrontations, issues of surrender or exchanging power. Individual lives and world affairs demand major overhaul.

PART III
Cycles in the World

The 1990s—The Reality Decade

The briefest glance at the "Megacycles" time line on page 260 should make people wonder if the cosmos is trying to send Earth a message. In fact the planetary cycles placed along the time line speak to "reality checks" and many realignments and changes under way throughout the world. In talking of a "reality decade," I refer to the economic and environmental challenges made more obvious as major cycles of thirty-six and forty-five years were renewing their energies as the 1980s ended. But the reality issue takes on broader meanings as it's applied to the stepped-up efforts on the part of ecologists, physicists, and physicians, as well as private planetary citizens, to get closer to a truer picture of reality in both its physical and metaphysical senses. The nature of reality has been under examination and in the process of being redefined throughout most of this century. It has a special urgency now as increased globalization and a greater need for global solutions forces people to change their worldview. Throughout the industrial and, now, postindustrial age, society has become increasingly fragmented, and the problem has been made dangerously evident with acid rain, shrinking forests, faltering economies, and health epidemics that relate to core issues.

The layers of earthly problems—the ozone being just one of them—cannot be tackled with our usual battery of experts. A total shift in consciousness, an overhaul of our concept of life, a new reality system in effect, is required before the change agents in society can do their work. Paradigm shifts unfortunately don't happen overnight, nor do they hold press conferences. Yet the active presence of people as different as Dr. Bernie Siegel, whose work with the terminally ill features a self-healing component that is being credited with keeping AIDS patients alive longer than traditional medicine had predicted, to glasnost and the dissolving of tariff borders among the European Economic Community are among the varying examples of how the world must be seen with different eyes.

Though there isn't a "Board of Paradigm Shifts" that can hold a State-of-the-Planet Address at prime time, evidence of the changing realities can be studied through Mundane Astrology. It focuses on the astrological factors affecting social, economic, and political trends, as well as the affairs of nations, cities, states, corporations, stock markets, and many other areas of human activity. Mundane Astrology usually takes a backseat to the astrology of individuals. But in addressing such matters as economic trends, astrology provides information about the needs of society as a unit. With the exception of some on Wall Street who combine conventional training with astrological knowledge, astrologers often lack the sociological, economic, and political backgrounds that would enable them to be a credible force in these areas.

But the astrological tools are there for people who want to take them in hand for study. Our "reality" decade is reflected in the appearance of Saturn, Uranus, and Neptune coming together in Capricorn, sign of structure, status quo, traditional business and government systems. Uranus, the planet that turns everything upside down, and Neptune, which dissolves whatever it touches with the aim of inspiring a new level of understanding, are coming together again for the first time in 172 years. Moving through Capricorn, these planets will be pushing around and spraying fog over everything—simultaneously exciting and dissolving all things having to do with that sign, from societal leaders and authority figures to each of us in our individual lives.

The following chapters will provide readers with much information on how the singular and combined impacts of the outer planets affect the world, as well as the generations that come into the world. The 172-year Uranus-Neptune cycle, the subject of an entire chapter, is not the final word. The years 1891–92 saw the renewal of a 492-year cycle involving the coming together of ideals-oriented Neptune with transformational Pluto. This cycle, which last renewed itself during the final years of the Middle Ages, before inventions such as the printing press and the spread of the Church's influence caused society to expand to another level of development, opened up the world through inventions, immigrations, and further exploration of spiritual ideals beyond the structure of organized religion. But the same cycle contains an ugliness profoundly personified by Adolf Hitler, born in 1889, and with the conjunction close though not exact in his chart. Whereas contemporaries Eugene O'Neill and Irving Berlin tapped the same sources and gave us art that spoke to aspects of the collective, Hitler evoked the grotesque. Though Pluto is the planet that excavates, it was hiding behind Neptune during the conjunction of 1891–92 and then showed its face in 1930 as Hitler's maniacal expression was attracting more and more followers. But

Pluto is not always the destroyer. Its ravages and destruction often lead to transformation—reforms, regeneration, and healing. The choice is always ours. We all have a connection to and responsibility for the actions of our leaders. The 1990s will make this truth more evident to everyone. Our survival depends on seeing and accepting this and then moving forward to act on the new knowledge.

Megacycles

```
                    Ju/Ur
          Ju/Pl  Ju/Ne                                         172 yrs                              20 yrs
   Ju/Sa Sa/Pl                           45 yrs  36 yrs              Ur/Ne Ju/Pl              Ju/Ne Ju/Ur        Ju/Sa
   1980  81  82  83  84  85  86  87  88  89  90  91  92  93  94  95  96  97  98  99  2000
                                  Sa/Ur Sa/Ne                       Sa/Pl         Ju/Sa              Sa/Ne Sa/Ur
                                  Ju/Sa                             Ju/Sa                                    Sa/Pl
                                  Ur/Pl                             Ju/Ur
                                                                    Ju/Ne
```

Cycles that are renewing themselves (conjunctions) are above the time line, while critical phases are below the time line.

Ju/Sa (20 years):	Restructuring of social/economic policies
Ju/Ur (14 years):	Expansion, breakaway, disruption
Ju/Ne (13 years):	Speculation, delusion, idealism
Ju/Pl (12 years):	Power mongering, tyranny
Sa/Pl (33 years):	Cultural restructuring, purgatory
Sa/Ne (36 years):	Malaise, fear, giving form to ideals
Sa/Ur (45 years):	Struggles between individual liberties and authoritarian forces
Ur/Pl (127 years):	Revolution
Ur/Ne (172 years):	Dissolving of old worlds, revelations
Ne/Pl (492 years):	Purging collective depths to bring ideals to life, 1891–92 conjunction

FOURTEEN

The Aquarian Conspiracy of 1992

If a 172-year cycle appears more overwhelming than the 7- or 11-year rhythms encountered earlier, it's with good reason. The 172-year cycle is the sponsor of major social and economic shifts. Some of these will include European Common Market and significant realignments in government and social structures, as well as new discoveries and expressions of art, science, and the way people see and experience reality. During 1992 and 1993 Uranus and Neptune will be together in the sky (conjunct), something that occurs every 172 years. The cycle we are completing right now started in 1820–21, a time that coincided with significant events, such as the retreat of Napoleon, the resurgence of the monarchy in France and elsewhere in Europe, and the rise of the proletariat and working classes around the world. The buildup of industrial mills in Lowell, Massachusetts, and other parts of the northeastern United States and Britain's passage of its first Factory Act, aimed at limiting abuses of employers, are examples of the kinds of socioeconomic redistributions associated with this cycle.

The coming together of Uranus, the great awakener and revolutionary, with Neptune, the planet of ideals, visions, and man's most elusive yearnings, represents the shifts in world thought that move society forward. We might even describe the two planets as "Aquarian conspirators," to borrow a term coined by author/researcher Marilyn Ferguson. She says that conspirators have the task of pointing out the flaws in the old worldview (paradigm) and showing that new ways, new visions, speak more aptly to the whole. A 492-year cycle involving Neptune/Pluto, which were conjunct in the late Middle Ages and conjunct again in 1891–92, will help the collective plumb its depths and sort out the good, the bad, and the ugly as it takes humankind to physical and metaphysical realms not yet fully realized or imagined. But that tall order can't be fulfilled without help from other planetary energies.

The conjunction of Uranus and Neptune may finally make it acceptable for people to start talking about a new American Revolution concerning the cosmic strings that tie the world together. We may even see astrology incorporated into university curricula and the World of business. More than a fad or short-term trend, Uranus/Neptune sets off waves of transfiguration that will reverberate throughout the world until the cycle renews itself again and takes Earth to still higher expressions of the ultimate visions offered by each of the planets.

When we begin to understand the influence of each planet individually, we can begin to guess at the fusion of their meanings caused by their interaction. Neptune is the ''somewhere over the rainbow,'' that we never get close to on Earth, not that we don't spend time trying. The result is often sublime music and art, as well as mystical experiences. The planet's desire to dissolve boundaries and meld all of life together often leads some people to devote themselves to serving the poor, sick, and helpless. More often than not, the planet is submerged in the consciousness, and the Neptunian state is reached through alcohol, drugs, or other forms of escapism and delusion. Yet the collective keeps trying for nirvana, and this results in efforts to set up communes, utopian societies, socialism, capitalism, and all manner of institutions that presumably lead humankind to the truth. Neptune was discovered in 1846, just before the publication of the Communist Manifesto, at a time when the working classes were becoming more agitated and Europe was about to experience a record wave of protests (1848) related to class strife and other discontent. The planet of divine discontent never produces the pot of gold. It serves up disappointment and confusion—much like the bittersweet experience of meeting the fantasy lover who ends up being just like everyone else—but new visions and understandings arise out of the disillusionment. Yet every veil lifted from Neptune's fog seems to produce another veil.

Uranus makes a more direct assault. It sounds its clarion call for individuality and freedom. While Neptune is intoxicating the masses with rounds of "We Shall Overcome," individuals, acting on their awakening to Uranus's call to break away from limits and structures, are throwing bombs (some of them real, others in a figurative sense) at all that the Saturnian culture values.

Moving Beyond Saturn

The discovery of a planet beyond Saturn meant that Saturnian authority—as personified by the likes of King George—was no longer an absolute. At the time of the American Revolution and the Declaration of Independence, Uranus, which was discovered in 1781, moving through the sign of Gemini, called for a revolution to bring about greater flexibility and freedom in attitudes, thinking, and environment. The as-yet-undiscovered Neptune was moving through the sign of Virgo, which represents servants, workers, the everyday man, and daily routine—all of whom were embittered enough under Neptune's illusory influence to yearn for something different.

Although the conjunction between Uranus and Neptune only occurs every 172 years, quartering this cycle (every 43 years) provides insight into the critical stages in the overall relationship. The shorter periods have always contained landmark events and other societal trends that speak to the shifts demanded by the planets. The cycle began in 1649 with the beheading of Charles I and Cromwell's crusades in England. The American Revolution was fought at the Last Quarter/Closing Square during the last 43 years of the cycle. The planets were three signs away from each other, with Uranus, the faster-moving planet, coming up from behind, having traveled three-quarters of the zodiac since the conjunction.

Once the cycle renewed itself, in 1820–21, America was flexing its muscles and becoming more concerned about intrusions into the Western Hemisphere, hence the Monroe Doctrine. The start of the First Quarter/Opening Square (planets three signs away, with faster-moving Uranus moving in front) coincided with the end of the American Civil War and the beginning of Reconstruction. The next phase—when the two planets were 180 degrees (six signs) away from each other—coincided with such breakthrough thinking as the 1905 paper in which Einstein first postulated his Theory of Relativity, and the telegraph, automobile, and other inventions were opening up the world. The Last Quarter Closing Square phase (once again, three signs separated the planets) coincided with the post–World War II period that changed the economic order all over the world and also pressed social and racial issues by realigning portions of society in China, America, and other nations.

Reality According to Capricorn

And now we're back at the starting point again, ready for changes that hit at the very expression of life on Earth. Like the 1820–21 renewal, the conjunction in 1992–93 will be in the sign of Capricorn, which is concerned with the fundamental structure of societies and reality. As guardian of tradition, the status quo, and the voice of authority (for example, government and business leaders), Capricorn's domain comprises all the accepted views. A major conjunction like Uranus/Neptune in the sign of Capricorn will work on all of our internal and external structures in ways both obvious and subtle. People in the late 1980s were still revering Capricornian ways of life and thought; there was a longing for the past that is represented by Capricorn and its polar-opposite sign, Cancer. By the time Uranus finishes upsetting Capricorn's applecart in 1996 and Neptune spreads its veil of illusion, glamour, and seduction over Capricornian areas throughout 1998, humankind won't be looking at the same world, because the framework from which we are viewing it—our reality system—will have changed.

That was part of the idea of the celebrations during the Harmonic Convergence of August 16–17, 1987, the date at which millennia-old Mayan and Aztec calendars ended, signaling, some believe, a change in world order. José Arguëlles, the art historian/anthropologist who helped popularize the event, described the time as being similar to moving into the eye of a hurricane. At least 144,000 people were needed to gather at sacred Earth sites around the world and commit themselves to the good of the planet and, in so doing, raise our collective consciousness and energy level. Arguëlles has said that a synchronization between Earth thinking and higher-galaxy intelligence will occur between 1987 and 1992, with the process refining itself through 2012, at which time a new world order will emerge. That Arguëlles's scenario includes visitations from "star people" (possibly former Mayans), whose job it is to help the Earth make the transition from isolation to membership in a galactic federation, often immediately causes people to stop examining the matter. But what if . . . ?

Most of the publicity surrounding the Harmonic Convergence ignored extensive research by Arguëlles and others that shows a correlation between the buildup of world civilizations since 3113 B.C. and cycles outlined by the Mayan calendar. The 5,125-year calendar contains thirteen major cycles that each contain subcycles of 394 years. The 394-year periods are broken into still-smaller twenty subages of about 19 years each. According to Mayan thought, each of the thirteen major periods is characterized by various advance by civilization. The first 394 years (3113–2718 B.C.) is presumably the point at which activation and preparation of Earth for future galactic membership began. At that time, ideas were being planted, the upper and lower portions of Egypt were merging, Sumeria was expanding, and the construction of Stonehenge began. The final 394 years of the cycle (A.D. 1618–2012) shows civilization making major industrial and technological gains and furthering the mechanistic paradigm to its extreme. Resulting Earth changes and other societal problems help deliver the message that a new way of viewing the Universe is needed. The problems presumably became most evident in 1987, as Earth, which Arguëlles says is passing through a galactic beam that is the equivalent of 5,125 years in diameter, moves through the eye of the storm en route to the final stages of synchronization.

What comes next is something that Arguëlles says causes even his imagination to stop in its tracks. But he and others speak of a global Earth civilization that learns to use its etheric body and senses, and to retrieve knowledge and tap other inner sources that are now only recognized in science fiction novels. Problems such as the growing energy shortage will be met as humankind learns to use its own "light body"—an internal system not yet generally recognized mainstream—to communicate with and harness power from the Sun. The rampant materialism and greed that squander Mother Earth's resources and set people against one another will be a mode of life that the entire planet works together to transform.

Not Ready for Prime Time

Even if one were to admit the possibility of only a few projections, it is obvious that human civilization has a very rocky trip on the way to any semblance of a global human family, never mind being able to live next door to "star people." This chapter and the ones that follow show how numerous cycles are conspiring to increasingly make such concepts as global government and telepathic/light bodies that harness power from the Sun not just plausible but inevitable stages in the process of our planet realizing its purpose. A subsequent chapter on Pluto describes the painful process of growth—death and transformation—under way in areas of life ranging from sexual and race relations to the collective use of financial and environmental resources.

For now, though, it's important to keep our discussion down to Earth. Talk of people beaming their "light bodies" up to the Sun to pick up a few quarts of energy is too far removed from the lives of people who must be in the office tomorrow at 8 A.M. But even if intergalactic scenarios seem too farfetched to accept, it's not difficult for people to look around them and see that most institutions—education, economic, therapeutic, religious, environmental—are beset with problems they can't solve. The more society advances in its high-technology achievements, the further back we seem to step in our ability to handle most other concerns. It is the view that Mother Earth is apart from "life," something to dominate and control, that has destroyed rain forests, promoted acid rain, and hurled so many pollutants into the air that we now must worry about the ozone layer. Those who see the functions of business and finance as separate from other human activities produce economic reports that are as useless as bubble-gum fortunes. Until recently physicians who dared to promote self-healing and a link between psychological and emotional states and terminal illnesses could be waved off as quacks. Pioneers such as Dr. Bernie Siegel are getting more respect from their colleagues, but physicians have a long way to go before accepting wider use of holistic care.

When Paradigms Shift

In an age when a killer disease such as AIDS can be transported around the world as quickly as the two-and-a-half-hour Concorde ride between New York and Paris, the message is clear: Problems with health epidemics, economies, education, and the environment are interconnected globally. And while the solution would obviously reveal itself to be global in scope, it is also becoming increasingly clear that a multidisciplinary approach that draws on what a range of fields have to say is needed. Biologists, sociologists, urban/rural planners, psychologists, economists—experts from all fields—must talk with one another. And from the synthesis of knowledge and intuition, and the common threads and patterns offered by each of the disciplines, they will help steer us to more integrated solutions to all of the Earth's problems.

What's under attack and being called up for an overhaul is the rationalistic, linear thinking that has dominated the Western world since Isaac Newton and René Descartes's works began pushing society in this direction in the seventeenth century. Without the legacy handed down from these men, the world would never have been able to step into a scientific revolution and launch the industrialization, computerization, and other benefits humankind knows today. As physicist Fritjof Capra observes in *The Tao of Physics*,

> It is now becoming apparent that overemphasis on the scientific method and on the rational, has led to attitudes that are profoundly anti-ecological. In truth, the understanding of ecosystems is hindered by the very nature of the rational mind. Rational thinking is linear, whereas ecological awareness arises from an intuition of nonlinear systems. One of the most difficult things for people in our culture to understand is the fact that if you do something that is good, then more of the same will not necessarily be better.

A move away from this rationalistic, linear approach is the "paradigm shift" associated with the 1992–93 Uranus/Neptune conjunction. A paradigm is a frame of thought or system for explaining reality. Since the seventeenth century the dominant paradigm has been a view that the Earth and the rest of the solar system work like a machine, which an ever-evolving humankind can study and learn to control. Physicists in the twentieth century increasingly began coming up against experimental results and other findings indicating that Newton's laws and paradigm were limited.

The paradigm shift that is making itself more evident in the 1990s has been working its way through various portions of society, changing the way we look at reality and our understanding of it, for most of the twentieth century. But as Thomas Kuhn, who coined the "paradigm shift" concept in science, has observed, it is in the nature of such shifts that the general public isn't aware of it for numerous decades, and those in science who witness the shift often ignore or deny it to their graves because they are overly vested in the old paradigms. Such has been the case within the field of physics, where those supporting Newton's view of a predictable clockwork Universe are at odds with the quantum-mechanics camp that argues for a degree of randomness. To some minds it is difficult to see how both the Newtonian and the quantum camps can be right. Einstein, for instance, while developing theories that opened up new ways of thinking for those who went on to develop quantum mechanics, rejected the idea of randomness, even in the case of minuscule bodies, or quanta. It was in his refutation of quantum mechanics that Einstein said, "I do not believe that God plays dice."

The new paradigm will eventually reconcile the Newtonian and quantum views, finally providing the unified field theory that eluded Einstein and that others chase today. The search for a unified theory, however, can be expanded to include numerous areas of knowledge, all which must be drawn on and integrated as humankind moves into the twenty-first century. Capra's *Tao of Physics* discusses the ways in which physicists confronted with the limitations of the Newtonian worldview began reassessing their work and have often come to see that their view of reality is coming closer and closer to that held by Eastern mystics, who are noted for their appreciation for the subtle interrelatedness between everything in the Universe. A similar journey must be taken by experts from other fields, as well as by private individuals. In his later work, *The Turning Point*, Capra writes of those physicists who had to "revise many of their basic concepts about reality."

The experience of questioning the very basis of their conceptual framework and of being forced to accept profound modifications of their most cherished ideas was dramatic and often painful for those scientists, especially during the first three decades of the century, but it was rewarded by deep insights into the nature of matter and the human mind.

Changing Realities Throughout Society

As the physicists continue their search in the 1990s, the Uranus/Neptune conjunction and the secondary Capricorn zodiacal influence will make the shift even more evident as others in society also seek to understand new realities. While the following issues are shaped by other planetary influences as well, the conjunction will be working in some of these key areas:

- The dissolving of tariff borders within the European Common Market is an example of the move toward synthesis and interconnectedness. The European Economic Community was founded at a critical point in the Uranus/Neptune cycle ending in 1992 (more on this later), so the re-creation of a new economic system as the cycle renews itself suggests the importance of this move to the evolving world order.
- Another "anniversary" related to the last Uranus/Neptune cycle poses both economic and defense concerns for the United States as it relates to Central and South America. The Monroe Doctrine, which claimed the Western Hemisphere as the United States' territory, was enacted two years after the 1820–21 Uranus/Neptune conjunction. With this configuration renewing itself in the same part of the zodiac as the adoption of the Doctrine, expect this "worldview" to undergo challenge and further realignment. U. S. activity will no doubt expand—as will communism—setting up situations that could lead to confrontations more difficult than those already experienced.
- While the United States will be a player as the economies of the world become even more intertwined, our country's spiraling trade deficit, a result of restrictive import rules in other nations as well as the United States' difficulty adjusting to changing economic realities, will continue to be a problem, particularly as the service economy expands while manufactured goods continue to be imported. Cor-

porate restructuring will continue to dissolve both blue- and white-collar jobs. A growing labor shortage caused by the small baby-bust generation (1965–75), in addition to the rising illiteracy among the nation's young, will decrease the country's competitiveness. Infrastructure (bridges, etc.) will increasingly demand costly repairs, but the bonds for such work may not look so attractive in the early 1990s.

- The economic interconnectedness throughout the world will make countries more readily see the need for international task forces to battle problems ranging from health epidemics to the environmental catastrophes that will continue to send smoke signals about its fragile state.

- The United States will make a series of alterations that will be the result of changing views and premises about the nature of our government. That most dreaded Constitutional Convention, with agenda items that strike at some of the country's founding principles, could happen in the second half of the decade.

- Life-style pressures such as the family/work concerns brought about by limited day care are certainly on the agenda for the nineties. Companies must accommodate employees who are being asked to care for aging parents. Work is dominating people's lives. But growing disillusionment indicates that American workers, particularly those born after World War II, are looking for changes in how they spend their workday.

- Neptune, the planet of escapism and drugs, moving through the sign of government and business, runs deals in the highest reaches of society. The National Institute on Alcohol Abuse estimates that substance abuse is costing the workplace more than *$80 billion*. Twenty percent of workers abuse drugs and alcohol. The war against drugs at the office and on the street continues. But nothing gets better until societal leaders address ethical and spiritual decay.

- Metaphysics: Some forms of astrology and related esoteric sciences will get more mainstream respect and attention. Astrology already integrates the Newtonian appreciation for mechanical laws with the quantum-mechanics preference for "probabilities" and approximations.

Shorter Cycles Help Put It Together

That many of the trends mentioned above are evident to most readers is a result of two important shorter-term (thirty-six- and forty-five-year) cycles working in tandem with the Uranus/Neptune conjunction. Saturn conjuncts Uranus every forty-five to forty-six years (most recently in 1988) and it conjuncts Neptune every thirty-five to thirty-six years (1989). The Saturn/Neptune conjunction has always been at critical points in its cycle during events that have resulted in collective depression, confusion, and sometimes irrationality. Brief examples are the Rosenburg trial, the John F. Kennedy assassination, and the taking of hostages in Iran. The U.S., like the rest of the world, doesn't feel good about itself during certain phases of this cycle. One's view of reality (Saturn) tends to become eroded, undermined by Neptune, while Neptunian ideals come up against the bitter demands and limitations of Saturn.

The Saturn/Uranus cycle—the conjunction occurred in 1988—is involved with confrontations between reform urges and attempts at suppression. Throughout history it has corresponded with a range of events that have included war actions and red scares, such as the McCarthy hearings and the clashes between the establishment and antiwar movements of the mid–1960s. Certainly there are positive manifestations of all these energies. The collective, however, does not move with as much conscious will as individuals do, which is why the negative manifestations are often realized more readily. Knowledge of Astrocycles could alter this course.

These shorter-term cycles (Saturn/Neptune and Saturn/Uranus) will be explored in more detail after the 172-year cycle and its quarter phases and zodiacal placement are examined further.

Uranus/Neptune and Signs of the Times

While the actual conjunction (every 172 years) of Uranus and Neptune is more significant than its zodiac placements, the sign does show specific areas of life where the conjunction will have the most influence:

Moving through Taurus, as it did during the so-called Gilded Age, Neptune related to the idealization of Taurean matters, such as wealth, property, and economic systems, which were all eventually dissolved and became sources of loss and disappointment before Neptune left the sign. Uranus in Taurus, most recently during the last half of the Great Depression, shook up world economic systems and produced a revolution with, for example, Social Security.

From 1971 to 1984 Neptune in Sagittarius coincided with the "me" decade. Sagittarius's rulership over the higher mind meant that Neptune in this sign coincided with the rise of cults and new religions, and it made a mishmash of the education system. Uranus moving through this sign from 1981 to 1988 sounded the call for reforms that Neptune's transit of Sagittarius had heightened the need for. Uranus got people talking about reforms in the Catholic church, about doing something about our schools, and about the need to treat the international business world—particularly the issues of imports and exports—more seriously. At the beginning of this century, when Uranus was in Sagittarius, sign of long-distance journeys, the Wright brothers took off from Kitty Hawk and car companies were being formed to move people around the world.

Now Uranus and Neptune are both in Capricorn, highlighting all matters associated with this sign (and indirectly its polarity, opposite sign Cancer). So while the Capricornian concerns for tradition, status, careers, and the workplace are undergoing changes, the emotional and personal lives of people, and the basic family unit itself—all of which are Cancerian—are feeling the Neptunian influence. Neptune moving into Capricorn, opposite Cancer (where it was in 1901–1914), marks times when the world is idealizing its national heritage, its sense of territory, and when people make a special effort to extol the virtues of home and hearth. (Mother's Day was founded when Neptune was in Cancer, and suffragettes were pushed back into the kitchen.). Although Capricorn is traditional and family-oriented, it's still much ado about business, which explains the booming increase that the U.S. Census Bureau is reporting in home-based businesses. Many of these businesses are being run by women, who are starting businesses at one-and-a-half times the rate of men. But even if people aren't working there, the home becomes more important when Neptune is moving through these traditional signs. Market researchers such as Faith Popcorn have helped spread the word that the couch potato is in, while manufacturers are producing more pastel—lavender, powder-blue, pink—home appliances. Pastels are Neptunian.

Neptune in Capricorn is the disillusionment people are having with work and large corporations, resulting in redefinitions of both. Demands for job sharing, part-time, temporary or free-lance opportunities have increased. But some of the changes people are making aren't voluntary. The restructuring of corporations and the continued buildup of factory closings or relocations are changing the lives of many, a trend that has been accelerating throughout the 1980s. More than three million white-collar jobs have been lost in the 1980s, despite the robust stock market activity, which people often mistakenly think is the true barometer of the nation's health.

Despite the farm crisis, increased homelessness, and other apparent problems, the country's leaders and forecasters, through most of the 1980s, chose not to look behind Neptune's veil. Instead they opted to focus on the trends that seem more positive. This was the general tack that economists took when assessing the effects of the October 19, 1987, stock market crash several months later. The experts chose to concentrate on the fact that the crash didn't move us into an immediate depression, a stance that is accurate on the surface, but that overlooks more long-term developing trends.

The increased layoffs and other growing economic problems have some relationship to the general economic disturbances that occur whenever the planet Neptune moves into Earth signs (Capricorn, Taurus, and Virgo). Astrologer Barry Lynes correlates Neptune's travels through Earth signs to the exacerbated economic problems that proponents of the Kondratieff Wave estimate occur every fifty-four years. Neptune in Capricorn from 1820 to 1834, in Taurus from 1875 to 1888, and in Virgo from 1929 to 1942 were all marked by the chaotic bank conditions, recessions, and problems that Lynes outlines in his book *Astro-Economics*.

Some of the more pressing needs for reform will be revealed by Uranus, which will be moving through Capricorn until 1996. Uranus may actually love upsetting Capricorn more than it does any other sign. While Uranus is the call of the wild, Capricorn can be, to put it bluntly, uptight and rigid. When Uranus is allowed to run Capricorn's show, the Earth sees radical government actions and legislation that hit at the very structure of the government, business, and the nation. While the Tax Code and the Federal Reserve Act were not enacted until Uranus moved into Aquarius, in 1912, the 1913 debate began when Uranus was in Capricorn. The 1905 paper on the Theory of

Relativity, like other scientific breakthroughs of the time, was concerned with the "structure" of the physical Universe. That was Capricorn's way of asking, "What's out there?"

When Uranus was in Capricorn's polar-opposite sign, Cancer, from 1949 to 1956, the world was just coming out of a world war, and everyone was concerned about rebuilding family, home, and state. In the United States the GI Bill and other government measures helped build up the suburbs and the home-with-the-picket-fence, a way of life that Neptune in Capricorn is currently idealizing. Expect attempts by many to restore this life-style, and a resulting bitterness from people who either can't afford the house or haven't yet found the right mate with whom to share a home. The increase in childbirths and the return of more women to their homes after battling in the workplace are indeed part of a trend. Though the Census Bureau reports that more than half of all new mothers return to work, many of these are deluded Neptunian attempts to actualize a perfect life and time that was never really there. Family units have merit and are necessary, but the nuclear family became a minority by the late 1970s, and cycles never reach backward. Elements of the past are taken forward and transformed into something new. Economic, social, and psychological changes under way are such that Mother, Father, Dick, Jane, and Sally will never be the same way we left them.

While the upcoming conjunction begins a cycle that will take 172 years to unfold, and for which the critical First Quarter won't be reached until the year 2033, a look at the cycle now being completed should illuminate our current place in history.

The Cycle's Phases

Some forty-three years after the conjunction of 1821, that ushered in the rapid growth of industrialization in America, Uranus and Neptune are 90 degrees away (three signs) from each other and form an Opening Square/First Quarter phase. This square was last in operation as the Civil War ended and the country was forced to rebuild in what was known as Reconstruction; Europe, too, underwent further industrialization.

Of special note here is that the United States, following Emancipation, was also forced for the first time to deal with a free black population. In addition to the more widely reported problems in the South, poor white immigrants in the North rallied against freedmen and recently freed slaves out of fear of losing their jobs. Issues of egalitarian relationships, whether between classes or between races, show up in other portions of the Uranus/Neptune cycle, though some of the more unconscious power struggles and interactions that are race-derived have a Pluto connection.

Uranus and Neptune in Opposition

When Uranus and Neptune reach the midpoint of the 172-year cycle and attempt to give a name and form to the radical ideals that started to form at the conjunction, these planets explode like a Fourth of July sky. The most recent opposition loosely took place from 1903 to 1910, though the tightest opposition was in 1905 to 1908, when Sigmund Freud was doing for the unconscious what Einstein was doing for the sky. By looking at the opposition in the years just before and just after exactitude, we take in activities such as the flight of the Wright brothers, the adoption of antitrust measures, as well as the beginning of union organizing and uprisings, and the founding of the National Association for the Advancement of Colored People (NAACP) as examples of the way society was being reorganized on social and economic levels in the United States. Various activities around the world were setting the stage for conflicts that hit directly at the ideologies and isms governing the world. With the Boer War over, the Union of South Africa declared its independence and was busy setting up racial and ethnic barriers. Separatist actions in Europe had nearly everyone ready to go to war once it came, only two to three years after the opposition period ended, while the Russians got their revolution a few years down the road. The upsurge of feminism (Neptune was in the domestic sign of Cancer) in the fight for the right to vote and other inroads into society, was an example of the social redistribution that is a critical aspect of Uranus/ Neptune phases.

The growth of Cubism, which through its geometric distortions reveals less apparent essences of art forms, captures the idea of colliding paradigms and world orders better than many of the special-interest movements of the time.

The phase was at its most potent during the final years around 1955 through 1957; Uranus and Neptune were in a loose square (three signs away) relationship to each other beginning in 1949.

World events reflect the animosity that planets in square have for one another. America and other countries were building up after World War II, but people in China and Korea were launching revolutions to free themselves. In America the race issue, which became unavoidable when the planets were in First Quarter/Opening Square phase after slavery, was now being addressed in the courts. The year 1949 saw the desegregation of the army, as well as the beginning of several civil rights–related cases that would ultimately give impetus to the *Brown* v. *Board of Education* desegregation decision issued in 1954. Rosa Parks, with the help of Martin Luther King, Jr., won victories in Montgomery, Alabama. In contrast, South Africa, its separatist cause being boosted further by Nazi and fascist affiliates no longer diverted by World War II, codified apartheid in 1950.

It would be nearly impossible to come up with precise predictions about the phases within the 172-year rhythm renewing itself in 1992. The midpoint of any cycle can be expected to host a repolarization of initiatives and concepts that were being birthed at the conjunction, and certainly the 1905 midpoint period of the Uranus/Neptune conjunction of 1820–21 was a turning-point period for the industrialist society still in its infancy in the early nineteenth century. But since the midpoint of the 1992–93 conjunction doesn't break out and reveal its intent until 2078, it's obvious there are many more immediate concerns for most people reading this book. People being born on the 1992–93 conjunction will have a special affinity with 2078, as the chapter on the ''Astrology of Generations'' will show. But they'll play a more active role as society goes through economic and social shifts in 2035, when Uranus and Neptune are three signs away from each other in the First Quarter/Opening Square phase of their 172-year cycle.

Whether there will be an Earth from which to experience this cycle in 2035 depends on more immediate challenges indicated by the 1992–93 conjunction and accompanying shorter-term rhythms. The 1989–92 corridor, and then again the final three years of the century, show some major cycles at their most intense. Saturn's encounters with Uranus and Neptune, and the subsequent renewal of thirty-six- and forty-five-year rhythms, are among the factors to consider.

Saturn Meets Uranus

(Conjunction, 1988–89; First Quarter, 1999–2000; Midpoint, 2011; Last Quarter, 2022)

Saturn meets (conjuncts) Uranus every forty-five to forty-six years. Some of the meaning of this rhythm can be found in the relationship between Chronos, the father of time, and Uranos, the free-spirited sky god. Chronos, as the story goes, castrated Uranos, making him creatively impotent. A similar correspondence between status quo, establishment groups, and reformers seems to be highlighted on Earth when Saturn and Uranus meet (conjunct) in the sky. New ideas and forms are trying to be born amid a struggle by more established systems and forms to exercise control.

Most recently the conjunction has correlated with Supreme Court attempts to restrict civil rights and freedom of speech, a trend that will continue as these rights get redefined. Court rulings restricting abortion, though having more Plutonian overtones, are a result of the Saturn/Uranus fight. Saturn's conjunction with Uranus took place in the final degrees of Sagittarius. Traveling in Sagittarius from 1986 to 1989, Saturn sought to redefine and regulate the airline industry, education, and religious organizations. It oversaw discussions on ethics and told public officials and other leaders that they'd better live by the belief systems they espouse. Saturn, in such a globe-trotting, expansionist sign as Sagittarius, helped pen legislation dealing with trade restrictions. It also started to push limitations on expansionist tendencies within businesses, setting the stage for the more extensive cutbacks and freezes that occur with Saturn in Capricorn. The media were among the notable Sagittarian casualties as decreased advertising caused newspapers and magazines, including normally deep-pocket and generous national media, to cut back budgets and lay off staff.

Past Saturn/Uranus conjunctions saw world powers begin moves toward a world economy and greater interconnectedness and communication (the conjunction was in late Taurus and early Gemini), goals that gained currency during the Depression and the war building in Europe. In addition to the worldwide struggles under way, the United States' attempts to block Japan's expansion into Southeast Asia, a conflict that eventually led to the attack at Pearl Harbor, represents the idea of authority in the form of the United States castrating Japan for its attempts at greater independence and individuality. The United States was involved in similarly motivated struggles in the Philippines in the late 1890s during a Saturn/Uranus conjunction. The 1896 *Plessy* v. *Ferguson* decision gave segregationists the ammunition they needed to keep separate bathrooms, schools, and other facilities until the mid-1950s. The Fugitive Slave Law in 1850, a year of other potent planetary energies, is another example of the assault on individual liberties that the conjunction can represent. The 1850 decision set the tone for the volatile *Dred Scot* Supreme Court decision three years later that, in its support of slavery even in a nonslave state, is viewed by scholars and historians as having made the Civil War inevitable.

And while astrologers in America were ridiculed when the Saturn/Uranus conjunction brought them into the news in 1988, the 1941 conjunction coincided with the Gestapo's rounding up of astrologers and throwing them into concentration camps after Rudolf Hess fled to Scotland, allegedly on the advice of his astrologer. Politicking and the support of Aryan astrology, or something of the sort, kept some astrologers out of jail, but the point is that simple freedoms, too often taken for granted, come under attack under this conjunction.

The Saturn/Uranus cycle every forty-five to forty-six years can also be quartered. The most recent First Quarter–Opening Square after the 1941 conjunction coincides with the McCarthy hearings, while the Last Quarter saw newly elected Jimmy Carter launching human-rights battles. Bhutto, accused of extensive assaults on human rights, was ousted in a coup. But Sadat went to Israel later in the year, which shows that the news isn't always bad when Saturn meets up with Uranus. This Last Quarter phase in particular shows some issues resolving themselves, or at least starting to move in that direction because of lessons learned at other points in the cycle.

During the Opposition phase of the mid-1960s, the opposing Saturn/Uranus principles seemed to be epitomized, though a range of more potent configurations were also at work. But the opposition (six signs away) of 1917, and the accompanying Bolshevik takeover in Russia, shows that revolutionaries and status-quo types can take many different forms.

Generational influences involving Saturn/Uranus are touched on in a later chapter. The lives of the many 1941–42 babies, who were born with the conjunction and came of age in the sixties, certainly show that there can be positive manifestations of any planetary configuration. The mass mind is harder to steer. The events that highlight the Saturn/Uranus struggle at its midpoint in 2011—many of the trade issues and civil liberties questions will be on the table—will take a more urgent form. And before that time the Opening Square of 1999 indicates that we'll be entering the twenty-first century struggling with the issue of how much freedom individuals are going to be given by their governments. Americans shouldn't think the issue is something that only those in more repressive societies need worry about. A restrictive trend through much of the nineties will cause those in the United States to be concerned about inherent rights as opposed to government-granted privileges. The following chapter elaborates on this.

Saturn Meets Neptune

(Conjunction, 1989; First Quarter, 1998; Midpoint, 2007; Last Quarter, 2016)

Saturn, the planet of restrictions, limitations, and sometimes-bitter reality, got together with the elusive discontent (Neptune), whose ideals and dreams are often hard to bring into focus, in 1989 to begin a thirty-six-year cycle. The result? Disappointment, manic stages, or as Jimmy Carter described one Saturn/Neptune time, "a national malaise."

Those were the words Carter used to describe the mood of the country in the summer of 1979—before he really knew how much malaise would overtake us—in a televised speech he gave after a few days away at Camp David. He had invited "just ordinary folk" to Camp David to help him put his finger on what was wrong with the country and his administration. Inflation was frustrating many, and the gas rationings (Neptune is gas, and Saturn in aspect to Neptune can limit the gas or oil supply) hadn't made Carter a popular person. In 1979 Saturn and Neptune were making a 90-degree angle (three signs apart) to each other and were in the last quarter of a cycle that had begun in 1953.

This cycle has had an interesting connection with efforts by people to give structure and form (Saturn) to an ideal (Neptune), such as communism. Both the 1847 publication of the Communist Manifesto and the Bolshevik Revolution in 1917–18 coincided with Saturn/Neptune conjunctions (with help from the Saturn/Uranus cycle, mentioned above). Since communism is obviously unworkable and controversial in the form that the world has seen it, it may be difficult for some to grasp the power that this planetary aspect has to give form to dreams. More positive examples can be found in the peace treaties signed following the Korean War in 1953 and World War I in 1918.

The frustration Carter experienced speaks to some features of this configuration that work on the psyches and confidence of the masses. The Opening Square, and its correlation with the Kennedy assassination, shows some of the lost faith and betrayal that difficult Saturn/Neptune configurations can represent. The Opposition (Saturn and Neptune six signs away) was at its most potent a few months before the Watergate break-in and coincided with droughts in Asia and Africa and increasing economic problems around the world. In the Last Quarter period, in 1979, Carter was dampening spirits with his talk about the loss of confidence that people had in the United States. "Say something good about America" he had exhorted in what became an infamous speech during that July 1979. He followed the speech with the firing of several cabinet members, got rid of Andrew Young at the United Nations, and was so blinded and unclear about the realities around him that he never recouped. The hostage takeover in November pretty much ended his presidency.

Knowledge of this cycle certainly can provide the impetus for the development of strategies to get through the crisis. Armed with an ephemeris, Carter could even have told viewers when the "malaise" would lift, because it would be seen in the context of all the other cycles (issues) on the table.

The Saturn/Neptune conjunction of 1989, which found the country dealing with a growing disillusionment and frustration with existing institutions, structures, and the people who run them, initiated a cycle that will be in effect for the next thirty-six years. It's difficult to separate this cycle, and the Saturn/Uranus cycle, from the big picture. But the Saturn/Neptune configuration speaks to a need to redefine realities as they're expressed in areas ranging from economics to spirituality. Saturn and Capricorn (the sign where the conjunction occurs) both build their life structures thinking that as long as they stick to certain rules, there won't be any surprises. Neptune, however, undermines everything it touches. Not being as direct as Uranus, it is able to pass out the drugs (narcotics, money, status, prestige, whatever you want) under the guise of glamour, ecstasy, transcendentalism.

The midpoint of the cycle, in 2007, will find society in a better position to assess the subsequent disillusionment, as well as some of the remedies and redefined structures that are emerging as a result of the conjunction. Efforts such as Polish Solidarity's government initiatives, launched under the Saturn/Neptune conjunction, would be at an important development phase (the Opening Square of 1998 would be of special interest also). Even George Bush's Drug Wars—as well as other vague initiatives of 1989—show the idealistic side of Neptune looking to be made manifest through Saturn. This is not a battle that this or any other country will win without doing some reevaluation and metaphysical reorientation (from the highest levels of society), so expect future points in the phase to magnify the problems. Although Sagittarius, too, is concerned with ethics, Capricorn has to be concerned about the actual conduct of society's leaders, so the conjunction of Saturn/Neptune in Capricorn hammers on the issue even more than Saturn did while traveling through Sagittarius. Neptune, as the planet of ideals, has some relation to ethics, but often it indicates deception and a lack of ethics, which is the face it is showing presently. Saturn and Neptune moving together can indicate bankruptcy in the literal sense, but the idea can be extended to society's moral fabric.

On a general note, Neptune's travels in Aquarius, and Saturn's in Leo, during 2007 suggests special tensions in societies where individual expression is valued over more collective policies. This seems to suggest shades of communism or more collective forms of government up against more libertarian tendencies.

The Opening Square of 1998, working with other configurations, can indicate ideals getting blindsided by external realities. This angle between the two planets would find the country at the same point it was in 1963, as the rhythm begun in 1953 hit its Opening Square. But none of the configurations can be viewed as being totally negative. Saturn and Neptune working together can give form to ideals and dreams, and this is what society must always keep as the ultimate goal when working with the more depressing indicators.

And On to 1992

But we have the 1990s to live through before thinking about how these cycles will shape up far into the twenty-first century. The upcoming Uranus/Neptune conjunction (once every 172 years) shows the outlines of the big picture. While we haven't yet imagined some of the challenges we face, increased concern about day care, the aged, and welfare reform, like many other issues outlined in this chapter, are already showing themselves to be increasing priorities. The economy has been toying with some of our leaders, making them think that it's going to continue to be strong, but that doesn't appear to be the coming trend. Shortsightedness will continue to get corporate America and the rest of the nation's businesses in trouble. While the Uranus/Neptune conjunction isn't official until the planets reach 19 degrees of Capricorn in February 1993, the effect of the upcoming conjunction is being felt around the world even now. Moreover, the shorter-term cycles that kicked off in 1989— particularly the Saturn/Neptune conjunction and the Jupiter/ Saturn opposition in mid-fall—point to forced adjustment and changes in relation to the economy, as well as foreign policy, throughout the early nineties. George Bush has major economic and moral problems piling up that will force major decisions during 1990–92. The victor of the 1992 presidential election will also be faced with major cleanups. Though the trends don't suggest easy times, periods of disintegration always pave the way for creative individuals to help implement new approaches and ideas. They become the men and woman whose actions synchronize with the needs of the time, which is how great times and great men and women are made.

FIFTEEN

Liberals, Conservatives, and the Jupiter/Saturn Cycle

There were many signs of a retreat from our obsession with acquisitions during the 1980s, even before George Bush went on record against rampant materialism in his inaugural address. *Newsweek* magazine made the pronouncement on its cover—THE 80s ARE OVER—during the last week of 1987. Some of this sentiment was certainly caused by the October 19, 1987, stock market crash, which forced Wall Streeters and many others to lower their expectations and scale back their more exorbitant displays of greed. But the shift in values had been brewing long before things went bad on Wall Street. Events like the October crash are held mainly for people who need literal warnings. Historians and social commentators, accustomed to taking a long view of societal changes, knew that Reaganomics was just a phase the country was going through. This camp was looking to the 1988 and 1992 elections to bring more moderate leaders in to oversee attempts to balance the extremes of the Reagan era and address the growing social and economic concerns. Elections to the House and Senate began reflecting this coming trend during the 1986 races held in Reagan's second term.

There was no crystal-ball gazing at work here. Academics and political commentators who saw the conservative and acquisitive 1980s giving way to a more moderate period were drawing on a historical rhythm. It is one that has seen Americans, at fairly predictable intervals, alternate their interest between government-sponsored social and economic initiatives, such as those in the 1960s, with the more private-sector interests of the 1980s. From this vantage point, the end of the 1980s and the move toward a more public-spirited 1990s was inevitable and necessary because of a range of socioeconomic factors.

A major proponent of this view is historian Arthur M. Schlesinger, Jr. Drawing on ideas formulated by his father and historian Henry Adams, he argues that the country experiences periods of "public purpose" when government and social programs for the overall good are favored by leaders and the public, and then the tide turns to a period of "private interest." Each period contains intensities and contradictions that will eventually pave the way for its antecedent to emerge. "People can never be fulfilled for long in the public or private sphere," Schlesinger writes. "As political eras, whether dominated by public purpose or by private interests, run their course, they infallibly invent the desire for something different." Usually societal circumstances—the economy, some social issue— emerge that can't be ignored and they help set the tone and provide the transition into the next era.

And that was essentially the scenario revealing itself in the late 1980s and setting the agenda for the 1990s. Housing, the budget deficit, trade imbalances, and other economic concerns were festering when Reaganomics was launched. The fortieth president was elected when the American people were fighting off inflation and the Ayatollah Khomeni, when the times demanded a buildup of private- and free-enterprise interests to make the country feel good about itself again. After the perceived weakness of Carter and liberal policies, Reagan was the man for the times. Once Reaganomics had its turn in Washington, the 1988 election indicated a need to move toward the middle again, and the 1992 election will carry this theme further. Increased concern about the economy and America's role in the world will necessitate more public involvement.

Though some are critical of Schlesinger's analysis because of his connections to Kennedy's Camelot, objective corroborations on the theory can be found in the cyclic relationships between Jupiter and Saturn. Moreover, this cycle, which is renewed every twenty years, when these two planets are conjunct, will also give insight into underlying trends and rhythms at work well into the twenty-first century. In other words, we can write our own political tipsheet—"Cycles in Future American History"—by knowing about the related cycles of Jupiter and Saturn. As the previous chapter indicated, much of the 1990s will be especially challenging on a number of social and economic fronts. While the ultimate trends are indicated further out in the solar system—through configurations involving Uranus, Neptune, and Pluto—Jupiter and Saturn show how we digest the trends, particularly in terms of policies and government.

The 1990s: Remaking Society

The trends associated with Jupiter and Saturn show America and other countries spending more time on "social engineering" and tinkering with the specifics of how their societies are run, applying more scrutiny to questions about individuals' and governments' relationship and responsibilities to society and community. This trend will be more apparent in 1991 as Saturn begins to move through its Aquarius/Pisces transits. This planetary movement parallels the period in American history that correlates to a time when the needs and demands of the masses require special attention. Saturn's ride through this portion of the sky has coincided with some of the most massive strikes in the country's history (500,000 plus), attempts to reform the Supreme Court, the passage of legislation such as the Food and Drug Administration Act, aimed at making life better for the masses, the making and adoption of the U.S. Constitution, and the inauguration of George Washington as the country's first president.

The focus is on the organization of society, community; the definition and shaping of goals for "the people." And this energy, on behalf of the masses, doesn't have to express itself in the most progressive ways. The conservative overlay that became evident in 1980–81, while undergoing some moderation, is the dominating influence in the 1990s. And some of the initiatives taken on behalf of society such as further protections for the flag or restrictions on abortion, reveal the conservative bent of the Saturnian influence. But simultaneously, economic concerns and other social problems, such as the homeless, the underclasses, and drug infestation, will have to be addressed, though not as expansively as was seen in the

1960s. We can't afford it, but moreover, we've learned that money isn't the only answer.

It's important to emphasize that the projections in this and other chapters are a synthesis of interpretations of a range of cycles and social commentary and analysis, all knit together with intuition and educated guesses. Detailed predictions are impossible because the cycles will never express themselves in exactly the same way they did in the past. Planetary configurations that might appear similar to those in effect during an event like the Great Depression must be viewed with caution because 1990s America is different socially, economically, and structurally than it was in 1930. But we are able to indicate the general direction of various trends in society.

Twenty-Year Rythms

So what is this twenty-year cycle? How does it work?

In putting forth his ideas, Schlesinger opted to describe the alternating trends as an average thirty-year cycle. The private sector dominated in the twenties, fifties, and eighties. He said that some of the more notable public-oriented phases, on the other hand, got their starts in 1901, with the election of Theodore Roosevelt; in 1933, with the election of FDR; and in 1961, with the election of John F. Kennedy. Previous cycle theorists have identified the same alternating phases, but describe the trend somewhat differently, often speaking of fifteen to twenty-year cycles.

The discrepancy is one of semantics more than substance. Studying the Jupiter/Saturn cycle in relation to this trend will actually help refine these theories and show that the rhythm is closer to a twenty-year alternating cycle, with a noticeable moderation period halfway into the twenty-year period. Each of the periods that the historians associate with measurable initiatives in either the public or the private arena, as well as the winding-down periods between such initiatives, coincide, without fail, with either the coming together (conjunction) of Jupiter and Saturn or the 180-degree halfway point in opposition between the two planets. Conjunctions 1921, 1940–41, 1960–61, and 1980–81, to name the most recent alignments, are followed by an opposition about ten years later. The oppositions coincide with the couch-potato fifties and the cooling-down seventies (at least in comparison to the heat of the sixties).

With the opposition in the fall of 1989—working along with other potent cycles—and the move back into orb through most of 1990, policy thrusts and attitudes from the 1980–81 conjunction were to be viewed with a more detached (and in many cases critical) eye. Bush's ''free-lance ad-hoc'' governing style (*Newsweek*'s description) has a hard time translating itself into strong policy direction, but early in his administration there were signs of quiet retreats from past policy. While Bush's savings-and-loan bailout is expected to work alongside domestic and trade-deficit problems to further threaten the country's economic health, Bush made early efforts, albeit mainly symbolic, to open up discussions with the advocates for the homeless and racial minorities, who felt Reagan ignored their concerns. These gestures showed he was aware on some level of a need to address growing alienation among sections of the population.

Governmental Ambassadors

The Jupiter/Saturn opposition—like other configurations between these two planets—has a way of putting specific issues before our politicians. While earlier chapters have addressed the personal rewards and obstacles that Jupiter and Saturn can represent in the lives of individuals, the planets also serve as bureaucrats dedicated to the cause of social organization and good government. Early on, astrologers viewed the planets of expansion and liberalism (Jupiter), and conservatism and restriction (Saturn), as playing a role in the question of political trends, associating the conjunction with changes in political administrations and policy. It was the Jupiter-Saturn conjunction in 6 B.C., working along with other cycles, including an eclipse, that summoned the Magi—aka astrologers, in some translations of the Bible—to Bethlehem to look for the baby Jesus. Johannes Kepler and others have hypothesized that a gathering of the Sun, Venus, and other planets near the conjunction in March or April was the ''Christmas Star'' that caused the ''wise men'' to travel to Bethlehem. Jupiter was the planet of kings, and Saturn was connected with time and the Hebrew people. The conjunctions of these planets, according to *Moore's Almanac* of 1762, ''have been constantly observed to dispose of times.''

Discoveries of Uranus, Neptune, and Pluto have given as-

trologers planets that coincide with bigger, more ultimate
trends, so today an astrologer would not assign such absolute
responsibility to Jupiter and Saturn, the way the *Moore's Almanac* does. Nonetheless these two planets still have a major
correlation with economic, social, and political trends. The
symbolism associated with the planets would demand nothing
less. Jupiter is the planet of expansion, assimilation, integration. It is the principle that embraces the individual's relationship to society. Saturn, in the most extreme sense, represents
tradition and structure. Working together on a social/political
level, Jupiter and Saturn perform a certain custodial service
for the longer-term, more psychological, and destiny-oriented
cycles. Their connection with laws and public administration
allows them to act as a check and balance to the operation of
society. While Neptune's ideals and Plutonian motivations may
not be as direct and obvious to us, Jupiter and Saturn speak to
the basic functioning of society. They help provide the plat-
form, through legislation and other vehicles, to implement the
vision of the three slower-moving planets. Uranus, Neptune,
and Pluto represent society's ultimate end. They show where
the collective is moving and the issues it must work through.
But in society at large, Jupiter and Saturn represent the shorter-
term trends and social adjustments we move through to reach
these ends.

And while the Jupiter/Saturn cycle can be more readily identified with American history because the election process and
two-party system of Democrats (Liberals) and Republicans
(Conservatives) often looks like a fight between the two planets,
the cycle resonates around the world. The last Jupiter/Saturn
conjunction (1980–81) corresponded to Margaret Thatcher's
overhauls in England, as well as to economic shifts all over
the world. Lech Walesa and the Solidarity movement in Poland
manifested with this conjunction. (And Solidarity was recognized officially as Jupiter and Saturn move toward the 180-
degree opposition six signs apart from one another.)

Everything derives from what has come before. Some people
like to talk about a pendulum shifting from the 1960s to the
1980s, but change doesn't work that way. It is more spirallike,
evolving, and there is no turning back. The 1960s never really
went away. Many ideas—food co-ops and social reforms—
became more legitimized in society. The 1970s politicians reflect the attempt to reconcile some of the more acceptable and
legitimate concerns of the 1960 conjunction with the more

controversial (and sometimes less valid) approaches and ideas. Liberal and Conservative leaders pander to the times and hence were more moderate in their expressions. The Fritz Mondale liberals began to decrease support and association with forced school busing and other social causes. Unlike the Goldwater or Ronald Reagan conservatives, Republican leaders in the early seventies included some of the new sixties thought in their agenda. The 1970s gave Richard Nixon a Democratic Congress, as well as the passage and signing of legislation such as the massive and expensive Section 8 housing program or the progressive Occupational Safety and Health Act, which are liberal by Reagan-era standards. In the same way, the 1988 and 1992 presidential victors are more moderate than Reagan and his men, but they won't be campaigning on giveaway platforms. They exhibit the 1980–81 conservative overlay but adopt proposals and approaches from the more public-oriented side of the scale.

Another warning: Drawing correlations between the 1980s and the 1960s gives more immediacy to the Jupiter/Saturn cycle, but the intense revolutionary changes brought about in the 1960s—the riots, the marches, the assassinations—are related to longer-term cycles. Specifically the 1965–68 period coincided with the conjunction of Uranus and Pluto, a cycle that last occurred in 1850–51 and that is tied to revolutions and sometimes violent transformations in society. Difficult configurations involving Saturn and Neptune, and Saturn and Uranus, also helped give the sixties its cutting edge.

The Jupiter/Saturn conjunction worked in tandem with this cycle in the form of civil rights legislation and other reforms that were rushed through in an effort to head off violence. Periods of reform that coincide with intense planetary conjunctions have an unreal sense of the process of change. The civil rights legislation, for instance, made it punishable by law to discriminate against people, and the 1960s saw a greater willingess on the part of some to accept these ideas. But the general segregation of society and more recent outbreaks of racial and anti-Semitic attacks show the limited level of intercultural understanding in America. Aberrations like the 1960s could be compared to the period following the Civil War. While a number of cycles were at work and coincided with aggravated war and economic activity, the war started around the time of the 1861 Jupiter/Saturn conjunction. The more dynamic cycles involving Uranus, Neptune, and Pluto helped the freed slaves make some immediate gains as the war ended. But the ongoing configurations between Jupiter and Saturn showed society's step-forward/step-backward attempts to incorporate the new world through legislation.

In America in the 1960s, the Uranus/Pluto cycle began in the mid-1960s with calls for the long-term overhaul of the individual and collective use of power. In the short term, calls for individual freedom and threats of revolution seemed to stampede anything in the way. As a result, the Jupiter/Saturn cycle, after moving on after its 1960–61 conjunction, then 1966 First Quarter Square, began reorienting itself for greater balance. By the 1980–81 conjunction the popular argument was that some of the 1960s initiatives may have gone too far; that the ranks of protected classes had grown to include too many ethnic groups; that minority programs were being abused; that despite much legislation few urban housing programs had worked in any long-term way.

The mid-60s Uranus/Pluto conjunction, and other potent cycles, had an urgency about it. But Jupiter and Saturn, working in the trenches, reflects the more gradual way that changes are implemented to bring about the balance necessary for both sides of an argument to flourish. The 1980s conservatives who launched the most aggressive attacks against the sixties would have ideally liked to wipe out all of the social programs and taken away gains such as the Voting Rights Act of 1965 and the protections for women. More liberal-minded activists were correct in fighting to retain basic civil rights legislation but often weren't willing to trash useless and expensive job programs. Time seems to have the real veto power.

The Cycle

Like most of the cycles studied, the Jupiter/Saturn relationship can be quartered so that some of the most dynamic critical periods can be understood in a fashion similar to the Sun/Moon phase. At each twenty-year point there is a conjunction, when new seeds are planted and initiatives launched. About five years after the conjunction comes the First Quarter/Opening Square, which coincides with a crisis and challenge. Ten years after conjunction is the 180-degree Opposition (Full Moon) phase where the cycle's purpose is made manifest in clear light and a retrenchment period begins. Fifteen years after the conjunction is the Last Quarter/Closing Square where old remnants from the cycle are discarded after being found wanting, and the need for a brand-new cycle (and its possibilities) is forming in the collective consciousness.

Conjunctions during presidential elections coincide with new orientations in policy, though certainly someone like William Harrison, who died after a month in office, didn't get a chance to implement many ideas. Harrison is the first of the infamous category of seven presidents who were elected in a zero-year (in this case 1840) that coincided with or was near a Jupiter/Satrun conjunction. But since Zachary Taylor died in office without having a Jupiter/Saturn connection, some people question whether or not there is a real correlation here. Harrison died in April 1841, whereas the conjunction didn't take place until January 1842. And Ronald Reagan's election on a conjunction confused matters more. Obviously Reagan made it through all eight years. Astrologers had long speculated that the so-called "curse" might not be operative for the winner of the 1980 election because Jupiter and Saturn would be in an Air sign (Libra), while other conjunctions had taken place in Earth signs, the last time being in Capricorn in 1960 (Kennedy). Most of the Jupiter/Saturn correlations are not as questionable as the Presidential Death Cycle. David Williams, the premier astroeconomist, has found that the conjunction has marked turning points in the economy more than 80 percent of the time since the 1761 conjunction, providing perhaps the best evidence of the intensification of the period as new trends are born.

Six years into the twenty-year cycle (for example, 1986) comes the First Quarter/Opening Square, when Jupiter is moving three signs ahead of Saturn. The time was characterized by a certain impulsiveness as leaders attempted to break away from the past by further implementing the seeds of the 1980s. Often, bad decisions made at the conjunction start catching up with leaders. Ronald Reagan's problems came in the form of spiraling deficits and confrontations in Libya, and then the scene shifted to Irangate. Lyndon Johnson "escalated" the war in Vietnam in 1966. The world started building itself back up on the Opening Square following World War II (1946). Economic disruptions occurred and dictatorships were coming to power (Pilsudski's iron fist over Poland in 1906, for instance), marking the Opening Squares of 1906 and 1926. Teddy Roosevelt's 1906 visit to see the work in progress on the Panama

Canal marked the first time an American president left the country to make such an inspection on our behalf.

The midpoint of the cycle has already been discussed, particularly in connection with 1989–90, 1971, and the 1950s. The polarization and subsequent calls for reconciliation in this century are also apparent in the 1930–31 buildup of the Depression. In 1910–11, the Liberal party's return to power in the British Parliament, South Africa's establishment of a new government, Japan's annexation of Korea, and the United States Congress' voting for direct election of senators, also mirror this midpoint's polarization and calls for reconciliation.

Jimmy Carter's term may be the best working definition of the Last Quarter/Closing Square phase. The odds are very strong that a challenger candidate (as opposed to an incumbent) who wins during the last four or five years of a soon-to-end cycle will only serve for one term. By 1980–81 it was time for something new. Had Carter been in office prior to the Last Quarter, his experience might have been different. Only James Monroe, who got a second term under other potent cycles, beat this trend. The Last Quarter phase of Jupiter/Saturn has not been good to first-termers who go in and try to show their stuff when the cycle is waning. The situation is similar to that of a third-string quarterback who finally gets a chance to play during the final two minutes of the game, but with little chance of affecting the point spread in either direction. The American Revolution, of course, was fought on a fitting Last Quarter Jupiter/Saturn, but the conjunction of 1781 helped provide direction as the fighting slowed down. The U.S. Constitution was written in the First Quarter/Opening phase, but the planets Jupiter and Saturn were making the trine aspect (120 degrees), easing the tension.

Trines and sextiles (60 degrees apart) are aspects through which planets try to cooperate. In connection with Jupiter and Saturn, these aspects have had some correlations to so-called economic booms, but usually with some help from other cycles. Jupiter and Saturn formed a trine a month after the October 19, 1987, stock market crash and may be the reason why it wasn't the "big one." The 1929 crash came with the two planets in 171-degree aspect to one another, which qualifies as an opposition.

Angles of 135 and 150 degrees are also important turning points and often represent breakdowns or warnings and calls for adjustments. While the aspects are beyond the scope of this book, the 150-degree aspect (called the inconjunct or quincunx) comes directly before and after the Opposition in demand for revisions and adjustments to specific situations. (There was one inconjunct in 1929 then again in 1933, while the actual Opposition took place in 1930.)

The 135, known as the sesquiquadorate, comes prior to the first inconjunct and then again following the second. It relates to sudden and unexpected shifts or breakdowns in situations. The inconjunct before the opposition says there is need to begin analyzing specific situations in need of repair. The one following the opposition coincided with the New Deal of FDR's administration.

An inconjunct coincided with the November 1988 election, preceding the 1989–90 opposition. An inconjunct will move into effect in February 1992, within the realm of time that this and subsequent chapters of this book highlight as marking discernible economic and social adjustments in this country and around the world.

Zodiac Connections

In studying individuals and world affairs, the zodiac placement of the Jupiter/Saturn cycle is also important. The 1940–41 conjunction in Taurus signified the need to begin integrating and restructuring new values into society. Since values to Taurus usually translate into things economic, the conjunction began a twenty-year cycle that, working along with more long-term cycles, produced governmental and other societal initiatives that created a larger middle class and a fairly possessive and materialistic society. The conjunction that brought in John F. Kennedy spoke to a call for Capricornian (the planets were in that sign) functions to be integrated into and defined by society. As a result, Capricornian ideas, such as government, took on larger roles and America's paternalism expanded and became more defined, both in this country and around the world.

In 1980–81 the conjunction occurred in Libra, so partnerships and our relations (both amiable and otherwise) with others got the Jupiter/Saturn treatment. While Pluto, among other forces, is sitting at the bottom of some of the deeper anxieties people have been harboring about male/female relations, the Jupiter/Saturn conjunction marked the beginning of the more obvious attempts, particularly in the broadcast publishing and media, to define the problem through documentaries, specials, and an avalanche of books. But this latest conjunction, which ironically began on the heels of the murder of Libran John Lennon, who was born on one conjunction and came to fame on another, is about much more than simply acquiring a mate. Libra represents one's relationship with others in a general sense: how we meet other people face-to-face, how we deal with them—all of which is connected to how we relate to ourselves. At the time of this conjunction Americans were pretty angry people. Inflation was high, the hostages had been in captivity for more than a year, and there was nothing Americans could do but vote out the seemingly impotent Libra in the White House. The launch of the Reagan Revolution allowed the release of the pent-up anger and frustration and helped sanction the antipoor and anti–civil rights tone that prevailed for several years. The emergence of a noveau riche, buoyed by the economic boom and increased expectations among others in the middle class, has contributed to a clash that was evident in some of the Yuppie-bashing that followed media focus on the life-styles of the professional paper-pushers. The glee with which some with lesser salaries eyed the losses logged in the 1987 crash is another example of the built-up resentment made more evident by the Opposition.

The Opposition of late fall 1989 is in effect throughout 1990 and into the spring and early summer of 1991. Most of the Opposition will involve the zodiac signs Cancer and Capricorn. It will relate to a need to negotiate a balance between calls for expansion of physical, economic, and emotional security (Jupiter moving through Cancer) with very immediate needs to check expansion and regulate and reorder governmental priorities (Saturn moving through Capricorn). The Jupiter/Saturn Opposition, working along with critical cycles involving Neptune and other planets, as well as the fact that the United States has its Sun sign in Cancer (and hence is especially affected by anything moving through Cancer and its opposite sign, Capricorn) all seem to suggest that the government will be forced to come to the aid of some groups in society but can't go overboard. Capricorn is the sign of "business," and Saturn moving through the sign indicates limitations, cutbacks, and more restructuring. The struggle between business interests and the personal life and home (Cancer) will be highlighted as debates over controversial (and expensive) day-care legislation and related issues are continued.

More immediate concerns for the country are related to the fact that Cancer and Capricorn rule agriculture, issues of land, and in particular real estate. Various nine-year cycles indicating real estate lows are coinciding with the 1990 Opposition, and this heightens the concern about depressed land values. Difficult times for the building/housing industry relate to trouble for other industries and increased concern about overall economic health in the country, so be warned. By the time the Jupiter/Saturn cycle that began with the 1980–81 conjunction winds down, it will leave no doubt what elements of the cycle need to be left behind.

The Reality Decade

The challenges (some will say threats) that current events, in areas ranging from economics to science and religion, have on humankind's take on "reality" have been outlined extensively. Entering the 1990s with major planets bearing down in reality-oriented Capricorn, signals that the very structure of life is high on the agenda of challenges for the decade.

Saturn's transit through Aquarius and Pisces from 1991 to 1996 will play an important role in the legislative and governmental actions that will be taken to address social concerns. As noted earlier in this chapter, Saturn's movement through this portion of the zodiac relates to "new deals" and changing roles for government and its relationship with the masses. The move into Aries in 1996–98 relates to individuals' attempts to break out of perceived restraints on their self-expression at the very same time that various authoritative forces—Russia's advance into Czechoslovakia, revolts in Mexico, the black athletes' protest at the 1968 Olympics, assassinations in the United States, Hitler's rampages—are making assaults on individual identity.

The Year 2000

As befitting a new decade and century, Jupiter and Saturn will make another conjunction in the year 2000. Prior to the conjunction, the mop-up Last Quarter phase between Jupiter and Saturn will occur in late 1994 and early 1995, closing out the cycle that began in 1980–81. With Jupiter bounding through its home sign of Sagittarius, and Saturn crimping Pisces, personal and world affairs will feature struggles between isolationist-expansionist/assimilationist factions. World trade matters would fit the bill for some of the symbolism. The United States, which started the twenty-year cycle trying to rebuild its spirits, has increasingly become more isolated from the rest of the world, despite its record foreign debt. There is also increasing concern in America—and Western European countries—about growing immigration by nonwhites. Studies projecting that whites will be a racial minority in the United States by 2030 have stirred rumblings among some population experts (and politicians). Events through the 1990s will force adjustments aimed at making Americans and others around the globe real citizens of the world.

Taurus will be the sign in which Jupiter and Saturn meet for the conjunction in the year 2000. Since a conjunction took place in this sign in 1941, there are some clues to the economic and values restructuring that will be called for by the year 2000. But don't expect concrete plans to surface and be implemented at this time, no matter who's spouting the political rhetoric and making the promises. If there's one thing this cycle—particularly in relation to American history—has shown, it is that it really does need twenty years to do its work, and it simply won't be hurried.

Major Planetary Conjunctions

The following list is offered for those who want to study major planetary conjunctions. To examine the critical phases within each cycle, divide the length of the cycle by four to determine the years in which the two planets would be making the First Square/Quarter-Opening (the faster-moving planet is moving three signs ahead of the slower-moving one); the Opposition (halfway through the cycle and six signs apart), and the Last Quarter/Square Closing (the faster-moving planet is three signs behind the slower moving one.

1. Neptune/Pluto: About every 492 years; last time in 1891–92, next, 2333–2334. Symbolizes higher ideals and human purposes of the time.

2. Uranus/Neptune: About every 172 years; most recently in 1820–21; next 1992–1993, and again in 2165. Marks periods when ideals and revolutions foment and lead to changes that redistribute society's wealth.

3. Uranus/Pluto: About every 115–125 years (Pluto's orbit is more erratic than other planets'); last conjunctions: 1965, 1850, 1710. Next, 2080–2085. Forces restructuring of society in ways that initially seem like overnight change.

4. Saturn/Uranus: About every 45 years; 2032, 1988, 1942, 1897. Clashes between the status quo/authoritarian leaders and reformist, progressive urges.

5. Saturn/Neptune: About every 36 years; most recently in 2025, 1989, 1953, 1917. Systems build around ideals, but also outbreaks of fear and paranoia (sometimes masked as influenza or other epidemics) that relate to economic or other social disappointments. Moral and spiritual bankruptcy.

6. Saturn/Pluto: About every 33 years; 2019–2020, 1982, 1947–1948, 1914–15. Breaks things down to basics. People and cultures go through transformative periods.

7. Jupiter/Saturn: About every 20 years; 2000, 1980–81, 1960–61, 1941. The development of new social structures, usually amid discernible competition between expansive and contractive tendencies.

8. Jupiter/Uranus: About every 14 years; 1997, 1983, 1969, 1955. Relates to expansion, invention, entrepreneurism. Rebellion against the status quo.

9. Jupiter/Neptune: About every 13 years; 1997, 1984, 1971, 1958. Characterized by idealism, humanitarianism, and the unfoldment of social activity and religious/spiritual beliefs.

10. Jupiter/Pluto: About every 12 years; 1994–95, 1981, 1968, 1955–56, 1943. The expansion of political power, wealth, and religious ideology, and more aggressive attempts (sometimes terrorism) to grab power.

SIXTEEN

Pluto in Scorpio

In a world where true change can only be affected through a series of often painful stages, somebody has to do the dirty work, and the task usually falls to Pluto, planet of death and rebirth. Uranus, planet of earthquakes of the mind and land, is in and out like a flash. It hurls people toward change, but doesn't provide a blueprint. Neptune gets glamourous assignments, such as advertising campaigns, but even as it spreads seeds of discontent and disillusionment, we keep making ourselves believe in its fairy tales. Change, however, requires purging people and situations of anger, resentments, repressed feelings, and attitudes that must be relinquished before new life can emerge.

So Pluto gets put on the case. The planet didn't show its face to humankind until 1930, as the United States sank deeper into the Great Depression and Adolf Hitler showed that the human species was capable of evil. Humankind's decision to use atomic weapons to destroy huge populations meant that the planet had taken irrevocable steps in a tragic direction. After introducing itself in such a vile manner, it shouldn't be surprising that Pluto's job is to drill the sewers and dredge up all the hidden matters that are never talked about, (sex, money, sex), in other words all the resentments, anger, hate, power

298

drives, unconscious motivations, and dirty little secrets that move through all of our lives.

In the late 1980s and early 90s, Pluto has been in the midst of a homecoming as it has moved through its natural sign, Scorpio. The high-powered meeting made it difficult to say anything good about anybody. The secrets of televangelists who solicited prostitutes, politicians with lusty drives, and evidence suggesting that many other leaders would not pass critical scrutiny were just the start of it. In the private arena, power struggles between the sexes and fears about sexually transmitted diseases (particularly AIDS) brought a new caution and wariness to interpersonal relationships. Extra doses of venom seemed to be injected into society as politicans, music groups, and other media seemed to be trying to push an invisible "hate button" within the mass psyche to get their messages across. Gang warfare and increasingly violent attacks and abductions of innocent people, most of them women; murder/suicides; contract killings; and out-of-control political terrorists were the most obvious symptoms of the inner turmoil in the collective mind. Subtle racial tension—and outright hatred demonstrated by attacks and killings of African Americans by mobs of white youths—as well as increased assaults on Jewish people, Asian Americans, gays, and lesbians also revealed the deep-seated hostility within the human psyche.

Personal Empowerment

Yet even as these ugly faces of humankind jumped out at us like demons in an amusement park's haunted-house tour, an instinct for reform and transformation was looking to fight its way through the layers of debris. Increasing numbers of people were making genuine efforts to rid themselves of the life patterns that had forced them to give up their lives to drugs, alcohol, gambling, food, lovers, anything being done to an unhealthy extreme. Personal empowerment was becoming an aim for many people, even if they were not battling more obvious addictions or other problems. And among people stricken with terminal illnesses, such as cancer or AIDS, there was a renewed sense and trust of life as they openly confronted the anger and resentments that had been blocking them from their true, healthy selves. The confrontations with the inner demons was leading to self-healing or, at the very least, much longer lives than had been anticipated when the diseases had first been diagnosed.

Those who had been victimized by crime or personal tragedies began channeling energies and anger into helping other people with similar problems. The abduction and murder of six-year-old Adam Walsh changed John Walsh's life forever. He took the pain and transformed it into a television show, *America's Most Wanted,* that has a more-than-50-percent success rate in helping police capture rapists, robbers, and other murderers who are pillaging society.

Intense—that's been one of the big words of the latter 1980s. Also *compulsive, fatal attraction, passion, excess, control,* and *obsession* (both the perfume ads and the psychological state). The nineties turns the heat up higher. Like Gotham City, the landscape in America and the rest of the world had a dark overcast, as if a shadow were moving across the Earth. The planet of destruction and elimination, which eventually clears the way for transformation and rebirth, is moving through the sign for which it has a natural affinity or is said to "rule." Scorpio is Pluto's familiar stomping ground, home court, so it knows where the bodies are buried. But Pluto knows where to find the secrets and weak spots even when it moves into alien territory.

Special Urgency in 1989–90

Pluto's more recent calls for the elimination of old ways in order to make room for new life also have special urgency for astronomical reasons related to Pluto's orbit and the section of the zodiac it is now visiting. Although it is traditionally the planet farthest from the Earth and the Sun, Pluto's orbit causes it to cut across Neptune's at certain points in its travel, making Neptune the outermost planet from 1978 to the year 2000. The celestial interchanges have special ramifications on Earth. The late Dane Rudhyar, perhaps the twentieth century's master astrologer, has described periods when Pluto's orbit shifts as being "fecundation" times for the planet. He noted that the worldwide Seven Years War and other accelerated societal changes, as well as the discoveries of Columbus and other explorers in the New World, have coincided with Pluto's penetration of Neptune's orbit. The Earth is apparently in a better position to receive messages from Pluto during these periods of fecundation. The phase also seems to include special points of emphasis. For instance, during 1989 Pluto was the closest it ever gets to the Sun in its 248-year orbit, giving especially intense messages to the Earth on matters ranging from impending financial problems (Pluto rules shared and global resources) to accelerated problems with international terrorism and domestic violence in the form of murder/suicides and gang-related attacks. Government scandals, natural disasters, and the mounting crisis with banks and other pooled resources of money escalated. (Continental Illinois, one of the first major public bank failings to get national attention, occurred as Pluto entered Scorpio for the first time in 1983–84).

Dane Rudhyar's theory about the accelerated rate of change during Pluto's current phase is instructive because it helps us look beyond 1996, when Pluto moves into Sagittarius, sign of journeys and truth seeking. And then it moves through Capricorn, where it will overhaul and create new forms of government and other societal structures in the second decade of the twenty-first century. After the Earth is purged of some of its unnecessary psychological and physical residue, we will be able to explore "new worlds," the way the fifteenth- and sixteenth-century discoverers did during the fecundation phase when Pluto last cut through the orbit of Neptune. Since we are now aware of the existence of Pluto and Neptune, and have even sent Voyager to Neptune for some up-close photographs, we are able to make more positive use of the planetary energies. Our explorations and journeys to inner and outer spaces in the twenty-first century will transform individuals and the planet on a larger scale.

An Elemental Force

But the purer side of Pluto's life-giving power—in the form of healed and new life situations, as well as new life itself—cannot be realized until all of its repressed ugliness is confronted and understood. While the planet represents primal Eve, mother of humankind, it is also reflected in Medea's revenge and her power over life and destruction. As the symbol for the process of change, Pluto contains within it many of the extremes that brought about the Holocaust, the unconscious fears and resentments, the hate, as well as the atomic forces that fell into the hands of world leaders in the decades after Pluto's discovery. In the same way that the world has never been the same since the first atomic bomb was dropped, people can never go back to the life they had before being touched by Pluto's irrevocable influence.

Pluto's goal is to transform people and situations. As a result its effects often seem ruthless. The planet is associated with the awful family legacies and tragedies that seem so unexplainable. Fate and karma are probably ideas one must accept in order to fully penetrate Pluto's meanings. Unlike Saturn, whose concern with karma involves more clearly defined societal rules, Pluto addresses the deeper meanings of "cause and effect." The circumstances of our lives, Buddhism holds, are all a direct result of "causes" we have made in past lives and that we continue to make every day in the present one. Sometimes we're not aware of causes when we make them. This chapter isn't intended to debate reincarnation and past lives, but the Buddhist idea of "cause" is being used to illustrate some of the retribution and so-called karmic concerns of Pluto. The sound and fury coinciding with Pluto signifies the old behaviors, situations, and relationships that must come to an end, usually painfully, so that a new plateau can be reached.

The Phoenix Rises from Its Ashes

After the old way of life has been destroyed and we've been forced to let go of possessions, people, and attitudes, the moment contains within itself the seeds for a new start. Then the real intent of Pluto is revealed. Pluto, after the fall, is elemental and raw, much the way the morning is after a major hurricane or tornado has wiped out the homes and lives of families. Survivors survey the scene with a sense of what has been lost and what must be done in order to go forward. The Pluto force doesn't say that the new beginning will be handled with aplomb or even that people will recognize that a way of life has ended. It simply puts the process into motion and will work with those who surrender to the time and move with it.

But don't think for a moment that this energy will be understanding toward those who want a raincheck or who claim not to be interested in change. Medical experts such as Dr. Bernie Siegel have helped pioneer the belief that cancer and other major illnesses appear in the bodies of people who refuse to go on after suffering major setbacks and losses in life. Pluto is related to this refusal to let go. It is also associated with the the stages of grief—denial, depression, anger, bargaining, acceptance—outlined by Elisabeth Kübler-Ross. People move through these stages at different paces and in different sequences, but the essence of the theory resonates with the stages of change held within Pluto. Successful passage through them can ultimately lead to the healing that Pluto holds as a reward. As alluded to earlier, it is Pluto at work in the life of a man like John Walsh, whose son, Adam, was abducted and murdered in 1981. Walsh subsequently started a nationwide campaign to find abducted children and put murderers and other criminals in jail. ''There's no way seeking revenge would have brought Adam back,'' Walsh said in an interview that focused on his highly successful television show. Mothers Against Drunk Driving (MADD), started by Candy Lightner, whose daughter was killed by a drunk driver, is another example. The victims'-rights movement in this country is becoming more fierce. People are fighting back, which explains some of the appeal of Batman, who lurked in the shadows as he fought crime. The Batman of the 1939 novel—and the more recent film version—is a vigilante, spurred on by inner demons and anger caused by the murder of his parents.

An About-face and Power Play

Pluto's change of direction, which occurs around the same time each year, highlights the way the planet lurks around in the shadows and steps forward in a display of manipulation and control that puts people on edge. In a fashion similar to Persephone's marital arrangement with the god of the Underworld, Pluto spends the first six months of the year moving backward—retrograde—and the following six months moving forward. During the week (usually in July) it makes its turnaround after lurking beneath the surface of consciousness, it spends a few days spewing out the excess residue before going out to kick us around again. The planet was preparing to move forward as Jesse Jackson and his supporters moved into Atlanta for the 1988 Democratic Convention, where racial undercurrents swirled all around. Pluto appears to move backward, generally for about the first six months in every year. During the week it appears to be stationary and then turns direct, life can often feel like a Russian-roulette game—which was the case during 1989 when terrorists threatened to kill American military personnel. In many ways Jesse Jackson took the Democratic Convention hostage. While he is not a statesman, he is a symbol to some people, and this forced the party leaders, including front-runner Dukakis, to give Jackson more due than may have been extended to a white candidate. The Democrats needed Jackson to work for the Dukakis/Bentsen team in November. They had to show Jackson and his supporters that they had the same goals, but the rest of America had to simultaneously get the message that Jackson wasn't a prime player for the ticket.

Pluto and Scorpio: Similar but Different

Since Scorpio is a sign in which people often experience crises that lead to transformation, it is easy to confuse the workings of a sign with its ruler, the planet Pluto. (Mars was the ruler of Scorpio before Pluto's discovery, and still has a strong connection with the sign. Pluto, in many ways, is a more universal expression, more impersonal than Mars.) But signs and planets do not serve the same cosmic role. Planets are the task, what must be done. With Mars, it's moving forward; with Jupiter, it's expansion. Signs show how one moves, for example: (aggressively in Aries, defensively in Cancer) or expands (flamboyantly and self-expressively in Leo, materially and persistently in Taurus). Pluto's task is to transform through death and regeneration. Like the lotus flower that blooms and seeds simutaneously, Pluto always holds death and rebirth in its hands. Moving through Cancer, the area undergoing the overhaul and new life are issues of emotional security, such as the family, home, one's personal foundations; through Virgo, the concept of work and one's daily routine are transformed. Scorpio lends qualities of intensity, passion, and tranformative instinct to whatever planet moves through it. And it insures that the planet concentrates on issues of power, in areas ranging from intimate relations (sex, shared resources) to the deaths, both large and small, that people meet up with every day.

Scorpio is the journey portrayed most poignantly in Inanna's descent to the Netherworld to confront her sister. What Inanna was doing, and what we all must do in Scorpio, is confront our power and our powerlessness. In doing so, we tap the inner resources that lead us toward self-mastery, which is the only true power we have on this planet. The sign's association with matters such as money—in particular one's creditworthiness and debts—can sometimes cause people to forget how aggressive inner creditors can be when payment is due.

But Scorpio's coming to self-mastery often involves intense interpersonal relationships in which issues of money, sex, and numerous matters of control and manipulation are constants. Ideally, those with a strong Scorpio influence learn to purge themselves of the unconscious and repressed motivations that lurk under their will to power and dealings with the world. Such purging ultimately makes Scorpio more powerful and resourceful than the lower forms of power they'd been seeking in the external world, where others are manipulated and often abused for Scorpio's own ends.

Because it involves the most intimate of our relations and associations, Scorpio matters are undercurrents that people repress and don't talk about. Usually they aren't even aware that there are "issues" under the table. As author Nancy Friday's study, *Jealousy*, illustrated, labeling various emotions as ugly and undesirable leaves the reasons for these emotions unexamined. In Scorpio, there's no getting around it—though everyone still tries—since the sign contains the unmasked motivations and desires that shape people's lives.

The sign deals with matters that at first don't seem to have much to do with each other: shared possessions (joint bank accounts and property), death, sex. But all of these issues are linked to the emotional connectedness between people and refer to situations that limit individual control. While Libra, the sign prior to Scorpio, is the sign of relationships, the unseen emotional matters in a relationship show up in the sign of the soul's battleground, because Scorpio is where two people merge and transcend their separateness. In Libra they're just together, relating, but they generally don't "know" each other in the Scorpio sense. In Scorpio, where relationships are consummated, interactions are more subtle and complex. Death and sex both force a confrontation with the interactions and meaning other people have had in one's life, but they also represent a "giving over" or giving up of control, a certain surrender and release.

Sex and Scorpio are tricky subjects. Taurus, the sign opposite Scorpio, deals with issues of possession and sex, but Taurean sex is aimed at serving bodily needs and demands, though some members of the sign can also have sexual matters tied up in power and control. In Scorpio, where many under the sign's heavy influence have been known to go through periods of enforced celibacy, sex and issues of control and power are intensified. But Scorpionic sex brings in more psychological, emotional, and spiritual issues than Taurean sex. In seeking to avoid overplaying the sexual side of Scorpio in light of the distortions wrought by popular astrology, astrologers often end up underplaying the connection between sexual energy and the creative and healing powers of insight natural to Scorpio.

The task for us, then, is to search the sewers and caves in our lives for the Plutonian issues that we must transform. While the planet acts upon every individual life in customized fashion, there are some general matters where Pluto's effect is most obvious. But we shouldn't spend all our time looking for Plutonian activities in newspaper reports about inner-city drug dealers or gang violence, for the planetary energy is at work right in our homes.

Battle of the Sexes

Courtship, marriage, and relationship rites between men and women may have been erroneously referred to as the battle of the sexes for many years, but now, with Pluto in Scorpio, it's hard to call it anything else. Shere Hite interviewed women to catalog their feelings about their relationships for her book, *Women and Love: A Cultural Revolution in Progress*. Hite's claim that more than 80 percent of the women who participated in her study were unhappy with their relationships shouldn't have come as a surprise, given the wide range of books throughout the eighties that were aimed at helping women find men and get men to treat them better.

Boy-meets-girl stories have always involved many negotiated rites. But when Pluto, which destroys old forms, moved through the relationship sign of Libra from 1971 to 1984, the rules of courtship and marriage changed forever. More people were divorcing, and others began postponing marriage while they pursued careers and explored themselves. Even when married and having children, economic necessity (and personal ambition and desire) in the late 1980s resulted in more than 50 percent of all new mothers returning to the workplace after giving birth. The U.S. Census Bureau announced that the statistics put working mothers into the category of an established social factor rather than a simple trend.

Some men have grown with the changes and openly prefer the independent woman of the 1990s to the more dependent woman of previous decades. Less-secure men have felt threatened and have helped to perpetuate the idea that women who use their brain lose their femininity.

But admittedly, relationships between men and women, as we move into the 1990s, are painful. There is anger, fear, and resentment. The sexes have been coming toward one another as warily as two superpowers who are negotiating the future of the world. People have been edgy, and suspicious. Nobody wants to get taken advantage of. Everybody wants to control. Pluto's nature is such that it is impossible for us to waltz merrily from Libra to Scorpio. Instead society must experience the same assault and overhaul in Scorpionic areas that Libran matters such as the law and relationships witnessed. While the end result can be deeply intimate unions—all Scorpios want a soul mate—such a goal can't be realized without first confronting the power-and-control issues that now have set many men and women at a standoff.

Underlying the standoff is the issue of the balance of power. Woman's changing role has made power—and the sharing of it within couples—an obvious agenda item, but such concerns have always been a key element in intimate relationships. Researcher/writer Maggie Scarf has observed that these power struggles are apparent in even the earliest encounters between new couples. ''The power struggles that go on in many intimate attachments—most particularly when the new relationship is crystallizing—frequently involve a contest about whose ideas about reality will be the stronger ones, the ones that will hold sway in their shared emotional territory.'' Common to alliances is an ''if you win, I lose'' attitude, but as Scarf observes, ''In relationships, there is never really one winner and one loser; two people either win—or lose—together.''

Sexuality is certainly one area where power and powerlessness are currently being confronted, as once-hidden issues from incest to date-rape get increasing attention. But the meaning of sex and the role it should have in life in general are also on the minds of people. When Neptune moved through Scorpio from 1956 to 1970, sex pervaded the culture in the form of *Playboy* magazine, more blatant pornography, orgies, and mainstream advertising. The publications of books such as *Lolita* and *Peyton Place*, as the period began, spoke to the hidden sexual dimension of the masses. Sex was romanticized, idealized, and some people thought they understood it so well that they could simply give it away. Uranus shook up Scorpio from

in sexually transmitted disease and other sexual dysfunctions.

Taking No Prisoners

Pluto in Scorpio couldn't have been expected to play along with the mass confusion. It had to take hostages in order to get people to take sexuality more seriously, to understand the way it must be integrated with the rest of a person's being and life. While the AIDS disease has been documented as existing for some decades before it became the scourge of the late 1980s and '90s, Pluto in Scorpio is related to the global shakeout under way. The focus on AIDS, however, has caused many people to overlook the rampant outbreak of syphilis and other sexually transmitted diseases. The threat of disease, as well as the ambivalence toward relationships and the perceived struggles that intimacy has come to represent, has driven many people into hibernation in the form of celibacy while they try to better understand sex and its role.

While many in society have come to view sex as being a form of recreation and separate it from love, this compartmentalization still confuses others. Complicating the matter further is a range of sexual/reproductive matters that raise the life-and-death issues posed by sex. The abortion-rights fight certainly has elements of the Saturn/Uranus conjunction (authority versus individual freedom), but Pluto and Scorpio relate to a number of the concerns raised by the abortion fight. Women's power over their bodies (and their lives) is obviously a major factor in the debate. That 500,000 of the 1.6 million annual abortions in America are conducted for teenagers, people who are not officially adults, makes discussions even trickier. But the question of when life begins—and who should be deciding that—is the most basic Plutonian association. Pluto is a custodian, a role connoting physical and moral responsibility and control. In the same way that the god of the Underworld was the steward of the dead, Pluto ushers people in and out of this life, which explains its connection to custody battles of children and frozen embryos, adoption and surrogate motherhood. Mary Beth Whitehead's surrogacy leaves unanswered moral and technical questions about what constitutes and creates life; whose baby is it really?

Hidden Consequences

While chastising Gary Hart for his infidelities, the country did an interesting sidestep around the issue of adultery. Hart's adultery, the general thinking went, was wrong because he was seeking a public trust. Underneath this attitude seemed to be an acceptance of adultery for private citizens, provided they aren't making a spectacle of themselves. Ever since Masters and Johnson began issuing their studies in the 1950s, there's been this "understanding" that men cheat on their wives, and most recently that more and more women run around, too.

But the rules are changing for many private citizens now as well. Even if they're put off by the concept of karma, most people will concede that the past affects the present. Pluto tells us that history has momentum, and this idea is being brought to bear in both the public and the private arenas. As people increase their use of therapy and take other steps to look inside themselves for the solutions to many of their life problems, they become more conscious of patterns in life, sexual and relationship patterns being just one area.

AIDS has worked on the human psyche in both covert and direct ways that indicate that the disease has more metaphysical significance than many other diseases and health problems besetting society. The fact that the 1980s version first became evident among social outcasts such as gays and then moved into inner-city ghettos allowed middle-class heterosexuals to overlook and deny the threat of the disease. While such complacency has been encouraged by segments of the medical establishment, some projections say that more than a million people will be infected by 1992. Some epidemiologists say the disease will spread in much the same way that venereal diseases spread throughout poor and more affluent populations.

AIDS is among the ills that are allowing humankind to more directly (and collectively) confront what it means to be human as well as the meaning of the shared experience of death. Groups around the country have adopted "AIDS buddies" to help patients with their daily routines. Volunteers are helping the sick get the most out of their final days, and the healthy people are healing parts of their lives at the same time. The approach furthers ideas that hospices are built upon. This collective healing, where both the sick and the healthy are sharing their vulnerabilities and strengths, is one of the more positive manifestations of Pluto and is related to the self-healing approaches that AIDS victims are taking as they undergo therapy to become more aware of various psychological issues that have held dominant roles in their lives.

It is still too early to judge the effectiveness of this holistic healing approach to AIDS. But the victims' efforts run parallel ... hological/spiritual approach that has allowed some ... ves of cancer. Individual therapy, group session... f faith underly these treatments. While some pe... f viewing faith as a medicine, biomedical scien... at the faith in various methods can work miracles. The ... roversial, but Dr. Bernie Siegel has predicted that such ... g approaches "will be science in five to ten years."

Roads to Recovery

Just as poignant as the trials of cancer survivors are the experiences of many individuals in the so-called recovery fields, which involve programs aimed at treating people who suffer from a variety of addictive and/or compulsive behaviors. Alcoholics Annoymous, which was founded in 1935, is the most popular recovery program, though many approaches, ranging from methadone treatment clinics to various forms of counseling, are getting increasing attention. Alcoholism and other addictions in a birthchart do not fall solely under the Pluto province about which we're now speaking. The alcoholic profile is very complex; people drink for different reasons. Collectively, Neptune's transiting through Capricorn is not only correlated to the selling of drugs and alcohol throughout the workplace and higher strata of society, it's also about getting people worried about the problem. Pluto, by contrast, more directly speaks to the road back, the process of recovery. And the widespread efforts to recover from situations ranging from family secrets and dysfunctions that have distorted "adult children's" sense of themselves, to efforts to rid life of substance abuse, have common links and are successfully being applied in many other seemingly unrelated areas. The Twelve Step program of Alcoholics Anonymous has been particularly instrumental in helping people with numerous problems—from overeating to gambling and so-called love addictions—to find their way back.

Alcoholics Anonymous, while viewing alcoholism as a "disease," prescribes a nonmedical remedy. At the core of the program is surrender to a Higher Power (God, the Universe, whatever an individual acknowledges) who will guide the alcoholic through the twelve steps of recovery. It is a lifelong process which includes taking a personal inventory of one's problems, failings, and transgressions of others, atonement, as well as assistance to other alcoholics, among other stages. The first of the twelve steps, presumably the most difficult, is to be able to make the statement "We admitted we were powerless over alcohol; that our lives had become unmanageable." By admitting that life had gotten out of control, people are better able to see the road back. This surrender is a process being invoked in support groups all around the country as people attempt to reclaim the parts of themselves that, in many cases, have been missing since birth. Whether the problem is overeating, gambling, victimization by sexual abuse, addictions, or crippling life experiences, the Twelve Step process, with its powerful First Step admission, is turning lives around in ways that have eluded trained professional therapists.

Race Relations

The pain that must be worked through rather than avoided is especially evident in the issue of race relations. Pluto's transit into Scorpio has coincided with an outbreak of racially motivated attacks on college campuses and city streets around the country. The increase in neo-Nazi and other anti-Semitic youth patrols and hostility toward Asians, are all evidence of the trend toward racial and ethnic power struggles, while increased gay-bashing also shows the fear and hatred simmering below the surface of society. It isn't just older white men in white hoods and sheets who are to be feared. America's youth, particularly its working class, are acting out many of the unresolved feelings that have always been simmering below the surface of society. Even more advantaged white youths were venting hostile feelings toward minorities as 250 racial incidents were reported on college campuses from 1986–89.

Race issues are highly complex and not easily grasped by most Americans. There are several astrological indicators related to race; the specific situation will determine the configurations. Individually, seemingly innocuous combinations like Moon and Jupiter raise issues of bigotry or indicate people being stuck in the prejudices of their upbringing. The succeeding chapter explains how the national horoscope relates to some of the more insidious forms of racism in America. Some sign combinations and patterns can pull people into racial matters. The Virgo/Pisces polarity, which deals with issues of the disadvantaged, as well as the Gemini/Sagittarius polarity, which can often involve the interaction of different cultures (usually different ethnicities rather than races), are examples. Saturn's concern with the past can also cause it to relate to racial identity or other matters in an individual birthchart. Neptune speaks to African Americans' experience, but astrologers who promote the idea that the planet "rules" African Americans generally aren't aware of the racial implications. What sign rules white people?

The history of slavery is so intertwined in America's future that no one planetary configuration can be isolated for its role in the race issue. The Uranus/Pluto conjunction of the mid-1960s certainly helped bring about initiatives, such as the 1965 Voting Rights Act. The 1850–51 conjunction coincided with the Fugitive Slave Law and the *Dred Scott* decision, which pushed the country closer to the Civil War. The ongoing cycle between Uranus and Neptune has always related to social realignment: in matters of both race and economics. In the same way that the coming together of Saturn and Neptune in 1989, and the 1992 Uranus/Neptune conjunction correlate to East Germans walking miles for freedom in the West, as well as some progress (albeit forced) in South Africa, American society can't help but experience some turmoil related to its social/economic fabric.

Pluto, however, plays a special role in interactions between races, in large part because of the history and issues of power, survival concerns, fear, and hate that often underlie these encounters. Some years back a series of observations I made as a member of a dream discussion group alerted me to the deep-seated, and often unconscious, racism in the American psyche. Several of the people in the dream group, when going through particularly stressful periods or major changes that caused fear and insecurity, often saw black people in their dreams. Sometimes these were people they knew from a distance or worked with; often the people were strangers. A nursery-school teacher who felt her family didn't understand her was dreaming about the sole black child in the nursery class who, it became apparent during some dream discussion, represented the teacher's feeling about her family's rejections. In so many words she said she felt they treated her as if she were black or something. A few group members, on occasion, reported dreams of sexual experiences with blacks, and one woman was chased by a black rapist several times.

The wonder here was not just that this was how their unconscious communicated to them but that none of these people were conscious enough to be embarrassed or to have second thoughts about relaying their dreams. Further experience with groups and some reading alerted me to the fact that these nightly enounters with blacks are common American dream motifs. Asians have no doubt been cast in stereotypical roles, too.

While it's trendy among presumed Jungians to unquestioningly relegate such dreams to revelations of people's "dark side," or "Shadow," the way this translates into an insidious racism cannot be overlooked. It also shows why various activists are fond of saying that the Ku Klux Klan and white supremacists who consciously promote racism are not as offensive as the more typical subtle forms of racism.

Part of the problem for the lack of understanding is that the American people have had limited experience working through the layers of debris surrounding race issues in America. While the sixties witnessed the legislation of laws intended to end discrimination and promote equal rights for African-Americans, the laws in many ways were years ahead of the racial understanding of the typical American. People were put on notice that racial epithets and slurs were not acceptable— and most were never inclined to use such slurs—but the laws couldn't wipe the racial attitudes and stereotypes from the collective mind. Stanley Elkin's classic work *Slavery* says that while numerous races and groups of people have held slaves, American practices have been the most brutal in human history. The residue can't be erased by the wave of a president's hand signing in new laws. Social niceties aside, slavery's legacy underlies all interracial encounters.

What this means is that the United States has not yet plunged itself into nitty-gritty racial issues. The typical American has not had the experiences that could illuminate their understanding of racial interactions, which in turn stimulates and increases their perceptions in other areas of life. Pluto moving through Scorpio is bringing us closer to the core issues, often in an angry fashion. Color battles are underneath many of the problems on the Earth. South Africa, with its white-minority-rule government, in many ways is a microcosm of the distribution of power on the globe: a small Caucasian population (represented most obviously by the two superpowers) fights for control of a planet that is mainly populated by people who are yellow, brown, and black. The South African situation also epitomizes the Pluto in Scorpio power struggles. After the changes brought about as Pluto traveled through Libra and now those brought on with Pluto in Scorpio men and women are asking whether one sex will always dominate the other. In the same way, beneath the talks of putting an end to apartheid is the question of whether those who once had power will be stripped of it entirely. As male/female relationships have shown, it's difficult to declare equality one day and have everyone walking down the street hand-in-hand a few days later. The racial situation and issues concerning balance of power in the United States were being aired throughout the early 1980s as the numbers of big-city black mayors increased. Ethnic whites, particularly in Chicago, were afraid they'd lose the patronage jobs and perks that came from having friends in office. With demographics moving away from their favor, the ethnic-white guards talked of wanting to "share" power. Since whites control the economics of most cities and also since the election of a black mayor doesn't preclude whites from holding the office, true power shifts have not taken place. Studies by the Joint Center for Political Studies that show black mayors picking up more white votes the second time around are also an indication that race becomes less of a factor once it is introduced.

These studies are important to our discussion of Pluto in Scorpio because both the planet and sign symbolize the baser power struggles and survival issues that come up when different races interact. As Pluto moved into Scorpio, the first black Miss America was crowned. Though she was forced to give up her crown after nude pictures from her past surfaced, the first runner-up who took her place was also African American, which puts more meaning behind the symbol. Jesse Jackson's run for the 1984 presidential ticket coincided with the move, and around the country even as leaders complained about Ronald Reagan, African Americans were seeing a renewed sense of cultural awareness. The interest is coming from all ages, but it is important to note that much of the increased cultural awareness comes from African-American youth, who are also increasingly choosing to attend predominantly black colleges because of the more supportive atmosphere. Trends such as the increased interest in African-American history, as well as the growing preferred use of the term *African American* as a way of acknowledging their roots in Africa, are examples of this will to power. History has a connection to the sign Capricorn and its ruling planet, Saturn, so . . . Neptune moving through Capricorn increases interest in history, but such histories tend to be the more traditional white-male versions. Scholars and others interested in the African-American past have had to excavate and dig through much Scorpionic waste, which is what Alex Haley did when Uranus, the scientist, was in Scorpio. The Scorpio connection is especially appropriate because of the empowerment that such efforts give people. America's predominantly white military/government/business leaders have indirect concerns about this awareness, even if they're not immediately conscious of this. Increased identification with Africa decreases the government's ability to send people of color into wars against other brown, yellow, and black people, especially in light of American history. The racial makeup of the military forces is an off-again on-again concern for these reasons.

With the tide of cultural awareness growing, it would seem that film director Spike Lee is a man of the times. Lee's *Do the Right Thing,* which focuses on racial hostility in a Brooklyn neighborhood, drew its critics, who felt he was inciting violence. But Lee appeared to be the person in the know; white youths gunned down a sixteen-year-old African-American youth in Brooklyn shortly after Lee's film aired. Unlike the 1960s films that featured pimps and other stereotypical characters, Lee's work is daring because it also addresses issues such as the tension between light-and dark-skinned African Americans. While some African Americans have chastised Lee for giving African Americans a critical look at themselves on this subject in his film *School Daze,* Lee's work has shown a consciousness that has often only been expressed in works by African-American women.

African-American women, meanwhile, have a special connection to Pluto in Scorpio. In many ways this planetary placement can be viewed as a "black feminist." The women's movement of the 1970s did not speak to the needs of most African-American women, who came to this country working, and generally weren't the stay-at-home women in the kitchen. The racism of white women also made it difficult for women of color to forge "sisterhood" links with them. At the same time, the sexism of African-American men, which has begun to transform itself in a manner similar to the more evolved white males, also cripples women of color. In the 1980s there were more public discussions and awareness of the special concerns of African-American women.

One taboo area in which African-American women (and other women of color) are ignoring the conditioning and manipulation of their culture is in the taboo realm of interracial dating and marriage. The number of black-female/white-male marriages in 1984 was around 60,000, up from 20,000 in the late 1970s. Until the 1980s it had generally been men of color who dated and married outside their race. While the number is currently at 112,000 marriages, it's decreasing slightly each year. African-American women had been conditioned to see white men as oppressors who have continued their devaluation of women of color. Yet, as an *Ebony* magazine exploration of this phenomenon revealed, the increase in professional women of color working alongside white men has changed racial attitudes. The changes in the workplace, coupled with some of the trickier aspects of intraracial sexual politics and the fact that there are fewer professional men of color than women (a trend that will increase because there are more African-American women in college than there are men) have also contributed to the changing attitudes.

It would be inaccurate, however, to assume that various increases in cross-racial marriages indicate an end to racism. A range of psychological patterns—sometimes unhealthy ones—can underlie these encounters, and it isn't uncommon to hear the white spouses or lovers of African Americans display much of the same racial ignorance as other whites. As Pluto in Scorpio (and Neptune more indirectly) tries to get people to understand, things often aren't how they seem.

Earthly Transformation

Life's mysteries are a special Plutonian project. When Neptune was in Scorpio, the story of Bridie Murphy's search for her past lives titillated the country, but few were willing to take reincarnation seriously at that time. Uranus in Scorpio in the 1970s, however, gave a more scientific cast to past-life studies. Research into near-death experiences laid the foundation. The general public is accepting of the idea that coma states and other forms of unconsciousness take people to another plane that seems to be between this life and another and that can give them a renewed understanding of their life purpose. The 1980s, however, now finds medical doctors writing books about reincarnation. Certainly, more research and information in this area will be forthcoming.

An instructive example of the Plutonian task awaiting humankind can be found in some of the solutions to the nationwide difficulty of finding places to dump refuse and the more hazardous, toxic waste. The problem has been on the minds of some leaders since the mid-1970s, when Uranus went into Scorpio, coinciding with the instructive, though tragic, problems at Love Canal and other environmental sites that had been ruined by the dumping of toxic wastes. Uranus dug up the poisonous underground materials. Increased regulations and the creation of plants that transform garbage to energy are among some of the possible solutions.

And that's the clue for all other areas of life being overhauled by Pluto. Like the refuse we're ready to throw out because it has no more use, or the noxious waste that is seeping up from the ground, our unexamined drives and "garbage" must be confronted and transformed into something that can benefit individuals and the world. As numerous examples in this chapter suggest, and as Pluto, custodian of life transitions, essentially decrees, the only way out of the storm is through it.

SEVENTEEN

The Astrology of National Horoscopes

That America is the land of Motherhood and Apple Pie is no accident. Back in July 1776, when representatives from the thirteen colonies convened in Philadelphia to declare their independence from England, the Sun was moving through the Cancer part of the zodiac, where concern about emotional security and "belonging" to a family, home, and country is paramount. Cancer looks at situations with a fairly subjective eye that is colored by personal experiences; "outsiders" are viewed through this lens as well. Cancer is patriotic, and sometimes nationalistic to the point of clannishness.

Just imagine the potential difficulties that Cancer would have integrating itself into an international vision, becoming a citizen of the world, a partner rather than a smothering parent or needy child. The problem, of course, wouldn't reveal itself immediately. But change the economic rules in other parts of the world, step up communication and mobility through technology, and live on a planet that is being sapped of many of its natural resources, and the need for a larger sense of citizenship becomes apparent.

The Sun in Cancer is just one piece to the puzzle that is the U.S.A.'s horoscope. Though the Cancer influence is especially strong—and hence always in evidence—the country was also born under planetary conditions indicating international stature

318

and power. Horoscope configurations are no less complex for nations, cities, and corporations than they are for humans. And nations wear their Sun signs in pretty much the same way as individuals, so it's not difficult to see the primary personality at work. The Soviet Union has been pretty faithful to the secretiveness, manipulation, and power concerns of its sign, Scorpio. But of late, the country is showing the Scorpionic ability to purge itself of the self-destructive and stagnant energies blocking its self-expression. When Taurean Israel digs its heels in the sand, we know it really means it. Japan has shown the Taurean knack for building a secure financial base and, more recently, its greed. The People's Republic of China is struggling with its Libra Sun's equality concerns, and its leaders don't hesitate to use some of the more violent Mars/Pluto energy in the horoscope to keep control.

While individuals have an element of control over their identity expression, national horoscopes have all sorts of characters to assimilate into their collective conscious and unconscious. As a result, configurations indicating difficulties in the horoscope of a nation or city usually correspond to literal circumstances, whereas an individual might deal with the configuration in a more spiritual or psychological manner. To complicate matters more, in attempting to cast the horoscope of a nation, city, or corporation, astrologers are faced with some rather sticky questions.

In Search of America's Birthtime

By now you have probably taken some steps to find the exact moment of your birth. But when was the United States born, really? Certainly the date July 4 has taken on a special mythology in our history. While the text of the Declaration was approved at this time, the colonists took the most crucial vote of all on July 2, when they declared themselves independent of England. This was the tension-filled vote, after which there was no turning back. Writing in his journal, John Adams remarked on the day as being momentous.

Yet Americans, and most astrologers, view July 4 as the birthday. From that point, the debate among astrologers settles on the exact hour and minute of the adoption and initial signing (the document was still being signed in August). The most popularly accepted time is 2:21 A.M., though evidence supporting this precise time has never been produced. Some astrologers claim that the Founding Fathers were knowledgeable about astrology and knew the importance of the exact moment, and hence hid it from public view. Next in popularity are various charts that have the Declaration being adopted in the early evening or late afternoon. The charts tend to be cast for times between 5:00 and 5:30 P.M., the later time having been recorded by the Philadelphia Historical Society.

Because the 2:00 A.M. and 5:00 P.M. times produce charts that are symmetrical in appearance—the signs on the Ascendant are polar opposites: Gemini/Sagittarius—proponents of both charts are successful in making similar assessments and predictions because of the reflex nature of the horoscope. This blurs the debate even more. Also, the July 2 and July 4 dates would contain common enough features that similar general forecasts could be derived from both. Given the dubious role that the country's Declaration has in our conduct of business—in comparison with that of the U.S. Constitution—it must be noted that a debate exists over whether dates such as the adoption of the Constitution or beginning of the federal government aren't more appropriate. Astrologers even include the study of horoscopes cast for the beginning of the Federal Reserve and New York Stock Exchange. The horoscope of national leaders, as well as charts for the time of inauguaration—in the United States this would produce a new chart every four years—must also be studied.

The problem of an exact "birth" is encountered when we seek to do charts for other countries, cities, and corporations as well. The Bolshevik's takeover between November 7 and 9, 1917, proposes several different charts for the Soviet Union, and other key dates must also be considered. Meanwhile coup d'états are another wild card. The difficulty in isolating precise times for charts is among the reasons why Mundane Astrology—which includes the study of affairs of state as well as sociological and political trends, and so on—lags behind the more personal areas of astrology. What we need are more astrology students who are interested in world affairs and who are willing to develop the socio/political/historic/economic background needed to become an authoritative voice in this area.

Astrology and Government Affairs

Real-world knowledge is especially important when astrology is being applied to world affairs. If the world ever gets to the point where it acknowledges input from Mundane astrologers, these experts will have the same traditional training and experience as their conventional counterparts. Such astrologers will simply be used to expand on their knowledge in the same way that those on Wall Street combine astrology with conventional techniques. Just as foreign-affairs experts have specialty areas, these astrologers will also concentrate on some specific bloc of countries. An example of some of the analysis and forecast possibilities can be found in *Cycles Research*, a newsletter published by Bill Meridian, a vice president at a major national brokerage firm in New York who uses astrology in his work. In a June 1988 issue, Meridian discusses the 1997 agreement through which Britain transfers Hong Kong to China. Meridian (a pseudonym used for professional reasons) analyzed charts keyed for the various dates throughout history and, in viewing China's upcoming role in Hong Kong, wrote,

The most vital piece of info that can be derived from this analysis is that the horoscope for the British lease on Hong Kong (which seems to be the most effective) gets hit hard much sooner than 1997. Neptune has been opposing the colony's Sun since the spring of 1987. Saturn moves up to join Neptune in January 1989, adding to the pressure throughout the year. As soon as Saturn moves away in late 1989, Uranus moves in to oppose the Sun in February 1990. This aspect persists throughout the year.

The Saturn/Neptune effect is a difficult influence. This pair is one of the least compatible combinations and is associated with depression, deflation, illness, and even bankruptcy in personal horoscopes. It will likely dampen spirits in general, leading to lower real estate prices and industrial activity. ... Because the Sun in a chart such as this represents leadership, Hong Kong's governor and legislature will likely see their power reduced or curtailed by their new masters. The Uranus opposition, which begins in 1990, symbolizes sudden changes in leadership or rebellion directed towards authority. It will likely agitate the population and hasten the exodus of people leaving Hong Kong for Australia and other parts of the world to avoid changes that will be enacted under China, which is against free markets and democratic rule. Meridian's Hong Kong forecast also foresaw a heavy set of hits starting in December 1989, and then again in April and October 1990. In short, Meridian recommended, "Move assets out of Hong Kong and avoid new investments." Singapore and Australia look better. The only players who should consider the Crown Colony are huge multinationals for whom investments would be a tiny percentage of their overall assets.

Meridian's work is an example of how detailed Mundane analysis can get. His Hong Kong examples are too complicated for newcomers and the purposes of this book, but they show the sense of history and numerous other data that people must have at their fingertips to produce effective reports. Meridian's newsletter takes many types of data into consideration, from the signing of the INF treaty—"an unseen disaster for U.S. defense"—to horoscopic analysis of world leaders. Astrologer Barry Lynes showed his powers of Mundane analysis by predicting the coming of Gorbachev, glasnost, and perestroika several years in advance. Lynes's projections were predicted overhauls, major changes, and rebirth. With the exception of dates, he didn't offer specifics. But Leonid Brezhnev's death in 1982, and the subsequent chain of events that it set off, all occurred in accord with Lynes's timing. Lynes has had similar success predicting the farm crisis and other problems in this country. He tried to get Paul Volcker, then head of the Federal Reserve Board, to give some of his ideas a hearing, but Volcker's office indicated they had the problem under control, thank you.

That Joan Quigley, the astrologer who advised Nancy Reagan, has boasted of her influential role in the White House and the power she wielded in setting times for events like the INF treaty, which Meridian criticizes, certainly suggests that astrological consulting can be subjective and poses many pitfalls for the country. The nation would certainly have the right to know the credentials and track record of any astrologer roaming the halls of officialdom. Yet one hopes the feds were just a little curious about some of the ideas Lynes outlined. Among them was the theory that Neptune's move through Capricorn from 1984 to 1998 (much like its move through the two other Earth signs) correlates to economic disturbances. Though Lynes has written extensively about the Neptune/Earth-sign connection to deflation, others, such as Norman Winski, a Chicago-based trader who combines conventional and astrological techniques, has also promoted the idea that Neptune's ride through Capricorn poses serious economic challenges and that the fourteen-year period relates to the deflation segment of the fifty-four-year Kondratieff Wave cycles.

Previous chapters have discussed the general effects of Neptune's move through Capricorn, as well as the movements of other planets on world affairs. But astrologers, in attempting to fine-tune their work and understand the specific challenges faced around the world, look to the national horoscopes for illumination. Because the elements of chart reading are beyond the scope of this book, this chapter is intended to give readers a general exposure to the field of Mundane Astrology. I will only briefly discuss some of the features and upcoming trends affecting the United States and key countries.

Cities and States

Cities, states, and corporations also have their own charts, but these are even more controversial. The problem lies not in the idea that a state is "born." Many would certainly agree that Louisiana's Gov. Edwin W. Edwards could probably not take his show on the road anyplace else. We were amused as we read about the New Year's Eve Concorde ride to Paris (at taxpayers' expense), and a range of other antics for which a jury acquitted him. Astrologers look on, knowing that Louisiana attained statehood when the Sun and Moon were in "I'm doing my own thing" Aries. But imagine the reaction that people in a Capricornian state like Connecticut, which is known as the "Land of Steady Habits," would have to such a character. To those in the Constitution State, a Leo neighbor like New York State can be too much. We all know that Leo needs to perform and hear applause, but those "I Love New York" ads can seem a little stale after all these years.

Louisiana's choice wouldn't even play elsewhere in the South. Connecticut and Texas don't seem to have much in common, but just as actress Susan Lucci, Richard Nixon, Ted Danson, and David Bowie are all different faces of Capricorn, Texas, like Connecticut, won statehood in Congress when the

Sun was in the sign of the status quo. Yet we can't overlook Texas's Independence Day celebrating its break from Mexico when the Sun and Moon were in Aries, which in many ways speaks to the Wild West image the state has.

Statehood charts may speak more to the type of legislators and laws affiliated with a state. California, for instance, would seem anything but virginal, but its Virgo statehood more accurately reflects the conservative voting habits of the entire state rather than fad-conscious southern California. Conservative leaders in the country are much more concerned about the "liberals" running around the Commonwealth of Massachusetts, which Congress voted in on a day when the Sun and Moon were in progressive, and often perverse and irreverent, Aquarius.

The dates on which Congress voted to grant statehood for each state are historic facts. Astrologers find general associations between these days and the perceived image of the state, but in truth, nobody is studying these charts in any depth. There are numerous questions about whether statehood charts should carry more weight than charts related to foundings and other activities. The matter is much more complex with the charts of cities, which, like corporations, exist for lengths of time preceding their incorporations or other legal sanctionings. The result is that there are several charts in use for most cities; charts based on charters, foundings, the building of forts, and incorporations. There is a general belief that each chart has some validity, but it is also obvious that one has to be more right than others. New York City is a perfect example. A popular chart in use gives the city a Sun in Cancer, which would have been under assault from constricting Saturn and regenerative Pluto, just to name a few of the explosive configurations associated with the bankruptcy of the mid-1970s. With Saturn moving into Capricorn, opposing the Cancer Sun from 1989 through 1991, one would expect the city to go through changes, as well as a reassessment of its direction and expression of itself. Since the Sun represents the leadership in a city, major changes in this symbol of the people would be expected.

The Cancer chart, which seems to reflect the emotional, defensive, containment, and food interests of the Big Apple, stems from the building of a fort in 1626. But astrologer Carolyn Dodson, who has compiled a collection of national horoscopes, argues that a fort or founding date isn't enough to make a city. Her book, *Horoscopes of the U.S. States & Cities*, offers an Aquarius Sun chart for the date (1653) of the first municipal form of government in New Amsterdam, and a Capricorn chart for the consolidation of the five boroughs. A Taurus chart based on the city's founding is also popular. Proponents of these and other charts back up their arguments by pointing to configurations they say relate to the financial crisis and other problems.

Cities and towns have different meanings, depending on the specific locale under discussion. Some cities only exist as a seat of government that holds together numerous outlying areas; other cities are more self-contained. As a journalist who once specialized in urban issues, I've had a special interest in tracking such activities astrologically. I don't think any of the city charts can be accepted without tracking planetary movements through the course of the city's entire history and not just the headline-grabbing events. It is also necessary to know something about how the city sees itself, to have a feel for the political alliances and debts involved. The faces of cities change over time; new industries evolve, others die. During some eras the activities seem to represent the chart quite literally. At other times it appears that different charts are in charge. It would seem impossible for a capital city, for instance, not to have an ongoing relationship with the state chart, particularly in cases where the state capitol and a range of other edifices have a bearing on the life of the city in which they're located.

The issue of city, state, and national horoscopes poses many philosophical and practical questions that can't be separated. Having lived in New England for more than twenty years, I know that it wouldn't be wise to ignore a city or town's founding date, even if all the settlers had done was to set up a fort on that date. The archetypes unleashed during the founding are something with which those who presume to keep the vigil for the city in modern times often identify. The earliest charts would provide a backdrop for the latter incorporation charts, which often may only speak to the various activities and attitudes of the city leaders rather than to the people themselves. Unlike the U.S.A. chart, which speaks to a nationality in effect, most people, particularly in these more mobile times, don't have an active relationship with the cities in which they live. The problem is the same for every American city. This is shaky ground, and not something that can be debated in depth here.

Born on the Fourth of July

For many of the reasons stated, and having given many words of caution, I'm using a July Fourth chart to help highlight some of the upcoming trends for the United States. This gives a limited, but solid, introductory view to newcomers to astrology. When it comes to the workings of government, the September 17, 1787, Constitution chart (which is appropriately a Virgo) and the Piscean federal government chart (March 4, 1789), which is concerned with maintaining an institution that dissolves competing interests and concerns into one citizenry, contain more specifics. The latter chart, interestingly, had a powerful connection with the birthchart of George Washington, who was also a Pisces. Pisces speaks more aptly to the concerns of a governing body (the real nitty-gritty workings) than the authoritarian sign of Capricorn, which mainly addresses structure and the hierarchy. Saturn was in Pisces in 1789, and its return to this sign in 1993 will be crucial to American-government structure (as it had been previously, most recently with Lyndon Johnson's Great Society and Franklin Roosevelt's New Deal).

To those familiar with the changing face of public opinion and current affairs, the differing messages presented by the federal government chart or the earlier 1776 chart should be no surprise. The American people are often at odds with the government and the Constitution. If decisions about issues like the abolition of slavery, military interventions, and other activities were truly left to the citizenry, the outcomes would be different. Ideally the 1787 and 1789 charts have a larger sense of purpose than the 1776 chart, which speaks to who we are as a collective people and indicates the trends that we must respond to. Astrologers use numerous charts before making their projections; these include charts of national leaders, as well as the Inauguration Day chart that launched the administration. More complexity is added when charts for the exact moment of equinoxes, solstices, and the entry of major planets into a given sign (Pluto in Scorpio, for instance) are introduced. But these are thumbnail sketches.

Since we've already established some of the Cancerian concerns indicated by astrology, it's important to note that some of these interpretations of the national character are held by scholars as well. Anthropologist Geoffrey Gorer touches on many aspects of the American character that relate to what astrologers would recognize as Cancerian traits. These personality traits range from the the peculiar use of food as both reward and punishment in the raising of children to a national character that Gorer says is decidedly "feminine."

Though Gorer's study was first published in 1948 (and later revised in 1964), some of his insights remain valid, despite changes in society. Mothers in America, Gorer observed, have had more control and say in the child's upbringing than in Europe and other parts of the world. While men control corporations and push for the country's prominence in the world, childrearing, until recently, was exclusively handled by the mother. Other strong adult role models, such as elementary-school teachers, are predominantly female, in contrast to many other cultures. Gorer contended that these strong feminine influences cause special confusions within the American male.

The fact that the rules for moral conduct are felt to emanate from a feminine source is a source of confusion to American men. They tend to resent such interference with their own behavior, and yet are unable to ignore it, since the insistent maternal conscience is a part of their personality. This frequently leads them into seemingly contradictory behavior, and is a major source of the bewilderment which most non-Americans feel when confronted with American men.

Gorer writes from a perspective of decades ago, but some of this influence continues today. Yet even as American men (and increasingly women) rebel against the psychological influence of "mother," the separation from the "rejected father," as Gorer describes it, leaves deeper psychological wounds and aptly explains some of the United States' efforts to make a place for itself in the world.

Astrologically the "rejected father" is indicated by the fact that the Sun (self) and Saturn (self-preservations, authority) are three signs away from one another in a ninety-degree angle. The configuration indicates that each energy is blocking the other one from thriving. It's as if they're saying to each other, "If I can't have the brass ring, neither can you." People born with this configuration are usually born into situations where they feel they must always prove themselves to a parent figure, or else are ashamed of a parent, a pattern that continues throughout life. It is appropriate, then, that as the colonists broke away from "father" King George and England, the configuration of the rejected father was in the sky. Gorer observes that the archetype is carried into modern times. American children are expected to do better economically than their fathers, which is not an expectation in other cultures. People who aren't economically mobile are considered failures. They didn't prove themselves. Talk in recent years of the dying American Dream, incidentally, is based on the presumption that all generations should "do better"—in terms of owning a home, cars, and other property—than the previous generation. Because such "dreams" are getting farther out of reach, Americans' Sun/ Saturn configuration is particularily anxiety-provoking.

The U.S.A.'s Moon Sign

While the Sun would have been in Cancer on July 2, a possible birthdate of the country, the Moon would have been in Capricorn on July 2, and in Aquarius on July 4. The Capricorn Moon, as noted in Part II of this book, would have produced a national emotional response programmed to react in a controlled, mature, and repressed way to various stimuli. There would be an emotional need to have authority and win respect from others, a conscious attempt to set oneself up in life (through career, relationships, or otherwise) in such a way as to be insulated from the more threatening and vulnerable position that comes from sharing emotions. The Moon in Aquarius that comes with the July Fourth date we're using is detached, but at the same time desirous (in need) of social participation and interaction with a community. They are concerned with social mores and often openly seek to write their own definition of them, the results of which can appear quite perverse to others. They are detached, hard to know, but move through many networks of people. Their approach to child-bearing and a range of other areas of life would be rational, based on scientific precepts (Americans created the market for how-to books on bringing up baby, lovemaking, living).

BEHIND THE AMERICAN DREAM It should be noted that the American Dream concept of emotional security, based on nurturing one's personal foundations—since New Deal initiatives of the 1930s, homeownership has been one prime way this is expressed—is linked to the placement of

Venus and Jupiter in Cancer (in addition to the Sun in Cancer placement). Venus and Jupiter enhance the sign they move through and bring benefits in these areas. In addition to larger living spaces and homes, this also relates to the abundance of food, and often its misuse.

Mercury in Cancer makes us foils for nostalgia and sales pitches that appeal to the emotions, sentiments, and remembrance of things past. The ad with Mrs. Cleaver and Mrs. Anderson—two Moms we grew up with—selling Milk of Magnesia makes this point. European advertising—even in firms with American affiliates—is more cerebral. Mercury opposition to Pluto also speaks to the unconscious legacies and power issues underlying the thought patterns and communications in the U.S.A. The Retrograde Mercury makes the situation less obvious because people are usually nurturing their own fears and insecurities. People don't feel that the country's bloodthirsty legacy of killing Native Americans, slavery, and other ills have anything to do with the American psyche and its present. But stereotypes, and our karma from the past, block much of our thinking. As a result, American minds are easily manipulated by scare campaigns, such as George Bush's Willie Horton advertisements. Certainly people around the world are vulnerable to various prejudices in their thinking, but American bigotry and racism in its unconscious forms permeate our culture. Americans are usually offended and surprised because they often equate racism with name-calling or openly hostile activities such as cross burnings and lynchings. While Europe isn't without its own problems, African-American businesspeople, some of whom have relocated to Europe, say they don't experience the same insidious racism they find in the United States. However, Mercury and Pluto are both retrograde in the U.S.A. chart, and this indicates a counterpoint, with an eventual escalation and illumination about the problem.

The United States has a strong Gemini influence that keeps it on the go but also makes us a superficial, scattered people. Gemini gets much credit for its intellectual interests and need for mental stimulation, but in most Geminis the concerns are very small. They are the people who repeat the gossip and little bits of information they take in during the course of their day. They immediately shorten new acquaintances' names or assign nicknames. Frequently they don't know what they're talking about. This energy, intermingled with Cancer, was demonstrated by Archie Bunker. Many people put the Gemini/Cancer

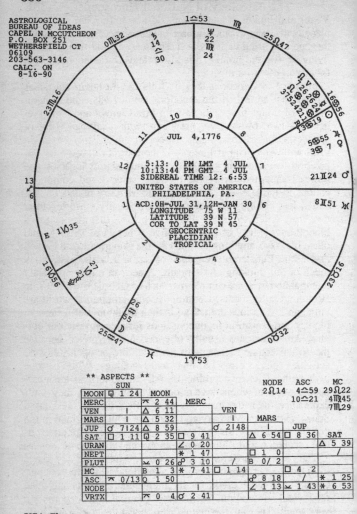

ASTROLOGICAL
BUREAU OF IDEAS
CAPEL N MCCUTCHEON
P.O. BOX 251
WETHERSFIELD CT
06109
203-563-3146
CALC. ON
8-16-90

1♎53
0♏32
25♌47
23♏16
13
6
E 1♑35
16♑56
25♒47

10
9
8
7
6
5
4
3
2
1
12
11

JUL 4, 1776

5:13: 0 PM LMT 4 JUL
10:13:44 PM GMT 4 JUL
SIDEREAL TIME 12: 6:53

UNITED STATES OF AMERICA
PHILADELPHIA, PA.

ACD:0H=JUL 31,12H=JAN 30
LONGITUDE 75 W 11
LATITUDE 39 N 57
COR TO LAT 39 N 45
GEOCENTRIC
PLACIDIAN
TROPICAL

16♌56
5♋55 ♃
3♋7 ♀
21♊24 ♂
8♊51 ♅
23♋16
0♋32
1♈53

♇
14
♎
30
♆
22
♏
24

25♒47 ☽

** ASPECTS **

	SUN		MOON		MERC		VEN		MARS		JUP		SAT
MOON	⊡ 1 24		MOON										
MERC			⊼ 2 44		MERC								
VEN	I		△ 6 11				VEN						
MARS	I		△ 5 32				I		MARS				
JUP	♂ 7 ⫯24		△ 8 59				♂ 21 ⫯48		I		JUP		
SAT	□ 1 11		⊡ 2 35		□ 9 41				△ 6 54		□ 8 36		SAT
URAN					∠ 0 20								△ 5 39
NEPT					* 1 47				□ 1 0				/
PLUT			⋎ 0 26		♂ 3 10				B 0/ 2				
MC			B 1 3		* 7 41		□ 1 14				□ 4 2		
ASC	⊼ 0/13		⊡ 1 50						♂ 8 18		/		* 1 25
NODE									∠ 1 13		⋎ 1 43		* 6 53
VRTX			⊼ 0 4		♂ 2 41		I						

	NODE	ASC	MC
	2♌14	4♎59	29♌22
		10♎21	4♏45
			7♏29

USA Chart:

These are the two most popular USA birthcharts; the first, calculated
at 2:13 A.M. July 4, 1776 (Gemini rising) gets the most extensive use,
though there is no documentation supporting this time; the chart for
5:13 P.M. (Sagittarius) was used by the late master astrologer, Dane

```
PLANET *DIG   SIGN      HSE DECLN   LAT TRAVL DS        GEOCENTRIC
SUN    B C   13CAN19    7   22.8    .0   0 57  1   N-NODE    S-NODE
MOON         26AQU55    3  -14.4  -1.6  14 27 97   7LEO37    7AQU37
MERC         24CAN11R   8   17.4  -3.9   0-29 93   0CAN26  10LEO 4
VEN    A      3CAN 7    7   23.6    .1   1 14  3   0CAN58  27LEO26
MARS   B     21GEM24    7   23.6    .4   0 41 11   9GEM 5   6LIB52
JUP    E      5CAN55    7   23.2   -.2   0 14 13   8CAN23   6CAP 2
SAT    E A   14LTB30   10  -3.4    2.5   0  2 50  19CAN58  21CAP30
URAN          8GEM51    6   21.7   -.1   0  3 24  12GEM38   9SAG26
NEPT   D     22VIR24    9    4.1    1.2   0  1 30   8LEO 0   9AQU38
PLUT   B     27CAP21R   2  -24.3  -3.7   0 -1 73  17CAN12  17CAP25
MC            1LIB53         .7
ASC          13SAG 6       -22.4    *R=RULE D=DETRIMENT E=EXALTED
NODE          7LEO37        18.4     F=FALL C=IN CRITICAL DEGREE
VRTX         26CAN52        20.8     A=ACCID DIGNITY BY HOUSE POS
EQ A          1CAP35       -23.5     B=ACCD DEBILITY BY HOUSE POS
```

```
FIRE NONE CAR SUN              ARABIC PARTS
ERTH   NEPT   6 MERC     FORTUNE  26 CANC 42
     2 PLUT     VEN      SPIRIT   29 ARIE 29
AIR  MARS      JUP       STATUS   15 TAUR 29
     4 SAT     SAT       DESTINY  18 AQUA 16
       URAN    PLUT
       MOON FIX MOON        * DYNAMIC FOCUS *
WATR   SUN    1         (CLOSEST SQUA OR OPPO)
     4 MERC MUT MARS     MARS SQUA NEPT 1  0
       VEN    3 URAN
       JUP     NEPT
```

```
ANG.  SUN    EAST             JULIAN DATE
    5 VEN                    2369916.426204
      MARS          MEAN OBLIQUITY OF ECLIPTIC
      JUP    WEST          23 DEG. 29 MIN
      SAT    7       SIDEREAL AYANAMSHA (SVP)
SUC.  MERC                   8 PISC 23
    2 PLUT   SOUTH
CAD.  URAN   3
    3 NEPT                ASPECTS     ANGLE ORB  NO
      MOON   NORTH    ♂=CONJUNCTION    0  10   4
      3              ⚹=SEMISEXTILE    30   2   2
                     ∠=SEMISQUARE     45   3   4
POS  4  NEG  6       ✱=SEXTILE        60   9   8
VOCATIONAL IND VEN   □=SQUARE         90  10   7
MUTUAL RECEPTION     △=TRINE         120  10   9
      NONE           ⚏=SESQUIQUAD    135   3   3
SOLE DISPOSITR NONE  ⚻=QUINCUNX      150   3   3
SINGLETON NONE       ☍=OPPOSITION    180  10   4
SUN/MOON ANG 223.61  Q=QUINTILE       72   2   2
                     B=BIQUINTILE    144   2   2
                     ∣=PARALLEL        0   1   8
                     /=CONTRAPARA    180   1   6
```

```
                           ** MID-POINTS **
      NEPT    URAN    SAT     JUP    MARS    VEN    MERC   MOON    SUN
LUT  Υ 7  24♌38  2♏51  5♏41  16♋23  9♋ 8  14♋59  25♋31  11♉54  20♌ 5  VRTX
♏29      0♏ 1  8♋14  11♏ 4  21♋46  14♋30  20♋22  0♋54  17♉16  25♋28  NODE
♏14   2♏45  10)(58  13♏48  24♏30  17♏15  23♏ 6  0♋24  1♏ 2  1♊12  ASC
♏37  27♏ 8  5♌22  8⚍11  18♌54  11♌38  17♌30  28♌ 2  14♒24  22♌36  MC
      24♏53  3Υ 6  5♐56  16Υ38  9Υ23  15Υ14  25Υ46  12♒ 8  20Υ20  PLUT
            0♌38  3⚍27  14♌ 9  6♌54  12♌45  23♌18  9♐40  17♌52  NEPT
                   11♌41  22♌23  15♊ 7  20♊59  1♋31  17Υ53  26♊ 5  URAN
                        25♌12  17♌57  23♌48  4♏21  20♐43  28♌55  SAT
                             28♊39  4♋31  15♋ 3  1♋25  9♋37  JUP
```

```
RAN       NEPT
         │△ 4 57│ PLUT
6 58│♂ 9 29│△ 4 31│ MC
3⚍14│∠ 9 18│∠ 0 44│Q 0 47│ ASC
1 14│∠ 0 13│      │✱ 5 45│△ 5 29│ NODE
1   │✱ 4 28│☍ 0 30│✱ 5 1│□ 1 14│
```

```
                    27♊15   7♋47  24Υ10  2♋21  MARS
                          13♋39   0♋ 1  8♋13  VEN
                                10♋33  18♋45  MERC
                                       5♉ 7  MOON
```

Rudhyar, and is based on records kept by the Philadelphia Historical Society. Astrologers using both charts have predicted events such as World War II, the assassination of John F. Kennedy, and the recession of 1989–90.

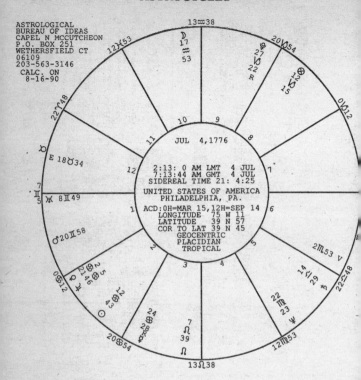

```
** ASPECTS **
```

	SUN	MOON	MERC	VEN	MARS	JUP	SAT
MOON	B 0 50						
MERC		/					
VEN	l	□ 0 33					
MARS	l	△ 3 5					
JUP	♂ 6157	□ 2 53		♂ 3126			
SAT	□ 1 46	△ 3 24	□ 9 58		△ 6 29	□ 8 43	
URAN		△ 9 4	∠ 0 38				△ 5 40
NEPT	B 1 30	⁎ 2 4	□ 9 57	□ 1 25			
PLUT		⚇ 2 55	/	B 0/24			
MC	⚹ 0 55	♂ 4115	/	△ 7 20	B 1 52	△ 0 51	
ASC			∠ 2 23		⚹ 1 19	△ 7 24	
NODE		l		∠ 1 41	⚹ 1 53	⚹ 6 50	
VRTX	△ 9 50		□ 8 25	△ 0 32	△ 2 53		

NODE	ASC	MC
20 ♏16	19 ♌59	23 ♐15
	7 ♋22	10 ♉39
		10 ♈21

```
PLANET *DIG  SIGN     HSE DECLN  LAT TRAVL DS      GEOCENTRIC
SUN     C  12CAN43   2  22.9   .0  0 57  1  N-NODE    S-NODE
MOON    B  17AQU53  10 -16.6  -.9 14 27 94  7LEO39   7AQU39
MERC    A  24CAN28R  3  17.5  -3.8 0-27 93 29GEM57   9LEO27
VEN     A   2CAN21   2  23.5   .1  1 14  3  0CAN37  26LEO36
MARS    A  20GEM58   1  23.6   .4  0 41 11  8GEM51   6LIB42
JUP   E B   5CAN46   2  23.2  -.2  0 14 13  8CAN17   6CAP10
SAT   E B  14LIB29   5  -3.4   2.5  0  2 50 19CAN54  21CAP34
URAN       8GEM49   1  21.7  -.1  0  3 24 12GEM36   9SAG27
NEPT  D   22VIR23   5  -4.1   1.2  0  1 30  7LEO59   9AQU39
PLUT      27CAP22R  9 -24.3  -3.7  0 -1 73 17CAN11  17CAP26
MC        13AQU38     -16.8
ASC        7GEM 5     21.5   *R=RULE D=DETRIMENT E=EXALTED
NODE       7LEO39     18.4   F=FALL C=IN CRITICAL DEGREE
VRTX       2SCO53    -12.5   A=ACCID DIGNITY BY HOUSE POS
EQ A      18TAU34     17.7   B=ACCD DEBILITY BY HOUSE POS
```

```
          FIRE NONE CAR SUN          ARABIC PARTS
          ERTH NEPT   6 MERC    FORTUNE  12 CAPR 15
           2  PLUT      VEN     SPIRIT    1 SCOR 55
          AIR  MARS      JUP    STATUS   18 VIRG 48
           4  SAT       SAT     DESTINY  .8 CANC 28
              URAN      PLUT
              MOON FIX MOON     * DYNAMIC FOCUS *
          WATR SUN   1       (CLOSEST SQUA OR OPPO)
           4  MERC MUT MOON     MARS SQUA NEPT 1 25
              VEN    3 URAN
              JUP      NEPT
```

```
          ANG. MARS EAST            JULIAN DATE
           3   URAN   7          2369915.801204
               MOON         MEAN OBLIQUITY OF ECLIPTIC
          SUC. SUN  WEST          23 DEG. 29 MIN
           5   VEN    3      SIDEREAL AYANAMSHA (SVP)
               JUP                 8 PISC 23
               SAT
               NEPT SOUTH
                      2
          CAD. MERC              ASPECTS    ANGLE ORB  NO
           2   PLUT NORTH      ☌=CONJUNCTION   0  10   4
                       8       ⩡=SEMISEXTILE  30   2   2
                               ∠=SEMISQUARE   45   3   4
          POS  4 NEG 6         ✳=SEXTILE      60   9   4
          VOCATIONAL IND VEN   □=SQUARE       90  10   8
          MUTUAL RECEPTION     △=TRINE       120  10  15
             NONE              ⚼=SESQUIQUAD  135   3   2
          SOLE DISPOSITR NONE  ⚻=QUINCUNX    150   4   1
          SINGLETON NONE       ☍=OPPOSITION  180  10   2
          SUN/MOON ANG 215.17  Q=QUINTILE     72   2   0
                               B =BIQUINTILE 144   2   6
                               |=PARALLEL      0   1   9
                               /=CONTRAPARA  180   1   5
```

```
                      ** MID-POINTS **
     NEPT   URAN   SAT    JUP    MARS   VEN    MERC   MOON   SUN
LUT  ♐ 8  12♏38 20♎51 23♎41  4♏20 26♌56  2♏37 13♏40 25♐23  7♏48 VRTX
♏31  0♏ 1  8♋14 11♏ 4 21♋43 14♋19 20♋ 0  1♌ 3 12♋46 25♋11 NODE
♈14 29♋44  7♏57 10♎47 21♏25 14♊ 2  7♈33  0♋46 12♈29 24♏54 ASC
≈30  3♈ 1 11♈14 14♐ 4 24♈42 17♈18 22♈59  4♌ 3 15≈46 28♈11 MC
     24♏53  3♈ 6  5♈56 16♈34  9♈10 14♈51 25♈55  7≈38 20♈ 7 PLUT
            0♌36  3♌26 14♌ 5  6♎41 12♌22 23♌25  5♐ 8 17♌33 NEPT
                 11♌39 22♏18 14♏54 20♊35  1♌38 13♈21 25♊46 URAN
                       25♌ 8 17♌44 23♌25  4♏28 16♏11 28♌36 SAT
```

```
RAN   NEPT  △ 4 59  PLUT          28♊22  4♏ 3 15♌ 7 26♈50  9♋15 JUP
      NEPT                              26♊39  7♏43 19♈26 16♋51 MARS
 4 49        MC                              13♋24 25♈ 7  7♋32 VEN
1144        △ 9 43 △ 6 33  ASC                    6♉10 18♋35 MERC
1 10 ∠ 0 16       ♂ 5 59 ✳ 0 34  NODE                  0♉18 MOON
0  4         □ 5 31       B 1 48 □ 4 46
```

energy to higher use. Bill Cosby has the Cancer/Gemini connection as well as a Mercury/Pluto conjunction that helps heal the Mercury/Pluto problems existing in the U.S.A. chart. Cosby's humor deals with everyday neighborhood concerns—from Fat Albert and his friends to the more recent sitcom—and focuses on issues that everyone can relate to.

The Gemini influence comes from the nation's Mars, which shows the country stepping forward into the world in a highly communicative, interactive, but also scattered fashion, and Uranus, which was discovered five years after the signing of the Declaration of Independence. Uranus, planet of awakening and revolution, moving through Gemini, was waking the world up to the need to break away from existing modes of thought and ways of connecting to their environment. Those who have adopted a "birthtime" of between 2:00 and 3:00 A.M. for the United States also recognize a Gemini Rising sign, which would emphasize the mobile, communicative tendencies of the nation. The evening times would give the country a Sagittarius Rising sign (Gemini's polar opposite), which is expansive and forward-looking and which seeks to explore and spread its beliefs to others.

The Declaration was signed when Neptune, moving through Virgo, was causing confusion and despair among the masses, who were becoming increasingly frustrated by the tax and other edicts from the overlords in England. Pluto moving through Capricorn indicated that it was time to transform the structures of authority that the people looked to for leadership. Pluto's return to Capricorn in the second decade of the twenty-first century will force the issue. This placement in its birthchart would also indicate that such structures would have to be continually transformed throughout the history of the country. Saturn in Libra showed the need to define relationships and to restructure contracts and partnerships.

That Was Then, This Is Now

Saturn in Libra is a good place to start in our attempt to "update" the chart and explain why the country entered the 1990s under such stress. The election of Ronald Reagan coincided with the country's seventh Saturn Return and represented a time when individuals and our government were restructuring and redefining ourselves. Saturn moving through

Capricorn (1989–91), three signs away from Libra, meant that the structures and soundness of the redefining that took place at the Saturn Return will be challenged. Jupiter in Cancer returned to the July 4, 1776, position during the summer of 1989, calling on the United States to integrate and assimilate new philosophies and knowledge as it starts another 11.8-year cycle. The country was responding to the expansionist tendencies of Jupiter, perhaps in an overly optimistic fashion, particularly in light of mounting debt and other fiscal problems. That Jupiter and Saturn were also midway through a 20-year socioeconomic cycle begun in 1980–81 has already been explored.

The importance to the country of late 1989 and the early 1990s is related to several configurations, all of which have been explored in previous chapters. However, further information is provided when the ongoing movement of the planets is compared to July 4, 1776. By the time Bush was elected, the country was like a person who has come out of the dark, fantasy land of the cinema, rubbing their eyes in an attempt to become reoriented to reality. Reagan, in many ways, wove cinematic untruths in front of our eyes. His second term proved to be particularly disoriented because Neptune, the fantasy master, had moved 180 degrees (six signs) across from the country's Venus (values, money) and Jupiter (faith and optimism). We were hoodwinked. When private individuals experience this configuration in their birthchart, they marry alcoholics or other helpless people, or hook up with people who say they're doctors and end up being wanted in several states for bigamy, credit-card theft, and other false claims.

It's fair to say that the love affair is over. The movements of Saturn, Uranus, and Neptune through Capricorn have a special significance for the country as the 1990s begin. Neptune, from late 1989 through 1990, will dissolve our sense of self as it depresses real estate values, the economy, and works to undermine authority figures and traditional values and procedures. Uranus, toward the end of 1990, will be shaking up the country and its leaders. Saturn finished out 1989 by applying extra pressures on the leadership, as represented by the country's Sun in Cancer.

Saturn's movements in relation to the country's Sun have always been critical. Its move through Capricorn puts it 180 degrees away from the country's Sun, an alignment that would relate to a refocusing or restructuring at the top. The country is midway in its 29.5-year self-definition cycle that began when

Saturn moved over the Sun in 1974 and Nixon resigned. (The cycle began in Cancer, and Saturn's movements through Libra, Capricorn, and Aries mark the important quarter phases of the cycle.) During the First Quarter season, seven years later, Ronald Reagan arrived. Bush is at the midpoint and is dealing with a changing economic world that, interestingly, began in the mid-1950s as Saturn moved through Cancer and OPEC and other changes created new realities that the country has never yet thoroughly faced. Saturn's move through Aries, the winter phase of the cycle, in 1996, will relate to fallout and reorientation as well.

Saturn's last move through Capricorn brought in John F. Kennedy, midway through a cycle that began as World War II ended, when Saturn was in Cancer. Saturn in Libra in 1952 brought Eisenhower, while the Saturn in Aries winter (and final) phase made Richard Nixon president.

These dates are significant for more than just the start of new presidential eras. All of them marked periods of economic and policy changes. Various scenarios can readily be intuited.

The importance of 1992–93, as well as dates through the remainder of the century, have already been explored. Without the exact birthtime of the United States, it is impossible to get a precise zodiacal position (degrees and minutes) for the country's Moon in Aquarius, which will be under orders to transform its collective emotional responses and security needs, as well as its experience of women, when Pluto moves into a square with it. Since Pluto leaves Scorpio (the offending sign to Aquarius, so to speak) by 1996, the 90-degree challenging experience will happen before that time. Since the sky changes every four minutes, the differences between the timing indicated by the early-morning July Fourth charts and the evening charts are significant and span a few years (1990 to 1994–95). Both dates could help pave the way for a woman in the White House by the 1996 election.

George Bush Meets the U.S.A. Chart

George Bush belongs to that tiny fraternity of Geminis—John F. Kennedy being the other—to hold the American presidency. The Gemini Sun/Libra Moon combination shows Bush to be a person for whom personal interactions and associations are very important. He needs stimulation and is open to discussion. He lacks the ideology of the Aquarian Sun/Taurus Moon of Ronald Reagan or even of the Aquarian Sun/Leo Moon of Dan Quayle. Bush's Virgo Rising sign also gives him some humility and task orientation, though it can be difficult for him to see the big picture or to get a handle on "this vision thing."

Bush was born under several potent configurations (His chart appears on page 338). The first, which involves the Sun, Jupiter, and Uranus, can make him erratic, scattered, pushing off in many directions, not necessarily certain where it's all leading. He's open to trying out new ideas and projects, but he can lack staying power. And even though he's not an ideologue, he is capable of running around with a certain feeling of "rightness" and being very wrong. He needs steadier and more stable advisers. Bush's chart is particularly interesting because it's very easy to see how, had he not been born an upper-middle-class white male, the more dynamic configurations in his chart could have been utilized to promote more progressive, effective changes within the system, or else to rebel against it entirely. A configuration involving his Moon, Venus, Saturn, and Pluto reflects the perception of his difficulties with women. At the very least the configuration indicates an emotional straitjacket. The Libra Moon's need for social approval and acceptance and its generally accommodating ways are emotionally restrictive and are felt as an obligation, as Saturn in the relationship-cautious sign of Libra suggests. The Moon/Saturn configuration is reflected in stories about the way his mother chastised him for schoolday tales that emphasized the first person (*I*). She stressed the need for the young Bush to speak of a *we*, to include others in his world, and to recognize their participation and abilities. This is at cross-purposes with Bush's Venus and Pluto in Cancer, which ultimately forces one to seek security within oneself. The sociability indicated by the Libra placements might lure a person into thinking that the Cancer needs are being met because there are all those smiling, pleasant people around. But Librans' continual edginess to achieve balance and see themselves reflected in others can exacerbate the emotional wariness and defensiveness that can result when Cancer isn't free to come from who it truly is.

Bush's chart has many direct links with the U.S.A. chart. The most obvious general connections involve the Gemini/Cancer energy. Cancer, it should be noted, is a popular sign for a number of political leaders and others in the limelight:

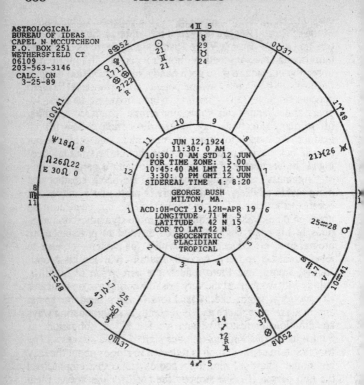

ASTROLOGICAL
BUREAU OF IDEAS
CAPEL N MCCUTCHEON
P.O. BOX 251
WETHERSFIELD CT
06109
203-563-3146
CALC. ON
3-25-89

JUN 12,1924
11:30: 0 AM
10:30: 0 AM STD 12 JUN
FOR TIME ZONE: 5.00
10:45:40 AM LMT 12 JUN
3:30: 0 PM GMT 12 JUN
SIDEREAL TIME 4: 8:20

GEORGE BUSH
MILTON, MA.

ACD:0H=OCT 19,12H=APR 19
LONGITUDE 71 W 5
LATITUDE   42 N 15
COR TO LAT 42 N 3
GEOCENTRIC
PLACIDIAN
TROPICAL

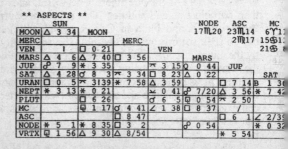

** ASPECTS **

	SUN		MOON		MERC		VEN		MARS		JUP		SAT	
MOON	△ 3 34													
MERC			□ 0 21											
VEN	I		△ 7 40		□ 3 56									
MARS	△ 4 6		△ 7 40		□ 3 56		⊼ 3 15		Q 0 44					
JUP	☍ 7 9		✳ 3 35				⊼ 3 15		Q 0 44					
SAT	△ 4 28		♂ 8 3		⊼ 3 34		□ 8 23		△ 0 22					
URAN	□ 0 5		⊼ 3139		✳ 7 58		△ 3 59				□ 7 14	B	△ 1 30	
NEPT	✳ 3 13		✳ 0 21				⋌ 0 41		☍ 7/20		△ 3 56	⊁	✳ 7 42	
PLUT			□ 6 26				♂ 6 5		Q 0 54		⊼ 2 50			
MC			Q 1 17		♂ 4 41		∠ 1 38		□ 8 37		/			
ASC					□ 8 47						□ 6 1		∠ 2/39	
NODE	✳ 5 1		✳ 8 35		△ 3 2				♂ 0 54				✳ 0 32	
VRTX	Q 1 56		△ 9 30		△ 8/54						✳ 5 54			

	NODE	ASC	MC
	17♏20	23♏14	6♈1
		2♏17	15♋1
			21♋

```
PLANET *DIG   SIGN    HSE DECLN  LAT TRAVL DS    GEOCENTRIC
  SUN        21GEM21  10  23.2   .0   0 57  3  N-NODE   S-NODE
  MOON   A   17LIB47   2  -3.1  4.1  14 23 87  26LEO22  26AQU22
  MERC   B   29TAU24   9  17.5 -2.6   1 27 51  13GEM25  13CAN23
  VEN        17CAN27R 11  23.1   .8   0 -7 94  19GEM 1   5CAN37
  MARS       25AQU28   6 -16.2 -3.4   0 55 88   1GEM48   1LIB31
  JUP  R A   14SAG12R  4 -21.8   .7   0 -8 85   6CAN53  13CAP40
  SAT  E   C 25LIB50R  2  -7.5  2.4   0 -2 63  19CAN45  26CAP 1
  URAN       21PIS26   7  -4.1 -1.8   0  1 27  13GEM35  12SAG43
  NEPT   A   18LEO 8  12  15.6   .3   0  1 28   9LEO26  12AQU20
  PLUT       11CAN22  11  20.6 -2.4   0  1 32  18CAN43  20CAP10
  MC          4GEM 5      21.0
  ASC         8VIR11       8.5        *R=RULE D=DETRIMENT E=EXALTED
  NODE       26LEO22      12.7        F=FALL C=IN CRITICAL DEGREE
  VRTX        8AQU17     -18.2        A=ACCID DIGNITY BY HOUSE POS
  EQ A       30LEO 0      11.5        B=ACCD DEBILITY BY HOUSE POS

        FIRE JUP  CAR VEN         ARABIC PARTS
         2   NEPT  4  SAT     FORTUNE   4 CAPR 37
        ERTH MERC     PLUT    SPIRIT   11 TAUR 45
         1            MOON    STATUS    0 LIBR 31
        AIR  SUN  FIX MERC    DESTINY   7 AQUA 39
         4   MARS  3  MARS
             SAT      NEPT      * DYNAMIC FOCUS *
             MOON MUT SUN     (CLOSEST SQUA OR OPPO)
        WATR VEN   3  JUP      SUN  SQUA URAN  0  5
         3   URAN     URAN
             PLUT
                   EAST
        ANG. SUN   6         JULIAN DATE
         3   JUP            2423949.145833
             URAN WEST    MEAN OBLIQUITY OF ECLIPTIC
        SUC. VEN   4       23 DEG. 27 MIN
         4   SAT          SIDEREAL AYANAMSHA (SVP)
             PLUT SOUTH         6 PISC 19
             MOON  6
        CAD. MERC
         3   MARS NORTH     ASPECTS      ANGLE ORB  NO
             NEPT  4       σ=CONJUNCTION    0  10   4
                          ⚹=SEMISEXTILE    30   2   1
        POS  6 NEG  4     ∠=SEMISQUARE     45   3   4
        VOCATIONAL IND MERC ⚹=SEXTILE      60   9  10
        MUTUAL RECEPTION   □=SQUARE        90  10  12
         VEN AND MOON      △=TRINE        120  10  10
        SOLE DISPOSITR NONE ⚼=SESQUIQUAD  135   3   3
        SINGLETON NONE     ⚻=QUINCUNX     150   4   7
        SUN/MOON ANG 116.43 ☍=OPPOSITION  180  10   4
                           Q=QUINTILE      72   2   2
                           B=BIQUINTILE   144   2   1
                           I=PARALLEL       0   1   3
                           /=CONTRAPARA   180   1   4
```

```
                      ** MID-POINTS **
*T  NEPT   URAN   SAT    JUP    MARS   VEN    MERC   MOON   SUN
50 13♏13 29♒52 17♐ 4 11♑15 16♒53 27♈52  3♈51 13♐ 2 14♈49 VRTX
52 22♌15  8♊54 26♏ 6 20♎17 25♏55  6♌54 12♋53 22♏ 5 23♋52 NODE
46 28♌10 14♊49  2♎ 1 26♐12  1♐49 12♌49 18♋48 27♍59 29♋46 ASC
43 11♋ 6 27♊45 14♌57  9♓ 8 14♈46 25♋46  1♊44 10♋56 12♋43 MC
   29♋45 16♉24  3♏36 27♏47  3♉25 14♋24 20♏23 29♏34  1♋21 PLUT
          4♊47 18♏59 16♋10 21♑48  2♎47  8♋46 17♏58 19♋45 NEPT
                 8♉38  2♒49  8♓27 19♋26 25♈25  4♒37  6♉24 URAN
18 NEPT              20♏ 1 25♐39  6♏38 12♌37 21♎49 23♌36 SAT
        PLUT               19♑50  0♎49  6♊48 16♏ 0 17♍47 JUP
39        I    MC                 6♏27 12♈26 21♐38 23♈25 MARS
      ⚹ 3 10 □ 4  6  ASC               23♊25  2♏37  4♋24 VEN
  σ 8 14 ∠ 0  0 □ 7 43     NODE                 8♌36 10♊23 MERC
51 ☍ 9 51 ⚻ 3  4 △ 4 13 ⚻ 0  6                       19♌34 MOON
```

From Jack Kemp to Elizabeth and Robert Dole to Thurgood Marshall, Geraldo Rivera, Ann Landers/Dear Abby, and George Steinbrenner. This is partly because July is often one of the country's most fertile birth months—it usually alternates with August. But the role that the sign Cancer plays in the formation of the American national character would also result in people born on the Fourth of July and other parts of the month having a special affinity with the collective.

Bush's Sun at 21 degrees 21 minutes Gemini is tightly conjunct the U.S.A.'s Mars, while Bush's Uranus is in the stressful 90 degree-angle (three signs away) from that same Mars. Some astrologers find this relationship fearful and speculate that this connection might result in Bush's impulsively hurling America into military actions or keeping the country on red alert for four years, as astrologer Mark Lerner has suggested in his column in *Welcome to Planet Earth,* an astrology magazine. It is certainly true that two individuals with such a connection between their birthcharts could expect an erratic relationship, possibly with much electricity and an element of danger. The energy, however, can also point to a leader who illuminates (his Sun) and awakens (his Uranus) us to make us act (our Mars) in a more dynamic fashion that is free of older ways of thinking. As Mark Lerner has also noted, Bush may literally take us to Mars.

Bush and the United States both have Venus in Cancer, indicating shared values. Like the United States, Bush was born with Saturn in Libra, a position stressing a heavy sense of responsibility toward partnerships and the ongoing redefinition of those relationships, a focused balancing of individual identity with the identity of the other. Bush was born as the United States went through its fifth Saturn Return, and he became vice president on the seventh, as the terms of both written and unwritten contracts in the spheres of individual, government, and general societal relations were being restructured. Saturn moving through Capricorn (particularly in late 1989 and early 1990) will be similar to the critical adjustments (sometimes forced by crisis or stressful circumstances) that force thirty-seven-year-olds to confront various challenges in their lives following decisions made at the Saturn Return at ages twenty-nine to thirty. Bush gets a double whammy; one is an age cycle affecting everyone seven years into their second Saturn return that comes at fifty-eight to sixty; the other is related to the U.S.A. chart, whose upcoming cycles for late

1989 and beyond were briefly outlined. On the personal level, January–February 1990 increases the stress as Bush's emotional nature (Moon) and his overall feeling of well-being and contentment (Venus) are also under Saturn's restrictive watch. Given the feminine nature of these planets, females in his life may feel the effects of the configuration.

J. Danforth Quayle

Unlike Bush, the vice president was born under a Sun sign, Aquarius, that has made its presence felt in long-term leadership roles (FDR, Ronald Reagan). Quayle's chart emphasizes the Aquarius/Leo polarity strongly (his chart appears on page 342.) (His Sun, Mercury, and Mars are in Aquarius; Moon and Pluto in Leo). This emphasis means that whenever he seeks to experience self through participation in the larger society, he is faced with his need to win approval and be on center stage. His Leo need to be self-expressive and be a star in his own right can often feel challenged by the more impersonal demands of Aquarius.

Quayle has the same Sun/Moon combination as the actor Tom Selleck. The energy (particularly with mass-media-minded Pluto in Leo thrown in) produces popular, creative people, media darlings. Quayle's ability to win votes and to appeal to some segments of voters has been evident, though he's yet to reveal any glimmers of the vision and individual uniqueness that are often exhibited by people with this combination.

The circle of people around Quayle say he is "teachable" and is not averse to hiring people who are smarter than he. Both Aquarius and Leo have a certain know-it-all pomposity about them, so this "insider" assessment is curious. Quayle's Mercury in Aquarius would certainly make him curious about new ideas and open to intellectual stimulation. The square (three signs away) to Jupiter is what causes him to ramble and sound dumber than he may actually be.

Yet there are some realities about the Quayle chart that even his more rabid critics will have to accept. His is a very high-powered chart. The heavy dosage of planets in fixed signs, as well as the way some of the personal features of his chart (the Sun, Moon, Mercury, Mars) interact with Pluto, the planet of power and generational empowerment, would indicate that he

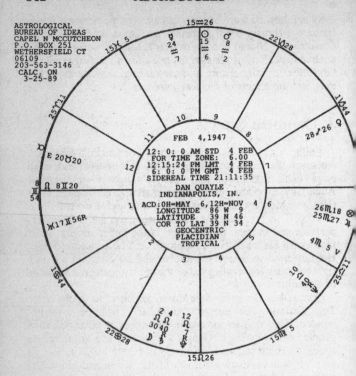

ASTROLOGICAL
BUREAU OF IDEAS
CAPEL N MCCUTCHEON
P.O. BOX 251
WETHERSFIELD CT
06109
203-563-3146
CALC. ON
3-25-89

FEB 4, 1947

12: 0: 0 AM STD 4 FEB
FOR TIME ZONE: 6.00
12:15:24 PM LMT 4 FEB
6: 0: 0 PM GMT 4 FEB
SIDEREAL TIME 21:11:35

DAN QUAYLE
INDIANAPOLIS, IN.

ACD:0H=MAY 6,12H=NOV
LONGITUDE 86 W 9
LATITUDE 39 N 46
COR TO LAT 39 N 34
GEOCENTRIC
PLACIDIAN
TROPICAL

** ASPECTS **

	SUN		MOON		MERC		VEN		MARS		JUP		SAT
MOON													
MERC	♂ 9 1												
VEN	∠ 1 40		* 4 19										
MARS	♂ 7 4		♂ 5 33		I								
JUP			△ 7 3		□ 1 19				Q 0 36				
SAT			♂ 2 10				B 0/14		♂ 3/23	△ 9 13			
URAN	△ 2 50		∠ 0127		△ 6 11				△ 9 54			∠ 1	
NEPT	△ 4 26		* 8 10		Q 1 33				△ 2 38	∠ 0 14		* 6	
PLUT	♂ 2 59		♂ 9138				Q 1 19		♂ 4 5			♂ 7	
MC	♂ 0120				∠ 8 41		∠ 2 0		♂ 7 24				
ASC	△ 6 12		* 6 24						△ 0 52			* 4	
NODE	△ 6 46		* 5 50						△ 0 18			* 3	
VRTX			□ 1 35		△ 9 58		* 5 39		△ 3 57			□ 0	

NODE   ASC   MC
21♌13 21♌30 24♐
8♊37 11♈
12♈

```
PLANET *DIG   SIGN      HSE DECLN  LAT TRAVL DS    GEOCENTRIC
 SUN  D      15AQU 6    9  -16.3    .0   1   1  92  N-NODE   S-NODE
 MOON        2LEO30     3  23.8    4.0  14  52  94   8GEM20  8SAG20
 MERC  E     24AQU 7   10 -15.1   -1.7   1  47  18   2PIS45 21CAP13
 VEN   A     28SAG26    7 -20.2    3.2   1   4  68  29PIS34 20CAP44
 MARS  C      8AQU 2    9 -19.3   -1.0   0  47  13  13ARI36 20SAG35
 JUP   B     25SCO27    6 -18.1    1.1   0   6  38   2CAN15 15CAP17
 SAT  D       4LEO40R   3  19.7     .6   0  -5  96  20CAN26 25CAP 2
 URAN  C     17GEM56R   1  23.0    -.1   0  -1  66  10GEM48 16SAG 4
 NEPT        10LIB40R   5  -2.8    1.5   0  -1  64  11LEO 2 11AQU18
 PLUT        12LEO 7R   3  23.8    6.9   0  -1  67  19CAN 3 20CAP23
 MC          15AQU26       -16.2
 ASC          8GEM54       21.8    *R=RULE  D=DETRIMENT  E=EXALTED
 NODE         8GEM20       21.7    F=FALL  C=IN CRITICAL DEGREE
 VRTX         4SCO 5      -12.9    A=ACCID DIGNITY BY HOUSE POS
 EQ A        20TAU20       17.8    B=ACCD DEBILITY BY HOUSE POS
```

```
      FIRE VEN  CAR NEPT            ARABIC PARTS
       4   SAT       1        FORTUNE  26 SCOR 18
           PLUT FIX SUN       SPIRIT   21 SAGG 30
           MOON      7 MERC   STATUS    2 LEO  50
      ERTH NONE         MARS  DESTINY  28 LEO   2
      AIR  SUN       JUP
       5   MERC      SAT          * DYNAMIC FOCUS *
           MARS      PLUT     (CLOSEST SQUA OR OPPO)
           URAN      MOON      MERC SQUA JUP  1 19
           NEPT MUT  VEN
      WATR JUP    2 URAN
       1
                     EAST              JULIAN DATE
      ANG. MERC      5            2432221.250000
           VEN              MEAN OBLIQUITY OF ECLIPTIC
           URAN WEST           23 DEG. 26 MIN
      SUC. NEPT      5       SIDEREAL AYANAMSHA (SVP)
       1                          6 PISC  0
      CAD. SUN   SOUTH
       6   MARS      4
           JUP              ASPECTS    ANGLE ORB  NO
           SAT   NORTH    d=CONJUNCTION   0  10  11
           PLUT      6    ⊻=SEMISEXTILE  30   2   0
           MOON          ∠=SEMISQUARE   45   3   5
                         ⋆=SEXTILE      60   9  12
      POS  9 NEG 1       □=SQUARE       90  10   5
      VOCATIONAL IND MARS △=TRINE      120  10  19
      MUTUAL RECEPTION   ⚼=SESQUIQUAD  135   3   3
        SUN  AND SAT     ⋔=QUINCUNX    150   2   0
        MERC AND URAN    ◦=OPPOSITION  180  10   5
      SOLE DISPOSITR NONE Q=QUINTILE    72   2   1
      SINGLETON NONE     B=BIQUINTILE  144   2   3
      SUN/MOON ANG 167.40 I=PARALLEL     0   1   6
                         /=CONTRAPARA  180   1   2
```

```
                   ** MID-POINTS **
 T   NEPT   URAN   SAT    JUP    MARS   VEN    MERC   MOON   SUN
 6  22♎23  26♌ 1  19♏22  14♏46  21♐ 4   1♐16  29♐ 6  18♏17  24♐36 VRTX
14   9♌30  13♊ 8   6♋30   1♏53   8♈11  18♓23  16♈14   5♋25  11♈43 NODE
31   9♌47  13♊25   6♋47   2♏10   8♈28  18♓40  16♈31   5♋42  12♈ 0 ASC
47  13♐ 3  16♈41  10♂ 3   5♑26  11♒44  21♑56  19♒47   8♉58  15♒16 MC
    11♏24  15♌ 2   8♑24   3♒47  10♏ 5  20♒17  18♂ 7   7♌19  13♂37 PLUT
          14♌18   7♏40   3♏ 3   9♒21  19♏33  17♐24  16♏35  12♐53 NEPT
                 11♋18   6♏41  12♐59  23♓11  21♈ 2  10♌13  16♈31 URAN
 AN
 16  NEPT          0♎ 3   6♑21  16♒33  14♉24   3♌35   9♌53 SAT
49 ⋆ 1 27  PLUT          1♑44  11♐56   9♒47  28♏58   5♌16 JUP
30 △ 4 46  ◦ 3 19  MC          18♑14  16♒ 5   5♉16  11♒34 MARS
 2 △ 1 46  ⋆ 3 13  △ 6 32  ASC         26♑17  15♎28  21♉46 VEN
36 △ 2 20  ⋆ 3 47  △ 7  6 d 0134  NODE        13♉19  19♒33 MERC
 9         □ 8 2         B 1 11 B 1 45               8♉48 MOON
```

isn't someone who will fade into the woodwork. His chart poignantly speaks to the growing up that the entire Pluto in Leo generation must accept, and contains configurations that one would expect of a 1947 person who achieved such a position. (There are similarities to configurations in the chart of Donald Trump, who was born in 1946.) His ascension to the vice presidency comes at a time when the planet Pluto is purging and overhauling much of his chart, and the result of this process will become more evident as 1992 nears. Saturn's travel over his Sun sign (and across from his Moon) in late 1991 starts a cycle of self-definition and crystallizes his sense of responsibility and of becoming a more visible leader.

Horoscopes Around the World

The controversy of birthtimes and dates extends to every nation, so only a smattering of examples and projections will be presented here.

The exact birthdate of Mikhail Gorbachev (March 2, 1931) is known and hence deserves some mention here. As a Pisces concerned with dissolving boundaries and serving and inspiring others, Gorbachev's apparent humanity is not a put-on. Pisces does have a gift for illusion and deceit, but it usually isn't on the power trips of other signs. A configuration between the Sun and Neptune increases visionary and perceptive powers, but it can also increase paranoia (Richard Nixon, too, had his Sun in an opposition—six signs apart—from Neptune). Combined with the proud Moon in Leo, the Sun/Neptune configuration, while providing charisma, can give one a messiah complex. Another result can be vision without implementation. The Sun/ Neptune combination along with the Moon in Leo, and a more hesitant, restrictive configuration involving Venus/Saturn across from a Retrograde Mars, would indicate a certain timidity and insecurity in the Gorbachev profile. A Jupiter/Uranus connection that is tied to other factors makes him a risk taker and gives him some entrepreneurial instincts.

Gorbachev shares the Leo Moon with the Soviet Union's birthchart. The Moon shows the haughtiness of the country. The Moon is in a stressful configuration with the Sun in Scorpio, which is secretive and manipulative but contains its own inner power to regenerate itself. The Scorpio/Leo combination is difficult to move. It's very stuck in its ideals and habits. This is why there has been such internal resistance to perestroika. But Russia also has a revolutionary and erratic side, which is why, dangers aside, it has always produced a stable of dissidents. (The country's birth, after all, bears the stamp of the Bolshevik Revolution.)

During most of its ride through Scorpio, Pluto will be knocking around planets in the Russian chart as if they were bowling pins. The 1990–91 period is particularly intense.

But it is a rare country that is not being shaken up by Pluto's current transit through Scorpio and Uranus and Neptune's through Capricorn. Even if many of the charts that astrologers study are invalid, the general nature of the Astrocycles in the sky is such that all countries are being forced to respond to the global connectedness of problems and common human-welfare concerns. The Saturn/Neptune conjunction that caused such turmoil in China in 1989 and in charts related to both sides of the Berlin Wall is also visiting the United States and showing up in South Africa. Some charts for South Africa are especially sensitive to the Uranus/Neptune conjunction, forcing a changing vision in 1992. Even Japan, which has been flexing its economic might of late, isn't immune. Its 1952 chart, representing the restoration of Japanese sovereignty (April 28), will see some Saturanian stress and restriction (as well as Uranian upsets around the mid-1990s). The 1992–93 Uranus/Neptune conjunction, which makes a precise square (three signs apart) to Neptune, planet of collective ideals, in the sovereignty chart, would make the economic changes indicated by Europe's unified market of particular interest to Japan, which, internal national problems aside, will probably gain a greater world presence with this energy. The European economic changes come at what increasingly are difficult economic times for the planet. But these difficulties will continually emphasize the need for a larger world economy and perhaps decrease the tendency of European countries to try to restrict the United States and other ''outsiders'' looking to do business in Europe.

It is the chart for the European Economic Community (effective January 1, 1958) that most compellingly speaks to the changing world all nations face. In 1989 the charts Venus (money, values) was being squared by Pluto and purged of its old concepts of value and worth, ending a series of other Plutonian upheavals that the chart experienced in the 1980s. Pluto

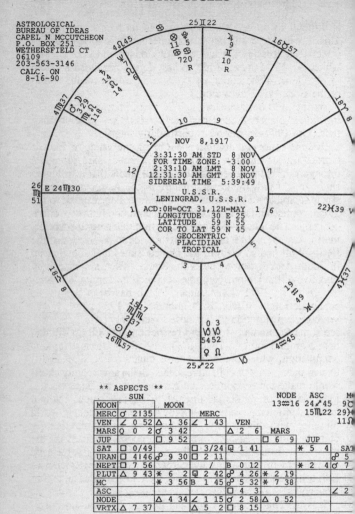

ASTROLOGICAL
BUREAU OF IDEAS
CAPEL N MCCUTCHEON
P.O. BOX 251
WETHERSFIELD CT
06109
203-563-3146
CALC. ON
8-16-90

NOV 8, 1917

3:31:30 AM STD 8 NOV
FOR TIME ZONE: -3.00
2:33:10 AM LMT 8 NOV
12:31:30 AM GMT 8 NOV
SIDEREAL TIME 5:39:49

U.S.S.R.
LENINGRAD, U.S.S.R.

ACD: 0H=OCT 31, 12H=MAY 1
LONGITUDE 30 E 25
LATITUDE 59 N 55
COR TO LAT 59 N 45
GEOCENTRIC
PLACIDIAN
TROPICAL

** ASPECTS **

	SUN		MOON		MERC		VEN		MARS		JUP		SAT	NODE 13♒16	ASC 24♐45	M 9♉
MOON														15♏22	29♋
MERC	♂ 2135														11♌
VEN	∠ 0 52	△ 1 36		∠ 1 43											
MARS	□ 0 2	♂ 3 42			△ 2 6									
JUP		□ 9 52						□ 6 9						
SAT	□ 0/49			□ 3/24		⊔ 1 41			* 5 4	SAT
URAN	□ 4146	♂ 9 30		□ 2 11							♂ 5
NEPT	□ 7 56					B 0 12				* 2 4	♂ 7
PLUT	△ 9 43	* 6 2		⊔ 2 42		♂ 4 26		* 2 19			
MC		* 3 56	B 1 45		♂ 5 32		* 7 38			
ASC						□ 4 3					∠ 2
NODE		△ 4 34	∠ 1 15		♂ 2 58	△ 0 52				
VRTX	△ 7 37			△ 5 2		□ 8 15				

Soviet Union:
Several charts for the Soviet Union exist; most are calculated for times between Nov 7–Nov 9, 1917, the Bolshevik takeover. This chart is

PLANET	*DIG	SIGN	HSE	DECLN	LAT	TRAVL		DS	GEOCENTRIC N-NODE	S-NODE
SUN		15SCO 2	2	-16.4	.0	1	0	78		
MOON		29LEO18	11	7.6	-4.4	11	51	1	3CAP52	3CAN52
MERC	A	17SCO37	3	-17.3	-2.2	1	35	4	14SCO 2	15SCO43
VEN	C	0CAP54	4	-26.4	-2.9	1	7	61	1LIB 2	27SCO51
MARS	C	3VIR 1	11	12.0	1.7	0	32	45	26TAU 0	17SCO12
JUP	D A	9GEM10R	9	20.9	-.9	0	-7	93	19CAN26	1CAP24
SAT	D A	14LEO14	11	17.1	.6	0	2	66	28CAN45	17CAP35
URAN	R B	19AQU49	5	-15.6	-.7	0	32		14GEM33	11SAG44
NEPT		7LEO 6	11	18.3	-.2	0	0	58	12LEO40	8AQU52
PLUT		5CAN20R	10	18.6	-4.7	0	-1	33	20CAN32	17CAP45
MC		25GEM22		23.4						
ASC		26VIR51		1.3						
NODE		3CAP52		-23.4						
VRTX		22PIS39		-2.9						
EQ	A	24VIR30		2.2						

```
*R=RULE  D=DETRIMENT  E=EXALTED
F=FALL  C=IN CRITICAL DEGREE
A=ACCID DIGNITY BY HOUSE POS
B=ACCD DEBILITY BY HOUSE POS
```

```
FIRE  SAT  CAR  VEN
  3   NEPT  2  PLUT
      MOON FIX  SUN
ERTH  VEN  6  MERC
  2   MARS     SAT
AIR   JUP      URAN
  2   URAN     NEPT
WATR  SUN      MOON
  3   MERC MUT MARS
      PLUT  2  JUP
```

ARABIC PARTS

FORTUNE	11	CANC	7
SPIRIT	12	SAGG	35
STATUS	9	ARIE	38
DESTINY	11	VIRG	6

```
* DYNAMIC FOCUS *
(CLOSEST SQUA OR OPPO)
SUN SQUA SAT  0 49
```

```
ANG.  VEN  EAST
 2    PLUT  7
SUC.  SUN
 6    MARS WEST
      SAT   3
      URAN
      NEPT SOUTH
      MOON  6
CAD.  MERC
 2    JUP  NORTH
           4
```

```
JULIAN DATE
2421540.521875
MEAN OBLIQUITY OF ECLIPTIC
23 DEG. 27 MIN
SIDEREAL AYANAMSHA (SVP)
6 PISC 24
```

```
POS 5  NEG 5
VOCATIONAL IND MARS
MUTUAL RECEPTION
  MERC AND MARS
SOLE DISPOSITR NONE
SINGLETON NONE
SUN/MOON ANG 284.26
```

ASPECTS		ANGLE	ORB	NO
♂=CONJUNCTION		0	10	5
⚹=SEMISEXTILE		30	2	1
∠=SEMISQUARE		45	3	5
✶=SEXTILE		60	9	6
□=SQUARE		90	10	13
△=TRINE		120	10	8
⚼=SESQUIQUAD		135	3	4
⚻=QUINCUNX		150	4	1
☍=OPPOSITION		180	10	7
Q=QUINTILE		72	2	1
B=BIQUINTILE		144	2	3
I=PARALLEL		0	1	3
/=CONTRAPARA		180	1	4

** MID-POINTS **

T	NEPT	URAN	SAT	JUP	MARS	VEN	MERC	MOON	SUN	
0	29♉53	6♓14	3♊26	0♉55	12♊50	11≈47	20♈ 8	10♊59	18♏51	VRTX
36	20≏29	26♏50	24≏ 3	21♓31	3♏26	2♈23	10♐45	1♏35	9♐27	NODE
5	1♏58	8♐20	5♏32	3♌ 0	14♏56	13♏53	22≏14	13♏ 5	20≏57	ASC
21	16♋14	22♈36	19♋48	17♊16	29♋12	28♓ 8	6♏30	27♋20	5♏12	MC
	21♋13	27♈34	24♋47	22♊15	4♌10	3≏ 7	11♏29	2♋19	10♏11	PLUT
		13♉27	10♌40	8♋ 8	20♋ 3	19≏ 0	27♏22	18♌12	26♏ 4	NEPT
			17♉ 1	14♈29	26♏25	25♏21	3♏43	24♏33	2♋26	URAN
				11♋42	23♌37	22≏34	0≏55	21♌46	29♏38	SAT
					21♋ 5	20♓ 2	28♏24	19♋14	27♌ 6	JUP
						1♏57	10≏19	1♏ 9	9≏ 2	MARS
							9♏16	0♏ 6	7✶58	VEN
								8≏28	16♏20	MERC
									7≏10	MOON

```
N   NEPT
31  ⚹ 1♏46   PLUT
34            ♂ 9 57   MC
 2            □ 8 29  □ 1 29  ASC
56  ⚻ 3 14  ☍ 1 28  ☍ 8/30  □ 7 1  NODE
    ⚼ 0 33           □ 2 43  ☍ 4 12
```

based on the time that Lenin's proclamation of Soviet power was read and is the chart preferred by Barry Lynes, an American astrologer who has successfully predicted the current Russian Revolution.

is the planet of death. In this case the figurative use of the term is overshadowed by the very real fact that the old ways have died (are dying) and a very definite new system is sprouting buds, giving birth to a new life and charts that will indirectly and directly affect most existing countries in the world.

EIGHTEEN

The Astrology of Generations

Everybody wants a chance to feel superior. Baby-boomers look at today's teenagers and decry their lack of social consciousness and obsession with malls and MTV. Today's teens—as well as those in their twenties—have gone on record with protests against the media's pandering to the so-called Woodstock Nation that came of age in the sixties. Those born in the Depression and earlier times in the country's history think the boomers, busters, and everything in between are all babies.

Is there anything to generation gaps? Are people who are born at different times in history really any different than those who've come earlier or are due to come later? This chapter attempts to address all of these issues. Astrologers take the age-old question of whether history makes Great Men or whether Great Men make history and shows that they are inexplicably linked.

The concept of generations has captured the interest of both philosophers and historians, though work in the area is not that extensive. The most reliable inquiries are now in the area of market research or opinion polls, most notably by Daniel Yankelovich, Louis Harris, and the Gallup Organization. While biological generations within one family line—father and son being two separate generations, for instance—are commonly spoken of under the heading of "generations," we will be concerning ourselves with sociological generations. These generations are made up of people born in the same year (1917 babies, for instance) or during specific time periods, such as the 75-million-strong baby-boom generation, born from 1946 to 1964. The idea of a baby-boom generation is a broad and misleading concept, but it embraces the idea of birth cohorts rather than biological family lines.

Actual research into sociological generations has left open the question of the life span of a generation. Philosopher José Ortega Y. Gasset believed that a generation spends about thirty years having an effect on society. Ortega contends that starting at about thirty (the Saturn Return), key players in a generation begin participating in more authoritative roles in political and corporate life, and for fifteen years they pay their dues and fight against the policies of the generation in power. At about age forty-five the younger generation begins coming into power and has another fifteen years to exercise its clout. Students of corporate power structures will recognize this "career path" as that commonly followed by those who move up the corporate and political ladders in society. The baby-boom generation, which is experiencing a bottleneck of bodies trying to push their way into a limited number of vice presidencies, may somewhat alter the timing for the passing of the torch. But forty-year-old CEOs are more common in small, entrepreneurial companies than in the Fortune 500. Even wunderkinds, as both popularized and academic life-cycle research show, are forced to make drastic career and life adjustments that often slow the "man in a hurry" down.

Students of generational theory seem to be subscribers to the "wait your turn" and "leave before you have to be thrown out" view. Ortega argued that exceptions to the generation-succession rule of fifteen years participation/fifteen years of authority—cases where the leader is severely older than his cabinet or team—often results in breakdowns in communication and policy implementation. The older leader is often alienated from the generational ethos of the people around him. The Reagan administration, where a 1911 baby was surrounded by a generation born in the mid-twenties to mid-thirties, is an example of the way in which an older leader can be distant from the day-to-day policy matters and other issues presumably under his authority. All insider accounts of the administration indicate that Reagan let men in their fifties and sixties run around with their own agendas. Reagan had some young staffers, most notably a 1946 baby, David Stockman, whose desire to decrease the power of the special-interest groups, and others who've helped swell the nation's budget, is typical of a younger generation that is pushing for room but that is not quite ready to lead.

George Bush has a number of baby-boomer advisers and a baby-boomer vice president, giving credence to the idea of people in their thirties and forties taking on fuller participation in life.. But it isn't certain whether Bush will be passing the torch to the generation born after World War II. There's an entire generation—those born in the 1930s and early '40s—in between Bush and Quayle. Yet the looseness of the issue of generation, at least when conventional sources are relied upon, is such that it isn't clear whether 1930s babies are in the same generation as those who, like Bush, were born in the 1920s.

Astrological Generations—Open to All

The study of astrological generations will show that Bush and Gorbachev, though separated by only six years, share some generational experiences—particularly the threat to personal and national security that was a result of World War II—but the two men belong to different subgenerations. Gorbachev was born at a time when certain planetary configurations were calling for reforms, whereas Bush's subgeneration was born into the more boisterous, secure time prior to the Great Depression. The differences, readers will come to understand, are not simply a matter of semantics. Substantial portions of the population have varying destinies, sometimes as noticeably different as people born only five years earlier. Moreover, the astrological generation perspective is extended to all people, in contrast to conventional studies that often view the artists, writers, and limited numbers of opinion makers of the day as "voices of their generation." It's as if a generation was a party to which only those from privileged backgrounds were sent an invitation. Social research certainly does indicate that lower-middle- and working-class people are less apt to have lives that are vastly different from those of their parents, unless they become movie or rock stars. But Yankelovich's inquiries during the late 1960s and 1970s found a closing gap between the attitudes of the college-educated and the non-college-educated. Meanwhile antidiscrimination laws and increased opportunities are giving more voices a chance to be heard. The changes that society has undergone in the past twenty years have made it possible for most people to tap into the energy that makes them and their generations unique. And this can be done in many ways, both positive and negative. People who took part in the burgeoning drug culture of the 1960s and '70s are just as representative of the generation that came of age at the time as students who channeled their energy into humanitarian and socially useful causes:

Astrologers recognize that everyone has a share in some generational destiny, but in varying degrees, depending on how the planets associated with generational influences relate to the rest of the birthchart. It should be obvious that most people, even when college-educated, stick to the status quo and make limited steps toward individuality. But even these lives show generational influences, even if its simply the issue of marrying and having babies later in life and balancing those aims with a career. Everyone has a vested interest in the generation cycles under which he or she was born. People are born when they are for a reason, and not just because there were a few extra seats on the airplane.

Generational Planets

Astrologers refer to Uranus, Neptune, and Pluto as generational planets. With orbits of 84, 168, and 248 years, respectively, the planets' slow drive through the zodiac signs means that hordes of people are born with each of these planets in the same sign. Jupiter and Saturn, which spend 1 and 2.5 years in signs, respectively, help form limited minigroups within generations. But it is the three planets discovered in 1781, 1846, and 1930 that show the evolving needs of society at large, as well as issues that will specifically be worked out by segments of the population. Pluto, the slowest, represents the process of change. It highlights the areas of life that must undergo a death if an individual is to exhibit the type of personal power that adds to the collective. Neptune represents the ideals held by a generation; some idealize work, others think that a perfect union or soul mate is the ultimate end. Uranus shows the areas that a generation breaks away from and gives new expression or form to in their behavior. The bulk of this chapter is intended to highlight issues facing the generations, with a special focus on the post–World War II and younger generations. However, a brief description showing the planets at work in all living generations follows. (Refer to the back-of-the-book tables to determine specific dates for planets' zodiac placements.) Because these planets move forward and then backtrack (retrogradation) before settling in a sign permanently, scan the tables carefully.

PLUTO Pluto and the zodiac sign it occupies indicates the process of change and area of life in which a generation will be forced to experience upheaval, the end of old forms and definitions, with the possibility of regeneration. While we will examine the **Pluto in Leo** generation (1937 to 1957) extensively later in this chapter, there are two older Pluto generations among us. **Pluto in Gemini** (1890 to 1914) came into a world where the concept of borders was widening through immigration, better developed transportation, and communications. The group held many common and small attitudes that were under attack as they aged. Nixon, born with Pluto in the last degrees of Gemini, helped break down our idea of neighborhoods (a Gemini word) by opening up communications with China before he was run out of office in 1974. (His leave-taking, however, did not end Pluto in Gemini's rule; Ronald Reagan was born with this placement.)

Pluto in Cancer (1912 to 1938) people came into the world when issues such as nationalism were sending countries to war and depressions around the globe threatened emotional security. Cancer is the primeval family, the clan; it's where we come from, in the sense of both our family lineage and our physical home. Emotional security and seemingly distant issues such as patriotism and nationalism in both its moderate and extreme dimensions are all tied up in the sign. Those born with Pluto in this position were forced into personal and generational situations aimed at purging some of the darker aspects to Cancer.

NEPTUNE The sign tenanted by Neptune, which spends about fourteen years in each zodiac sector, shows the areas of life that society is idealizing during a given period. It describes the ideals, illusions, and some of the seemingly unreachable yearnings of a generation. As was demonstrated with the quick look at Pluto (which we'll return to later on in the chapter), there will be a close association between the events that took place during a given time period and the children being born. An example: Given the excesses of the "me" seventies—the religious cults, growth-groups and other examples of self-involvement—should it surprise anyone that the children of **Neptune in Sagittarius** (1970 to 1984) are fixated on MTV and video rentals, or that they think the Vietnam war happened back in the 1800s and are hooked on shopping? The Neptune placement suggests a lifetime of overidealized philosophies and unrealistic attitudes and ideas about freedom, religion, education, and other concepts that take people out of their environment and into the bigger world. And don't expect the even younger **Neptune in Capricorn** (1984 to 1998) children to grow up with much faith in established institutions like Congress or the business world. Most of the traditional structures are dissolving all around those now being born, but we can hope that the search will get them closer to more ideal and humane governments and systems.

But while the jury won't be in on Neptune's effect on those born in the 1970s and '80s for sometime, it has cast its verdict on other Neptune generations. The **Neptune in Cancer** (1902 to 1916) generation has a yearning for the "way it was." Motherhood, apple pie and country, and the nuclear family make up this group's dreams. While Neptune in Cancer people have included John Adams and Thomas Jefferson, whose Neptunian ideals gave birth to this nation, the twentieth-century transit brought on Ronald Reagan and many of the older leaders in society, whose nationalism and paternalism was better suited to bygone days. Neptune, moving through Capricorn six signs away from Neptune in Cancer, will make these older people even more disillusioned and confused, but not before there's one last attempt to show what's right about their way of seeing the world.

George Bush and many world leaders were born when **Neptune in Leo** (1915 to 1928–29) celebrated the cult of personality. The flappers and jazz men were associated with the age, which produced glamorous characters from John F. Kennedy to free spirits like the beatniks (the latter often took the idealized support of self-expression to extremes). The Neptune in Leo party came to an end with the Depression. **Neptune in Virgo** (1929 to 1943) people have a special yearning for order, routine, regularity, some of the very aspects of life that dissolved in front of them as the Depression got under way. Paradoxically, as they seek order, this generation also has a desire to transcend the "dailiness" of living, with all of its external details and demands.

Most talked about among the Neptunian generations is **Neptune in Libra** (1942 to 1956–57). They want the perfect union and won't settle for less, as will be discussed in more detail later in this chapter. **Neptune in Scorpio** (1955–57 to 1970) were born when sex and drugs were being romanticized and explored, and as a result this generation is just as confused about mating and sexual intimacy as the Neptune in Libra crowd. Incidentally, some from this era talk of feeling cheated by the outbreak of sexual disease because it coincided with their coming of age. They had their own apartments and credit cards, but the sexual/dating climate had become more conservative.

URANUS: HOW GENERATIONS BREAK OUT

This planet strikes blows for individuality that can then be utilized toward societal aims. Uranus forces revolutions in the use and expression of the zodiac sign through which it travels and indicates various "behaviors" common to a subgeneration. **Uranus in Aries** (1927 to 1935) called for the discovery of identity and the projection of it for societal good. Aries' celebration of courage and "heroes" is reflected by Neil Armstrong and Gloria Steinem, among others born under this influence. Charles Lindbergh's transatlantic trip, Babe Ruth, and Amelia Earhart accomplished feats during these times that reflect the pioneering, ground-breaking spirit in the air. **Uranus in Taurus** (1935 to 1942) represents a generation's desire to break away from old existing values and build new ones. It produced Jerry Rubin, Abbie Hoffman, and Jesse Jackson, to name just a few of the people who acted out their Uranian urges in the 1960s. **Uranus in Gemini** (1942 to 1949) brought in a generation desiring to break away from existing attitudes, particularly those held by their parents. This generation is the first to go to college in large numbers, but it also has a notable superficiality, which coincides with the increase in television and mass media. **Uranus in Cancer** (1949 to 1956) acted out by breaking away from more traditional expressions of emotional security, particularly the nuclear-family unit. Many in this generation have yet to marry and may elect forms of families that depart from the more traditional idea. Estrangement from the families they grew up in has caused many to define their "family" as being friends at work, the larger community, or other single people.

Uranus in Leo (1955 to 1962). When the planet first dipped into the sign in the fall of 1955—it moved back into Cancer and then became a regular in Leo in June 1956—television shows such as *The Mickey Mouse Club* and *Leave It to Beaver* were airing for the first time. The television programming was part of an attempt to play to "kids" who were in abundance and whose uninhibited self-expression reflects some of the meaning of Leo. Teen dance shows and other television shows also played the Leo theme, while James Dean's *Rebel Without a Cause* epitomizes the way many Uranus in Leo people fail to find true self-expression that allows participation in the larger human community. During this portion of the 1950s society was very much concerned with "juvenile delinquents," who couldn't find a channel for their energies. Madonna and Sean Penn, and many young actors in the so-called brat pack, bear the stamp of these times. The need here is to tap individual creativity and express it, but at the same time to channel the energy into activities and expressions that further societal and collective aims.

It's not that the **Uranus in Virgo** (1962 to 1969) isn't a rebel. After all, they were born in the sixties, a time when people were going for looser routines and life-styles, something Virgo isn't known to endorse. Many in this generation have readily shown the Virgo ability to be efficient and to adapt by getting the business or computer degrees that will lead to a job. But there's also a segment of this generation that has been slow to get into the job market or adult routine. Many of them are either floating around or still living with parents. For both the workaholics and the loafers there's a need to break away from the more traditional concepts of work and routine and create a more individualized rhythm and at the same time to stay in harmony with changing external realities. The increased use of flextime, work-at-home arrangements, and even more frequent job-hopping speaks to some of the needs of this subgeneration.

The many teenagers and young adults with **Uranus in Libra** (1969 to 1976) were born when the divorce rate began to zoom upward and the word *marriage* took on new meaning. This subgroup (along with the younger Scorpio and Sagittarius) might be the first to produce significant statistics for the "never married" column. They may be able to develop more equal partnerships than older Neptune in Libra people, who, despite their yearnings for equality, have the imprint of the 1940s- and 1950s-style relationships in their heads. Most of the Neptune in Libra generation wants to be coupled—and most have married at least once—while the issues may be different with Uranus in Libra. Already a segment of this generation opt for group dating, as opposed to high-pressure couples dating. When the first of this group were in high school, media reports featured several cases where women challenged the "couples only" rule for junior and senior proms. A group of women in Rhode Island sued for the right to go to the senior prom together because they wanted to spend their final high school days together.

Uranus was in Libra in the late 1880s and early 1890s, but society was so different that we can't make direct comparisons, though Uranus in Libra (and Libra Sun) Eugene O'Neill's work certainly dramatized the "self versus the other" issues that arise in relationships. Adolf Hitler is another man of the times who experienced some of the more disruptive energies of this Uranus placement.

Women in today's Uranus in Libra generation will have careers in much greater numbers than their late nineteenth-century counterparts, because of both economic need and their own sense of individuality. The nineteenth-century generation did not produce unusual marriage statistics. Another obvious place from which to seek information about the meaning and behaviors of Uranus in Libra would be from Uranus in Aries (1927–1935) since Aries is the sign opposite Libra. When this comparison is made, the individuality of both of these generations comes across strongly. Uranus in Aries Neil Armstrong walked on the Moon when Uranus first moved into Libra in 1969. Uranus's travel through Aries corresponded to the 1927 Lindbergh flight across the Atlantic. Uranus combined with other planets to correlate to the feats, but the heroic individuality of the 1927 placement in Aries and then that of 1969 in Libra, is the "one small step for man" that ultimately advances all of life on the planet. Gloria Steinem, a Uranus in Aries with the Sun and Mars in Aries as well, came into the spotlight in the women's movement and with *Ms*. magazine when Uranus was in Libra. Once again, the message that came through to society, especially to women at the time, was that to be a good partner one first needs to be a strongly developed individual. Initially this may manifest as sudden breaks in relationships or in a desire to avoid commitments. But Uranus in Libra may be the first truly liberated generation.

The **Uranus in Scorpio** cohorts (1975 to 1982) will also exhibit different approaches to interpersonal relations as we know them. Experimentation with sex, and many other taboo areas, has great appeal to those born with the awakener planet moving through the sign concerned with life's mysteries. Scorpio's concerns with confronting one's power and powerlessness forces it to plunge into some of life's more hidden realms, particularly sex and intimate relations in which resources are shared with another person. Those born to this subgeneration will attempt to reveal hidden aspects of Scorpio and will go through many breaks from interpersonal commitments that seem to overtake and rob them of power. Uranus in Scorpio could produce tireless investigators into artificial intelligence, gene research, or reincarnation, the mysteries of life that fall under Scorpio's watch. Additionally, Pluto's transit through Scorpio, the sign of self-transformation (1984 to 1996), will produce healers and magicians, as well as those with more destructive tendencies.

Uranus in Sagittarius (1982 to 1989) people of the past have included Mark Twain, Margaret Mead, Joseph Campbell, George Gallup, and many others who have helped us discover the big picture or break out of old philosophies and worldviews. The current crop can be expected to add its insights in areas ranging from religion to education. They'll be working closely with people born with **Uranus in Capricorn** (1988 to 1996), which is concerned with overturning the more traditional structures in life, as it proved from 1906 to 1913, while the **Uranus in Aquarius** (1913 to 1920 and 1996 to 2003) is concerned with reorganizing society and their own place within it. George Bush's **Uranus in Pisces** (1920 to 1927 and 2003 to 2011) attempts to break down barriers and connect with the universal, but often results in the generation being contagious with belief systems that are inaccurate or inappropriate, such as the confusion planted during the Roaring Twenties.

A generation's Plutonian, Neptunian, and Uranian concerns are challenged throughout life. Most critical are the times when each of the planets are in stressful configurations that are part of its own cyclic orbit. Transiting Pluto, moving in relation to the planet's position during the birth of groups of people, corresponds to tremendous shifts in consciousness in generational activity. The following discussion focuses on key issues affecting generations born after World War II.

PLUTO: THE POWER OF GENERATIONS Pluto in Leo (1937 to 1957): Yes, the *Y*-word has been overused. When market researchers and others started throwing around the term *Yuppie*, a lot of people didn't want to be talked about that way. And then there were the nitpickers who pointed out that in terms of income, few people made the minimum forty thousand dollars that a single person would need to qualify for pure Yuppiedom. Daniel Yankelovich, the pollster who was among those who popularized the Yuppie idea, added some insight to the debate by noting that he and his colleagues hadn't used the term to pinpoint a specific income bracket. Most baby-boomers, he conceded, didn't fit into the category. The expression was used to connote an attitude, a life-style, an aspiration. The Yuppie was the person in Yankelovich's studies in the late 1970s and early '80s who was looking for "self-fulfillment," greater freedom of self-expression, and time to do his or her own thing. The people who Yankelovich interviewed and studied generally fell in the category that we shall call the Pluto in Leo generation. Because the Pluto in Virgo generation is work-oriented and has a segment of young M.B.A.s it's easy to mistake the groups. But the Pluto in Virgo types are more clinical in their approach to life, as we'll be discussed later in this chapter. The two Pluto groups have different karmas.

Leo is the sign where we love and play and do things that help us make statements about who we are. Leo loves to put its stamp on things, and this means everything from the loved one, to creative endeavors such as writing and art, to one's children. Do I dare bring up that word and risk seeing the pictures or hearing about the French lessons, the competitive nursery schools, the parenting classes that Pluto in Leo people who are giving birth to the baby-boomlet are going through? Your child is an extension of you, so people who don't have a family often try to adopt and even kidnap to have children of their own.

Not everyone will face their Pluto in Leo issues through children. For others the most pressing issue will be blockages to love and to understanding what love is. Remember that most of the Pluto in Leo group also has Neptune in Libra, adding to confusion in the area of sexual expression and love. Many in this generation are learning to tap their personal power of love and share it with AIDS victims. The increase in people starting their own businesses is, in part, fueled by Pluto in Leo babies, who want to have a greater arena in which to express themselves, especially since this group isn't too keen on bosses and authority figures.

This generation can see their issues highlighted across the Atlantic in the person of Prince Charles. He is a Pluto in Leo baby who is undergoing something all the Pluto in Leo people will have experienced by 1996: Pluto in Scorpio will make a square (three signs away) to the Leo placements and will co-incide with crises that will force this generation to get a better hold on who they are and how they demonstrate that identity.

Several periodicals have featured articles about Charles's blockage of self-expression and his inability to utilize his personal power. Charles, the most educated British prince to date, has ideas and plans he'd like to implement, but tradition places him in the role of a man-in-waiting until his mother dies. And even when he takes the throne, Charles will be discouraged from actually doing anything. The man who would be king wants a real job, a chance to make a difference, whereas everybody else wants him to just keep an eye on his wife and be quiet.

With Pluto in Scorpio squaring Charles's natal Pluto position with special intensity in 1989–90, the Prince will be forced to tap his inner resources and deal with his power concerns. His more conservative advisers may not like the results. Previous generations of kings, world leaders, and commoners experienced the Pluto-square-Pluto aspect in their fifties and sixties. Nixon resigned shortly after the Pluto Square at age sixty-one. But since the planet has been moving more quickly, people born at the end of Pluto in Leo will experience the cycle around age thirty-six or thirty-seven. Charles is just entering his forties and is a relatively young man. It will be hard for him not to make some difficult choices and changes under this Pluto cycle (never mind the mid-life crisis). Pluto isn't going to let a grown man sit around and twiddle his thumbs.

Back in America, Oliver North's Pluto Square brought to light the way North overstepped some power lines, while Donald Trump was acquiring a higher profile and was embroiled in financial duels with Merv Griffin and other kingpins. Cher and other actresses were out looking for more clout. The intensity of Pluto, in confrontation with a life of privilege and lack of extensive accomplishment, was forcing J. Danforth Quayle to get serious and develop substance.

The bottom-line task for all the Pluto in Leo babies is self-affirmation and self-love, which is then shared with the rest of the world. Unfortunately the crisis in relationships, infertility problems, and other ailments reported by this demographic group reflect an inability to understand what their special place is on the planet. In his *The Last Intellectuals* social commentator Robert Jacoby touches on some truths about the post—World War II generation that have perplexed many social observers. Why is it, Jacoby and others wonder, that the most educated generation in American history, as well as the most outspoken during its college years, has failed to produce significant numbers of intellectuals and highly innovative or productive people? There are the artistic and scientific exceptions, of course. But Jacoby argues that the generation's limited output in terms of real creativity and discovery—which of course is separate from simply having a good-paying job—is in noticeable disproportion to its numbers. And, while some baby-boomers have not yet reached their thirties, the late 1940s group is old enough to have shown more results. Jacoby contends that there hasn't been a strong intellectual wave since the generation that was spawned in the mid-1920s (Norman Mailer, George Bush, the beatniks, and some jazz greats). Prior to that group the late-nineteenth-century babies dominated the intellectual scene.

Pluto in Leo tries very hard to fit in. The 1960s was a paint-by-numbers form of rebellion. The dare to be different was easy to accept, since everyone's friends were already in line. Everybody bought guitars and wore tie-dyed shirts. Once that period died down, the generation went out to become "professionals," though such work often doesn't allow the creative expression that Pluto in Leo demands. Jacoby says that careerism and the desire to play it safe and stay in favor have had a stifling effect on the country. People want tenure and a limited amount of hassle.

While not all Pluto in Leo babies can be expected to be twenty-first-century versions of Benjamin Franklin, who was born under this Pluto sign, the crisis confronting this generation as Pluto moves through Scorpio will involve tearing away the trappings and props they have used for self-expression. Then the task will be to touch their personal core and move out into the world. Sociologist Joseph Conlin argues that the youth participation in the Civil Rights movement and other '60s revolts was limited. Most protest energy was aimed at the Vietnam War and died down when the war did. Conlin said that the typical American youth was too self-absorbed and insensitive to run with the Freedom Riders, which is why most of the college-student involvement in that movement only lasted one summer. He, like others, also notes that most of the generational rebels were actually born in the late 1930s or early 1940s and weren't baby-boomers.

But there is hope. Check out this generation once Pluto leaves Scorpio. Bona fide world healers and leaders will emerge who can really lead a revolution.

Pluto in Virgo (1958 to 1970–71): They are the siblings of the Pluto in Leo generation and, as has been noted, can often be confused with them. But these younger siblings started their business and computer training early, often at ages when Pluto in Leo was still trying to find itself. Some have made it to Wall Street by now where they've exhibited well-documented greed. But the baby bankers and M.B.A.s should not be viewed as the final statement on the Pluto in Virgo group, though the number-crunching and other technical details that are the reality of most of the young Wall Streeters' lives are illustrative of Virgoan details.

Virgo is often minutiae, details, and points that often in themselves seem like nothing at all. Virgo seeks to give order to such information, to develop systems and routines that allow people to move with a certain rhythm in their lives. When this rhythm is not understood or realized, the Virgo energy manifests as stress and illnesses that block the rhythmic flow of life. When we apply these ideas to a generation, we find people who have developed systems of success—a business degree or computer training—and who seem to have eagerly embraced the idea of adjusting to external reality, a routine. But the challenge for this group of people (and they got a hint of this with the first crash on Wall Street) is their need for the daily routine to have more meaning in their lives. Work must be more than functional. The Buddhist idea of right livelihood, where people fuse with a routine and from it develop a worldview that helps them ask the more ontological questions—even if the work is a lower-level service job as opposed to a high-powered glamour-money job—is what will be demanded of Pluto in Virgo people. Changes in corporate work, mergers, and the dissolution of many professional jobs, will force this group of people to rethink their schedules and work routines.

The Virgo area of the zodiac also deals with interactions between various classes, which also underwent transformation with this generation. Since Pluto was in Virgo when the country was confronted with risings of oppressed groups, this generation will carry some of these ideas along with it. Neptune in Scorpio was also involved. The outbreak of racial incidents on college campuses and around the country in the mid-1980s has been sparked by youths bearing this Pluto in Virgo and Neptune in Scorpio combination (see the Uranus/Pluto generations below). Like the business majors, the neo-Nazi and racist groups are a small portion of the generation, but their presence shows some of the ways the outer planets are working.

Pluto in Libra (1971 to 1984): These people were born as the whole country was undergoing Plutonian upheavals in areas ranging from male/female relationships, as well as broader relationships, to legal rights and other contracts. Watch for them to distinguish themselves by negotiating different ways of interacting with others, as a result of crises related to identity and relationships. Some of these youths are showing difficulties in adjusting to the blended families—stepparents and siblings—that have developed as a result of their parents' divorces. Gang activity (Pluto rules gangs) is the way some youths, particularly in inner cities, are fostering relationships. Police in Los Angeles, where gangs are killing an average of a person a day, estimate that some seventy thousand youths are involved with gangs. Similar examples of alienation can be found among statistics of runaways. Suicides continue to rise, though they've been rising in the fifteen-to-twenty-four age group since the mid-1970s.

"We Went to Different High Schools Together"—Mini-Generations

Mini-generations are two-year influences created when Saturn interacts with the slower-moving planets (Jupiter creates some mini-groups over a year's time, but those won't be studied here).

Saturn/Uranus (1941 to 42): Maybe one of the reasons Jesse Jackson was doing so well in the early 1988 primaries and caucuses is that he is in sync with the start of the new Saturn/Uranus cycle that began in 1988. Jackson was born at the start of the last Saturn/Uranus cycle, which renews itself every forty-five to forty-six years. The cycle demands that some structures be undone and replaced with something new, but these reforms are not pushed through without struggle. Jackson is too Uranian, without demonstrated Saturnian discipline, responsibility, and dues-paying, to sit in the White House in this century, but his fight illustrates various aspects of the Saturn/Uranus rhythm. Since Saturn and Uranus don't respect each other, they each push their extreme agendas—and Uranus initially loses, since Saturn writes the rules—before finally going to the table to talk. Saturn and Uranus in Taurus in 1941 called for a reordering of value systems ranging from the personal to the economic, while the 1942 conjunction took place at the beginning of the sign Gemini and indicated a need to reorder attitudes and connections to one's immediate environment.

Like Jackson, those born with the 1941–42 conjunctions came of age when Saturn and Uranus were opposite each other 180 degrees, six signs apart in the sky. Many felt a special need to mediate the restrictive, more cautious tendencies within themselves with their more rebellious, break-out urges. Bob Dylan, Joan Baez, John Lennon, and others born under the conjunction showed a special gift for using a traditional medium (the rules of music) to express their generation's more individualistic urges. The pattern continues. A segment of those born in the mid-sixties, when Saturn and Uranus were opposite each other (Pluto and Uranus were also in difficult aspects) are active in environmental and antinuclear concerns. Sociologists have identified an interest in social activism among this age group, even if it isn't as visible as activities among youth in the 1960s.

Being born on a Saturn/Pluto conjunction or opposition may indicate that a generation will come of age at a time when urgent reforms are pressing society. For instance, the 1896–87 generation would have been old enough to have fought in wars and to be affected by numerous changes under way in the world when Saturn and Uranus were in opposition in 1917. The 1917 opposition babies fought in World War II, and some of them helped usher in the 1960s reforms. The latter is an example of the more positive aspects of the Saturn/Uranus conjunction. This configuration gives us some of society's most productive and creative people. In the same way that the 1941–42 conjunction brought in a band of social leaders and musicians, the 1896–87 conjunction brought us a cluster of writers:

F. Scott Fitzgerald, Thomas Wolfe, and William Faulkner.

Uranus/Pluto (1964 to 1967): This was a revolutionary configuration that was most potent in the mid-1960s. It has produced youths who are passionately involved with causes, such as antinuclear protests, as well as some who are guilty of the increased violence aimed at gays and racial and ethnic minorities. Others, like Princess Stephanie of Monaco, are simply rebellious. The conjunction was in Virgo, a sign that deals with the underclasses and the oppressed, and it coincided with many of the civil rights reforms and the Great Society programs of the 1960s. (A Saturn/Uranus opposition was also in effect.) The last was in 1850–51 in Aries, the sign of fight and innovation. While the mid-nineteenth-century conjunction correlates to American industrial expansion and inventions, such as the harvesting machines that expanded the farm economy, the Fugitive Slave Law, and other slavery-related controversies, the year didn't produce the avalanche of dynamic leaders that might be expected. Some revolutionaries were born in 1850— a few Haymarket rioters, for instance—but the year is not known for being a vintage one for major historical figures. Some especially potent personalities, such as inventors Thomas Edison and Alexander Graham Bell, were born in the years just prior to the exact conjunction. The watershed revolutionary year of 1848, which saw more than fifty uprisings worldwide, is also among the events that preceded the precise conjunction and that correlate more to other influences. But the Uranus/Pluto configuration, as a generational influence, seems to have been more pronounced at other points in the cycle. Einstein was born on the First Quarter Uranus/Pluto Square following the conjunction; the Opposition in 1900 was also fertile. Michael Dukakis, who has always been known as a reform politician, was born during the Last Quarter of the cycle and shows some of the more practical, everyday ways the energy can express itself. Gorbachev was born then as well.

Saturn/Pluto (1947 to 48): They seethe, many astrologers say. These people have a strong authoritarian streak, but they also hate authority figures. It's almost as if they were born with the memory of the Nazi dictators and the darkness that filled the years just prior to their birth.

Saturn/Neptune (1953): They seem panicky as they move back and forth between Saturnine caution and pessimism and Neptunian ideals. Their Saturn Return stories are often marked by an especially disappointing relationship that spurred them on to greater self-esteem and understanding. They have the ability to ground their ideals and dreams.

Uranus in Cancer/Neptune in Libra (1949 to 56, most potent 1955 to 56 and mid-1957): They will produce the first statistical evidence showing whether ideas like middle-class single mothers, or older-woman/younger-men trends, will really take hold. The larger numbers of women born in comparison to men in the mid-1950s, as well as the smaller numbers of 1952–53 male babies born in comparison to mid-1950s women, will mean that these women will marry men either substantially older or quite a bit younger. This demographic change will require American women to abandon the longtime practice of marrying a man approximately three years older, who makes more money and is taller. A quarter of the women marrying today are marrying men who are younger—nearly 50 percent of those remarrying take younger husbands—but early conditioning dies hard, and this is why so many women talk of a so-called male shortage. The truth is that there are many men, but American women, particularly professional women, have very specific criteria.

Generational history seems to indicate that groups born under significant configurations between Uranus and Neptune give birth to life-styles or trends that move against the mainstream culture. The mid-1920s, and Uranus in the inconjunct (five signs away) aspect to Neptune, hosted the Jazz Age and gave birth to beatniks. As Jacoby argues, the last intellectual generation came from this era. The period from 1905 to 1910, when Uranus and Neptune were making the opposition (six signs away), produced a generation of women who, as Landon Y. Jones notes in a study on the baby-boom generation, have a life-style and fertility-rate pattern that are similar to those of women born in the 1950s. About 22 percent of the women born in 1908 never gave birth to children, while about 25 percent of woman now in their thirties have not given birth. Two wars and a depression played a role in the demographics from the 1908 group, and some of these women married later and helped contribute to the baby boom. The babies born around 1908 and 1910 came in at a time when talk of women's rights was strong—Uranus in Capricorn was shaking up the status quo and challenging the idealization of motherhood and home that was taking place with Neptune in Cancer at the same time. Bette Davis and Katharine Hepburn are examples of women born at this time who grew up to give birth to the changing status quo. And many other nonfamous women born in the same generation fought against the traditional roles assigned to them.

The 1950s Uranus in Cancer/Neptune in Libra generation should be viewed as being in a pivotal position in history. The women in this generation in particular showed the differences between themselves and earlier generations very early in their lives. While all but 17 percent of women who were born in 1946 (when Uranus was in Gemini and Neptune was in Libra) were married by age twenty-four, some 34 percent of women born in 1956 (when the Uranus in Cancer/Neptune in Libra square was especially tight) were not married by age 24, preferring to pursue careers and lives of independence. Today, the United States Census Bureau reports that 25 percent of the women born in the 1950s still have not had their first child. Those born in the 1950s and with the Uranus/Neptune square will provide the first large bulk of women whose lives differed from pre-feminist tradition.

Lost Generations

There's one more issue to take up in our discussion on generations: it's the plight of lost generations. Many of us who were forced to sit out Woodstock but who were technically teenagers in the late 1960s were born during a period between 1955 and 1957 when all three generational planets were changing signs. Pluto moved from Leo to Virgo, Uranus from Cancer to Leo, and Neptune from Libra to Scorpio, each after a long stretch of time in the previous sign.

The problem with planets changing signs is that they don't go peacefully—nor all at once. Instead a planet like Neptune moves from Libra to Scorpio in December 1955, and goes back to 29 degrees of Libra in March 1956, and then back to Scorpio in October 1956. In 1957 it spent June 17 to August 5 in Libra, before moving into Scorpio for good. The other planets are just as slow about making a commitment, and that's how generations get lost. The result is groups of people who don't feel linked to either what has gone right before or to what is about to come on their heels. Author David Leavitt discussed this precarious position in an article in *Esquire* magazine, and other writers have also spoken of the frustration of watching the 1960s from the sidelines or on television like Kevin Arnold, lead character in the popular *Wonder Years* television show. Arnold would be a cohort of the 1955–57 "lost generation."

The transitional periods produce chasms that are interesting to watch. As an editor on a college daily, I'd been involved in providing coverage of some of the protest activities of the handful of campus radicals still hanging around in 1977. One protest activity—campus radicals went to Ohio to protest plans by Kent State officials to build a gym on the site where four students had been shot down by National Guardsmen in 1970—annoyed younger students (Pluto in Virgo, Uranus in Leo, Neptune in Scorpio). A number wrote letters asking, "Don't they know the sixties are over?" and characterized the sixties as a waste of time. More recently adults in their twenties have been criticizing the media for this obsession with baby-boomers who refuse to concede that many of them are now middle-aged. Such frustrations caused a group of men in their twenties to start the National Association for the Advancement of Time, which, during a campaign aimed at getting media and others to decrease nostalgia about Woodstock and other sixties events, adopted the slogan "Just Say Now." Leader Eugene Dillenberg argues that people who came of age in the 1970s and 1980s cannot experience their own culture, but are forced to relive distorted memories of the past that have been handed down by the older baby-boomers. Being born at a point where generational destinies were changing allows an appreciation for the arguments on both sides, but it might have been nice to "belong" to one of the camps.

Generations get lost frequently, since the slower-moving planets always do a two-step between two signs. The lost generations include people whose predicaments are often obvious. Jane Fonda was born on the very last degree of Pluto in Cancer (after it had already visited Leo), and it's probably fair to venture that the nationalistic, home-loving Pluto in Cancer generation has "problems" with Jane, though she's not quite Pluto in Leo. Richard Nixon is a tentative member of the Pluto in Gemini generation, though his foreign policies helped open up the world for the Gemini crowd. Elisabeth Kübler-Ross was born with Uranus at the end of Pisces, and her pioneering work has taken the world deeper into the question of man's connection to the Universal One, which is symbolized by Pisces. Jesse

Jackson is a 29-degree Uranus in Taurus who is certainly look-ing to shake up old Taurean values. Prince Charles's 29 degrees of Uranus in Gemini shows his fight against old thinking patterns and attitudes and his attempts to simply have more freedom to think and move around.

Since a number of the events—the walk on the Moon, Lind-bergh's crossing, desegregation of schools in Little Rock, Ar-kansas—took place within the month that generational planets changed signs, it seems that some of the meaning of the pla-netary cycles will make themselves known during these times. In the case of the walk on the Moon, transatlantic flight, or school desegregation, the meaning was just being hinted at since the planet was just starting to move through a sign. The death of Marilyn Monroe, whose glory days took place with Uranus in Leo, came in the weeks before childish Uranus in Leo gave way to Virgo in August 1962, the sign that knows how to keep a day job. Kennedy's Camelot would not have played well with Uranus in Virgo.

The business that the lost generation with Neptune in Libra square Uranus in Cancer—those born with the planets in the very last degrees—is being asked to finish involves a range of interpersonal and emotional matters. Neptune in Capricorn, of course, will make a square to Neptune in Libra (ideals and illusions) by 1998. (Those born earlier in the 1950s will feel the effects of Neptune in Capricorn in the early part of the 1990s). What is being dissolved are current ideas about emo-tional ties, home, family, the foundations that were so impor-tant in the 1950s. The Uranus in Cancer group's fortieth to forty-second birthdays will involve Uranus in Capricorn making an opposition and shaking up the more certain, established structures in their personal lives and around them in society. Given trends discussed in other portions of the book, it will appear that some economic shifts and changes will play a role in helping the Neptune in Libra/Uranus in Cancer group plunge forward and create the new paradigms that society needs.

We're All in This Together

This chapter has focused on the broader issues that connect us to others born around the same time. An astrological reading would show how the relationships between these generational planets are personalized. Having any of these planets making significant aspects to your Sun, Moon, or personal planets (Mercury, Venus, and Mars) would bring many of the collective issues right to your front door and force you to confront them more directly.

The Sun with Neptune would make one more idealistic and spiritual, but also easily confused and often not able to fend off the collective's psychic energy. The result can be a weak sense of identity. Gorbachev has Sun in configuration with Neptune, planet of a generation's ideals. The Sun in a potent picture with Neptune helped FDR illuminate the nation.

Uranus with the Sun can coincide with a courageous reformer or else just someone with a bad attitude. Beatniks Jack Kerouac and Allen Ginsberg both had the Sun in configuration with Uranus. Generation cohort George Bush's Gemini Sun is 90 degrees from erratic and rebellious Uranus, but he chose to represent the generation in a more traditional fashion.

Bush's Moon and Venus, plus other important points, acquire extra transformative power for himself and the country by an alliance with Pluto. Quayle's Sun in close opposition to Pluto helps his political efforts. Founding Father John Adams had a similar connection. Being born with the planet Pluto at the top of the chart would put one in the company of Thomas Jefferson, Richard Nixon and Jimmy Carter, as well as major industrial leaders.

Politician Albert Gore's personal planets are strongly configured with the Uranus/Neptune generational energy of the late 1940s, a connection that may help further his national political aims. But artists looking to build long-term careers depend on a certain empathy and communication with the masses that is indicated by having the Sun, Moon, and personal planets intermingled with generational themes: Steven Spielberg, Stephen King, Michael Jackson, and Madonna—literally most of the names in *Who's Who* in the library. Actress Meryl Streep's Sun in Cancer fits right into the Uranus in Cancer/Neptune in Libra square of 1949–56, making her especially appealing to those born under the same configuration. Bill Cosby's Moon is conjunct Neptune, enhancing his ability to draw on public moods. Industrialist Henry Ford's dreams to build an auto company that would supply the masses with transportation was in harmony with his generation's Pluto in Taurus need to build new resources and values. Both his Sun and his Moon were in a potent alignment with Pluto, giving him extra strength to work both his own will and the will of the times. The astrology of generations shows how the times and its people depend on each other to evolve and move forward.

PART IV
The Advanced Class

Your Personal Cycles

I hope that the introduction to age cycles and rhythms, as they relate to individual birthdates, has whetted your appetite for a more detailed, personalized study. The succeeding sections address this interest.

The first section will allow individuals to pinpoint a seven-year rhythm that relates to major shifts in life direction. This indicates periods of withdrawal and sometimes even "bottoming out," as well as very definite times of expansion and special public recognition. The cycle involves the ongoing movement of Saturn through the twelve-spoked horoscope wheel. Periods when Saturn crosses the Ascendant and moves through the First House, and also when it's moving through the Tenth House, are especially important. Saturn moving through the sign at the top of your chart (Tenth House) marks a special culmination of life and career goals. Saturn moving through the First House marks career and other life changes and a preparation period that starts building for special success once Saturn starts moving through the Seventh House 14 years later. The Fourth House, or Nadir, is a new start, often following a bottoming-out or crisis period.

There's a chance that the Tenth House in your official horoscope won't match the loose placement on your general chart. In actual practice the houses are not broken down into twelve even pieces. Also, portions of more than one sign can fall in a house. However, location of Saturn's movement, within a year or two, should be possible if the instructions for setting up a general chart are followed carefully.

Once the chart has been set up, find the sign in which Saturn was located at birth and place it in the chart. Saturn will come back to this point in the chart every twenty-nine years. Next find where Saturn is currently located (see page 197 for Saturn's movements) and place it in the chart. If you are reading this book between 1989 and 1991, Saturn is moving through your Capricorn house, which it visits every twenty-nine years.

Where were you during Watergate (1972–74), when Saturn

375

moved through Gemini and then Cancer? The point in the chart should be nearly opposite the 1988–91 position. Every fourteen years Saturn is opposite the point where it was located fourteen years earlier. Sometimes there is a symmetry of events. When was Saturn in your Ascendant sign? Your Fourth House? Your Seventh House?

Once the rhythm is generally understood, you can use the approximate birthchart you have set up to chart Saturn's movements. Some individuals will want to leave nothing to guesswork, however, and they will use a computer-calculated birthchart. (A list of companies that sell such charts is provided on page 416).

While Chapter 10 introduced the idea of a planet (in this case, Saturn) transiting a portion of the birthchart (the Sun), the importance of the Sun may cause some to wonder about cycles such as Jupiter's visit to the Sun sign every 11.8 years, or Mars's regular visit every 2 years. A brief section will help you begin to examine this issue. While the same principle can be applied to other points in the horoscope (Moon, Venus, etc.), the complexity of such analysis is not one newcomers are ready to tackle.

The contents of this "advanced class," however, will further alert students to the lifelong possibilities of astrological studies.

NINETEEN

The Rise and Fall of
Saturn: A Personalized
Timing System

Here he is—again.

That, in essence, is how the media was describing the return (again) of Richard Nixon in the mid-1980s as he began making speeches before civic groups, newspaper publishers, and other opinion leaders after some ten years of exile. Unanswered details about the intricacies of the Watergate scandal aside, Nixon, the author of several books about governing and foreign policy, had emerged as a statesman. He was someone for other political leaders to turn to—even if surreptitiously—for advice about world affairs. And who isn't fascinated by the cycles of ups and downs he has weathered. The writers of made-for-TV movies should be so imaginative and deft at designing such complex characters.

We don't have to look at the lives of the powerful or to prime-time television to follow these rhythmic periods, from external activity, to retrenchment and withdrawal, and then to rebuilding. This is the path of Everyman. We all can look to times in life when the general concerns and priorities moved—quite inevitably—in and out of high profile and into withdrawn periods, when concerns were more private and personal.

Such marked changes in a life coincide with the movements of Pluto, Neptune, and Uranus in relation to the contents of individual birthcharts. But it is Saturn, the timer and inner taskmaster, that acts as the place keeper, showing the general structure and direction one is moving in and toward at any given time. There are periods when the general structure favors climbing with outward signs of prestige and success. There are also periods of retreat and work on goals in a more self-identified and quiet way. They all fall under Saturn's rule.

Part II of this book included two chapters about how the general use of Saturn in charting seven-year cycles was geared to age as well as to the month of birth. This advanced class lets you get more personal, provided you're willing to take a few calculation steps or order a computerized birthchart for a cost of approximately $2.50 to $5.00 (see page 408 for details and guidelines for setting up a chart when a birthtime isn't known).

The timing of busts and booms that has brought Nixon both in and out of the public eye, and the timing that can bring a fairly anonymous employee into management and possibly even a career change another seven years down the road, are tied to Saturn's travel around the twelve-sector birthmap. Each one of the sectors stands for specific areas of life, such as identity, posessions, relationships, status. Involvement with each of these areas is colored according to the way the planets were placed in these houses at birth.

But life and the planets all continued to move on after the first breath. The relationships that these moving planets (transits) make to birth planetary positions coincide with various issues and changes that must be confronted. When planets are transiting (moving through a chart), the movement is counter-clockwise. Mars energizes every house it moves through, and the energy is particularly pronounced if planets were placed in the house at birth. An emotionally rocky day or two might be the result if Mars were to move over the Moon, and the picture would be even more complex if Mars was moving three or six signs away from another point in the horoscope. Jupiter expands what it touches and can spend a year in a house. The Sun's annual counterclockwise trip through the chart causes it to stay in each house for about a month. Since it always enters a house at the same time each year, it relates to those personal rhythms through which we regularly find ourselves giving some attention to careers, relationships, or home life around the same time each year. Mercury and Venus move quickly and may often only correlate to an especially communicative and pleasant day. Uranus upsets things and breaks people out of routines over a seven-year span, though changes will be more sudden when it moves over a planet in a house. Neptune dissolves, inspires new visions, but its fourteen-year stay in a house is often subtle. Pluto tears down, overhauls, with an eye toward empowering and transforming.

It is Saturn, giver of the structure of life and timer of maturation, that gives us information about the outline of timing in a life. The planet's 29.5-year orbit also means that the average person can experience at least two rounds of the planet through the houses. Saturn always corresponds to specific situations as it moves through each house. It announces itself and then spends 2.5 years guiding its students through specific lessons intended to clarify a given area of life. The situation brings to mind a twelve-section Wheel of Fortune or game board of life. Moving through the Second House, Saturn forces clarification about money and one's general values and how they relate to who we are. Experiences can relate to activities from the start of a new business that will pay off in the long term to bankruptcy. Saturn in the Sixth House of daily routine can relate to changes in work schedules, diets, as well as illnesses that might be a result of a failure to tap into a personal rhythm and routine.

Everybody starts with Saturn in one of the twelve houses, and this placement shows the area of life where people are the most insecure and suffer from feelings of inferiority. Through the course of life the house where Saturn is located often becomes the strong suit because people, out of a sense of incompleteness, put much energy into improving themselves there. As a result someone like Cher, born with Saturn in the First House, a position that indicates worries about oneself and body image and an initial fear of projecting the personality, gets a hold of her Saturnine fear and becomes someone with an image she is proud to project to others. (Her chart appears on page 380) It is this personal placement of Saturn in one of the twelve sectors that adds the color—and often the pathos—to turning-thirty stories. A person starting with Saturn in the Sixth House will be on a different schedule than someone born with Saturn in the Twelfth House. A Twelfth House Saturn, for instance, might be in a better position to take on a role of responsibility (a career) at twenty-two or twenty-three, when Saturn hits the highest point (the Tenth House). A person starting with Saturn in the Sixth House would experience Saturn reaching the highest point in his chart the first time at around at age eight and

ASTROLOGICAL
BUREAU OF IDEAS
CAPEL N MCCUTCHEON
P.O. BOX 251
WETHERSFIELD CT
06109
203-563-3146
CALC. ON
5-27-88

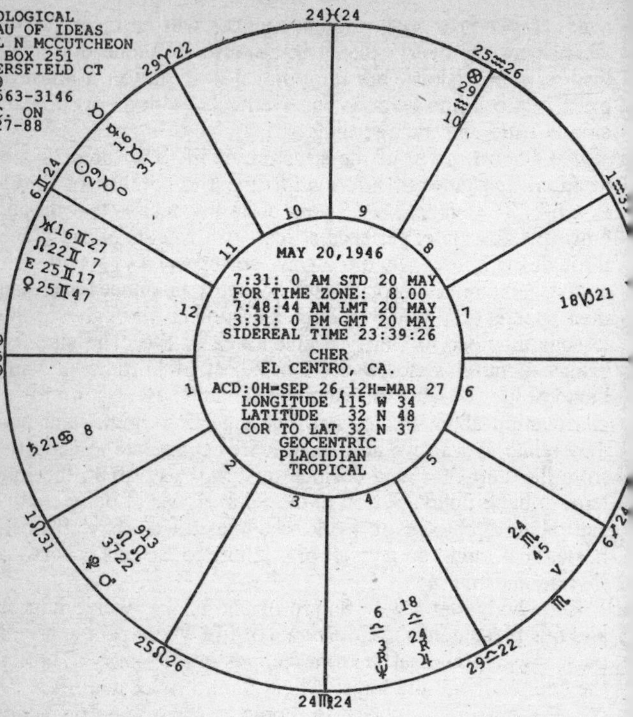

MAY 20,1946
7:31: 0 AM STD 20 MAY
FOR TIME ZONE: 8.00
7:48:44 AM LMT 20 MAY
3:31: 0 PM GMT 20 MAY
SIDEREAL TIME 23:39:26
CHER
EL CENTRO, CA.
ACD:0H=SEP 26,12H=MAR 27
LONGITUDE 115 W 34
LATITUDE 32 N 48
COR TO LAT 32 N 37
GEOCENTRIC
PLACIDIAN
TROPICAL
24♓24
25♒26
29♈22
6♊24
18♑21
24♍24
25♌26
29♎22
1♌31

** ASPECTS **

	SUN	MOON	MERC	VEN	MARS	JUP	SAT
MOON							
MERC		△ 1 51					
VEN		/					
MARS			□ 3 9	∠ 2 35			
JUP		□ 0 2	⚻ 1 53	△ 7 23	* 5 2		
SAT	* 7 52	☍ 2 47	* 4 38			□ 2 45	
URAN		⚻ 1 54	⚺ 0 3	☌ 9 20	* 3 6	△ 1 57	1
NEPT	△ 7 3				* 7 18		
PLUT	Q 1 24	/	□ 6 54	∠ 1110	☌ 3 45	* 8 47	
MC	* 4 37	* 6 3	* 7 53	□ 1 23			△ 3
ASC		☍ 8 32	* 6 41			□ 8 34	
NODE		⚻ 3 45		☌ 3 40	* 8 45	△ 3 43	⚺ 0
VRTX	☍ 4/15	* 6 24	☍ 8 15	⚻ 1 2	/		△ 3

NODE	ASC	MC
8♍26	17♍17	24♑
	0♋58	8♉
		17♉

PLANET	*DIG	SIGN	HSE	DECLN	LAT	TRAVL	DS	GEOCENTRIC	
SUN	B	29TAU 0	11	19.9	.0	0 58	14	N-NODE	S-NODE
MOON	D	18CAP21	7	-24.9	-2.6	12 10	21	22GEM 7	22SAG 7
MERC	A	16TAU31	11	15.6	-1.3	1 59	24	26TAU18	8GEM 6
VEN	A	25GEM47	12	24.6	1.3	1 13	19	6GEM 8	24ARI17
MARS	B	13LEO22	2	18.4	1.6	0 31	46	23TAU 2	1SCO58
JUP	A	18LIB24R	4	-5.8	1.5	0 -4	72	3CAN31	18CAP 9
SAT	D B	21CAN 8	1	21.9	.1	0 6	46	18CAN16	27CAP58
URAN	C	16GEM27	12	22.8	.0	0 3	25	12GEM46	14SAG16
NEPT		6LIB 3R	4	-1.0	1.5	0 -1	66	9LEO22	13AQU 0
PLUT	B C	9LEO37	2	23.9	6.3	0 1	60	18CAN36	21CAP 0
MC		24PIS24		-2.2					
ASC		9CAN49		23.1	*R=RULE D=DETRIMENT E=EXALTE[				
NODE		22GEM 7		23.2	F=FALL C=IN CRITICAL DEGREE				
VRTX		24SCO45		-19.0	A=ACCID DIGNITY BY HOUSE POS				
EQ	A	25GEM17		23.4	B=ACCD DEBILITY BY HOUSE POS				

	FIRE	MARS	CAR	JUP		ARABIC PARTS	
	2	PLUT	4	SAT	FORTUNE	29 AQUA	10
	ERTH	SUN		NEPT	SPIRIT	20 SCOR	29
	3	MERC		MOON	STATUS	13 SCOR	45
		MOON	FIX	SUN	DESTINY	5 LEO	3
	AIR	VEN	4	MERC			
	4	JUP		MARS	* DYNAMIC FOCUS *		
		URAN		PLUT	(CLOSEST SQUA OR OPPO)		
		NEPT	MUT	VEN	MOON SQUA JUP 0 2		
	WATR	SAT	2	URAN			
	1						

```
                    EAST
ANG.  JUP        7              JULIAN DATE
 4    SAT                    2431961.146528
      NEPT   WEST      MEAN OBLIQUITY OF ECLIPTIC
      MOON        3         23 DEG. 26 MIN
SUC.  VEN              SIDEREAL AYANAMSHA (SVP)
 4    MERC  SOUTH            6 PISC 1
      MARS        5
      PLUT
CAD.  VEN   NORTH
 2    URAN        5
```

ASPECTS	ANGLE	ORB	NO
♂=CONJUNCTION	0	10	4
⚼=SEMISEXTILE	30	2	3
∠=SEMISQUARE	45	3	3
✳=SEXTILE	60	9	14
□=SQUARE	90	10	9
△=TRINE	120	10	8
⚼=SESQUIQUAD	135	3	2
⚻=QUINCUNX	150	4	5
♌=OPPOSITION	180	10	4
Q =QUINTILE	72	2	1
B =BIQUINTILE	144	2	0
|=PARALLEL	0	1	7
/=CONTRAPARA	180	1	4

```
POS  6  NEG  4
VOCATIONAL IND MERC
  MUTUAL RECEPTION
  MERC AND VEN
  SAT  AND MOON
SOLE DISPOSITR NONE
SINGLETON NONE
SUN/MOON ANG 229.35
```

** MID-POINTS **

	NEPT	URAN	SAT	JUP	MARS	VEN	MERC	MOON	SUN	
:1	0♏24	5♍36	22♍57	6♏34	4♎ 3	10♏16	20♒38	21♐33	26♌53	VRTX
:2	14♌ 5	19♌17	6♋38	20♌15	17♍44	23♊57	4♊19	5♐14	10♊34	NODE
:3	22♌56	28♊ 8	15♋29	29♌ 7	26♋35	2♋48	13♊10	14♈ 5	19♊25	ASC
0	0♑14	5♋26	22♋46	6♋24	3♋53	10♉ 5	20♈27	21♒23	26♈42	MC
	7♏50	13♋ 2	0♋23	14♍ 0	11♌29	17♋42	28♊ 4	28♎59	4♋19	PLUT
		11♌15	28♌36	12♋13	9♍42	15♌55	26♊17	27♍12	2♌32	NEPT
N			3♋48	17♌25	14♍54	21♌ 7	1♊29	2♈24	7♊44	URAN
	NEPT			4♍46	2♌15	8♋28	18♊50	19♎45	25♊ 4	SAT
:51	* 3 33	PLUT			15♍53	22♌ 5	2♋27	3♈23	8♌42	JUP
:57		⚼ 0 13	MC			19♍34	29♊56	9♍51	6♋11	MARS
	□ 3 46	⚻ 0113		ASC			6♊ 9	7♈ 4	12♊24	VEN
:39		∠ 2130	□ 2 17			NODE		17♓26	22♉46	MERC
			△ 0 21	⚼ 0	4	⚻ 2 39			23♓41	MOON

would obviously not have the career or public-reputation opportunities of the twenty-two-year-old. The first time around for the eight-year-old, however, might coincide with special problems with parents or other authority figures.

Knowing where we started with our Saturn will immediately show the fallacy of the idea of "late bloomers," since everyone is on a different Saturn schedule. While we've compared Saturn's movements to a board game where you throw a die and move, everybody is moving at his or her own pace. People "pass Go" or "go directly to jail" pretty much on their own timing. Saturn moving through certain portions—in particular its rise to the top or noon position—of the chart more often correlates to the assumption of highly public responsibilities and positions of authority. Periods when the planet is moving down toward the Nadir, or lowest point in the chart—also called the midnight position, since the Sun is here at this time of night—are more inwardly directed times.

Nixon, born with Saturn in the "philosophy of life" Ninth House, was elected and reelected president as Saturn came home and approached the top of his chart. But his confrontation with Saturnian reality and justice (as well as other planets' ire) forced him to leave the White House soon after Saturn moved out of the Tenth House of reputation, career, and status. His mid-1980s comeback came as Saturn crossed the lowest point in the chart, started rebuilding in the Fourth House, and began climbing again.

The Rise and Fall of Saturn

Nixon's age, and the fact that we have a fairly precise birthtime for him, makes him an ideal main character for this study of Saturn's move through twelve houses. His chart appears on page 384. Saturn's counterclockwise travel through the twelve houses outlines twelve separate areas. It can also be viewed as containing four time blocks of about seven years each, which depict the broader trends in a life.

Quadrant One. Moving counterclockwise through the first quadrant, which consists of Houses One through Three, Saturn is associated with new starts. The period of time when Saturn first started moving through the Ascendant/Rising sign until it crosses the Nadir marks a withdrawal/preparation phase in which concerns are more inwardly directed. People tend to move away from the activities—careers, shorter-term goals, associations—that were so consuming as Saturn moved through Houses Ten, Eleven, and Twelve.

The change under way is most obvious as Saturn moves across the Ascendant and into the First House. People characteristically leave careers, relocate, make some of the most significant structural changes in their lives. The new sense of identity gets built upon as Saturn moves through the rest of this quadrant, which is concerned with developing one's essential being. It's a slow build as people become acquainted with a new identity (First House) and new values (Second House) and change the way they interact with their environment (Third House). The young Nixon's family moved from Yorba Linda to Whittier, forcing him to adjust to a new environment, during Saturn's first trek through this part of the birthchart. The next time around, Nixon was elected to the Senate and then the vice-presidency. The most recent time, nearly thirty years later, from 1979 to 1986, marked a period of reading and writing and exile as a private citizen.

Quadrant Two allows for experimentation in the environment through building a foundation (Fourth House), changing modes of self-expression (Fifth House), and dealing with a daily routine (Sixth House). Nixon is now in this period. Saturn's previous transit through this area marked the start of his vice-presidency and the loss of his presidential bid and campaign to be governor of California. The earliest time that Saturn went through this area corresponded to Nixon's school years.

Quadrant Three consists of Houses Seven, Eight, and Nine and involves stepping out to relate to others, form emotional connections, and develop a worldview and position in the world. There is often an increasing sense of responsibility and prestige. Since Nixon's Saturn is placed in the third quadrant, he has already experienced two Saturn Returns in his Ninth House (ages thirty and sixty). The first Return coincided with his marriage and law school, while the second involved his remaking his image and running for president and winning twice.

Quadrant Four is for the public record, since a person is on view, obtaining goals, and having an impact on the world, as symbolized by Houses Ten, Eleven, and Twelve. People reap the seeds that were sown in the First House. But just as Saturn gets comfortable in the Twelfth House, this high-profile cycle will start to dissolve, because it will soon be time to

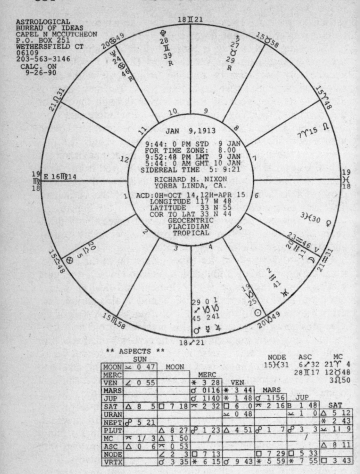

ASTROLOGICAL
BUREAU OF IDEAS
CAPEL N MCCUTCHEON
P.O. BOX 251
WETHERSFIELD CT
06109
203-563-3146
CALC: ON
9-26-90

JAN 9,1913

9:44: 0 PM STD 9 JAN
FOR TIME ZONE: 8.00
9:52:48 PM LMT 9 JAN
5:44: 0 AM GMT 10 JAN
SIDEREAL TIME 5: 9:21

RICHARD M. NIXON
YORBA LINDA, CA.

ACD:0H=OCT 14,12H=APR 15
LONGITUDE 117 W 48
LATITUDE 33 N 55
COR TO LAT 33 N 44
GEOCENTRIC
PLACIDIAN
TROPICAL

** ASPECTS **

	SUN	MOON	MERC	VEN	MARS	JUP	SAT	NODE 15)(31	ASC 6✗32 28Ⅱ17	MC 21Υ 4 12♉48 3♌50
MOON	⊼ 0 47									
MERC										
VEN	∠ 0 55		✶ 3 28							
MARS			✶ 3 44	σ 0116						
JUP			✶ 1 48	σ 1140	σ 1156					
SAT	△ 8 5	□ 7 18	⊼ 2 32	□ 6 0	⊼ 2 16	B 1 48				
URAN				∠ 0 48		∠ 1 0	✶ 2 43			
NEPT	⊗ 5 21						⊼ 11 9			
PLUT		△ 8 27	⊗ 1 23	△ 4 51	⊗ 1 7	⊗ 3 3				
MC	⊼ 1/ 3	△ 1 50		/		/	△ 8 11			
ASC	△ 0 6	⊼ 0 53			□ 7 29	□ 5 33				
NODE		∠ 2 3	□ 7 13							
VRTX		σ 3 35	✶ 6 15	σ 9 43	✶ 5 59	✶ 7 55	□ 3 43			

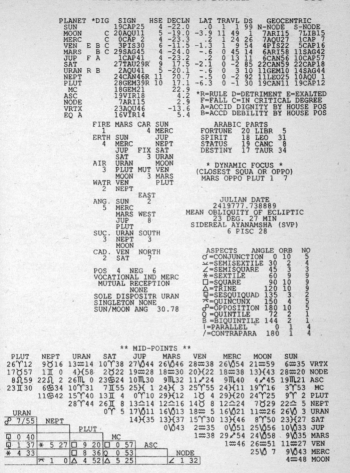

```
PLANET *DIG  SIGN    HSE DECLN  LAT TRAVL DS   GEOCENTRIC
SUN          19CAP25  4 -22.0   .0   1  1 99 N-NODE  S-NODE
MOON       C 20AQU11  5 -19.0 -3.9  11 49  1  7ARI15  7LIB15
MERC       C  0CAP 2  4 -23.3   .2   1 24 26  7AQU27  1CAP 7
VEN    E B C  3PIS30  6 -11.5 -1.3   1  9 54  4PIS22  5CAP16
MARS   B C 29SAG45  4 -24.0  -.6   0 45 14  6ARI58 11SAG42
JUP    F A  1CAP41  4 -23.2  -.2   0 13 11  6CAN56 10CAP57
SAT         27TAU29R  9  17.5 -2.1   0 -2 85 22CAN59 22CAP18
URAN   R B  2AQU41  5 -20.1  -.6   0  3 10 11GEM10 14SAG44
NEPT         24CAN46R 11  20.7  -.6   0 -2 92 11LEO25 10AQU11
PLUT         28GEM59N 10  17.1 -6.3   0 -1 30 19CAN11 19CAP12
MC           18GEM21     22.9
ASC          19VIR18      4.2 *R=RULE  D=DETRIMENT E=EXALTED
NODE          7ARI15      2.9 F=FALL  C=IN CRITICAL DEGREE
VRTX         23AQU46    -13.6 A=ACCID DIGNITY BY HOUSE POS
EQ A         16VIR14      5.4 B=ACCD DEBILITY BY HOUSE POS
```

```
FIRE MARS CAR SUN         ARABIC PARTS
 1        4  MERC      FORTUNE  20 LIBR  5
ERTH SUN    SUN        SPIRIT   18 LEO  31
 4   MERC   JUP        STATUS   19 CANC  8
     JUP FIX NEPT      DESTINY  17 TAUR 34
     SAT    SAT
AIR  URAN  3 URAN
 3   PLUT MUT MOON    * DYNAMIC FOCUS *
     MOON    VEN      (CLOSEST SQUA OR OPPO)
WATR VEN  3 MARS      MARS OPPO PLUT 1  7
 2   NEPT    PLUT
```

```
          EAST
ANG. SUN    2              JULIAN DATE
 5   MERC               2419777.738889
     MARS WEST     MEAN OBLIQUITY OF ECLIPTIC
     JUP    8          23 DEG. 27 MIN
     PLUT           SIDEREAL AYANAMSHA (SVP)
SUC. URAN SOUTH          6 PISC 28
 3   NEPT    3
     MOON
CAD. VEN  NORTH        ASPECTS     ANGLE ORB NO
 2   SAT    7       ♂=CONJUNCTION   0  10  5
                    ✶=SEMISEXTILE  30   2  4
POS  4  NEG 6       ∠=SEMISQUARE   45   2  3
VOCATIONAL IND MERC  ✶=SEXTILE     60   9  9
     MUTUAL RECEPTION □=SQUARE      90  10  9
          NONE       △=TRINE       120 10  9
SOLE DISPOSITR URAN  ⚷=SESQUIQUAD  135  3  2
SINGLETON NONE       ⚻=QUINCUNX    150  4  5
SUN/MOON ANG 30.78   ♂=OPPOSITION  180 10  5
                     Q=QUINTILE    72   2  1
                     B=BIQUINTILE  144  2  1
                     I=PARALLEL     0   1  4
                     /=CONTRAPARA  180  1  4
```

```
                        ** MID-POINTS **
PLUT   NEPT   URAN   SAT    JUP    MARS   VEN    MERC   MOON   SUN
26♈12  9♓16  13♒14 10♈38 27♐44 26♐46 28♒38 26♐54 21♒59  6♒35 VRTX
17♉57  1♊ 0  4♓58  2♉22 19♒28 18♒30 20♓22 18♒38 13♓43 28♒20 NODE
 8♌59 22♒ 2 26♏ 0 23♋24 10♏30  9♏32 11♈24  9♏40  4♍45 19♊21 ASC
23♊30  6♋34 10♈31  7♊15 25♓ 1 24♓ 1 25♈55 24♓11 19♈16  3♈53 MC
      11♓42 15♈40 13♊ 4  0♈10 29♓12  1♉ 4 29♓20 24♈25  9♈ 2 PLUT
            28♈44 26♊ 8 13♒14 12♒16 14♉ 8 12♒24  7♋29 22♎ 5 NEPT
                   0♈ 5 17♐11 16♐13 18♒ 5 16♒21 11♒26 26♍ 3 URAN
                        14♓35 13♓37 15♈30 13♓46  8♈50 23♓27 SAT
                              0♐43  1♒38 0♒51 25♒56 10♍33 JUP
                                    1♒38 29♒54 24♒58  9♒35 MARS
                                         1♒46 26♒51 11♒27 VEN
                                              25♒ 7  9♒43 MERC
                                                     4♒48 MOON
```

```
URAN
♂ 7/55 NEPT
          PLUT
⚷ 0 40
⚷ 1 37 ✶ 5 27 □ 9 20 □ 0 57 ASC
✶ 4 33         □ 8 36 Q 0 53   NODE
       ⚻ 1  0 △ 4 52 △ 5 25   ∠ 1 32
```

rebuild the identity and life as Saturn returns to the First House. Nixon first entered public office when Saturn went through this fourth quadrant. He was forced out of public life as Saturn moved through the same area some thirty years later. Numerous cycles, among them Pluto and Neptune, as well as some of the complexes in Nixon's birthmap, were involved in his downfall. But he was forced to resign from office when Saturn was in the Eleventh House, about midway between the highest point in his chart and his Rising sign/First House, en route to the Twelfth House of self-undoing. Saturn's movement across the highest point in Nixon's chart, when he went to China and during the Watergate break-in, and at the start of his entry into public life thirty years earlier, is a perfect example of the personal rhythms to which each individual character resonates.

And Then the Cycle Starts All Over Again

There is a tendency in astrological circles to wrongly assume that people are totally in hiding and don't have any success as Saturn moves through their first three houses. Candice Bergen's successful life as Murphy Brown came with Saturn moving from her First House and into her Second. A television sitcom was a new life (and risk) for the former photographer-author-model-film actress.

While popular theory holds that people's biggest successes or public dishonor come when Saturn hits the top of the chart, Nixon's chart is one of those literal extremes. Metaphysically speaking, success takes many forms, and its meaning in a life differs with each individual. Age and the Saturn placement at the time of birth are all factors that will determine how literally the traditional success formula should be understood.

Saturn was in the Tenth House as Gelsey Kirkland became a prima ballerina with the New York City Ballet at age nineteen. A more typical nineteen-year-old would have just started coming into a career or dealing with issues of public authority. But for Kirkland's life, Saturn was able to mean more; people don't become prima ballerinas at thirty-five. Frank Sinatra, who was born with Saturn in the Fourth House, was fifteen the first time Saturn moved across the top of his chart and coincided with problems with authorities and school. Sinatra is a high school dropout. The second time Saturn moved through this house, Sinatra was concerned about his public image after the Kennedy family began limiting associations with him because of his Mafia connections, author Kitty Kelly reports. Saturn will next be in this house around 1989–90.

Sinatra announced his retirement in 1971, when Saturn was in the first quadrant. But as Saturn moved down to the Nadir and also coincided with his second Saturn Return as he entered his sixties, Sinatra made plans for a comeback. Despite his continued popularity, Sinatra has never reclaimed the appeal he had in 1949, particularly in the period when Saturn moved through his second quadrant. At that time Sinatra was in his thirties and was essentially releasing the skill and singing ability he'd gathered and refined when he launched his career with Saturn moving through the first three houses of his horoscope.

Bette Davis started collecting Oscars with Saturn in her first quadrant, the presumably "obscure" period. When Saturn returned to this area thirty years later, Hollywood moguls put up a fight against financing *Whatever Happened to Baby Jane?*, claiming that Davis and Joan Crawford were no longer bankable names. As usual, Davis proved them wrong. Hollywood gave her a Lifetime Achievement Award in 1977 as Saturn moved through her Eighth House, a few years away from the top of her chart.

Around the Wheel a Few Times

While the use of Davis and Sinatra—as well as some older public figures—may seem dated to some readers, it is for that reason that these people make better study subjects. Saturn has moved through these birthcharts at least twice, allowing the cycle to be viewed with more perspective. Today's popular actresses' and actors' successes will be better understood after a few more bouts with Saturn. An exact birthtime is also crucial to these types of study. And very few of the birthcharts for famous people have been verified.

Saturn also doesn't take well to America's version of fame and success. It prefers to work with people who build over a stretch of time and isn't patient with people who are looking to get their fifteen minutes of fame the easy way. Saturn eventually pulls the switch, particularly as the planet is moving through the first quadrant, when people refuse to specify and clarify the issues that are on the table. When Saturn is moving through the first quadrant is the time when many seem to disappear for years at a time. The truly successful ones are working quietly, slowly building new ideals, careers, lives. It can sometimes be the perfect "vice-presidential" time. Witness Gerald Ford, who was a vice president when he got the bigger job. George Bush held the number-two spot during this time as well and came out to run for the big office with Saturn trying to gain momentum in the second quadrant. Carter took on the new career of "private citizen" as Saturn moved through his first quadrant. But as it crossed over the Nadir and started building momentum in his Fourth House (the beginning of the second quadrant) in 1989, he was being lauded in national publications for his statesmanship and continued diplomatic activities around the world.

The first quadrant demands that work and other activities be a clear reflection of one's true identity. People must stand on their own feet and be willing to take responsibility for their lives. Cher, who has Saturn in the First House in her birthmap, began to go it alone (sans Sonny or Greg Allman) when Saturn came back to this quadrant as her Saturn Return began. Her television show was canceled, then rescheduled again, before going off the air. Cher sang, performed, and continued to build her career, setting a tone that would help carry her through the rest of the cycle. With Saturn traveling through her Fifth and Sixth Houses she was in several movies. She won an Academy Award as Saturn was in the latter part of the Sixth House of hard work, soon to cross into the Seventh House of the public and really start moving toward the top.

A similar phenomenon has been experienced by Bill Cosby, whose first brush with success came with Saturn moving through Houses Ten and Eleven. (His chart appears on page 390.) With Saturn having gone the distance through busy, but sometimes quieter times, Cosby was being touted as a rich businessman, author, and father figure as climbing Saturn crossed the setting area (House Seven of the public). Like Cher, Cosby had been working especially hard during Houses Four through Six. He underwent a period of disfavor as Saturn moved through the Twelfth House/Ascendant area, but began developing educational programs for children as Saturn moved farther through quadrant one, where new lives are created.

But none of this is as easy as it might look.

The first quadrant, while aimed at inner direction, is a place where people often experience a crisis as Saturn approaches the Nadir. They actually bottom out, which is often necessary to get them back on track. While there is some dispute about whether Michael Dukakis was born precisely at 6:00 P.M., as his mother reports, his dramatic failure to win reelection as governor in 1978 coincides with Saturn in the lower portion of either a 5:30 or 6:00 P.M. chart. The 1978 election is commonly described as having been a "life-changing" experience for Dukakis, who then took three years off to teach and understand the reasons for the loss before coming back to win again. He did this by restructuring his foundation, trying not to isolate himself from aides and the political process, and making an effort to at least appear to listen to others more. Like many Scorpios, Dukakis had been acting as a law unto himself and had felt himself above the politic king needed to get legislation and programs approved up at the statehouse.

Dukakis chased the presidency with Saturn approaching his Tenth House, often a transit that can indicate a big new job. George Bush, on the other hand, was running with Saturn moving through the beginning of the second quadrant. This period calls for a new start, and while it has not been a popular post from which to win the presidency—John F. Kennedy is one of the notable few who was elected president with Saturn moving through the bottom part of the chart—it made sense for Bush, given his "first quadrant" vice presidency. While Dan Quayle's exact birthtime is in dispute, one of the two popular choices (noon) would see Saturn moving through the top of Quayle's chart in 1992. Jack Kemp will experience the same Saturn transit in 1993–96, along with a second Saturn Return. Richard Gephart sees Saturn moving through his career/status house in 1996–1998, right before a Saturn Return. Robert Dole is still riding high with Saturn moving through his Eleventh House of benefits and societal involvement from 1991 to 1993.

But Saturn moving through the top of the chart is just a piece of the puzzle. Saturn approaching the Tenth didn't help Walter Mondale. Gary Hart would have had Saturn going through his Tenth House around Inauguration Day 1989, but a lot of other cycles obviously weren't in his favor. He tripped himself up with Saturn at the height of his reaping period. Mario Cuomo will experience Saturn into and up through his third quadrant (beginning with the Seventh House) in 1992. Lloyd Bentsen is moving farther into the lower, key first quadrant. Youngblood Albert Gore will see Saturn move through his Tenth House from 1997 to 1999.

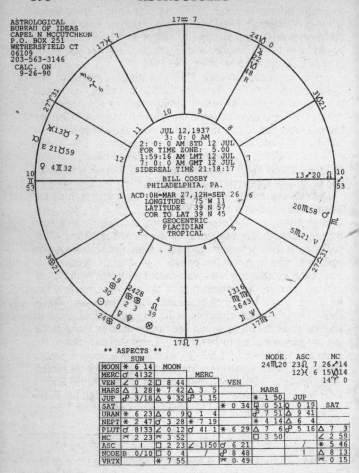

ASTROLOGICAL
BUREAU OF IDEAS
CAPEL N MCCUTCHEON
P.O. BOX 251
WETHERSFIELD CT
06109
203-563-3146
CALC. ON
9-26-90

JUL 12, 1937
3: 0: 0 AM
2: 0: 0 AM STD 12 JUL
FOR TIME ZONE: 5.00
1:59:16 AM LMT 12 JUL
7: 0: 0 AM GMT 12 JUL
SIDEREAL TIME 21:18:17

BILL COSBY
PHILADELPHIA, PA.

ACD:0H=MAR 27,12H=SEP 26
LONGITUDE 75 W 11
LATITUDE   39 N 57
COR TO LAT 39 N 45
GEOCENTRIC
PLACIDIAN
TROPICAL

** ASPECTS **

	SUN	MOON	MERC	VEN	MARS	JUP	SAT
MOON	* 6 14						
MERC	♂ 4132						
VEN	∠ 0 2	□ 8 44					
MARS	△ 1 28	* 7 42	△ 3 5				
JUP	♂ 3/18	△ 9 32	♂ 1 15				
SAT				* 0 34	□ 0 51	♂ 0 19	
URAN	* 6 23	△ 0 9	∠ 1 4		♂ 7 51	△ 9 41	
NEPT	* 2 47	△ 3 28	* 7 19		* 4 14	△ 6 4	
PLUT	♂ 8133	∠ 0 12	♂ 41 1	* 6 29	△ 7 6	♂ 5 16	△ 7 3
MC	⊼ 2 23	⊼ 3 52			□ 3 50		∠ 2 59
ASC	/	□ 2 23	∠ 1150	♂ 6 21		/	* 5 46
NODE	B 0/10	□ 0 4	/	♂ 8 48		/	△ 8 13
VRTX		* 7 55		⊼ 0.49			⊼ 0 15

	NODE	ASC	MC
	24♏20	23♌ 7	26♐14
		12♓ 6	15♑14
			14♈ 0

PLANET	*DIG	SIGN	HSE	DECLN	LAT	TRAVL	DS	N-NODE	S-NODE
SUN		19CAN30	2	22.0	.0	0 57	1		
MOON	A	13VIR16	4	1.6	-5.2	12 59	48	13SAG20	13GEM20
MERC	A	24CAN 2	3	23.0	1.7	2 6	16	5CAN54	16LEO22
VEN	A C	4GEM32	12	18.1	-3.0	1 2	62	5CAN31	4VIR52
MARS	R C	20SCO58	6	-20.5	-2.6	0 12	88	12GEM48	9LIB32
JUP	F	22CAP48R	8	-21.8	-.3	0 -8	92	11CAN16	7CAP21
SAT	F A	5ARI 6	11	-.1	-2.3	0 0	60	22CAN36	23CAP19
URAN	F	13TAU 7	12	15.4	-.4	0 2	26	15GEM 2	11SAG30
NEPT	D C	16VIR43	4	6.2	1.0	0 1	23	10LEO22	11AQU46
PLUT		28CAN 3	3	23.0	2.5	0 2	16	29CAN32	29CAP32
MC		17AQU 7		-15.7					
ASC		10GEM53		22.1					
NODE		13SAG20		-22.4					
VRTX		5SCO21		-13.3					
EQ	A	21TAU59		18.3					

*R=RULE D=DETRIMENT E=EXALTED
F=FALL C=IN CRITICAL DEGREE
A=ACCID DIGNITY BY HOUSE POS
B=ACCD DEBILITY BY HOUSE POS

Elements / Modes

FIRE 1: SAT
ERTH 4: JUP, URAN, NEPT, MOON
AIR 1: VEN
WATR 4: SUN, MERC, MARS, PLUT

CAR 5: SUN, MERC, JUP, PLUT, SAT
FIX 2: URAN, MARS
MUT 3: VEN, NEPT, MOON

EAST 6 / WEST 4
SOUTH 4 / NORTH 6

ANG. 2: NEPT, MOON
SUC. 3: SUN, JUP, SAT
CAD. 5: MERC, MARS, URAN, PLUT, VEN

POS 2   NEG 8
VOCATIONAL IND VEN
MUTUAL RECEPTION
 MERC AND MOON
SOLE DISPOSITR NONE
SINGLETON NONE
SUN/MOON ANG 53.76

ARABIC PARTS

FORTUNE 4 LEO 39
SPIRIT 17 ARIE 7
STATUS 10 ARIE 53
DESTINY 23 SAGG 21

* DYNAMIC FOCUS *
(CLOSEST SQUA OR OPPO)
MERC OPPO JUP 1 15

JULIAN DATE
2428726.791667
MEAN OBLIQUITY OF ECLIPTIC
23 DEG. 26 MIN
SIDEREAL AYANAMSHA (SVP)
6 PISC 8

ASPECTS

Aspect	ANGLE	ORB	NO
☌=CONJUNCTION	0	10	5
⚺=SEMISEXTILE	30	2	0
∠=SEMISQUARE	45	3	5
⚹=SEXTILE	60	9	12
□=SQUARE	90	10	8
△=TRINE	120	10	11
Q=SESQUIQUAD	135	3	2
⚻=QUINCUNX	150	4	6
☍=OPPOSITION	180	10	7
Q=QUINTILE	72	2	2
B=BIQUINTILE	144	2	2
I=PARALLEL	0	1	7
/=CONTRAPARA	180	1	7

** MID-POINTS **

PLUT	NEPT	URAN	SAT	JUP	MARS	VEN	MERC	MOON	SUN	
16♏42	11♌ 2	9♌14	20♑14	14♐ 4	13♏ 9	19♌56	14♍42	9♋18	12♍25	VRTX
5♋42	0♏ 2	28♒13	9♒13	3♈ 4	2♐ 9	8♓56	3♋41	28♋18	1♋25	NODE
4♋28	28♋48	27♉ 0	8♉ 0	1♉50	0♏55	7♊42	2♋28	27♋ 4	0♊11	ASC
7♉35	1♐55	0♈ 7	11♑ 7	4♋57	4♋ 2	10♈50	5♉35	0♈11	3♉19	MC
	22♌23	20♊35	1♊35	25♋25	24♍30	1♌18	26♋ 3	20♌39	23♋47	PLUT
		14♋55	25♋55	19♍45	18♋50	25♋38	20♋23	14♍59	18♋ 7	NEPT
			24♈ 6	17♓57	17♒ 2	23♉49	18♍34	13♋11	16♊18	URAN
				28♋57	28♒ 2	4♉49	29♋34	24♊11	27♋18	SAT
					21♐53	28♓40	23♎25	18♍ 2	21♈ 9	JUP
						27♎45	22♏30	17♎ 7	20♍14	MARS
							29♊17	23♋54	27♊ 1	VEN
								18♌39	21♋46	MERC
									16♌23	MOON

Mid-point aspect grid:

```
          URAN
  △ 3 37   NEPT
  □ 4/ 1   ⚻ 0 24                    PLUT
           □ 5 51   ∠ 2111   △ 6 15   MC
                                       ASC
  ⚻ 0 13   □ 3 24   Q 0/17   ⚹ 3 47   ⚹ 2/27   NODE
  ☍ 7 46             □ 7 18             B 0 28
```

Dukakis will experience his second Saturn Return in 1991 with the planet near the top of his chart, but presently is swearing off politics once his gubernatorial term expires. Dukakis won his first political office—as state representative in Massachusetts—with Saturn rising through this part of his chart. A failed run for lieutenant governor in 1970, at age thirty-seven, forced Dukakis out of public office for the first time since 1963. But he characteristically put the time to good use. He practiced law full-time and in 1971–72 started gathering support for what became his successful push for the governorship in 1974.

Saturn Through the First House

Dukakis's quiet maneuvering is illustrative of the way some people go about making changes as Saturn moves through the Twelfth House at the end of quadrant four and into the First House. The 6:00 P.M. time for Dukakis would have had Saturn going over the First House through the spring of 1972.

Once again, the move from the Twelfth House to the First House is one of the most significant times in a person's life. Whatever one was doing before—when Saturn was in the Twelfth House—has often ended, and it's time to redefine one's identity. While this cycle can happen at any age, it's put to greater practical use by someone older than twenty-eight.

Since the Rising sign and the First House are related to the body, and Saturn to the skeletal system, people often go through major weight losses or image changes at this time. They can also feel cut off, separated from others. Such isolation is necessary in order to build a new identity. Increased personal and career responsibility often come with this cycle. An increased sense of authority—or desire for authority—is also felt. William Rehnquist became chief justice, after serving as an associate on the court for fifteen years. The first appointment had been made as Saturn moved into his Seventh House, which is directly across from the First House. Clint Eastwood became a politician—mayor—when Saturn went through his First House. Bruce Springsteen cut his first album. Bette Midler left Hawaii and started performing in clubs and bathhouses in New York as Saturn moved through her First House. Her bankability continues to rise as Saturn moves toward the top of her chart.

The nonfamous have similar experiences. One woman left a marriage and moved across country; another began therapy and, as she began changing her life-style, was forced to endure hostility from people who had been more comfortable with her old self-deprecating ways. Jan explains: "I would say things like, 'I'm going to go back to school,' and these people would tell me, 'You're not the school type.' It made me angry. They were reacting to me in very superficial, taken-for-granted ways, and I had to walk away and stand up for myself. I was working a full-time job, going to school, and just really focusing in on myself, my needs, who I was."

Reginald became a manager in a pharmaceutical sales company and, for the first time in his life, had to deal with the sense of authority and increased self-awareness that such a position often brings. "I was in my early thirties and still kind of a play-around guy, but now I had to always be setting off on the right foot, taking responsibility, being more grown up."

Reginald's experiences, which were marked by reprimands and some dressing down by higher-ups, who felt he needed somewhat of an image change, are instructive for people moving into this period. It's important to "set off on the right foot" and realize that you're moving in a period where you must be more self-aware, self-identified. Since the Rising sign tells how you start things and approach life, Saturn wants some of those attitudes redefined for the next 29.5-year cycle that will coincide with its movement through all twelve houses.

Natal Saturns

Natal Saturn in the First House

The move of Saturn into the First House was also especially important for Reginald because he was born with the planet in that house. A person born with Saturn in this house spends a lifetime fighting for the right to his or her identity and with feeling comfortable in authority roles. They may start life feeling criticized, rejected, ridiculed, afraid to assert themselves. One First House Saturn woman says "I never felt I had the right to wear red. I thought it was reserved for glamorous people." Saturn Return turning-thirty stories for these people often involve situations that showed them how much of themselves they'd been afraid to show to the world. They learn they have the right to take themselves seriously.

After leaving the First House, Saturn builds on the ideas that started struggling for life as the new 29.5-year cycle began.

Saturn Through the Second House

Saturn in the Second House has to be somewhat related to what was going on when it was in the First House. The new identity that broke through must now renegotiate its values, what it deems to be worthwhile. A common manifestation is situations in which money—particularly a limited supply of money—forces people to develop ways of enhancing their cash flow and also to rethink some of their attitudes about possessions. Some people may be financially comfortable, but at this time they're particularly concerned with building a nest egg for the future. The Second Houses's connection with inner resources also results in thoughts about how a person wants to employ these resources to sustain him or her in life. "I decided that I would never squander money anymore, and that was the time in life when I was really taking bills seriously, trying to get financially free and secure," says Maureen, who spent half of this period out of work. "At first it really worried me—I never thought I'd ever have to work as a temp—but then I really got into increasing my word-processing skills and understanding that that would help me survive." Thoughts of surviving can bog people down and keep them from seeing the bigger concern, which has to do with one's value system.

Natal Saturn in the Second House

When people talk behind the backs of people born with Saturn in the Second House, they invariably mention the way they pull out the calculator to divide the lunch check so precisely. Some friends just cut the flowery stuff and say they're cheap. At the very least, their worries about the costs of things is noticeable. Both the rich and the poor with this placement worry about becoming bag ladies. Some are highly acquisitive and equate possessions with self-worth. Clothes, houses, cars don't make the man (or woman) and this placement spend lifetimes trying to develop a healthy relationship between their things and themselves without confusing the two.

Saturn Through the Third House

Even if they relocated when Saturn moved over the Ascendant, people will start talking about how much they dislike their neighborhood or immediate environment when Saturn moves into the Third House. "It's so limiting. I really believe it's possible to die of boredoom. I actually get headaches just thinking about living here," was how one man described his feeling about the city where he'd relocated to for work. While it's important to be honest and point out that many people have this to say about the Insurance City, this man was particularly upset and angry. He was having trouble with landlords and neighbors, and it's a wonder nobody had organized a block-watch group just to protect everyone else from his negativity. Saturn moving through the Third House of one's immediate environment was trying to get him to develop better ways of communicating and interacting with others, but all he could see was a dull city. He was becoming more frustrated, depressed, and blocked in his thinking. While some people use this period for reflection, night classes, activities that will help restructure the way they use their minds and move around in their immediate world, this man was succumbing to the mental exhaustion and depression that can coincide with this Saturn placement.

Natal Saturn in the Third House

Many born with Saturn in the Third House grow up apprehensive about their ability to communicate and be understood. They sometimes feel stupid or are self-conscious about educational limitations. These areas of life may have suffered setbacks in their youth. Relations with siblings may have been impaired. Symbolically speaking, being cut off from a sister or brother is like not being able to access a part of ourselves. When this group learns to focus their thoughts and gain more confidence, they're celebrated for their depth, profundity, and their wry sense of humor.

Saturn Through the Fourth House

Saturn reaching the Nadir of the chart is indicative of the end of one phase and the start of another, though often not without crisis (as we have seen). Saturn's crossing of the Nadir and transit into the Fourth House is highly discernible, since it usually relates to a move from one life structure to another. George Wallace emerged in this house declaring himself a new man—no longer a bigot—after spending the time that Saturn traveled through his first quadrant recuperating from the attempt on his life. James moved across country within a month of Saturn's entry into this house, after being particularly depressed as Saturn had moved through his Third House. Kathy left her marriage and began building a career and a self-sufficient lifestyle. The Fourth House is the home, both in a physical and an emotional sense. It also represents what each individual comes from (family, spiritual heritage) and the movement of Saturn through this house calls for people to deal with the very foundations of their physical and emotional life. Parental and family concerns may be especially pressing for some, while others must do inner regrouping, much the way Dukakis was forced to after losing reelection as governor.

Natal Saturn in the Fourth House

Growing up was especially difficult and restrictive for people born with Saturn in the Fourth. One parent may have been particularly unnurturing and rejecting. There is a legacy that may result in a Saturn Return that is similar to Marjorie's, whose parents stopped speaking to her when she married a non-Jew. Astrologers sometime hate to see this Saturn placement come for a visit because many will insist that they had an idyllic childhood. Many of them are like Alan, who says that he was thirty-five before he realized that the beatings and punishments he received as a child went beyond his parents' claim—and his long-held belief—that they were simply strict disciplinarians.

Saturn Through the Fifth House

Some astrology books describe this as being a period when creativity doesn't come as readily, but the activities of Cher and members of rock bands suggest that the key to harnessing this period is true self-expression. None of that trendy stuff. The problem is that too many people adopt styles and manners from others instead of tapping into their own individual essence. When people fail to do this, the common experiences that Saturn through the Fifth House can bring—trouble with children and lovers and other such downers—will be more likely. Saturn always involves a little discomfort, no matter what the chart. But rising to its requirements also results in a certain amount of freedom.

Natal Saturn in the Fifth House

Saturn in the Fifth House represents people who feel they have to work hard to make the rest of us love them. When Fifth House Saturn people learn self-love, they find they don't have to put on a show for the rest of the world. Some are frightened by spontaneity and never let themselves go and be truly creative. This estrangement from the "inner child" often results in special difficulties with one's real flesh-and-blood children.

Saturn Through the Sixth House

People during this time are engaged in long-term tasks that require much detail and attention. A developer who rehabilitated a Victorian building explained it this way: "I learned that big things get done a little bit each day." People learn to see God in the details and daily routine of life. People who aren't careful can bring about health problems, such as the man who was forced to change his diet because of hypertension. Since the Sixth House is the last one Saturn rides through before crossing the horizon and moving into the Seventh House and the growing influence of quadrant three, the Sixth House corresponds to physical and other self-improvement phases that, like the extra work hours, seem to be trying to help pull it all together.

Natal Saturn in the Sixth House

What those born with a Sixth House Saturn must learn to do is to develop a more flowing rhythm and routine that allows them to put work, health, and all areas of their lives into perspective. Through meditation and self-awareness they can become living proof of the spirituality and beauty of life's rhythms as they allow the right work and daily routine to flow into one another.

Saturn Through the Seventh House

With Saturn moving through the house of relationships and into quadrant three, people find themselves reassessing their relationships. Often there's been a promotion—or in Cher's case an Academy Award—that has taken a person out of the rank and file. The rules are different now. Nancy, who got her first significant promotion at this time, says she found it difficult to balance relationships now that she was a boss and had workers who reported to her. The balancing act is evident in personal affairs as well. Marriages and divorces can come at this time—though such events can also happen at other times around the wheel. John DeLorean's legal problems were aired in court with Saturn moving through this house.

Natal Saturn in the Seventh House

Relationships seem to be something this group has to work at harder than other people. They do have a tendency to go overboard trying to define the parameters of relationships. They're also known to put a damper on social interactions because of their often poor social skills. Eventually they take these faults and become a shining example of refinement, a real Ms. (Mr.) Manners who reads all the cues.

Saturn Through the Eighth House

Your personal connections with others were highlighted in the previous house, and now, with Saturn through the Eighth, even more nitty-gritty interpersonal matters seem to crop up. Saturn was heading into this house as Bruce Springsteen's marriage was breaking up, forcing him to confront the consequences of his relations and commitments. Pat and Doug started having sexual problems that they couldn't talk about when Saturn moved through this house. Pat dragged her husband into counseling. Nobody's saying much about what happened—or didn't happen—but Pat complains about discovering that "we hadn't really come together as a couple." There was no "real intimacy or sense of oneness." They're divorcing and going through the power struggles that the Eighth House can also get you into. "When this is over, I don't want anything in my house or anything else in my life to show any sign that he was in my life."

Natal Saturn in the Eighth House

The problems of people born with this placement are subtle and are not as obvious to the rest of us as, say, the problems of Saturn in the Seventh House. But Eighth House Saturn has many fears about getting close to people, emotionally and sexually. They're struggling with issues of their own power and powerlessness. Once they understand and utilize their inner resources, their external interrelationships with others are easier to handle.

Saturn Through the Ninth House

This is the time to develop a philosophy and worldview that help you operate as Saturn moves through the fourth quadrant. It is also a time when people are beginning to understand and realize some of their larger goals, and they are taking on a more public role, which is why it's important to have some idea about how one plans to play the game of life. Saturn moving through this house helps provide the momentum that allows one to push on out and into the Tenth House.

Natal Saturn in the Ninth House

People born with Saturn in the Ninth are particularly concerned about the way the "game of life" is played. Some constantly question their early religious teachings; others hold to them rigidly. Education is sometimes interrupted, causing discomfort. Others are especially learned. Richard Nixon was born with this placement and has undergone several public crises that have forced him to reassess and realign his philosophy of life.

Saturn Through the Tenth House

You've been in training for this moment ever since Saturn moved through your First House. Now you should be moving in on your goal. You're taking on more responsibility, and more people know who you are. If you've learned your lessons and are prepared, this can be the height of your career, depending on your age and so forth. Others will get the kick out the door that they deserve. It's important to be aboveboard, because everything done in this house is on view. The whole world is watching.

Natal Saturn in the Tenth House

People with this position at birth are especially ambitious, but they must make sure that their goals are self-defined rather than simply something that the family in which they were born demands. People with this position—John F. Kennedy for one—often have a parent who tries to control their activities and futures, even if it's simply via a telephone call every Sunday afternoon.

Saturn Through the Eleventh House

After getting more responsibility in the Tenth House, it's now time to become part of the larger community. People often find themselves joining organizations and interacting with larger networks of people at this time. This is still a reaping cycle, so promotions—or deserved demotions—are also associated with this time.

Natal Saturn in the Eleventh House

People born with this Saturn placement often like to make a big deal about not wanting to have anything to do with the rest of us human creatures, especially if we belong to organizations. But this Saturn group is usually insecure about its ability to fit in. When they work on themselves, they can show us all something about how one can be part of the family of man and still retain his or her sense of individuality.

Saturn Through the Twelfth House

Life is pretty diffuse right now. That high-profile, Saturn-about-town life that people were living is coming to an end. The cycle that started with Saturn in the First House must be cleared away and new seeds planted. People don't recognize this at first. They keep trying the same old routines—Carter was planning a second term during this time—and the same old forms of expression and they can't understand why the tried-and-true ways are no longer working. Some people get sick or depressed. Others get hospitalized.

Natal Saturn in the Twelfth House

The lives of people born with Saturn in the Twelfth House are particularly instructive about some of the downfalls of this time. Many of these people have difficulties projecting their identities and are often paranoid and fearful (Emily Dickinson is an example). Those born with Saturn in the Twelfth House, as well as people who have it moving through their Twelfth House, must not give in to the pain and fear. Instead it's important to develop a feeling for the threads that weave all of life together and that speak to the continuity within that which is ever-constant—change. Times of abundance and going outward always give way to times of retreat. In the words of Rudyard Kipling, the trick is to "treat those two imposters just the same."

The Twelfth House is the best vantage point from which to view the seeming victories and defeats in our lives and to understand how we brought each one about. When the time is right, the curtains that now appear to be drawn will open to a stage that has been redesigned and made ready so that yet another story can unfold.

TWENTY

Transits to the Sun

The Sun is the center of being and hence, the most important point in the birthchart. Transits to the Sun, particularly the long-term ones, play a major role in self-development and expression.

Minor transits to the Sun—those of Mercury or Venus, for instance—have been mentioned only in passing. The only major transit to the Sun we've discussed is Saturn's. This is because that cycle is compact, and Saturn is the indisputable maker of life structures. Saturn's influence, as it makes its 29.5-year orbit, is one of specifics, definition, crystallization; its concerns are more concrete than are the subtle influences from Neptune, for example.

Though the scope of this book is not to teach transits—this segment of astrology cannot be tackled fully until students gain an understanding of how all the planets work in the natal chart—students may want to test the effects of Mars and other planets moving through the Sun sign. To accomplish this, check the ephemeris to determine when each given planet is moving through the Sun sign as well as the signs that stand in critical relation to the Sun sign. The same rules involving aspects— planets three and six signs away are stressful; two and four signs away, less so—apply. The appearance of a planet in the same sign as one's Sun indicates the start of a new cycle involving the Sun's embodiment of the principles represented by the planet. For instance, Jupiter conjuncting the Sun sign (or self-sign, one might say) starts a new eleven-year cycle of self-expansion and self-integration in areas related to it. Mars moving over the Sun calls for a new cycle of self-assertion.

Those looking to track the phases within the transit can refer to the chart (a replica of one encountered earlier in this book) on page 50 showing the sign-to-sign aspect relationship. In all cases, the important aspects are the conjunction (same sign), First Quarter/Opening Square (planet moving three signs ahead of Sun); Last Quarter/Closing Square (three signs behind the Sun), and the midpoint of the cycle, the opposition (six signs, or 180 degrees away). Less stressful aspects (two and four signs apart) can also be studied, but often don't correlate to dynamic energy or turning points.

Here are the general meanings of transits to the Sun:

Sun transits to the natal Sun: Self-renewal. This cycle was taken up in the discussion of the Solar Return, or birthday chart. The Sun transiting through signs three and six away from the birth Sun are critical points in this cycle.

Mercury transits to the Sun: Though annual, it is not a major cycle. Maybe a day of increased communicative exchanges.

Venus transits to the Sun: Again, this annual cycle is passive. May correlate to a day of pleasant contacts.

Mars transits to the Sun: An energizer, a call for greater self-assertion once every two years. The cycle can cause people to overdo activity, resulting in illnesses or setbacks. Though this isn't a major cycle, it can have correlations to new activities, particularly if the Mars-to-Mars cycle is renewing itself around the same time. Critical phases of this rhythm are Mars's placement three and six signs away from the Sun sign.

Jupiter transits to the Sun: An 11.8-year cycle related to greater self-expansion and integration. Good time for promotions, taking on larger societal roles, education, travel, publishing, any activity that takes people out of their smaller world. Energy is often wasted if a more stable Saturn transit is not in effect at the same time. Once again, Jupiter's move to three and six signs away from the Sun are the critical phases in the rhythm.

Saturn transits to the Sun: A 29-year rhythm related to

self-definition. Important intervals every seven years. See Chapter 9.

Uranus transits to the Sun: A wild card; a call for self-awakening that aims to pull people out of their personal ruts and move them toward greater individuality. A hard cycle to predict because the unexpected always happens. The planet only comes to the Sun sign once every eighty-four years. Its critical phases, in relation to the birth Sun, come every twenty-one years. Uranus moving near Jimmy Carter's Sun sign helped bring about his unexpected decision to seek (and win) the governorship of Georgia; William Rehnquist turned around one day and was appointed to the Supreme Court under this aspect.

Neptune transits to the Sun: A disorienting phase that often finds people trying hard to stay afoot on things that are melting underneath them. But the same transit illumines and inspires. While many people report highly disillusioning, faith-breaking experiences, some reach for the stars and get pretty close. Neptune returns to a Sun sign every 168 years. So while people may never experience it moving right over their Sun, they'll most likely have the planet moving three or six signs away from it at some point in their life, and the effects are similar to moves over the Sun. George Bush dissolved his profile as political appointee/agency head and began making stabs at a larger role of "statesmen" when Neptune in Sagittarius opposed his Sun in the late 1970s and early 1980s. After he failed to capture enough support for his presidential bid, he altered his political views and signed on as Reagan's vice president.

Pluto transits to the Sun: Not for everybody—the planet takes 248 years to return to any given Sun sign and has only moved through Gemini, Cancer, Leo, Virgo, Libra, and now Scorpio in the twentieth century. Following a Pluto transit to the Sun, people always say things like "I felt like I was dead." That's almost not an exaggeration; the planet destroys and uproots all parts of the life that defined the self. Ego issues, struggles for power, and the role of sexuality as it relates to one's experience with life are all matters that Pluto dredges from beneath the surface of life. The goal is to strip the self of its false skins and make it ready for a new life. The purge is on, as the life of Michael Dukakis, who experienced this transit during the 1988 election and the year afterward, can attest. Pluto's move to points three and six signs away from the Sun sign are just as empowering as Dan Quayle's rise in 1988 demonstrates.

Pluto's move five signs away (an inconjunct or quincunx) can also force people to make major adjustments and changes in their life. Though not considered a major aspect, the inconjunct, particularly between Pluto and the Sun, can relate to significant life events such as career turnarounds or relationships that are aimed at overhauling one's purest sense of self.

Sometimes the minor aspects, such as the inconjunct, can be even more important to a life than some of the more obvious aspects because people undergoing the inconjunct may have already experienced the opposition (six signs away) or other Pluto-to-Sun transits and this makes them more ready than other signs to accept the current challenge. For instance, Pluto moving through Scorpio from 1984 to 1996 was moving 180 degrees (six signs) from Taurus, forcing this sign to deal with power issues, matters of control, sexuality, and shared resources right up front in their dealings with the world. Leo and Aquarius, both of which sit three signs away from Scorpio, were finding such issues coming up alongside them in their lives as well.

Aries, which is five signs away from Pluto in Scorpio, was being called on to deal with both physical and psychological crises related to their coming into their true selves. The sign, however, had faced showdowns with Pluto throughout the 1970s, when it was moving through Libra, which is six signs (180 degrees) from Aries. In the same way that the seven-year phases in the Saturn cycle work together, the Pluto in Scorpio experience of Aries individuals would contain some of the same issues faced when Pluto was moving directly across from it in Libra. Bette Davis literally died of cancer with Pluto in Scorpio making an inconjunct to her Sun in Aries, but numerous other points in Davis's chart were activated when she passed on as well. These configurations were unique to her chart; people pass over on a variety of different aspects depending on the issues of their lives.

Those with the Sun in Gemini, it should be noted, are also experiencing the inconjunct from Pluto five signs away. One woman with this Sun sign is just beginning to face her alcoholism and says that she feels "as if I'm being stripped to the core." Gemini George Bush will face this special Plutonian stress in 1991–92.

Whether it's moving three, six, or five signs away, Pluto can have a death/rebirth effect. The planet can even be seen having a transformative effect on areas of life when it is moving two or four signs from the Sun sign. Gorbachev's rise to power and glasnost was helped along by Pluto in Scorpio moving four signs away from his Sun. The friendly position makes the needed overhaul a little easier, most likely because people are not resisting and fighting the chances so angrily.

Encouragement—and Caution

Fairly astute readers will be aware that the same ephemeris used to find transits to the Sun can be used to locate transits to the Moon, Mercury, Venus, and other planets. Those willing to supplement this book with astrological textbooks may derive some helpful information from studying transits to other points in the chart. Such information, however, may be confusing and do more harm than good without proper astrological foundations. Information on transits to the Sun was included here because of the Sun's primary importance and because of previous discussions of Saturn transits of the Sun.

APPENDIX I

How to Find Your Ascendant/Rising Sign and Set Up an Approximate Chart

Having a birthchart calculated by a computer service will provide the most precise information. But this section will help you locate your approximate Ascendant/Rising sign and set up the basic outlines of a birthchart.

The exact zodiac degree that was coming up on the horizon at your time of birth is one of the most sensitive points in the horoscope. The Ascendant, or Rising sign, changes every two hours, but the specific angular relationship (and zodiac degree, such as 19 Scorpio changing to 20 Scorpio) changes every four minutes. A baby in Manhattan might conceivably draw its first breath at the same time as a baby born up the highway in suburban Connecticut, but the different locations relate to changes in latitude variations that result in differing horizons and subsequently different zodiac degrees.

In this section we're only going to be dealing with the sign that was rising; it is impossible to delineate degrees without extensive tables. It's important to remember that what we're doing is loose, and in some cases factors such as war time, daylight saving time, and the peculiarities of certain Ascendants will cause the chart to be off by one sign placement.

But the chart will help with general timing.

To find your Ascendant, or Rising sign, find the Ascendant/Rising Sign Table on page 417 and scan the left-hand horizontal column designating the Sun sign. Once you've located your Sun sign, follow the line to the vertical line designating the approximate two-hour period in which you were born. This is your Ascendant. You must remember to subtract an hour from the birthtime if you were born during daylight saving time (usually between April 24 and October 28 in most parts of the country). Remember that the entire country observed daylight saving time (or war time) from February 9, 1942, to September 30, 1945, and during the 1974–75 oil crisis. People born within the first ten days of the Sun sign and/or within an hour of a Ascendant sign change may want to try out the Ascendant before or after the one listed in the chart, whichever seems to fit best. Those born near the beginning or end of daylight saving time should also be cautious. While the chart states that an Aries born between 10:00 P.M. and midnight will have Capricorn rising, many 10:00–11:00 P.M. babies may still be within the Sagittarius period. Sending away for a precisely calculated chart is best. Information on mail-order companies can be found on page 416. Special instructions for those who don't know their actual birthtime are also included.

Rising Signs

The Ascendant, or Rising sign, which is the point where the horizon and zodiac belt (or ecliptic) meet, shows a person's orientation toward life, his or her overall approach. The sign on the Ascendant shows the coping mechanisms developed to get through life. These are usually adaptive strategies learned as a result of conditions in the early environment.

The planet that rules the Rising sign is said to be one's life "ruler." A Sagittarius Ascendant would have Jupiter as ruler; Taurus rising would be ruled by Venus. The ruler's condition in a horoscope (the house in which it is located and the configurations it makes with other planets) is especially important in a person's life.

APPENDIX II

Ascendant Descriptions

Aries: A confident personality that moves out in the world seeking to thrust itself into experience. Take-charge approach, sometimes brusque, with Mars as ruler of the chart. Seeks to break apart from the others and experience self.

Taurus: They usually have a fleshy or thick build. Sturdy, reliable. Some of these Venus-ruled people are noted for liking to talk about money and their possessions. Physical-security and survival issues color their approach to life. Sometimes too caught up in pleasures and only the most concrete view of reality.

Gemini: They are known for the way they can be in so many places at one time around the community. (Fleet-footed Mercury is the ruler) Many are facile communicators with quick minds. Others form many superficial alliances and get side-tracked by gossip and the short-term affairs under way in their environment. Scatteredness is often evident.

Cancer: Emotional security is a prime concern, causing them to approach people and circumstances with a defensiveness or touchiness. Can display extreme emotionalism or be stuck on their own shelf. May want to be babied, or else attempt to play mother to those around them. Moody, changeable; the Moon rules this chart.

Leo: More than any other Rising sign, these Sun-ruled people look the part, with manes of hair and often a regalness of bearing. They adapt to their environment by being creative, self-expressive, seeking love. This need for self-affirmation can cause them to put much energy into seeking the applause and the "love" of others. All the world's a stage.

Virgo: They try to bring order to the environment around them so they usually keep busy. Their ruler, Mercury, makes them critical, often petty, failing to see issues in context. Their desire to seek order and establish a routine often brings them into contact with people whose heavy dependencies or addictions make them prime candidates for "makeovers." The low self-esteem of the sign sometimes makes them view these types of relationships as being either safe or all they deserve.

Libra: Pleasant, tactful, social, these Venus-ruled people have the perfect public relations persona. Many are so intent on being fair and balancing life situations that you can see it in their faces, which seem to be more symmetrical than most. But this group also has an aggressive, angry side that, if not acknowledged, will result in attractions to and relationships with overbearing people. At the very least, they usually have partners who are strong individuals.

Scorpio: Secretive, intense, mysterious. People are usually conscious of the passionate undercurrents contained within these personalities, which is why many are thought of as being "sexy." They smile as they're mentally drawing up the battle plans; they don't show their hand. They're mistrustful of others and are ever conscious of the power balance in negotiations and relations. Their will and inner strength allow them to endure much, and they transform their lives frequently, with the help of ruler Pluto.

Sagittarius: They come at the world with their philosophies, lectures, and tales of adventure. Their Jupiter-expansiveness is often apparent in their gait and speech, which is sometimes known for being especially blunt. Their personalities are usually upbeat and gregarious as they spread themselves about.

They fight off urges to fence them in or typecast them, though they often aren't as respectful of others' freedom urges.

Capricorn: Most have a hesitancy in their demeanor, a certain reticence and caution. It takes many years for them to build self-confidence. They're generally viewed as conservative, responsible people, Saturnian, like their ruler Saturn. Building structures and a place in the world are important. Their early upbringing and relationship to their parents have left a more-profound-than-usual stamp on their relation to today's world. Often they're trying to prove their worth to a parent or authority figure.

Aquarius: They often have an unusual look. Sometimes it seems to be the domelike head, other times it's nothing you can quite put your finger on. Like ruler Uranus, they usually have an approach to life that is different from anybody else, are known for their eccentricity, and have goals that are linked to society and the future. While they seem to attract many friends and acquaintances, they're hard to know and are characterized by their detachment. They can sometimes make their many friends feel shut out.

Pisces: They are a caring, compassionate bunch that want to inspire and help others. Some of these children of Neptune have an elusive quality; others come across as just plain wishy-washy, sad sacks. This Rising sign has a certain elusive and spongy quality that allows it to adapt to roles, whether in real life or on the silver screen. Relationships are often characterized by self-sacrifice (either on their part or by their mates). Problems with addictions or other handicaps are common.

How to Set Up a General Chart

This section is for those of you who wish to set up a general chart to study. This chapter includes the outline of a birthchart broken into twelve sections (see page 414).

Working with this blank chart wheel, place your Ascendant on the First House and, moving counterclockwise, fill in the rest of the houses in the order in which they follow your Ascendant. If the Ascendant is Taurus, the Second House is Gemini, the Third House Cancer, and so on (see "Ascendant/Rising Sign" chart on page 417).

Check your work in this manner: The Seventh House, across from the Ascendant, should hold the opposite sign, which is six signs away from the Ascendant. Libra is opposite Aries; Sagittarius is opposite Gemini.

What to Do If You Don't Know What Time You Were Born

Professional astrologers have many techniques under the heading of "rectification" that can determine an approximate birthtime. Rectification methods require that the astrologer take an extensive case history—dates of marriages, parents' deaths,

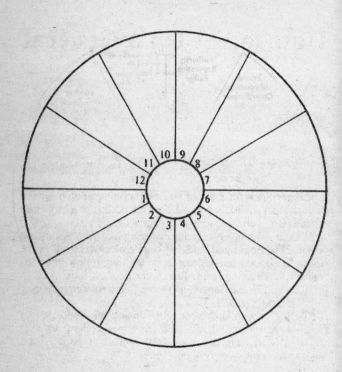

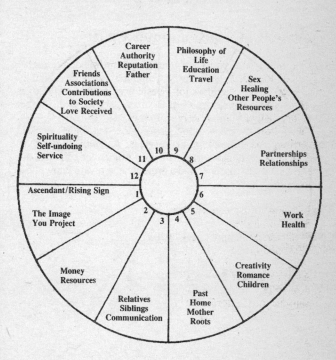

and other key events—and apply various astrological techniques, to come up with a birthtime. Without benefit of an astrologer who knows how to do this, readers without their exact birthtime can assume a birthtime somewhere between 4:00 and 6:00 A.M. set up their charts with the Ascendant/ Rising sign (First House) being the same as that of the Sun.

How to Order a Computer Chart

First make sure you have your exact birthtime, preferably right off the birth certificate. Computer services generally charge two to three dollars for a basic horoscope, and the ones listed here have either same- or next-day service. Don't forget to state whether your were born in the A.M. or P.M.

The following list is brief; astrological magazines contain advertisements from numerous services. A computerized chart may also be obtainable right in your hometown, though not everyone with a computer and astrological software knows how to use it correctly.

Astrological Bureau of Ideas
P.O. Box 251
Wethersfield, Connecticut 06109
(203) 563–3146

Astro Computer Services
Box 16297
San Diego, California 92116
(714) 297–5648

Astrolabe
Box 28
Orleans, Massachusetts 02653
(617) 255–0510

Matrix Software
315 Marion Avenue
Grand Rapids, Michigan 49307
(616) 796–2483

Ascendant/Rising Sign Table

Sun Sign	Birth Hours (A.M. in boldface)											
	4–6	**6–8**	**8–10**	**10–12**	**12–2**	**2–4**	4–6	6–8	8–10	10–12	12–2	2–4
ARIES	Ar	Tau	Gem	Can	Leo	Vir	Lib	Sco	Sag	Cap	Aqu	Pis
TAURUS	Tau	Gem	Can	Leo	Vir	Lib	Sco	Sag	Cap	Aqu	Pis	Ar
GEMINI	Gem	Can	Leo	Vir	Lib	Sco	Sag	Cap	Aqu	Pis	Ar	Tau
CANCER	Can	Leo	Vir	Lib	Sco	Sag	Cap	Aqu	Pis	Ar	Tau	Gem
LEO	Leo	Vir	Lib	Sco	Sag	Cap	Aqu	Pis	Ar	Tau	Gem	Can
VIRGO	Vir	Lib	Sco	Sag	Cap	Aqu	Pis	Ar	Tau	Gem	Can	Leo
LIBRA	Lib	Sco	Sag	Cap	Aqu	Pis	Ar	Tau	Gem	Can	Leo	Vir
SCORPIO	Sco	Sag	Cap	Aqu	Pis	Ar	Tau	Gem	Can	Leo	Vir	Lib
SAGITTARIUS	Sag	Cap	Aqu	Pis	Ar	Tau	Gem	Can	Leo	Vir	Lib	Sco
CAPRICORN	Cap	Aqu	Pis	Ar	Tau	Gem	Can	Leo	Vir	Lib	Sco	Sag
AQUARIUS	Aqu	Pis	Ar	Tau	Gem	Can	Leo	Vir	Lib	Sco	Sag	Cap
PISCES	Pis	Ar	Tau	Gem	Can	Leo	Vir	Lib	Sco	Sag	Cap	Aqu

APPENDIX V

Setting Up the House/Sign Wheel

The following table shows the counterclockwise order of signs along the horoscope wheel. Find Rising Sign (First House) in left-hand column, then move across to determine the approximate sign on each of the twelve houses in the horoscope.

Rising Sign/First House	2	3	4	5	6	7	8	9	10	11	12
Ar	Ta	Ge	Ca	Le	Vi	Li	Sc	Sa	Cp	Aq	Pi
Ta	Ge	Ca	Le	Vi	Li	Sc	Sa	Cp	Aq	Pi	Ar
Ge	Ca	Le	Vi	Li	Sc	Sa	Cp	Aq	Pi	Ar	Ta
Ca	Le	Vi	Li	Sc	Sa	Cp	Aq	Pi	Ar	Ta	Ge
Le	Vi	Li	Sc	Sa	Cp	Aq	Pi	Ar	Ta	Ge	Ca
Vi	Li	Sc	Sa	Cp	Aq	Pi	Ar	Ta	Ge	Ca	Le
Li	Sc	Sa	Cp	Aq	Pi	Ar	Ta	Ge	Ca	Le	Vi
Sc	Sa	Cp	Aq	Pi	Ar	Ta	Ge	Ca	Le	Vi	Li
Sa	Cp	Aq	Pi	Ar	Ta	Ge	Ca	Le	Vi	Li	Sc
Cp	Aq	Pi	Ar	Ta	Ge	Ca	Le	Vi	Li	Sc	Sa
Aq	Pi	Ar	Ta	Ge	Ca	Le	Vi	Li	Sc	Sa	Cp
Pi	Ar	Ta	Ge	Ca	Le	Vi	Li	Sc	Sa	Cp	Ar

APPENDIX VI

Meanings of the Twelve Houses

1. Image, approach to life
2. Money, possessions, values
3. Communication, attitudes
4. Home, parents, private life
5. Self-expression, love affairs
6. Daily survival, routine
7. Relations with others
8. Shared resources, regeneration
9. Worldview, education, journeys
10. Public standing, life direction
11. Friends, associations, benefits, rewards
12. Self-undoing, limitations, hidden enemies

Ephemeris

Sun Table for Year 1900

Date	Zodiac Sign	Time
01/20	Aquarius	11:30
02/19	Pisces	02:00
03/21	Aries	01:37
04/20	Taurus	13:24
05/21	Gemini	13:13
06/21	Cancer	21:35
07/23	Leo	08:30
08/23	Virgo	15:12
09/23	Libra	12:12
10/23	Scorpio	20:48
11/22	Sagittarius	17:44
12/22	Capricorn	06:42

Sun Table for Year 1901

Date	Zodiac Sign	Time
01/20	Aquarius	17:20
02/19	Pisces	07:49
03/21	Aries	07:26
04/20	Taurus	19:13
05/21	Gemini	19:01
06/22	Cancer	03:23
07/23	Leo	14:18
08/23	Virgo	21:01
09/23	Libra	18:01
10/24	Scorpio	02:37
11/22	Sagittarius	23:34
12/22	Capricorn	12:32

Sun Table for Year 1902

Date	Zodiac Sign	Time
01/20	Aquarius	23:10
02/19	Pisces	13:39
03/21	Aries	13:15
04/21	Taurus	01:01
05/22	Gemini	00:49
06/22	Cancer	09:11
07/23	Leo	20:06
08/24	Virgo	02:49
09/23	Libra	23:49
10/24	Scorpio	08:26
11/23	Sagittarius	05:23
12/22	Capricorn	18:21

Sun Table for Year 1903

Date	Zodiac Sign	Time
01/21	Aquarius	04:59
02/19	Pisces	19:28
03/21	Aries	19:04
04/21	Taurus	06:50
05/22	Gemini	06:38
06/22	Cancer	14:59
07/24	Leo	01:54
08/24	Virgo	08:37
09/24	Libra	05:38
10/24	Scorpio	14:15
11/23	Sagittarius	11:12
12/23	Capricorn	00:11

Greenwich Mean Time (GMT)
24-Hour Clock

Note: Eastern Standard Time (EST), add 5 hrs.
Central Standard Time (CST), add 6 hrs.
Mountain Standard Time (MST), add 7 hrs.
Pacific Standard Time (PST), add 8 hrs.
Daylight Saving Time/War Time, minus 1 hr. from total.

Sun Table for Year 1904

Date	Zodiac Sign	Time
01/21	Aquarius	10:49
02/20	Pisces	01:17
03/21	Aries	00:53
04/20	Taurus	12:38
05/21	Gemini	12:26
06/21	Cancer	20:47
07/23	Leo	07:42
08/23	Virgo	14:25
09/23	Libra	11:26
10/23	Scorpio	20:04
11/22	Sagittarius	17:02
12/22	Capricorn	06:00

Sun Table for Year 1905

Date	Zodiac Sign	Time
01/20	Aquarius	16:38
02/19	Pisces	07:07
03/21	Aries	06:42
04/20	Taurus	18:27
05/21	Gemini	18:14
06/22	Cancer	02:35
07/23	Leo	13:30
08/23	Virgo	20:13
09/23	Libra	17:15
10/24	Scorpio	01:53
11/22	Sagittarius	22:51
12/22	Capricorn	11:50

Sun Table for Year 1906

Date	Zodiac Sign	Time
01/20	Aquarius	22:28
02/19	Pisces	12:56
03/21	Aries	12:31
04/21	Taurus	00:15
05/22	Gemini	00:02
06/22	Cancer	08:23
07/23	Leo	19:18
08/24	Virgo	02:01
09/23	Libra	23:03
10/24	Scorpio	07:42
11/23	Sagittarius	04:40
12/22	Capricorn	17:39

Sun Table for Year 1907

Date	Zodiac Sign	Time
01/21	Aquarius	04:17
02/19	Pisces	18:45
03/21	Aries	18:20
04/21	Taurus	06:04
05/22	Gemini	05:50
06/22	Cancer	14:11
07/24	Leo	01:06
08/24	Virgo	07:50
09/24	Libra	04:52
10/24	Scorpio	13:31
11/23	Sagittarius	10:30
12/22	Capricorn	23:29

Greenwich Mean Time (GMT)
24-Hour Clock

Note: Eastern Standard Time (EST), add 5 hrs.
Central Standard Time (CST), add 6 hrs.
Mountain Standard Time (MST), add 7 hrs.
Pacific Standard Time (PST), add 8 hrs.
Daylight Saving Time/War Time, minus 1 hr. from total.

Sun Table for Year 1908

Date	Zodiac Sign	Time
01/21	Aquarius	10:07
02/20	Pisces	00:35
03/21	Aries	00:09
04/20	Taurus	11:53
05/21	Gemini	11:39
06/21	Cancer	19:59
07/23	Leo	06:54
08/23	Virgo	13:38
09/23	Libra	10:40
10/23	Scorpio	19:20
11/22	Sagittarius	16:19
12/22	Capricorn	05:19

Sun Table for Year 1909

Date	Zodiac Sign	Time
01/20	Aquarius	15:57
02/19	Pisces	06:24
03/21	Aries	05:58
04/20	Taurus	17:41
05/21	Gemini	17:27
06/22	Cancer	01:46
07/23	Leo	12:41
08/23	Virgo	19:26
09/23	Libra	16:29
10/24	Scorpio	01:09
11/22	Sagittarius	22:08
12/22	Capricorn	11:08

Sun Table for Year 1910

Date	Zodiac Sign	Time
01/20	Aquarius	21:46
02/19	Pisces	12:14
03/21	Aries	11:47
04/20	Taurus	23:30
05/21	Gemini	23:15
06/22	Cancer	07:34
07/23	Leo	18:29
08/24	Virgo	01:14
09/23	Libra	22:18
10/24	Scorpio	06:58
11/23	Sagittarius	03:58
12/22	Capricorn	16:58

Sun Table for Year 1911

Date	Zodiac Sign	Time
01/21	Aquarius	03:36
02/19	Pisces	18:03
03/21	Aries	17:36
04/21	Taurus	05:18
05/22	Gemini	05:03
06/22	Cancer	13:22
07/24	Leo	00:17
08/24	Virgo	07:02
09/24	Libra	04:06
10/24	Scorpio	12:47
11/23	Sagittarius	09:47
12/22	Capricorn	22:47

Greenwich Mean Time (GMT)
24-Hour Clock

Note: Eastern Standard Time (EST), add 5 hrs.
Central Standard Time (CST), add 6 hrs.
Mountain Standard Time (MST), add 7 hrs.
Pacific Standard Time (PST), add 8 hrs.
Daylight Saving Time/War Time, minus 1 hr. from total.

Sun Table for Year 1912

Date	Zodiac Sign	Time
01/21	Aquarius	09:25
02/19	Pisces	23:52
03/20	Aries	23:25
04/20	Taurus	11:07
05/21	Gemini	10:51
06/21	Cancer	19:10
07/23	Leo	06:05
08/23	Virgo	12:50
09/23	Libra	09:55
10/23	Scorpio	18:36
11/22	Sagittarius	15:36
12/22	Capricorn	04:37

Sun Table for Year 1913

Date	Zodiac Sign	Time
01/20	Aquarius	15:15
02/19	Pisces	05:42
03/21	Aries	05:14
04/20	Taurus	16:55
05/21	Gemini	16:39
06/22	Cancer	00:58
07/23	Leo	11:53
08/23	Virgo	18:38
09/23	Libra	15:43
10/24	Scorpio	00:25
11/22	Sagittarius	21:26
12/22	Capricorn	10:26

Sun Table for Year 1914

Date	Zodiac Sign	Time
01/20	Aquarius	21:04
02/19	Pisces	11:31
03/21	Aries	11:03
04/20	Taurus	22:44
05/21	Gemini	22:28
06/22	Cancer	06:46
07/23	Leo	17:41
08/24	Virgo	00:27
09/23	Libra	21:32
10/24	Scorpio	06:14
11/23	Sagittarius	03:15
12/22	Capricorn	16:16

Sun Table for Year 1915

Date	Zodiac Sign	Time
01/21	Aquarius	02:54
02/19	Pisces	17:20
03/21	Aries	16:52
04/21	Taurus	04:33
05/22	Gemini	04:16
06/22	Cancer	12:34
07/23	Leo	23:29
08/24	Virgo	06:15
09/24	Libra	03:20
10/24	Scorpio	12:03
11/23	Sagittarius	09:04
12/22	Capricorn	22:06

Greenwich Mean Time (GMT)
24-Hour Clock

Note: Eastern Standard Time (EST), add 5 hrs.
Central Standard Time (CST), add 6 hrs.
Mountain Standard Time (MST), add 7 hrs.
Pacific Standard Time (PST), add 8 hrs.
Daylight Saving Time/War Time, minus 1 hr. from total.

Sun Table for Year 1916

Date	Zodiac Sign	Time
01/21	Aquarius	08:44
02/19	Pisces	23:10
03/20	Aries	22:41
04/20	Taurus	10:21
05/21	Gemini	10:04
06/21	Cancer	18:22
07/23	Leo	05:17
08/23	Virgo	12:03
09/23	Libra	09:09
10/23	Scorpio	17:52
11/22	Sagittarius	14:54
12/22	Capricorn	03:55

Sun Table for Year 1917

Date	Zodiac Sign	Time
01/20	Aquarius	14:33
02/19	Pisces	04:59
03/21	Aries	04:30
04/20	Taurus	16:10
05/21	Gemini	15:52
06/22	Cancer	00:10
07/23	Leo	11:05
08/23	Virgo	17:51
09/23	Libra	14:57
10/23	Scorpio	23:41
11/22	Sagittarius	20:43
12/22	Capricorn	09:45

Sun Table for Year 1918

Date	Zodiac Sign	Time
01/20	Aquarius	20:23
02/19	Pisces	10:49
03/21	Aries	10:19
04/20	Taurus	21:58
05/21	Gemini	21:40
06/22	Cancer	05:58
07/23	Leo	16:53
08/23	Virgo	23:39
09/23	Libra	20:46
10/24	Scorpio	05:30
11/23	Sagittarius	02:33
12/22	Capricorn	15:34

Sun Table for Year 1919

Date	Zodiac Sign	Time
01/21	Aquarius	02:12
02/19	Pisces	16:38
03/21	Aries	16:08
04/21	Taurus	03:47
05/22	Gemini	03:28
06/22	Cancer	11:46
07/23	Leo	22:41
08/24	Virgo	05:27
09/24	Libra	02:34
10/24	Scorpio	11:19
11/23	Sagittarius	08:22
12/22	Capricorn	21:24

Greenwich Mean Time (GMT)
24-Hour Clock

Note: Eastern Standard Time (EST), add 5 hrs.
Central Standard Time (CST), add 6 hrs.
Mountain Standard Time (MST), add 7 hrs.
Pacific Standard Time (PST), add 8 hrs.
Daylight Saving Time/War Time, minus 1 hr. from total.

Sun Table for Year 1920

Date	Zodiac Sign	Time
01/21	Aquarius	08:02
02/19	Pisces	22:27
03/20	Aries	21:57
04/20	Taurus	09:35
05/21	Gemini	09:17
06/21	Cancer	17:34
07/23	Leo	04:29
08/23	Virgo	11:16
09/23	Libra	08:23
10/23	Scorpio	17:08
11/22	Sagittarius	14:11
12/22	Capricorn	03:13

Sun Table for Year 1921

Date	Zodiac Sign	Time
01/20	Aquarius	13:52
02/19	Pisces	04:17
03/21	Aries	03:46
04/20	Taurus	15:24
05/21	Gemini	15:05
06/21	Cancer	23:22
07/23	Leo	10:17
08/23	Virgo	17:04
09/23	Libra	14:11
10/23	Scorpio	22:57
11/22	Sagittarius	20:01
12/22	Capricorn	09:03

Sun Table for Year 1922

Date	Zodiac Sign	Time
01/20	Aquarius	19:41
02/19	Pisces	10:06
03/21	Aries	09:35
04/20	Taurus	21:13
05/21	Gemini	20:53
06/22	Cancer	05:10
07/23	Leo	16:05
08/23	Virgo	22:52
09/23	Libra	20:00
10/24	Scorpio	04:46
11/23	Sagittarius	01:50
12/22	Capricorn	14:53

Sun Table for Year 1923

Date	Zodiac Sign	Time
01/21	Aquarius	01:31
02/19	Pisces	15:55
03/21	Aries	15:24
04/21	Taurus	03:01
05/22	Gemini	02:41
06/22	Cancer	10:58
07/23	Leo	21:53
08/24	Virgo	04:40
09/24	Libra	01:49
10/24	Scorpio	10:35
11/23	Sagittarius	07:39
12/22	Capricorn	20:42

Greenwich Mean Time (GMT)
24-Hour Clock

Note: Eastern Standard Time (EST), add 5 hrs.
Central Standard Time (CST), add 6 hrs.
Mountain Standard Time (MST), add 7 hrs.
Pacific Standard Time (PST), add 8 hrs.
Daylight Saving Time/War Time, minus 1 hr. from total.

Sun Table for Year 1924

Date	Zodiac Sign	Time
01/21	Aquarius	07:20
02/19	Pisces	21:45
03/20	Aries	21:13
04/20	Taurus	08:50
05/21	Gemini	08:29
06/21	Cancer	16:46
07/23	Leo	03:41
08/23	Virgo	10:28
09/23	Libra	07:37
10/23	Scorpio	16:24
11/22	Sagittarius	13:29
12/22	Capricorn	02:32

Sun Table for Year 1925

Date	Zodiac Sign	Time
01/20	Aquarius	13:10
02/19	Pisces	03:34
03/21	Aries	03:02
04/20	Taurus	14:38
05/21	Gemini	14:18
06/21	Cancer	22:34
07/23	Leo	09:28
08/23	Virgo	16:16
09/23	Libra	13:26
10/23	Scorpio	22:13
11/22	Sagittarius	19:18
12/22	Capricorn	08:21

Sun Table for Year 1926

Date	Zodiac Sign	Time
01/20	Aquarius	18:59
02/19	Pisces	09:24
03/21	Aries	08:51
04/20	Taurus	20:27
05/21	Gemini	20:06
06/22	Cancer	04:22
07/23	Leo	15:16
08/23	Virgo	22:05
09/23	Libra	19:14
10/24	Scorpio	04:02
11/23	Sagittarius	01:07
12/22	Capricorn	14:11

Sun Table for Year 1927

Date	Zodiac Sign	Time
01/21	Aquarius	00:49
02/19	Pisces	15:13
03/21	Aries	14:40
04/21	Taurus	02:15
05/22	Gemini	01:54
06/22	Cancer	10:09
07/23	Leo	21:04
08/24	Virgo	03:53
09/24	Libra	01:03
10/24	Scorpio	09:51
11/23	Sagittarius	06:57
12/22	Capricorn	20:00

Greenwich Mean Time (GMT)
24-Hour Clock

Note: Eastern Standard Time (EST), add 5 hrs.
Central Standard Time (CST), add 6 hrs.
Mountain Standard Time (MST), add 7 hrs.
Pacific Standard Time (PST), add 8 hrs.
Daylight Saving Time/War Time, minus 1 hr. from total.

Sun Table for Year 1928

Date	Zodiac Sign	Time
01/21	Aquarius	06:39
02/19	Pisces	21:02
03/20	Aries	20:29
04/20	Taurus	08:04
05/21	Gemini	07:42
06/21	Cancer	15:57
07/23	Leo	02:52
08/23	Virgo	09:41
09/23	Libra	06:51
10/23	Scorpio	15:40
11/22	Sagittarius	12:46
12/22	Capricorn	01:50

Sun Table for Year 1929

Date	Zodiac Sign	Time
01/20	Aquarius	12:28
02/19	Pisces	02:52
03/21	Aries	02:18
04/20	Taurus	13:53
05/21	Gemini	13:30
06/21	Cancer	21:45
07/23	Leo	08:40
08/23	Virgo	15:29
09/23	Libra	12:40
10/23	Scorpio	21:29
11/22	Sagittarius	18:35
12/22	Capricorn	07:39

Sun Table for Year 1930

Date	Zodiac Sign	Time
01/20	Aquarius	18:18
02/19	Pisces	08:41
03/21	Aries	08:07
04/20	Taurus	19:41
05/21	Gemini	19:18
06/22	Cancer	03:33
07/23	Leo	14:28
08/23	Virgo	21:17
09/23	Libra	18:28
10/24	Scorpio	03:18
11/23	Sagittarius	00:25
12/22	Capricorn	13:29

Sun Table for Year 1931

Date	Zodiac Sign	Time
01/21	Aquarius	00:07
02/19	Pisces	14:30
03/21	Aries	13:56
04/21	Taurus	01:30
05/22	Gemini	01:07
06/22	Cancer	09:21
07/23	Leo	20:16
08/24	Virgo	03:05
09/24	Libra	00:17
10/24	Scorpio	09:07
11/23	Sagittarius	06:14
12/22	Capricorn	19:19

Greenwich Mean Time (GMT)
24-Hour Clock

Note: Eastern Standard Time (EST), add 5 hrs.
Central Standard Time (CST), add 6 hrs.
Mountain Standard Time (MST), add 7 hrs.
Pacific Standard Time (PST), add 8 hrs.
Daylight Saving Time/War Time, minus 1 hr. from total.

Sun Table for Year 1932

Date	Zodiac Sign	Time
01/21	Aquarius	05:57
02/19	Pisces	20:20
03/20	Aries	19:45
04/20	Taurus	07:18
05/21	Gemini	06:55
06/21	Cancer	15:09
07/23	Leo	02:04
08/23	Virgo	08:53
09/23	Libra	06:05
10/23	Scorpio	14:56
11/22	Sagittarius	12:03
12/22	Capricorn	01:08

Sun Table for Year 1933

Date	Zodiac Sign	Time
01/20	Aquarius	11:46
02/19	Pisces	02:09
03/21	Aries	01:34
04/20	Taurus	13:07
05/21	Gemini	12:43
06/21	Cancer	20:57
07/23	Leo	07:52
08/23	Virgo	14:42
09/23	Libra	11:54
10/23	Scorpio	20:45
11/22	Sagittarius	17:53
12/22	Capricorn	06:58

Sun Table for Year 1934

Date	Zodiac Sign	Time
01/20	Aquarius	17:36
02/19	Pisces	07:59
03/21	Aries	07:23
04/20	Taurus	18:55
05/21	Gemini	18:31
06/22	Cancer	02:45
07/23	Leo	13:40
08/23	Virgo	20:30
09/23	Libra	17:42
10/24	Scorpio	02:34
11/22	Sagittarius	23:42
12/22	Capricorn	12:47

Sun Table for Year 1935

Date	Zodiac Sign	Time
01/20	Aquarius	23:26
02/19	Pisces	13:48
03/21	Aries	13:12
04/21	Taurus	00:44
05/22	Gemini	00:19
06/22	Cancer	08:33
07/23	Leo	19:28
08/24	Virgo	02:18
09/23	Libra	23:31
10/24	Scorpio	08:23
11/23	Sagittarius	05:31
12/22	Capricorn	18:37

Greenwich Mean Time (GMT)
24-Hour Clock

Note: Eastern Standard Time (EST), add 5 hrs.
Central Standard Time (CST), add 6 hrs.
Mountain Standard Time (MST), add 7 hrs.
Pacific Standard Time (PST), add 8 hrs.
Daylight Saving Time/War Time, minus 1 hr. from total.

Sun Table for Year 1936

Date	Zodiac Sign	Time
01/21	Aquarius	05:15
02/19	Pisces	19:37
03/20	Aries	19:01
04/20	Taurus	06:33
05/21	Gemini	06:08
06/21	Cancer	14:21
07/23	Leo	01:16
08/23	Virgo	08:06
09/23	Libra	05:20
10/23	Scorpio	14:11
11/22	Sagittarius	11:21
12/22	Capricorn	00:26

Sun Table for Year 1937

Date	Zodiac Sign	Time
01/20	Aquarius	11:05
02/19	Pisces	01:27
03/21	Aries	00:50
04/20	Taurus	12:21
05/21	Gemini	11:56
06/21	Cancer	20:09
07/23	Leo	07:04
08/23	Virgo	13:54
09/23	Libra	11:08
10/23	Scorpio	20:00
11/22	Sagittarius	17:10
12/22	Capricorn	06:16

Sun Table for Year 1938

Date	Zodiac Sign	Time
01/20	Aquarius	16:54
02/19	Pisces	07:16
03/21	Aries	06:39
04/20	Taurus	18:10
05/21	Gemini	17:44
06/22	Cancer	01:57
07/23	Leo	12:52
08/23	Virgo	19:42
09/23	Libra	16:57
10/24	Scorpio	01:49
11/22	Sagittarius	22:59
12/22	Capricorn	12:06

Sun Table for Year 1939

Date	Zodiac Sign	Time
01/20	Aquarius	22:44
02/19	Pisces	13:05
03/21	Aries	12:28
04/20	Taurus	23:58
05/21	Gemini	23:32
06/22	Cancer	07:45
07/23	Leo	18:40
08/24	Virgo	01:30
09/23	Libra	22:45
10/24	Scorpio	07:38
11/23	Sagittarius	04:49
12/22	Capricorn	17:55

Greenwich Mean Time (GMT)
24-Hour Clock

Note: Eastern Standard Time (EST), add 5 hrs.
Central Standard Time (CST), add 6 hrs.
Mountain Standard Time (MST), add 7 hrs.
Pacific Standard Time (PST), add 8 hrs.
Daylight Saving Time/War Time, minus 1 hr. from total.

Sun Table for Year 1940

Date	Zodiac Sign	Time
01/21	Aquarius	04:33
02/19	Pisces	18:55
03/20	Aries	18:17
04/20	Taurus	05:47
05/21	Gemini	05:20
06/21	Cancer	13:33
07/23	Leo	00:27
08/23	Virgo	07:19
09/23	Libra	04:34
10/23	Scorpio	13:27
11/22	Sagittarius	10:38
12/21	Capricorn	23:45

Sun Table for Year 1941

Date	Zodiac Sign	Time
01/20	Aquarius	10:23
02/19	Pisces	00:44
03/21	Aries	00:06
04/20	Taurus	11:36
05/21	Gemini	11:09
06/21	Cancer	19:21
07/23	Leo	06:15
08/23	Virgo	13:07
09/23	Libra	10:22
10/23	Scorpio	19:16
11/22	Sagittarius	16:27
12/22	Capricorn	05:34

Sun Table for Year 1942

Date	Zodiac Sign	Time
01/20	Aquarius	16:13
02/19	Pisces	06:34
03/21	Aries	05:55
04/20	Taurus	17:24
05/21	Gemini	16:57
06/22	Cancer	01:09
07/23	Leo	12:03
08/23	Virgo	18:55
09/23	Libra	16:11
10/24	Scorpio	01:05
11/22	Sagittarius	22:17
12/22	Capricorn	11:24

Sun Table for Year 1943

Date	Zodiac Sign	Time
01/20	Aquarius	22:02
02/19	Pisces	12:23
03/21	Aries	11:44
04/20	Taurus	23:13
05/21	Gemini	22:45
06/22	Cancer	06:57
07/23	Leo	17:51
08/24	Virgo	00:43
09/23	Libra	21:59
10/23	Scorpio	06:54
11/23	Sagittarius	04:06
12/22	Capricorn	17:13

Greenwich Mean Time (GMT)
24-Hour Clock

Note: Eastern Standard Time (EST), add 5 hrs.
Central Standard Time (CST), add 6 hrs.
Mountain Standard Time (MST), add 7 hrs.
Pacific Standard Time (PST), add 8 hrs.
Daylight Saving Time/War Time, minus 1 hr. from total.

Sun Table for Year 1944

Date	Zodiac Sign	Time
01/21	Aquarius	03:52
02/19	Pisces	18:12
03/20	Aries	17:33
04/20	Taurus	05:01
05/21	Gemini	04:33
06/21	Cancer	12:45
07/22	Leo	23:39
08/23	Virgo	06:31
09/23	Libra	03:48
10/23	Scorpio	12:43
11/22	Sagittarius	09:55
12/21	Capricorn	23:03

Sun Table for Year 1945

Date	Zodiac Sign	Time
01/20	Aquarius	09:41
02/19	Pisces	00:02
03/20	Aries	23:22
04/20	Taurus	10:50
05/21	Gemini	10:21
06/21	Cancer	18:32
07/23	Leo	05:27
08/23	Virgo	12:19
09/23	Libra	09:36
10/23	Scorpio	18:32
11/22	Sagittarius	15:45
12/22	Capricorn	04:52

Sun Table for Year 1946

Date	Zodiac Sign	Time
01/20	Aquarius	15:31
02/19	Pisces	05:51
03/21	Aries	05:11
04/20	Taurus	16:38
05/21	Gemini	16:09
06/22	Cancer	00:20
07/23	Leo	11:15
08/23	Virgo	18:07
09/23	Libra	15:25
10/24	Scorpio	00:21
11/22	Sagittarius	21:34
12/22	Capricorn	10:42

Sun Table for Year 1947

Date	Zodiac Sign	Time
01/20	Aquarius	21:20
02/19	Pisces	11:40
03/21	Aries	11:00
04/20	Taurus	22:27
05/21	Gemini	21:58
06/22	Cancer	06:08
07/23	Leo	17:03
08/23	Virgo	23:56
09/23	Libra	21:13
10/24	Scorpio	06:10
11/23	Sagittarius	03:24
12/22	Capricorn	16:32

Greenwich Mean Time (GMT)
24-Hour Clock

Note: Eastern Standard Time (EST), add 5 hrs.
Central Standard Time (CST), add 6 hrs.
Mountain Standard Time (MST), add 7 hrs.
Pacific Standard Time (PST), add 8 hrs.
Daylight Saving Time/War Time, minus 1 hr. from total.

Sun Table for Year 1948

Date	Zodiac Sign	Time
01/21	Aquarius	03:10
02/19	Pisces	17:30
03/20	Aries	16:49
04/20	Taurus	04:16
05/21	Gemini	03:46
06/21	Cancer	11:56
07/22	Leo	22:51
08/23	Virgo	05:44
09/23	Libra	03:02
10/23	Scorpio	11:59
11/22	Sagittarius	09:13
12/21	Capricorn	22:21

Sun Table for Year 1949

Date	Zodiac Sign	Time
01/20	Aquarius	09:00
02/18	Pisces	23:19
03/20	Aries	22:38
04/20	Taurus	10:04
05/21	Gemini	09:34
06/21	Cancer	17:44
07/23	Leo	04:39
08/23	Virgo	11:32
09/23	Libra	08:50
10/23	Scorpio	17:48
11/22	Sagittarius	15:02
12/22	Capricorn	04:11

Sun Table for Year 1950

Date	Zodiac Sign	Time
01/20	Aquarius	14:49
02/19	Pisces	05:09
03/21	Aries	04:27
04/20	Taurus	15:53
05/21	Gemini	15:22
06/21	Cancer	23:32
07/23	Leo	10:27
08/23	Virgo	17:20
09/23	Libra	14:39
10/23	Scorpio	23:37
11/22	Sagittarius	20:52
12/22	Capricorn	10:00

Sun Table for Year 1951

Date	Zodiac Sign	Time
01/20	Aquarius	20:39
02/19	Pisces	10:58
03/21	Aries	10:16
04/20	Taurus	21:41
05/21	Gemini	21:10
06/22	Cancer	05:20
07/23	Leo	16:15
08/23	Virgo	23:08
09/23	Libra	20:27
10/24	Scorpio	05:26
11/23	Sagittarius	02:41
12/22	Capricorn	15:50

Greenwich Mean Time (GMT)
24-Hour Clock

Note: Eastern Standard Time (EST), add 5 hrs.
Central Standard Time (CST), add 6 hrs.
Mountain Standard Time (MST), add 7 hrs.
Pacific Standard Time (PST), add 8 hrs.
Daylight Saving Time/War Time, minus 1 hr. from total.

Sun Table for Year 1952

Date	Zodiac Sign	Time
01/21	Aquarius	02:28
02/19	Pisces	16:47
03/20	Aries	16:05
04/20	Taurus	03:30
05/21	Gemini	02:59
06/21	Cancer	11:08
07/22	Leo	22:03
08/23	Virgo	04:56
09/23	Libra	02:16
10/23	Scorpio	11:15
11/22	Sagittarius	08:30
12/21	Capricorn	21:39

Sun Table for Year 1953

Date	Zodiac Sign	Time
01/20	Aquarius	08:18
02/18	Pisces	22:37
03/20	Aries	21:54
04/20	Taurus	09:18
05/21	Gemini	08:47
06/21	Cancer	16:56
07/23	Leo	03:51
08/23	Virgo	10:45
09/23	Libra	08:04
10/23	Scorpio	17:04
11/22	Sagittarius	14:20
12/22	Capricorn	03:29

Sun Table for Year 1954

Date	Zodiac Sign	Time
01/20	Aquarius	14:08
02/19	Pisces	04:26
03/21	Aries	03:43
04/20	Taurus	15:07
05/21	Gemini	14:35
06/21	Cancer	22:44
07/23	Leo	09:39
08/23	Virgo	16:33
09/23	Libra	13:53
10/23	Scorpio	22:53
11/22	Sagittarius	20:09
12/22	Capricorn	09:18

Sun Table for Year 1955

Date	Zodiac Sign	Time
01/20	Aquarius	19:57
02/19	Pisces	10:15
03/21	Aries	09:33
04/20	Taurus	20:56
05/21	Gemini	20:23
06/22	Cancer	04:32
07/23	Leo	15:26
08/23	Virgo	22:21
09/23	Libra	19:42
10/24	Scorpio	04:42
11/23	Sagittarius	01:58
12/22	Capricorn	15:08

Greenwich Mean Time (GMT)
24-Hour Clock

Note: Eastern Standard Time (EST), add 5 hrs.
Central Standard Time (CST), add 6 hrs.
Mountain Standard Time (MST), add 7 hrs.
Pacific Standard Time (PST), add 8 hrs.
Daylight Saving Time/War Time, minus 1 hr. from total.

Sun Table for Year 1956

Date	Zodiac Sign	Time
01/21	Aquarius	01:47
02/19	Pisces	16:05
03/20	Aries	15:22
04/20	Taurus	02:44
05/21	Gemini	02:11
06/21	Cancer	10:20
07/22	Leo	21:14
08/23	Virgo	04:09
09/23	Libra	01:30
10/23	Scorpio	10:31
11/22	Sagittarius	07:48
12/21	Capricorn	20:58

Sun Table for Year 1957

Date	Zodiac Sign	Time
01/20	Aquarius	07:36
02/18	Pisces	21:54
03/20	Aries	21:11
04/20	Taurus	08:33
05/21	Gemini	07:59
06/21	Cancer	16:08
07/23	Leo	03:02
08/23	Virgo	09:57
09/23	Libra	07:19
10/23	Scorpio	16:20
11/22	Sagittarius	13:37
12/22	Capricorn	02:47

Sun Table for Year 1958

Date	Zodiac Sign	Time
01/20	Aquarius	13:26
02/19	Pisces	03:44
03/21	Aries	03:00
04/20	Taurus	14:21
05/21	Gemini	13:48
06/21	Cancer	21:56
07/23	Leo	08:50
08/23	Virgo	15:45
09/23	Libra	13:07
10/23	Scorpio	22:09
11/22	Sagittarius	19:26
12/22	Capricorn	08:37

Sun Table for Year 1959

Date	Zodiac Sign	Time
01/20	Aquarius	19:15
02/19	Pisces	09:33
03/21	Aries	08:49
04/20	Taurus	20:10
05/21	Gemini	19:36
06/22	Cancer	03:44
07/23	Leo	14:38
08/23	Virgo	21:33
09/23	Libra	18:56
10/24	Scorpio	03:58
11/23	Sagittarius	01:16
12/22	Capricorn	14:26

Greenwich Mean Time (GMT)
24-Hour Clock

Note: Eastern Standard Time (EST), add 5 hrs.
Central Standard Time (CST), add 6 hrs.
Mountain Standard Time (MST), add 7 hrs.
Pacific Standard Time (PST), add 8 hrs.
Daylight Saving Time/War Time, minus 1 hr. from total.

Sun Table for Year 1960

Date	Zodiac Sign	Time
01/21	Aquarius	01:05
02/19	Pisces	15:22
03/20	Aries	14:38
04/20	Taurus	01:58
05/21	Gemini	01:24
06/21	Cancer	09:32
07/22	Leo	20:26
08/23	Virgo	03:22
09/23	Libra	00:44
10/23	Scorpio	09:47
11/22	Sagittarius	07:05
12/21	Capricorn	20:16

Sun Table for Year 1961

Date	Zodiac Sign	Time
01/20	Aquarius	06:55
02/18	Pisces	21:12
03/20	Aries	20:27
04/20	Taurus	07:47
05/21	Gemini	07:12
06/21	Cancer	15:20
07/23	Leo	02:14
08/23	Virgo	09:10
09/23	Libra	06:33
10/23	Scorpio	15:36
11/22	Sagittarius	12:54
12/22	Capricorn	02:05

Sun Table for Year 1962

Date	Zodiac Sign	Time
01/20	Aquarius	12:44
02/19	Pisces	03:01
03/21	Aries	02:16
04/20	Taurus	13:36
05/21	Gemini	13:00
06/21	Cancer	21:08
07/23	Leo	08:02
08/23	Virgo	14:58
09/23	Libra	12:21
10/23	Scorpio	21:25
11/22	Sagittarius	18:44
12/22	Capricorn	07:55

Sun Table for Year 1963

Date	Zodiac Sign	Time
01/20	Aquarius	18:34
02/19	Pisces	08:50
03/21	Aries	08:05
04/20	Taurus	19:24
05/21	Gemini	18:49
06/22	Cancer	02:56
07/23	Leo	13:50
08/23	Virgo	20:46
09/23	Libra	18:10
10/24	Scorpio	03:14
11/23	Sagittarius	00:33
12/22	Capricorn	13:45

Greenwich Mean Time (GMT)
24-Hour Clock

Note: Eastern Standard Time (EST), add 5 hrs.
Central Standard Time (CST), add 6 hrs.
Mountain Standard Time (MST), add 7 hrs.
Pacific Standard Time (PST), add 8 hrs.
Daylight Saving Time/War Time, minus 1 hr. from total.

Sun Table for Year 1964

Date	Zodiac Sign	Time
01/21	Aquarius	00:23
02/19	Pisces	14:40
03/20	Aries	13:54
04/20	Taurus	01:13
05/21	Gemini	00:37
06/21	Cancer	08:43
07/22	Leo	19:38
08/23	Virgo	02:34
09/22	Libra	23:58
10/23	Scorpio	09:02
11/22	Sagittarius	06:22
12/21	Capricorn	19:34

Sun Table for Year 1965

Date	Zodiac Sign	Time
01/20	Aquarius	06:13
02/18	Pisces	20:29
03/20	Aries	19:43
04/20	Taurus	07:01
05/21	Gemini	06:25
06/21	Cancer	14:31
07/23	Leo	01:26
08/23	Virgo	08:22
09/23	Libra	05:47
10/23	Scorpio	14:51
11/22	Sagittarius	12:12
12/22	Capricorn	01:24

Sun Table for Year 1966

Date	Zodiac Sign	Time
01/20	Aquarius	12:02
02/19	Pisces	02:19
03/21	Aries	01:32
04/20	Taurus	12:50
05/21	Gemini	12:13
06/21	Cancer	20:19
07/23	Leo	07:14
08/23	Virgo	14:10
09/23	Libra	11:35
10/23	Scorpio	20:40
11/22	Sagittarius	18:01
12/22	Capricorn	07:13

Sun Table for Year 1967

Date	Zodiac Sign	Time
01/20	Aquarius	17:52
02/19	Pisces	08:08
03/21	Aries	07:21
04/20	Taurus	18:39
05/21	Gemini	18:01
06/22	Cancer	02:07
07/23	Leo	13:02
08/23	Virgo	19:59
09/23	Libra	17:24
10/24	Scorpio	02:29
11/22	Sagittarius	23:50
12/22	Capricorn	13:03

Greenwich Mean Time (GMT)
24-Hour Clock

Note: Eastern Standard Time (EST), add 5 hrs.
Central Standard Time (CST), add 6 hrs.
Mountain Standard Time (MST), add 7 hrs.
Pacific Standard Time (PST), add 8 hrs.
Daylight Saving Time/War Time, minus 1 hr. from total.

Sun Table for Year 1968

Date	Zodiac Sign	Time
01/20	Aquarius	23:42
02/19	Pisces	13:57
03/20	Aries	13:10
04/20	Taurus	00:27
05/20	Gemini	23:49
06/21	Cancer	07:55
07/22	Leo	18:50
08/23	Virgo	01:47
09/22	Libra	23:12
10/23	Scorpio	08:18
11/22	Sagittarius	05:40
12/21	Capricorn	18:52

Sun Table for Year 1969

Date	Zodiac Sign	Time
01/20	Aquarius	05:31
02/18	Pisces	19:47
03/20	Aries	18:59
04/20	Taurus	06:16
05/21	Gemini	05:38
06/21	Cancer	13:43
07/23	Leo	00:37
08/23	Virgo	07:35
09/23	Libra	05:01
10/23	Scorpio	14:07
11/22	Sagittarius	11:29
12/22	Capricorn	00:42

Sun Table for Year 1970

Date	Zodiac Sign	Time
01/20	Aquarius	11:21
02/19	Pisces	01:36
03/21	Aries	00:48
04/20	Taurus	12:04
05/21	Gemini	11:26
06/21	Cancer	19:31
07/23	Leo	06:25
08/23	Virgo	13:23
09/23	Libra	10:49
10/23	Scorpio	19:56
11/22	Sagittarius	17:18
12/22	Capricorn	06:31

Sun Table for Year 1971

Date	Zodiac Sign	Time
01/20	Aquarius	17:10
02/19	Pisces	07:25
03/21	Aries	06:37
04/20	Taurus	17:53
05/21	Gemini	17:14
06/22	Cancer	01:19
07/23	Leo	12:13
08/23	Virgo	19:11
09/23	Libra	16:38
10/24	Scorpio	01:45
11/22	Sagittarius	23:08
12/22	Capricorn	12:21

Greenwich Mean Time (GMT)
24-Hour Clock

Note: Eastern Standard Time (EST), add 5 hrs.
Central Standard Time (CST), add 6 hrs.
Mountain Standard Time (MST), add 7 hrs.
Pacific Standard Time (PST), add 8 hrs.
Daylight Saving Time/War Time, minus 1 hr. from total.

Sun Table for Year 1972

Date	Zodiac Sign	Time
01/20	Aquarius	23:00
02/19	Pisces	13:15
03/20	Aries	12:26
04/19	Taurus	23:41
05/20	Gemini	23:02
06/21	Cancer	07:07
07/22	Leo	18:01
08/23	Virgo	00:59
09/22	Libra	22:26
10/23	Scorpio	07:34
11/22	Sagittarius	04:57
12/21	Capricorn	18:11

Sun Table for Year 1973

Date	Zodiac Sign	Time
01/20	Aquarius	04:49
02/18	Pisces	19:04
03/20	Aries	18:15
04/20	Taurus	05:30
05/21	Gemini	04:50
06/21	Cancer	12:55
07/22	Leo	23:49
08/23	Virgo	06:47
09/23	Libra	04:15
10/23	Scorpio	13:23
11/22	Sagittarius	10:46
12/22	Capricorn	00:00

Sun Table for Year 1974

Date	Zodiac Sign	Time
01/20	Aquarius	10:39
02/19	Pisces	00:54
03/21	Aries	00:04
04/20	Taurus	11:19
05/21	Gemini	10:39
06/21	Cancer	18:43
07/23	Leo	05:37
08/23	Virgo	12:36
09/23	Libra	10:03
10/23	Scorpio	19:12
11/22	Sagittarius	16:36
12/22	Capricorn	05:50

Sun Table for Year 1975

Date	Zodiac Sign	Time
01/20	Aquarius	16:29
02/19	Pisces	06:43
03/21	Aries	05:53
04/20	Taurus	17:07
05/21	Gemini	16:27
06/22	Cancer	00:31
07/23	Leo	11:25
08/23	Virgo	18:24
09/23	Libra	15:52
10/24	Scorpio	01:01
11/22	Sagittarius	22:25
12/22	Capricorn	11:39

Greenwich Mean Time (GMT)
24-Hour Clock

Note: Eastern Standard Time (EST), add 5 hrs.
Central Standard Time (CST), add 6 hrs.
Mountain Standard Time (MST), add 7 hrs.
Pacific Standard Time (PST), add 8 hrs.
Daylight Saving Time/War Time, minus 1 hr. from total.

Sun Table for Year 1976

Date	Zodiac Sign	Time
01/20	Aquarius	22:18
02/19	Pisces	12:32
03/20	Aries	11:42
04/19	Taurus	22:56
05/20	Gemini	22:15
06/21	Cancer	06:19
07/22	Leo	17:13
08/23	Virgo	00:12
09/22	Libra	21:41
10/23	Scorpio	06:50
11/22	Sagittarius	04:14
12/21	Capricorn	17:29

Sun Table for Year 1977

Date	Zodiac Sign	Time
01/20	Aquarius	04:08
02/18	Pisces	18:22
03/20	Aries	17:31
04/20	Taurus	04:44
05/21	Gemini	04:03
06/21	Cancer	12:07
07/22	Leo	23:01
08/23	Virgo	06:00
09/23	Libra	03:29
10/23	Scorpio	12:39
11/22	Sagittarius	10:04
12/21	Capricorn	23:18

Sun Table for Year 1978

Date	Zodiac Sign	Time
01/20	Aquarius	09:57
02/19	Pisces	00:11
03/20	Aries	23:20
04/20	Taurus	10:33
05/21	Gemini	09:51
06/21	Cancer	17:55
07/23	Leo	04:49
08/23	Virgo	11:48
09/23	Libra	09:18
10/23	Scorpio	18:28
11/22	Sagittarius	15:53
12/22	Capricorn	05:08

Sun Table for Year 1979

Date	Zodiac Sign	Time
01/20	Aquarius	15:47
02/19	Pisces	06:00
03/21	Aries	05:09
04/20	Taurus	16:22
05/21	Gemini	15:40
06/21	Cancer	23:43
07/23	Leo	10:37
08/23	Virgo	17:36
09/23	Libra	15:06
10/24	Scorpio	00:17
11/22	Sagittarius	21:42
12/22	Capricorn	10:57

Greenwich Mean Time (GMT)
24-Hour Clock

Note: Eastern Standard Time (EST), add 5 hrs.
Central Standard Time (CST), add 6 hrs.
Mountain Standard Time (MST), add 7 hrs.
Pacific Standard Time (PST), add 8 hrs.
Daylight Saving Time/War Time, minus 1 hr. from total.

Sun Table for Year 1980

Date	Zodiac Sign	Time
01/20	Aquarius	21:36
02/19	Pisces	11:50
03/20	Aries	10:58
04/19	Taurus	22:10
05/20	Gemini	21:28
06/21	Cancer	05:31
07/22	Leo	16:25
08/22	Virgo	23:24
09/22	Libra	20:55
10/23	Scorpio	06:06
11/22	Sagittarius	03:32
12/21	Capricorn	16:47

Sun Table for Year 1981

Date	Zodiac Sign	Time
01/20	Aquarius	03:26
02/18	Pisces	17:39
03/20	Aries	16:47
04/20	Taurus	03:59
05/21	Gemini	03:16
06/21	Cancer	11:19
07/22	Leo	22:13
08/23	Virgo	05:13
09/23	Libra	02:43
10/23	Scorpio	11:55
11/22	Sagittarius	09:21
12/21	Capricorn	22:37

Sun Table for Year 1982

Date	Zodiac Sign	Time
01/20	Aquarius	09:16
02/18	Pisces	23:29
03/20	Aries	22:36
04/20	Taurus	09:47
05/21	Gemini	09:04
06/21	Cancer	17:06
07/23	Leo	04:01
08/23	Virgo	11:01
09/23	Libra	08:32
10/23	Scorpio	17:44
11/22	Sagittarius	15:10
12/22	Capricorn	04:26

Sun Table for Year 1983

Date	Zodiac Sign	Time
01/20	Aquarius	15:05
02/19	Pisces	05:18
03/21	Aries	04:25
04/20	Taurus	15:36
05/21	Gemini	14:52
06/21	Cancer	22:54
07/23	Leo	09:48
08/23	Virgo	16:49
09/23	Libra	14:20
10/23	Scorpio	23:33
11/22	Sagittarius	21:00
12/22	Capricorn	10:16

Greenwich Mean Time (GMT)
24-Hour Clock

Note: Eastern Standard Time (EST), add 5 hrs.
Central Standard Time (CST), add 6 hrs.
Mountain Standard Time (MST), add 7 hrs.
Pacific Standard Time (PST), add 8 hrs.
Daylight Saving Time/War Time, minus 1 hr. from total.

Sun Table for Year 1984

Date	Zodiac Sign	Time
01/20	Aquarius	20:55
02/19	Pisces	11:07
03/20	Aries	10:14
04/19	Taurus	21:24
05/20	Gemini	20:40
06/21	Cancer	04:42
07/22	Leo	15:36
08/22	Virgo	22:37
09/22	Libra	20:09
10/23	Scorpio	05:22
11/22	Sagittarius	02:49
12/21	Capricorn	16:05

Sun Table for Year 1985

Date	Zodiac Sign	Time
01/20	Aquarius	02:44
02/18	Pisces	16:57
03/20	Aries	16:03
04/20	Taurus	03:13
05/21	Gemini	02:29
06/21	Cancer	10:30
07/22	Leo	21:24
08/23	Virgo	04:25
09/23	Libra	01:57
10/23	Scorpio	11:10
11/22	Sagittarius	08:38
12/21	Capricorn	21:55

Sun Table for Year 1986

Date	Zodiac Sign	Time
01/20	Aquarius	08:34
02/18	Pisces	22:46
03/20	Aries	21:52
04/20	Taurus	09:02
05/21	Gemini	08:17
06/21	Cancer	16:18
07/23	Leo	03:12
08/23	Virgo	10:13
09/23	Libra	07:46
10/23	Scorpio	16:59
11/22	Sagittarius	14:27
12/22	Capricorn	03:44

Sun Table for Year 1987

Date	Zodiac Sign	Time
01/20	Aquarius	14:23
02/19	Pisces	04:36
03/21	Aries	03:41
04/20	Taurus	14:50
05/21	Gemini	14:05
06/21	Cancer	22:06
07/23	Leo	09:00
08/23	Virgo	16:01
09/23	Libra	13:34
10/23	Scorpio	22:48
11/22	Sagittarius	20:17
12/22	Capricorn	09:34

Greenwich Mean Time (GMT)
24-Hour Clock

Note: Eastern Standard Time (EST), add 5 hrs.
Central Standard Time (CST), add 6 hrs.
Mountain Standard Time (MST), add 7 hrs.
Pacific Standard Time (PST), add 8 hrs.
Daylight Saving Time/War Time, minus 1 hr. from total.

Sun Table for Year 1988

Date	Zodiac Sign	Time
01/20	Aquarius	20:13
02/19	Pisces	10:25
03/20	Aries	09:30
04/19	Taurus	20:39
05/20	Gemini	19:53
06/21	Cancer	03:54
07/22	Leo	14:48
08/22	Virgo	21:50
09/22	Libra	19:23
10/23	Scorpio	04:37
11/22	Sagittarius	02:06
12/21	Capricorn	15:23

Sun Table for Year 1989

Date	Zodiac Sign	Time
01/20	Aquarius	02:03
02/18	Pisces	16:14
03/20	Aries	15:19
04/20	Taurus	02:27
05/21	Gemini	01:41
06/21	Cancer	09:42
07/22	Leo	20:36
08/23	Virgo	03:38
09/23	Libra	01:11
10/23	Scorpio	10:26
11/22	Sagittarius	07:55
12/21	Capricorn	21:13

Sun Table for Year 1990

Date	Zodiac Sign	Time
01/20	Aquarius	07:52
02/18	Pisces	22:04
03/20	Aries	21:08
04/20	Taurus	08:16
05/21	Gemini	07:30
06/21	Cancer	15:30
07/23	Leo	02:24
08/23	Virgo	09:26
09/23	Libra	07:00
10/23	Scorpio	16:15
11/22	Sagittarius	13:45
12/22	Capricorn	03:03

Sun Table for Year 1991

Date	Zodiac Sign	Time
01/20	Aquarius	13:42
02/19	Pisces	03:53
03/21	Aries	02:57
04/20	Taurus	14:05
05/21	Gemini	13:18
06/21	Cancer	21:18
07/23	Leo	08:12
08/23	Virgo	15:14
09/23	Libra	12:48
10/23	Scorpio	22:04
11/22	Sagittarius	19:34
12/22	Capricorn	08:52

Greenwich Mean Time (GMT)
24-Hour Clock

Note: Eastern Standard Time (EST), add 5 hrs.
Central Standard Time (CST), add 6 hrs.
Mountain Standard Time (MST), add 7 hrs.
Pacific Standard Time (PST), add 8 hrs.
Daylight Saving Time/War Time, minus 1 hr. from total.

Sun Table for Year 1992

Date	Zodiac Sign	Time
01/20	Aquarius	19:31
02/19	Pisces	09:42
03/20	Aries	08:46
04/19	Taurus	19:53
05/20	Gemini	19:06
06/21	Cancer	03:06
07/22	Leo	14:00
08/22	Virgo	21:02
09/22	Libra	18:37
10/23	Scorpio	03:53
11/22	Sagittarius	01:24
12/21	Capricorn	14:42

Sun Table for Year 1993

Date	Zodiac Sign	Time
01/20	Aquarius	01:21
02/18	Pisces	15:32
03/20	Aries	14:35
04/20	Taurus	01:42
05/21	Gemini	00:54
06/21	Cancer	08:54
07/22	Leo	19:48
08/23	Virgo	02:50
09/23	Libra	00:25
10/23	Scorpio	09:42
11/22	Sagittarius	07:13
12/21	Capricorn	20:31

Sun Table for Year 1994

Date	Zodiac Sign	Time
01/20	Aquarius	07:10
02/18	Pisces	21:21
03/20	Aries	20:24
04/20	Taurus	07:30
05/21	Gemini	06:42
06/21	Cancer	14:42
07/23	Leo	01:36
08/23	Virgo	08:38
09/23	Libra	06:14
10/23	Scorpio	15:31
11/22	Sagittarius	13:02
12/22	Capricorn	02:21

Sun Table for Year 1995

Date	Zodiac Sign	Time
01/20	Aquarius	13:00
02/19	Pisces	03:11
03/21	Aries	02:13
04/20	Taurus	13:19
05/21	Gemini	12:31
06/21	Cancer	20:30
07/23	Leo	07:24
08/23	Virgo	14:26
09/23	Libra	12:02
10/23	Scorpio	21:20
11/22	Sagittarius	18:51
12/22	Capricorn	08:10

Greenwich Mean Time (GMT)
24-Hour Clock

Note: Eastern Standard Time (EST), add 5 hrs.
Central Standard Time (CST), add 6 hrs.
Mountain Standard Time (MST), add 7 hrs.
Pacific Standard Time (PST), add 8 hrs.
Daylight Saving Time/War Time, minus 1 hr. from total.

Sun Table for Year 1996

Date	Zodiac Sign	Time
01/20	Aquarius	18:50
02/19	Pisces	09:00
03/20	Aries	08:02
04/19	Taurus	19:08
05/20	Gemini	18:19
06/21	Cancer	02:18
07/22	Leo	13:11
08/22	Virgo	20:15
09/22	Libra	17:51
10/23	Scorpio	03:09
11/22	Sagittarius	00:41
12/21	Capricorn	14:00

Sun Table for Year 1997

Date	Zodiac Sign	Time
01/20	Aquarius	00:39
02/18	Pisces	14:49
03/20	Aries	13:51
04/20	Taurus	00:56
05/21	Gemini	00:07
06/21	Cancer	08:06
07/22	Leo	18:59
08/23	Virgo	02:03
09/22	Libra	23:39
10/23	Scorpio	08:58
11/22	Sagittarius	06:30
12/21	Capricorn	19:49

Sun Table for Year 1998

Date	Zodiac Sign	Time
01/20	Aquarius	06:29
02/18	Pisces	20:39
03/20	Aries	19:40
04/20	Taurus	06:45
05/21	Gemini	05:55
06/21	Cancer	13:54
07/23	Leo	00:47
08/23	Virgo	07:51
09/23	Libra	05:28
10/23	Scorpio	14:47
11/22	Sagittarius	12:19
12/22	Capricorn	01:39

Sun Table for Year 1999

Date	Zodiac Sign	Time
01/20	Aquarius	12:18
02/19	Pisces	02:28
03/21	Aries	01:29
04/20	Taurus	12:33
05/21	Gemini	11:43
06/21	Cancer	19:42
07/23	Leo	06:35
08/23	Virgo	13:39
09/23	Libra	11:16
10/23	Scorpio	20:36
11/22	Sagittarius	18:09
12/22	Capricorn	07:28

Greenwich Mean Time (GMT)
24-Hour Clock

Note: Eastern Standard Time (EST), add 5 hrs.
Central Standard Time (CST), add 6 hrs.
Mountain Standard Time (MST), add 7 hrs.
Pacific Standard Time (PST), add 8 hrs.
Daylight Saving Time/War Time, minus 1 hr. from total.

Sun Table for Year 2000

Date	Zodiac Sign	Time
01/20	Aquarius	18:08
02/19	Pisces	08:17
03/20	Aries	07:18
04/19	Taurus	18:22
05/20	Gemini	17:32
06/21	Cancer	01:29
07/22	Leo	12:23
08/22	Virgo	19:27
09/22	Libra	17:05
10/23	Scorpio	02:25
11/21	Sagittarius	23:58
12/21	Capricorn	13:18

Greenwich Mean Time (GMT)
24-Hour Clock

Note: Eastern Standard Time (EST), add 5 hrs.
Central Standard Time (CST), add 6 hrs.
Mountain Standard Time (MST), add 7 hrs.
Pacific Standard Time (PST), add 8 hrs.
Daylight Saving Time/War Time, minus 1 hr. from total.

WORLD TIME ZONES
Western Hemisphere

Time Zone Name	Abbrev.	Meridian		Add
Greenwich Mean Time	GMT	0	W 00	0
West Africa Time	WAT	15	W 00	1
Azores Time	AT	30	W 00	2
Brazil Zone 2	BZ2	45	W 00	3
Newfoundland Std. Time	NST	52	W 30	3.5
Atlantic Standard Time	AST	60	W 00	4
Eastern Standard Time	EST	75	W 00	5
Central Standard Time	CST	90	W 00	6
Mountain Standard Time	MST	105	W 00	7
Pacific Standard Time	PST	120	W 00	8
Yukon Standard Time	YST	135	W 00	9
Alaska-Hawaii Std. Time	AHST	150	W 00	10
Hawaii Standard Time	HST	157	W 30	10.5
Nome Time	NT	165	W 00	11
Bering Standard Time	BST	165	W 00	11
International Date Line	——	180	W 00	12

Zones on Daylight Saving Time/War Time → subtract 1 hr.
Zones on Double Summer Time → subtract 2 hrs.

WORLD TIME ZONES
Eastern Hemisphere

Time Zone Name	Abbrev.	Meridian	Sub.
Central European Time	CET	15 E 00	−1
Middle European Time	MET	15 E 00	−1
Eastern European Time	EET	30 E 00	−2
Baghdad Time	BT	45 E 00	−3
USSR Zone 3	UZ3	60 E 00	−4
USSR Zone 4	UZ4	75 E 00	−5
Indian Standard Time	IST	82 E 30	−5.5
USSR Zone 5	UZ5	90 E 00	−6
North Sumatra Time	NST	97 E 30	−6.5
South Sumatra Time	SST	105 E 00	−7
Java Time	JT	112 E 30	−7.5
China Coast Time	CCT	120 E 00	−8
Japan Standard Time	JST	135 E 00	−9
So. Australia Std. Time	SAST	142 E 30	−9.5
Guam Standard Time	GST	150 E 00	−10
		165 E 00	−11
New Zealand Standard Time	NZT	180 E 00	−12

Zones on Daylight Saving Time/War Time → subtract 1 hr.
Zones on Double Summer Time → subtract 2 hrs.

Mercury Table for Year 1900

Date	Zodiac Sign	Time
01/09	Capricorn	02:05
01/28	Aquarius	17:02
02/14	Pisces	23:57
03/03	Aries	21:22
03/29	Aries*	22:53
04/17	Aries	01:03
05/11	Taurus	00:08
05/26	Gemini	10:41
06/09	Cancer	09:19
06/27	Leo	09:14
09/03	Virgo	00:31
09/18	Libra	23:07
10/07	Scorpio	08:14
10/30	Sagittarius	06:34
11/18	Sagittarius*	20:26
12/12	Sagittarius	14:52

Mercury Table for Year 1901

Date	Zodiac Sign	Time
01/02	Capricorn	12:21
01/21	Aquarius	06:23
02/07	Pisces	10:31
04/15	Aries	17:03
05/03	Taurus	13:47
05/17	Gemini	19:59
06/01	Cancer	23:28
08/10	Leo	04:31
08/25	Virgo	22:15
09/11	Libra	06:11
10/01	Scorpio	04:27
12/06	Sagittarius	23:27
12/26	Capricorn	09:21

Mercury Table for Year 1902

Date	Zodiac Sign	Time
01/13	Aquarius	19:27
02/01	Pisces	16:05
02/18	Pisces*	06:51
03/19	Pisces	03:00
04/09	Aries	11:58
04/25	Taurus	08:30
05/09	Gemini	12:04
05/29	Cancer	08:34
06/26	Cancer*	06:32
07/13	Cancer	09:15
08/02	Leo	21:13
08/17	Virgo	16:28
09/04	Libra	02:24
09/28	Scorpio	07:25
10/15	Scorpio*	23:30
11/10	Scorpio	14:55
11/30	Sagittarius	01:18
12/19	Capricorn	02:47

Mercury Table for Year 1903

Date	Zodiac Sign	Time
01/06	Aquarius	19:22
03/14	Pisces	21:41
04/02	Aries	00:16
04/16	Taurus	21:40
05/02	Gemini	13:38
07/10	Cancer	12:54
07/25	Leo	12:03
08/09	Virgo	17:44
08/29	Libra	05:33
11/04	Scorpio	04:44
11/22	Sagittarius	19:09
12/11	Capricorn	24:00

Greenwich Mean Time (GMT)
24-Hour Clock

Note: * Indicates retrograde motion.

Eastern Standard Time (EST), add 5 hrs.

Central Standard Time (CST), add 6 hrs.

Mountain Standard Time (MST), add 7 hrs.

Pacific Standard Time (PST), add 8 hrs.

Daylight Saving Time/War Time, minus 1 hr. from total.

Mercury Table for Year 1904

Date	Zodiac Sign	Time
01/02	Aquarius	09:35
01/14	Aquarius*	03:36
02/15	Aquarius	10:45
03/07	Pisces	07:50
03/23	Aries	23:23
04/07	Taurus	19:04
06/14	Gemini	06:12
07/01	Cancer	22:01
07/16	Leo	00:15
08/01	Virgo	13:16
08/28	Libra	08:24
09/07	Libra*	20:19
10/09	Libra	01:36
10/26	Scorpio	20:00
11/14	Sagittarius	13:33
12/04	Capricorn	14:01

Mercury Table for Year 1905

Date	Zodiac Sign	Time
02/09	Aquarius	05:20
02/27	Pisces	21:51
03/15	Aries	19:19
04/01	Taurus	18:13
04/28	Taurus*	13:12
05/15	Taurus	19:37
06/08	Gemini	17:44
06/23	Cancer	09:39
07/07	Leo	21:55
07/27	Virgo	06:41
10/01	Libra	23:04
10/19	Scorpio	07:31
11/07	Sagittarius	16:15
12/02	Capricorn	05:00
12/10	Capricorn*	00:47

Mercury Table for Year 1906

Date	Zodiac Sign	Time
01/12	Capricorn	20:41
02/02	Aquarius	11:49
02/20	Pisces	03:15
03/08	Aries	01:56
05/15	Taurus	02:49
05/31	Gemini	22:33
06/14	Cancer	19:08
06/30	Leo	21:16
09/07	Virgo	21:38
09/24	Libra	03:13
10/11	Scorpio	23:21
11/01	Sagittarius	19:20
12/06	Sagittarius*	22:37
12/12	Sagittarius	23:16

Mercury Table for Year 1907

Date	Zodiac Sign	Time
01/07	Capricorn	00:38
01/26	Aquarius	04:44
02/12	Pisces	08:23
03/03	Aries	20:47
03/14	Aries*	04:54
04/18	Aries	10:23
05/08	Taurus	15:05
05/23	Gemini	10:25
06/06	Cancer	16:32
06/27	Leo	08:02
07/26	Leo*	14:48
08/12	Leo	15:50
08/31	Virgo	06:40
09/16	Libra	06:43
10/05	Scorpio	04:20
12/11	Sagittarius	03:19
12/31	Capricorn	03:37

Greenwich Mean Time (GMT)
24-Hour Clock

Note: * Indicates retrograde motion.
Eastern Standard Time (EST), add 5 hrs.
Central Standard Time (CST), add 6 hrs.
Mountain Standard Time (MST), add 7 hrs.
Pacific Standard Time (PST), add 8 hrs.
Daylight Saving Time/War Time, minus 1 hr. from total.

451

Mercury Table for Year 1908

Date	Zodiac Sign	Time
01/18	Aquarius	17:04
02/05	Pisces	04:12
04/12	Aries	22:34
04/29	Taurus	18:44
05/13	Gemini	20:39
05/30	Cancer	04:23
08/06	Leo	23:32
08/22	Virgo	01:15
09/07	Libra	18:01
09/28	Scorpio	19:24
11/01	Scorpio*	22:49
11/11	Scorpio	17:09
12/03	Sagittarius	17:39
12/22	Capricorn	22:15

Mercury Table for Year 1909

Date	Zodiac Sign	Time
01/10	Aquarius	08:45
03/17	Pisces	11:13
04/06	Aries	01:12
04/21	Taurus	09:45
05/05	Gemini	21:33
07/13	Cancer	05:39
07/30	Leo	00:24
08/13	Virgo	21:16
08/31	Libra	23:49
11/07	Scorpio	17:48
11/26	Sagittarius	14:44
12/15	Capricorn	16:17

Mercury Table for Year 1910

Date	Zodiac Sign	Time
01/03	Aquarius	21:14
01/31	Aquarius*	02:59
02/15	Aquarius	12:41
03/11	Pisces	21:18
03/29	Aries	06:34
04/13	Taurus	00:13
04/30	Gemini	15:48
06/02	Gemini*	00:08
06/11	Gemini	24:00
07/07	Cancer	03:14
07/21	Leo	12:26
08/06	Virgo	04:26
08/27	Libra	06:33
09/28	Libra*	13:33
10/12	Libra	04:16
10/31	Scorpio	17:55
11/19	Sagittarius	07:57
12/08	Capricorn	18:10

Mercury Table for Year 1911

Date	Zodiac Sign	Time
02/13	Aquarius	03:47
03/04	Pisces	20:58
03/21	Aries	03:13
04/05	Taurus	08:57
06/13	Gemini	01:14
06/28	Cancer	23:48
07/13	Leo	03:09
07/30	Virgo	13:35
10/06	Libra	20:36
10/24	Scorpio	06:20
11/12	Sagittarius	04:42
12/03	Capricorn	01:37
12/27	Capricorn*	16:33

Greenwich Mean Time (GMT)
24-Hour Clock

Note: * Indicates retrograde motion.

Eastern Standard Time (EST), add 5 hrs.

Central Standard Time (CST), add 6 hrs.

Mountain Standard Time (MST), add 7 hrs.

Pacific Standard Time (PST), add 8 hrs.

Daylight Saving Time/War Time, minus 1 hr. from total.

Mercury Table for Year 1912

Date	Zodiac Sign	Time
01/15	Capricorn	07:00
02/07	Aquarius	02:13
02/25	Pisces	06:21
03/12	Aries	01:15
05/16	Taurus	19:44
06/05	Gemini	04:57
06/19	Cancer	08:50
07/04	Leo	08:52
07/26	Virgo	08:15
08/21	Virgo*	03:19
09/10	Virgo	16:43
09/28	Libra	07:14
10/15	Scorpio	18:46
11/04	Sagittarius	14:33

Mercury Table for Year 1913

Date	Zodiac Sign	Time
01/10	Capricorn	05:11
01/30	Aquarius	01:33
02/16	Pisces	10:34
03/04	Aries	22:29
04/07	Aries*	15:32
04/14	Aries	02:43
05/12	Taurus	06:04
05/28	Gemini	00:17
06/10	Cancer	21:23
06/28	Leo	05:30
09/04	Virgo	10:48
09/20	Libra	09:53
10/08	Scorpio	14:46
10/30	Sagittarius	18:03
11/23	Sagittarius*	12:27
12/13	Sagittarius	08:35

Mercury Table for Year 1914

Date	Zodiac Sign	Time
01/03	Capricorn	19:11
01/22	Aquarius	15:40
02/08	Pisces	19:04
04/16	Aries	15:53
05/05	Taurus	00:49
05/19	Gemini	09:52
06/03	Cancer	05:48
08/11	Leo	06:14
08/27	Virgo	10:38
09/12	Libra	15:38
10/02	Scorpio	05:50
12/08	Sagittarius	04:42
12/27	Capricorn	17:30

Mercury Table for Year 1915

Date	Zodiac Sign	Time
01/15	Aquarius	04:17
02/02	Pisces	10:35
02/23	Pisces*	14:57
03/19	Pisces	08:38
04/10	Aries	19:14
04/26	Taurus	21:33
05/10	Gemini	23:40
05/29	Cancer	10:46
08/04	Leo	08:49
08/19	Virgo	04:32
09/05	Libra	08:56
09/28	Scorpio	08:12
10/21	Scorpio*	01:05
11/11	Scorpio	13:55
12/01	Sagittarius	09:06
12/20	Capricorn	11:03

Greenwich Mean Time (GMT)
24-Hour Clock

Note: * Indicates retrograde motion.

Eastern Standard Time (EST), add 5 hrs.

Central Standard Time (CST), add 6 hrs.

Mountain Standard Time (MST), add 7 hrs.

Pacific Standard Time (PST), add 8 hrs.

Daylight Saving Time/War Time, minus 1 hr. from total.

Mercury Table for Year 1916

Date	Zodiac Sign	Time
01/08	Aquarius	01:13
03/15	Pisces	00:01
04/02	Aries	10:49
04/17	Taurus	10:51
05/02	Gemini	16:14
07/10	Cancer	18:09
07/26	Leo	01:33
08/10	Virgo	03:58
08/29	Libra	04:48
11/04	Scorpio	12:18
11/23	Sagittarius	03:31
12/12	Capricorn	07:05

Mercury Table for Year 1917

Date	Zodiac Sign	Time
01/01	Aquarius	17:15
01/18	Aquarius*	04:18
02/15	Aquarius	03:12
03/08	Pisces	15:23
03/25	Aries	11:24
04/09	Taurus	05:36
06/14	Gemini	18:00
07/03	Cancer	10:16
07/17	Leo	13:18
08/02	Virgo	19:26
08/26	Libra	22:54
09/14	Libra*	11:50
10/10	Libra	04:36
10/28	Scorpio	05:15
11/15	Sagittarius	21:20
12/05	Capricorn	16:50

Mercury Table for Year 1918

Date	Zodiac Sign	Time
02/10	Aquarius	09:15
03/01	Pisces	07:40
03/17	Aries	07:15
04/02	Taurus	13:15
06/10	Gemini	01:14
06/24	Cancer	23:42
07/09	Leo	08:36
07/28	Virgo	01:28
10/03	Libra	08:53
10/20	Scorpio	16:41
11/08	Sagittarius	22:00
12/01	Capricorn	16:25
12/15	Capricorn*	12:34

Mercury Table for Year 1919

Date	Zodiac Sign	Time
01/13	Capricorn	18:04
02/03	Aquarius	19:18
02/21	Pisces	13:57
03/09	Aries	10:37
05/16	Taurus	02:14
06/02	Gemini	10:56
06/16	Cancer	08:37
07/02	Leo	01:59
09/09	Virgo	03:35
09/25	Libra	14:10
10/13	Scorpio	07:18
11/02	Sagittarius	19:04

Greenwich Mean Time (GMT)
24-Hour Clock

Note: * Indicates retrograde motion.

Eastern Standard Time (EST), add 5 hrs.
Central Standard Time (CST), add 6 hrs.
Mountain Standard Time (MST), add 7 hrs.
Pacific Standard Time (PST), add 8 hrs.
Daylight Saving Time/War Time, minus 1 hr. from total.

Mercury Table for Year 1920

Date	Zodiac Sign	Time
01/08	Capricorn	05:47
01/27	Aquarius	13:41
02/13	Pisces	18:33
03/02	Aries	19:35
03/19	Aries*	16:10
04/17	Aries	17:58
05/08	Taurus	23:47
05/24	Gemini	00:23
06/07	Cancer	02:53
06/26	Leo	12:32
08/02	Leo*	22:36
08/10	Leo	08:10
08/31	Virgo	18:18
09/16	Libra	17:05
10/05	Scorpio	09:18
10/30	Sagittarius	12:56
11/10	Sagittarius*	19:17
12/11	Sagittarius	04:28
12/31	Capricorn	11:11

Mercury Table for Year 1921

Date	Zodiac Sign	Time
01/19	Aquarius	02:20
02/05	Pisces	10:08
04/14	Aries	02:04
05/01	Taurus	06:49
05/15	Gemini	10:00
05/31	Cancer	05:03
08/08	Leo	07:27
08/23	Virgo	13:43
09/09	Libra	02:29
09/29	Scorpio	15:57
12/05	Sagittarius	00:21
12/24	Capricorn	06:34

Mercury Table for Year 1922

Date	Zodiac Sign	Time
01/11	Aquarius	16:49
02/01	Pisces	18:13
02/09	Pisces*	03:48
03/18	Pisces	06:17
04/07	Aries	10:08
04/22	Taurus	23:05
05/07	Gemini	06:55
06/01	Cancer	03:02
06/10	Cancer*	22:35
07/13	Cancer	19:41
07/31	Leo	13:13
08/15	Virgo	08:47
09/02	Libra	04:11
10/01	Scorpio	10:45
10/05	Scorpio*	01:19
11/08	Scorpio	22:19
11/27	Sagittarius	22:55
12/17	Capricorn	00:15

Mercury Table for Year 1923

Date	Zodiac Sign	Time
01/04	Aquarius	23:31
02/06	Aquarius*	16:18
02/13	Aquarius	23:18
03/13	Pisces	02:25
03/30	Aries	17:57
04/14	Taurus	12:48
05/01	Gemini	05:18
07/08	Cancer	12:32
07/23	Leo	01:57
08/07	Virgo	13:23
08/27	Libra	22:18
10/04	Libra*	12:52
10/11	Libra	21:51
11/02	Scorpio	02:31
11/20	Sagittarius	16:12
12/10	Capricorn	00:05

Greenwich Mean Time (GMT)
24-Hour Clock

Note: * Indicates retrograde motion.

Eastern Standard Time (EST), add 5 hrs.

Central Standard Time (CST), add 6 hrs.

Mountain Standard Time (MST), add 7 hrs.

Pacific Standard Time (PST), add 8 hrs.

Daylight Saving Time/War Time, minus 1 hr. from total.

Mercury Table for Year 1924

Date	Zodiac Sign	Time
02/14	Aquarius	03:08
03/05	Pisces	05:41
03/21	Aries	15:25
04/05	Taurus	16:18
06/13	Gemini	01:32
06/29	Cancer	13:08
07/13	Leo	15:28
07/30	Virgo	16:37
10/07	Libra	03:57
10/24	Scorpio	15:43
11/12	Sagittarius	11:52
12/02	Capricorn	23:30
12/31	Capricorn*	16:11

Mercury Table for Year 1925

Date	Zodiac Sign	Time
01/14	Capricorn	06:48
02/07	Aquarius	08:00
02/25	Pisces	16:41
03/13	Aries	12:25
04/01	Taurus	15:39
04/15	Taurus*	23:18
05/17	Taurus	01:17
06/06	Gemini	15:06
06/20	Cancer	22:53
07/05	Leo	17:40
07/26	Virgo	11:38
08/27	Virgo*	06:45
09/11	Virgo	04:35
09/29	Libra	17:49
10/17	Scorpio	03:34
11/05	Sagittarius	18:37

Mercury Table for Year 1926

Date	Zodiac Sign	Time
01/11	Capricorn	07:09
01/31	Aquarius	09:47
02/17	Pisces	21:17
03/06	Aries	02:46
05/13	Taurus	10:39
05/29	Gemini	13:36
06/12	Cancer	09:58
06/29	Leo	04:54
09/05	Virgo	20:20
09/21	Libra	20:43
10/09	Scorpio	21:44
10/31	Sagittarius	10:47
11/28	Sagittarius*	05:23
12/13	Sagittarius	20:13

Mercury Table for Year 1927

Date	Zodiac Sign	Time
01/05	Capricorn	01:40
01/24	Aquarius	00:53
02/10	Pisces	04:13
04/17	Aries	12:04
05/06	Taurus	11:14
05/20	Gemini	23:50
06/04	Cancer	13:32
06/28	Leo	19:37
07/14	Leo*	03:47
08/12	Leo	03:27
08/28	Virgo	22:54
09/14	Libra	01:22
10/03	Scorpio	08:27
12/09	Sagittarius	09:08
12/29	Capricorn	01:31

Greenwich Mean Time (GMT)
24-Hour Clock

Note: * Indicates retrograde motion.
Eastern Standard Time (EST), add 5 hrs.
Central Standard Time (CST), add 6 hrs.
Mountain Standard Time (MST), add 7 hrs.
Pacific Standard Time (PST), add 8 hrs.
Daylight Saving Time/War Time, minus 1 hr. from total.

Mercury Table for Year 1928

Date	Zodiac Sign	Time
01/16	Aquarius	13:16
02/03	Pisces	10:15
02/29	Pisces*	06:13
03/18	Pisces	02:22
04/11	Aries	01:40
04/27	Taurus	10:21
05/11	Gemini	11:57
05/28	Cancer	22:57
08/04	Leo	19:45
08/19	Virgo	16:46
09/05	Libra	16:05
09/27	Scorpio	18:02
10/24	Scorpio*	21:44
11/11	Scorpio	08:40
12/01	Sagittarius	16:40
12/20	Capricorn	19:21

Mercury Table for Year 1929

Date	Zodiac Sign	Time
01/08	Aquarius	07:53
03/16	Pisces	00:52
04/03	Aries	21:03
04/19	Taurus	00:09
05/03	Gemini	21:21
07/11	Cancer	20:54
07/27	Leo	14:58
08/11	Virgo	14:39
08/30	Libra	05:51
11/05	Scorpio	19:17
11/24	Sagittarius	11:52
12/13	Capricorn	14:29

Mercury Table for Year 1930

Date	Zodiac Sign	Time
01/02	Aquarius	10:21
01/23	Aquarius*	00:34
02/15	Aquarius	14:45
03/09	Pisces	22:24
03/26	Aries	23:20
04/10	Taurus	16:52
05/01	Gemini	05:18
05/17	Gemini*	11:39
06/14	Gemini	19:39
07/04	Cancer	21:58
07/19	Leo	02:31
08/04	Virgo	02:31
08/26	Libra	18:04
09/20	Libra*	02:12
10/11	Libra	04:28
10/29	Scorpio	14:24
11/17	Sagittarius	05:17
12/06	Capricorn	20:45

Mercury Table for Year 1931

Date	Zodiac Sign	Time
02/11	Aquarius	12:12
03/02	Pisces	17:15
03/18	Aries	19:18
04/03	Taurus	13:36
06/11	Gemini	07:12
06/26	Cancer	13:38
07/10	Leo	19:46
07/28	Virgo	23:18
10/04	Libra	18:15
10/22	Scorpio	01:57
11/10	Sagittarius	04:14
12/01	Capricorn	23:47
12/20	Capricorn*	07:49

Greenwich Mean Time (GMT)
24-Hour Clock

Note: * Indicates retrograde motion.
Eastern Standard Time (EST), add 5 hrs.
Central Standard Time (CST), add 6 hrs.
Mountain Standard Time (MST), add 7 hrs.
Pacific Standard Time (PST), add 8 hrs.
Daylight Saving Time/War Time, minus 1 hr. from total.

Mercury Table for Year 1932

Date	Zodiac Sign	Time
01/14	Capricorn	12:32
02/05	Aquarius	02:24
02/23	Pisces	00:38
03/09	Aries	20:11
05/15	Taurus	22:40
06/02	Gemini	22:53
06/16	Cancer	22:18
07/02	Leo	08:08
07/27	Virgo	20:28
08/10	Virgo*	07:10
09/09	Virgo	07:05
09/26	Libra	01:03
10/13	Scorpio	15:32
11/02	Sagittarius	20:22

Mercury Table for Year 1933

Date	Zodiac Sign	Time
01/08	Capricorn	10:16
01/27	Aquarius	22:30
02/14	Pisces	04:56
03/03	Aries	10:56
03/25	Aries*	21:43
04/17	Aries	15:07
05/10	Taurus	07:28
05/25	Gemini	14:13
06/08	Cancer	14:03
06/27	Leo	01:01
09/02	Virgo	05:32
09/18	Libra	03:37
10/06	Scorpio	14:56
10/30	Sagittarius	04:33
11/16	Sagittarius*	01:55
12/12	Sagittarius	03:35

Mercury Table for Year 1934

Date	Zodiac Sign	Time
01/01	Capricorn	18:31
01/20	Aquarius	11:36
02/06	Pisces	17:16
04/15	Aries	04:05
05/02	Taurus	18:32
05/16	Gemini	23:34
06/01	Cancer	08:19
08/09	Leo	13:36
08/25	Virgo	02:10
09/10	Libra	11:24
09/30	Scorpio	14:42
12/06	Sagittarius	06:35
12/25	Capricorn	14:50

Mercury Table for Year 1935

Date	Zodiac Sign	Time
01/13	Aquarius	01:14
02/01	Pisces	11:31
02/15	Pisces*	02:46
03/18	Pisces	21:46
04/08	Aries	18:32
04/24	Taurus	12:18
05/08	Gemini	17:17
05/29	Cancer	19:33
06/20	Cancer*	17:49
07/13	Cancer	22:18
08/02	Leo	01:41
08/16	Virgo	20:32
09/03	Libra	09:29
09/28	Scorpio	16:02
10/12	Scorpio*	17:38
11/10	Scorpio	01:17
11/29	Sagittarius	06:59
12/18	Capricorn	08:21

Greenwich Mean Time (GMT)
24-Hour Clock

Note: * Indicates retrograde motion.
    Eastern Standard Time (EST), add 5 hrs.
    Central Standard Time (CST), add 6 hrs.
    Mountain Standard Time (MST), add 7 hrs.
    Pacific Standard Time (PST), add 8 hrs.
    Daylight Saving Time/War Time, minus 1 hr. from total.

Mercury Table for Year 1936

Date	Zodiac Sign	Time
01/06	Aquarius	03:31
03/13	Pisces	06:35
03/31	Aries	05:03
04/15	Taurus	01:39
05/01	Gemini	01:31
07/08	Cancer	20:38
07/23	Leo	15:32
08/07	Virgo	22:51
08/27	Libra	17:40
11/02	Scorpio	10:49
11/21	Sagittarius	00:31
12/10	Capricorn	06:31

Mercury Table for Year 1937

Date	Zodiac Sign	Time
01/01	Aquarius	17:10
01/09	Aquarius*	20:58
02/14	Aquarius	00:27
03/06	Pisces	13:59
03/23	Aries	03:35
04/07	Taurus	01:04
06/13	Gemini	22:23
07/01	Cancer	02:11
07/15	Leo	04:05
07/31	Virgo	21:01
10/08	Libra	10:02
10/26	Scorpio	01:04
11/13	Sagittarius	19:18
12/03	Capricorn	23:45

Mercury Table for Year 1938

Date	Zodiac Sign	Time
01/06	Capricorn*	21:36
01/12	Capricorn	22:27
02/08	Aquarius	13:11
02/27	Pisces	02:52
03/14	Aries	23:56
04/01	Taurus	13:38
04/23	Taurus*	13:52
05/16	Taurus	17:32
06/08	Gemini	00:25
06/22	Cancer	12:59
07/07	Leo	03:16
07/26	Virgo	22:51
09/03	Virgo*	02:51
09/10	Virgo	14:54
10/01	Libra	04:11
10/18	Scorpio	12:34
11/06	Sagittarius	23:24

Mercury Table for Year 1939

Date	Zodiac Sign	Time
01/12	Capricorn	07:44
02/01	Aquarius	17:47
02/19	Pisces	07:59
03/07	Aries	09:12
05/14	Taurus	13:36
05/31	Gemini	02:39
06/13	Cancer	22:55
06/30	Leo	06:42
09/07	Virgo	04:47
09/23	Libra	07:39
10/11	Scorpio	05:09
11/01	Sagittarius	06:54
12/03	Sagittarius*	07:55
12/13	Sagittarius	18:50

Greenwich Mean Time (GMT)
24-Hour Clock

Note: * Indicates retrograde motion.
   Eastern Standard Time (EST), add 5 hrs.
   Central Standard Time (CST), add 6 hrs.
   Mountain Standard Time (MST), add 7 hrs.
   Pacific Standard Time (PST), add 8 hrs.
   Daylight Saving Time/War Time, minus 1 hr. from total.

Mercury Table for Year 1940

Date	Zodiac Sign	Time
01/06	Capricorn	07:42
01/25	Aquarius	10:00
02/11	Pisces	13:49
03/04	Aries	11:26
03/08	Aries*	01:16
04/17	Aries	04:48
05/06	Taurus	21:05
05/21	Gemini	13:50
06/04	Cancer	22:22
06/26	Leo	14:40
07/21	Leo*	01:32
08/11	Leo	16:48
08/29	Virgo	11:00
09/14	Libra	11:25
10/03	Scorpio	12:05
12/09	Sagittarius	12:34
12/29	Capricorn	09:24

Mercury Table for Year 1941

Date	Zodiac Sign	Time
01/16	Aquarius	22:24
02/03	Pisces	13:04
03/07	Pisces*	02:37
03/16	Pisces	11:31
04/12	Aries	07:04
04/28	Taurus	22:57
05/13	Gemini	00:39
05/29	Cancer	17:29
08/06	Leo	05:45
08/21	Virgo	05:08
09/06	Libra	23:47
09/28	Scorpio	09:16
10/29	Scorpio*	20:42
11/11	Scorpio	19:45
12/02	Sagittarius	23:58
12/22	Capricorn	03:41

Mercury Table for Year 1942

Date	Zodiac Sign	Time
01/09	Aquarius	15:10
03/16	Pisces	23:57
04/05	Aries	06:49
04/20	Taurus	13:28
05/05	Gemini	04:27
07/12	Cancer	20:12
07/29	Leo	04:14
08/13	Virgo	01:39
08/31	Libra	08:21
11/07	Scorpio	01:32
11/25	Sagittarius	20:11
12/14	Capricorn	22:07

Mercury Table for Year 1943

Date	Zodiac Sign	Time
01/03	Aquarius	08:16
01/27	Aquarius*	23:51
02/15	Aquarius	18:35
03/11	Pisces	04:44
03/28	Aries	11:01
04/12	Taurus	04:44
04/30	Gemini	15:50
05/26	Gemini*	10:38
06/14	Gemini	00:29
07/06	Cancer	08:50
07/20	Leo	15:56
08/05	Virgo	10:25
08/27	Libra	00:25
09/25	Libra*	10:01
10/11	Libra	23:15
10/30	Scorpio	23:24
11/18	Sagittarius	13:23
12/08	Capricorn	01:35

Greenwich Mean Time (GMT)
24-Hour Clock

Note: * Indicates retrograde motion.
Eastern Standard Time (EST), add 5 hrs.
Central Standard Time (CST), add 6 hrs.
Mountain Standard Time (MST), add 7 hrs.
Pacific Standard Time (PST), add 8 hrs.
Daylight Saving Time/War Time, minus 1 hr. from total.

Mercury Table for Year 1944

Date	Zodiac Sign	Time
02/12	Aquarius	14:00
03/03	Pisces	02:31
03/19	Aries	07:27
04/03	Taurus	17:22
06/11	Gemini	11:25
06/27	Cancer	03:25
07/11	Leo	07:27
07/28	Virgo	23:30
10/05	Libra	03:01
10/22	Scorpio	11:19
11/10	Sagittarius	10:53
12/01	Capricorn	15:22
12/23	Capricorn*	23:18

Mercury Table for Year 1945

Date	Zodiac Sign	Time
01/14	Capricorn	02:48
02/05	Aquarius	09:02
02/23	Pisces	11:09
03/11	Aries	06:31
05/16	Taurus	15:00
06/04	Gemini	10:09
06/18	Cancer	12:13
07/03	Leo	15:25
07/26	Virgo	14:42
08/17	Virgo*	08:43
09/10	Virgo	06:59
09/27	Libra	11:54
10/15	Scorpio	00:00
11/03	Sagittarius	22:54

Mercury Table for Year 1946

Date	Zodiac Sign	Time
01/09	Capricorn	13:57
01/29	Aquarius	07:06
02/15	Pisces	15:27
03/04	Aries	09:20
04/01	Aries*	18:49
04/16	Aries	14:03
05/11	Taurus	14:10
05/27	Gemini	03:56
06/10	Cancer	01:46
06/27	Leo	18:54
09/03	Virgo	16:15
09/19	Libra	14:20
10/07	Scorpio	21:08
10/30	Sagittarius	11:19
11/20	Sagittarius*	20:13
12/12	Sagittarius	23:49

Mercury Table for Year 1947

Date	Zodiac Sign	Time
01/03	Capricorn	01:34
01/21	Aquarius	20:52
02/08	Pisces	01:20
04/16	Aries	04:16
05/04	Taurus	05:49
05/18	Gemini	13:33
06/02	Cancer	13:35
08/10	Leo	17:20
08/26	Virgo	14:38
09/11	Libra	20:39
10/01	Scorpio	15:12
12/07	Sagittarius	12:15
12/26	Capricorn	23:02

Greenwich Mean Time (GMT)
24-Hour Clock

Note: * Indicates retrograde motion.
Eastern Standard Time (EST), add 5 hrs.
Central Standard Time (CST), add 6 hrs.
Mountain Standard Time (MST), add 7 hrs.
Pacific Standard Time (PST), add 8 hrs.
Daylight Saving Time/War Time, minus 1 hr. from total.

Mercury Table for Year 1948

Date	Zodiac Sign	Time
01/14	Aquarius	09:53
02/02	Pisces	00:36
02/20	Pisces*	11:02
03/18	Pisces	08:00
04/09	Aries	02:14
04/25	Taurus	01:26
05/09	Gemini	04:29
05/28	Cancer	10:47
06/28	Cancer*	18:35
07/11	Cancer	20:27
08/02	Leo	13:38
08/17	Virgo	08:32
09/03	Libra	15:34
09/27	Scorpio	07:08
10/17	Scorpio*	03:31
11/10	Scorpio	02:04
11/29	Sagittarius	14:55
12/18	Capricorn	16:33

Mercury Table for Year 1949

Date	Zodiac Sign	Time
01/06	Aquarius	08:45
03/14	Pisces	09:40
04/01	Aries	15:50
04/16	Taurus	14:43
05/02	Gemini	02:11
07/10	Cancer	03:03
07/25	Leo	05:06
08/09	Virgo	08:53
08/28	Libra	15:38
11/03	Scorpio	18:43
11/22	Sagittarius	08:52
12/11	Capricorn	13:22

Mercury Table for Year 1950

Date	Zodiac Sign	Time
01/01	Aquarius	12:45
01/15	Aquarius*	07:21
02/14	Aquarius	18:58
03/07	Pisces	21:51
03/24	Aries	15:40
04/08	Taurus	11:05
06/14	Gemini	14:19
07/02	Cancer	14:44
07/16	Leo	17:00
08/02	Virgo	02:36
08/27	Libra	14:35
09/10	Libra*	18:52
10/09	Libra	14:25
10/27	Scorpio	10:24
11/15	Sagittarius	02:58
12/05	Capricorn	01:43

Mercury Table for Year 1951

Date	Zodiac Sign	Time
02/09	Aquarius	17:37
02/28	Pisces	12:48
03/16	Aries	11:42
04/02	Taurus	03:23
05/01	Taurus*	21:31
05/15	Taurus	01:40
06/09	Gemini	08:34
06/24	Cancer	03:04
07/08	Leo	13:35
07/27	Virgo	15:21
10/02	Libra	14:16
10/19	Scorpio	21:41
11/08	Sagittarius	04:50
12/01	Capricorn	20:45
12/12	Capricorn*	12:01

Greenwich Mean Time (GMT)
24-Hour Clock

Note: * Indicates retrograde motion.
Eastern Standard Time (EST), add 5 hrs.
Central Standard Time (CST), add 6 hrs.
Mountain Standard Time (MST), add 7 hrs.
Pacific Standard Time (PST), add 8 hrs.
Daylight Saving Time/War Time, minus 1 hr. from total.

Mercury Table for Year 1952

Date	Zodiac Sign	Time
01/13	Capricorn	06:32
02/03	Aquarius	01:28
02/20	Pisces	18:42
03/07	Aries	17:05
05/14	Taurus	14:32
05/31	Gemini	15:17
06/14	Cancer	12:15
06/30	Leo	10:26
09/07	Virgo	11:47
09/23	Libra	18:37
10/11	Scorpio	12:55
11/01	Sagittarius	05:28

Mercury Table for Year 1953

Date	Zodiac Sign	Time
01/06	Capricorn	13:13
01/25	Aquarius	19:01
02/11	Pisces	23:47
03/02	Aries	19:28
03/15	Aries*	21:10
04/17	Aries	16:36
05/08	Taurus	06:11
05/23	Gemini	03:49
06/06	Cancer	08:17
06/26	Leo	11:08
07/28	Leo*	13:49
08/11	Leo	13:41
08/30	Virgo	22:51
09/15	Libra	21:39
10/04	Scorpio	16:35
10/31	Sagittarius	16:29
11/06	Sagittarius*	21:45
12/10	Sagittarius	14:42
12/30	Capricorn	17:05

Mercury Table for Year 1954

Date	Zodiac Sign	Time
01/18	Aquarius	07:35
02/04	Pisces	17:58
04/13	Aries	11:22
04/30	Taurus	11:12
05/14	Gemini	13:48
05/30	Cancer	16:08
08/07	Leo	14:34
08/22	Virgo	17:35
09/08	Libra	08:02
09/29	Scorpio	04:05
11/04	Scorpio*	13:10
11/11	Scorpio	09:42
12/04	Sagittarius	06:56
12/23	Capricorn	12:00

Mercury Table for Year 1955

Date	Zodiac Sign	Time
01/10	Aquarius	22:57
03/17	Pisces	20:42
04/06	Aries	16:06
04/22	Taurus	02:49
05/06	Gemini	13:03
07/13	Cancer	14:30
07/30	Leo	17:15
08/14	Virgo	13:02
09/01	Libra	12:04
11/08	Scorpio	06:47
11/27	Sagittarius	04:26
12/16	Capricorn	05:58

Greenwich Mean Time (GMT)
24-Hour Clock

Note: * Indicates retrograde motion.
   Eastern Standard Time (EST), add 5 hrs.
   Central Standard Time (CST), add 6 hrs.
   Mountain Standard Time (MST), add 7 hrs.
   Pacific Standard Time (PST), add 8 hrs.
   Daylight Saving Time/War Time, minus 1 hr. from total.

Mercury Table for Year 1956

Date	Zodiac Sign	Time
01/04	Aquarius	09:12
02/02	Aquarius*	12:41
02/15	Aquarius	06:24
03/11	Pisces	10:20
03/28	Aries	22:33
04/12	Taurus	17:03
04/29	Gemini	22:40
07/06	Cancer	18:51
07/21	Leo	05:26
08/05	Virgo	18:59
08/26	Libra	13:29
09/29	Libra*	21:25
10/11	Libra	07:10
10/31	Scorpio	08:12
11/18	Sagittarius	21:35
12/08	Capricorn	07:07

Mercury Table for Year 1957

Date	Zodiac Sign	Time
02/12	Aquarius	14:23
03/04	Pisces	11:26
03/20	Aries	19:38
04/04	Taurus	23:31
06/12	Gemini	13:25
06/28	Cancer	16:56
07/12	Leo	19:32
07/30	Virgo	01:36
10/06	Libra	10:58
10/23	Scorpio	20:42
11/11	Sagittarius	17:52
12/02	Capricorn	11:20
12/28	Capricorn*	17:31

Mercury Table for Year 1958

Date	Zodiac Sign	Time
01/14	Capricorn	09:48
02/06	Aquarius	15:11
02/24	Pisces	21:35
03/12	Aries	17:22
04/02	Taurus	19:44
04/10	Taurus*	13:22
05/17	Taurus	01:46
06/05	Gemini	20:49
06/20	Cancer	02:13
07/04	Leo	23:39
07/26	Virgo	10:18
08/23	Virgo*	14:20
09/11	Virgo	01:02
09/28	Libra	22:37
10/16	Scorpio	08:44
11/05	Sagittarius	02:27

Mercury Table for Year 1959

Date	Zodiac Sign	Time
01/10	Capricorn	16:39
01/30	Aquarius	15:29
02/17	Pisces	02:06
03/05	Aries	11:50
05/12	Taurus	19:39
05/28	Gemini	17:24
06/11	Cancer	14:06
06/28	Leo	16:29
09/05	Virgo	02:18
09/21	Libra	01:08
10/09	Scorpio	03:52
10/31	Sagittarius	01:06
11/25	Sagittarius*	11:58
12/13	Sagittarius	15:25

Greenwich Mean Time (GMT)
24-Hour Clock

Note: * Indicates retrograde motion.
Eastern Standard Time (EST), add 5 hrs.
Central Standard Time (CST), add 6 hrs.
Mountain Standard Time (MST), add 7 hrs.
Pacific Standard Time (PST), add 8 hrs.
Daylight Saving Time/War Time, minus 1 hr. from total.

Mercury Table for Year 1960

Date	Zodiac Sign	Time
01/04	Capricorn	08:16
01/23	Aquarius	06:05
02/09	Pisces	10:07
04/16	Aries	02:13
05/04	Taurus	16:35
05/19	Gemini	03:16
06/02	Cancer	20:25
07/01	Leo	01:24
07/06	Leo*	01:09
08/10	Leo	17:29
08/27	Virgo	03:00
09/12	Libra	06:16
10/01	Scorpio	17:05
12/07	Sagittarius	17:14
12/27	Capricorn	07:08

Mercury Table for Year 1961

Date	Zodiac Sign	Time
01/14	Aquarius	18:45
02/01	Pisces	21:34
02/24	Pisces*	20:14
03/18	Pisces	10:02
04/10	Aries	09:08
04/26	Taurus	14:20
05/10	Gemini	16:23
05/28	Cancer	17:20
08/04	Leo	01:02
08/18	Virgo	20:41
09/04	Libra	22:20
09/27	Scorpio	12:12
10/22	Scorpio*	02:25
11/10	Scorpio	23:42
11/30	Sagittarius	22:38
12/20	Capricorn	00:49

Mercury Table for Year 1962

Date	Zodiac Sign	Time
01/07	Aquarius	14:54
03/15	Pisces	11:27
04/03	Aries	02:17
04/18	Taurus	03:56
05/03	Gemini	05:56
07/11	Cancer	07:20
07/26	Leo	18:36
08/10	Virgo	19:19
08/29	Libra	15:38
11/05	Scorpio	02:07
11/23	Sagittarius	17:14
12/12	Capricorn	20:34

Mercury Table for Year 1963

Date	Zodiac Sign	Time
01/02	Aquarius	00:57
01/20	Aquarius*	05:04
02/15	Aquarius	09:43
03/09	Pisces	05:10
03/26	Aries	03:38
04/09	Taurus	21:52
05/03	Gemini	04:59
05/10	Gemini*	20:05
06/14	Gemini	23:10
07/04	Cancer	02:48
07/18	Leo	06:08
08/03	Virgo	09:12
08/26	Libra	20:26
09/16	Libra*	20:31
10/10	Libra	16:21
10/28	Scorpio	19:39
11/16	Sagittarius	10:50
12/06	Capricorn	05:00

Greenwich Mean Time (GMT)
24-Hour Clock

Note: * Indicates retrograde motion.

Eastern Standard Time (EST), add 5 hrs.

Central Standard Time (CST), add 6 hrs.

Mountain Standard Time (MST), add 7 hrs.

Pacific Standard Time (PST), add 8 hrs.

Daylight Saving Time/War Time, minus 1 hr. from total.

Mercury Table for Year 1964

Date	Zodiac Sign	Time
02/10	Aquarius	21:12
02/29	Pisces	22:32
03/16	Aries	23:40
04/02	Taurus	00:44
06/09	Gemini	15:29
06/24	Cancer	17:04
07/09	Leo	00:25
07/27	Virgo	11:26
10/02	Libra	23:57
10/20	Scorpio	06:56
11/08	Sagittarius	10:48
11/30	Capricorn	19:20
12/16	Capricorn*	14:18

Mercury Table for Year 1965

Date	Zodiac Sign	Time
01/13	Capricorn	02:57
02/03	Aquarius	08:46
02/21	Pisces	05:22
03/09	Aries	02:06
05/15	Taurus	12:55
06/02	Gemini	03:30
06/16	Cancer	01:49
07/01	Leo	15:43
07/31	Virgo	11:47
08/03	Virgo*	07:34
09/08	Virgo	16:53
09/25	Libra	05:34
10/12	Scorpio	20:59
11/02	Sagittarius	05:51

Mercury Table for Year 1966

Date	Zodiac Sign	Time
01/07	Capricorn	18:09
01/27	Aquarius	03:54
02/13	Pisces	10:00
03/03	Aries	02:49
03/22	Aries*	02:49
04/17	Aries	21:06
05/09	Taurus	14:28
05/24	Gemini	17:43
06/07	Cancer	18:58
06/26	Leo	19:01
09/01	Virgo	10:22
09/17	Libra	08:08
10/05	Scorpio	21:49
10/30	Sagittarius	07:38
11/13	Sagittarius*	03:16
12/11	Sagittarius	15:09

Mercury Table for Year 1967

Date	Zodiac Sign	Time
01/01	Capricorn	00:34
01/19	Aquarius	16:49
02/06	Pisces	00:22
04/14	Aries	14:21
05/01	Taurus	23:10
05/16	Gemini	03:14
05/31	Cancer	17:51
08/08	Leo	21:56
08/24	Virgo	06:04
09/09	Libra	16:43
09/30	Scorpio	01:33
12/05	Sagittarius	13:29
12/24	Capricorn	20:18

Greenwich Mean Time (GMT)
24-Hour Clock

Note: * Indicates retrograde motion.
Eastern Standard Time (EST), add 5 hrs.
Central Standard Time (CST), add 6 hrs.
Mountain Standard Time (MST), add 7 hrs.
Pacific Standard Time (PST), add 8 hrs.
Daylight Saving Time/War Time, minus 1 hr. from total.

Mercury Table for Year 1968

Date	Zodiac Sign	Time
01/12	Aquarius	07:07
02/01	Pisces	13:17
02/11	Pisces*	18:27
03/17	Pisces	14:29
04/07	Aries	00:51
04/22	Taurus	16:04
05/06	Gemini	22:46
05/29	Cancer	22:29
06/13	Cancer*	22:56
07/13	Cancer	01:10
07/31	Leo	05:57
08/15	Virgo	00:38
09/01	Libra	16:49
09/28	Scorpio	14:56
10/07	Scorpio*	22:43
11/08	Scorpio	10:44
11/27	Sagittarius	12:36
12/16	Capricorn	13:58

Mercury Table for Year 1969

Date	Zodiac Sign	Time
01/04	Aquarius	12:11
03/12	Pisces	15:06
03/30	Aries	09:46
04/14	Taurus	05:43
04/30	Gemini	15:16
07/08	Cancer	03:43
07/22	Leo	19:01
08/07	Virgo	04:10
08/27	Libra	06:46
10/07	Libra*	04:31
10/09	Libra	14:31
11/01	Scorpio	16:43
11/20	Sagittarius	05:52
12/09	Capricorn	13:13

Mercury Table for Year 1970

Date	Zodiac Sign	Time
02/13	Aquarius	13:00
03/05	Pisces	19:59
03/22	Aries	07:48
04/06	Taurus	07:34
06/13	Gemini	12:32
06/30	Cancer	06:11
07/14	Leo	08:00
07/31	Virgo	05:14
10/07	Libra	17:54
10/25	Scorpio	06:06
11/13	Sagittarius	01:08
12/03	Capricorn	10:13

Mercury Table for Year 1971

Date	Zodiac Sign	Time
01/02	Capricorn*	23:22
01/14	Capricorn	02:09
02/07	Aquarius	20:46
02/26	Pisces	07:49
03/14	Aries	04:39
04/01	Taurus	14:37
04/18	Taurus*	21:36
05/17	Taurus	03:28
06/07	Gemini	06:37
06/21	Cancer	16:18
07/06	Leo	08:51
07/26	Virgo	17:07
08/29	Virgo*	20:41
09/11	Virgo	06:15
09/30	Libra	09:10
10/17	Scorpio	17:38
11/06	Sagittarius	06:49

Greenwich Mean Time (GMT)
24-Hour Clock

Note: * Indicates retrograde motion.
Eastern Standard Time (EST), add 5 hrs.
Central Standard Time (CST), add 6 hrs.
Mountain Standard Time (MST), add 7 hrs.
Pacific Standard Time (PST), add 8 hrs.
Daylight Saving Time/War Time, minus 1 hr. from total.

Mercury Table for Year 1972

Date	Zodiac Sign	Time
01/11	Capricorn	18:09
01/31	Aquarius	23:39
02/18	Pisces	12:46
03/05	Aries	16:58
05/12	Taurus	23:42
05/29	Gemini	06:37
06/12	Cancer	02:49
06/28	Leo	16:51
09/05	Virgo	11:25
09/21	Libra	12:04
10/09	Scorpio	11:03
10/30	Sagittarius	19:21
11/29	Sagittarius*	07:21
12/12	Sagittarius	23:18

Mercury Table for Year 1973

Date	Zodiac Sign	Time
01/04	Capricorn	14:34
01/23	Aquarius	15:15
02/09	Pisces	19:26
04/16	Aries	21:14
05/06	Taurus	02:48
05/20	Gemini	17:15
06/04	Cancer	04:38
06/27	Leo	06:49
07/16	Leo*	07:50
08/11	Leo	12:03
08/28	Virgo	15:14
09/13	Libra	16:09
10/02	Scorpio	20:07
12/08	Sagittarius	21:21
12/28	Capricorn	15:06

Mercury Table for Year 1974

Date	Zodiac Sign	Time
01/16	Aquarius	03:46
02/02	Pisces	22:38
03/02	Pisces*	17:51
03/17	Pisces	19:59
04/11	Aries	15:11
04/28	Taurus	03:04
05/12	Gemini	04:49
05/29	Cancer	08:13
08/05	Leo	11:34
08/20	Virgo	09:01
09/06	Libra	05:45
09/28	Scorpio	00:22
10/26	Scorpio*	23:12
11/11	Scorpio	15:49
12/02	Sagittarius	06:08
12/21	Capricorn	09:07

Mercury Table for Year 1975

Date	Zodiac Sign	Time
01/08	Aquarius	21:47
03/16	Pisces	11:40
04/04	Aries	12:17
04/19	Taurus	17:13
05/04	Gemini	11:55
07/12	Cancer	08:50
07/28	Leo	07:58
08/12	Virgo	06:09
08/30	Libra	17:17
11/06	Scorpio	08:51
11/25	Sagittarius	01:35
12/14	Capricorn	04:02

Greenwich Mean Time (GMT)
24-Hour Clock

Note: * Indicates retrograde motion.

Eastern Standard Time (EST), add 5 hrs.

Central Standard Time (CST), add 6 hrs.

Mountain Standard Time (MST), add 7 hrs.

Pacific Standard Time (PST), add 8 hrs.

Daylight Saving Time/War Time, minus 1 hr. from total.

Mercury Table for Year 1976

Date	Zodiac Sign	Time
01/02	Aquarius	20:19
01/25	Aquarius*	01:34
02/15	Aquarius	18:50
03/09	Pisces	11:53
03/26	Aries	15:25
04/10	Taurus	09:25
04/29	Gemini	23:11
05/19	Gemini*	19:18
06/13	Gemini	19:07
07/04	Cancer	14:09
07/18	Leo	19:27
08/03	Virgo	16:38
08/25	Libra	20:49
09/21	Libra*	07:15
10/10	Libra	14:26
10/29	Scorpio	04:47
11/16	Sagittarius	18:51
12/06	Capricorn	09:17

Mercury Table for Year 1977

Date	Zodiac Sign	Time
02/10	Aquarius	23:45
03/02	Pisces	07:57
03/18	Aries	11:44
04/03	Taurus	02:39
06/10	Gemini	20:53
06/26	Cancer	06:57
07/10	Leo	11:52
07/28	Virgo	10:15
10/04	Libra	09:07
10/21	Scorpio	16:16
11/09	Sagittarius	17:11
12/01	Capricorn	06:42
12/21	Capricorn*	07:09

Mercury Table for Year 1978

Date	Zodiac Sign	Time
01/13	Capricorn	19:58
02/04	Aquarius	15:41
02/22	Pisces	15:57
03/10	Aries	11:59
05/16	Taurus	08:01
06/03	Gemini	15:09
06/17	Cancer	15:37
07/02	Leo	22:17
07/27	Virgo	06:14
08/13	Virgo*	06:38
09/09	Virgo	19:11
09/26	Libra	16:30
10/14	Scorpio	05:20
11/03	Sagittarius	07:40

Mercury Table for Year 1979

Date	Zodiac Sign	Time
01/08	Capricorn	22:22
01/28	Aquarius	12:36
02/14	Pisces	20:25
03/03	Aries	21:27
03/28	Aries*	10:50
04/17	Aries	12:20
05/10	Taurus	21:51
05/26	Gemini	07:30
06/09	Cancer	06:23
06/27	Leo	09:47
09/02	Virgo	21:27
09/18	Libra	18:46
10/07	Scorpio	03:42
10/30	Sagittarius	07:03
11/18	Sagittarius*	03:05
12/12	Sagittarius	13:14

Greenwich Mean Time (GMT)
24-Hour Clock

Note: * Indicates retrograde motion.
Eastern Standard Time (EST), add 5 hrs.
Central Standard Time (CST), add 6 hrs.
Mountain Standard Time (MST), add 7 hrs.
Pacific Standard Time (PST), add 8 hrs.
Daylight Saving Time/War Time, minus 1 hr. from total.

Mercury Table for Year 1980

Date	Zodiac Sign	Time
01/02	Capricorn	07:47
01/21	Aquarius	02:05
02/07	Pisces	07:54
04/14	Aries	15:43
05/02	Taurus	10:39
05/16	Gemini	16:54
05/31	Cancer	21:53
08/09	Leo	03:12
08/24	Virgo	18:34
09/10	Libra	01:46
09/30	Scorpio	01:03
12/05	Sagittarius	19:32
12/25	Capricorn	04:33

Mercury Table for Year 1981

Date	Zodiac Sign	Time
01/12	Aquarius	15:36
01/31	Pisces	17:34
02/16	Pisces*	07:55
03/18	Pisces	04:16
04/08	Aries	08:55
04/24	Taurus	05:15
05/08	Gemini	09:32
05/28	Cancer	16:47
06/22	Cancer*	23:41
07/12	Cancer	20:31
08/01	Leo	18:14
08/16	Virgo	12:33
09/02	Libra	22:25
09/27	Scorpio	10:53
10/14	Scorpio*	02:12
11/09	Scorpio	12:56
11/28	Sagittarius	20:38
12/17	Capricorn	22:05

Mercury Table for Year 1982

Date	Zodiac Sign	Time
01/05	Aquarius	16:39
03/13	Pisces	18:53
03/31	Aries	20:45
04/15	Taurus	18:39
05/01	Gemini	13:25
07/09	Cancer	11:07
07/24	Leo	08:37
08/08	Virgo	13:55
08/28	Libra	03:11
11/03	Scorpio	00:55
11/21	Sagittarius	14:13
12/10	Capricorn	19:48

Mercury Table for Year 1983

Date	Zodiac Sign	Time
01/01	Aquarius	13:39
01/12	Aquarius*	06:37
02/14	Aquarius	09:19
03/07	Pisces	04:06
03/23	Aries	19:54
04/07	Taurus	16:52
06/14	Gemini	07:48
07/01	Cancer	19:02
07/15	Leo	20:45
08/01	Virgo	10:10
08/29	Libra	05:49
09/06	Libra*	02:47
10/08	Libra	23:28
10/26	Scorpio	15:30
11/14	Sagittarius	08:40
12/04	Capricorn	11:10

Greenwich Mean Time (GMT)
24-Hour Clock

Note: * Indicates retrograde motion.
Eastern Standard Time (EST), add 5 hrs.
Central Standard Time (CST), add 6 hrs.
Mountain Standard Time (MST), add 7 hrs.
Pacific Standard Time (PST), add 8 hrs.
Daylight Saving Time/War Time, minus 1 hr. from total.

Mercury Table for Year 1984

Date	Zodiac Sign	Time
02/09	Aquarius	01:40
02/27	Pisces	17:53
03/14	Aries	16:15
03/31	Taurus	20:22
04/25	Taurus*	12:02
05/15	Taurus	12:03
06/07	Gemini	15:28
06/22	Cancer	06:24
07/06	Leo	18:45
07/26	Virgo	06:35
09/30	Libra	19:27
10/18	Scorpio	02:42
11/06	Sagittarius	11:52
12/01	Capricorn	16:45
12/07	Capricorn*	21:37

Mercury Table for Year 1985

Date	Zodiac Sign	Time
01/11	Capricorn	18:06
02/01	Aquarius	07:29
02/18	Pisces	23:29
03/06	Aries	23:56
05/14	Taurus	01:55
05/30	Gemini	19:29
06/13	Cancer	15:58
06/29	Leo	19:25
09/06	Virgo	19:23
09/22	Libra	23:01
10/10	Scorpio	18:36
10/31	Sagittarius	16:32
12/04	Sagittarius*	20:03
12/12	Sagittarius	10:11

Mercury Table for Year 1986

Date	Zodiac Sign	Time
01/05	Capricorn	20:26
01/25	Aquarius	00:19
02/11	Pisces	05:09
03/03	Aries	07:38
03/11	Aries*	17:14
04/17	Aries	12:18
05/07	Taurus	12:19
05/22	Gemini	07:14
06/05	Cancer	13:58
06/26	Leo	14:13
07/23	Leo*	21:59
08/11	Leo	20:53
08/30	Virgo	03:16
09/15	Libra	02:17
10/04	Scorpio	00:06
12/10	Sagittarius	00:21
12/29	Capricorn	22:55

Mercury Table for Year 1987

Date	Zodiac Sign	Time
01/17	Aquarius	12:53
02/04	Pisces	02:23
03/11	Pisces*	23:05
03/13	Pisces	17:31
04/12	Aries	20:13
04/29	Taurus	15:29
05/13	Gemini	17:44
05/30	Cancer	04:22
08/06	Leo	21:10
08/21	Virgo	21:25
09/07	Libra	13:43
09/28	Scorpio	17:14
11/01	Scorpio*	02:09
11/11	Scorpio	21:30
12/03	Sagittarius	13:20
12/22	Capricorn	17:27

Greenwich Mean Time (GMT)
24-Hour Clock

Note: * Indicates retrograde motion.
   Eastern Standard Time (EST), add 5 hrs.
   Central Standard Time (CST), add 6 hrs.
   Mountain Standard Time (MST), add 7 hrs.
   Pacific Standard Time (PST), add 8 hrs.
   Daylight Saving Time/War Time, minus 1 hr. from total.

Mercury Table for Year 1988

Date	Zodiac Sign	Time
01/10	Aquarius	05:15
03/16	Pisces	09:56
04/04	Aries	21:52
04/20	Taurus	06:32
05/04	Gemini	19:35
07/12	Cancer	06:29
07/28	Leo	21:09
08/12	Virgo	17:21
08/30	Libra	20:17
11/06	Scorpio	14:45
11/25	Sagittarius	09:54
12/14	Capricorn	11:45

Mercury Table for Year 1989

Date	Zodiac Sign	Time
01/02	Aquarius	19:35
01/29	Aquarius*	04:16
02/14	Aquarius	17:58
03/10	Pisces	17:57
03/28	Aries	03:03
04/11	Taurus	21:26
04/29	Gemini	19:47
05/28	Gemini*	23:20
06/12	Gemini	08:24
07/06	Cancer	00:46
07/20	Leo	08:55
08/05	Virgo	00:47
08/26	Libra	06:11
09/26	Libra*	15:32
10/11	Libra	05:53
10/30	Scorpio	13:44
11/18	Sagittarius	02:59
12/07	Capricorn	14:22

Mercury Table for Year 1990

Date	Zodiac Sign	Time
02/12	Aquarius	01:02
03/03	Pisces	17:04
03/19	Aries	23:53
04/04	Taurus	07:33
06/12	Gemini	00:21
06/27	Cancer	20:38
07/11	Leo	23:42
07/29	Virgo	11:14
10/05	Libra	17:37
10/23	Scorpio	01:39
11/10	Sagittarius	23:57
12/02	Capricorn	00:07
12/25	Capricorn*	22:50

Mercury Table for Year 1991

Date	Zodiac Sign	Time
01/14	Capricorn	07:48
02/05	Aquarius	22:10
02/24	Pisces	02:26
03/11	Aries	22:30
05/16	Taurus	22:41
06/05	Gemini	02:14
06/19	Cancer	05:34
07/04	Leo	06:01
07/26	Virgo	13:14
08/19	Virgo*	21:24
09/10	Virgo	17:02
09/28	Libra	03:19
10/15	Scorpio	13:57
11/04	Sagittarius	10:37

Greenwich Mean Time (GMT)
24-Hour Clock

Note: * Indicates retrograde motion.
   Eastern Standard Time (EST), add 5 hrs.
   Central Standard Time (CST), add 6 hrs.
   Mountain Standard Time (MST), add 7 hrs.
   Pacific Standard Time (PST), add 8 hrs.
   Daylight Saving Time/War Time, minus 1 hr. from total.

Mercury Table for Year 1992

Date	Zodiac Sign	Time
01/10	Capricorn	01:42
01/29	Aquarius	21:07
02/16	Pisces	06:57
03/03	Aries	21:43
04/03	Aries*	23:36
04/14	Aries	17:20
05/11	Taurus	04:04
05/26	Gemini	21:07
06/09	Cancer	18:22
06/27	Leo	05:07
09/03	Virgo	07:55
09/19	Libra	05:33
10/07	Scorpio	10:09
10/29	Sagittarius	17:07
11/21	Sagittarius*	19:38
12/12	Sagittarius	07:55

Mercury Table for Year 1993

Date	Zodiac Sign	Time
01/02	Capricorn	14:42
01/21	Aquarius	11:18
02/07	Pisces	16:15
04/15	Aries	15:08
05/03	Taurus	21:45
05/18	Gemini	06:44
06/02	Cancer	03:50
08/10	Leo	05:37
08/26	Virgo	07:01
09/11	Libra	11:13
10/01	Scorpio	02:08
12/07	Sagittarius	00:59
12/26	Capricorn	12:42

Mercury Table for Year 1994

Date	Zodiac Sign	Time
01/14	Aquarius	00:20
02/01	Pisces	10:33
02/21	Pisces*	15:08
03/18	Pisces	11:54
04/09	Aries	16:19
04/25	Taurus	18:16
05/09	Gemini	21:00
05/28	Cancer	14:54
07/02	Cancer*	23:37
07/10	Cancer	11:51
08/03	Leo	05:59
08/18	Virgo	00:37
09/04	Libra	04:49
09/27	Scorpio	08:54
10/19	Scorpio*	06:07
11/10	Scorpio	12:36
11/30	Sagittarius	04:30
12/19	Capricorn	06:18

Mercury Table for Year 1995

Date	Zodiac Sign	Time
01/06	Aquarius	22:13
03/14	Pisces	21:31
04/02	Aries	07:21
04/17	Taurus	07:46
05/02	Gemini	15:20
07/10	Cancer	16:47
07/25	Leo	22:10
08/10	Virgo	00:05
08/29	Libra	02:00
11/04	Scorpio	08:39
11/22	Sagittarius	22:35
12/12	Capricorn	02:46

Greenwich Mean Time (GMT)
24-Hour Clock

Note: * Indicates retrograde motion.
  Eastern Standard Time (EST), add 5 hrs.
  Central Standard Time (CST), add 6 hrs.
  Mountain Standard Time (MST), add 7 hrs.
  Pacific Standard Time (PST), add 8 hrs.
  Daylight Saving Time/War Time, minus 1 hr. from total.

473

Mercury Table for Year 1996

Date	Zodiac Sign	Time
01/01	Aquarius	18:12
01/17	Aquarius*	09:20
02/15	Aquarius	02:38
03/07	Pisces	11:44
03/24	Aries	07:54
04/08	Taurus	03:10
06/13	Gemini	21:35
07/02	Cancer	07:24
07/16	Leo	09:47
08/01	Virgo	16:09
08/26	Libra	05:20
09/12	Libra*	09:18
10/09	Libra	02:59
10/27	Scorpio	00:49
11/14	Sagittarius	16:25
12/04	Capricorn	13:39

Mercury Table for Year 1997

Date	Zodiac Sign	Time
02/09	Aquarius	05:46
02/28	Pisces	03:44
03/16	Aries	04:05
04/01	Taurus	13:47
05/05	Taurus*	02:15
05/12	Taurus	09:38
06/08	Gemini	23:15
06/23	Cancer	20:27
07/08	Leo	05:18
07/27	Virgo	00:28
10/02	Libra	05:25
10/19	Scorpio	11:55
11/07	Sagittarius	17:30
11/30	Capricorn	19:05
12/13	Capricorn*	17:53

Mercury Table for Year 1998

Date	Zodiac Sign	Time
01/12	Capricorn	16:03
02/02	Aquarius	15:01
02/20	Pisces	10:07
03/08	Aries	08:22
05/15	Taurus	01:59
06/01	Gemini	07:57
06/15	Cancer	05:24
06/30	Leo	23:45
09/08	Virgo	01:46
09/24	Libra	10:02
10/12	Scorpio	02:30
11/01	Sagittarius	15:52

Mercury Table for Year 1999

Date	Zodiac Sign	Time
01/07	Capricorn	01:45
01/26	Aquarius	09:15
02/12	Pisces	15:11
03/02	Aries	22:38
03/18	Aries*	09:29
04/17	Aries	21:53
05/08	Taurus	21:09
05/23	Gemini	21:12
06/07	Cancer	00:08
06/26	Leo	15:40
07/31	Leo*	19:13
08/11	Leo	03:52
08/31	Virgo	15:01
09/16	Libra	12:41
10/05	Scorpio	04:57
10/30	Sagittarius	19:56
11/09	Sagittarius*	20:01
12/11	Sagittarius	01:55
12/31	Capricorn	06:31

Greenwich Mean Time (GMT)
24-Hour Clock

Note: * Indicates retrograde motion.
Eastern Standard Time (EST), add 5 hrs.
Central Standard Time (CST), add 6 hrs.
Mountain Standard Time (MST), add 7 hrs.
Pacific Standard Time (PST), add 8 hrs.
Daylight Saving Time/War Time, minus 1 hr. from total.

Mercury Table for Year 2000

Date	Zodiac Sign	Time
01/18	Aquarius	22:05
02/05	Pisces	07:57
04/13	Aries	00:04
04/30	Taurus	03:38
05/14	Gemini	06:59
05/30	Cancer	04:17
08/07	Leo	05:26
08/22	Virgo	09:56
09/07	Libra	22:08
09/28	Scorpio	13:13
11/07	Scorpio*	13:19
11/08	Scorpio	16:16
12/03	Sagittarius	20:10
12/23	Capricorn	01:45

Greenwich Mean Time (GMT)
24-Hour Clock

Note: * Indicates retrograde motion.
Eastern Standard Time (EST), add 5 hrs.
Central Standard Time (CST), add 6 hrs.
Mountain Standard Time (MST), add 7 hrs.
Pacific Standard Time (PST), add 8 hrs.
Daylight Saving Time/War Time, minus 1 hr. from total.

Venus Table for Year 1900

Date	Zodiac Sign	Time
01/20	Pisces	01:32
02/13	Aries	14:06
03/10	Taurus	18:09
04/06	Gemini	04:18
05/05	Cancer	15:54
09/08	Leo	20:46
10/08	Virgo	13:26
11/03	Libra	21:24
11/28	Scorpio	21:50
12/23	Sagittarius	07:44

Venus Table for Year 1901

Date	Zodiac Sign	Time
01/16	Capricorn	11:24
02/09	Aquarius	13:02
03/05	Pisces	14:46
03/29	Aries	17:58
04/22	Taurus	23:25
05/17	Gemini	07:21
06/10	Cancer	17:23
07/05	Leo	05:09
07/29	Virgo	19:02
08/23	Libra	12:24
09/17	Scorpio	11:20
10/12	Sagittarius	19:06
11/07	Capricorn	19:18
12/05	Aquarius	13:28

Venus Table for Year 1902

Date	Zodiac Sign	Time
01/11	Pisces	17:57
02/06	Pisces*	22:59
04/04	Pisces	19:27
05/07	Aries	07:01
06/03	Taurus	23:52
06/30	Gemini	06:19
07/25	Cancer	18:50
08/19	Leo	18:19
09/13	Virgo	07:11
10/07	Libra	11:59
10/31	Scorpio	11:40
11/24	Sagittarius	08:51
12/18	Capricorn	05:16

Venus Table for Year 1903

Date	Zodiac Sign	Time
01/11	Aquarius	02:02
02/04	Pisces	00:31
02/28	Aries	02:48
03/24	Taurus	11:39
04/18	Gemini	06:31
05/13	Cancer	16:17
06/09	Leo	03:06
07/07	Virgo	20:40
08/17	Libra	21:57
09/06	Libra*	01:43
11/08	Libra	14:29
12/09	Scorpio	14:29

Greenwich Mean Time (GMT)
24-Hour Clock

Note: * Indicates retrograde motion.
Eastern Standard Time (EST), add 5 hrs.
Central Standard Time (CST), add 6 hrs.
Mountain Standard Time (MST), add 7 hrs.
Pacific Standard Time (PST), add 8 hrs.
Daylight Saving Time/War Time, minus 1 hr. from total.

Venus Table for Year 1904

Date	Zodiac Sign	Time
01/05	Sagittarius	03:29
01/30	Capricorn	09:16
02/24	Aquarius	02:57
03/19	Pisces	15:51
04/13	Aries	03:15
05/07	Taurus	14:39
06/01	Gemini	02:14
06/25	Cancer	13:14
07/19	Leo	22:45
08/13	Virgo	06:35
09/06	Libra	13:31
09/30	Scorpio	20:45
10/25	Sagittarius	05:21
11/18	Capricorn	16:27
12/13	Aquarius	08:57

Venus Table for Year 1905

Date	Zodiac Sign	Time
01/07	Pisces	14:27
02/03	Aries	04:36
03/06	Taurus	05:10
05/09	Taurus*	11:20
05/28	Taurus	10:10
07/08	Gemini	11:47
08/06	Cancer	08:05
09/01	Leo	20:03
09/27	Virgo	03:47
10/21	Libra	18:15
11/14	Scorpio	22:24
12/08	Sagittarius	21:17

Venus Table for Year 1906

Date	Zodiac Sign	Time
01/01	Capricorn	18:09
01/25	Aquarius	14:55
02/18	Pisces	12:52
03/14	Aries	13:18
04/07	Taurus	17:36
05/02	Gemini	02:51
05/26	Cancer	17:56
06/20	Leo	16:16
07/16	Virgo	01:02
08/11	Libra	03:08
09/07	Scorpio	15:23
10/09	Sagittarius	10:21
12/15	Sagittarius*	12:42
12/25	Sagittarius	23:09

Venus Table for Year 1907

Date	Zodiac Sign	Time
02/06	Capricorn	16:09
03/06	Aquarius	20:26
04/02	Pisces	01:09
04/27	Aries	12:10
05/22	Taurus	15:02
06/16	Gemini	12:59
07/11	Cancer	06:26
08/04	Leo	18:50
08/29	Virgo	02:10
09/22	Libra	05:31
10/16	Scorpio	06:33
11/09	Sagittarius	06:44
12/03	Capricorn	07:01
12/27	Aquarius	08:29

Greenwich Mean Time (GMT)
24-Hour Clock

Note: * Indicates retrograde motion.
Eastern Standard Time (EST), add 5 hrs.
Central Standard Time (CST), add 6 hrs.
Mountain Standard Time (MST), add 7 hrs.
Pacific Standard Time (PST), add 8 hrs.
Daylight Saving Time/War Time, minus 1 hr. from total.

Venus Table for Year 1908

Date	Zodiac Sign	Time
01/20	Pisces	13:31
02/14	Aries	02:40
03/10	Taurus	07:54
04/05	Gemini	20:45
05/05	Cancer	17:34
09/08	Leo	22:12
10/08	Virgo	05:55
11/03	Libra	11:13
11/28	Scorpio	10:28
12/22	Sagittarius	19:45

Venus Table for Year 1909

Date	Zodiac Sign	Time
01/15	Capricorn	23:02
02/09	Aquarius	00:23
03/05	Pisces	01:55
03/29	Aries	04:55
04/22	Taurus	10:15
05/16	Gemini	18:08
06/10	Cancer	04:13
07/04	Leo	16:09
07/29	Virgo	06:22
08/23	Libra	00:16
09/17	Scorpio	00:04
10/12	Sagittarius	09:13
11/07	Capricorn	11:58
12/05	Aquarius	12:48

Venus Table for Year 1910

Date	Zodiac Sign	Time
01/15	Pisces	20:25
01/29	Pisces*	10:03
04/05	Pisces	09:26
05/07	Aries	02:10
06/03	Taurus	14:40
06/29	Gemini	19:14
07/25	Cancer	06:45
08/19	Leo	05:42
09/12	Virgo	18:16
10/06	Libra	22:57
10/30	Scorpio	22:37
11/23	Sagittarius	19:51
12/17	Capricorn	16:19

Venus Table for Year 1911

Date	Zodiac Sign	Time
01/10	Aquarius	13:09
02/03	Pisces	11:43
02/27	Aries	14:08
03/23	Taurus	23:16
04/17	Gemini	18:41
05/13	Cancer	05:32
06/08	Leo	18:43
07/07	Virgo	19:04
11/09	Libra	00:39
12/09	Scorpio	09:09

Greenwich Mean Time (GMT)
24-Hour Clock

Note: * Indicates retrograde motion.
Eastern Standard Time (EST), add 5 hrs.
Central Standard Time (CST), add 6 hrs.
Mountain Standard Time (MST), add 7 hrs.
Pacific Standard Time (PST), add 8 hrs.
Daylight Saving Time/War Time, minus 1 hr. from total.

Venus Table for Year 1912

Date	Zodiac Sign	Time
01/04	Sagittarius	18:27
01/29	Capricorn	22:36
02/23	Aquarius	15:21
03/19	Pisces	03:39
04/12	Aries	14:37
05/07	Taurus	01:42
05/31	Gemini	13:04
06/24	Cancer	23:58
07/19	Leo	09:29
08/12	Virgo	17:25
09/06	Libra	00:34
09/30	Scorpio	08:08
10/24	Sagittarius	17:10
11/18	Capricorn	04:52
12/12	Aquarius	22:15

Venus Table for Year 1913

Date	Zodiac Sign	Time
01/07	Pisces	05:21
02/02	Aries	23:17
03/06	Taurus	17:07
05/02	Taurus*	05:34
05/31	Taurus	09:21
07/08	Gemini	09:09
08/05	Cancer	23:25
09/01	Leo	09:11
09/26	Virgo	15:54
10/21	Libra	05:51
11/14	Scorpio	09:44
12/08	Sagittarius	08:29

Venus Table for Year 1914

Date	Zodiac Sign	Time
01/01	Capricorn	05:16
01/25	Aquarius	01:58
02/17	Pisces	23:51
03/14	Aries	00:16
04/07	Taurus	04:35
05/01	Gemini	13:57
05/26	Cancer	05:20
06/20	Leo	04:14
07/15	Virgo	14:03
08/10	Libra	18:09
09/07	Scorpio	11:00
10/10	Sagittarius	01:50
12/05	Sagittarius*	23:37
12/30	Sagittarius	22:58

Venus Table for Year 1915

Date	Zodiac Sign	Time
02/06	Capricorn	15:46
03/06	Aquarius	13:05
04/01	Pisces	15:10
04/27	Aries	00:50
05/22	Taurus	02:53
06/16	Gemini	00:18
07/10	Cancer	17:25
08/04	Leo	05:39
08/28	Virgo	12:56
09/21	Libra	16:20
10/15	Scorpio	17:31
11/08	Sagittarius	17:53
12/02	Capricorn	18:23
12/26	Aquarius	20:07

Greenwich Mean Time (GMT)
24-Hour Clock

Note: * Indicates retrograde motion.
Eastern Standard Time (EST), add 5 hrs.
Central Standard Time (CST), add 6 hrs.
Mountain Standard Time (MST), add 7 hrs.
Pacific Standard Time (PST), add 8 hrs.
Daylight Saving Time/War Time, minus 1 hr. from total.

Venus Table for Year 1916

Date	Zodiac Sign	Time
01/20	Pisces	01:31
02/13	Aries	15:19
03/09	Taurus	21:47
04/05	Gemini	13:32
05/05	Cancer	20:44
09/08	Leo	22:23
10/07	Virgo	22:06
11/03	Libra	00:54
11/27	Scorpio	23:02
12/22	Sagittarius	07:44

Venus Table for Year 191

Date	Zodiac Sign	Time
01/15	Capricorn	10:39
02/08	Aquarius	11:44
03/04	Pisces	13:02
03/28	Aries	15:53
04/21	Taurus	21:06
05/16	Gemini	04:55
06/09	Cancer	15:03
07/04	Leo	03:09
07/28	Virgo	17:43
08/22	Libra	12:12
09/16	Scorpio	12:53
10/11	Sagittarius	23:28
11/07	Capricorn	04:58
12/05	Aquarius	13:14

Venus Table for Year 1918

Date	Zodiac Sign	Time
04/05	Pisces	19:57
05/06	Aries	20:48
06/03	Taurus	05:17
06/29	Gemini	08:04
07/24	Cancer	18:38
08/18	Leo	17:03
09/12	Virgo	05:21
10/06	Libra	09:54
10/30	Scorpio	09:34
11/23	Sagittarius	06:50
12/17	Capricorn	03:22

Venus Table for Year 191

Date	Zodiac Sign	Time
01/10	Aquarius	00:17
02/02	Pisces	22:56
02/27	Aries	01:30
03/23	Taurus	10:56
04/17	Gemini	06:54
05/12	Cancer	18:55
06/08	Leo	10:36
07/07	Virgo	18:26
11/09	Libra	07:59
12/09	Scorpio	03:22

Greenwich Mean Time (GMT)
24-Hour Clock

Note: * Indicates retrograde motion.
Eastern Standard Time (EST), add 5 hrs.
Central Standard Time (CST), add 6 hrs.
Mountain Standard Time (MST), add 7 hrs.
Pacific Standard Time (PST), add 8 hrs.
Daylight Saving Time/War Time, minus 1 hr. from total.

Venus Table for Year 1920

Date	Zodiac Sign	Time
01/04	Sagittarius	09:13
01/29	Capricorn	11:49
02/23	Aquarius	03:42
03/18	Pisces	15:24
04/12	Aries	01:58
05/06	Taurus	12:45
05/30	Gemini	23:54
06/24	Cancer	10:42
07/18	Leo	20:12
08/12	Virgo	04:16
09/05	Libra	11:38
09/29	Scorpio	19:32
10/24	Sagittarius	05:02
11/17	Capricorn	17:21
12/12	Aquarius	11:39

Venus Table for Year 1921

Date	Zodiac Sign	Time
01/06	Pisces	20:27
02/02	Aries	18:31
03/07	Taurus	09:14
04/26	Taurus*	00:13
06/02	Taurus	03:59
07/08	Gemini	05:48
08/05	Cancer	14:32
08/31	Leo	22:13
09/26	Virgo	03:57
10/20	Libra	17:25
11/13	Scorpio	21:03
12/07	Sagittarius	19:40
12/31	Capricorn	16:23

Venus Table for Year 1922

Date	Zodiac Sign	Time
01/24	Aquarius	13:01
02/17	Pisces	10:51
03/13	Aries	11:14
04/06	Taurus	15:34
05/01	Gemini	01:05
05/25	Cancer	16:46
06/19	Leo	16:16
07/15	Virgo	03:10
08/10	Libra	09:22
09/07	Scorpio	07:13
10/10	Sagittarius	22:33
11/28	Sagittarius*	21:21

Venus Table for Year 1923

Date	Zodiac Sign	Time
01/02	Sagittarius	07:15
02/06	Capricorn	14:24
03/06	Aquarius	05:26
04/01	Pisces	05:04
04/26	Aries	13:26
05/21	Taurus	14:41
06/15	Gemini	11:35
07/10	Cancer	04:23
08/03	Leo	16:27
08/27	Virgo	23:42
09/21	Libra	03:10
10/15	Scorpio	04:29
11/08	Sagittarius	05:02
12/02	Capricorn	05:46
12/26	Aquarius	07:47

Greenwich Mean Time (GMT)
24-Hour Clock

Note: * Indicates retrograde motion.
Eastern Standard Time (EST), add 5 hrs.
Central Standard Time (CST), add 6 hrs.
Mountain Standard Time (MST), add 7 hrs.
Pacific Standard Time (PST), add 8 hrs.
Daylight Saving Time/War Time, minus 1 hr. from total.

Venus Table for Year 1924

Date	Zodiac Sign	Time
01/19	Pisces	13:34
02/13	Aries	04:02
03/09	Taurus	11:48
04/05	Gemini	06:40
05/06	Cancer	01:43
09/08	Leo	21:28
10/07	Virgo	13:59
11/02	Libra	14:27
11/27	Scorpio	11:32
12/21	Sagittarius	19:40

Venus Table for Year 1925

Date	Zodiac Sign	Time
01/14	Capricorn	22:14
02/07	Aquarius	23:03
03/04	Pisces	00:10
03/28	Aries	02:50
04/21	Taurus	07:56
05/15	Gemini	15:43
06/09	Cancer	01:53
07/03	Leo	14:11
07/28	Virgo	05:06
08/22	Libra	00:10
09/16	Scorpio	01:46
10/11	Sagittarius	13:52
11/06	Capricorn	22:18
12/05	Aquarius	14:55

Venus Table for Year 1926

Date	Zodiac Sign	Time
04/06	Pisces	03:40
05/06	Aries	14:58
06/02	Taurus	19:44
06/28	Gemini	20:49
07/24	Cancer	06:28
08/18	Leo	04:22
09/11	Virgo	16:24
10/05	Libra	20:51
10/29	Scorpio	20:31
11/22	Sagittarius	17:50
12/16	Capricorn	14:26

Venus Table for Year 1927

Date	Zodiac Sign	Time
01/09	Aquarius	11:25
02/02	Pisces	10:10
02/26	Aries	12:53
03/22	Taurus	22:37
04/16	Gemini	19:11
05/12	Cancer	08:24
06/08	Leo	02:45
07/07	Virgo	18:54
11/09	Libra	13:07
12/08	Scorpio	21:08

Greenwich Mean Time (GMT)
24-Hour Clock

Note: * Indicates retrograde motion.
Eastern Standard Time (EST), add 5 hrs.
Central Standard Time (CST), add 6 hrs.
Mountain Standard Time (MST), add 7 hrs.
Pacific Standard Time (PST), add 8 hrs.
Daylight Saving Time/War Time, minus 1 hr. from total.

Venus Table for Year 1928

Date	Zodiac Sign	Time
01/03	Sagittarius	23:49
01/29	Capricorn	00:57
02/22	Aquarius	15:59
03/18	Pisces	03:08
04/11	Aries	13:17
05/05	Taurus	23:46
05/30	Gemini	10:44
06/23	Cancer	21:25
07/18	Leo	06:56
08/11	Virgo	15:07
09/04	Libra	22:43
09/29	Scorpio	06:58
10/23	Sagittarius	16:55
11/17	Capricorn	05:53
12/12	Aquarius	01:10

Venus Table for Year 1929

Date	Zodiac Sign	Time
01/06	Pisces	11:46
02/02	Aries	14:19
03/08	Taurus	07:05
04/20	Taurus*	02:26
06/03	Taurus	09:15
07/08	Gemini	01:47
08/05	Cancer	05:26
08/31	Leo	11:09
09/25	Virgo	15:58
10/20	Libra	04:56
11/13	Scorpio	08:21
12/07	Sagittarius	06:50
12/31	Capricorn	03:29

Venus Table for Year 1930

Date	Zodiac Sign	Time
01/24	Aquarius	00:04
02/16	Pisces	21:51
03/12	Aries	22:12
04/06	Taurus	02:35
04/30	Gemini	12:14
05/25	Cancer	04:14
06/19	Leo	04:21
07/14	Virgo	16:23
08/10	Libra	00:48
09/07	Scorpio	04:05
10/12	Sagittarius	02:45
11/22	Sagittarius*	07:28

Venus Table for Year 1931

Date	Zodiac Sign	Time
01/03	Sagittarius	19:46
02/06	Capricorn	12:09
03/05	Aquarius	21:31
03/31	Pisces	18:50
04/26	Aries	01:58
05/21	Taurus	02:26
06/14	Gemini	22:51
07/09	Cancer	15:21
08/03	Leo	03:15
08/27	Virgo	10:28
09/20	Libra	14:00
10/14	Scorpio	15:28
11/07	Sagittarius	16:13
12/01	Capricorn	17:10
12/25	Aquarius	19:28

Greenwich Mean Time (GMT)
24-Hour Clock

Note: * Indicates retrograde motion.
Eastern Standard Time (EST), add 5 hrs.
Central Standard Time (CST), add 6 hrs.
Mountain Standard Time (MST), add 7 hrs.
Pacific Standard Time (PST), add 8 hrs.
Daylight Saving Time/War Time, minus 1 hr. from total.

Venus Table for Year 1932

Date	Zodiac Sign	Time
01/19	Pisces	01:40
02/12	Aries	16:49
03/09	Taurus	01:59
04/05	Gemini	00:10
05/06	Cancer	08:56
07/13	Cancer*	11:09
07/28	Cancer	11:35
09/08	Leo	19:36
10/07	Virgo	05:38
11/02	Libra	03:54
11/26	Scorpio	23:58
12/21	Sagittarius	07:33

Venus Table for Year 193

Date	Zodiac Sign	Time
01/14	Capricorn	09:47
02/07	Aquarius	10:22
03/03	Pisces	11:16
03/27	Aries	13:47
04/20	Taurus	18:46
05/15	Gemini	02:31
06/08	Cancer	12:45
07/03	Leo	01:14
07/27	Virgo	16:31
08/21	Libra	12:11
09/15	Scorpio	14:45
10/11	Sagittarius	04:27
11/06	Capricorn	16:02
12/05	Aquarius	18:05

Venus Table for Year 1934

Date	Zodiac Sign	Time
04/06	Pisces	09:10
05/06	Aries	08:43
06/02	Taurus	10:01
06/28	Gemini	09:29
07/23	Cancer	18:15
08/17	Leo	15:39
09/11	Virgo	03:26
10/05	Libra	07:48
10/29	Scorpio	07:27
11/22	Sagittarius	04:49
12/16	Capricorn	01:29

Venus Table for Year 193

Date	Zodiac Sign	Time
01/08	Aquarius	22:33
02/01	Pisces	21:24
02/26	Aries	00:18
03/22	Taurus	10:21
04/16	Gemini	07:32
05/11	Cancer	22:00
06/07	Leo	19:13
07/07	Virgo	20:39
11/09	Libra	16:26
12/08	Scorpio	14:30

Greenwich Mean Time (GMT)
24-Hour Clock

Note: * Indicates retrograde motion.
      Eastern Standard Time (EST), add 5 hrs.
      Central Standard Time (CST), add 6 hrs.
      Mountain Standard Time (MST), add 7 hrs.
      Pacific Standard Time (PST), add 8 hrs.
      Daylight Saving Time/War Time, minus 1 hr. from total.

Venus Table for Year 1936

Date	Zodiac Sign	Time
01/03	Sagittarius	14:14
01/28	Capricorn	14:00
02/22	Aquarius	04:13
03/17	Pisces	14:50
04/11	Aries	00:35
05/05	Taurus	10:47
05/29	Gemini	21:33
06/23	Cancer	08:08
07/17	Leo	17:40
08/11	Virgo	01:58
09/04	Libra	09:49
09/28	Scorpio	18:25
10/23	Sagittarius	04:51
11/16	Capricorn	18:29
12/11	Aquarius	14:47

Venus Table for Year 1937

Date	Zodiac Sign	Time
01/06	Pisces	03:18
02/02	Aries	10:45
03/09	Taurus	13:33
04/14	Taurus*	03:58
06/04	Taurus	06:35
07/07	Gemini	21:10
08/04	Cancer	20:09
08/31	Leo	00:01
09/25	Virgo	03:55
10/19	Libra	16:26
11/12	Scorpio	19:37
12/06	Sagittarius	18:00
12/30	Capricorn	14:34

Venus Table for Year 1938

Date	Zodiac Sign	Time
01/23	Aquarius	11:06
02/16	Pisces	08:51
03/12	Aries	09:11
04/05	Taurus	13:36
04/29	Gemini	23:24
05/24	Cancer	15:45
06/18	Leo	16:30
07/14	Virgo	05:42
08/09	Libra	16:29
09/07	Scorpio	01:43
10/13	Sagittarius	18:57
11/15	Sagittarius*	16:16

Venus Table for Year 1939

Date	Zodiac Sign	Time
01/04	Sagittarius	21:36
02/06	Capricorn	09:09
03/05	Aquarius	13:20
03/31	Pisces	08:29
04/25	Aries	14:25
05/20	Taurus	14:10
06/14	Gemini	10:06
07/09	Cancer	02:17
08/02	Leo	14:02
08/26	Virgo	21:14
09/20	Libra	00:50
10/14	Scorpio	02:27
11/07	Sagittarius	03:24
12/01	Capricorn	04:36
12/25	Aquarius	07:12

Greenwich Mean Time (GMT)
24-Hour Clock

Note: * Indicates retrograde motion.
Eastern Standard Time (EST), add 5 hrs.
Central Standard Time (CST), add 6 hrs.
Mountain Standard Time (MST), add 7 hrs.
Pacific Standard Time (PST), add 8 hrs.
Daylight Saving Time/War Time, minus 1 hr. from total.

Venus Table for Year 1940

Date	Zodiac Sign	Time
01/18	Pisces	13:49
02/12	Aries	05:42
03/08	Taurus	16:19
04/04	Gemini	18:06
05/06	Cancer	18:50
07/05	Cancer*	16:02
08/01	Cancer	02:22
09/08	Leo	16:53
10/06	Virgo	21:01
11/01	Libra	17:14
11/26	Scorpio	12:20
12/20	Sagittarius	19:25

Venus Table for Year 1941

Date	Zodiac Sign	Time
01/13	Capricorn	21:19
02/06	Aquarius	21:39
03/02	Pisces	22:22
03/27	Aries	00:43
04/20	Taurus	05:36
05/14	Gemini	13:19
06/07	Cancer	23:36
07/02	Leo	12:18
07/27	Virgo	03:58
08/21	Libra	00:15
09/15	Scorpio	03:49
10/10	Sagittarius	19:11
11/06	Capricorn	10:10
12/05	Aquarius	22:58

Venus Table for Year 1942

Date	Zodiac Sign	Time
04/06	Pisces	12:50
05/06	Aries	02:06
06/02	Taurus	00:09
06/27	Gemini	22:04
07/23	Cancer	05:59
08/17	Leo	02:55
09/10	Virgo	14:27
10/04	Libra	18:43
10/28	Scorpio	18:23
11/21	Sagittarius	15:49
12/15	Capricorn	12:33

Venus Table for Year 1943

Date	Zodiac Sign	Time
01/08	Aquarius	09:42
02/01	Pisces	08:40
02/25	Aries	11:44
03/21	Taurus	22:07
04/15	Gemini	19:58
05/11	Cancer	11:45
06/07	Leo	12:00
07/07	Virgo	23:54
11/09	Libra	18:13
12/08	Scorpio	07:31

Greenwich Mean Time (GMT)
24-Hour Clock

Note: * Indicates retrograde motion.
Eastern Standard Time (EST), add 5 hrs.
Central Standard Time (CST), add 6 hrs.
Mountain Standard Time (MST), add 7 hrs.
Pacific Standard Time (PST), add 8 hrs.
Daylight Saving Time/War Time, minus 1 hr. from total.

Venus Table for Year 1944

Date	Zodiac Sign	Time
01/03	Sagittarius	04:30
01/28	Capricorn	02:57
02/21	Aquarius	16:25
03/17	Pisces	02:29
04/10	Aries	11:52
05/04	Taurus	21:47
05/29	Gemini	08:22
06/22	Cancer	18:52
07/17	Leo	04:25
08/10	Virgo	12:50
09/03	Libra	20:56
09/28	Scorpio	05:54
10/22	Sagittarius	16:50
11/16	Capricorn	07:09
12/11	Aquarius	04:32

Venus Table for Year 1945

Date	Zodiac Sign	Time
01/05	Pisces	19:05
02/02	Aries	07:55
03/11	Taurus	10:45
04/07	Taurus*	20:09
06/04	Taurus	22:28
07/07	Gemini	16:00
08/04	Cancer	10:40
08/30	Leo	12:46
09/24	Virgo	15:49
10/19	Libra	03:55
11/12	Scorpio	06:52
12/06	Sagittarius	05:09
12/30	Capricorn	01:40

Venus Table for Year 1946

Date	Zodiac Sign	Time
01/22	Aquarius	22:08
02/15	Pisces	19:51
03/11	Aries	20:10
04/05	Taurus	00:38
04/29	Gemini	10:35
05/24	Cancer	03:17
06/18	Leo	04:42
07/13	Virgo	19:08
08/09	Libra	08:25
09/07	Scorpio	00:11
10/16	Sagittarius	10:48
11/08	Sagittarius*	08:19

Venus Table for Year 1947

Date	Zodiac Sign	Time
01/05	Sagittarius	16:32
02/06	Capricorn	05:28
03/05	Aquarius	04:55
03/30	Pisces	22:01
04/25	Aries	02:49
05/20	Taurus	01:51
06/13	Gemini	21:19
07/08	Cancer	13:13
08/02	Leo	00:49
08/26	Virgo	07:59
09/19	Libra	11:40
10/13	Scorpio	13:26
11/06	Sagittarius	14:36
11/30	Capricorn	16:03
12/24	Aquarius	18:57

Greenwich Mean Time (GMT)
24-Hour Clock

Note: * Indicates retrograde motion.
Eastern Standard Time (EST), add 5 hrs.
Central Standard Time (CST), add 6 hrs.
Mountain Standard Time (MST), add 7 hrs.
Pacific Standard Time (PST), add 8 hrs.
Daylight Saving Time/War Time, minus 1 hr. from total.

Venus Table for Year 1948

Date	Zodiac Sign	Time
01/18	Pisces	02:01
02/11	Aries	18:40
03/08	Taurus	06:49
04/04	Gemini	12:30
05/07	Cancer	08:15
06/29	Cancer*	08:34
08/03	Cancer	01:55
09/08	Leo	13:27
10/06	Virgo	12:11
11/01	Libra	06:27
11/26	Scorpio	00:39
12/20	Sagittarius	07:14

Venus Table for Year 1949

Date	Zodiac Sign	Time
01/13	Capricorn	08:49
02/06	Aquarius	08:56
03/02	Pisces	09:27
03/26	Aries	11:40
04/19	Taurus	16:26
05/14	Gemini	00:07
06/07	Cancer	10:29
07/01	Leo	23:23
07/26	Virgo	15:27
08/20	Libra	12:23
09/14	Scorpio	16:58
10/10	Sagittarius	10:07
11/06	Capricorn	04:45
12/06	Aquarius	06:00

Venus Table for Year 1950

Date	Zodiac Sign	Time
04/06	Pisces	14:58
05/05	Aries	19:07
06/01	Taurus	14:08
06/27	Gemini	10:35
07/22	Cancer	17:41
08/16	Leo	14:09
09/10	Virgo	01:27
10/04	Libra	05:39
10/28	Scorpio	05:19
11/21	Sagittarius	02:48
12/14	Capricorn	23:38

Venus Table for Year 1951

Date	Zodiac Sign	Time
01/07	Aquarius	20:52
01/31	Pisces	19:56
02/24	Aries	23:11
03/21	Taurus	09:55
04/15	Gemini	08:27
05/11	Cancer	01:38
06/07	Leo	05:08
07/08	Virgo	04:58
11/09	Libra	18:41
12/08	Scorpio	00:12

Greenwich Mean Time (GMT)
24-Hour Clock

Note: * Indicates retrograde motion.
Eastern Standard Time (EST), add 5 hrs.
Central Standard Time (CST), add 6 hrs.
Mountain Standard Time (MST), add 7 hrs.
Pacific Standard Time (PST), add 8 hrs.
Daylight Saving Time/War Time, minus 1 hr. from total.

Venus Table for Year 1952

Date	Zodiac Sign	Time
01/02	Sagittarius	18:37
01/27	Capricorn	15:50
02/21	Aquarius	04:33
03/16	Pisces	14:07
04/09	Aries	23:08
05/04	Taurus	08:46
05/28	Gemini	19:10
06/22	Cancer	05:35
07/16	Leo	15:09
08/09	Virgo	23:43
09/03	Libra	08:04
09/27	Scorpio	17:24
10/22	Sagittarius	04:51
11/15	Capricorn	19:53
12/10	Aquarius	18:24

Venus Table for Year 1953

Date	Zodiac Sign	Time
01/05	Pisces	11:07
02/02	Aries	05:53
03/14	Taurus	18:35
03/31	Taurus*	05:33
06/05	Taurus	10:18
07/07	Gemini	10:22
08/04	Cancer	01:02
08/30	Leo	01:27
09/24	Virgo	03:40
10/18	Libra	15:21
11/11	Scorpio	18:06
12/05	Sagittarius	16:17
12/29	Capricorn	12:45

Venus Table for Year 1954

Date	Zodiac Sign	Time
01/22	Aquarius	09:11
02/15	Pisces	06:51
03/11	Aries	07:09
04/04	Taurus	11:40
04/28	Gemini	21:48
05/23	Cancer	14:51
06/17	Leo	16:57
07/13	Virgo	08:42
08/09	Libra	00:37
09/06	Scorpio	23:37
10/23	Sagittarius	22:19
10/27	Sagittarius*	08:21

Venus Table for Year 1955

Date	Zodiac Sign	Time
01/06	Sagittarius	06:42
02/06	Capricorn	01:10
03/04	Aquarius	20:17
03/30	Pisces	11:26
04/24	Aries	15:09
05/19	Taurus	13:30
06/13	Gemini	08:31
07/08	Cancer	00:08
08/01	Leo	11:36
08/25	Virgo	18:45
09/18	Libra	22:31
10/13	Scorpio	00:26
11/06	Sagittarius	01:48
11/30	Capricorn	03:31
12/24	Aquarius	06:44

Greenwich Mean Time (GMT)
24-Hour Clock

Note: * Indicates retrograde motion.
Eastern Standard Time (EST), add 5 hrs.
Central Standard Time (CST), add 6 hrs.
Mountain Standard Time (MST), add 7 hrs.
Pacific Standard Time (PST), add 8 hrs.
Daylight Saving Time/War Time, minus 1 hr. from total.

Venus Table for Year 1956

Date	Zodiac Sign	Time
01/17	Pisces	14:16
02/11	Aries	07:43
03/07	Taurus	21:30
04/04	Gemini	07:23
05/08	Cancer	02:16
06/23	Cancer*	12:11
08/04	Cancer	09:41
09/08	Leo	09:21
10/06	Virgo	03:08
10/31	Libra	19:34
11/25	Scorpio	12:54
12/19	Sagittarius	19:01

Venus Table for Year 1957

Date	Zodiac Sign	Time
01/12	Capricorn	20:18
02/05	Aquarius	20:12
03/01	Pisces	20:32
03/25	Aries	22:36
04/19	Taurus	03:17
05/13	Gemini	10:56
06/06	Cancer	21:22
07/01	Leo	10:30
07/26	Virgo	02:57
08/20	Libra	00:33
09/14	Scorpio	06:13
10/10	Sagittarius	01:14
11/05	Capricorn	23:49
12/06	Aquarius	15:37

Venus Table for Year 1958

Date	Zodiac Sign	Time
04/06	Pisces	15:47
05/05	Aries	11:48
06/01	Taurus	03:58
06/26	Gemini	23:02
07/22	Cancer	05:21
08/16	Leo	01:22
09/09	Virgo	12:27
10/03	Libra	16:33
10/27	Scorpio	16:15
11/20	Sagittarius	13:48
12/14	Capricorn	10:42

Venus Table for Year 1959

Date	Zodiac Sign	Time
01/07	Aquarius	08:02
01/31	Pisces	07:13
02/24	Aries	10:40
03/20	Taurus	21:46
04/14	Gemini	21:01
05/10	Cancer	15:39
06/06	Leo	22:39
07/08	Virgo	12:11
09/20	Virgo*	04:53
09/25	Virgo	06:10
11/09	Libra	18:01
12/07	Scorpio	16:33

Greenwich Mean Time (GMT)
24-Hour Clock

Note: * Indicates retrograde motion.
Eastern Standard Time (EST), add 5 hrs.
Central Standard Time (CST), add 6 hrs.
Mountain Standard Time (MST), add 7 hrs.
Pacific Standard Time (PST), add 8 hrs.
Daylight Saving Time/War Time, minus 1 hr. from total.

Venus Table for Year 1960

Date	Zodiac Sign	Time
01/02	Sagittarius	08:36
01/27	Capricorn	04:38
02/20	Aquarius	16:38
03/16	Pisces	01:44
04/09	Aries	10:23
05/03	Taurus	19:45
05/28	Gemini	05:58
06/21	Cancer	16:18
07/16	Leo	01:54
08/09	Virgo	10:36
09/02	Libra	19:13
09/27	Scorpio	04:56
10/21	Sagittarius	16:55
11/15	Capricorn	08:42
12/10	Aquarius	08:23

Venus Table for Year 1961

Date	Zodiac Sign	Time
01/05	Pisces	03:26
02/02	Aries	04:47
06/05	Taurus	19:06
07/07	Gemini	04:17
08/03	Cancer	15:13
08/29	Leo	14:03
09/23	Virgo	15:29
10/18	Libra	02:46
11/11	Scorpio	05:20
12/05	Sagittarius	03:24
12/28	Capricorn	23:49

Venus Table for Year 1962

Date	Zodiac Sign	Time
01/21	Aquarius	20:13
02/14	Pisces	17:51
03/10	Aries	18:10
04/03	Taurus	22:44
04/28	Gemini	09:02
05/23	Cancer	02:28
06/17	Leo	05:17
07/12	Virgo	22:22
08/08	Libra	17:08
09/07	Scorpio	00:08

Venus Table for Year 1963

Date	Zodiac Sign	Time
01/06	Sagittarius	17:15
02/05	Capricorn	20:18
03/04	Aquarius	11:26
03/30	Pisces	00:46
04/24	Aries	03:26
05/19	Taurus	01:07
06/12	Gemini	19:41
07/07	Cancer	11:02
07/31	Leo	22:22
08/25	Virgo	05:30
09/18	Libra	09:21
10/12	Scorpio	11:26
11/05	Sagittarius	13:02
11/29	Capricorn	15:00
12/23	Aquarius	18:34

Greenwich Mean Time (GMT)
24-Hour Clock

Note: * Indicates retrograde motion.
Eastern Standard Time (EST), add 5 hrs.
Central Standard Time (CST), add 6 hrs.
Mountain Standard Time (MST), add 7 hrs.
Pacific Standard Time (PST), add 8 hrs.
Daylight Saving Time/War Time, minus 1 hr. from total.

Venus Table for Year 1964

Date	Zodiac Sign	Time
01/17	Pisces	02:35
02/10	Aries	20:51
03/07	Taurus	12:22
04/04	Gemini	02:49
05/09	Cancer	02:57
06/17	Cancer*	18:13
08/05	Cancer	08:32
09/08	Leo	04:39
10/05	Virgo	17:53
10/31	Libra	08:35
11/25	Scorpio	01:06
12/19	Sagittarius	06:45

Venus Table for Year 1965

Date	Zodiac Sign	Time
01/12	Capricorn	07:46
02/05	Aquarius	07:26
03/01	Pisces	07:37
03/25	Aries	09:32
04/18	Taurus	14:07
05/12	Gemini	21:45
06/06	Cancer	08:16
06/30	Leo	21:37
07/25	Virgo	14:30
08/19	Libra	12:47
09/13	Scorpio	19:35
10/09	Sagittarius	16:35
11/05	Capricorn	19:27
12/07	Aquarius	04:29

Venus Table for Year 1966

Date	Zodiac Sign	Time
02/06	Aquarius*	14:08
02/25	Aquarius	10:07
04/06	Pisces	15:29
05/05	Aries	04:12
05/31	Taurus	17:41
06/26	Gemini	11:24
07/21	Cancer	16:58
08/15	Leo	12:34
09/08	Virgo	23:25
10/03	Libra	03:28
10/27	Scorpio	03:10
11/20	Sagittarius	00:48
12/13	Capricorn	21:47

Venus Table for Year 1967

Date	Zodiac Sign	Time
01/06	Aquarius	19:13
01/30	Pisces	18:32
02/23	Aries	22:11
03/20	Taurus	09:40
04/14	Gemini	09:39
05/10	Cancer	05:50
06/06	Leo	16:35
07/08	Virgo	22:01
09/09	Virgo*	11:59
10/01	Virgo	17:44
11/09	Libra	16:22
12/07	Scorpio	08:38

Greenwich Mean Time (GMT)
24-Hour Clock

Note: * Indicates retrograde motion.
Eastern Standard Time (EST), add 5 hrs.
Central Standard Time (CST), add 6 hrs.
Mountain Standard Time (MST), add 7 hrs.
Pacific Standard Time (PST), add 8 hrs.
Daylight Saving Time/War Time, minus 1 hr. from total.

Venus Table for Year 1968

Date	Zodiac Sign	Time
01/01	Sagittarius	22:27
01/26	Capricorn	17:22
02/20	Aquarius	04:41
03/15	Pisces	13:18
04/08	Aries	21:36
05/03	Taurus	06:43
05/27	Gemini	16:46
06/21	Cancer	03:01
07/15	Leo	12:39
08/08	Virgo	21:30
09/02	Libra	06:23
09/26	Scorpio	16:30
10/21	Sagittarius	05:02
11/14	Capricorn	21:35
12/09	Aquarius	22:31

Venus Table for Year 1969

Date	Zodiac Sign	Time
01/04	Pisces	20:03
02/02	Aries	04:44
06/06	Taurus	01:29
07/06	Gemini	21:48
08/03	Cancer	05:15
08/29	Leo	02:34
09/23	Virgo	03:15
10/17	Libra	14:09
11/10	Scorpio	16:32
12/04	Sagittarius	14:31
12/28	Capricorn	10:53

Venus Table for Year 1970

Date	Zodiac Sign	Time
01/21	Aquarius	07:15
02/14	Pisces	04:52
03/10	Aries	05:10
04/03	Taurus	09:48
04/27	Gemini	20:17
05/22	Cancer	14:07
06/16	Leo	17:41
07/12	Virgo	12:11
08/08	Libra	09:57
09/07	Scorpio	01:55

Venus Table for Year 1971

Date	Zodiac Sign	Time
01/07	Sagittarius	01:01
02/05	Capricorn	14:55
03/04	Aquarius	02:23
03/29	Pisces	13:59
04/23	Aries	15:39
05/18	Taurus	12:41
06/12	Gemini	06:51
07/06	Cancer	21:56
07/31	Leo	09:08
08/24	Virgo	16:15
09/17	Libra	20:12
10/11	Scorpio	22:27
11/05	Sagittarius	00:16
11/29	Capricorn	02:31
12/23	Aquarius	06:25

Greenwich Mean Time (GMT)
24-Hour Clock

Note: * Indicates retrograde motion.
Eastern Standard Time (EST), add 5 hrs.
Central Standard Time (CST), add 6 hrs.
Mountain Standard Time (MST), add 7 hrs.
Pacific Standard Time (PST), add 8 hrs.
Daylight Saving Time/War Time, minus 1 hr. from total.

Venus Table for Year 1972

Date	Zodiac Sign	Time
01/16	Pisces	14:56
02/10	Aries	10:06
03/07	Taurus	03:27
04/03	Gemini	22:52
05/10	Cancer	14:00
06/11	Cancer*	19:57
08/06	Cancer	01:27
09/07	Leo	23:25
10/05	Virgo	08:27
10/30	Libra	21:32
11/24	Scorpio	13:15
12/18	Sagittarius	18:28

Venus Table for Year 1973

Date	Zodiac Sign	Time
01/11	Capricorn	19:12
02/04	Aquarius	18:41
02/28	Pisces	18:41
03/24	Aries	20:28
04/18	Taurus	00:58
05/12	Gemini	08:34
06/05	Cancer	19:11
06/30	Leo	08:46
07/25	Virgo	02:05
08/19	Libra	01:05
09/13	Scorpio	09:03
10/09	Sagittarius	08:08
11/05	Capricorn	15:41
12/07	Aquarius	21:40

Venus Table for Year 1974

Date	Zodiac Sign	Time
01/29	Aquarius*	20:07
02/28	Aquarius	14:15
04/06	Pisces	14:11
05/04	Aries	20:18
05/31	Taurus	07:17
06/25	Gemini	23:43
07/21	Cancer	04:33
08/14	Leo	23:44
09/08	Virgo	10:23
10/02	Libra	14:21
10/26	Scorpio	14:06
11/19	Sagittarius	11:47
12/13	Capricorn	08:53

Venus Table for Year 1975

Date	Zodiac Sign	Time
01/06	Aquarius	06:24
01/30	Pisces	05:51
02/23	Aries	09:44
03/19	Taurus	21:36
04/13	Gemini	22:22
05/09	Cancer	20:11
06/06	Leo	10:58
07/09	Virgo	11:21
09/02	Virgo*	15:22
10/04	Virgo	05:28
11/09	Libra	13:52
12/07	Scorpio	00:27

Greenwich Mean Time (GMT)
24-Hour Clock

Note: * Indicates retrograde motion.
Eastern Standard Time (EST), add 5 hrs.
Central Standard Time (CST), add 6 hrs.
Mountain Standard Time (MST), add 7 hrs.
Pacific Standard Time (PST), add 8 hrs.
Daylight Saving Time/War Time, minus 1 hr. from total.

Venus Table for Year 1976

Date	Zodiac Sign	Time
01/01	Sagittarius	12:10
01/26	Capricorn	06:01
02/19	Aquarius	16:42
03/15	Pisces	00:51
04/08	Aries	08:49
05/02	Taurus	17:41
05/27	Gemini	03:34
06/20	Cancer	13:45
07/14	Leo	23:24
08/08	Virgo	08:25
09/01	Libra	17:34
09/26	Scorpio	04:06
10/20	Sagittarius	17:12
11/14	Capricorn	10:34
12/09	Aquarius	12:49

Venus Table for Year 1977

Date	Zodiac Sign	Time
01/04	Pisces	13:00
02/02	Aries	05:54
06/06	Taurus	05:50
07/06	Gemini	14:56
08/02	Cancer	19:08
08/28	Leo	15:01
09/22	Virgo	14:59
10/17	Libra	01:31
11/10	Scorpio	03:43
12/04	Sagittarius	01:38
12/27	Capricorn	21:57

Venus Table for Year 1978

Date	Zodiac Sign	Time
01/20	Aquarius	18:17
02/13	Pisces	15:52
03/09	Aries	16:11
04/02	Taurus	20:53
04/27	Gemini	07:34
05/22	Cancer	01:48
06/16	Leo	06:09
07/12	Virgo	02:08
08/08	Libra	03:06
09/07	Scorpio	05:11

Venus Table for Year 1979

Date	Zodiac Sign	Time
01/07	Sagittarius	06:29
02/05	Capricorn	09:06
03/03	Aquarius	17:09
03/29	Pisces	03:07
04/23	Aries	03:49
05/18	Taurus	00:14
06/11	Gemini	17:59
07/06	Cancer	08:49
07/30	Leo	19:53
08/24	Virgo	03:00
09/17	Libra	07:03
10/11	Scorpio	09:28
11/04	Sagittarius	11:31
11/28	Capricorn	14:03
12/22	Aquarius	18:19

Greenwich Mean Time (GMT)
24-Hour Clock

Note: * Indicates retrograde motion.
Eastern Standard Time (EST), add 5 hrs.
Central Standard Time (CST), add 6 hrs.
Mountain Standard Time (MST), add 7 hrs.
Pacific Standard Time (PST), add 8 hrs.
Daylight Saving Time/War Time, minus 1 hr. from total.

Venus Table for Year 1980

Date	Zodiac Sign	Time
01/16	Pisces	03:22
02/09	Aries	23:27
03/06	Taurus	18:44
04/03	Gemini	19:37
05/12	Cancer	20:12
06/05	Cancer*	06:39
08/06	Cancer	13:58
09/07	Leo	17:41
10/04	Virgo	22:51
10/30	Libra	10:22
11/24	Scorpio	01:21
12/18	Sagittarius	06:09

Venus Table for Year 1981

Date	Zodiac Sign	Time
01/11	Capricorn	06:37
02/04	Aquarius	05:54
02/28	Pisces	05:45
03/24	Aries	07:24
04/17	Taurus	11:48
05/11	Gemini	19:24
06/05	Cancer	06:07
06/29	Leo	19:56
07/24	Virgo	13:41
08/18	Libra	13:26
09/12	Scorpio	22:37
10/08	Sagittarius	23:55
11/05	Capricorn	12:35
12/08	Aquarius	20:51

Venus Table for Year 1982

Date	Zodiac Sign	Time
01/23	Aquarius*	03:31
03/02	Aquarius	11:02
04/06	Pisces	12:00
05/04	Aries	12:08
05/30	Taurus	20:46
06/25	Gemini	11:58
07/20	Cancer	16:06
08/14	Leo	10:53
09/07	Virgo	21:20
10/02	Libra	01:15
10/26	Scorpio	01:01
11/18	Sagittarius	22:47
12/12	Capricorn	19:58

Venus Table for Year 1983

Date	Zodiac Sign	Time
01/05	Aquarius	17:37
01/29	Pisces	17:12
02/22	Aries	21:18
03/19	Taurus	09:35
04/13	Gemini	11:11
05/09	Cancer	10:42
06/06	Leo	05:50
07/10	Virgo	05:08
08/27	Virgo*	12:26
10/05	Virgo	19:05
11/09	Libra	10:36
12/06	Scorpio	16:00

Greenwich Mean Time (GMT)
24-Hour Clock

Note: * Indicates retrograde motion.
Eastern Standard Time (EST), add 5 hrs.
Central Standard Time (CST), add 6 hrs.
Mountain Standard Time (MST), add 7 hrs.
Pacific Standard Time (PST), add 8 hrs.
Daylight Saving Time/War Time, minus 1 hr. from total.

Venus Table for Year 1984

Date	Zodiac Sign	Time
01/01	Sagittarius	01:46
01/25	Capricorn	18:37
02/19	Aquarius	04:39
03/14	Pisces	12:23
04/07	Aries	20:01
05/02	Taurus	04:38
05/26	Gemini	14:21
06/20	Cancer	00:28
07/14	Leo	10:10
08/07	Virgo	19:20
09/01	Libra	04:46
09/25	Scorpio	15:43
10/20	Sagittarius	05:24
11/13	Capricorn	23:37
12/09	Aquarius	03:15

Venus Table for Year 1985

Date	Zodiac Sign	Time
01/04	Pisces	06:18
02/02	Aries	08:30
06/06	Taurus	08:33
07/06	Gemini	07:43
08/02	Cancer	08:53
08/28	Leo	03:24
09/22	Virgo	02:40
10/16	Libra	12:51
11/09	Scorpio	14:53
12/03	Sagittarius	12:43
12/27	Capricorn	09:01

Venus Table for Year 1986

Date	Zodiac Sign	Time
01/20	Aquarius	05:19
02/13	Pisces	02:53
03/09	Aries	03:13
04/02	Taurus	08:00
04/26	Gemini	18:53
05/21	Cancer	13:32
06/15	Leo	18:41
07/11	Virgo	16:14
08/07	Libra	20:38
09/07	Scorpio	10:11

Venus Table for Year 1987

Date	Zodiac Sign	Time
01/07	Sagittarius	10:06
02/05	Capricorn	02:51
03/03	Aquarius	07:44
03/28	Pisces	16:09
04/22	Aries	15:56
05/17	Taurus	11:45
06/11	Gemini	05:06
07/05	Cancer	19:41
07/30	Leo	06:38
08/23	Virgo	13:45
09/16	Libra	17:54
10/10	Scorpio	20:30
11/03	Sagittarius	22:48
11/28	Capricorn	01:37
12/22	Aquarius	06:15

Greenwich Mean Time (GMT)
24-Hour Clock

Note: * Indicates retrograde motion.
Eastern Standard Time (EST), add 5 hrs.
Central Standard Time (CST), add 6 hrs.
Mountain Standard Time (MST), add 7 hrs.
Pacific Standard Time (PST), add 8 hrs.
Daylight Saving Time/War Time, minus 1 hr. from total.

497

Venus Table for Year 1988

Date	Zodiac Sign	Time
01/15	Pisces	15:51
02/09	Aries	12:54
03/06	Taurus	10:16
04/03	Gemini	17:08
05/17	Cancer	17:03
05/27	Cancer*	06:10
08/06	Cancer	23:18
09/07	Leo	11:30
10/04	Virgo	13:04
10/29	Libra	23:08
11/23	Scorpio	13:23
12/17	Sagittarius	17:48

Venus Table for Year 1989

Date	Zodiac Sign	Time
01/10	Capricorn	18:01
02/03	Aquarius	17:06
02/27	Pisces	16:48
03/23	Aries	18:19
04/16	Taurus	22:39
05/11	Gemini	06:14
06/04	Cancer	17:03
06/29	Leo	07:07
07/24	Virgo	01:21
08/18	Libra	01:51
09/12	Scorpio	12:20
10/08	Sagittarius	15:58
11/05	Capricorn	10:13
12/10	Aquarius	04:59

Venus Table for Year 1990

Date	Zodiac Sign	Time
01/16	Aquarius*	16:01
03/03	Aquarius	17:43
04/06	Pisces	09:04
05/04	Aries	03:44
05/30	Taurus	10:08
06/25	Gemini	00:10
07/20	Cancer	03:37
08/13	Leo	22:00
09/07	Virgo	08:16
10/01	Libra	12:07
10/25	Scorpio	11:56
11/18	Sagittarius	09:47
12/12	Capricorn	07:04

Venus Table for Year 1991

Date	Zodiac Sign	Time
01/05	Aquarius	04:50
01/29	Pisces	04:34
02/22	Aries	08:54
03/18	Taurus	21:37
04/13	Gemini	00:04
05/09	Cancer	01:24
06/06	Leo	01:15
07/11	Virgo	05:16
08/21	Virgo*	14:34
10/06	Virgo	21:23
11/09	Libra	06:39
12/06	Scorpio	07:20
12/31	Sagittarius	15:15

Greenwich Mean Time (GMT)
24-Hour Clock

Note: * Indicates retrograde motion.
Eastern Standard Time (EST), add 5 hrs.
Central Standard Time (CST), add 6 hrs.
Mountain Standard Time (MST), add 7 hrs.
Pacific Standard Time (PST), add 8 hrs.
Daylight Saving Time/War Time, minus 1 hr. from total.

Venus Table for Year 1992

Date	Zodiac Sign	Time
01/25	Capricorn	07:08
02/18	Aquarius	16:35
03/13	Pisces	23:53
04/07	Aries	07:11
05/01	Taurus	15:34
05/26	Gemini	01:08
06/19	Cancer	11:11
07/13	Leo	20:56
08/07	Virgo	06:16
08/31	Libra	15:59
09/25	Scorpio	03:23
10/19	Sagittarius	17:40
11/13	Capricorn	12:45
12/08	Aquarius	17:51

Venus Table for Year 1993

Date	Zodiac Sign	Time
01/03	Pisces	23:58
02/02	Aries	12:46
06/06	Taurus	09:51
07/06	Gemini	00:12
08/01	Cancer	22:31
08/27	Leo	15:43
09/21	Virgo	14:19
10/16	Libra	00:09
11/09	Scorpio	02:02
12/02	Sagittarius	23:49
12/26	Capricorn	20:04

Venus Table for Year 1994

Date	Zodiac Sign	Time
01/19	Aquarius	16:21
02/12	Pisces	13:55
03/08	Aries	14:15
04/01	Taurus	19:07
04/26	Gemini	06:13
05/21	Cancer	01:19
06/15	Leo	07:18
07/11	Virgo	06:30
08/07	Libra	14:35
09/07	Scorpio	17:17

Venus Table for Year 1995

Date	Zodiac Sign	Time
01/07	Sagittarius	12:10
02/04	Capricorn	20:13
03/02	Aquarius	22:10
03/28	Pisces	05:06
04/22	Aries	04:01
05/16	Taurus	23:15
06/10	Gemini	16:12
07/05	Cancer	06:32
07/29	Leo	17:23
08/23	Virgo	00:31
09/16	Libra	04:45
10/10	Scorpio	07:33
11/03	Sagittarius	10:05
11/27	Capricorn	13:12
12/21	Aquarius	18:13

Greenwich Mean Time (GMT)
24-Hour Clock

Note: * Indicates retrograde motion.
Eastern Standard Time (EST), add 5 hrs.
Central Standard Time (CST), add 6 hrs.
Mountain Standard Time (MST), add 7 hrs.
Pacific Standard Time (PST), add 8 hrs.
Daylight Saving Time/War Time, minus 1 hr. from total.

Venus Table for Year 1996

Date	Zodiac Sign	Time
01/15	Pisces	04:23
02/09	Aries	02:28
03/06	Taurus	02:02
04/03	Gemini	15:31
08/07	Cancer	06:00
09/07	Leo	04:55
10/04	Virgo	03:08
10/29	Libra	11:48
11/23	Scorpio	01:23
12/17	Sagittarius	05:25

Venus Table for Year 1997

Date	Zodiac Sign	Time
01/10	Capricorn	05:24
02/03	Aquarius	04:18
02/27	Pisces	03:51
03/23	Aries	05:15
04/16	Taurus	09:30
05/10	Gemini	17:05
06/04	Cancer	04:00
06/28	Leo	18:20
07/23	Virgo	13:02
08/17	Libra	14:20
09/12	Scorpio	02:09
10/08	Sagittarius	08:18
11/05	Capricorn	08:42
12/12	Aquarius	04:27

Venus Table for Year 1998

Date	Zodiac Sign	Time
01/09	Aquarius*	21:35
03/04	Aquarius	15:57
04/06	Pisces	05:26
05/03	Aries	19:06
05/29	Taurus	23:23
06/24	Gemini	12:18
07/19	Cancer	15:05
08/13	Leo	09:06
09/06	Virgo	19:11
09/30	Libra	23:00
10/24	Scorpio	22:50
11/17	Sagittarius	20:47
12/11	Capricorn	18:11

Venus Table for Year 1999

Date	Zodiac Sign	Time
01/04	Aquarius	16:03
01/28	Pisces	15:57
02/21	Aries	20:31
03/18	Taurus	09:43
04/12	Gemini	13:03
05/08	Cancer	16:18
06/05	Leo	21:17
07/12	Virgo	15:09
08/15	Virgo*	14:10
10/07	Virgo	16:31
11/09	Libra	02:05
12/05	Scorpio	22:27
12/31	Sagittarius	04:37

Greenwich Mean Time (GMT)
24-Hour Clock

Note: * Indicates retrograde motion.
Eastern Standard Time (EST), add 5 hrs.
Central Standard Time (CST), add 6 hrs.
Mountain Standard Time (MST), add 7 hrs.
Pacific Standard Time (PST), add 8 hrs.
Daylight Saving Time/War Time, minus 1 hr. from total.

Venus Table for Year 2000

Date	Zodiac Sign	Time
01/24	Capricorn	19:36
02/18	Aquarius	04:28
03/13	Pisces	11:21
04/06	Aries	18:21
05/01	Taurus	02:30
05/25	Gemini	11:55
06/18	Cancer	21:55
07/13	Leo	07:42
08/06	Virgo	17:12
08/31	Libra	03:14
09/24	Scorpio	15:04
10/19	Sagittarius	05:59
11/13	Capricorn	01:59
12/08	Aquarius	08:38

Greenwich Mean Time (GMT)
24-Hour Clock

Note: * Indicates retrograde motion.
Eastern Standard Time (EST), add 5 hrs.
Central Standard Time (CST), add 6 hrs.
Mountain Standard Time (MST), add 7 hrs.
Pacific Standard Time (PST), add 8 hrs.
Daylight Saving Time/War Time, minus 1 hr. from total.

Mars Table for Year 1900

Date	Zodiac Sign	Time
01/21	Aquarius	18:40
02/28	Pisces	22:01
04/08	Aries	03:39
05/17	Taurus	08:41
06/27	Gemini	09:01
08/10	Cancer	00:59
09/26	Leo	18:04
11/23	Virgo	09:02

Mars Table for Year 1901

Date	Zodiac Sign	Time
03/01	Virgo*	18:37
05/11	Virgo	06:33
07/13	Libra	20:00
08/31	Scorpio	18:10
10/14	Sagittarius	12:41
11/24	Capricorn	04:41

Mars Table for Year 1902

Date	Zodiac Sign	Time
01/01	Aquarius	23:51
02/08	Pisces	23:53
03/19	Aries	04:28
04/27	Taurus	10:37
06/07	Gemini	11:05
07/20	Cancer	17:27
09/04	Leo	14:35
10/23	Virgo	22:45
12/20	Libra	03:43

Mars Table for Year 1903

Date	Zodiac Sign	Time
04/19	Libra*	18:43
05/30	Libra	18:18
08/06	Scorpio	16:37
09/22	Sagittarius	13:44
11/03	Capricorn	05:18
12/12	Aquarius	09:36

Mars Table for Year 1904

Date	Zodiac Sign	Time
01/19	Pisces	15:32
02/27	Aries	02:58
04/06	Taurus	17:50
05/18	Gemini	03:20
06/30	Cancer	14:36
08/15	Leo	03:00
10/01	Virgo	13:24
11/20	Libra	06:02

Mars Table for Year 1905

Date	Zodiac Sign	Time
01/13	Scorpio	19:27
08/21	Sagittarius	20:21
10/08	Capricorn	00:32
11/18	Aquarius	04:23
12/27	Pisces	13:44

Greenwich Mean Time (GMT)
24-Hour Clock

Note: * Indicates retrograde motion.
Eastern Standard Time (EST), add 5 hrs.
Central Standard Time (CST), add 6 hrs.
Mountain Standard Time (MST), add 7 hrs.
Pacific Standard Time, (PST), add 8 hrs.
Daylight Saving Time/War Time, minus 1 hr. from total.

Mars Table for Year 1906

Date	Zodiac Sign	Time
02/04	Aries	23:29
03/17	Taurus	11:24
04/28	Gemini	16:25
06/11	Cancer	19:01
07/27	Leo	13:37
09/12	Virgo	12:13
10/30	Libra	03:43
12/17	Scorpio	11:25

Mars Table for Year 1907

Date	Zodiac Sign	Time
02/05	Sagittarius	08:47
04/01	Capricorn	17:58
10/13	Aquarius	15:03
11/29	Pisces	04:55

Mars Table for Year 1908

Date	Zodiac Sign	Time
01/11	Aries	04:57
02/23	Taurus	03:29
04/07	Gemini	03:56
05/22	Cancer	13:49
07/08	Leo	03:22
08/24	Virgo	06:04
10/10	Libra	05:20
11/25	Scorpio	13:30

Mars Table for Year 1909

Date	Zodiac Sign	Time
01/10	Sagittarius	03:00
02/24	Capricorn	01:14
04/09	Aquarius	19:22
05/25	Pisces	21:38
07/21	Aries	06:46
09/27	Aries*	00:18
11/20	Aries	19:31

Mars Table for Year 1910

Date	Zodiac Sign	Time
01/23	Taurus	01:45
03/14	Gemini	07:06
05/01	Cancer	20:33
06/19	Leo	03:12
08/06	Virgo	00:34
09/21	Libra	23:47
11/06	Scorpio	13:11
12/20	Sagittarius	11:45

Mars Table for Year 1911

Date	Zodiac Sign	Time
01/31	Capricorn	20:57
03/13	Aquarius	23:24
04/23	Pisces	07:36
06/02	Aries	20:51
07/15	Taurus	14:53
09/05	Gemini	13:40
11/30	Gemini*	07:27

Greenwich Mean Time (GMT)
24-Hour Clock

Note: * Indicates retrograde motion.
Eastern Standard Time (EST), add 5 hrs.
Central Standard Time (CST), add 6 hrs.
Mountain Standard Time (MST), add 7 hrs.
Pacific Standard Time, (PST), add 8 hrs.
Daylight Saving Time/War Time, minus 1 hr. from total.

Mars Table for Year 1912

Date	Zodiac Sign	Time
01/30	Gemini	19:38
04/05	Cancer	11:06
05/28	Leo	07:57
07/17	Virgo	02:22
09/02	Libra	16:38
10/18	Scorpio	02:15
11/30	Sagittarius	07:17

Mars Table for Year 1913

Date	Zodiac Sign	Time
01/10	Capricorn	13:28
02/19	Aquarius	07:48
03/30	Pisces	05:39
05/08	Aries	02:44
06/17	Taurus	00:12
07/29	Gemini	10:01
09/15	Cancer	16:34

Mars Table for Year 1914

Date	Zodiac Sign	Time
05/01	Leo	20:07
06/26	Virgo	04:33
08/14	Libra	13:56
09/29	Scorpio	10:25
11/11	Sagittarius	10:26
12/22	Capricorn	03:29

Mars Table for Year 1915

Date	Zodiac Sign	Time
01/30	Aquarius	05:53
03/09	Pisces	12:39
04/16	Aries	20:32
05/26	Taurus	03:02
07/06	Gemini	06:18
08/19	Cancer	09:05
10/07	Leo	20:41

Mars Table for Year 1916

Date	Zodiac Sign	Time
05/28	Virgo	18:36
07/23	Libra	05:23
09/08	Scorpio	17:49
10/22	Sagittarius	02:59
12/01	Capricorn	17:10

Mars Table for Year 1917

Date	Zodiac Sign	Time
01/09	Aquarius	12:49
02/16	Pisces	13:19
03/26	Aries	17:21
05/04	Taurus	21:51
06/14	Gemini	20:34
07/28	Cancer	03:43
09/12	Leo	10:37
11/02	Virgo	10:43

Greenwich Mean Time (GMT)
24-Hour Clock

Note: * Indicates retrograde motion.
   Eastern Standard Time (EST), add 5 hrs.
   Central Standard Time (CST), add 6 hrs.
   Mountain Standard Time (MST), add 7 hrs.
   Pacific Standard Time (PST), add 8 hrs.
   Daylight Saving Time/War Time, minus 1 hr. from total.

Mars Table for Year 1918

Date	Zodiac Sign	Time
01/11	Libra	08:44
02/25	Libra*	19:25
06/23	Libra	19:08
08/17	Scorpio	04:14
10/01	Sagittarius	07:42
11/11	Capricorn	10:21
12/20	Aquarius	09:15

Mars Table for Year 1919

Date	Zodiac Sign	Time
01/27	Pisces	11:29
03/06	Aries	18:54
04/15	Taurus	04:58
05/26	Gemini	09:27
07/08	Cancer	17:02
08/23	Leo	06:04
10/10	Virgo	03:38
11/30	Libra	12:00

Mars Table for Year 1920

Date	Zodiac Sign	Time
01/31	Scorpio	22:55
04/23	Scorpio*	21:42
07/10	Scorpio	17:24
09/04	Sagittarius	19:58
10/18	Capricorn	13:01
11/27	Aquarius	13:26

Mars Table for Year 1921

Date	Zodiac Sign	Time
01/05	Pisces	07:33
02/13	Aries	05:23
03/25	Taurus	06:29
05/06	Gemini	01:43
06/18	Cancer	20:29
08/03	Leo	10:52
09/19	Virgo	11:28
11/06	Libra	16:06
12/26	Scorpio	11:47

Mars Table for Year 1922

Date	Zodiac Sign	Time
02/18	Sagittarius	16:22
09/13	Capricorn	12:40
10/30	Aquarius	18:29
12/11	Pisces	12:43

Mars Table for Year 1923

Date	Zodiac Sign	Time
01/21	Aries	09:46
03/04	Taurus	00:27
04/16	Gemini	02:40
05/30	Cancer	21:07
07/16	Leo	01:13
09/01	Virgo	00:37
10/18	Libra	03:56
12/04	Scorpio	01:48

Greenwich Mean Time (GMT)
24-Hour Clock

Note: * Indicates retrograde motion.
Eastern Standard Time (EST), add 5 hrs.
Central Standard Time (CST), add 6 hrs.
Mountain Standard Time (MST), add 7 hrs.
Pacific Standard Time (PST), add 8 hrs.
Daylight Saving Time/War Time, minus 1 hr. from total.

Mars Table for Year 1924

Date	Zodiac Sign	Time
01/19	Sagittarius	18:47
03/06	Capricorn	18:55
04/24	Aquarius	15:55
06/24	Pisces	16:50
08/24	Pisces*	14:56
10/19	Pisces	18:17
12/19	Aries	10:38

Mars Table for Year 1925

Date	Zodiac Sign	Time
02/05	Taurus	09:50
03/24	Gemini	00:10
05/09	Cancer	22:14
06/26	Leo	08:41
08/12	Virgo	20:43
09/28	Libra	18:32
11/13	Scorpio	13:29
12/28	Sagittarius	00:02

Mars Table for Year 1926

Date	Zodiac Sign	Time
02/09	Capricorn	03:01
03/23	Aquarius	04:06
05/03	Pisces	16:32
06/15	Aries	00:29
08/01	Taurus	08:56

Mars Table for Year 1927

Date	Zodiac Sign	Time
02/22	Gemini	00:12
04/17	Cancer	00:59
06/06	Leo	11:08
07/25	Virgo	07:21
09/10	Libra	13:57
10/25	Scorpio	23:58
12/08	Sagittarius	10:38

Mars Table for Year 1928

Date	Zodiac Sign	Time
01/19	Capricorn	01:37
02/28	Aquarius	06:02
04/07	Pisces	13:50
05/16	Aries	20:57
06/26	Taurus	08:26
08/09	Gemini	03:33
10/03	Cancer	03:01
12/20	Cancer*	06:20

Mars Table for Year 1929

Date	Zodiac Sign	Time
03/10	Cancer	22:25
05/13	Leo	01:54
07/04	Virgo	09:27
08/21	Libra	21:24
10/06	Scorpio	12:05
11/18	Sagittarius	13:14
12/29	Capricorn	10:37

Greenwich Mean Time (GMT)
24-Hour Clock

Note: * Indicates retrograde motion.
Eastern Standard Time (EST), add 5 hrs.
Central Standard Time (CST), add 6 hrs.
Mountain Standard Time (MST), add 7 hrs.
Pacific Standard Time (PST), add 8 hrs.
Daylight Saving Time/War Time, minus 1 hr. from total.

Mars Table for Year 1930

Date	Zodiac Sign	Time
02/06	Aquarius	18:17
03/17	Pisces	05:47
04/24	Aries	17:15
06/03	Taurus	02:59
07/14	Gemini	12:30
08/28	Cancer	11:04
10/20	Leo	14:17

Mars Table for Year 1931

Date	Zodiac Sign	Time
02/16	Leo*	15:14
03/30	Leo	03:05
06/10	Virgo	14:27
08/01	Libra	16:07
09/17	Scorpio	08:09
10/30	Sagittarius	12:11
12/10	Capricorn	02:41

Mars Table for Year 1932

Date	Zodiac Sign	Time
01/18	Aquarius	00:15
02/25	Pisces	02:23
04/03	Aries	06:57
05/12	Taurus	10:55
06/22	Gemini	09:20
08/04	Cancer	19:56
09/20	Leo	19:42
11/13	Virgo	21:24

Mars Table for Year 1933

Date	Zodiac Sign	Time
07/06	Libra	22:02
08/26	Scorpio	06:21
10/09	Sagittarius	11:13
11/19	Capricorn	06:52
12/28	Aquarius	03:17

Mars Table for Year 1934

Date	Zodiac Sign	Time
02/04	Pisces	03:46
03/14	Aries	08:44
04/22	Taurus	15:24
06/02	Gemini	16:10
07/15	Cancer	21:34
08/30	Leo	13:48
10/18	Virgo	05:12
12/11	Libra	10:00

Mars Table for Year 1935

Date	Zodiac Sign	Time
07/29	Scorpio	17:57
09/16	Sagittarius	13:13
10/28	Capricorn	18:26
12/07	Aquarius	04:34

Greenwich Mean Time (GMT)
24-Hour Clock

Note: * Indicates retrograde motion.
Eastern Standard Time (EST), add 5 hrs.
Central Standard Time (CST), add 6 hrs.
Mountain Standard Time (MST), add 7 hrs.
Pacific Standard Time, (PST), add 8 hrs.
Daylight Saving Time/War Time, minus 1 hr. from total.

Mars Table for Year 1936

Date	Zodiac Sign	Time
01/14	Pisces	13:51
02/22	Aries	03:56
04/01	Taurus	21:15
05/13	Gemini	08:58
06/25	Cancer	21:40
08/10	Leo	09:31
09/26	Virgo	14:47
11/14	Libra	14:56

Mars Table for Year 1937

Date	Zodiac Sign	Time
01/05	Scorpio	20:55
03/13	Sagittarius	04:33
05/14	Sagittarius*	20:46
08/08	Sagittarius	23:01
09/30	Capricorn	09:34
11/11	Aquarius	18:55
12/21	Pisces	18:04

Mars Table for Year 1938

Date	Zodiac Sign	Time
01/30	Aries	12:53
03/12	Taurus	07:50
04/23	Gemini	18:29
06/07	Cancer	01:15
07/22	Leo	22:09
09/07	Virgo	20:09
10/25	Libra	06:11
12/11	Scorpio	23:19

Mars Table for Year 1939

Date	Zodiac Sign	Time
01/29	Sagittarius	09:50
03/21	Capricorn	07:33
05/25	Aquarius	00:05
07/21	Aquarius*	20:32
09/24	Aquarius	00:56
11/19	Pisces	15:51

Mars Table for Year 1940

Date	Zodiac Sign	Time
01/04	Aries	00:04
02/17	Taurus	01:56
04/01	Gemini	18:36
05/17	Cancer	14:36
07/03	Leo	10:12
08/19	Virgo	15:33
10/05	Libra	13:56
11/20	Scorpio	16:52

Mars Table for Year 1941

Date	Zodiac Sign	Time
01/04	Sagittarius	19:30
02/17	Capricorn	23:25
04/02	Aquarius	11:47
05/16	Pisces	05:03
07/02	Aries	05:09

Greenwich Mean Time (GMT)
24-Hour Clock

Note: * Indicates retrograde motion.
Eastern Standard Time (EST), add 5 hrs.
Central Standard Time (CST), add 6 hrs.
Mountain Standard Time (MST), add 7 hrs.
Pacific Standard Time (PST), add 8 hrs.
Daylight Saving Time/War Time, minus 1 hr. from total.

Mars Table for Year 1942

Date	Zodiac Sign	Time
01/11	Taurus	21:29
03/07	Gemini	07:27
04/26	Cancer	05:45
06/14	Leo	03:21
08/01	Virgo	07:51
09/17	Libra	09:31
11/01	Scorpio	21:49
12/15	Sagittarius	16:07

Mars Table for Year 1943

Date	Zodiac Sign	Time
01/26	Capricorn	18:28
03/08	Aquarius	12:12
04/17	Pisces	10:03
05/27	Aries	09:14
07/07	Taurus	23:06
08/24	Gemini	00:05

Mars Table for Year 1944

Date	Zodiac Sign	Time
03/28	Cancer	09:19
05/22	Leo	13:37
07/12	Virgo	02:16
08/28	Libra	23:45
10/13	Scorpio	11:24
11/25	Sagittarius	15:24

Mars Table for Year 1945

Date	Zodiac Sign	Time
01/05	Capricorn	18:39
02/14	Aquarius	09:08
03/25	Pisces	02:56
05/02	Aries	19:44
06/11	Taurus	11:20
07/23	Gemini	08:34
09/07	Cancer	20:47
11/11	Leo	21:14
12/26	Leo*	14:11

Mars Table for Year 1946

Date	Zodiac Sign	Time
04/22	Leo	19:12
06/20	Virgo	08:05
08/09	Libra	12:53
09/24	Scorpio	16:07
11/06	Sagittarius	17:56
12/17	Capricorn	10:24

Mars Table for Year 1947

Date	Zodiac Sign	Time
01/25	Aquarius	11:11
03/04	Pisces	16:08
04/11	Aries	22:19
05/21	Taurus	02:58
07/01	Gemini	02:55
08/13	Cancer	20:54
10/01	Leo	02:02
12/01	Virgo	11:29

Greenwich Mean Time (GMT)
24-Hour Clock

Note: * Indicates retrograde motion.
Eastern Standard Time (EST), add 5 hrs.
Central Standard Time (CST), add 6 hrs.
Mountain Standard Time (MST), add 7 hrs.
Pacific Standard Time (PST), add 8 hrs.
Daylight Saving Time/War Time, minus 1 hr. from total.

Mars Table for Year 1948

Date	Zodiac Sign	Time
02/12	Virgo*	10:17
05/18	Virgo	20:39
07/17	Libra	05:07
09/03	Scorpio	13:35
10/17	Sagittarius	05:24
11/26	Capricorn	21:41

Mars Table for Year 1949

Date	Zodiac Sign	Time
01/04	Aquarius	17:38
02/11	Pisces	17:53
03/21	Aries	21:42
04/30	Taurus	02:07
06/10	Gemini	00:24
07/23	Cancer	05:20
09/07	Leo	04:19
10/27	Virgo	00:35
12/26	Libra	05:19

Mars Table for Year 1950

Date	Zodiac Sign	Time
03/28	Libra*	10:36
06/11	Libra	20:31
08/10	Scorpio	16:39
09/25	Sagittarius	19:36
11/06	Capricorn	06:18
12/15	Aquarius	08:38

Mars Table for Year 1951

Date	Zodiac Sign	Time
01/22	Pisces	12:47
03/01	Aries	21:46
04/10	Taurus	09:23
05/21	Gemini	15:18
07/03	Cancer	23:26
08/18	Leo	10:37
10/05	Virgo	00:04
11/24	Libra	06:02

Mars Table for Year 1952

Date	Zodiac Sign	Time
01/20	Scorpio	01:50
08/27	Sagittarius	19:29
10/12	Capricorn	05:01
11/21	Aquarius	19:44
12/30	Pisces	21:30

Mars Table for Year 1953

Date	Zodiac Sign	Time
02/08	Aries	00:51
03/20	Taurus	06:34
05/01	Gemini	05:45
06/14	Cancer	03:28
07/29	Leo	19:04
09/14	Virgo	17:40
11/01	Libra	13:56
12/20	Scorpio	11:03

Greenwich Mean Time (GMT)
24-Hour Clock

Note: * Indicates retrograde motion.
Eastern Standard Time (EST), add 5 hrs.
Central Standard Time (CST), add 6 hrs.
Mountain Standard Time (MST), add 7 hrs.
Pacific Standard Time, (PST), add 8 hrs.
Daylight Saving Time/War Time, minus 1 hr. from total.

Mars Table for Year 1954

Date	Zodiac Sign	Time
02/09	Sagittarius	17:14
07/03	Capricorn*	03:27
08/24	Capricorn	15:52
10/21	Aquarius	12:57
12/04	Pisces	08:24

Mars Table for Year 1955

Date	Zodiac Sign	Time
01/15	Aries	05:02
02/26	Taurus	10:38
04/10	Gemini*	23:11
05/26	Cancer	00:43
07/11	Leo	09:08
08/27	Virgo	09:57
10/13	Libra	10:56
11/29	Scorpio	01:02

Mars Table for Year 1956

Date	Zodiac Sign	Time
01/14	Sagittarius	01:54
02/28	Capricorn	19:22
04/14	Aquarius	22:57
06/03	Pisces	07:10
12/06	Aries	11:35

Mars Table for Year 1957

Date	Zodiac Sign	Time
01/28	Taurus	14:35
03/17	Gemini	21:48
05/04	Cancer	15:25
06/21	Leo	12:11
08/08	Virgo	05:18
09/24	Libra	04:18
11/08	Scorpio	20:47
12/23	Sagittarius	01:13

Mars Table for Year 1958

Date	Zodiac Sign	Time
02/03	Capricorn	18:32
03/17	Aquarius	06:38
04/27	Pisces	01:47
06/07	Aries	05:28
07/21	Taurus	06:09
09/21	Gemini	02:48
10/29	Gemini*	03:09

Mars Table for Year 1959

Date	Zodiac Sign	Time
02/10	Gemini	13:27
04/10	Cancer	09:36
06/01	Leo	02:17
07/20	Virgo	10:55
09/05	Libra	22:33
10/21	Scorpio	09:22
12/03	Sagittarius	17:55

Greenwich Mean Time (GMT)
24-Hour Clock

Note: * Indicates retrograde motion.
Eastern Standard Time (EST), add 5 hrs.
Central Standard Time (CST), add 6 hrs.
Mountain Standard Time (MST), add 7 hrs.
Pacific Standard Time (PST), add 8 hrs.
Daylight Saving Time/War Time, minus 1 hr. from total.

Mars Table for Year 1960

Date	Zodiac Sign	Time
01/04	Capricorn	04:48
02/23	Aquarius	04:01
04/02	Pisces	06:12
05/11	Aries	06:58
06/20	Taurus	08:39
08/02	Gemini	03:58
09/21	Cancer	03:26

Mars Table for Year 196[1]

Date	Zodiac Sign	Time
05/06	Leo	00:50
06/28	Virgo	23:31
08/17	Libra	00:25
10/01	Scorpio	19:39
11/13	Sagittarius	21:26
12/24	Capricorn	17:23

Mars Table for Year 1962

Date	Zodiac Sign	Time
02/01	Aquarius	22:42
03/12	Pisces	07:39
04/19	Aries	16:39
05/28	Taurus	23:29
07/09	Gemini	03:34
08/22	Cancer	11:16
10/11	Leo	23:28

Mars Table for Year 196[3]

Date	Zodiac Sign	Time
06/03	Virgo	06:18
07/27	Libra	04:03
09/12	Scorpio	08:56
10/25	Sagittarius	17:15
12/05	Capricorn	08:39

Mars Table for Year 1964

Date	Zodiac Sign	Time
01/13	Aquarius	05:44
02/20	Pisces	07:01
03/29	Aries	10:48
05/07	Taurus	14:04
06/17	Gemini	11:12
07/30	Cancer	17:52
09/15	Leo	04:54
11/06	Virgo	02:51

Mars Table for Year 196[5]

Date	Zodiac Sign	Time
06/29	Libra	00:41
08/20	Scorpio	11:59
10/04	Sagittarius	06:39
11/14	Capricorn	07:14
12/23	Aquarius	05:33

Greenwich Mean Time (GMT)
24-Hour Clock

Note: * Indicates retrograde motion.
Eastern Standard Time (EST), add 5 hrs.
Central Standard Time (CST), add 6 hrs.
Mountain Standard Time (MST), add 7 hrs.
Pacific Standard Time, (PST), add 8 hrs.
Daylight Saving Time/War Time, minus 1 hr. from total.

Mars Table for Year 1966

Date	Zodiac Sign	Time
01/30	Pisces	06:57
03/09	Aries	12:41
04/17	Taurus	20:12
05/28	Gemini	21:40
07/11	Cancer	02:43
08/25	Leo	15:24
10/12	Virgo	18:10
12/04	Libra	00:26

Mars Table for Year 1967

Date	Zodiac Sign	Time
02/12	Scorpio	11:36
03/31	Scorpio*	06:56
07/19	Scorpio	22:14
09/10	Sagittarius	01:13
10/23	Capricorn	01:52
12/01	Aquarius	19:58

Mars Table for Year 1968

Date	Zodiac Sign	Time
01/09	Pisces	09:46
02/17	Aries	03:18
03/27	Taurus	23:42
05/08	Gemini	14:11
06/21	Cancer	04:50
08/05	Leo	16:51
09/21	Virgo	18:20
11/09	Libra	05:51
12/29	Scorpio	21:57

Mars Table for Year 1969

Date	Zodiac Sign	Time
02/25	Sagittarius	06:20
09/21	Capricorn	06:14
11/04	Aquarius	18:26
12/15	Pisces	14:04

Mars Table for Year 1970

Date	Zodiac Sign	Time
01/24	Aries	21:16
03/07	Taurus	01:17
04/18	Gemini	18:52
06/02	Cancer	06:42
07/18	Leo	06:36
09/03	Virgo	04:48
10/20	Libra	10:44
12/06	Scorpio	16:26

Mars Table for Year 1971

Date	Zodiac Sign	Time
01/23	Sagittarius	01:32
03/12	Capricorn	10:14
05/03	Aquarius	21:10
11/06	Pisces	12:22
12/26	Aries	17:50

Greenwich Mean Time (GMT)
24-Hour Clock

Note: * Indicates retrograde motion.
Eastern Standard Time (EST), add 5 hrs.
Central Standard Time (CST), add 6 hrs.
Mountain Standard Time (MST), add 7 hrs.
Pacific Standard Time (PST), add 8 hrs.
Daylight Saving Time/War Time, minus 1 hr. from total.

Mars Table for Year 1972

Date	Zodiac Sign	Time
02/10	Taurus	13:49
03/27	Gemini	04:21
05/12	Cancer	13:03
06/28	Leo	16:00
08/15	Virgo	00:51
09/30	Libra	23:09
11/15	Scorpio	22:02
12/30	Sagittarius	15:56

Mars Table for Year 1973

Date	Zodiac Sign	Time
02/12	Capricorn	05:38
03/26	Aquarius	20:48
05/08	Pisces	04:07
06/20	Aries	20:56
08/12	Taurus	15:03
10/29	Taurus*	23:11
12/24	Taurus	07:40

Mars Table for Year 1974

Date	Zodiac Sign	Time
02/27	Gemini	09:55
04/20	Cancer	08:01
06/09	Leo	00:43
07/27	Virgo	13:58
09/12	Libra	19:00
10/28	Scorpio	06:55
12/10	Sagittarius	21:51

Mars Table for Year 1975

Date	Zodiac Sign	Time
01/21	Capricorn	18:32
03/03	Aquarius	05:07
04/11	Pisces	18:50
05/21	Aries	07:48
07/01	Taurus	03:32
08/14	Gemini	20:34
10/17	Cancer	08:11
11/25	Cancer*	18:55

Mars Table for Year 1976

Date	Zodiac Sign	Time
03/18	Cancer	12:53
05/16	Leo	10:48
07/06	Virgo	23:07
08/24	Libra	05:35
10/08	Scorpio	20:09
11/20	Sagittarius	23:44

Mars Table for Year 1977

Date	Zodiac Sign	Time
01/01	Capricorn	00:39
02/09	Aquarius	11:53
03/20	Pisces	02:15
04/27	Aries	15:34
06/06	Taurus	02:39
07/17	Gemini	14:51
08/31	Cancer	23:50
10/26	Leo	18:13

Greenwich Mean Time (GMT)
24-Hour Clock

Note: * Indicates retrograde motion.
    Eastern Standard Time (EST), add 5 hrs.
    Central Standard Time (CST), add 6 hrs.
    Mountain Standard Time (MST), add 7 hrs.
    Pacific Standard Time, (PST), add 8 hrs.
    Daylight Saving Time/War Time, minus 1 hr. from total.

Mars Table for Year 1978

Date	Zodiac Sign	Time
01/26	Leo*	02:49
04/10	Leo	17:55
06/14	Virgo	02:02
08/04	Libra	08:29
09/19	Scorpio	20:20
11/02	Sagittarius	00:45
12/12	Capricorn	17:10

Mars Table for Year 1979

Date	Zodiac Sign	Time
01/20	Aquarius	16:46
02/27	Pisces	20:13
04/07	Aries	01:03
05/16	Taurus	04:19
06/26	Gemini	01:51
08/08	Cancer	13:19
09/24	Leo	21:09
11/19	Virgo	21:19

Mars Table for Year 1980

Date	Zodiac Sign	Time
03/11	Virgo*	20:51
05/04	Virgo	01:59
07/10	Libra	17:24
08/29	Scorpio	05:13
10/12	Sagittarius	05:44
11/22	Capricorn	00:59
12/30	Aquarius	21:45

Mars Table for Year 1981

Date	Zodiac Sign	Time
02/06	Pisces	22:08
03/17	Aries	02:04
04/25	Taurus	06:43
06/05	Gemini	05:01
07/18	Cancer	08:32
09/02	Leo	01:36
10/21	Virgo	01:41
12/16	Libra	00:06

Mars Table for Year 1982

Date	Zodiac Sign	Time
08/03	Scorpio	11:43
09/20	Sagittarius	01:04
10/31	Capricorn	22:42
12/10	Aquarius	05:43

Mars Table for Year 1983

Date	Zodiac Sign	Time
01/17	Pisces	12:32
02/24	Aries	23:38
04/05	Taurus	13:18
05/16	Gemini	21:03
06/29	Cancer	06:17
08/13	Leo	16:25
09/29	Virgo	23:44
11/18	Libra	10:05

Greenwich Mean Time (GMT)
24-Hour Clock

Note: * Indicates retrograde motion.
Eastern Standard Time (EST), add 5 hrs.
Central Standard Time (CST), add 6 hrs.
Mountain Standard Time (MST), add 7 hrs.
Pacific Standard Time, (PST), add 8 hrs.
Daylight Saving Time/War Time, minus 1 hr. from total.

Mars Table for Year 1984

Date	Zodiac Sign	Time
01/11	Scorpio	03:12
08/17	Sagittarius	20:05
10/05	Capricorn	06:10
11/15	Aquarius	18:09
12/25	Pisces	06:32

Mars Table for Year 1985

Date	Zodiac Sign	Time
02/02	Aries	17:08
03/15	Taurus	04:42
04/26	Gemini	08:42
06/09	Cancer	10:03
07/25	Leo	03:30
09/10	Virgo	01:00
10/27	Libra	14:50
12/14	Scorpio	18:43

Mars Table for Year 1986

Date	Zodiac Sign	Time
02/02	Sagittarius	06:16
03/28	Capricorn	03:37
10/09	Aquarius	00:47
11/26	Pisces	02:29

Mars Table for Year 1987

Date	Zodiac Sign	Time
01/08	Aries	12:20
02/20	Taurus	14:40
04/05	Gemini	16:30
05/21	Cancer	02:44
07/06	Leo	16:26
08/22	Virgo	19:25
10/08	Libra	18:59
11/24	Scorpio	02:59

Mars Table for Year 1988

Date	Zodiac Sign	Time
01/08	Sagittarius	15:09
02/22	Capricorn	10:10
04/06	Aquarius	21:39
05/22	Pisces	07:38
07/13	Aries	19:42
10/24	Aries*	10:03
11/01	Aries	02:53

Mars Table for Year 1989

Date	Zodiac Sign	Time
01/19	Taurus	07:39
03/11	Gemini	08:24
04/29	Cancer	04:11
06/16	Leo	13:46
08/03	Virgo	13:09
09/19	Libra	14:06
11/04	Scorpio	05:00
12/18	Sagittarius	04:29

Greenwich Mean Time (GMT)
24-Hour Clock

Note: * Indicates retrograde motion.
Eastern Standard Time (EST), add 5 hrs.
Central Standard Time (CST), add 6 hrs.
Mountain Standard Time (MST), add 7 hrs.
Pacific Standard Time, (PST), add 8 hrs.
Daylight Saving Time/War Time, minus 1 hr. from total.

Mars Table for Year 1990

Date	Zodiac Sign	Time
01/29	Capricorn	13:54
03/11	Aquarius	15:42
04/20	Pisces	22:08
05/31	Aries	07:21
07/12	Taurus	14:58
08/31	Gemini	12:02
12/14	Gemini*	07:00

Mars Table for Year 1991

Date	Zodiac Sign	Time
01/21	Gemini	01:22
04/03	Cancer	00:40
05/26	Leo	12:09
07/15	Virgo	12:23
09/01	Libra	06:19
10/16	Scorpio	18:42
11/29	Sagittarius	01:48

Mars Table for Year 1992

Date	Zodiac Sign	Time
01/09	Capricorn	09:17
02/18	Aquarius	04:08
03/28	Pisces	01:40
05/05	Aries	21:22
06/14	Taurus	15:50
07/26	Gemini	19:08
09/12	Cancer	06:26

Mars Table for Year 1993

Date	Zodiac Sign	Time
04/27	Leo	23:53
06/23	Virgo	07:43
08/12	Libra	01:08
09/27	Scorpio	02:13
11/09	Sagittarius	05:19
12/20	Capricorn	00:21

Mars Table for Year 1994

Date	Zodiac Sign	Time
01/28	Aquarius	03:44
03/07	Pisces	10:33
04/14	Aries	17:32
05/23	Taurus	22:07
07/03	Gemini	22:09
08/16	Cancer	19:05
10/04	Leo	15:56
12/12	Virgo	12:40

Mars Table for Year 1995

Date	Zodiac Sign	Time
01/22	Virgo*	21:57
05/25	Virgo	16:20
07/21	Libra	09:20
09/07	Scorpio	06:57
10/20	Sagittarius	20:55
11/30	Capricorn	13:53

Greenwich Mean Time (GMT)
24-Hour Clock

Note: * Indicates retrograde motion.
Eastern Standard Time (EST), add 5 hrs.
Central Standard Time (CST), add 6 hrs.
Mountain Standard Time (MST), add 7 hrs.
Pacific Standard Time, (PST), add 8 hrs.
Daylight Saving Time/War Time, minus 1 hr. from total.

Mars Table for Year 1996

Date	Zodiac Sign	Time
01/08	Aquarius	10:56
02/15	Pisces	11:41
03/24	Aries	15:00
05/02	Taurus	17:56
06/12	Gemini	14:17
07/25	Cancer	18:08
09/09	Leo	19:41
10/30	Virgo	06:58

Mars Table for Year 1997

Date	Zodiac Sign	Time
01/03	Libra	08:34
03/08	Libra*	18:49
06/19	Libra	08:41
08/14	Scorpio	08:37
09/28	Sagittarius	22:06
11/09	Capricorn	05:17
12/18	Aquarius	06:20

Mars Table for Year 1998

Date	Zodiac Sign	Time
01/25	Pisces	09:11
03/04	Aries	16:06
04/13	Taurus	00:49
05/24	Gemini	03:24
07/06	Cancer	08:40
08/20	Leo	18:53
10/07	Virgo	12:05
11/27	Libra	09:58

Mars Table for Year 1999

Date	Zodiac Sign	Time
01/26	Scorpio	12:18
05/05	Scorpio*	19:02
07/05	Scorpio	05:09
09/02	Sagittarius	19:40
10/17	Capricorn	01:32
11/26	Aquarius	06:42

Mars Table for Year 2000

Date	Zodiac Sign	Time
01/04	Pisces	02:36
02/12	Aries	00:37
03/23	Taurus	00:54
05/03	Gemini	18:45
06/16	Cancer	11:56
08/01	Leo	00:45
09/16	Virgo	23:37
11/04	Libra	01:20
12/23	Scorpio	14:05

Greenwich Mean Time (GMT)
24-Hour Clock

Note: * Indicates retrograde motion.
Eastern Standard Time (EST), add 5 hrs.
Central Standard Time (CST), add 6 hrs.
Mountain Standard Time (MST), add 7 hrs.
Pacific Standard Time (PST), add 8 hrs.
Daylight Saving Time/War Time, minus 1 hr. from total.

Jupiter Table

Year	Day	Zodiac Sign	Time
1901	01/19	Capricorn	08:12
1902	02/06	Aquarius	18:34
1903	02/20	Pisces	07:16
1904	03/01	Aries	02:07
1904	08/08	Taurus	21:15
1904	08/31	Taurus*	11:17
1905	03/07	Taurus	17:34
1905	07/21	Gemini	00:08
1905	12/04	Gemini*	21:06
1906	03/09	Gemini	21:51
1906	07/30	Cancer	22:44
1907	08/18	Leo	22:12
1908	09/12	Virgo	08:39
1909	10/11	Libra	22:09
1910	11/11	Scorpio	15:42

Jupiter Table

Year	Day	Zodiac Sign	Time
1911	12/10	Sagittarius	10:05
1913	01/02	Capricorn	18:07
1914	01/21	Aquarius	13:43
1915	02/03	Pisces	23:53
1916	02/12	Aries	06:44
1916	06/26	Taurus	01:46
1916	10/26	Taurus*	13:30
1917	02/12	Taurus	16:28
1917	06/29	Gemini	23:51
1918	07/13	Cancer	06:06
1919	08/02	Leo	09:01
1920	08/27	Virgo	05:29

Greenwich Mean Time (GMT)
24-Hour Clock

Note: * Indicates retrograde motion.
Eastern Standard Time (EST), add 5 hrs.
Central Standard Time (CST), add 6 hrs.
Mountain Standard Time (MST), add 7 hrs.
Pacific Standard Time (PST), add 8 hrs.
Daylight Saving Time/War Time, minus 1 hr. from total.

Jupiter Table

Year	Day	Zodiac Sign	Time
1921	09/25	Libra	22:36
1922	10/26	Scorpio	18:10
1923	11/24	Sagittarius	15:53
1924	12/18	Capricorn	04:39
1926	01/05	Aquarius	23:41
1927	01/18	Pisces	09:52
1927	06/06	Aries	08:11
1927	09/11	Aries*	04:41
1928	01/23	Aries	01:20
1928	06/04	Taurus	03:33
1929	06/12	Gemini	11:41
1930	06/26	Cancer	22:22

Jupiter Table

Year	Day	Zodiac Sign	Time
1931	07/17	Leo	07:33
1932	08/11	Virgo	06:48
1933	09/10	Libra	04:34
1934	10/11	Scorpio	04:29
1935	11/09	Sagittarius	02:22
1936	12/02	Capricorn	07:43
1937	12/20	Aquarius	02:52
1938	05/14	Pisces	06:13
1938	07/30	Pisces*	03:27
1938	12/29	Pisces	17:36
1939	05/11	Aries	13:37
1939	10/29	Aries*	23:37
1939	12/20	Aries	16:28
1940	05/16	Taurus	07:30

Greenwich Mean Time (GMT)
24-Hour Clock

Note: * Indicates retrograde motion.
Eastern Standard Time (EST), add 5 hrs.
Central Standard Time (CST), add 6 hrs.
Mountain Standard Time (MST), add 7 hrs.
Pacific Standard Time (PST), add 8 hrs.
Daylight Saving Time/War Time, minus 1 hr. from total.

Jupiter Table

Year	Day	Zodiac Sign	Time
1941	05/26	Gemini	12:24
1942	06/10	Cancer	09:33
1943	06/30	Leo	21:02
1944	07/26	Virgo	00:10
1945	08/25	Libra	04:49
1946	09/25	Scorpio	08:40
1947	10/24	Sagittarius	01:01
1948	11/15	Capricorn	08:36
1949	04/12	Aquarius	16:37
1949	06/27	Aquarius*	19:41
1949	11/30	Aquarius	18:41
1950	04/15	Pisces	07:37
1950	09/15	Pisces*	03:29
1950	12/01	Pisces	18:08

Jupiter Table

Year	Day	Zodiac Sign	Time
1951	04/21	Aries	13:54
1952	04/28	Taurus	20:25
1953	05/09	Gemini	15:21
1954	05/24	Cancer	05:10
1955	06/13	Leo	00:40
1955	11/17	Virgo	05:54
1956	01/17	Virgo*	23:22
1956	07/07	Virgo	19:13
1956	12/13	Libra	03:00
1957	02/19	Libra*	13:30
1957	08/07	Libra	01:54
1958	01/13	Scorpio	12:41
1958	03/20	Scorpio*	17:52
1958	09/07	Scorpio	08:06
1959	02/10	Sagittarius	13:05
1959	04/24	Sagittarius*	13:43
1959	10/05	Sagittarius	13:32
1960	03/01	Capricorn	12:09
1960	06/10	Capricorn*	02:39
1960	10/26	Capricorn	01:36

Greenwich Mean Time (GMT)
24-Hour Clock

Note: * Indicates retrograde motion.

Eastern Standard Time (EST), add 5 hrs.
Central Standard Time (CST), add 6 hrs.
Mountain Standard Time (MST), add 7 hrs.
Pacific Standard Time (PST), add 8 hrs.
Daylight Saving Time/War Time, minus 1 hr. from total.

Jupiter Table

Year	Day	Zodiac Sign	Time
1961	03/15	Aquarius	06:02
1961	08/12	Aquarius*	11:15
1961	11/03	Aquarius	23:41
1962	03/25	Pisces	20:14
1963	04/04	Aries	02:07
1964	04/12	Taurus	05:45
1965	04/22	Gemini	13:48
1965	09/21	Cancer	05:04
1965	11/17	Cancer*	03:21
1966	05/05	Cancer	13:58
1966	09/27	Leo	12:21
1967	01/16	Leo*	01:53
1967	05/23	Leo	07:26
1967	10/19	Virgo	10:14
1968	02/27	Virgo*	01:53
1968	06/15	Virgo	14:14
1968	11/15	Libra	22:00
1969	03/30	Libra*	20:39
1969	07/15	Libra	12:54
1969	12/16	Scorpio	15:09

Jupiter Table

Year	Day	Zodiac Sign	Time
1970	04/30	Scorpio*	06:06
1970	08/15	Scorpio	17:15
1971	01/14	Sagittarius	07:47
1971	06/05	Sagittarius*	02:36
1971	09/11	Sagittarius	14:07
1972	02/06	Capricorn	18:22
1972	07/24	Capricorn*	17:38
1972	09/25	Capricorn	16:39
1973	02/23	Aquarius	08:38
1974	03/08	Pisces	10:43
1975	03/18	Aries	16:11
1976	03/26	Taurus	10:11
1976	08/23	Gemini	12:02
1976	10/16	Gemini*	17:36
1977	04/03	Gemini	15:13

Greenwich Mean Time (GMT)
24-Hour Clock

Note: * Indicates retrograde motion.
Eastern Standard Time (EST), add 5 hrs.
Central Standard Time (CST), add 6 hrs.
Mountain Standard Time (MST), add 7 hrs.
Pacific Standard Time (PST), add 8 hrs.
Daylight Saving Time/War Time, minus 1 hr. from total.

Jupiter Table

Year	Day	Zodiac Sign	Time
1977	08/20	Cancer	13:16
1977	12/30	Cancer*	21:05
1978	04/12	Cancer	00:44
1978	09/05	Leo	08:44
1979	02/28	Leo*	20:35
1979	04/20	Leo	09:16
1979	09/29	Virgo	09:53
1980	10/27	Libra	09:02
1981	11/27	Scorpio	00:50
1982	12/26	Sagittarius	00:22
1984	01/19	Capricorn	13:43
1985	02/06	Aquarius	13:51
1986	02/20	Pisces	14:24
1987	03/02	Aries	17:39
1988	03/08	Taurus	15:08
1988	07/22	Gemini	00:19
1988	11/30	Gemini*	18:54
1989	03/11	Gemini	04:09
1989	07/31	Cancer	00:00
1990	08/18	Leo	07:16

Jupiter Table

Year	Day	Zodiac Sign	Time
1991	09/12	Virgo	05:57
1992	10/10	Libra	13:14
1993	11/10	Scorpio	07:44
1994	12/09	Sagittarius	10:03
1996	01/03	Capricorn	05:58
1997	01/21	Aquarius	13:42
1998	02/04	Pisces	09:37
1999	02/13	Aries	00:01
1999	06/28	Taurus	08:31
1999	10/23	Taurus*	05:46
2000	02/14	Taurus	20:52
2000	06/30	Gemini	06:29

Greenwich Mean Time (GMT)
24-Hour Clock

Note: * Indicates retrograde motion.

Eastern Standard Time (EST), add 5 hrs.

Central Standard Time (CST), add 6 hrs.

Mountain Standard Time (MST), add 7 hrs.

Pacific Standard Time (PST), add 8 hrs.

Daylight Saving Time/War Time, minus 1 hr. from total.

Saturn Table

Year	Day	Zodiac Sign	Time
1900	01/21	Capricorn	07:50
1900	07/18	Capricorn*	14:30
1900	10/17	Capricorn	04:48
1903	01/19	Aquarius	20:55
1905	04/13	Pisces	05:59
1905	08/17	Pisces*	00:21
1906	01/08	Pisces	10:02
1908	03/19	Aries	11:29
1910	05/17	Taurus	04:28
1910	12/15	Taurus*	02:52
1911	01/20	Taurus	01:41
1912	07/07	Gemini	03:47
1912	11/30	Gemini*	18:39

Saturn Table

Year	Day	Zodiac Sign	Time
1913	03/26	Gemini	10:53
1914	08/24	Cancer	16:41
1914	12/07	Cancer*	04:52
1915	05/11	Cancer	20:39
1916	10/17	Leo	18:05
1916	12/07	Leo*	14:52
1917	06/24	Leo	13:32
1919	08/12	Virgo	13:48
1921	10/07	Libra	17:00
1923	12/20	Scorpio	03:08
1924	04/06	Scorpio*	06:21
1924	09/13	Scorpio	21:01
1926	12/02	Sagittarius	20:39
1929	03/15	Capricorn	10:50
1929	05/05	Capricorn*	04:50
1929	11/30	Capricorn	02:10

Greenwich Mean Time (GMT)
24-Hour Clock

Note: * Indicates retrograde motion.
    Eastern Standard Time (EST), add 5 hrs.
    Central Standard Time (CST), add 6 hrs.
    Mountain Standard Time (MST), add 7 hrs.
    Pacific Standard Time (PST), add 8 hrs.
    Daylight Saving Time/War Time, minus 1 hr. from total.

Saturn Table

Year	Day	Zodiac Sign	Time
1932	02/24	Aquarius	00:53
1932	08/13	Aquarius*	10:30
1932	11/20	Aquarius	00:25
1935	02/14	Pisces	12:48
1937	04/25	Aries	04:58
1937	10/18	Aries*	03:32
1938	01/14	Aries	10:19
1939	07/06	Taurus	03:39
1939	09/22	Taurus*	04:46
1940	03/20	Taurus	08:22
1942	05/08	Gemini	17:23
1944	06/20	Cancer	05:35
1946	08/02	Leo	13:07
1948	09/19	Virgo	03:34
1949	04/03	Virgo*	00:25
1949	05/29	Virgo	11:24

Saturn Table

Year	Day	Zodiac Sign	Time
1950	11/20	Libra	16:06
1951	03/07	Libra*	09:59
1951	08/13	Libra	16:11
1953	10/22	Scorpio	15:09
1956	01/12	Sagittarius	18:57
1956	05/14	Sagittarius*	00:16
1956	10/10	Sagittarius	15:22
1959	01/05	Capricorn	12:27
1962	01/03	Aquarius	16:21
1964	03/24	Pisces	00:52
1964	09/16	Pisces*	22:42
1964	12/16	Pisces	00:57

Greenwich Mean Time (GMT)
24-Hour Clock

Note: * Indicates retrograde motion.
      Eastern Standard Time (EST), add 5 hrs.
      Central Standard Time (CST), add 6 hrs.
      Mountain Standard Time (MST), add 7 hrs.
      Pacific Standard Time (PST), add 8 hrs.
      Daylight Saving Time/War Time, minus 1 hr. from total.

Saturn Table

Year	Day	Zodiac Sign	Time
1967	03/03	Aries	18:12
1969	04/29	Taurus	19:52
1971	06/18	Gemini	14:56
1972	01/10	Gemini*	02:21
1972	02/21	Gemini	14:46
1973	08/01	Cancer	22:07
1974	01/07	Cancer*	17:31
1974	04/18	Cancer	22:36
1975	09/17	Leo	04:55
1976	01/14	Leo*	09:57
1976	06/05	Leo	05:23
1977	11/17	Virgo	03:04
1978	01/04	Virgo*	20:23
1978	07/26	Virgo	11:51
1980	09/21	Libra	09:56
1982	11/29	Scorpio	08:57
1983	05/06	Scorpio*	18:05
1983	08/24	Scorpio	09:22

Year	Day	Zodiac Sign	Time
1985	11/17	Sagittarius	00:18
1988	02/13	Capricorn	22:47
1988	06/10	Capricorn*	03:41
1988	11/12	Capricorn	08:19
1991	02/06	Aquarius	18:04
1993	05/21	Pisces	04:01
1993	06/30	Pisces*	07:29
1994	01/28	Pisces	22:48
1996	04/07	Aries	07:07
1998	06/09	Taurus	03:31
1998	10/25	Taurus*	20:06
1999	02/28	Taurus	22:02
2000	08/09	Gemini	22:25
2000	10/16	Gemini*	02:34

Greenwich Mean Time (GMT)
24-Hour Clock

Note: * Indicates retrograde motion.

Eastern Standard Time (EST), add 5 hrs.

Central Standard Time (CST), add 6 hrs.

Mountain Standard Time (MST), add 7 hrs.

Pacific Standard Time (PST), add 8 hrs.

Daylight Saving Time/War Time, minus 1 hr. from total.

Uranus Table

Year	Day	Zodiac Sign	Time
1904	12/20	Capricorn	11:04
1912	01/30	Aquarius	19:27
1912	09/04	Aquarius*	13:23
1912	11/12	Aquarius	06:05
1919	04/01	Pisces	01:04
1919	08/16	Pisces*	16:12
1920	01/22	Pisces	17:31
1927	03/31	Aries	12:20
1927	11/04	Aries*	12:40
1928	01/13	Aries	02:08
1934	06/06	Taurus	13:50
1934	10/09	Taurus*	20:37
1935	03/28	Taurus	01:18
1941	08/07	Gemini	10:23
1941	10/05	Gemini*	02:23
1942	05/14	Gemini	23:30

Year	Day	Zodiac Sign	Time
1948	08/30	Cancer	08:57
1948	11/12	Cancer*	14:34
1949	06/09	Cancer	23:24
1955	08/24	Leo	16:52
1956	01/27	Leo*	20:39
1956	06/10	Leo	00:15
1961	11/01	Virgo	09:51
1962	01/10	Virgo*	06:35
1962	08/09	Virgo	20:52
1968	09/28	Libra	13:23
1969	05/20	Libra*	17:21
1969	06/24	Libra	09:47
1974	11/21	Scorpio	09:40
1975	05/01	Scorpio*	12:39
1975	09/08	Scorpio	05:46

Greenwich Mean Time (GMT)
24-Hour Clock

Note: * Indicates retrograde motion.

Eastern Standard Time (EST), add 5 hrs.

Central Standard Time (CST), add 6 hrs.

Mountain Standard Time (MST), add 7 hrs.

Pacific Standard Time (PST), add 8 hrs.

Daylight Saving Time/War Time, minus 1 hr. from total.

Uranus Table

Year	Day	Zodiac Sign	Time
1975	05/01	Scorpio*	12:39
1975	09/08	Scorpio	05:46
1981	02/17	Sagittarius	05:36
1981	03/20	Sagittarius*	23:06
1981	11/16	Sagittarius	08:35
1988	02/14	Capricorn	23:56
1988	05/26	Capricorn*	21:31
1988	12/02	Capricorn	14:42
1995	04/01	Aquarius	14:14
1995	06/08	Aquarius*	19:28
1996	01/12	Aquarius	06:24

Greenwich Mean Time (GMT)
24-Hour Clock

Note: * Indicates retrograde motion.
Eastern Standard Time (EST), add 5 hrs.
Central Standard Time (CST), add 6 hrs.
Mountain Standard Time (MST), add 7 hrs.
Pacific Standard Time (PST), add 8 hrs.
Daylight Saving Time/War Time, minus 1 hr. from total.

Neptune Table

Year	Day	Zodiac Sign	Time
1901	07/19	Cancer	22:34
1901	12/25	Cancer*	06:35
1902	05/21	Cancer	11:07
1914	09/23	Leo	18:47
1914	12/14	Leo*	13:37
1915	07/19	Leo	11:20
1916	03/19	Leo*	03:16
1916	05/02	Leo	13:50
1928	09/21	Virgo	04:52
1929	02/19	Virgo*	10:21
1929	07/24	Virgo	08:25
1942	10/03	Libra	10:53
1943	04/17	Libra*	10:28
1943	08/02	Libra	11:50

Neptune Table

Year	Day	Zodiac Sign	Time
1955	12/24	Scorpio	16:09
1956	03/11	Scorpio*	16:25
1956	10/19	Scorpio	07:11
1957	06/15	Scorpio*	10:05
1957	08/06	Scorpio	10:19
1970	01/04	Sagittarius	15:38
1970	05/02	Sagittarius*	21:24
1970	11/06	Sagittarius	12:52
1984	01/18	Capricorn	18:11
1984	06/23	Capricorn*	03:13
1984	11/21	Capricorn	03:52
1998	01/28	Aquarius	19:39
1998	08/23	Aquarius*	02:41
1998	11/27	Aquarius	14:09

Greenwich Mean Time (GMT)
24-Hour Clock

Note: * Indicates retrograde motion.
Eastern Standard Time (EST), add 5 hrs.
Central Standard Time (CST), add 6 hrs.
Mountain Standard Time (MST), add 7 hrs.
Pacific Standard Time (PST), add 8 hrs.
Daylight Saving Time/War Time, minus 1 hr. from total.

Pluto Table

Year	Day	Zodiac Sign	Time
1912	09/10	Cancer	05:01
1912	10/20	Cancer*	08:11
1913	07/09	Cancer	15:40
1913	12/27	Cancer*	21:10
1914	05/26	Cancer	14:49
1937	10/07	Leo	15:17
1937	11/24	Leo*	20:41
1938	08/03	Leo	15:44
1939	02/07	Leo*	05:08
1939	06/14	Leo	01:28
1956	10/20	Virgo	05:25
1957	01/14	Virgo*	17:50
1957	08/19	Virgo	01:12

Pluto Table

Year	Day	Zodiac Sign	Time
1958	04/11	Virgo*	10:49
1958	06/10	Virgo	14:19
1971	10/05	Libra	03:56
1972	04/17	Libra*	02:06
1972	07/30	Libra	11:09
1983	11/05	Scorpio	14:05
1984	05/18	Scorpio*	14:32
1984	08/27	Scorpio	21:18
1995	01/17	Sagittarius	11:29
1995	04/20	Sagittarius*	17:45
1995	11/10	Sagittarius	17:57

Greenwich Mean Time (GMT)
24-Hour Clock

Note: * Indicates retrograde motion.
Eastern Standard Time (EST), add 5 hrs.
Central Standard Time (CST), add 6 hrs.
Mountain Standard Time (MST), add 7 hrs.
Pacific Standard Time (PST), add 8 hrs.
Daylight Saving Time/War Time, minus 1 hr. from total.

About the Author

Vivan B. Martin, an Aries, lives a double life as a journalist and astrologer. In the early 1980s, as a reporter for the *Hartford Courant*, Martin was one of the first reporters in the United States to draw attention to the problems of urban housing and homelessness. A contributor to *Woman's World* and such diverse publications as *Black Enterprise* and *Woman's Day of Australia*, Martin has written extensively about race relations and social trends. Today she continues to report on business and law and is writing her first novel.

Her professional astrological activities, which span twelve years, have focused on research, career counseling, and lectures to groups unfamiliar with astrology's more serious and practical sides. During a particularly group-oriented phase of her life, Martin helped found a local chapter of the National Council for Geocosmic Research (NCGR) in Connecticut. As the chapter's education chairperson, she promoted NCGR proficiency tests and organized a series of innovative programs, such as an astronomy-for-astrologers planetarium show. Martin's current research interest is "astrotwins," unrelated people who share the same birthdate and location, a topic about which she is planning to lecture and write in the future.

Go Beyond the Limits of Mind and Body...